# Studies in Power and Class in Africa

# Studies in Power and Class in Africa

EDITED BY

## Irving Leonard Markovitz

New York • Oxford
OXFORD UNIVERSITY PRESS
1987

Oxford University Press

Oxford    New York    Toronto
Delhi    Bombay    Calcutta    Madras    Karachi
Petaling Jaya    Singapore    Hong Kong    Tokyo
Nairobi    Dar es Salaam    Cape Town
Melbourne    Auckland

and associated companies in

Beirut    Berlin    Ibadan    Nicosia

Library of Congress Cataloging-in-Publication Data

Studies in power and class in Africa.

Bibliography: p.
Includes index.
1. Africa—Politics and government.    2. Power
(Social sciences) 3.  Elite (Social sciences)
4. Social classes—Africa. 5. Women—Africa—
Political activity. 6. Africa—Economic conditions.
I Markovitz, Irving Leonard, 1934–        .
JQ1872.S78   1987        306'.2'096        86-8573
ISBN 0-19-504129-1
ISBN 0-19-504130-5 (pbk.)

2 4 6 8 9 7 5 3 1

Printed in the United States of America

For Rita and Harvey

# Preface

More fleeting than an English summer, most books about Africa are little read and less remembered. Even so, the coauthors of this volume labored over their articles as if chiseling in stone. Lengthy correspondences filed in thick manila folders, arguments that filled long seminar mornings, costly long distance telephone calls, and as many as four revisions attested to the seriousness of their effort. For their patience in attending the publication of this book, and for bearing with my constant nudging in matters large and small, I am grateful.

Contributors did not have to pay the price of any intellectual orthodoxy to gain admission to these pages. Although they differed in their approaches to problems of power and class, they all agreed that the subject of this volume was too important for the simple application of sterile formulas or automatic categorizations. My colleagues also had enough confidence in the significance of their ideas so as to want to express themselves clearly. The results in the words of one prepublication reviewer—and I hope that the reader will agree—are "clear and comprehensive description" coupled with "sophisticated analysis of technical and theoretical matters."

The contributors have agreed to donate all royalties to Oxfam America to support Oxfam's efforts in relief and rehabilitation as well as in African constructive development.

Kenneth Erickson, Douglas Friedman, Athumani J. Liviga, Janet Mac-Gaffey, Francis Fox Piven, Dessalegn Rahmato, and Stuart Schaar read, and through their disagreements, improved my arguments in "Continuities in the Study of Power and Class in Africa."

Queens College is fortunate to have a community of scholars—much more so than most institutions of higher learning—people who continuously and critically discuss ideas and politics with each other, who teach together and who willingly put aside their own work to read carefully their colleagues' endeavors. John R. Bowman, John Gerassi, Alem Habtu, Michael Krasner, Peter T. Manicas, W. Ofuatey-Kodjoe, and Carl A. Riskin clarified my writing and my thinking. Henry W. Morton in his stewardship of the department of political science helped in many ways, above all through creating a deep calm which scholarship needs to flourish. Norma Sileo's friendly warmth and special competence enhanced the office atmosphere and made the department a pleasant place in which to work. Iris Braun and Florence B. Friedman willingly offered every possible assistance.

A Faculty Research Award from the City University Research Foundation, in conjunction with a Mellon Fellowship, and Faculty Fellowship in Residence, enabled travel and the study of problems of rural development in Senegal, Ghana, Tanzania, Kenya, and Ethiopia. A Presidential Research Award, introduced by Shirley Strum Kenny of Queens College, provided a full semester free of all teaching and administrative responsibilities and facilitated the final writing and editing of this volume.

James N. Jordan, Dean of the Social Sciences at Queens College, Helen S. Cairns, Dean of Graduate Studies and Research also at Queens College, and Solomon Goldstein, Dean for Research and University Programs at the Graduate Center of CUNY offered significant material aid and encouragement. Michael R. Dohan made available the services of the Social Science Laboratory. Janet Gingold skillfully reconstructed and computerized the bibliography. Julia E. Kwartler, Eugenie P. Pagano, and Arlene Diamond, of the Office of Word Processing headed by Pearl Sigberman, once more uncomplainingly deciphered my handwriting and produced grant proposals, correspondence, and manuscript copy, rapidly and with exceptional accuracy.

Well thought out and properly grounded in effective administrative and financial resources, the National Endowment for the Humanities Summer Seminars provide a unique opportunity for advanced study and research with colleagues in areas of mutual interest. Every encounter was warm, courteous, and helpful. I would like to recall the aid of Richard Emmerson, Karen Fuglie, April R. Hall, Ronald Herzman, Peter MacDonald, Michael Roman, Connie Matthews, Jane Schumate, Steven Tigner, and Dorothy Wartenberg.

The "Power and Class in Africa" seminars brought together an outstanding group of scholars and teachers, men and women of remarkably diverse personal and disciplinary backgrounds. Somehow during each of the seminars, everyone brought out the best in everybody else. The net result was a series of most stimulating conversations and an intellectual experience remarkable for its intensity. When, for the first time, I tried out some of the ideas in the introduction of this volume during one of our sessions, my colleagues probed my unstated assumptions, queried the logic of my arguments, and wondered about the significance of my interests. They challenged, they cajoled, they argued, they gave advice. They improved my paper. I can only hope that I was of equal service in advancing their scholarly interests.

It was my privilege to direct three of the college seminars. Members of the 1981 group included Yohannis Abate, Agostino Almeida, Gary Baker, Risa Ellovich, Richard W. Franke, Robert D. Grey, Mary Ann Hanley, Ndiva Kofele-Kale, Anne Lippert, Deborah A. Sanders, and Jeffrey M. Schulman.

The 1983 seminar consisted of Patrick D. Bellegarde-Smith, Achameleh Debela, Donald R. Floyd, Barbara H. Chasin, Susan L. Gasster, Wendy Kindred, Lorna McDaniel, Alan L. McLeod, Gordon D. Morgan, Aihawa Ong, Frank A. Salamone, and Janice E. Weaver.

The 1985 members were Victoria Bernal, Sheila H. Carapico, Carolyn M. Clarke, Mohamed Diakite, Lawrence P. Frank, Diane S. Isaacs, Girma Kebbede, Craig N. Murphy, James A. Quirin, Penelope M. Roach, William H. Shaw, and Tekle Mariam Woldemikael.

The NEH Seminar for High School Teachers on "Great Issues of African Politics, Philosophy, and Literature" also provided the opportunity to try out some of my ideas and to expand my interests. These seminars for secondary school teachers raised for critical discussion classic issues of African political thought and literature within their social context and in terms of their historical development. Africa still receives a cursory place in secondary instruction. Evenworse, too frequently much of what is offered strengthens rather than diminishes old stereotypes, and the "traditional" approaches of both the liberal arts and schools of education have not remedied this situation.

The college seminars had not prepared me for the enthusiasm, commitment, relish for intellectual confrontation, and simply the hard work that the high school and junior high school teachers devoted to the study of our African materials. Members of the 1984 group who lived in the New York–New Jersey area continued to meet for over a year after our last formal session. The members of the 1984 seminar were Joseph Ball, Beverly G. Bond, Jeffrey Feinberg, Charlene Jassim, Esther Liberman, Andrea Libresco, Atiba Mbiwan, Michael Putman, Raymond Russo, Goldie B. Seiderman, Barry Smith, Robert Smithwick, Deanne Vandevert, Susan Weliky, and Marvin Williams.

Finally, members of my last seminar in 1986 include Joan H. Cohen, Thomas J. Determan, Barbara S. Ellery, Victor O. Emumwen, David P. Freudenburg, Patrick J. Gallo, Carl M. Gussin, Kate Hepner, Patricia Lyon, Brian C. Morrison, Scott P. Newkirk, Patrick G. O'Brien, Daniel H. Perlstein, Nicholas H. Spencer, and Jennifer J. Squires.

I would also like to note the special help with the preparation and conduct of the seminars of Alem Habtu, Thomas G. Karis, Michael Krasner, Jane R. Moore, W. Ofuatey-Kodjoe, William A. Proefriedt, Allan Stein, and Susan Weliky, as well as the special support of Sheila H. Carapico, Robert D. Grey, Mary Ann Hanley, Martin Kilson, Esther Liberman, Peter T. Manicas, James H. Mittelman, Henry W. Morton, Carl G. Rosberg, and Burton Zwiebach.

Susan Rabiner of Oxford University Press was a sensitive editor who strongly supported this volume from its inception.

Doris Suarez ably assisted in the preparations for both the seminar and the book.

My last—and first—obligation is to Ruth, my wife, who challenged me to think one step further than I otherwise would have done, who caused me to dig up the evidence for propositions that were less than self-evident, and who blue-penciled some of my most poetic images merely because of their vulgar grandiloquence.

Poetry aside, responsibility for matters of judgment, fact, and interpretation remain the editor's and the coauthors.

*Bayside, New York*                                                                 I. L. M.

# Contents

# Contributors

**George C. Bond** is a professor of applied anthropology at Teachers College, Columbia University. He is the author of *The Politics of Change in a Zambian Community* (Chicago: University of Chicago Press, 1976), co-editor of *African Christianity* (New York: Academic Press, 1979) and the guest editor of a special issue, *African Education and Social Stratification,* of the *Anthropology and Education Quarterly.* He has published articles on topics as diverse as education, kinship, politics, and religion.

**Thomas M. Callaghy** is assistant professor of political science, associate director of the Research Institute on International Change, and research associate at the Institute of African Studies at Columbia University. He received his Ph.D. in political science from the University of California, Berkeley, in 1979. He is co-editor and contributor to *Socialism in Sub-Saharan Africa: A New Assessment* (Berkeley: Institute of International Studies, 1979); editor and contributor to *South Africa in Southern Africa: The Intensifying Vortex of Violence* (New York: Praeger, 1983); and author of *The State-Society Struggle: Zaire in Comparative Perspective* (New York: Columbia University Press, 1984). He has also contributed to several journals and edited volumes.

**Richard W. Franke** received his Ph.D. from Harvard University. He is currently professor of anthropology at Montclair State College, where he has taught since 1972. Professor Franke has carried out fieldwork in Surinam, Bougainville, Indonesia, and West Africa and has held grants from the National Science Foundation, National Institute of Mental Health, Harvard School of Public Health, and National Endowment for the Humanities. He has published several articles on underdevelopment, food production in the Third World, and ecology. In 1980 he co-authored (with Barbara H. Chasin) *Seeds of Famine: Ecological Destruction and the Development Dilemma in the West African Sahel* (Montclair, N.J.: Allanheld, Osmun, 1980). He is currently on the editorial board of the *Bulletin of Concerned Asian Scholars*.

**Robert D. Grey,** who received his Ph.D. from Yale University, is a professor of political science at Grinnell College. A longtime student of Ethiopian politics, he has published articles in such journals as *The African Review* and *Northeast African Studies.* He has branched out into the study of both comparative communism and African international relations. His latest research focuses on the autonomy of African states in the international order.

**Beverly Carolease Grier,** who holds a Ph.D. from Yale University, was Fulbright Lecturer in the Faculté des Lettres et Sciences Humains at the University of Niamey in Niger. She has published several articles on the political economy of Ghana and is working on a full-length manuscript on that subject. Her current research interests are in the area of legal change under capitalist development in colonial and postcolonial Africa.

**Hermann Giliomee** is a professor of government at the University of Cape Town, formerly lecturing in history at the University of Stellenbosch. His books include *Ethnic Power Mobilized* (with Heribert Adam), *Afrikaner Political Thought: Analysis and Documents 1780–1850* (with Andre DuToit), *The Shaping of South African Society 1652–1820* (with R. Elphick), and, most recently, *Parting of the Ways: South African Politics 1976–82*. He is at present preparing a manuscript on the development of Afrikaner politics and ideology in late nineteenth-century South Africa.

**Stanley B. Greenberg** is associate director of the Southern African Research Program at Yale University and has held visiting appointments in political science at Wesleyan University and at the University of Witswatersrand. His books include *Politics and Poverty: Modernization and Response in Five Poor Neighborhoods* and, most recently, *Race and State in Capitalist Development: Comparative Perspectives,* a study of Alabama, South Africa, Northern Ireland, and Israel. His present work, *Legitimating the Illegitimate,* focuses on the state and labor markets in divided societies.

**Martin Kilson,** professor of government at Harvard University, received his B.A. from Lincoln University in Pennsylvania and his Ph.D. from Harvard. He is author of *Political Change in a West African State African Diaspora: Interpretive Essays* (1976), and *African Autocracy: Patterns and Crises in Modernization* (forthcoming).

**Ndiva Kofele-Kale** received his Ph.D. and J.D. from Northwestern University. He is an attorney-at-law and professor of political science, Governors State University, Illinois. In addition to over thirty articles, his major publications include: *Comparative Political Culture and Socialization* (1976); *An African Experiment in Nation-Building: The Bilingual Cameroon Republic Since Reunification* (1980); and *Tribesmen and Patriots: Political Culture in a Polyethnic African State* (1981).

**Sonia Kruks** has a doctorate from the London School of Economics and has taught at colleges in London, New York, and at the Eduardo Mondlane University in Mozambique. As well as participating in research at the Centre for African Studies at the Eduardo Mondlane University, she has served as a consultant on projects in Tanzania and Kenya. She is currently assistant professor of political science at the New School for Social Research. Her research interests encompass not only African politics but also feminist theory and recent French political philosophy. Among her publications are a book, *The Political Philosophy of Merleau-Ponty* (1981), and two articles on women in Mozambique: "Mozambique: Some Reflections on the Struggle for Women's Emancipation," *Frontiers* (1983), and "The State, the Party and the Female Peasantry in Mozambique" (co-author), *Journal of Southern African Studies* 11,1 (1984).

**Ronald T. Libby,** formerly senior lecturer in government at the University of the West Indies (Jamaica), was visiting professor of political science at Northwestern University during 1985–86. He is the author of *The Economics of Power and Struggle in Southern Africa* (forthcoming) and *Toward an African-*

*ized U.S. Policy Towards Southern Africa* (1980). He is a contributor to *The Political Economy of Zimbabwe* (1984) and has published numerous articles on international political economy, African politics, and Central America in scholarly journals such as *World Politics, International Organization, Comparative Politics, The Journal of Commonwealth and Comparative Politics, Foreign Policy, The African Review,* and *African Studies Review.* He is currently engaged in research on the power of subnational political authorities to influence the major transnational corporations to restructure the world aluminum industry.

**Anne Lippert,** professor of French at Ohio Northern University, received her Ph.D. from Indiania University in (1971). She has held the NEH Younger Humanist Award as well as an NEH seminar grant. From 1973 to 1975 Professor Lippert was a Fulbright Senior Lecturer in Algeria and has continued to visit Africa frequently, most recently in 1982, under the auspices of a Department of Education grant through the Indiana Consortium of International Programs. She has written numerous articles on Africa and has testified as an expert witness at the Hearings before the Subcommittee on Africa and International Organizations of the Committee on Foreign Affairs of the U.S. House of Representatives. In 1984–85 she held the Ridenour Humanities Chair at Ohio Northern University.

**Irving Leonard Markovitz,** who received his Ph.D. from the University of California at Berkeley, is a professor of political science at Queens College and the Graduate Center of the City University of New York. He has written *Léopold Sédar Senghor and the Politics of Negritude* (New York: Atheneum, 1969; London: Heinemann, 1970); *African Politics and Society* (editor and contributor) (New York: Free Press, 1970); and *Power and Class in Africa,* (Englewood Cliffs, N.J.: Prentice-Hall, 1977). His articles have appeared in major African journals.

**Jeffrey M. Schulman** is an attorney-at-law and part-time instructor of political science and law at Urbana College, Urbana, Ohio. He is a member of the International Law Section of the American Bar Association. In 1978, the author received the Rutgers Society Award for International Law and in 1981 was awarded an NEH grant to attend a seminar on "Power and Class in Africa," where this article was conceived. The author has visited the Western Sahara and written several articles on the war, including papers presented at the Hearings before the Subcommittee on Africa and International Organizations of the Committee on Foreign Affairs of the U.S. House of Representatives in 1979 and at the *Colloque sur les fondements juridiques et institutionnels de la RASD* at the French National Assembly in Paris in October 1984.

**Kathleen Staudt** has her Ph.D. from the University of Wisconsin. She is an associate professor of political science at the University of Texas at El Paso. Professor Staudt has published articles in *Comparative Politics, Development and Change, Journal of Politics, Policy Studies Journal, Rural Africana, Western Political Quarterly,* and *Women and Politics.* She co-edited, with Jane Jaquette, *Women in Developing Countries: A Policy Focus* (New York: Haworth, 1983), and her book manuscript, *Redistribution Between the Sexes: Obstacles to Policy Implementation and Institutionalization,* is forthcoming from Praeger.

# Studies in Power
# and Class in Africa

MELILLA
CEUTA
TUNIS
Rabat
Algiers
TUNISIA
MOROCCO
Tripoli
Benghazi
Cairo
El-Ayoun
ALGERIA
LIBYA
EGYPT
WESTERN
SAHARA
CAPE
VERDE
IS.
Praia
MAURITANIA
Nouakchott
Khartoum
DJIBOUTI
MALI
NIGER
CHAD
Djibouti
SENEGAL
Dakar
Bamako
Niamey
SUDAN
THE
GAMBIA
Banjul
BURKINA FASO
Ndjamena
GUINEA-BISSAU
Bissau
GUINEA
Conakry
Ouagadougou
ETHIOPIA
SIERRA LEONE
Freetown
BENIN
Porto Novo
NIGERIA
CENTRAL AFRICAN
REPUBLIC
Addis Ababa
Monrovia
IVORY
COAST
GHANA
Accra
Lagos
SOMALIA
LIBERIA
Abidjan
TOGO
Lome
CAMEROON
Bangui
UGANDA
Kampala
KENYA
Mogadishu
EQUATORIAL GUINEA
Malabo
Yaounde
RWANDA
Kigali
Nairobi
SAO TOME E
PRINCIPE
Libreville
GABON
CONGO
ZAIRE
BURUNDI
Bujumbura
ZANZIBAR
Dar es Salaam
Brazzaville
Kinshasa
TANZANIA
SEYCHELLES IS.
Victoria
Luanda
Moroni
COMORO IS.
ANGOLA
Lilongwe
MALAWI
ZAMBIA
Lusaka
Antananarivo
MAURITIUS
Port Louis
Harare
MOZAMBIQUE
MADAGASCAR
NAMIBIA
ZIMBABWE
REUNION
BOTSWANA
Windhoek
Gaborone
Pretoria
Maputo
SWAZILAND
Mbabane
SOUTH
AFRICA
LESOTHO
Maseru

# Introduction:
# Continuities in the Study
# of Power and Class in Africa

The studies in this volume demonstrate the explanatory power which a sophisticated framework focusing on social class brings to the analysis of contemporary African politics. Although most of these studies deal with class, they recognize the importance of the state, religion, ideology, gender, ethnicity, language, and international relations in the determination of policy and in the understanding of the real world. The authors address problems of major concern in the daily lives of ordinary people.

These essays show graphically how precarious life was for the mass of the population during and after the colonial period. They reveal how most people suffered an absolute decline in their standard of living, lived at the edge of economic dependence, and were bound in servile relations. They explain the thirst for education as a way out of exploitative economic and political conditions in the villages. They show how class conflict intensified with war and depression, how farmers fled to the city to maintain their independence, and how migrant workers struggled to protect their meager, declining standards of living. They picture the colonial governors, heirs of the Magna Carta and the Revolution of 1789, worrying that African nationalism signified "democracy gone mad," and that independence would "open the way for mob rule."

Above all, these analyses challenge the conventional wisdom about Africa as it appears in both the popular press and the mainstream social science literature. They also have clear implications which, if heeded, could affect policy as well as academic judgments. We can find only too vivid examples of what happens when even the well intentioned fail to consider the crucial power and class variables brought out in this volume. A tragic case in point is most of the television and press discussion of the recent drought and famine.[1]

I have found even the "best" analysis in the press disturbing. A front-page article by Alan Cowell in the *New York Times,* for example, is entitled "African War Against Famine: Dependence on Aid is Villain."[2] As compassionate and competent an observer as Cowell, blind to the social, political, and economic realities which provide the context for agricultural failure in Africa, ends by positing a seemingly hopeless dilemma. He appears to endorse a Social Darwinist perspective when he declares:

> Western consciences dictate that people should not be allowed to starve; but the specialist contends that by saving them, without finding a key to greater food production on fragile lands, too much pressure is placed on that land and it dies while dependence on outsiders increases.[3]

He goes on to point out that "it is acknowledged" that "the billions of dollars that have flowed into the Continent in the last ten years have worsened the plight of millions of people, and no one has found a solution."[4] I would acknowledge no such thing. The "billions of dollars" do not have a life of their own. We must question who uses these monies, for what purposes, and who benefits. By Cowell's own account, less than eight percent of the $7.5 billion in aid monies poured into the Sahel by Western governments and international agencies actually reached "the poor peasants most affected by the drought." Who received the funds? Did those vast sums, like desert showers, simply evaporate?

There is no mystery. Africa's ruling classes and their foreign allies were the recipients.[5] Cowell knows that the World Bank pushed the expansion of cash crops for export, rather than food crops for immediate, local consumption, but he misses the link between indigenous decision makers and their foreign friends. He says that the tenfold increase of Africa's foreign debt between 1970 and 1982 led to policies which promote starvation.[6] But the "debt" didn't do that; Africa's rulers did. Again the problem is neither that "aid" projects are "ill conceived," nor that modern techniques of agriculture have failed because of an arrogant disregard for the practice of traditional farming. The famine is not due to "mistakes," plentiful though they might have been. Certain classes *did* benefit, and that was *no* mistake.

Cowell tells us that there is a "neglect" of small farmers and "an indifference by government towards the governed," but he doesn't tell us why, and he makes this neglect and indifference seem almost accidental. He gives the impression that if anybody is to blame, it is the "volatile poor" who live in shantytowns and whose threatened rebellion forces governments to feed them cheaply, which in turn robs the peasant farmer of incentive to produce for the market. This kind of presentation could easily lead the casual reader to the conclusion that "the volatile poor" are the basic cause of Africa's poverty, that aid is useless, and that it is pointless to try to save Africa's starving today because long-run solutions are impossible.

What is missing in Cowell's article is an understanding of the nature of Africa's ruling classes and their interested interrelationship with external agencies, including multinational corporations and the World Bank.[7] Without such an analysis, we are as likely to blame free sacks of grain and greedy cows, chomping those tufts of grass that hold back the desert, for a tragedy which *does* have identifiable human agents.[8] In contrast, Richard Franke, in his contribution to this volume, clearly demonstrates the value of a class analysis not only to understand the drought, but also to arrive at a series of remedial measures.[9]

The example of drought and famine is particularly vivid, but our understanding of other African developments—from the consolidation of nonparticipatory state structures to the continued exploitation of women—suffers as badly from lack of attention and outright hostility to class analysis.

## BACKGROUND AND ORIGIN OF THIS VOLUME

The thirteen original studies of this volume all deal with aspects of a single theme: the "authoritative allocation of values" or, more simply, the question of who gets what, when, where, and why—and who gets left out.[10] Although they differ in their political perspectives and their disciplinary backgrounds, they focus on some aspect of "class" as a key variable.

Five of the thirteen studies resulted from a National Endowment for the Humanities (NEH) sponsored seminar on "Power and Class in Africa." Members of the original group later agreed to invite as participants a selected number of prominent authorities whose work complemented our own.

The NEH seminar and the book after which it was named, *Power and Class in Africa*,[11] originally grew out of my teaching and research requirements. I needed a sensible framework within which to synthesize the vast outpouring of scholarly studies and other writing produced about Africa during the 1960s and 1970s. Existing theories and frameworks were unsatisfactory, first because of their preoccupation with law and order. This concern with ordinarily highly desirable objectives turned out too frequently to be a way to justify the perpetuation of establishment forces, no matter what their policies and nature.

Second, at the time most analysts, African and non-African alike, from Léopold Sédar Senghor[12] to Aristide Zolberg,[13] denied the existence of classes in Africa and talked instead of "status groups" or "elites" or "technicoprofessional" interests. Thus, they were unable to explain the "smoldering discontent" which followed independence, and were unprepared for the rapid demise of bourgeois political parties and the seemingly endless succession of military coups.[14]

Third, "modernization" theory held sway. Today we can clearly label modernization theorists, a school of thought which includes people of as diverse politics as Rupert Emerson, C. E. Black, W. W. Rostow, and Herbert Butterfield.[15] They all believed that the less developed countries would evolve along lines similar to those of the "advanced" countries as a result of the diffusion of Newtonian science and technology. This approach appeared to be objective and ideologically neutral, a simple description of the necessary path and tools of progress, no matter what the ultimate political end.

In *Power and Class in Africa,* I rejected these approaches and argued that class conflict existed in contemporary Africa and was rooted in traditional social structure; that, from any historical perspective, what was remarkable about political life was not disorder, but the rapidity with which a pattern of *stability* had been achieved. This stability, however, was not necessarily a reason to rejoice, because finally, far from successfully following "a path of evolutionary-diffusionist development," conditions for the vast majority of Africans had worsened both relatively and absolutely.

Since the publication of that study in 1977, the expulsion of "foreigners" from Nigeria and the misery of the citizens of Zaire clearly demonstrate that "stability" is not the major problem of contemporary Africa. Famine in Ethiopia and Somalia resulted not only from drought, but was part of a broader deterioration in the conditions of daily existence. The new widespread necessity to import food vividly underlines problems deeper than mainstream concerns with "modernization." Many scholars have turned to class analysis. The terms of the debate have indeed gone beyond "world systems" and "dependency" theory,[16] and both their radical and conservative challengers now require a new perspective. Yet, leading social scientists and Africanists have recently renewed their attacks against the validity and significance of any type of class analysis.

Robert H. Jackson and Carl G. Rosberg, for example, in *Personal Rule in Black Africa,*[17] view *personal rule* as a distinctive kind of political system with generic characteristics and processes. While African leaders differ in style of rule, they argue, personality counts more than constitutional restraints or institutional offices. Their book is important because of the clarity with which it states its basic assumptions, the rigor with which it pursues its theme. While we might quarrel with the practical differences between "prince," "autocrat," "prophet," and "tyrant" as distinctive types of personal rule, the more fundamental issue is whether a decline of political institutions has in fact occurred in postcolonial African states. Jackson and Rosberg assume such a decline and ask why there was no commensurate disintegration in political order. Their answer is that personal rule can provide peace, security, and stability—political goods which, analysts like Samuel Huntington once argued, only effective political institutions could provide.[18]

Personalities do matter. The sources of political order do not depend solely on the effects of the underlying social and economic environment. However, we must carefully analyze the extent that the continued postcolonial development of social class provides the context, the limitations, and opportunities within which personalities operate. *Personal Rule in Black Africa* forces us to a more precise evaluation of the role of leadership (and the degree of institutionalization) in African politics.[19]

Similarly, an important challenge to class interpretations comes from those who emphasize ethnic identity or communal solidarity. In the African context, class models must certainly be modified by factors of cultural values and communal concern, as well as those of race and ideology.[20] The normal and historical logic of the social sciences is that of an either/or situation, to think in terms of class and community as mutually exclusive categories. Yet the political facts of the real world indicate the need for a different logic or a more subtle formulation. Sometimes a given population acts in unity on the basis of a perceived common identity; at other times "a people" splits into clashing classes. When and why does this happen? Are appeals to ethnic or tribal loyalties simply another device of the dominant classes to strengthen their rule? What are the alternative explanations?

## NEW LINES OF STUDY

The studies in this volume help to answer some of these questions and pose additional problems for investigation. I have organized this work on the same principles that guided my original essay, *Power and Class in Africa*. My underlying assumption was then, and still is, that since the end of the Second World War, almost all African states have experienced three phases of political development: (1) gaining formal independence; (2) consolidating power—that is, creation of the fundamental framework, institutions, and political limits of the new state; and (3) restructuring society and forging a new bureaucratic apparatus necessary to establish the psychological and technological framework for development.[21]

In terms of key issues of the preindependence phase, P. T. Bauer, in a volume published as recently as 1984, flatly asserted that, contrary to "stereotype," "British Colonial rule before the 1970's benefited a great majority of Africans."[22] In Part I of our present volume, "Revolution and the Struggle for Independence," Beverly Grier more than confronts Bauer's contention with concrete evidence from the capitalist development of Ghana prior to 1948. She demonstrates, in Claus Offe's terms, that the colonial state could not make enough Africans full participants in commodity relationships, and that this inability underlay the delegitimization and destabilization of the colonial state.[23]

Grier also addresses herself to a problem not asked in *Power and Class in Africa:* Are there differences in state formation and in the mechanisms through which foreign capitalism underdeveloped both "settler" and "peasant" Africa?[24] Martin Kilson, in the same vein, goes on to ask: If populism in Africa embodied a burgeoning class awareness and a revolutionary potential, how did it become diverted from revolution to rebellion? Jeffrey Schulman addresses political movements firmly committed to independence when he wants to know: Can the Polisario and Swapo succeed in overcoming internal class division, as did FRELIMO, the MPLA, and the PAIGC before them, to meet the real needs of their potential constituency before the advent of formal independence? Can they achieve international legitimacy by demonstrating that they offer alternative institutional arrangements of demonstrated capacity and growing effectiveness?[25]

In those sections of the book dealing with "The Consolidation of Power," Thomas Callaghy raises the questions of how the formation of African ruling classes compares with the processes of consolidation of power in early European nations from the sixteenth century and with Latin American countries from the time of their breaks with Spain and Portugal. What conditions must facilitate the political autonomy of the state and enable it to accumulate power at the expense of class interest? Robert Grey wants to know when a precariously situated class will become aware of its vulnerability, and under what circumstances it will turn to what types of action. Ndiva Kofele-Kale shows us how fractions of the organizational bourgeoisie manipulate ethnicity, religion, and regional loyalties in order more tightly to integrate themselves into state and bureaucratic power structures. George Bond provides graphic evidence that kinship, an ideology which once served the community, became, with the increasing commercialization of the countryside, an ideology serving as the basis for capital accumulation.

Addressing a problem in the "Consolidation of Power" not raised in *Power and Class in Africa,* that of women's role in political and economic transformations, Kathleen Staudt asks how African women, who in precolonial precapitalist Africa were full participants in a wider economy beyond that of the household and who played significant roles in the political decision-making process, ended up dependent and subservient. How was the *process* of the *domination* of women related to economic growth and the rise of complex political organizations? Anne Lippert enquires: Although women's access to wealth and power will vary with social class, in what ways does gender, as an independent variable, affect people's life chances?

The study by Sonia Kruks leads us to ask how ideology can be of changing significance in the *encadrement* of the population. Richard Franke poses the problem of how a range of differences in power relationships between traditional producing classes and ruling classes in the Sahel affected the environment. Finally, the last section again expands the scope of the original volume by turning to South Africa. Ronald Libby considers how regional and international forces have encouraged class fragmentation in both the South African white national bourgeoisie and the South African black working class. In the last study, Stanley Greenberg and Hermann Giliomee speculate about the function of the Bantustans, maintaining that their function is neither "super exploitation," nor to provide agricultural reserves for the production of cheap

African labor, nor to keep "tribal" structures intact, nor to control populations through African bureaucracies, nor to legitimatize "separate" African development.

## PROBLEMS FOR FUTURE INVESTIGATION: ON THE NATURE OF AFRICA'S RULING CLASSES, DIFFERENCES BETWEEN THE ORGANIZATIONAL BOURGEOISIE AND THE NEW CLASS

The studies in this collection, and in the work of those scholars who have focused on class analysis, have improved our understanding of African politics. Nevertheless, great gaps remain in our theoretical understanding of the nature of class in Africa and in the factual knowledge necessary to answer the important questions they have raised. The work already accomplished has clearly highlighted key problems for further investigation.

In *Power and Class in Africa,* for example, I used the term "organizational bourgeoisie" to refer to a combined ruling group consisting of the top political leaders and bureaucrats, the traditional rulers and their descendants, the leading members of the liberal professions, the rising business bourgeoisie, and top members of the military and police forces. Over time, leading elements in this coalition changed. The organizational bourgeoisie was not simply a collection of individuals; neither did it consist of only managers, or racketeers, or a comprador class, as other analysts have asserted. While the definition and existence of this class were highly disputed, I maintained, first, that its members derived their power from organization. They were located at pivotal points of control in those overarching systems of political, social, and economic power analyzed by Hobbes, Marx, and Weber—the nation-state and capitalism. These systems incorporated the most diverse, parochial, and isolated elements in rationalizing organizations that stopped only tangentially at the national boundaries.

The organizational bourgeoisie was more than a "new class" in Djilas's sense, more than either a bureaucratic or "state" bourgeoisie, because it included elements of private business as well as the managers of public enterprises and top state officials. The organizational bourgeoisie was also more than a "managerial bourgeoisie" or "elite" because it not only managed, it exploited. It was willing to innovate in its own interest; it increasingly did create wealth-producing enterprises, and it was as hungry as any previous ascendant class. To draw sharp distinctions between the administrative bourgeoisie, the politicians, and businessmen could mislead because power and class were not necessarily attributes of individuals, but of families. Thinking in terms of families also better enabled us to picture continuities between traditional leaders and their modern successors. *Power and Class in Africa* asked whether this organizational bourgeoisie could be independent or whether it was simply the tool of imperial interests—indeed, what was the range of possibilities?[26]

Social scientists still disagree about the nature of Africa's ruling classes. However, we now have enough empirical and theoretical materials to provide some ideas towards a new categorization of African states based upon our perceptions of the nature of Africa's ruling classes and their relations to the forces of production. A theory of power in contemporary African regimes must consider transformations in the institutionalization of office, differences in the positions of postindependence African officeholders from those in apparently similar positions under colonialism, and the nature of the connections between politicians, bureaucrats, producers, and merchants.[27]

In this volume, Beverly Grier and Martin Kilson detail how change came about in state officers, and how a new "public" with a rising class consciousness forced policy outcomes with consequences extending beyond colonialism to contemporary regimes. Thomas Callaghy demonstrates the terrible autonomy of a modern political aristocracy from both domestic economic class forces and powerful international agencies. Robert Grey lets us see how uneasily sit even long-established traditional regimes when key fractions of the petite bourgeoisie become apprehensive. Ndiva Kofele-Kale tells us that ethnicity, language, religion, and region will not prevent factions of the organizational bourgeoisie from consolidating their power. George Bond shows how a rising merchant class can convert traditional beliefs into a modern ideology justifying its actions. Kathleen Staudt and Anne Lippert provide evidence that the dependent position of women developed over time and served the purposes of state building and capitalism. Sonia Kruks and Richard Franke illustrate the social basis of ideology and planning. Stanley Greenberg and Hermann Giliomee analyze how bureaucracies foster "protective" (for the regime) working-class schisms. Finally, Jeffrey Schulman shows how the need for international recognition can pressure internal unity, even as Ronald Libby reminds us of the significance of external economic forces in creating growing divisions within South Africa's ruling class.

What else can we say about the nature of Africa's rulers? In the remainder of this introduction I would like simply to suggest several additional propositions for further research about the nature of the organizational bourgeoisie that go beyond the original formulations in *Power and Class in Africa*. Since writing that study, new evidence indicates (and additional empirical work is certainly necessary to substantiate what at this point is little more than informed speculation) the rise of a "new" type of government entrepreneur.[28]

Government actions and policies might always have served dominant class interests, but civil servants in the West are not only supposed to be politically neutral—they are expected to be full-time government employees devoted to public concerns. Most Western states have even frowned upon second wage-earning jobs for bureaucrats. Governments have codified these restrictions and enacted into legislation expectations about the behavior of their officeholders and civil servants. Everywhere, of course, civil servants deviate from these obligations and requirements. In fact, a common definition of corruption is behavior of government officials which deviates from accepted norms to serve private purposes.

Social scientists, as well as the general public, have noticed that African government officials frequently hold what look like dual positions: they are primarily civil servants, but they are also those who deal in business. Observers have generally focused on the illegal aspects of the business arrangements, and either denounced this "graft on the side" or learnedly discussed the "functional advantages" of corruption in a developing society. Samuel Huntington, for example, maintains that corruption was more common in "modernizing" societies because of "the absence of effective political institutionalization" and the rise of new groups with new resources and new values who wished "to make themselves effective within the political sphere." Huntington tells us that in Africa, corruption threw a bridge between those who held power and those who controlled wealth, enabling the two groups—far apart during the initial stages of nationalist development—to assimilate each other. Huntington's general point is that through bribing government officials, the business classes can facilitate—at this stage of development, until legitimate channels of effective representation are created—getting on with their creative, productive activity. Only in a significantly modernized society can the difference between public role and private interest gain recognition because: "If the culture of the society does not distinguish between the king's role as a private person and the king's role as king, it is impossible to accuse the king of corruption in the use of public monies."[29] Huntington clearly expects that with "modernization" the public and private spheres will increasingly become clearly separated, and that politicians and businessmen will go their separate ways as their functional division of labor becomes ever better defined.

In Africa, these expectations have not been borne out. The two spheres of the public and the private—nowhere really separate—have if anything, become, in certain ways, at all levels more tightly bound together. Businessmen and politicians have not become separated by a growing division of labor, but have become instead more closely integrated for productive purposes. This does not mean simply an increase of graft and corruption or personal enrichment. *African civil servants don't just use their offices for private gain any more than a corporation officer in a private business can pocket customer payments. Those offices have come to combine an institutional governmental position and an institutional private position. The result is a new type of government entrepreneur, a new social position, not simply random, independently acting individuals.* Over time, offices of government come to embody entrepreneurial functions and powers. Anybody who sits in those offices could engage in the same types of activities and, I suspect, for logical and empirical reasons, does so. If enough government entrepreneurs act jointly and consciously for similar ends, the result would be a new form of government, although one with enormous variations from Tanzania to Zaire.[30]

Control of the political apparatus guarantees control over productive forces of society. This is not just a matter of "superstructure" controlling "substructure." The control of productive forces in advanced industrial societies as well as in modernizing *organized* societies is always accomplished through the occupation of certain strategically located offices. Sometimes they are the offices of corporations and sometimes they are the offices of government ministries. In either case, those who occupy these offices make both political and economic decisions. They can expand or contract the productive forces; they affect the life chances of millions of individuals. Old distinctions between the economic sphere and the political sphere become blurred. Especially in recent years throughout the world, in both developed and underdeveloped countries, the state has played an increasingly large role in every aspect of human activities. This role has become so large that the state is obviously more than simply a "committee of the ruling class." The state plays an independent role in originating policy which cannot be ignored.[31]

All of the new theorists of the growing power of the state, despite their differences, agree at a minimum that the state plays primarily a *political* role, that in addition to advancing its own interests it intervenes in the economy on behalf of other, economic, fractions of the dominant classes. As a starting point for further research, however, I would turn a different face to the study of power. I will begin with the assumption that the postcolonial state plays a dominant economic role in expanding the forces of production and is defined in terms of its relationship not only to the bureaucratic or political apparatus, but in terms of its relationship to the forces of production, distribution, and exchange as well. I differ with Warren, Syzmanski, and other neo-Marxist postdependency modernization theorists[32] in that I believe that African states are not evolving along the lines Marx predicted in the *Communist Manifesto* or his essay on India. Capitalism by itself does not produce cheap commodities which batter down Chinese walls and reorganize entire societies. The situation of contemporary African states, I believe, is different because although the business bourgeoisie can be important, it is not simply the "bourgeoisie" but the *state bourgeoisie* and the *organizational bourgeoisie* who have introduced historically new uses of the state for purposes of economic expansion. The organizational bourgeoisie differs from the classical bourgeoisie described by Marx because they are *in* state office and *in* political power and they do not simply use the state and politicians as their allies or instruments. Thus, for example, the *state* manages foreign corporations; that is, the *state* controls the terms of their activities, attracts capital, and puts multinational corporations to productive use. Members of the organizational bourgeoisie might demand their personal percentage, but they do further the process of industrialization.[33]

## CONTRAST BETWEEN THE POSTINDEPENDENCE MODE OF PRODUCTION AND THE NEW STATE, AND THE COLONIAL MODE OF PRODUCTION AND THE COLONIAL STATE

To comprehend fully the difference between the African organizational bourgeoisie and its antecedents, consider, for example, the difference between officeholders in the new state and officeholders in the colonial state structures.

In the 1950s and 1960s the prevalent social science image of independence portrayed Africans as simply taking over the roles and stepping into the shoes of the colonialists. Western liberals and Africans alike celebrated this assumption of power as long overdue. African leaders, the Thomas Jeffersons and George Washingtons of their countries, presumably would advance the cause of parliamentary democracy as well as of economic development. They would "develop" their nations to become like "us," the United States and other Western industrialized states. Those expectations were not fulfilled, in large measure because the original set of assumptions about the nature of power in African societies was false.

In the colonial state, governing officials were civil servants; that is, they were paid salaries by "somebody else." The colonial state itself served "somebody else's" interest, for example, that of the English ruling class. In England, the big business bourgeoisie dominated the economic sector; the government acted "responsibly" as a political agency, the colonial state performed primarily a political role. When the colonial state played an economic role, it did so at the behest of someone else, usually for English overseas interests, sometimes for indigenous economic interests (such as building roads in Ghana for cocoa farmers). The point is that the colonial state did not, for the most part or primarily, *originate* economic activity. The colonial state played a major role in African class formation. For example, taxation policies of the state forced proletarianization because Africans had to turn to wage labor in order to get money to pay taxes. However, the taxation policies and the creation of a labor force served the interests of European capital and capitalists who *used* the state for their economic purposes. In the same way, the state used economic interests for its *political* purposes, that is, the state was never simply an instrument of economic dominant classes but had its distinct and special purposes, even if as mundane as guaranteeing their own salaries and pensions.

The officers of the colonial state were not only salaried employees; paid by the metropolitan governments, they were temporary. They served for a term, as did elected officials. This is a major difference between colonial and African postcolonial states. Some theorists contend that the new states are weak, with limited powers in terms of their grandiose sets of objectives. However, African officials, in comparison with their colonial predecessors, and in terms of other Africans, are far more powerful in the sense that they are not removable from office; or, to put the point more precisely, they can be turned out only with the greatest difficulty. Even those governments which are responsive to public concerns are not necessarily *responsible* to a constituency with the power to turn them out.

Above all, African postcolonial states, in contrast to preindependence re- gimes, take the lead in organizing the forces of production. They organize markets through a generalized control over labor and capital, but, more spe- cifically, they organize the labor process, that is, engage in actual production. The organizational bourgeoisie acts as an economic class in its role as manager, sometimes as the owner, of the basic means of production, distribution, and exchange. This ruling class uses its position of control over the economy, and not just its political power, moreover, first to control wage labor and, second, to siphon off surplus. The organizational bourgeoisie siphons off surpluses through a vast variety of mechanisms including salaries and bonuses; perquisites of office including cars, houses, clothing, food, servants, education, vacations, foreign travel and expenses abroad, medical care, etc., for wives, children, relatives, cronies, and dependents; goverment loans, including the use of gov- ernment monies of the general treasury as well as those of special agencies such as marketing boards; graft and corruption; and positions on the boards of private and government corporations through their own businesses or through partnership in the businesses of others.[34]

## CLASS ANALYSIS AND DEPENDENCY THEORY

Unlike the alleged "new class" of Eastern bloc countries, the organizational bourgeoisie does not simply rest upon the political and bureaucratic mecha- nisms of coercion, or upon formal offices.[35] Its power may be based, or can come to rest, upon control over the forces of production, which ultimately means its control over the organization of wage labor and marketing. Even if, for example, the organizational bourgeoisie does not own land—and frequently it does—it can nevertheless control agricultural production and therefore a large percentage of the surplus production of the entire economy through its ability to manipulate and control marketing boards, exchange rates, import licensing, food policy, government subsidies, etc.[36] Also, unlike the dominant classes in Communist countries, component elements of the organizational bourgeoisie do engage in exchange relations with the open and avowed intent of making profits.

The capitalist state in the West has always had a role in labor control, in accumulation, in repression, and in the regulation of enterprise when capitalist entrepreneurs could not agree on essential matters of self-discipline. Some might argue that the extent to which these roles became *apparent* varied depending on historical conditions, and that only the transparency of state interventionism distinguishes African countries from those in the West; that the basic functions of the state have not changed, nor become larger, nor do they differ in any real way in Africa and the West. Yet the nature of the state in Africa has certainly changed fundamentally since the colonial era.

Within the first two decades after the end of the Second World War, African states enormously expanded the scope and size of their activities and the number of bureaucratic employees. As I argued in *Power and Class in Africa,* three major developments forced this new growth and range of involvements: (1) "Africanization" as the result of progress towards independence; (2) the expansion of governmental activities in response to the rising demands of an expanded "politically relevant" population; and (3) an extension of the bureaucracy into rural areas and to other previously deprived and exploited social groups.

At the time of Africa's "nationalist movement," every regime, no matter how conservative, seemed bound to do something, if not about the misery of the mass of the population then at least about the fact that fewer and fewer people seemed willing to accept their "historical lot" and threatened to rise in rebellion. However, predictions of progressive policies did not in most cases turn out to be true. Organizations and bureaucracies designed in the interest of the poor serviced only the technicians and civil servants. These new organizations did, however, strengthen the state; they buttressed, reinforced, and institutionalized the power of the organizational bourgeoisie. They co-opted the most vocal critics and expanded the intermediary layers of well-paid class allies into the cities, towns, and villages.

The state fraction of the organizational bourgeoisie depended on its allies in these expanded bureaucracies, among other reasons, because of the relative weakness of an indigenous business bourgeoisie. The absence or dearth of African business has always been vastly exaggerated. However, in modern times the nation-state, like the church and the corporation in previous eras, is the organizational embodiment, the modal form, of the greatest potential of concentrated power.

Colonialism strengthened the "natural" rise of state power through policies that inhibited the development of competitive African commerce, and that tamed "antagonistic" traditional authorities. When Africans captured the colonial heights of power, they overlooked a plain empty of serious adversaries.

Although Western governments engage, or appear to engage, in "business' or in the encouragement of business in ways that seem similar to actions of African governments, the context, history, size, and significance of the relative institutions produce qualitative differences in policy outcomes, in the nature of the relationships between business and state, and in the ultimate nature of the respective dominant classes. American governments, for example, *can* help business in an enormous variety of ways, from the Small Business Administration to the Taft-Hartley Law. However, Western governments in no way threaten to incorporate, overwhelm, overthrow, outsell, outproduce, or in any way dominate business as a distinctive and separate entity.

Contemporary international forces, in addition to colonialism, have helped shape the distinctive nature of the organizational bourgeoisie. The last group of developing nations, the African states, emerged into independence at another distinctive conjuncture of national and international forces. Today, for example, is not only the age of the nation-state, it is also the age of the transnational corporation (TNC). The TNC is an organizational factor of such size and power and of such control over markets and technology that the state is the only institution in Third World countries which can stand up to it or negotiate with it. This fact alone would guarantee a qualitatively unique role for African states in both the domestic and international marketplace. Even at their friendliest, the TNCs need negotiating partners of comparable capacity; the state alone in Africa can meet this challenge.

Earnest Wilson, in his study of public enterprises in Africa, tells us that the scope of African public enterprise activity is the highest in the world: Africa "tops the charts" in all areas of state economic intervention; Africa, of all the developing areas, had by far the greatest percentage of the commercial work force employed by public enterprises; and, in terms of capital accumulation allocation, Africa differed from the rest of the Third World in the huge role of the state.[37]

Here also is where the limited truths of "dependency"[38] and "world systems" theories are relevant.[39] Capital, technology, and the marketing arrangements of transnational corporations directly affect productivity and the distribution of surplus production of African countries. World systems and dependency theorists have shown how the apparent autonomy of the market and of economic systems in a world of seemingly autonomous and independent nation-states leads in fact to an increasingly interdependent capitalist world economic system.[40]

Marxist critics of dependency theory[41] have, however, voiced two objections which should be considered most seriously: first, that dependency theory does not adequately take into account class and class conflict;[42] second, that capitalism is in fact a progressive force throughout the world, as Marx had originally indicated, and not the primarily regressive force that leads to the "development of underdevelopment."[43]

My own feeling is that it is necessary first to distinguish between different types of Third World countries and, second, between different historical periods for each of the countries. Peter Evans, in his path-breaking book *Dependent Development,* has suggested the evolution of some major Third World countries like Brazil and Nigeria into "sub-imperial centers," able to use the surplus value of their less fortunate neighbors for their own advancement. Evans feels that even though countries such as Brazil can succeed in achieving substantial economic growth, economic development in the sense of a widespread sharing of those benefits, that is, an improving mass standard of living, will not be possible.[44] My reading of the currently available social science literature is that both economic growth and economic development are possible for some countries for some of the time. All countries may have gone through a "dependency" stage at some time in their development. Some countries may remain in a condition of "dependency" forever. The historical evidence seems to demonstrate that not only did some once dependent countries grow out of their dependency and become full partners with their previous economic masters, but some seem to have themselves become dominant centers. We need a great deal more empirical work to establish the truth of these competing generalizations. However, the importance of class and class conflict and the growing importance of state-aided African capitalism seem clear.

## INDIGENIZATION AND OTHER MEASURES OF AND FOR THE ORGANIZATIONAL BOURGEOISIE

"Indigenization" is one common label given to African state efforts to reduce dependence on external forces, or at least to gain the most favorable terms of participation for a significant minority of their leading nationals. African governments have designed public policies to achieve "citizen ownership" or "local equity participation" in formerly foreign-controlled enterprises. According to K. A. Owusu-Ansah, various African states have exercised the following options:

> (1) outright nationalization, whereby the state by legislation, either confiscates, seizes, or compulsorily controls certain foreign enterprises; (2) establishment of state economic organizations to complement and/or compete with or oust alien enterprise; (3) discriminatory administrative practices, such as import control through import licensing, immigration control though a quota system, *exchange* control through allocation of foreign exchange, and credit control; and (4) the direct transfer of ownership to citizens as well as the local equity participation in alien enterprises.[45]

All of these measures have expanded the role of the governmental entrepreneur, productive enterprises undertaken by the state, and the admixture of government and business.

Through the trauma of "Zairianization," Zaire's version of indigenization, Crawford Young and Thomas Turner tell us, "the class character" of Mobutu's state became "fully manifest."[46] The Zairian state undertook to develop the industrial and energy potential of Kinshasa and Bas-Zaire; to expand the mineral output of the Shaba copperbelt; and to encourage agriculturally based industries in Kisangani. Mobutu in fact fulfilled his pledges to produce the first steel in Zaire and to develop the Inga hydroelectric site in Bas-Zaire. The Zairianization measures of November 30, 1973, placed most commerce and all foreign-owned plantations in the hands of Zairians; this was an enormous windfall. The state converted an enormous array of private enterprises into "public goods." The top political leaders took over the most lucrative business.

The most fundamental contradiction of the November 30 measures, Young and Turner tell us, was the

> conflict between the public and private interests of the top cadres. The state assumed the responsibility for administering the process of confiscation and the distribution of the assets, ostensibly as guardians of the interests of society as a whole. The prime beneficiaries, members of the ruling political class, were expected to use their public capacities to maximize their private gains and at the same time to police the operation so that it truly benefited the entire populace. The unfolding of these measures, more than any other event, dramatized to civil society the moral vacuum in which the state operated.[47]

Young and Turner's analysis in a way misses the point, for Zairianization demonstrates the intermingling, at this stage of Zaire's development, of the public and the private. This unity of the state and business (private) bourgeoisie goes beyond "patrimonial linkages" or a system of "personal rule."[48] Young and Turner come closer to the mark when they point to the "rapidly congealing politico-commercial Zairian bourgeoisie."[49] Access to state power "opened the doors to accumulation" for some elements of the commercial bourgeoisie and enabled others vastly to expand their economic enterprises.[50]

"Power," state power, might indeed have been "the constitutive field for emergent class relations"[51] for significant fractions of the bourgeoisie in many, if not all, African countries. As Fernand Braudel has pointed out: "of the various social hierarchies—the hierarchies of wealth, of state power or of culture, that oppose yet support each other—which is the most important? The answer as we have already seen, is that it may depend on the time, the place and who is speaking."[52]

Braudel warns us against false assumptions that society is a simple matter, against the use of "such familiar formulae" as "an ordered society" or "a class society" without first thinking of the overall analysis such expressions imply. "It will help us," he declares, "to be on guard against facile equations such as merchants = bourgeois; or merchants = capitalists; . . . as if these words referred unequivocally to clearly defined entities, as if the borderlines between categories or classes were unmistakable, whereas such frontiers really have the fluidity of water."[53]

In Zaire, also, it is true that increasingly significant elements of the bourgeoisie have succeeded, especially in the informal sector and in the secondary cities, without the aid of the state. The difficulty of the Zairian bourgeoisie is not, as detractors of African business have alleged, that they are "lazy," "incompetent," "compradors," or, in Fanon's term, "racketeers." They are as much interested in profit making as any other historical capitalist class. They invest in urban property, taxis, trucking, and the export-import trade—enterprises which offer quick returns, as well as in production, in plantations, ranches, processing of agricultural products, and some manufacturing enterprises. The Zairian business bourgeoisie is, for good reason, above all insecure, constantly threatened by Mobutu's erratic and self-protective policies. Overseas investments offered the only long-range safety. Yet the new, politically unconnected commercial class, particularly visible in regional and secondary centers, less under the thumb of the state, consistently dismissed as non-existent or insignificant by many observers, has grown significantly.[54] And if those with high political positions entered business, it was also true that successful businessmen gained entry into politics. Young and Turner point out that few members of "the ruling class" have command over productive resources that are not tied, indirectly or directly, "to either exercise of a political role or immediate access to political influence and protection." Yet they also show that if political position can lead to economic success, those who have succeeded most brilliantly and independently in business can enter political office and are prime candidates for cooptation in the Political Bureau or other major office.[55]

Senegal offers another excellent example of the dramatic rise of an indigenous bourgeoisie and the dramatic new role of the state. "Colonial trade" dominated commerce and agriculture until independence. A few French corporations had exercised a monopoly through import offices, wholesale stores, and networks of retail depots. In 1960 the government broke this arrangement though the creation of the Office Commercialization des Arachides (Groundnut Marketing Board) and the establishment of cooperatives. Large Senegalese corporations easily filled the vacuum left by the French, for example, the Compagnie Sénégalaise du Sud-Est grew to a network of forty-eight stores and imported directly. This was also true of the Chaine Africaine d'Importation et de Distribution (CHAIDIS), the Consortium Africaine, and the enterprises of certain great *marabouts*, particularly the Mourides.[56]

As Hassatou Diallo has pointed out, "Senegalese capitalism, like all emerging capitalisms, needs state protection. Senegalese businessmen solicit this assistance, conscious of the fact that Senegalese capital is very weak."[57] The Senegalese state determined the outcome of the struggle between the new Senegalese "greats" of commerce and the former colonial corporations "traders." By 1967 the government had finished the process of nationalization of the groundnut trade, which wreaked havoc on the mainly small Senegalese traders who had acted as middlemen between the rural producers and the marketing board. However, through its control of rice imports, the country's basic foodstuff, the government allocation of quotas aided the largest Senegalese firms and almost a hundred major Senegalese traders.

Samir Amin estimates that, aided in large measure by government intervention, out of the thousands of traders in Senegal, almost fifty dominate commerce in Dakar and some sixty stand out in the large-scale general trade of the hinterland. The state also guided the creation of SIDICO, an international association of some twenty large dealers in kola nuts from the Ivory Coast, where the nuts are grown, and Senegal, where they are consumed. This broke the monopoly controlled by the Lebanese. Amin labels as "equally spectacular" the government-aided "break-through" of a dozen wholesale butchers who eliminated foreigners and created a monopoly in supplying the country's slaughterhouses. The Dakar wholesale fishmongers, similarly assisted by the state, created the same type of enterprise, as did the leading dealers in fruits and vegetables who grouped nearly 5000 large market gardeners together in a syndicate.[58]

The state in Senegal has, since independence, invested in over 135 joint stock companies, four public establishments, and four regional development companies. These corporations include the two largest enterprises in the country, ONCAD in the commercial sector and C.S. Phosphates de Taiba in mining. These companies have employed more than one-quarter of the wage earners in their respective sectors. Direct state participation has amounted to more than 40 percent of the capital of the 135 joint stock companies. The state also provided annual subsidies to meet the operating deficits of some of these companies. The state participated in the decisions of board of directors of companies through the financial involvement of state-dominated banks including the Union Sénégalaise de Banques, la Banque Nationale de Développement du Sénégal, la Société Financière Sénégalaise pour le Développement de l'Industrie et du Tourisme, etc.[59]

The Société National de Garantie et d'Assistance au Commerce (SONAGA) was a joint stock company with state majority participation linking together local banks and chambers of commerce to give grants and technical assistance to small and medium Senegalese industrial and trading businesses. The Société National d'Etudes et de Promotion Industrielle (SONEPI), a state corporation, evaluated projects, invited investors, and promoted national small-scale industry by, among other ways, making funds available on a participation and guarantee basis. The government established the Comité des Investissements Industriels to facilitate easier credit to Senegalese businessmen, to centralize feasibility studies, to coordinate decision making, and to direct and to control projects.

Finally, Senegal offered its own version of "indigenization." The purpose of the Investment Code of 1972 was to attract foreign capital and to promote the establishment and extension of "national entrepreneurs" in small- and medium-scale enterprises. The state extended tax exemption benefits, customs and fiscal privileges, and an investment program for both industrial and agricultural activities. SONEPI provided "national entrepreneurs" with management assistance and banking guarantees.

Although many of these activities parallel measures taken by Western governments, the results in Senegal were qualitatively different. Although far more modest in intent than the proposals in Zaire, government-promoted economic activity resulted in more than a doubling of Senegalese in managerial positions from 1962 to 1974. The number of Senegalese "cadres" and "experts" more than quadrupled.[60]

These examples taken from Zaire and Senegal typify a range of actions taken by Ghana, Nigeria, Kenya, the Ivory Coast, Uganda, and many other African states.[61]

## THE GROWTH OF THE STATE
## AND BUREAUCRATIC NETWORKS

The growth of the power of the postcolonial African state and its willingness to assume new economic roles, along with the growing partnership between the state and key elements in the economy, have hastened the liberation of some Third World countries from their conditions of dependency. We cannot fully understand these processes without once more considering the organizational bourgeoisie not only in terms of their aid to and alliance with indigenous business, but as part of a new mode of production including state fractions of the expanding bureaucratic networks.

Marvin Harris has vividly depicted the interrelationship between bureaucratic and political consolidation of power and the intensification of economic production. The power of the state increases through the creation of reinforcing networks:

> Once the state becomes a functional reality, its components resonate within a single gigantic amplifier. The more powerful the ruling class, the more it can intensify production, increase population, wage war, expand territory, mystify the peasants, and increase its powers still further. All neighboring chieftains must either rapidly pass across the threshold of state formation, or succumb to the triumphant armies of the new social leviathan.[62]

How and why are the component bureaucratic networks built? For further investigation we might consider the constriction of bureaucratic structures as a series of generational waves of civil servants. Broken loose from their traditional niches in society by the processes of modernization, impatient youths— strident, strong, energetic, hard to satisfy, hard to accommodate—confront a dominant class. For its own protection, the dominant class creates jobs and opportunities to buy off at least a portion of this discontented, potentially dangerous, rising petite bourgeoisie: it builds bureaucracies for them. When the next generational wave comes along, bureaucracies expand but also change in a number of subtle ways in order to accommodate the new onslaught. The older bureaucrats become more easily accommodated. Weaker, older, more isolated, more compromised by their identification with and participation in the structures of the ruling classes, the older bureaucrats are more easily retired or contained within another circle of the bureaucracy, part of the expanding net which grows to contain new potential dissenters.

"Animation Rurale" in Senegal and "Community Development"[63] in Ghana, for example, over several decades changed their mission from political activism and creation of community organizations, to providing expert technicians, neutral administrators, and professional social workers. Their ultimate purpose changed from mass organization to increase the standard of living and political activism of the rural peasantry, to the originally unintended function of providing jobs for a growing and ever more dangerous class of better-educated, technically proficient members of a rising petite bourgeoisie. Originally, those organizations were created to carry a message; ultimately, the medium *became* the message. The story of "Animation Rurale" and "Community Development" is part of the process of state formation, part of the development of loyalty to the state and of false consciousness. To the extent that organizations like "Community Development" and "Animation Rurale" are extended to the most remote areas of the nation, they serve the function of cementing elements of the organizational petite bourgeoisie of the regions into a foundation of support for the regime. Different types of states (for example, to use Crawford Young's categories, Afro-Marxist, Socialist, and Afro-Capitalist states) will use these organizational networks for different purposes, and therefore their impact on the mass of the population will vary. And this will again require further study, even though one almost certain outcome of the process will be the strengthening of the power of the state and of the organizational bourgeoisie, the dominant ruling class.[64]

If all of this is still ill defined, studies like those by Richard Jeffries, *Class, Power and Ideology in Ghana*,[65] and W. G. Clarence-Smith, *Slaves, Peasants and Capitalists in Southern Angola 1840–1926*,[66] add to our precision about the processes of class formation in Africa. We still need additional case studies for every African country to answer basic questions, such as what happened to the descendants of traditional rulers.[67] We also need more monographs like that of Andrew Beveridge and Anthony Oberschall, who have given us not only a detailed account of African businessmen in Zambia, but also analyzed the nature of their relationship with other key groups such as civil servants and politicians.[68] Above all, lest the organizational bourgeoisie, and especially its state and business fractions, appears to develop according to its own natural laws of motion, we need to understand those painful conflicts through which Africa's working classes struggled for a fair share of their own societies. We think our work in this volume helps raise important new questions for understanding problems of "Power and Class in Africa"—and we have made some limited progress.

# PART I

# Revolution and the Struggle for Independence: Capitalist Development, Class Consciousness, and the State in World Perspective

Capitalism, the sorcerer's apprentice of social change in Africa as elsewhere, conjured up whole populations out of the ground, melted the bonds between peasants and lords, scarred the countryside with railway tracks and roads, swept away sacred forest to make room for cotton and cocoa, gouged Africa's harbors for the safe berthing of ocean going vessels, fused the Demba and Nyakyusa into copper miners and the Wolof and Serer into peanut farmers, and redivided the continent on the basis of new loyalties and new appetites. In nationalistic challenges to colonial rule, Sierra Leone barristers filed legal briefs, Nigerian journalists wrote flaming editorials, Senegalese railroad workers went on strike, Gold Coast dockworkers stopped loading ships, and Gambian women boycotted imported goods. Slogans of self-determination and songs of rebellion rose from the throats of people with a new awareness of themselves as oppressed members of new classes. The conflicts were always there, but they intensified, became more visible, and took the form of public confrontations. New classes arose to confront the state, and the colonial state itself changed, affecting the evolution of African states down to the present day.

While we know all of this in a general way, relatively few serious scholars have given us both the detail necessary to explain the difficulties of people living in the real world and the theoretical abstractions we need to understand the mechanisms of social control. Beverly Grier, Martin Kilson, and Jeffrey Schulman add to our knowledge of the processes that led to independence and to the later difficulties of a more advanced stage of political development.

Beverly Grier, in "Contradiction, Crisis, and Class Conflict: The State and Capitalist Development in Ghana Prior to 1948," builds upon the work of social scientists who have dealt with "settler Africa,"[1] countries where the existence of permanent white settler communities was the single most important political variable. Based upon her study of agriculture and class formation in the Gold Coast (which she calls "peasant Africa," in contrast to "settler Africa"), she offers a new synthesis to explain the mechanism through which foreign "capitalism" underdeveloped both settler and peasant Africas. She attacks the common assumption that colonial penetration in settler Africa and in peasant Africa differed fundamentally. In so doing, she provides additional empirical materials for a general theory of capitalist development and state building.

In every country, successful European-dominated capitalism, she argues, required that the full proletarianization of African workers *not* take place. The preservation of cheap African labor and cheap raw materials necessitated "the preservation of noncapitalist relations of production" so that the poorest Africans in the subsistence sector of the economy would subsidize Western capitalist development. This analysis in part resembles that of Andre Gundar Frank, but Grier refines his categories. Consider, for example, the notion of *super exploitation*.

The most impoverished sector of the economy, by supporting the cost of raising workers and by providing for them in their old age, transfers value to the capitalist economy and directly subsidizes the dominant classes.[2] In this way, labor-intensive capitalist enterprise in Third World countries proved especially profitable in certain historical periods. Capitalists could drive wages below the cost of worker subsistence, because kin and other precapitalist social structures met the expenses of reproduction. While a great deal of debate and technical vocabulary have developed around theories of super exploitation, the basic reality is commonsensical and simple and it immediately and directly affected colonial policy.

In *Crisis: In the Third World*,[3] Frank argued that super exploitation had always existed and is on the increase. Frank's notion of super exploitation goes hand in hand with his rejection of the idea of the "dual economy," this is, the idea of the side-by-side existence of capitalism and some form of feudal or subsistence economy. From the first, Frank maintained, capitalism almost instantaneously captured the precapitalist economic form and so dominated it that it is meaningless to talk about independent noncapitalist economic forms.

Grier delimits more carefully the process of integration of precapitalist and capitalist economies, and shows how a single social formation evolved, how super exploitation was most characteristic of a *limited* period in the development of the Ghanaian state and economy. Above all, she contends, capitalist expansion required a transient African work force no matter what the form—no matter whether the mass of Africans retained control as peasant producers over their own land or whether agricultural laborers hired themselves out for European commercial farming or mining (as in South Africa). African labor could not become permanently settled, full-time wage labor because the noncapitalist relations of production which supported the subsistence needs of a large part of the African work force guaranteed both the cheap African labor and the cheap raw materials necessary for European commerce.

Thus, in Ghana the colonial state sought to stop the breakdown of the peasantry, to maintain agricultural labor "in its place," and to preserve enough of a shell of "traditional societies" so that they could continue to produce and maintain cheap labor. The resulting policies often exacerbated conflicts and produced even more "dangerous" contradictions leading to agricultural stagnation, migration to the cities, and intensified class conflict, which continue to bedevil the current Ghanaian government. To the extent that British agricultural policy succeeded in maintaining cheap labor, cheap land, and cheap prices for agricultural products, it made farming less productive and therefore less attractive; it shifted economic resources away from the countryside and into the hands of the organizational bourgeoisie.

By focusing on class as her key variable, and by examining the interaction between changing class relations and the constant evolution of the embryonic colonial state, Grier succeeds in reinterpreting Ghanaian history, a history which makes no sense without an appreciation of the precapitalist class structure of Ghanaian society. Grier outlines how Asanti dominant classes intensified "traditional" forms of the appropriation of labor power (such as slavery and pawnage) as they rushed to increase production of cash crops demanded by European firms. Simultaneously, the "historically dominated classes" sought to loosen their bonds by themselves producing for the external market. The colonial state tried first to break the chiefs whom they originally considered the keystone of "barbarism." Later, however, colonial officials changed their policies as they came to fear that "elements from the lower classes" would overthrow the chiefs and threaten chaos. With increased buying and selling of land, peasant indebtedness grew and extremes of wealth intensified as small peasants suffered the loss of their lands and wealthy farmers added to their accumulated acreage.

Historians of the Gold Coast long have puzzled over why colonial officials originally disparaged the expansion of cocoa production, the indigenous crop which generated the necessary revenues for the state apparatus. Grier rejects the prevailing explanation of Kay and others[4] that the colonials feared the emergence of an African class of capitalist producers who might challenge British commercial domination. The problem as the colonial state saw it, she believes, was not one of a European capitalist class against an African capitalist class. Rather, the state rulers feared that the rise of African capitalists on the land and in the market threatened the more rapid erosion of the *African peasantry*. A peasantry firmly anchored to the land, knowing its place and compliant in fixed village societies, and willing to turn an eye to the market but self-sufficient in food guaranteed cheap raw materials and social peace. The British wished to maintain this system of production at all costs lest they risk the political and social order of the countryside. Grier enables us to see how nevertheless, from 1900 to 1930, expanded peasant production went hand in hand with what she calls "the maturation of the colonial state."

The *abusa* sharecropper turned over at least one-third of his produce to the farm owner in return for the right to till a plot of land. No wonder constant conflict marred the countryside. In addition—and this provides essential background for an understanding of Martin Kilson's analysis—"commoners" or "young men" of unfree or poor lineage, some of whom had gained some wealth through cocoa or education, challenged the traditional ruling class of royals and other privileged lineages. Grier briefly shows how the *asafo*, a traditional association of young men, crystalized into permanent organizations furthering the interests of the lower classes and a rising petite bourgeoisie. Her account agrees with Kilson's that the demands of the *asafo* were not for an end to chieftainship, but for its "democratization" through new constitutional procedures of election and accountability.

Martin Kilson's study, "Anatomy of Class Consciousness: Agrarian Populism in Ghana," complements Grier's work with an analysis of the difficulties involved in the development of class consciousness, of "classes for themselves." In his case study of the Kwahu, a people who lived along the main road linking Accra and Kumasi during the period between the First and Second world wars, Kilson also speculates on how agrarian-linked movements in Ghana and elsewhere in Africa could result in Ayatollah-type movements such as the one which overthrew the Shah of Iran in 1979. Kilson describes populism as a reaction by the weak and the least powerful people in society to their exploitation and deprivation, embodying a burgeoning class awareness and a revolutionary potential. He explains, however, how populism can become diverted from revolution to rebellion.

To understand why revolutionary momentum becomes detoured into merely rebellious activity, and why potential class consciousness does not rise above the level of a general populist reaction, Kilson stresses the constraints of tradition and traditional religious commitments to long-established political hierarchies. The "populist dilemma," as Kilson describes it, constitutes a fundamental psychological barrier to a full recognition of class interests and full-fledged class action: the leaders and peasant masses psychologically cannot accept the abolition of fundamental religious and traditional institutions, for example, chieftaincy.

The chiefs abandoned some facets of the ancient principles of divine rule by allowing ordinary peasants to participate in the selection of local government authorities. Peasants selected their new political leaders on the basis of their perceptions of their secular and economic interests. But, by reasserting their fidelity to the customary religious obligations of their office, the chiefs continued to hold great power long beyond the point when many "modernization theorists" have expected their disintegration. Kilson contends that success in overthrowing corrupt or inept individual chiefs diverted the populace from trying to eliminate the institution of chieftaincy and the old ruling classes. Kilson thus explains the "psycho-cultural underpinning" of a ruling class which persists long after the disintegration of its economic basis, contributing to the type of understanding of the noneconomic forces of African rule that Eugene Genovese provided for the cultural and psychological basis of planter domination in the South at the time of the American Civil War.[5] Kilson helps us fill in a mosaic that will one day show us a total picture of social structures of domination.

He contends as well that African rulers seek to manipulate popular consciousness away from secularized awareness and individual self-improvement because they have been inept in creating wealth-producing skills and an ethos of productivity. Turning people's attention towards the past and nurturing "tribalism" are cynical manipulations which diminish the possibility of rapid economic growth. But recently, agrarian masses have joined with members of the petite bourgeoisie, trade unions, and junior-rank military officers who have shared grievances against this type of domination. Kilson concludes by arguing that something akin to this combination of social classes characterized the 1979 coup d'etat in Ghana led by Flight Captain Jerry Rawlings, as well as the coup d'etat in Liberia led by Master Sergeant Samuel Doe.

He predicts that, to the extent that Samuel Doe and Jerry Rawlings are not successful, the next stage of political development might very well be a turn towards African versions of Ayatollah-led movements seeking the reimposition of traditional types of controls over modern processes. The net result would be both an advance and a negation of agrarian class consciousness. Even an "Ayatollah" leadership would at first encourage peasant consciousness to overthrow the organizational bourgeoisie. When successful, however, it would naturally reassert the dominance of religious and communal constraints as the basis of its political authority. Manipulating the popular consciousness, however, is a dangerous game, for it can create a "progressive" revolutionary potential.

Jeffrey Schulman, in "Wars of Liberation in the International System: Western Sahara—a Case in Point," analyzes a very different dimension of the struggle for independence. His essay informs us that international factors always impinge on the emergence of national liberation movements. Schulman spells out the ways in which the Polisario Front in the Western Sahara systematically sought legitimacy at the international level. Above all, according to Schulman, the revolutionaries sought to establish a state within a state to meet the real needs of their potential constituency before fomal independence. Little by little, the revolutionaries destroyed the competing organization of the dominant state. They sought to demonstrate that the old regime could not meet its basic responsibilities or carry out its routine duties, and that the revolutionaries offered alternative institutional arrangements of demonstrated capacity and growing effectiveness. The Polisario also tried to outmaneuver the Moroccan state on the international level. On February 27, 1976, when Spain surrendered Spanish Sahara to Morocco and Mauritania, the Polisario announced the creation of the Saharan Arab Democratic Republic and launched an intense diplomatic effort to gain recognition. By gaining legitimacy, it could use the norms as well as the organizations of "international systems" to exert pressure on Morocco for concessions and ultimately end the hostilities. The Polisario sought to present the conflict with Morocco as one between two equal national systems, rather than an illegitimate domestic rebellion confronting state authority. International pressure would help overcome the military weaknesses by bringing an added political dimension to the conflict. Schulman argues that the tactics of the Polisario were akin to those used by the FLN in Algeria against France and the Haganah in Israel against Great Britain. Once the liberation party succeeds in gaining international recognition as a state, it can turn to international organizations such as the Organization of African Unity for support. It can also demand the invocation of multilateral treaties which limit hostilities and regulate the conduct between states. The embattled state is denied the protection of the assertion of sovereignty and claim of the right of nonintervention by the other nations in domestic affairs. The Polisario Front's most dramatic success on the diplomatic front, in addition to gaining full admission for the Saharan Arab Democratic Republic as a full member of the OAU, was the decision by the Organization of African Unity and the United Nations to demand that Morocco hold a referendum in the Western Sahara.

Although Schulman does not analyze the class basis of the Polisario, he does show how, during the stage of nationalist political development, those liberation parties that can achieve a unified purpose and comprehensive support can project the right of self-determination into the international arena. Schulman shows how and why the Polisario, like other nationalist movements, insisted on at least temporarily deemphasizing the importance of class in order better to combat a common enemy.

Schulman, who spent months touring the Western Sahara and interviewing military commanders responsible for different regions of the territory, writes as a partisan of the Polisario. Even so, the Moroccan and Mauritanian assertions at the time that their Saharan "kin" welcomed the annexations were clearly dubious. Since 1976, the divergence between these assertions and reality has widened, international support for Morocco has decreased, and Schulman's case that the Polisario engaged in a defensive war against "colonial" conquest appears increasingly convincing.

Morocco has asserted its claim to the Western Sahara on the grounds of precolonial ethnic ties. African leaders have feared that legitimizing claims such as these would threaten their own historical integrity and sovereign dominance. Overlapping ethnic communities exist everywhere in Africa. If Morocco's claim were upheld, Mauritania could claim parts of Senegal; Nigeria, parts of Niger, etc. Schulman's analysis, therefore, not only helps us to understand the international factors involved in the struggle for independence, but leads us as well to a further consideration of some of the difficulties involved in the consolidation of power in the postindependence period.

# CHAPTER 1

# Contradiction, Crisis, and Class Conflict: The State and Capitalist Development in Ghana Prior to 1948

**Beverly Grier**

The purpose of this essay is to use the historical experience of Ghana to begin to build upon a more general theoretical approach to the study of capitalist development and the state in peasant Africa. The theoretical literature and empirical research linking capitalist development in peasant Africa with the development of the state lags far behind similar kinds of thinking and research on settler Africa.[1] Yet this linkage, fully explored, is key to understanding the current agricultural and political crises in those countries in which the mass of Africans retained control of the bulk of the land and, as peasant producers, formed the base upon which metropolitan accumulation took place. The general assumption is that the historical experience of peasant and settler forms of colonial penetration had very little in common and that the tools developed for the analysis of one are of very little relevance for the analysis of the other. While differences were (and continue to be) profound, the similarities were so significant as to make the study of historical change in one most illuminating to the study of historical change in the other.

Perhaps the most fundamental of these similarities was that no matter which form capitalist penetration took—the expansion of peasant agricultural production for export or internal sale, as in colonial Ghana, the use of African labor in European commercial farming or mining, as in South Africa, or both, as in colonial Kenya and Zimbabwe—it was essential that the full proletarianization of the African population, either by European capitalists or by an emerging bourgeoisie of African farmers, not take place. The acquisition of cheap raw materials produced by Africans and the acquisition of cheap African labor for use in the European sector required that part of the subsistence needs of the African population be met by the preservation or creation of "noncapitalist" relations of production. The form and function of the colonial state were shaped in large part by these requirements and by the response of the African population for whom the new context meant intensified economic and political hardship.

The needs of capital, on the one hand, and the actions of capital, on the other, were very much in opposition. This opposition or contradiction constituted the dynamic that, in turn, shaped the apparatus of the colonial state.[2] In colonial Ghana, it was to the advantage of metropolitan capital that the bulk of the African population remain wedded to "traditional" forms of economic, social, and political organization. Cocoa could be produced much more cheaply if it was based on the use of nonalienable family or lineage land and on the use of family or other forms of unpaid or cheap labor. Labor for the mines and for the development and maintainance of the state's physical infrastructure could be obtained much more cheaply if it took the form of seasonal or long-term migrant labor from the colony and surrounding territories. However, with respect to the cocoa-dominated south of the colony, there was a tendency for the forces that were responsible for the emergence of a cash-cropping peasantry to be responsible simultaneously for the erosion of that peasantry. Political unrest, in the form of local class conflict and anticolonial sentiments, was the usual consequence. The task of the colonial state was to find ways of blocking or retarding the disintegration of the peasantry and shape or reshape rural social relations in ways that were advantageous to metropolitan capital. What very often happened instead was the exacerbation of the very social and political tensions and contradictions that policy aimed at containing or eliminating and/ or the emergence of new and potentially more dangerous tensions and contradictions. The result for Ghana, long before independence, was an ever deepening crisis involving agricultural stagnation, rural depopulation, and intensified local and national social and political conflict.

The focus of this study is on the colonial period prior to the 1948 riots most often associated in the literature with the earliest phase of mass nationalism in Ghana. We have identified three major subperiods that coincide with fairly distinct phases in the development of the capitalist mode of production in the colony and with the development of the colonial state's administrative, legal, coercive, and ideological apparatus. The first subperiod began in the first half of the nineteenth century and lasted until about 1900–1910. During this time, many aspects of the preexisting precapitalist lineage mode of production that dominated social relations in southern Ghana underwent considerable disintegration as opportunities for the export of slaves declined, as the demand and price in Europe for African agricultural exports rose, and as the Industrial Revolution of the previous century made possible greater quantities of basic consumer items at prices that were actually falling. Many of the older forms of appropriation of labor power, such as slavery and pawnage, were simultaneously intensified and weakened as the historically privileged sought to take advantage of the external market for agricultural products by increasing the amounts of land and labor they exploited and while the historically dominated classes sought to free themselves or, at least, to loosen the bonds, by producing for the external market as well. Increasing amounts of land and labor went over to producing, first the oil palm tree, followed briefly by the collection of wild rubber (in Ashanti) and the cultivation of coffee, and, finally, the cultivation of cocoa. Land rapidly became a commodity in southernmost Ghana, bought and sold freely and held by individuals rather than by lineage-based groups. What we call the "infant" or "embryonic" colonial state was instrumental in the disintegration of preexisting forms of relations, largely through its policy of breaking the backs of the chiefs and through its tendency, in the colonial courts, to reinforce the changes in land tenure relations and inheritance already taking place at the level of social reality. By 1900, however, colonial officials were beginning to look on with fear at the "chaos" of politics and society in the rural districts of the south. They saw the power of both large and small chiefs being overturned and replaced daily by elements from the lower classes. There were also signs of land loss and growing peasant indebtedness.

The British experience in India had taught officials much about the effects of pauperization of the peasantry and its transformation into a rural proletariat. They were determined that the same would not occur in British West Africa. In addition, as the twentieth century progressed, many officials were becoming convinced of the twin economic advantages of colonial exploitation based on expanded peasant production rather than large-scale European agriculture: cheap raw materials and a market for European manufactured goods. The present century and our second subperiod, therefore, opened with the growing predominance of a radically different view of the chiefs and of a noncapitalist order in general. But since so much of the latter was unsuitable or had already been eroded, it had to undergo a process of redefinition and re-creation. The cornerstone of this process was indirect rule, which included new regulations governing land tenure relations as well as new forms of political control over the lower classes. The reformation of the state's structure was consolidated with the Guggisberg Native Administrative reforms of the 1920s.

Our third and final subperiod began about 1930, when the effects of the Great Depression began to make themselves felt in Ghana. It lasted until early 1948, when several large cities and towns in the colony were rocked by serious rioting. As in South Africa, Kenya, and elsewhere, however, it is important to see this postwar political unrest as the culmination or climax to a long period of unrest whose source was rural but whose effects were beginning to spill over into the major towns during the 1930s. The unrest of the 1930s, which took the form of an intensified rural conflict, migration to the cities and towns, and labor unrest, was linked directly to previous attempts to structure or restructure rural social and political relations through indirect rule. In the state's attempt to maintain the small cash-cropping peasantry as the predominant rural social group, agricultural stagnation, growing rural poverty, rural depopulation (semi-proletarianization), and urban unemployment confronted the colonial state as the war drew to a close. The way in which the state sought to resolve this new crisis was through the co-optation of the most vocal and potentially the most political dangerous of the lower-class elements—the rising rural petite bourgeoisie that had been in the forefront of the political unrest of the 1930s. The expansion of the state sector, to soak up the unemployed, had the effect of linking the interests of this class with the interest of the metropole as well as of creating the need for greater and greater state revenues. The appropriation of cocoa surpluses by way of the cocoa marketing board system (introduced in 1939) could only take place if the peasantry remained wedded to a particular set of social relations in agriculture. The untransformed nature of agriculture after independence (either in an orthodox capitalist or socialist direction) has meant an intensification of the very problems that confronted colonial officials in the period immediately before self-government and independence.

## DISINTEGRATION OF PRECAPITALIST SOCIETY IN NINETEENTH-CENTURY GHANA

Two modes of production combined to give shape to the social formation of early-nineteenth-century southern Ghana: the dominant lineage mode and the subordinate slave mode. So intimately connected were these two modes of production and forms of labor exploitation that the existence and reproduction of one cannot be explained without reference to the other.[3]

At the village level, society was organized on the basis of matrilineages or patrilineages, extended family groupings that traced their origins (theoretically) to a common ancestor. Each lineage, along with its constituent family groupings, claimed rights to a definite parcel of land which it used for subsistence crop production on a rotation or long fallow basis.[4] A certain amount of reserve land was set aside to accommodate the expansion of the lineage by natural or other increase. A head or elder presided over each lineage. In consultation with lineage elders and members, he held all lineage lands in trust and made decisions about the disposal of the reserve lands. Lineage membership entitled one to clear and cultivate as much land as one's resources allowed, a system that favored those with control over the labor of others, such as women, youths, slaves, and pawns. As long as this new land was used on a routine basis, it was considered family land and devolved according to customary rules of inheritance; if not, it reverted to the category of lineage reserve land. While the fruits of the land belonged to the individual or family that cultivated them, the land itself was conceived of as belonging to the lineage as a whole. Land, however, could be permanently alienated. The customary ceremony giving legal effect to sales was known as "cutting the *guaha*" or *foyibah*, and it required the prior permission of family or lineage members.[5] The occasions for such outright sales were somewhat rare: land was sold or given away permanently to political exiles, refugees fleeing war or famine, and stranger traders. The entrenchment in customary Akan and Ga-Adangbe law of provisions for outright sales goes a long way toward explaining the ease with which Krobo and other migrant farmers were able to acquire land from Akim chiefs for the expansion of oil palm cultivation in the first half of the nineteenth century.

A number of parcels of land and the lineages to which the land belonged constituted a village over which a chief presided. The chief, usually head of one of the constituent lineages of the village, along with the other heads made up the council of elders that managed the "stool" or reserve lands of the village as a whole, as distinct from lineage reserve lands. The chief and his elders were not the owners of stool lands, merely the trustees. Nor could they claim ownership of or make decisions about lineage lands even though they could demand the political allegiance of members of all lineages in the village.[6] In addition to holding in trust stool lands, the chief and his elders adjudicated disputes between villagers and had the power to impose fines and prison sentences on persons who violated customary law. There were constitutional ways in which chiefs could be deposed ("destooled") and, according to Ivor Wilks, these were increasingly taken advantage of in the second half of the nineteenth century in Ashanti by the lower classes of poor but free-born males, pawns, and descendants of slaves.[7]

Perhaps as much as fifty percent of the population at the village level were free-born persons engaged in subsistence production and in the production of homemade handicrafts for local consumption and for short- and long-distance trade. A substantial proportion of the population was not free but was subject to a variety of forms of bondage or dependence. Slaves captured in wars or raids or received as tribute were subjected to the greatest exploitation and received the least amount of protection under customary law. However, slaves could marry, purchase their freedom, and trade on their own account. Most captives were attached in small or large numbers to village households where they performed labor and received subsistence, shelter, and clothing from their masters. Within a generation or two, they were absorbed theoretically into their master's lineage. Captives and their descendants might be given a plot of land by their master on which to cultivate subsistence crops. In some cases, a portion (one-third) of the crop and continued labor services were required of them. The plot of land so granted devolved to the captive's descendants according to customary law, but the rights and privileges attached were not equal to the rights and privileges of the free-born. Connected to wealthy households were large numbers of slaves, so many that separate villages, inhabited entirely by slaves, were established on reserve lineage or stool land. These slaves and their descendants farmed for themselves or for their masters. Their status, as that of individual captives, remained a subordinate one even if they were absorbed into their masters' lineage and took his name.

It was estimated by two nineteenth-century European travelers that persons in some form of bondage or servitude formed between two-thirds and three-quarters of the population of southern Ghana.[8] These are accurate only if they included, in addition to captives or slaves of foreign origin, slaves of local origin. Lower-class but free-born persons or families that fell into debt or incurred heavy fines imposed by the chief might "pawn" a family member to a creditor in order to secure a loan. If the family fell onto even harder times, the pawn might be sold into outright slavery with the understanding that he or she could be redeemed if the money could be found. Pawns enjoyed some legal protections that slaves did not, but their labor was appropriated by the creditor just the same to meet interest payments.[9]

Control over the labor power of others was fundamental to the accumulation of wealth and to the concentration of political power in rural southern Ghana. It was a source of social tension and conflict in the precolonial era and it would become a source of heightened tension and conflict in the era of expanded oil palm and cocoa production. Chiefs, heads of important lineages, traders, and elders in general were well positioned to exploit the labor power of others (women, youths, pawns, and slaves) and to concentrate the benefits of the newly emerging economy in their hands.

Beginning in the 1830s, many Krobo began a westward move in search of virgin land on which to plant oil palm trees.[10] Palm oil, which was used as a lubricant for machinery and as a base for soap and candles, was in great demand in Europe. The Krobo purchased land outright from chiefs in eastern Akim and northern Akwakpim, paying in installments or lump sums. They were joined later by Akwapim, Shai, Ga, and Fanti farmers in search of agricultural export opportunities.

By the 1860s, the twin processes of commercialization of lineage and stool lands and individualization of purchased or allotted holdings were well under way both in the migrants' home areas and in the areas to which they migrated.[11] Individual cultivators, both in the homelands and in the purchased areas, pressed for secure individual rights over land now planted with permanent tree crops with economic value. They wanted to be able to mortgage and sell their holdings as well even though they were fought at every turn by fellow lineage members in whose interest it was to reinforce the corporate nature of land ownership and disposition. Indebtedness and land loss, however, went hand in hand with commercial agricultural expansion for a number of reasons. The land itself might have been purchased with borrowed funds that could not be repaid in time. Market prices fluctuated wildly in this era and export routes to the coast were not always secure. Moreover, after the 1874 British orders abolishing slave trading, slavery, and pawning, farms under an economically valuable crop or land that was suitable for cash crop cultivation began to replace the pawn as security for loans.[12]

Two aspects of the expansion of agricultural production for export are worth noting before proceeding. First, this expansion was encouraged by the declining prices and increasing volume of European manufactured goods over the century.[13] The cheapness of European manufactured textiles, brass and copper goods, hardware, cutlery, and iron and steel undermined the self-sufficiency of African communities with respect to the most basic household items.[14] Second, for the first time thousands of small producers and collectors were able to participate directly in overseas trade, the trans-Atlantic trade having been the monopoly of the military aristocracies of the participating states.[15] Oil palms, for example, grew wild in the forests of southern Ghana, so that persons of all social classes could collect the wild produce and sell it as their own. With an income or a potential income, the poorer and middle classes had an alternative to pawning relatives when they fell into debt or when they were fined by the chief. The largest gains, however, were made not by the collectors but by those who could clear virgin forests and plant acreages with oil palm trees and by those who bought up the produce of others and transported it to trading stations. Both deliberate cultivation and trading in produce could be carried out on a large scale only by the wealthy, that is, by those who had control over large amounts of unfree or dependent labor. When the external demand for slaves declined in the nineteenth century, the internal demand actually picked up, a partial explanation for the large proportions of the population reported by European travelers to be in one form or another of servitude.[16] In nineteenth-century southern Ghana, a very small proportion of the total population controlled the bulk of the palm oil that was produced and exported. Thus, on the one hand, expanded overseas trade opened opportunities for the lower classes, affording many a cash income. On the other hand, however, many of the old forms of exploitation of labor were intensified. By the time of the cocoa boom, which involved far more people and at higher stakes, the stage was set for an intensified class conflict in the rural areas and in the towns of southern Ghana.

We refer to the colonial state apparatus as "infant" or "embryonic" during this subperiod because official views of the shape social relations should take had not yet crystallized. Prior to 1900 or so, there were many officials who believed that the backs of the chiefs should be broken because they were the key agents in slavery, slave trading, and pawning. According to this view, the growth of an independent and prosperous peasantry governed by forms and procedures of English law should be encouraged. There were others who believed that, while these goals might be desirable, they were not feasible at the present time. There were not the financial or human resources to staff every district with a white officer, and the sudden abolition of slavery and pawning might result in widespread economic, social, and political chaos.[17] Still others believed that the proper form of rule was through the indigenous chiefs, "the most respectable persons in the community and 'the expression of the native mind in favour of social order and rights of property.' "[18] While each viewpoint found expression at the legislative, administrative, and judicial levels of the state, the overall impact of the British presence in this subperiod was such that the decline of the precapitalist order was greatly reinforced. Thus, the first, or precapitalist, viewpoint tended to predominate on the whole before 1900. It was said that even before the middle of the nineteenth century people in and around the coastal fort settlements were flocking to the British courts to seek relief from the judicial hand of cruel and unfair chiefs and that the majority of customary courts in these areas had fallen into disuse except for matters of little importance.[19] Slavery and pawning were ignored very often, but, at the same time, there was a tendency for English law and rules of evidence and procedures to prevail in matters involving property, debt, and murder.

A series of orders and ordinances passed between 1874 (the year in which the area to the south of Ashanti became the Crown Colony of the Gold Coast) and 1900 intensified and gave wider expression to early destructive tendencies. It is important to keep in mind that this was precisely the geographical area in which significant economic and social changes associated with the expansion of commodity production for export were taking place. During this subperiod, much of the power of the chiefs was destroyed and/or appropriated by colonial officials and by the colonial courts and the initial process of redefinition of customary law got underway. By the turn of the century, it would have been impossible to conceive of a dual legal system in which customary law and English law coexisted side by side, each with its separate sphere of operations. Expressing in the legal arena the articulation of three modes of production (the two indigenous modes and the capitalist mode), the two forms of law were by this time intimately intertwined. This can best be illustrated by looking at land tenure law.

The West African Lands Committee (WALC), which sat from 1912 to 1915, found that by the early 1870s the judicial assessor had begun to sanction the practice of land sales, holding that the chief or head of the family could sell stool or family land provided the consent of the requisite parties was obtained.[20] The Supreme Court Ordinance of 1876 lent further weight to this practice. The practice was growing rapidly whereby the parties involved not only performed the customary ceremony for selling land but signed papers (which they believed to be legal documents of title) to affect land sales. In the case of a grant of land by a chief to a stool subject, the courts also acted in a way that reinforced the erosion of the precapitalist order. The decision that gave greatest expression to this was made in 1907 under Chief Justice Brandford Griffith. In the case of *Lokko* v. *Konklofi*, Konklofi used as security for a loan from Lokko a piece of land that had been granted by the stool to his father some forty years prior. The farm contained some palm trees, sugar cane, and some recently planted cocoa trees. When Konklofi defaulted on the loan, Lokko took out a writ of *fi. fa.* and Konklofi's hamlet and his farms were attached in execution. The chief put in an interpleader claiming that stool land could not be seized in execution of debts incurred by stool subjects. Brandford Griffith, however, held that the occupation had been of such continuance and of such character that the land must now be deemed to be the individual property of Konklofi and therefore seizable in execution. In other words, when it came to the question of stool land under permanent cultivation for a certain duration, such land ceased to fall into the sphere of stool land and became the individual *and* alienable property of the stool subject and grantee of the land. Family and lineage land continued to receive some protection from conversion to individual property by the Supreme Court Ordinance (the permission of certain parties had to be obtained), but, given the pressures at the time on land for cocoa cultivation, it was only a matter of time before these would undergo erosion.

## EXPANDED PEASANT PRODUCTION AND THE MATURATION OF THE COLONIAL STATE: 1900–1930

The changes that emerged only in embryonic form during the nineteenth-century expansion of oil palm cultivation were consolidated and elaborated upon with the expansion of cocoa cultivation. As is well known, in 1891 the colony exported only 80 pounds of raw cocoa beans; by 1930, exports had reached more than 200,000 tons, making the Gold Coast the leading world producer with a market share of more than 40 percent. The 1930 Census estimated that some 300,000 persons were engaged in the production and sale of cocoa in the colony. Directly and indirectly, the export of cocoa provided the bulk of the state's revenue and paid for the rapidly rising volume of imported goods, mostly British in origin.

It is surprising, then, to find that the attitude of officials throughout the colonial period was at best ambivalent and very often contemptuous and disparaging of nearly everything associated with the expansion of cocoa production.[21] Indeed, as Geoffrey Kay argues, the state faced a perplexing dilemma. It depended upon the revenue generated by expanded cocoa production to finance its own apparatus and the social and economic infrastructure which British capital needed to do business in the colony.[22] But the forces generated by expanded cocoa production—African traders and export merchants—were challenging the position of British merchant capital in the colony. However, this dilemma was more apparent than real. By the turn of the century, large European firms were on the road to eliminating competition from smaller firms, African and European alike. The real basis for the ambivalence lay in three closely related fears: the decline of the peasantry as an emerging social class, the decline in food self-sufficiency, and the growing challenge to the rural political and social order from newly emerging and historically dominated classes. It was becoming increasingly clear to officials that the colony's economic prosperity depended upon the consolidation of the position of the partially self-sufficient, partially cash-crop-oriented peasantry and on the creation of a political order that would guarantee the peasantry's position. Economic prosperity for the British was defined in large measure by the cheapness with which cocoa could be obtained.

The British made no secret of the reasons it was important to "safeguard against the destruction of the present unique position the Gold Coast peasant-proprietor enjoys and his decline to that of a hired labourer."[23] The director of agriculture wrote in 1919:

> There is no doubt that land has shown a tremendous appreciation in value due to cocoa; nevertheless the bulk of the cocoa is grown on family or stool lands for which no such outlay was necessary, and, I have no hesitation in saying,—without minimising the expense and labour entitled,—that cocoa can be more cheaply produced in this country than in any other country with which I am acquainted.[24]

The director cited usury as the main threat to the peasant: in every district there was one or more wealthy cocoa brokers who accumulated their wealth through land purchase, price speculation, moneylending, and foreclosure. He recommended the introduction of a system of state-controlled cooperatives that would provide, among other things, credit, and a system of state-controlled produce-buying stations in the rural areas, both of which were to involve the chiefs directly. He did not seem to be aware that chiefs played a contradictory role in the emerging system of rural social relations, being at the center of the simultaneous destruction and preservation of the precapitalist modes of production.

But it was the WALC that went to the core of the problem. The WALC had been set up to investigate the impact of the cash crop economy on the indigenous producers of Sierra Leone, the Gambia, Nigeria, and the Gold Coast. Like others that looked into the question, it found that in the Gold Coast Colony, where the cash crop economy was most advanced, the peasant producer was rapidly losing his independence to the wealthy few. It was individual ownership and outright sale of land that were responsible for what it felt to be the gradual emergence of a rural proletariat and for the rising tide of rural unrest. Its recommendations fit in neatly with official concern over increasing rural violence directed at chiefs and with the need to restructure the colonial state apparatus to deal with the violence. "Native rule," the WALC wrote,

> depends upon the native land system. If it is the policy of the Government to govern the natives through themselves, subject to European supervision, retaining what is useful in their institutions, the native system of land tenure must be preserved at all costs.[25]

And what was the "native system of land tenure"? According to the WALC, "pure native tenure," that is, the system that existed before the introduction of cash crops and of British courts and British-trained African lawyers, was based on three principles: the rights of first clearance, the lineage basis of land use, and the nonalienability of land. Because "the land carries with it the responsibility or charge of supporting the sick, the indigent, infirm, and old," rights to its use were of a usufructuary nature only and, by extension, the land could not be bought or sold.[26] In defining customary land rights in this way, the WALC was going against the weight of the evidence presented to it by numerous missionaries, colonial officials, European traders, and Africans. These testified overwhelmingly that in previous times land was bought, sold, and held individually. What the WALC was doing, in fact, was redefining customary law with respect to land in an attempt to alter the direction of social change, and it is perhaps for this reason primarily that the entire WALC document, including evidence, correspondence, minutes, and the *Draft Report*, were not released from the British official secret documents list until the 1950s. By the end of the First World War, this redefinition had become the standard definition used by colonial officials and chiefs alike.

In Ashanti, the situation evolved somewhat differently. Cocoa cultivation spread to that region at about the same time that the British were establishing their formal presence in the area, roughly 1900–1905. The Orders in Council and the Administrative Ordinances incorporating Ashanti and the Northern Territories into the British sphere placed them from the beginning, on a legal footing different from the Colony: in Ashanti and the Northern Territories, the governor, not the Legislative Council, was empowered to make laws; justice was administered by colonial officials rather than meted out in colonial courts where English law as well as customary law applied; barristers and solicitors were specifically excluded from these administrative courts, except by leave of the governor; and the chiefs' courts constituted the courts of first instance for all land cases and all land was deemed to fall under the sphere of "customary law." An executive order was issued in 1905 affirming the prohibition on the mortgaging and sale of Ashanti land to non-Ashanti. Chiefs were encouraged instead to rent land to strangers at reasonable rates. The WALC noted a decade later that strict executive control over land in Ashanti had prevented a repetition of the massive alienations that had occurred in the south and had helped to reinforce the power and authority of traditional rulers during a time when land was very much in demand.

It is important to note the fears concerning food shortages because they entered also into the emerging ideal of the shape rural social relations should take. In 1930, the colony imported nearly £1.5 million in food, mostly flour, fish, sugar, and dairy products. The secretary of native affairs had told the WALC more than fifteen years earlier that "in the cocoa districts the agricultural reports say there is a very serious scarcity of foodstuffs, and people are living almost entirely on tinned foods—tinned sardines, and that sort of thing. They are sent in enormous quantities [from the coast]."[27] While it is not clear how accurate these reports were, two things, at least, were clear. First, agricultural officials were discovering that so much land was under cocoa in the Colony, as distinct from Ashanti and the Northern Territories, that fallow periods for food plots were drastically reduced. This meant that the soil's fertility was falling through overuse and that not only were yields falling but heartier but less nutritious crops, such as cassava, were being planted. Second, food shortages, even if only periodic, placed upward pressures on cocoa prices. It was no coincidence that cocoa holdups occurred when cocoa prices were down and when imported foodstuffs were in short supply. The most serious of these holdups occurred during and shortly after the First World War, in 1930–1931, and in 1937–1938.

Officials recorded 112 successful destoolments of paramount or head chiefs between 1904 and 1926: seven between 1904 and 1908, twenty-three in 1909–1913, thirty-eight in 1914–1918, forty-one between 1919 and 1924, and three in 1925–1926.[28] These figures do not include the large number of lesser chiefs successfully destooled or the large number of unsuccessful destoolment attempts of major and minor chiefs. In part, the numbers reflect more accurate recording of such events but they also reflect, upon the admission of the chiefs themselves, an intensified social and political conflict in the rural cocoa-growing districts. At the heart of the conflict was the struggle between the traditional ruling class of royals and other privileged lineages, on the one hand, and the "commoners" or "young men," persons of unfree or poor lineage, on the other. Some of the commoners had become moneyed through cocoa and some had obtained an education or a partial education. We refer to this latter group as an emerging petite bourgeoisie. The grievances of nearly all commoners against the privileged classes were rooted in the past and in the rapidly changing present: excessive fines, court fees, and prison sentences imposed by the chiefs and their elders, as well as extortion and bribery, all designed to "confiscate part of the money gains made by the commoners in the new economy";[29] burdensome levies to meet debts incurred by chiefs in litigation over boundaries and land sales; lack of assessable stool land because of land sales to stranger farmers; misuse of revenue from mining concessions and sales of stool land.

It was in Akim Abuakwa, in the Eastern Province of the Colony, where efforts to overturn the old order were concentrated in this period. It was also in Akim Abuakwa (at Begoro, Tafo, Asafo, Apedwa, Apapam, and Kibi) where chiefs had alienated the greatest amounts of land to stranger farmers. In this area more than elsewhere, the *asafo* crystallized into a permanent organization to further the interests of the lower classes, the rising petite bourgeoisie, in particular. The demand was not for an end to the chieftaincy as such. It was, at times, for the democratization of the chieftaincy through new constitutional procedures of election and accountability; at other times it was for the simple replacement of unpopular chiefs by the more popular contenders, many of them coming from the common classes. Clashes between rival factions were often violent. When, for example, the Kwaben *asafo* lost its destoolment case against the Gyasehene or stool treasurer before the Omanhene of Akim Abuakwa in 1918, the *asafo* members assaulted their chief in the street, tore off his clothes, kicked him, and promised to flog him. [30] The district commissioner wrote of the growth of a revolutionary spirit which through the introduction of mob law was tending to undermine the existing system of government. After serious rioting in Apam (Akim Abuakwa) in 1930, the government commissioned J. C. de Graft Johnson, a Fanti assistant secretary of native affairs, to make a comprehensive study of the *asafo* as an organization of the lower classes. De Graft Johnson recommended that the *asafo* be given legal recognition and be integrated into the system of village government alongside the chiefs and elders. Officials in the Native Affairs Department rejected this recommendation because, to them, the *asafo* represented "democracy gone mad" and because the *asafo* would ultimately undermine the native administration system by opening the way for "mob rule." The government was wise not to ban these organizations altogether, as some officials recommended. Instead, they were outlawed on a local basis whenever they became a threat to established law and order.

It is within the context of rapid change and growing instability that we should place the reformation of the colonial state's apparatus between 1900 and 1930. Indirect rule was more than an administrative system of governing through the chiefs. Its structures were legal, coercive, and ideological as well. Moreover, indirect rule aimed at preserving or, to be more accurate, creating a system of rural social relations that would guarantee the economic prosperity of the Colony. That prosperity could be guaranteed by ensuring the numerical predominance of a small cash-cropping peasantry that farmed on lineage land, used family or other forms of cheap labor, and grew most of its own food crops.

The cornerstone of indirect rule was the chieftaincy, and a new place was carved out for it at the local, regional, and national levels. By the end of the 1920s, chiefs were the most important tool of the colonial state. The administrative, coercive, and legal powers they exercised were not traditional at all, as colonial officials sometimes admitted, but were designed to equip chiefs with the weapons they needed to control social and political change. However, far from bringing change under control, indirect rule's effect was to exacerbate the tensions and contradictions of rural society and to speed up the pressures for change. As we will see in the next section, by the early 1930s, officials were beginning to search for new forms of state that would contain old and now more recently emerged contradictions.

At the village level, in the Colony, the expansion of chiefly power began in 1910 when the Native Jurisdiction Ordinance of 1883 was amended. The 1883 ordinance sought to exclude customary courts from the judicial framework it set up by stripping chiefs of the power to enforce their decisions. Subjects were not obligated to take their cases to the chiefs' courts, with the result that "the young men ran to the British courts with every complaint." The 1910 amendments established the customary courts as the courts of first instance for certain matters, prescribed limits for court fees, fines and prison sentences, and allowed chiefs and elders to keep and share out the fees and fines collected. The reforms of the 1920s enhanced jurisdiction in criminal and civil matters. Criminal jurisdiction extended to matters such as petty assault, defamation, disobeying the lawful order of a chief, fouling the water, using or composing insulting songs or drumming, causing a nuisance, quarreling, refusing homage to a chief, adultery, selling unwholesome food, swearing an oath unlawfully, offences against by laws, theft, extortion, and cheating. Clearly aimed at political opponents and at uncontrollable younger men, the punishment for several specified criminal offences, such as insulting the chief, was banishment from the area. The civil jurisdiction of customary courts extended to matters such as custody of children, ownership, possession or occupation of land, matrimonial causes under customary law, personal suits for debt, damage or demand, and succession of property.

At the regional level, reforms introduced in the 1920s redrew customary political boundaries, established state and provincial councils of chiefs, and gave these councils the power to decide stool disputes and to make declarations of customary law. The latter was done through pronouncement or through the decisions of state or provincial-level courts. Chiefs who governed large areas were empowered to issue orders and make by laws. Finally, at the level of the colony as a whole, beginning in 1911, chiefs were appointed to the Legislative Council. The Legislative Council had always consisted of African as well as European members, but the Africans historically had been drawn from the educated coastal elite of merchants and lawyers. From 1925 onward, chiefs (elected by the provincial councils) outnumbered the coastal elites on the Legislative Council by as much as two to one.

While the power of the traditional aristocracy over the rural population was being reinforced and strengthened, the power of the state to control the chiefs was also being increased as part of a process of power centralization. At every step of the way, the state reaffirmed the ultimate nature of its power. In 1904, a Chiefs (Colony) Ordinance was passed empowering the governor to appoint a secretary of state to inquire into the circumstances surrounding the destoolment of any chief. The ordinance also conferred upon the governor the legal power to dismiss a chief and to recognize or withhold recognition of any chief enstooled by his people. Refusal to recognize a chief's enstoolment deprived him of revenue accruing from the court system after the reforms of 1910. Although the 1927 Native Administrative Ordinance gave the provincial councils the power to decide stool disputes, the governor remained the final arbiter in stool disputes and his decisions could not be appealed in any court of law in the colony. Finally, the governor's approval was required of any declaration or modification of customary law made by the chiefs.

At the ideological level, the aim of indirect rule was "the preservation of native institutions."[31] These were said to be "essentially democratic" because the power to elect and destool chiefs rested in the hands of the people. The chiefs were "in the fullest sense of the word the representative of their people" and it was for this reason that they were being incorporated into the new administrative and judicial structures. However, by enhancing the power of the chiefs, by backing up the chiefs with the full coercive might of the state, and by redefining customary law, indigenous institutions were not being preserved but distorted. Moreover, the democratic aspects of the precapitalist order (such as the constitutional provision for destooling) and the democratic tendencies of the precapitalist under the disintegrating effects of the modern economy (such as the *asafo*) were held in check and even reversed by the reformed state apparatus.

## GENERALIZED CRISIS AND THE INTENSIFICATION OF CLASS CONFLICT, 1930–1948

Within the framework of indirect rule, four forces combined in the 1930s to produce an almost intolerable situation for the lower classes of rural southernmost Ghana: the depression, land shortages, declining cocoa farm yields, and the swollen shoot disease of cocoa. The combined effects of these forces created a downward pressure on the peasantry, *abusa* sharecroppers, and farm laborers that made survival on the land alone very difficult. Because these forces had an impact on every phase of rural life in the south, because they affected the home villages of farm laborers from the Northern Territories, and because they were at the base of growing urban unrest, we refer to the situation during this third subperiod as one of "generalized crisis."

During the first five years of the Great Depression, cocoa prices declined sharply. They averaged less than half the average level of prices during the five years before 1930. The absolute decline in farm income during these years was exacerbated by three additional factors. The first of these was deteriorating terms of trade for cocoa producers. As noted earlier, Ghana exchanged raw materials (oil palm, rubber, coffee, and then cocoa) for imported manufactured goods on favorable terms during the nineteenth century. This pattern was reversed in the twentieth century, beginning about 1914, and adverse terms were more painfully felt when prices declined sharply. Second, in order to maintain profit levels and to reduce or eliminate competition, the large European import-export firms agreed among themselves to fix floor prices for imported manufactured goods and ceiling prices for exported raw materials.[32]. Price-fixing was a well-established practice in West African trade, but the incentive to do so was increased during economic downturns. The cocoa holdups of 1930–

1931 and 1937–1938 were organized in large part in response to price-fixing. Third, African produce buyers in the interior systematically appropriated surpluses from peasant producers by advancing sums of money during the off-season and buying up the debtors' crops at low prices at harvest time. During the holdups mentioned above, African produce buyers bought up large stocks of cocoa in anticipation of price rises. In several areas, chiefs attempted to establish stool monopolies, using their positions to try to force producers to sell their crops to the chiefs' buying agents alone.[33]

By about 1930 it was difficult to find new land on which to plant cocoa in the pioneering areas of the Eastern Province of the Colony. While new plantings had not ceased in Akwapim and Akim Abuakwa, the purchase of new land had all but ceased.[34] The areas still unoccupied consisted of land that was too dry or swampy or hilltops and slopes too steep for agricultural use. Fresh opportunities for expansion existed now only in Ashanti-Akim, Ashanti, Brong-Ahafo, and in parts of the Western and Central provinces. Many producers from the Eastern Province did find their way to these virgin areas, but migration and purchase were limited by the distances involved and by the insecure nature of tenure. The prohibition on land sales combined with the redefinition of customary land tenure had the effect of slowing down the process of alienation. Most land in the possession of stranger farmers was rented and land that migrants thought they had purchased outright from local chiefs or lineage heads was the subject of litigation by stool subjects or lineage members. It is reasonable to assume that because land for new cocoa cultivation was no longer available in the Eastern Province and because of the problems involved in obtaining land elsewhere economic opportunities were disappearing in the Eastern Province, particularly for the young who were from lower-class or slave lineages. When we add to this the onslaught of the lorry age (a post–World War I phenomenon), which involved the displacement of many men and women who previously had been engaged as carriers, we can conclude that the search for economic opportunities must have heated up in this part of the colony.

The third force that affected the population of the southernmost part of the colony was aging trees. Declining yields in the Eastern Province were noticeable and they were believed to be due to the fact that "appreciable areas have already passed the stage of maximum productivity and that very large areas are at or are approaching their peak of production."[35] New planting was not keeping pace with the number of trees yearly approaching their peak. Incomes had already begun to fall due to declining yields in the oldest areas, and they would continue to fall on an increasing scale. C. Y. Shephard wrote, in his 1936 *Report on the Economics of Peasant Agriculture in the Gold Coast,* that "The phase of effortless exploitation is coming to an end and the Gold Coast farmer must accordingly adjust his standard of living and his methods of cultivation."[36] All of the recommended changes in methods of production—spacing, pruning, draining, supplying new trees for old or dead ones, windbelting, and manuring—required greater inputs of capital and labor and, most probably, a consolidation of holdings to make the investments economic. Farm holdings tended to be widely scattered in the Eastern Province, small tracts being interspersed among larger holdings.[37] Some of the changes would have so altered the organization of extant relations of production that cocoa produced in colonial Ghana would not have been as cheap as it had been previously. Moreover, the consolidation of holdings would have helped to generate the rural proletariat, or semiproletariat, that officials always feared. Officials opted, at this time, for a future that promised stagnation instead.

While some of the decline in yields was attributable to aging trees, the better part of it was due to disease. This realization dawned on agricultural officials in the years after 1936 when the virus disease swollen shoot was first spotted. Transmitted by the mealybug and by wind, the disease, according to early surveys, was already widely distributed in one of the oldest and most extensively cultivated cocoa-growing districts of the Eastern Province, centered around Nankese, where cocoa farms were almost continuous over several hundred square miles. If left unchecked, swollen shoot spread at the alarming rate of 15 million trees per year. The tree population in the colony as a whole (i.e., the Gold Coast Colony and Ashanti/Brong-Ahafo) was roughly 400 million in the mid-1940s. The only known treatment at the time involved cutting out the infected trees and establishing a security zone between infected and healthy areas. Replanting could follow, but at the time it was not known with what results. Since an infected tree can continue to bear healthy cocoa pods for two or three years after the disease has been detected, there was a great deal of opposition, sometimes violent, to the Department of Agriculture's cutting-out program. This program was begun in the early 1940s but was suspended because of the war and because of the level of opposition to it. Introduced on a voluntary basis, officials soon afterward made cutting out compulsory because farm owners ignored their appeals. Compulsory cutting out involved the entry of department inspectors and laborers onto farms and the removal of infected trees without the farm owners' permission. There were widespread accusations of corruption. Apparently, department workers accepted bribes and even extorted money from owners in exchange for leaving farms untouched. By the mid-1940s, swollen shoot had spread into southeastern Ashanti and into the northern part of the Central Province. It had its most devastating effect, however, in the historic cocoa-growing area—southern Akim Abuakwa and northwestern Akwapim—where it is estimated that by 1951 nearly all of the trees had been cut out or were eventually destroyed by the disease.[38]

Reaction to the generalized crisis took two forms. Increasing numbers of people, mostly semieducated young men, left the rural areas for the towns, where they sought wage and other forms of nonagricultural labor. Most people remained in the rural areas, where clashes between established authority and the "youngmen" and between propertied and nonpropertied interests were intensified. These reactions suggest to us a growing perception that the rural areas could not sustain their populations under existing economic, social, and political relationships and that those relationships would have to be altered.

The 1948 census revealed that the major towns—Accra, Kumasi, and Sekondi-Takoradi—had doubled or more than doubled in size and that the smaller coastal and hinterland towns also had experienced pronounced growth. This growth has been attributed largely to the stepped-up economic activity in the colony during the war. Unfortunately, there is no way of being precise about urban population growth during this period because no census was taken between 1930 and 1948. However, there is evidence which suggests that the war only accelerated the movement to the towns and that the movement to the towns stemmed from the generalized crisis. First, there is the report issued by Major Orde Browne, labor advisor to the secretary of state for the colonies, on his tour of British West Africa in 1939–1940. Browne wrote:

> During the last decade prices have fluctuated considerably with a general downward tendency, and the money received for the crops was sometimes little more than half the earlier figures; this seriously affected the spending power of the people. . . .
>
> There were thus few alternative means of obtaining ready money, since opportunities for wage-earning were restricted to industry, with certain limited openings in mines and timber concessions. The mining development which has taken place (except in the Gambia) on a considerable scale during the last ten years was therefore very welcome both to the Governments and to the peoples concerned; the peasant proprietor who found his cocoa or palm kernels providing him with a moiety of his former profit, was glad to go to work for a few months for regular wages which enabled him to save a small, though welcome, sum of ready money. . . . [39]

Indeed, the production of gold, diamonds, and manganese in the colony did expand during the 1930s due to new discoveries, improvements in technology, and good prices. Gold production increased by 100 percent and diamond production by 400 percent. The number of laborers employed in all types of mining grew from 12,140 in 1929–1930 to 41,012 in 1939–1940.[40] Up to 1930, Department of Mines annual reports echoed the complaints of mining companies that labor, both skilled and unskilled, was in short supply. Beginning with the 1930 report, remarks concerning labor were just the reverse: the supply was more than adequate to meet current needs and the needs of the foreseeable future. While a considerable proportion of mine laborers was of nonsouthern origin (the Northern Territories and adjacent French territories), the reports reveal that during the years of labor force growth, southerners held on to their one-third share of the jobs. The 1938 report made note of this fact with some surprise and pointed out that wage increases could not have been responsible for the increase in the number of men looking for mines employment because, when the cost of living was taken into account, wages had fallen rather than risen over the period 1914–1938.

But it was not only to the mining centers that men (along with some women and children) were flocking. Here, again, precise data is lacking, but if we are to place any weight on official concerns, it seems that the major cities and smaller towns were experiencing a kind of growth that was alarming. By the mid-1930s, the drift of the young educated and semieducated away from agriculture and into the towns and cities was resulting in what officials called a serious "unemployment" problem for the first time. One suggestion was that educational opportunities should be limited and that those already in school should have it drilled into their heads that "their careers must be on the land." In 1937, a set of amendments made to the Immigration Restriction Ordinance sought to keep out of the colony political agitators, criminals, prostitutes, the insane, and paupers and destitutes coming from elsewhere in West Africa. The attorney general remarked, in support of the amendments, that it was essential "to give jobs in the Gold Coast to Gold Coast people as far as possible" and that persons coming from outside in search of work should be barred, except by leave of the governor.[41] And, in response to the suggestion made by an African member of the Legislative Council that the state should employ those out of work, as in Europe, the governor replied that "the economic conditions of Africa, with its vast unoccupied spaces and warm climate, are not, and never will be, the same as those of Europe with its cramped, crowded environments and cruel winters. In this country there is work and occupation for every unemployed man if he will only go to the land. He may not be able to make a large sum of money, but he can certainly provide a living until times improve."[42]

But it was precisely survival on the land that was becoming less and less possible for many people. It is important to remember that the bulk of the population of southern Ghana, both before and during the colonial period, was on the edge of economic dependence. In spite of the loosening of old bonds and the emergence of new social groups, old and new forms of servile or semi-servile relationships prevented many groups from exercising control over their own labor power: *abusa* sharecroppers who were descendents of slaves, indebted peasant farmers, hired laborers, pawns, and women. Swollen shoot disease, shrinking opportunities for geographical expansion, declining yields due to old age, and low world market prices for cocoa had their most severe effects upon these groups and their families, forcing many, especially those who had received some education in one of the privately funded, substandard village primary schools, to search for nonagricultural supplemental income. The WALC had feared the emergence of a fully proletarianized wage labor force. Here was an only partially proletarianized wage labor force for whom dependence solely on the land meant impoverization and political subordination.

It is within the context of rural impoverization that the rise of labor militancy in the commercial, administrative, and mining centers of the colony must be seen. In the early 1930s, labor began to organize in ways that were quite distinct from previous years. Demands began to go beyond wage increases to include conditions of employment, conditions of work, sick leave, annual leave, and retirement. As late as 1930, most wage laborers in the colony were hired and paid on a daily rated basis. In other words, there were very few permanent workers, even in government railway yards and harbors. The number of strikes, strike threats, work slowdowns, and downings of tools by government and mines workers greatly increased between 1935 and 1938, prompting certain reforms of the state's apparatus. Up to this point, the criminal code was used to prosecute strikers. When it became clear that arrests and killings would not curb labor unrest, a Labor Department was created (1938) and workers were given the right to unionize (1940) and strike (1941). As the chief inspector of labor noted, the new legislation was intended to make unions "legal and an endeavour would be made to educate them and see that they develop on right lines. In that way persons with grievances will be able to put them forward in an orderly and peaceful manner."[43]

Labor's militancy during this period was connected to the rural crisis in a number of senses. Those persons already employed saw their insecure position threatened by the influx of unskilled laborers from the rural areas. And, because of the nature of the forces expelling part of the rural population, those persons already employed began to look upon wage labor as essential to their long-term survival. While they were by no means landless, they could no longer look completely to the land to sustain them in sickness, unemployment, and old age.

What of the majority, that is, those people who remained in the rural areas? It should not be surprising to find tensions running high between employers and employees during this period of depressed income. The Department of Labor reported in the late 1930s and throughout much of the 1940s that a major problem outside the industrial, commercial, and administrative centers was the refusal of employers to pay their laborers. The problem first came to the attention of officials during the 1937–1938 holdup but most probably predated this specific event. During the holdup, *abusa* sharecroppers were stoned and beaten for attempting to sell their cocoa shares clandestinely.[44] Many were able to survive the season by depending on the earnings of their wives and children, who collected and sold firewood and charcoal. *Abusa* sharecroppers could also grow their own food on plots provided by their employers. The same could not be said for hired laborers. Certain types of hired labor depended upon the employer for food, shelter, and clothing. Many were forced to return home in 1937–1938 without any of their year's earnings. In the early 1940s, Department of Agriculture officials reported attempts by hired laborers and sharecroppers to alter the terms under which they were contracted.[45]

It was the struggle between the traditional aristocracy and lower-class elements that was the source of most of the period's unrest. Guggisberg would have shuddered at the contradictory effects his Native Administrative Ordinances had on rural politics in the 1930s and 1940s. Immediately after the passage of the 1924 and 1927 ordinances the number of successful destoolings declined. However, by 1930, conflict had risen to the surface again and it was more intense than before. The activities of the *asafo* in Apam (Akim Abuakwa) have been mentioned. Disputes continued to center on the struggle between rival stool candidates but, increasingly, challengers for the stool came from the lower (i.e., nonroyal) classes and such challengers often had the backing of the local youngmen's organization. At the forefront of these attempts to overturn the traditional aristocracy was the emerging petite bourgeoisie of medium- to large-scale cocoa farmers and farmer-traders, small shopkeepers, school teachers, and clerks. The interests of this newly emerging group were not identical to the interests of the ordinary people and it was not always clear whether the petite bourgeoisie wanted to transform political relations or merely replace those in power. But all could agree that the chiefs had too much power over them. The reforms of the 1920s had paved the way for ordinances in the 1930s that gave chiefs the power to levy and collect taxes. The revenue was to be used for local improvements, but charges were made that the chiefs added tax revenue to court fees and fines as a source of wealth. Tax delinquents could be prosecuted in traditional courts and fined for nonpayment. A new charge was that the aristocracy, in particular the head, or paramount, chiefs, were artificial creations over whom the people had no control. As one Ashanti trader put it: "Every day we see the chiefs going to the council. We have no say in what they discuss. When they come out, they give us laws to obey. Most of these are in their own interest."[46] So dangerous a thread had lower-class elements become in certain parts of Ashanti in the mid-1930s that the Ashanti Confederacy Council (the joint council of head chiefs in Ashanti) passed a resolution barring stools to all persons of nonroyal lineage and banned all *asafo* organizations. In 1941, a riot occurred in Teshie, a town just outside Accra, involving the followers of rival stool candidates. The young men were reported by police to have been carrying guns, cutlasses, sticks, and other weapons. They set houses on fire and knocked in doors and windows. At least six persons were killed. In 1942, the Police Department reported that its responsibilities had greatly increased during the war, not because of an increase in serious crime, but because of "the number of riots and disturbances which turbulent members of the community have misguidedly seen fit to stage."[47] Later that same year, the new governor summed up the political climate in the colony during the depression and early war years in the following way:

> As a new-comer to this country I have been struck—and struck with dismay—by the large number of interminable stool disputes which disturb the peaceful life of the community . . . within the last ten years no less than 22 Paramount Chiefs have been destooled, in addition to 22 others who have abdicated in that period—in most cases in order to forestall destoolment; that seven stools of Paramount Chiefs are now vacant and that in many States no Paramount Chief has succeeded in maintaining his place on the stool for more than a very short time. In the case of subordinate chiefs I understand that the position is as bad or worse and since my arrival in the colony rioting has occurred in small villages in stool disputes. Now I want to make it quite clear that such disorders will not be permitted and will be put down with a strong hand. It is intolerable that the peaceful life of the community should be disturbed by irresponsible minorities or by a few irreconcilables who will agree to no reasonable solution of any problem however trifling.[48]

What the governor neglected to add was that now rural unrest was anticolonial as well as antichief.

As the events of the 1930s unfolded, the ability of the existing state apparatus to contain the pressures for change was increasingly called into question. A number of officials were coming to the conclusion that indirect rule should be abandoned and replaced by a form of state whose primary agents would come from the educated community. Most officials, however, remained committed to indirect rule and believed that, with certain modifications, the level of tension and violence in the villages and small towns could be reduced. The modifications made to meet the challenge from the lower classes took three forms primarily. The first involved addressing some of the grievances of the lower classes against the abuses of the aristocracy. An amendment to the Native Jurisdiction Ordinance in 1935 gave district commissioners the power to review the proceedings of customary courts and to revise any decisions they considered unfairly arrived at. Stools that became the intense focus of discontent risked forfeiting their administrative, judicial, and legislative powers to the district commissioner. The precedent for this was set in 1935 when an ordinance was passed stripping the chief and elders of the Asamangkese division of Akim Abuakwa of their authority. Finally, an effort was made to make stools accountable for the revenues they collected when, in 1936, stool treasuries were introduced. Regulations made in 1939 and 1940 for the operation of stool treasuries were strict. Treasuries could be established compulsorily by the district commissioner, if he saw fit. They were to have paid treasurers and staffs and were to be managed by finance boards appointed by the stool but answerable to the district commissioner. Accounts were subject to audits, and checks on treasury accounts had to be signed by the district commissioner before they could be cashed. Those stools with treasuries were required to draw up annual estimates of revenue and expenditures. Among their revenue sources were all fees and fines collected by the customary courts.

The second form that modifications took had a much more radical appearance. It was the view of many that the only way indirect rule could be saved was by incorporating into its structures the more "progressive elements" of the community, that is, the emerging petite bourgeoisie of the rural districts and small towns. As early as 1932, state councils were being encouraged to include among their members young men of nonaristocratic origin. In 1939, an ordinance was passed establishing the legal basis for the appointment of persons holding no hereditary office to hereditary councils such as the Joint Provincial Council of Chiefs. In 1936, the latter had issued an invitation to the heads of *asafo* companies in the Colony to begin attending council meetings on a regular basis. In 1944, amendments to the Native Administration Ordinance empowered the governor, in case of a prolonged stool dispute or other disorders, to appoint an African council to be responsible for local administration and justice until a chief was elected. The amendments specifically stated that persons of nonhereditary backgrounds were eligible for such a council. The 1944 amendments also opened up membership on stool treasury finance boards to the lower classes and provided for the setting up of advisory committees, again with lower-class members, to advise chiefs on matters such as education and village development. Finally, it was recommended, though not implemented until after the war, that the lower classes be allowed to sit on customary courts "to render them more representative."[49]

As radical as these changes appear, they could not, nor was it their aim to, transform and democratize the system of local government. Their aim was to incorporate the most vocal and articulate of the lower-class elements so as to absorb the pressures for change. Co-optation could work with a group such as the petite bourgeoisie because it was interested as much in personal and material advancement as it was in justice. Governor Burns made his objectives clear when he stated in 1942:

> I am a great believer in the value of Native administrations, and I feel that these administrations are strengthening themselves very greatly by introducing into their Councils and Finance and other Committees a number of the younger and progressive elements of the population as they have done in a large number of cases in the Colony. Such a step strengthens—not weakens—a State Council. It gives those better educated persons, apart from the traditional rulers, an opportunity for more direct participation in the administration of their country, and it provides a useful outlet for the constructive energies of responsible men who might otherwise take up an attitude of irresponsible opposition to the traditions of native administration.[50]

To reemphasize the commitment to the aristocracy, the 1946 Burns Constitution provided for a chiefly majority when it gave the Legislative Council an unofficial African majority.

When combined with the third form that modifications took, efforts to co-opt the petite bourgeoisie had grave implications for the future of Ghana. In 1938, serious rioting erupted in the West Indies. Unemployment, general impoverization, and the lack of democratic forms of expression could be pinpointed as the causes of the unrest. There was unrest elsewhere in the British Empire and the fear was that the demands for democratic reforms, such as were coming out of India and a few African territories, especially the Gold Coast, would be linked with economic issues. Coming on the heels of the 1937–1938 holdup and in a general atmosphere of political discontent, the West Indian disturbances were of particular concern to officials in the colony. As part of a general rethinking of colonial policy prompted by the West Indian disturbances, Lord Hailey was sent out to British Africa in 1939. In his confidential report to the Colonial Office (*Native Administration and Political Development in British Tropical Africa, 1940–1942*) Hailey echoed a viewpoint that was gaining ground with increasing rapidity. The British government, he wrote, must now direct its energies "to encouraging the conception of the states' organisations [i.e., the local apparatus of indirect rule] as agencies for the extension of the social services."[51] In the following year, the Colonial Development and Welfare Act was passed. Along with the revenues collected by local authorities and by central governments in the colonies, grants under the Colonial Development and Welfare Act would put the emphasis where it was really needed in the colonies now—in the improvement of education, health, sanitation, and agricultural techniques in the rural areas. Technical staffs, manned by Africans and attached to local authorities, would have to be developed and Africans would have to be appointed to an enlarged bureaucracy at the central government level as well (the so-called European posts). The first ten-year development plan for the colony was submitted in 1947.

Efforts to reconceptualize native administration, to curb the abuses of the chiefs, and to incorporate lower-class elements amounted to an important shift away from indirect rule as a form of political control and domination. It was hoped that these efforts would help to establish a new political basis upon which to maintain the social relations of the "peasant mode of production." It is within the context of shoring up the peasantry that the introduction of cocoa marketing and credit cooperatives were introduced and statutory controls on the export of cocoa imposed in the 1930s. State-controlled cooperatives expressly barred from membership or discouraged from joining the "capitalist farmer."[52] The objective was to establish a wedge between the wealthy African creditor-trader and the peasant farmer. More important was the statutory produce marketing board introduced in 1939 for all British West African export crops. The details of how this board operated need not be repeated here.[53] Suffice it to say that the British government purchased, on a monopoly basis, all of the cocoa, oil palm, ground nuts, cotton, etc., of the West African colonies, guaranteeing producers a price (and an income) fixed at the beginning of each season. One of the aims was to cushion producer prices in years when they were low by building up a price stabilization reserve fund. It was feared that raw materials prices would collapse during the war and with them the peasant producers who would have little alternative to going deeper into debt and losing their farms. As it turned out, the demand for these and other raw materials was particularly strong during the war and the West African Produce Control Board accumulated large trading surpluses in every year of its operation save one between 1939 and 1947. The British government borrowed heavily on these funds during the war and made use of the hard currency colonial exports earned.[54]

It was following the riots of February and March 1948 that the state apparatus in Ghana underwent its most radical reformation since the introduction of indirect rule earlier in the century. The aim remained that of ensuring the dominance of the social relations of peasant production. However, it was realized that in order to save the peasantry, agriculture and rural life would have to be "revitalized." There were several aspects to this revitalization project. The first involved creating a new political framework to replace indirect rule. This was "representative government," a form of "democracy" for the localities said to be more suited to the African situation than were British political forms.[55] Under representative government, a system of local councils was to coexist with state councils. Local councils were to consist of popularly elected members and hereditary members and to concern themselves with matters such as welfare and social services. State councils were to remain predominantly hereditary and were to continue to have jurisdiction over marriage, divorce, certain aspects of justice, stool disputes, land, and other "customary" matters. These reforms only incorporated the lower classes at a certain level, giving them discretion over public funds that would yield many opportunities for corruption and graft while leaving beyond their reach control over questions such as property, debt collection, and landlord-sharecropper relationships. For example, pawning continued as a form of debt payment and labor control.[56] It was important, the Coussey Committee on constitutional reform wrote, to maintain "the existing community of interests" and the predominance of "customary law"; " . . . the social structure of a society should not be disturbed unduly."[57]

Other aspects of revitalization included soaking up the politically volatile "unemployed," that is, the semiproletarianized educated and semieducated youth of the cocoa districts, largely through state employment; introducing certain rural social services, such as schools, pipe-borne water, sanitation and health facilities, and electricity; making infrastructural improvements, such as building good roads and a modern harbor, to reduce the costs of transportation; extending credit to cocoa producers through state-controlled cooperatives; and rehabilitating the areas of the colony devastated by swollen shoot and generally improving cocoa-growing techniques. Efforts were made to rehabilitate the swollen shoot areas by giving replanting grants to producers whose farms had been affected by the cutting-out program. Improvements in agricultural techniques included the introduction of improved varieties of cocoa seeds designed to yield fruit earlier and the introduction of fertilizers and insecticides. The aim of these improvements—all government funded—was to increase the yield of the individual producer without altering the existing relations of production. In other words, the peasant mode was being intensified.

It was to the Cocoa Marketing Board (CMB) that officials turned to finance the revitalization of the peasant mode of production. In 1947, the surplus funds of the West African board were divided among the various colonies concerned and statutory marketing boards for the individual colonies were created. The Gold Coast (later Ghana) CMB began operations in 1947 with £13 million. In April 1948, one month after the riots, the government passed legislation enabling it to borrow £4 million from the CMB to construct a new harbor at Takoradi. This was the first in a long line of CMB loans for "development" purposes. By 1949, the CMB price stabilization reserve fund had become the main source of government funding and producer prices were being set with the revenue the government needed in mind. As a consequence, producers received half or less of the world market price for their cocoa. Most of the CMB loans were never repaid, and in the 1950s the CMB loans became outright grants to the government. By the end of the 1950s, the CMB's funds were exhausted and the government began to search abroad for money to finance development.

The contradictions that emerged from development, that is, from the efforts to revitalize the peasant mode of production, in the last decade of colonial rule go a long way toward explaining the tensions of the immediate post independence period in Ghana. A petite bourgeoisie which was predominantly state employed was being consolidated and many other lower-class elements found unskilled employment in the state sector. The material basis for incorporating the petite bourgeoisie and for absorbing lower-class tensions in general lay in appropriating surpluses from the peasant producers. However, only if rural social and political relations remained untransformed could this appropriation take place. It was essential that land not take a commodity form, that labor relations remain dependent, that peasant producers grow most of their own food, and that all independent forms of political expression and social reorganization be blocked. We can see here the emergence of a correspondence between the interests of foreign capital and the interests of the local ruling group, a fraction of the petite bourgeoisie. But the consequences were agricultural stagnation and rural impoverization, along with intensified rural flight (semiproletarianization). The specific efforts made to revitalize cocoa production only reinforced these processes as the wealthier and the politically more powerful of the rural community reaped a disproportionate share of the inputs. It was not long after independence in 1957 that the Nkrumah regime began its own search for new forms of political control that would contain urban and rural discontent and opposition, potential and real. It is within the context of coping with inherited and new contradictions that we should understand the restructuring of the state's legal, coercive, and ideological apparatus in the late 1950s and early 1960s, namely, the introduction of the one-party state and the "socialist" development strategy.

# CHAPTER 2

# Anatomy of African Class Consciousness: Agrarian Populism in Ghana from 1915 to the 1940s and Beyond

### Martin Kilson

**CHARACTER OF AFRICAN POPULISM**

A good starting point for thinking about the character of African populism is John Saul's typology of African populism. Saul distinguishes between two modes of populist assertion—one he calls "communalistic," the other, "individualistic." The former is concerned with "defending the traditional unit of solidarity at the first impact of capitalism [modernization]," while the latter is "essentially market oriented, defending itself [agrarian interest] against the further 'rationalization' of an expansive capitalism."[1]

Insofar as Saul's definition of African populism in the agrarian sector emphasizes primarily *defensive responses* to modernization (that is, to capitalism and the bureaucratic state), his framework for analyzing agrarian populism focuses attention mainly on the intrusive role of capitalist commercial and bureaucratic practices. Another view of agrarian populism in Africa is possible, however—one that focuses on the *offensive posture* of agrarian actors. This posture among agrarian populists is concerned with adjusting agrarian society to or integrating it with capitalist modernization, hopefully on terms respectful of some traditional norms while co-opting the benefits of modernization, a populist process that Naomi Chazan refers to as "reconciling communal needs and predilections with material concerns associated with the [modernizing] state." Chazan suggests, correctly I think, that this has been a constant feature of agrarian populism in twentieth-century Ghana: "this process of populist normative reconciliation led to the careful amalgamation of traditional and modern concerns in a syncretistic quest of a neo-traditionalist sort."[2]

In general, "populism" is the assertion or articulation (in action and structure) of what I call embryonic class consciousness. Though there is a variety of uses of this term, I suggest that the generic meaning of "populism" or "populist" is that it refers to the context and modes of formative agrarian and working-class political thrusting, modes predicated on a shallow structure of group or class awareness.

In modernizing African societies, the "integrative" populist response referred to above is always culturally ambivalent, seeking as it were both a greater conformity of agrarian society to the cash nexus as well as the selective preservation of the sacred nexus of kinship, lineage, and reciprocal authority. This situation, when confronted with the expanding dynamics of modern development, produces a curious form of political-cultural schizophrenia. The actions of African populists invariably intertwine atavistic and modern demands. For example, when they mount attacks upon the political action of chiefs, the thrust of such attacks is both secular and sacred in substance. Agrarian populists in Africa are seldom able functionally to disentangle such assaults against the political actions of chiefs, letting a criticism of their modern political function such as tax practices stand alone. Instead, any such modern criticism is, as it were, overlapped and given efficacy by a parallel criticism of some sacred function associated with chiefs, such as ritual acts, land litigation functions, etc. Furthermore, neither the modern nor the traditional criticism the populists mount against chiefs involves attacks upon the office or institution of chieftaincy as such, but rather are attacks on actions of a given chief. The embryonic class consciousness that defines agrarian populism cannot psychically assimilate abolition of an institution which, like chieftaincy, mediates numerous life-cycle functions that are culturally fundamental to African peasants. A more intricate involvement in modern society—at the psychic and normative levels—is required before this can occur.

*Put another way, while African agrarian populism has a capacity for rebellious action, it lacks a revolutionary capability.* This *populist dilemma* constitutes a constraint upon both the level and quality of politicization in African agrarian society. For example, whenever chiefs face populist pressures during the process of modernization, they are often able to respond by satisfying populist criticism of their sacred function while neglecting criticism of their modern actions. This is possible because, owing to the embryonic class consciousness that defines African populism, the agrarian populists perceive the sacred nexus they share with chiefs (Saul's "unit of solidarity") as superior to the evolving secular nexus (money, wealth, mobility) associated with development. There is, therefore, good reason to think that the process by which African agrarians transfer their psychic investment from the sacred nexus to the secular nexus (a process that inevitably risks a fundamental societal upheaval) is going to be protracted and rather complex.[3] The analysis of agrarian populism in colonial Ghana bears this out.

Thus much of the political militancy associated with African populism constitutes a form of what Max Gluckman called "rituals of rebellion."[4] For Gluckman, rebellious rituals, while militant in form, are essentially restorative of customary class or authority patterns, and as such are not necessarily revolutionary (system changing) in outcome. Indeed, even when colonial administrations attempt to reinforce certain agrarian populist actions—which they did when replacing a chief's autocratic role in local tax policies with a representative body that included commoner agrarians—the agrarian populists proceed with moderation, seldom using their new political clout to uproot their customary sacred nexus with chiefs. Gutkind suggests that a similar moderation of

class struggle characterizes the relations of the African urban working class—
itself of rural agrarian origins—and the African capitalist class, for the sacred
nexus they share in common (kinship, tribe, and religion) may have primacy
over the wealth-producing and wealth-appropriating relationships associated with
modernization.[5] A similar perspective of a sacred-cultural crosscutting of modern social stratification in Africa has been offered recently by Peter Lloyd, who
observes that "obvious differences in wealth among the urban poor and the
relationships produced by their work situation are . . . cross-cut by ties of
ethnicity and residence [with the result that] marked stratification of the urban
poor is thus prevented."[6] At any rate, a full-fledged secularization of peasants'
class consciousness in African societies, even a generation after colonialism,
remains in its formative stage.

   The following analysis of agrarian populism in Africa is a case study of the
evolution of populism in a district of Ghana during the era between the two
world wars. This analysis attempts to illuminate the difficulties surrounding the
secularization of class consciousness in African societies.

## SOCIAL SETTING OF KWAHU POPULISM

Kwahu District, situated at the northern part of the Eastern Province, underwent
significant social and economic change in the first two decades of the twentieth
century. The Kwahu took readily to cocoa and palm oil growing for the world
market. Located along the main road route (and, from 1923, the railway route)
linking Accra and Kumasi, Kwahu District spawned several "big towns existing at Nkawkaw, Akwaseho, and Kwahu Prashu."[7] Nkawkaw, the major town,
had a population of 8000 in 1923 and was a prominent center of trade, in which
Kwahu themselves played a major role: "The Kwahus were always renowned
as petty traders," observed the district commissioner in 1923, "and are to be
seen throughout the Colony—even going to Ashanti and the Northern Territories."[8]

   Data from the 1921 census of Ghana illustrate the context of sociological
differentiation of Kwahu society consequent upon the growth of cash crop
farming, commerce, education, and mining.[9] By 1921, Kwahu District had a
population of 41,693, of which some 22,000 were sixteen years of age and
over. Some 2600, or 12 percent, of the adult population were occupied in the
modern economy and thus experienced modern social relations. Of this group,
about 200 were artisans, nearly 500 were in small-scale trade, 1857 in cash
crop farming, and perhaps 100 held "elite-type" jobs, that is, jobs requiring
primary to middle schooling, and the largest group in this category were clerks.
When compared to other districts in the Eastern Province, the Kwahu District
had a marked advantage in cash crop farmers and traders: for example, Kwahu
District had nearly three times as many traders as Akim Abuakwa (population
90,306 in 1921), twice as many as Addah-Quittah District (population 177,625),
and more than three times as many traders as Akwapim (population 79,917).
Kwahu District also had nearly three times as many cash crop farmers as Akim
Abuakwa, more than three times the farmers in Addah-Quittah, and slightly
more than the farmers in Akwapim.

   Moreover, social change in Kwahu District occurred within a traditional system which had a comparatively low ratio of chiefs per head of adult population.
For example, Kwahu District had 65 chiefs (paramount, town, and village) for

an adult population of 22,000—or about 1 chief for every 3500 adults—compared to 250 chiefs for an adult population of 48,000 in Akim Abuakwa, or 1 chief for every 2000. The comparatively low ratio of chiefs per head of adult population in Kwahu District might indicate that the area was also more loosely organized in its customary sociopolitical relationships than other areas in the Eastern Province (for example, Akim Abuakwa) and in Ashanti. This situation, reinforced by high rates of social change throughout the first thirty years of this century, was conducive to a high degree of political assertiveness and innovation on the part of emergent modern groups.

## ASAFO: INSTRUMENT OF KWAHU POPULISM

During the period between the two world wars, populist politics in Kwahu, and elsewhere in Ghana, was often organized along informal lines. Persons new to modern political economy—akin to those described by John Iliffe in *The Emergence of African Capitalism* (small cash crop farmers, petty traders, semiskilled artisans, school dropouts, etc.)—would cohere for the specific purpose of leveling charges against a paramount chief and, if necessary, press these charges, often with the aid of violence, to the point of dethroning a chief.[10]

As noted above, the term "populism," as used in this case study of political development in Kwahu District, is used to denote the assertion and articulation of a primitive class consciousness among African agrarians. In Kwahu District between the two world wars, there was a tendency for populist activity to fluctuate between informal and formal arrangements; and when an explicit instrument of populist assertion was utilized, that agency displayed attributes more traditional than modern, thereby complicating the perception of populist activity by colonial officialdom. The typical instrument of populist politics in southern and central Ghana during the interwar era was the *asafo,* a traditional association of commoner males whose original functions centered on warfare but also on building public works. The use of *asafo* as a sustained agency of agrarian (and urban) populist assertion first appeared in Kwahu District in 1915, though *asafo* had been evident in populist form in the Agona Division of Ashanti in 1905, in Akim Abuakwa in 1910–1911, and in Elmina, Central Province, in 1914.[11]

The precise origins of *asafo* in traditional politics are obscure, though it was prevalent in southern Ghana—in Fanti areas—in the seventeenth century and had spread as far as Ashanti by the eighteenth century.[12] It performed a variety of functions, often military in nature but including public works like road clearing. At the time colonial rule was being established in the late nineteenth century, the role of *asafo* as an integral part of the traditional politics in most of southern Ghana and Ashanti had lapsed. Only in the Central Province, especially Winneba District, was *asafo* still functioning, though in a rather curious manner. Commoner males among the Fanti had fashioned the *asafo* into a bizarre agency of fratricidal violence, a situation that persisted sporadically throughout the first forty years of this century. Late-nineteenth-century fratricidal encounters between Fanti men organized into *asafo* associations or companies were common events. For example, one fratricidal encounter occurred in 1914, at Senya Beraku, Central Province, resulting in ninety-eight deaths. As late as 1941, a commission of inquiry reported on fratricidal *asafo* encounters in the Central Province:

Tatum Legu Riot resulted in very serious loss of life—30 people were killed and a number wounded arising out of a dispute between different *asafo* Companies of two towns. Mumfort Riot—over 40 persons were killed. This was a dispute between *asafo* Companies of the same town. Appam Riot—numbers were killed and wounded. Half the town was burnt, a large number of people tied up and burnt in their houses. The dispute was between two *asafo* Companies of the same town. Cape Coast Riot— a dispute between two or three *asafo* Companies and another Company. A large number wounded, and three persons last their lives.[13]

Outside of Fanti areas, however, the use of *asafo* by emergent groups seldom displayed this murderous and pathological form of intergroup contest. Instead, the use of *asafo* was more functional to the efforts of emergent groups to assert a political presence in Native Administrations. Such use of *asafo* was a central feature of populist politics in Dwahu District from 1915 through the 1930s. In Fanti areas, on the other hand, such populism was less frequent, though in 1914 there was an *asafo*-based effort to destool the paramount chief at Elmina, resulting in physical assaults on the chief and the burning of his modern property—car and home.[14]

From its inception, the *asafo*-based populist politics in Kwahu District was as much concerned with shoring up customary norms and relations, in face of the corrosive forces of modernity, as with removing traditional impediments to modern change, especially those emanating from the position of chiefs in local administration. Thus the rules and regulations of the Kwahu *asafo* movement, issued in December 1915, favor strengthening the authority of chiefs' oaths controlling adultery—especially chiefs' cohabitation with young men's wives—and the sexual exploitation of young girls. One such oath provided that "whoever shall be found guilty of violating Omanhene's oath shall be liable to a fine not exceeding 2.8s., inclusive of pacification of the judgment creditor and 2 sheep."

The same rules, however, contain forward-looking or progressive proposals seeking to adjust traditional relationships to the requirements of secular evolution. For example, the rules favor limiting the coercive powers of chiefs and demand a position for young men, through *asafo,* in the exercise of these powers. The rules also demand better wages for artisans and the regulation of prices for consumer goods, goods exchanged in both the traditional and modern economy. The authors of the rules, who were clearly semiliterate, seemed to presume that the paramount chief had authority over wages and prices in the context of Native Administrations.[15]

Here, then, was a bid by early-twentieth-century Ghanaian agrarians to fashion a political posture which, as it were, straddled antithetical social and political worlds—the traditional and the secular. They sought, with limited skills and experience, to influence the character of secularization emanating from the capitalist political economy while simultaneously shoring up traditional authority precepts.

## FISSION AND FUSION IN KWAHU MODERNIZATION

For the most part, this description of the *asafo* populists in Kwahu District was not shared at the time by either the chiefs or the colonial government. The paramount chief in Kwahu District, Omanhene Kwaku Akuamoa V, saw the movement as an attempt to destroy his authority and that of chiefly office as such, feeling quite helpless in face of the *asafo* bid for influence. Appealing to the colonial government for assistance, he informed the district commissioner, in semiliterate English, that "I am afraid to use my influence in them for abolition of this *asafo* Company."[16] He also appealed to his influential and educated counterpart in the neighboring Akim Abuakwa District, Nana Ofori Atta I, who articulated the fears of Kwahu chiefs more effectively than they could. "The '*asafo*' . . . have gone to the extent of interfering with the power of the Omanhene and his Chiefs," he wrote the provincial commissioner, "consequently the Chiefs are not listened to; any orders emanating from them being liable to immediate condemnation. . . . The Kwahu Chiefs are dispossessed of their powers as Chiefs, and notwithstanding the provisions of the Native Jurisdiction Ordinance which apply to Kwahu, the Omanhene and the Chiefs have been made to recognize the laws of the '*asafo*.' . . . It is very much feared that unless the Government supported the recognized native authority in Kwahu the radical changes which are now heard of will be developed to such an extent that the real native Institutions will be utterly discarded. . . ."[17]

The colonial government was equally alarmist in its reation to the Kwahu *asafo* movement in 1915. The district commissioner in Kwahu District remarked in his Quarterly Reports that "The power and influence of this organization [*asafo*] constitute a dangerous and most undesirable element in the politics of the district. . . . Its policy appears to be a consistent opposition to all established authority."[18] In like vein, the colonial secretary characterized the Kwahu *asafo* movement as "a sort of Bolshevist movement . . . a striking commentary on . . . the disintegrating influences at work in Kwahu Affairs at the present moment."[19] And the provincial commissioner described the movement as a "Third Estate" and felt it had "virtually taken over the reins of government."[20]

These descriptions of the character of the Kwahu populist movement in 1915 were not altogether incorrect. This use of *asafo* by emergent modernizing groups in agrarian society was, in one of its dimensions, very much a defiance of established authority within colonial Native Administrations. But these official descriptions of *asafo* were wrong in assuming that the goal of such defiance was the utter destruction of both chiefly authority and office. The emergent groups responsible for the populist opposition were not, after all, capable of dispensing with chiefly authority. They needed the sacred authority associated with chiefs and other traditional rulers for a major part of their life's needs— religious, ritual, kinship, etc.

This discrepancy between the Kwahu populists' defiance of chiefly authority while clinging to this authority created, in its turn, a unique field of interaction between these contesting groups. For in criticizing chiefs' traditional and modern malpractices, the Kwahu populists provided chiefs a broad leeway in their response to these charges. In particular, chiefs could choose—and often did choose—to rectify their traditional behavior while ignoring their violations under colonial governance. Thus, by allowing chiefs to rectify traditional malpractices as a trade-off for their modern transgressions, the agrarian populists were affording the indi-political culture a measure of renewal and stability in face of the long-run secularizing dynamics of modernization. Equally important is that those chiefs wishing to experiment with the participatory political values associated with modern governance could do so on win-win rather than win-lose terms. In this way, then, the populists' style of oppositionary politics afforded Kwahu chiefs a unique opportunity, as it were, to have their political cake and eat it too. Many Kwahu chiefs perceived this win-win opportunity and seized it.

## POPULISM, CHIEFS, AND POLITICAL CHANGE

More so than in other areas of southern Ghana and Ashanti, the politics of emergent groups in Kwahu District in the period 1915–1930s facilitated basic changes in the role of chiefs in colonial governance. Why was this so?

Traditional political relations in Kwahu society were probably less rigidly organized than in other Akan-speaking areas like Akim Abuakwa. This meant that both chiefs and commoners in Kwahu were more free to adapt to changing situations. Furthermore, the Kwahu traditionally displayed a marked entrepreneurial proclivity. "The Kwahus were always renowned as petty traders," remarked the district commissioner in the 1920s, which might be interpreted as a cultural tendency toward innovation.[21] Thus an adaptive response by Kwahu chiefs to the politics of emergent groups might be seen as an outgrowth of the traditional cultural orientations of Kwahu society.

In any event, it happened that rather than adamantly resist the politics of emergent groups in Native Administrations, as Ashanti chiefs were inclined to do,[22] Kwahu chiefs—including the Omanhene of Kwahu—attempted to adapt to this politics, treating it, if not as legitimate, at least as deserving of a hearing. The process through which Kwahu chiefs fashioned their political response to the *asafo* movement was not, of course, without its hitches and setbacks, including some chiefs opposing the movement's claim for recognition as a participant in the emergent modern-type politics of Native Administrations. But, then, political development or modernization—conceived as the extension of access of persons or groups to sources of influence and authority in a political system—never proceeds without hitches.

The colonial government had a rather different conception of the way most Kwahu chiefs responded to the *asafo* movement. Government saw this response as a sign of weakness and political on the part of Kwahu chiefs. For example, in 1918, three years after the appearance of the *asafo* movement, the provincial commissioner complained to his superior, the colonial secretary, that the Omanhene of Kwahu was incapable of crushing the movement: "[He] sits shivering on his stool, preferring for some to me at present rather obscure reason to retain a very empty semblance of power to the risk of being destooled."[23] But this view of the behavior of the Omanhene and other Kwahu chiefs in relation to the *asafo* movement was mistaken.

What government officials saw as signs of cowardice and political ineptitude on the part of Kwahu chiefs were, in fact, merely facets of the dialectics of political development in Kwahu Native Administrations. As the politics of the dissident groups evolved through the 1920s and 1930s, the semiliterate leaders of this politics acquired the attributes of incipient politicians. They were vigilant in attending issues their politics defined as relevant; chiefs who were believed to be corrupt, privy to maladministration of Native Administrations, and disrespectful of customary obligations found themselves exposed to *asafo*-initiated public criticism as well as to threats of destoolment. For example, in 1925 the *asafo* movement directed charges of corruption at a leading Kwahu chief, the Nifahene of Obo Division, whom the district commissioner described as "a strong and very unpopular Chief." The *asafo*'s pursuit of this charge caused the government to enquire into the matter, and though the findings of the inquiry exonerated the Nifahene, his educated clerk in the Native Administration was found guilty and sentenced by government to two months' imprisonment at hard labor.[24]

The same chief was again confronted, in 1933, with a similar charge from the Kwahu populists. In pressing the charge, the *asafo* leader, who had been a clerk to the Omanhene of Kwahu, "paid propaganda visits to the various villages of the Nifahene stirring up the people against their chief and trying to get them to destool him."[25] The Nifahene, one of the Kwahu chiefs who never accepted the populists as legitimate participants in the politics of Native Administration, cultivated his peers in the central Kwahu Native Administration—the so-called Kwahu State Council—in order to squash the *asafo* charges. But, alas, his fellow chiefs failed to respond, a position the district commissioner interpreted as merely another instance, among many since 1915, of the cowardice and indecisiveness of Kwahu chiefs when faced with populist dissidents: "Owing to the lack of cohesion between the Kwahu Chiefs the Nifahene has realized that it would be useless to take action against Mosi [the *asafo* leader] in the State Council. . . ."[26]

But what the district comissioner saw as a "lack of cohesion" among Kwahu chiefs was in actuality a more complex phenomenon. The behavior of Kwahu chiefs was now susceptible to the increasingly subtle dialectics of political modernization, especially the tendency of interest groups to differentiate not merely along self-serving lines but also along institutionally functional (efficiency) lines, a principle of differentiation more salient in modern than traditional society.

By the 1930s many Kwahu chiefs were now recognizing the political capacity of the *asafo* populists, especially their ability to immobilize the local political system. In a word, the militants' veto capacity was now apparent. And as long as the colonial oligarchy used representative principles in regulating agrarian conflicts, participatory reforms were only a matter of time. Kwahu chiefs, therefore, had increasingly fewer options: face perpetual political instability in the agrarian political economy of colonial Ghana or devise means, however fitful, for adapting to the expansive populist politics. Insofar as Kwahu society traditionally sanctions innovating proclivities—in contrast to Ashanti society—the latter option was well within reach, involving fewer long-run risks to the political salience of Kwahu chiefs than a last-ditch defense of the status quo.

Moreover, *asafo* populists did not oppose the participation of chiefs in the modernization process, especially the conversion of traditional authority into modern sources of power.[27] But this applied with a condition: that chiefs neither impede the interests of the emergent groups nor brazenly disregard the customary obligations of their office—the latter representing a normative revolution the populists could not endure.

Thus, by the late 1930s the increasing evidence of political accommodation between Kwahu chiefs and the populists prepared the way for reformation in the character of colonial local government. The groundwork was now virtually ready for a qualitative metamorphosis in the direction of representative politics, involving of course the surrender by chiefs of some facets of the ancient principles of divine rule, allowing the commoners in agrarian society to select local government authorities on the basis of secular and functional criteria.

## FORGING REPRESENTATIVE GOVERNMENT IN KWAHU

A fundamental feature of the process of forging representative government in Kwahu District during the 1930s was the recognition by chiefs and populists of shared concerns and interests, a mutual awareness that is basic to a more functional type of politics. The great Depression provided a number of social and political crises which afforded these groups opportunities for political alliance. In particular, the greatly depressed market prices offered by European firms for Ghana's primary cash crop, cocoa, sparked widespread cocoa farmers' boycotts of cocoa-buying firms.

Kwahu chiefs played a major role in Ghana's most extensive cocoa boycotts in 1937, much more so than the chiefs in other cocoa-growing districts. Kwahu chiefs also joined a boycott movement of European consumer goods, a movement sparked by Kwahu populists. Furthermore, the exercise of Kwahu chiefs' influence in behalf of the cocoa boycott was modernist in character, free of traditionalist forms of pressure and clout. This contrasted markedly with the practices of chiefs in Ashanti and the Central Province, where such traditionalist instruments as swearing oaths against the sale of cocoa were widely employed. "The holdup of this District," wrote the Kwahu district commissioner in December 1973, "appears to be quite voluntary and no cases were reported of compulsion being used on farmers not to sell. The boycott of European firms is also strong and apart from a case early in November when two Native Administration Police brought before the [district commissioner's] Court were charged with interfering with a woman who was making a purchase from a store in Nkawkaw, no cases of attempted force have been reported."[28]

Another instance of the ability of Kwahu chiefs to adapt their neo-traditional politics to changing realities occurred in 1939, when the colonial government, after more than twenty years of vacillation, enacted the Native Administration Treasuries Ordinance of 1939.[29] This legislation empowered the government to require Native Administrations to establish treasuries and to account for revenue and expenditures, subject to supervision by government officials. But chiefs were allowed some initiative in approaching the government to establish treasuries in their Native Administrations.

Kwahu chiefs were among the first in Ghana to establish Native Administration treasuries under the 1939 ordinance. By March 1939 the central Native Administration in kwahu District, located at Obomeng, boasted a state treasury and eight additional treasuries in subordinate Native Administrations. Moreover, the chiefs in the central treasury were surrendering much of their financial authority to a Financial Committee, which was initially composed solely of educated persons, including an educated representative of the *asafo* populists.[30]

Some Kwahu chiefs later felt that they had let go of too much authority in financial matters, and in 1940 they moved successfully to reconstitute the Financial Committee. But the restructuring was not meant to serve uneducated or conservative chiefs. Rather, it allowed for several educated nominees of chiefs.

The reconstituted Financial Committee, now called the Financial Board, gained widespread acceptance and was effective at increasing the revenue of the central Native Administration. In particular, the board persuaded numerous Kwahu chiefs to divulge and surrender incomes from customary sources like court fees, fines, land incomes, and customary levies. The Financial Board also facilitated popular participation in its affairs, holding annual public audits of the Native Administration's finances attended by farmers, artisans, wage laborers, etc. The district commissioner commented on one such public audit held in 1943 as follows: "The public audit on the State Treasury Accounts were held at Abetifi on the 12th of April. The meeting was well attended and numerous questions were asked."[31]

Few chiefly strata elsewhere in Ghana compared to the Kwahu chiefs in the adaptability of neo-traditional politics. In Ashanti few, if any, Native Administrations experienced the spread of representative tendencies before the mid-1940s. For example, the central Native Administration in the Ejisu Division did not acquire a Financial Committee with popular representation until 1945–1946. Advances in the financial administration of central Native Administration in Ejisu were registered within less than a year of the Financial Committee's creation: "Their [the Financial Committee's] efforts led to the detection of irregularities in collection of the cocoa tribute for last year [1945] and the matter is in the hands of the Police. It was also propaganda by the Financial Board which had a considerable effect in including the young men to agree to the increase in levy. . . ."[32]

This development did not take place in the Kumasi Division until 1948. In the same year the first limitations were placed upon the share of revenue from customary land payments claimed by chiefs in Kumasi Division, thus enabling the Native Administrations to increase their revenues. As the district commissioner remarked in his annual report: "The share of land revenue payable to land-owning Chiefs has been reduced from 60 percent to 40 percent. This may still be considered too high but it is a definite improvement."[33]

## CHARACTER OF AFRICAN POPULISM: GENERALIZING THE GHANAIAN EXPERIENCE

It is, of course, never easy to discern a general political process or dynamic from a single manifestation. Yet our case study of the political dynamics of agrarian populism in the Kwahu District of Colonial Ghana reveals an exceptionally variegated pattern of rural politicization. Thus, while aware of the limits imposed on us by a single case study, it is possible to distill from it some of the *generic attributes* of African populism.

The political style of African populism seems to be intricately atavistic. This preference among African populists for grafting a traditional ethos (and the anxieties related to it) onto social and political choices that emerge in the context of modernization renders the rationalization of these choices difficult.

These features of African populism were widespread during the rash of populist-instigated dethronements of chiefs in the Ashanti areas of Ghana during World War I. For instance, the senior British commissioner of Ashanti remarked in his annual report for 1920 that "one common feature in these destoolments is the charge of mal-administration of [modern] Stool revenue. There is no proper system of dealing with these (modern) revenues, and most of the Stools are in debt." However, these same Ashanti populists were equally motivated by atavistic concerns: "There are also charges that the Chief violates native custom; that he breaks the [customary] laws to which he assented on his enstoolment; that he does not add to the Stool [traditional] property; and that he does not keep up [traditionalistic] appearances."[34] Furthermore, in the Agona

Division of Ashanti in 1918 a group of dissident young agrarians boycotted the election of a new paramount chief, charging him with violation of "certain rules—one of which concerned the number of wives the Omanhene should possess."[35] And in the Akim Abuakwa District in 1911 the emergent populists drew up an extensive list of charges, essentially traditionalistic in character, that they considered bona fide grounds for his dethronement: "(1) Excessive drinking. (2) Illicit intercourse with other people's wives, including those of his paternal uncles. (3) Being disrespectful and insulting to his sub-chiefs. (4) Purchasing things without paying for them." They also tacked on complaints of modern character, including "misappropriation of £800 entrusted to him."[36]

Thus it seems that while it is relatively easy to realize the usual manifest function of agrarian populism in Ghana—namely, dethroning a norm-breaking chief—the successive political step of dispensing with chiefly authority in a modernizing agrarian society was unacceptable.[37] This was so, moreover, despite the fact that the general context of populist politics in Ghana was sometimes rather conducive to political reformation of a revolutionary variety, owing to what might be called secondary politicizing spin-offs from primary populist assertions. It happens that a frequent political outcome of the populists' attack on paramount chiefs was a widespread populist-type disaffection of these chiefs' subordinates—so-called section or village chiefs. The senior British commissioner for Ashanti remarked in 1926, for instance, that "subchiefs are very much inclined to break away from their head stools, thereby declaring their independence."[38] Thus it seems that African populism is not lacking a potential to stimulate a pattern of political upheaval that might well sustain a political revolution in agrarian society. But revolution is, of course, fundamentally a matter of perception, not simply one of objective reality. The basic reason why Ghanaian populists did not push their oppositionary politics towards chiefs to revolutionary limits was that they were cross-pressured, so to speak, by deep-rooted ideological nexus with traditional authority.

Another dimension of the connection between Ghanaian and African populism requires attention. Viewed over the long run, populism in Ghana displays an interesting and curious *latent function*. Populism's persistent critique of chiefs' distortion of customary obligations stimulates some chiefs to restore legitimacy to their role and office; this, in turn, protects the traditional policy, especially its authority and deference patterns, from threats of basic political reformation. The senior commissioner for the Ashanti region was cognizant of this paradoxical feature of agrarian populism, as evidenced by his observation in 1920 that, when "judged in the light of the [social] changes that are taking place," the ubiquitous populist dethroning of chiefs is best understood not as a threat to the viability of chiefly office but is "rather a symptom of the vitality of native institutions. . . . Among the charges in the cases of destoolment are often charges of violation of native custom of which the 'youngmen' pose as the jealous guardian."[39]

Yet populism remains the fundamental cutting edge of change in the agrarian sector in much of Africa. And though African populism paradoxically reinforces certain traditional authority moorings while simultaneously critiquing and upending the dead hand of precapitalist forms upon African modernization, populism is nonetheless a persistent agent of at least quasi-secular and class awareness in the agrarian sector of African societies.[40] This is so, moreover, even though the rise of African nationalist movements and independent regimes in the 1950s and 1960s has brought more sophisticated agencies of modern politics to African societies. In general, the new political ruling classes in African societies utilize the new state power more to extend their own leverage than to advance that of popular society, especially the agrarian sector. On the other hand, the instrumentalities of African populism, while co-opted by the new rulers in most states for their own purposes, have nonetheless continued to be controlled by the agrarian sector, owing in part to the fact that to launch a viable populist thrust the African agrarians (and urban proletarians too) depend upon a unique syncretistic ideological format. This sphere of populist ideological sovereignty out of which African populist politics springs forth is put into motion typically by crises in the modern political economy of African states.[41]

Yet it is still doubtful how far along the sacred-secular continuum the populist outbursts by the crisis-riddled African masses will travel. For example, the extensive populist outbursts by the Maitatsine religious sect in northern Nigeria in December 1980 (resulting in some 5000 deaths) and more recently in February 1984 (again resulting in over 4000 deaths) display a persistent tendency of African populism to package claims against the modern state in syncretistic terms that emphasize restoring certain cultural forms while critiquing new inequities. These populist outbursts in northern Nigeria sought simultaneously to reduce class privileges brought about by modern wealth as well as to purify Islamic religious practices, and the leaders of the Maitatsine sect tried to realize these goals in the first instance not by seizing a state agency but by capturing the Central Mosque in Kano, using bows, arrows, swords, and antique guns.[42] Surely an effective differentiation in the sacred and secular constituents of class and political consciousness in African populism is not yet in the offing.

## SECULARIZING CLASS CONSCIOUSNESS: A NEO-MARXIST PERSPECTIVE

What is particularly baffling about African populism is the persistence, since the early 1900s, of the embryonic class consciousness that defines it. *Changes in this pattern of class consciousness are extremely slow.*

The crux of the problem, I think, is that African political development proceeds within a societal milieu (a normative and sociocultural context) wherein neither the traditionalist nor modernist norms are viably ascendant. Thus the status of *societal metamorphosis* in African states is highly syncretistic and the choices required of individual Africans are deeply ambiguous—so much so that the French sociologist Georges Balandier characterizes emergent African culture as *Afrique ambique.*[43]

This standoff between sacred and secular normative patterns results in a problematic process of political development or modernization for agrarian and working-class Africans, owing to the fact that African ruling classes hesitate to cultivate the secularization of African normative patterns because they fear a concomitant secularization of class consciousness.[44] During the period of nationalist party politics in the 1950s to early 1960s, African political rulers closely regulated the politicization of the agrarian masses, especially the *normative dimensions* of such politicization. This control of the normative dimensions of politicization was intensified under African authoritarian governance—the African one-party and military regimes that commenced in the middle 1960s.[45]

Thus, in the typical African state, the politically effective linkages between the ruling classes and the masses are mediated by tribal, lineage, kinship, religious, and other traditional norm-mediating agencies. This is so, moreover, even when the more modernized segments among the masses fashion secularizing interest groups—such as trade unions and farmers' associations—because these modern interest groups qualify or checkmate secularization.

Furthermore, sacred modalities of politicization in African systems are everywhere shrouded in a *collectivist ethos* which discourages the individual from acting (making choices) outside the boundaries of primordial collectivities. Sacred modalities of politicization are also shrouded in a presumptive (phony) *equalitarian ethos* which, when linked to the collectivist ethos, implies that there is parity in life-cycle circumstances in African societies, regardless of whether one's status is high rank or commoner. Joan Vincent perceptively delineates this phenomenon in her analysis of modern leadership patterns among the Gondo tribe in Uganda, observing that there prevails "an equalitarian myth that permitted leadership to pass unresented."[46]

*Thus it would seem that sacred modalities of politicization in African systems tend to ritualize rather than objectify power, protecting the ruling classes in their power monopoly.* Put another way, minimizing secular modalities of social perception and political choice—especially the values of belief systems that emphasize the efficacy of the individual, his capacity to innovate and fashion solutions to problems—militates in favor of the ruling classes. Almost everywhere in contemporary Africa the ruling classes have implicitly understood this.

Finally, this helps us to grasp, from a cultural and hence multidimensional perspective, an important feature of African politics during the 1960s and 1970s— the decline of competitive politics. Democracy, as a method of modernization and politicization, has a long-run tendency to secularize popular consciousness; it enhances the growth of individuals who believe in self-efficacy.[47] Perceiving this, the African bourgeoisie scuttles democracy or competitive politics, closing off by force and stealth the avenues available to the masses to power and influence at both the center and periphery of African states, much like what Marx had in mind when he remarked that "during the very first storms of the [French] revolution, the French bourgeoisie dared to take away from the workers the right of association but just acquired."[48]

This preference on the part of the ruling classes in African states for sustaining an atavistic popular mind-set or consciousness represents a profoundly cynical approach to political development. It is also a costly perspective, because in the long run the quality of modern development is jeopardized, owing to the fact that the character of modernization in crucial secular spheres like technology, science, production, and bureaucracy depends upon a popular mind-set that can deal with these components of modernization on their own terms. The popular mind-set must be encouraged to surrender some of its primordial attachment to the sacred nexus, a task that politics has performed in other parts of the world that have experienced effective modernization.

But rulers in a modernizing society who exercise political hegemony for its own sake—or, what amounts to the same thing, for sake of the wealth-appropriating monopoly such hegemony allows—run the risk of almost certainly condemning that state and its people to an inferior position on the developmental trajectory. This has been amply demonstrated in the cynical type of elite hegemonic regimes in Latin America and in Caribbean regimes like Haiti[49]—regimes characterized by massive kleptocratic and coercive governance—and equally in some African governments like Uganda, Zaire, Guinea, Upper Volta, Liberia, Central African Republic, Equatorial Guinea, Ghana, and Niger.[50]

## REBELLION SCENARIOS

### Proxy Rebellion

What role can agrarian populism play in the future in upending the dead hand of kleptocratic ruling class governance in African societies? This, of course, is one of the most baffling issues confronting analysts of African political systems. In general, radicalizing or rebellious pressures from the agrarian sector in African regimes have not been abundant during the past twenty years of authoritarian governance. This is so despite the disastrous neglect of the agrarian sector. Kleptocratic rulers have so mismanaged the developmental priorities between the urban and agrarian sectors in African states, distorting the agrarian sector's capacity to contribute to economic and social development and sparking a food production crisis of enormous proportion, that a recent World Bank study predicts that "Under any but the most favorable circumstances, people in sub-Saharan Africa will be poorer in 1990 than they are now."[51]

What, then, can be expected in the way of rebellious agrarian pressures in African politics? Perhaps not much. Thus I would agree with Gavin Williams's suggestion that "Peasants have not usually sought to transform their society either along lines of their own choosing or on the lines willed for them by socialist intellectuals. They have sought [instead] to defend their gains within the frontiers of peasant society, but have not acted of their own accord to seize state power and thus control the instrument of their own exploitation. . . . In particular, African peasants lack access to the literate culture through which the contemporary state is administered and legitimated."[52]

Though Gavin Williams is correct in his realist assessment of the prospects of agrarian rebellion in African regimes, his assessment might be somewhat more pessimistic than it need be. By focusing mainly on the capacity of the agrarian sector to launch rebellious responses *in its own right* and through its own machinations, Williams neglects the more likely prospect of agrarian allies launching rebellion *in the name of populist concerns*. This populist rebellious scenario would involve leadership roles by elements from marginal groups like minor bureaucrats, trade union officials, junior-rank military officers, etc. In sparking a rebellious outbreak, these elements would be fashioning a *populist-rebellion-in-proxy* for the alienated agrarians.

Indeed, something resembling this proxy-rebellion scenario characterized the coups d'état in 1979 and 1981 in Ghana, led by Flight Lieutenant Jerry Rawlings, and in 1980 in Liberia, led by Master Sergeant Samuel Doe. Victoria Brittain, a keen observer of Ghanaian politics, delineates this populist-rebellious feature of these coups when she remarks that "When Flight Lieutenant Rawlings seized power . . . it was, like similar coups in Liberia and Ethiopia (1972), under the pressure of intolerable economic crisis which has brought in its wake social and political crises of equally daunting proportions. . . . Under [previous civilian and military] regimes the economic slide continued downwards; corruption continued upwards. The common soldier lived as poorly as peasants and urban workers, but close enough to those in power to know only too well how exploitative [the regimes] were."[53]

The coups d'état in Ghana and Liberia displayed a distinctly populist ambience, occurring as they did at the lower ranks of the armed forces. They also displayed fierce bloodletting, directed against the chief figures who controlled the kleptocratic oligarchies the coups overturned. But neither Rawlings's nor Doe's coups was able to sustain its populist aura, failing to elaborate a viable populist reorganization of state power. Rawlings's junta—the Armed Forces Revolutionary Council—Surrendered power to a civilian government after four months, and the Doe Junta coalesced with a new segment of domestic oligarchic rulers and multinational firms, thereby effectively negating the distinctly populist forces which propelled it into power. But while Sergeant Doe eventually inflated his military rank to that of "General" and donned a scholarly rank of "Doctor," Flight Lieutenant Rawlings remained a low-rank officer and in December 1981 seized power again, this time pushed by expansive populist forces that saw to it that "the traditional authority and privilege of [elite] groups were frontally challenged." And even though the enormous economic dislocation in Ghana has forced the Rawlings regime to compromise with the established bourgeoisie, foreign firms, and especially international financial forces associated with the International Monetary Fund, some fundamental features of this regime's populism, like the Public Tribunals, have survived. Clearly linked to Rawlings's governing Provisional National Defense Council, the Public Tribunals, according to their chairman, "have come to stay and need to stay. . . . Many lawyers . . . also see the objective need for a system of dispensing justice that includes those people without the 'traditional legal training.' . . . There will be community, district, and regional tribunals."[54]

### Restorationist Rebellion

Another rebellion scenario for agrarian upheaval is plausible. This scenario involves a populist outbreak akin to the Ayatollah-led rebellion that forced the fall of the Shah in Iran in 1979. The Ayatollah-type populist scenario is initiated by, or at least executed with the aid of, religious leaders and other arbiters of traditionalist values. This type of populist upheaval seeks, at the very least, the restoration of traditionalist-type controls (or the aura of such controls) over modern power and processes. This scenario is made possible by the marked degree of alienation of the agrarian masses (about 80 percent of the population in the typical African state) from the postcolonial modernization process. Such stark alienation reflects a vacuum in regard to popular authority in African regimes, a vacuum likely to be intensified by the contemporary economic crisis in African states.

Leaders of the Ayatollah-type populist upheaval, best described perhaps as neo-traditionalist in orientation, will be radical perforce. They will, that is, be required to reject, at least symbolically, much of the pseudoideologies (e.g., Nkrumahism, Mobutuism, etc.) that have been used to legitimate the African ruling classes, replacing them with neo-traditionalist forms. However, while denying legitimacy to the pseudoideologies that the ruling classes have opportunistically fashioned for themselves, the tradition-restorationist process associated with the Ayatollah-type populist upheaval will probably permit modern wealth-producing patterns. Modernization is not, after all, precluded by the restorationist aura of a traditionalist-skewed political order, as evidenced in early twentieth-century Japan and elsewhere.[55] So the agrarian masses, accustomed to restorationist assertions during the colonial phase of modernization, might very well find the Ayatollah-type populist thrusts appealing.

In practice, the Ayatollah-type populist upheaval is likely to occur in African regimes as a by-product or a second stage of a rebellious populist scenario of the Rawlings type whereby counterelites ally with peasants to produce a populist-rebellion-in-proxy for the agrarian sector. The counterelites who succeed with this rebellious populist option will turn to african variants of Ayatollahs—to chiefs, witch-cult leaders, Koranic teachers, and syncretistic religious leaders—for assistance in extending their regime's political authority.[56]

A prototype of the kind of traditionalistic leadership and populist organization capable of sustaining a restorationist rebellion against kleptocratic governance in African states emerged in northern Nigeria in the late 1970s and early 1980s. Known popularly as the Maitatsine sect, this militant muslim movement was founded by Mohammed Marwa, a Koranic teacher, whose followers, residing in both small towns and cities of northern Nigeria, are "mainly peasants and urban poor . . . adept with knives, matchets, bows, and arrows and would gladly launch suicidal assaults in defence of their cause. They [are] dogmatically opposed to many aspects of modern life and some of them reportedly regarded their charismatic leader and mystic as the true prophet of Allah. After their founder Maitatsine [Marwa's religious name] was killed in the Kano disturbances [1980], there were reports that copies of the Koran had been found in his house with Mohammed's name crossed out and maitatsine inserted."[57]

During the last five years the Maitatsine sect has launched five major riots (in Kano State, 1980; Borno state and Kaduna State, 1982; Gongola State, 1984; and Bauchi State, 1985), in the course of which Maitatsine spokesmen pronounced their opposition to class privileges brought about by modern wealth as well as their wish to purify Islamic religious practices in Nigerian society. The realization of this syncretistic agenda—modern class equity and religious restoration—was to be accomplished in the first instance not by seizing state power directly but by capturing, in the 1980 Kano riots, the Central mosque in Kano, using bows, arrows, swords, and antique guns. The Nigerian army intervened in the Kano riots, resulting in nearly 5000 deaths, and subsequent riots have added some 4000 deaths to the toll.[58] There is clearly a fervent tenacity in restorationist-type populist groups.

Restorationist sects or organizations with populist capability are common enough in African states (e.g., Lenshina Movement in Zambia, Bwiti Cult in Gabon, Mau Mau in Kenya, etc.), so that there is presently a widespread potential for the Ayatollah-type populist rebellion.[59] The key variable in such a rebellion would appear to be the appearance of viable counterelites—most likely dissident military officers or soldiers—who entertain a deep-rooted emotional disenchantment with the moral and political decay of African governance and modernization. This *trauma of modernist disenchantment* compels such counterelites to ally with restorationist groups, forging an emotively complex marriage of coercive state authority and rigid cultural authority. The current regime in Iran fits this characterization, and it is not idle speculation to suggest that a number of African regimes currently dislocated systemically by moral and political decay (e.g., Zaire, Uganda, Guinea, Central African Republic, Sudan, Chad, Ethiopia, etc.) are ready-made candidates for this metamorphosis.

## CONCLUDING NOTE

While either populist-rebellion-in-proxy for the agrarian masses or Ayatollah-type restorationist rebellion is a possible development in the near future in a number of African states, the typical populist responses in today's authoritarian African regimes will evolve well below the rebellion threshold. For one thing, the African populists' seemingly endemic attachment to atavistic behavior is likely to persist. At the same time, a protracted but distinctive acquisition of secularizing norms, especially in areas of economic modernization, will also characterize the agrarian populists. This is suggested by an analysis of agrarian adaptive responses to economic change and political modernization during the years between the two world wars in Ghana, and during the postwar era as well.[60] An analysis of the 1970s by Naomi Chazan also supports the expectation of protracted acquisition of secularizing norms by African agrarian populists. For Ghana, Chazan found that

> The populist political culture that crystallized in the 1970s exhibited . . . a coherence, an inclusivity, and a specificity not easily found in [Nkrumahist] political thought. They were also much more change-oriented and secular than their state counterparts. . . . Populist notions sprung from below and flourished on the basis of indigenously rooted ideas that addressed changing conditions. . . .[61]

Chazan's view of the secular tendencies in Ghanaian populism is, I think, rather overstated, suggesting a unilinear trajectory of secular transformation. The reality is, in fact, far more uneven and diffuse, with each secularizing breakthrough checkmated, as it were, by an atavistic commitment or imperative. What Chazan fails to grasp is that the embryonic class consciousness that defines African agrarian populism (and proletarian populism too) has not yet reached the stage of a sustained sense of class-power interests.

This means, in particular, that it has not proved easy for African populism to integrate and institutionalize popular grievances and concerns across ethnic and class contours, as Catherine Newberry has recently shown in a perceptive analysis of price riots among Tembo women cassava traders in eastern Zaire. Newberry also remarks on another crucial constraint on the radicalization of African populism, *namely, the localistic territorial isolation of many populist assertions.*[62] Thus, without some kind of dynamic whereby a more politically viable leadership aggregates and allies with localized populist proclivities, African populism's political potential will for the most part continue to lack a system-changing capability.

# CHAPTER 3

# Wars of Liberation and the International System: Western Sahara—a Case in Point

**Jeffrey M. Schulman**

In the past quarter of a century, the world has witnessed a proliferation of liberation parties and wars of liberation. While all liberation parties have as an ultimate goal the successful completion of the war, certain liberation parties have a radically different method of achieving this. These parties, such as the Polisario Front in Western Sahara and the National Liberation Front in Algeria, create an entity that can vie for legitimacy on the international level with the state from which they are seeking independence. With the announcement of the creation of a new sovereign state, the Saharan Arab Democratic Republic in Western Sahara and the Popular and Democratic Republic in Algeria, the respective liberation parties launched a deliberate, concerted effort to gain access to the units, and their norms and organizations, that comprise the international system for utilization in exerting pressure on the state they were fighting. The adoption of this tactic, in turn, mandates that the liberation party suppress differences based upon class, ethnicity, and gender, in order to present itself as the representative of a unified society. This paper will examine this tactic and its ramifications through the current situation in Western Sahara.

## ESTABLISHING THE WAR'S CONTEXT

Joel Migdal, when describing peasant participation in revolutions, stated that revolutionaries "seek to supply an increasing number of components leading to the development of a new network, autonomous from the existing national system."[1] In short, the revolutionaries attempt to create a quasi-state within an already existing state, that is capable of meeting all the needs of the revolution and its participants until it is sufficiently strong enough to destroy the competing organization of the old national system and assume control over the entire state. The Polisario Front and the National Liberation Front, however, also sought to outmaneuver the existing state on the international level. These parties seek direct access to the international system through the announcement of the creation of a new sovereign state followed by a concerted effort to have the new state accepted as such. This process entails the actual creation of a government with a diplomatic corps and bureaucracy to represent the new state in the international forum. To the degree that this diplomatic corps can succeed in gaining recognition and acceptance for the newly proclaimed state in the international community, the liberation party gains legitimacy and can utilize the norms and organizations of the international system to exert pressure on the state it is fighting to achieve concessions and ultimately a termination of the hostilities. Moreover, this tactic of carrying the battle to the diplomatic plane provides a means for the liberation party for surmounting the realities and constraints of military weakness. Thus liberation parties that adopt this tactic seek to have the conflict viewed as one between two equal units of the international system rather than an established state authority suppressing insurrection or guerilla incursions.

The creation of the State of Israel is illustrative of the commencement of this process of internationalization. In April 1948, the Zionist General Council adopted the following resolution:

> In accordance with the decision of the World Zionist Organization and with the approval of Jews everywhere we resolve that with the termination of the British Mandate and the end of foreign rule, the Jewish people will establish an independent regime in their homeland.[2]

On the basis of this resolution, a provisional government was formed. While David Ben-Gurion noted that the "Zionist General Council's decision had no legal standing vis-à-vis the outside world since the Mandatory Government was still in power,"[3] it is significant that the liberation party made the decision to announce the creation of their state.[4] Accordingly, on May 14, 1948, upon the departure of the British, the Provisional State Council announced the creation of the State of Israel.[5] In reality, there had already been fierce fighting between Jews and Arabs in Palestine. Moreover, upon the departure of the British the territory would be subject to invasion by neighboring states. Thus the liberation party sought to prevent a political vacuum with the departure of the British. Through the announcement of the creation of the State of Israel, the liberation party attempted to have the conflict viewed as one where they were the lawful authority of the territory and were engaging in self-defense rather than resisting other states attempting to restore order to a territory torn by civil strife. By adopting this tactic, the liberation party laid claim to the territory and established the framework and context within which the fighting took place.

The course of action adopted by the Polisario Front in the former Spanish Sahara was identical to the policy adopted by the Zionists in Palestine. In August 1974, the first goal adopted as part of a National Action Program by the Second Popular Congress of the Polisario Front was national liberation and complete independence of the Western Sahara.[6] Accordingly, on February 27, 1976, when Spain withdrew from the territory and surrendered it to Morocco and Mauritania, the Polisario Front announced the creation of the Saharan Arab Democratic Republic with the Saharan National Provisional Council to be the legislative assembly.[7] In reality, there had already been fierce fighting between the Polisario front and the invading forces of Morocco in the north and Mauritania in the south. Yet, once again, the liberation party, in this case the Polisario Front, through the announcement of the creation of their state, laid claim to the territory and established the framework and context of the current conflict in Western Sahara.[8]

The quick actualization of the state of Israel, in contrast to the Saharan Arab Democratic Republic, is primarily attributable to two factors. The Zionists had a worldwide network of support and had feverishly prepared for war.[9] Moreover, when the state of Israel was announced, there was no other competing entity claiming title to the same territory. Thus the swift military victories of the Israeli forces insured international recognition of their creation. The absence of these favorable factors determined that the struggle in the Western Sahara would be protracted. Not only was the Polisario Front not as militarily prepared as the Israelis, but Morocco and Mauritania laid claim to the territory through the Madrid Accords, a tripartite agreement with Spain which transferred the administration of this non-self-governing territory to Morocco and Mauritania.[10] Thus, upon the announcement of the Saharan Arab Democratic Republic, the Polisario Front faced the situation where vast parts of the territory were occupied by states who laid claim to the territory and whose forces were militarily superior to those of the liberation party. This situation, though, was not without precedent.

On September 19, 1958, the National Liberation Front proclaimed their state, the Algerian Republic, while France occupied vast parts of Algeria and claimed title to Algeria.[11] As Mohammed Bedjaoui stated when discussing the Algerian Republic's diplomatic relations, "The Algerian people's struggle against an imperialism militarily and politically more powerful than themselves forced them to pay considerable attention to the struggle on the diplomatic plane."[12] In Algeria, the French were firmly in control of the metropolitan area with the National Liberation Front in firm control only of part of the hinterland. The reality of the situation was one of military stalemate whereby neither side was of sufficient strength to dislodge or destroy the other in its respective area. Thus, in order to carry the struggle forward past the reality of military weakness and the prospect of a stalemate, the National Liberation Front internationalized the conflict by announcing the creation of the Algerian Republic and then seeking recognition of their state. The alternative to the adoption of this tactic, in the event of a protracted military stalemate, could have been political stagnation of the National Liberation Front with a forced accommodation with the French. Such an accommodation would most probably have meant partitionment of the territory.[13]

The situation in the Western Sahara was identical. Morocco and Mauritania were in control of the cities and towns. Only the interior of the territory was under the control of the Polisario Front when they announced the creation of the Saharan Arab Democratic Republic. Again the situation was one of military weakness on the part of the liberation party. Thus, as the National Liberation Front had done, the Polisario Front internationalized the conflict by announcing the creation of the Saharan Arab Democratic Republic and then seeking recognition of their state. Similarly, the alternative to announcing a state which encompassed the entire territory would most probably have meant permanent partitionment of the territory.[14]

## THE DIPLOMATIC FRONT

With the announcement of the Saharan Arab Democratic Republic, and the subsequent initiatives by the Polisario front to achieve international recognition of their state, a clear understanding of the Polisario Front's actions becomes mandatory. Unfortunately, this topic has been obscured by several misconceptions. In one book, the authors state that "in setting up the RASD with the trappings of a sovereign state the Polisario lost the chance of being recognized by the OAU as a liberation movement, while not improving the prospect of its being admitted as an independent nation to membership in that body."[15] The rationale offered was that "to become a member required a two-thirds affirmative vote by OAU heads of state, whereas recognition by the OAU of the Polisario as a liberation movement needed only a simple majority."[16] In reality, Article XXVIII of the Charter of the Organization of African Unity clearly states that admission of a state shall be decided by a simple majority of the member states,[17] and in 1982, by a simple majority, the Saharan Arab Democratic Republic became the fifty-first member of that organization.[18]

Similar misconceptions concern the nature of the conflict. Certain authors acknowledge the forcible occupation of the Western Sahara, but state that within the creation of their state, "the Polisario . . . added a disruptive political dimension to what until then had been applauded as the challenge by an African David to a European Goliath."[19] In short, with the Saharan Arab Democratic Republic in opposition to Morocco and Mauritania, as opposed to a colonial power, infighting and confusion is mandated because the parties are "all Arabs and Africans."[20] Accordingly, these authors conclude "by early 1976, therefore, the stakes in the Western Sahara had been so altered by both parties to the dispute that the Third World in general and the Polisario in particular were cast into disarray."[21] Yet such reasoning seems specious. To acknowledge the forcible occupation and yet criticize the creation of the Saharan Arab Democratic Republic for the dissension it will cause in the Arab and African family of nations is to oppose rape and yet chastize the victim for resisting because of the rapist's lineage. Moreover, by early 1976, the one item that had not been altered in the Western Sahara was the "stakes." For Morocco,[22] Mauritania,[23] and the Polisario Front,[24] the stakes had been and still were the Western Sahara.

What is evident, though, is that these authors have chosen to focus on certain effects of, and reactions to, decisions made by the Polisario Front rather than the underlying causes of those decisions. Thus, by stating that "in setting up the RASD with the trappings of a sovereign state the Polisario lost the chance of being recognized by the OAU as a liberation movement," it is implied, through the use of the word "trappings," that the Saharan Arab Democratic Republic is not a real state and that status as a liberation movement was preferable. Yet if this is true, why did the Polisario Front create the Saharan Arab Democratic Republic? The above question becomes even more intriguing in the light of the fact that at the time of the announcement of the Saharan Arab Democratic Republic, the Western Sahara had already been invaded by two states militarily and politically more powerful than the Polisario Front. Thus the Polisario Front knew that they would have great difficulty in making their announcement a reality and yet still chose to announce the creation of their state. While these authors do not provide a clear understanding or appreciation of exactly what it is that the Polisario Front is attempting to do, they do provide a clue. The clue is contained in their characterization of the Saharan Arab Democratic Republic as a "disruptive" influence.

With the announcement of a sovereign state by the liberation party, the conflict is thrust into the international system and the embattled state which is seeking to maintain control over the disputed territory suddenly finds itself engaged in a struggle against the international system. As Mohammed Bedjaoui noted:

> On the day after the Algerian Republic was proclaimed, the French Government warned all countries with which it maintains diplomatic relations that any subsequent recognition by them of the Algerian Provisional Government would be considered most 'unfriendly.'

> Since September 19, 1958, French diplomacy can be said to have been in a permanent state of alert, exerting pressure and making numerous overtures and protests. Threats of reprisals have even been formulated.[25]

With slight modifications, these statements describe the diplomatic mobilization of Morocco against the Saharan Arab Democratic Republic.[26] These defensive responses are an acknowledgment of the structure of the international system wherein all the units are sovereign independent states. To the degree that the liberation party succeeds in having its proclaimed state accepted as such, international organizations comprised of states, such as the Arab League or the Organization of African Unity, and norms regulating conduct between states, such as multilateral treaties which limit hostilities, become accessible for utilization in exerting pressure on the state which is seeking to maintain control over the territory. Moreover, acceptance of the libertion party's state converts the conflict into one between two equal members of the system and the justification the embattled state proffers for the fighting, such as suppressing insurrection or guerrilla incursions, is eroded or destroyed. Consequently, the embattled state is forced to adopt an aggressive defensive posture as organizations and states friendly to the newly proclaimed state become sources of condemnation.

One of the most basic tenets of international law is that all states are sovereign and equal.[27] From this concept of sovereignty, that each state alone is responsible for what transpires within its territory, arises the principle that no state should intervene in the internal affairs of another state.[28] These two concepts, sovereignty and nonintervention in the domestic affairs of another state, are the focal point of the diplomatic struggle which ensues when liberation parties seek access to the international system. The embattled state continually asserts that the conflict is solely a domestic issue. After the proclamation of the Algerian Republic, the French continually asserted to any and all who would listen that the situation in Algeria was one of rebellion. On April 30, 1959, from the rostrum of the French National Assembly, the French Prime Minister stated:

> I wish as from this evening to say that friendly Governments, neutral Governments and responsible powers have been warned by our Ambassadors, and are constantly kept informed by our Minister of Foreign Affairs, both of our wishes and the consequences of any aid which they might give to the rebellion.[29]

In 1976, following the announcement of the Saharan Arab Democratic Republic, Morocco and Mauritania asserted that "the people of Western Sahara are their brothers who welcome the annexations,"[30] and "the question of Western Sahara is an internal one."[31] Morocco even went so far as to characterize the hostilities as raids by Algerian guerrillas.[32] These responses of embattled states are attempts to keep the conflict at a level below cognizance of the international system. Thus resolution of the issue will fall solely within the jurisdiction of the embattled state, and actions by other states can be labeled as intervention or affronts to sovereignty. Conversely, the liberation party, by gaining recognition of its state as a member of the international system, legitimizes its position at the expense of the embattled state and elevates the conflict to where it can utilize institutional structures and norms increasingly to put pressure on the embattled state as a recalcitrant member of the system and seek a termination of the conflict. Illustrative is the Polisario Front's success in getting the Organization of African Unity and the United Nations to insist that Morocco hold a referendum in the Western Sahara.[33]

## THE PSYCHOLOGICAL FRONT

It is this attempt to internationalize the conflict which clearly differentiates the National Liberation Front in Algeria and the Polisario Front in Western Sahara from other liberation parties such as the Palestine Liberation Organization in Lebanon and the South-West African People's Organization in Namibia. The Algerian Revolution commenced in November 1954, and yet it was not until September 1958 that the National Liberation Front proclaimed the Algerian Republic. This fact, as well as Algeria's own literature on the subject, demonstrates that the decision to internationalize the conflict was a well-thought-out strategy.[34] For the announcement of a new state by the liberation party is not only a method of attempting to win the war of liberation, it is also a method of transforming the issues involved. A clear example of this is the issue of decolonization and the right of self-determination for non-self-governing peoples.

Since the lowest unit in the international system is a sovereign state, those liberation parties, such as the Palestine Liberation Organization or the South-West African People's Organization, who do not claim to be states are left in an ambiguous position. Because these entities are of a status lower than that of the lowest unit within the international system, even if they are recognized as the legitimate representative of their people, the question remains as to what their exact status is. Thus embattled states can use derogatory and inflammatory appellations, such as "Marxist" or "terrorist organization," to characterize these liberation parties, while professing willingness to discuss the issue with any state or legitimate entity. The result of this tactic is that any attempt to resolve these conflicts gets bogged down over technical matters such as what status should be afforded these liberation parties and how the non-self-governing people will exercise their right of self-determination. Partially out of frustration with this seemingly intractable morass, a Middle East observer urged the following:

> After the recent cease-fire, Yasir Arafat has a new political strength.
>
> He should feel able now to do what he has never yet dared, to proclaim a provisional government in exile. . . .

By forming a government . . . Mr. Arafat would dramatically transform his claim
to international recognition of the P.L.O.[35]

While Afif Safeih, aide to Yasir Arafat, stated, "Today the PLO is a pre-
governmental organization which is already assuming the responsibilities of a
state,"[36] the Palestine Liberation Organization still lacks unity. This was clearly
demonstrated when radical factions initially ignored the call for a cease-fire
and even shelled Yasir Arafat's headquarters in Tripoli, Lebanon. Only after
increased pressure was brought to bear on these elements was a cease-fire ef-
fectuated. Similarly, due to the lack of status of the South-West African People's Organization, the political situation in Namibia has devolved into inter-
minable technical discussions on decolonization. There, however, the problem
is not one of lack of unity but of support. In Namibia, as was the case with
Zimbabwe, there is more than one liberation party. Consequently, in Lebanon
and Namibia, any present claim to be a government would probably lack credibility, cause interfactional conflicts, and buttress the position of the embattled
state. However, those liberation parties that can achieve a unity of purpose and
support seek to internationalize the conflict and transmute the entire issue of
decolonization and the right of self-determination for non-self-governing peoples.

When the state of Israel was proclaimed, within the proclamation was the
following language:

On November 29, 1947, the General Assembly of the United Nations adopted a
resolution calling for the establishment of a Jewish State in the Land of Israel, and
required the inhabitants themselves to take all measures necessary on their part to
carry out the resolution. This recognition by the United Nations of the right of the
Jewish people to establish their own State is irrevocable.

It is the natural right of the Jewish people, like any other people to control their
own destiny in their sovereign State.[37]

Similarly the Preamble of the Statutes of the National Liberation Front states
that the

struggle of the Algerian people is taking place within the vast movement of liberation
of the African and Asian peoples. It is taking place as part of the historic process
of the liberation of colonial peoples. The victory of the Algerian people will contribute to strengthening the idea of peace and liberty throughout the world.[38]

So, too, with the Polisario Front, who asserted that their goal was one of "National liberation from all forms of colonialism and the achievement of complete
independence."[39] While the language differs, what is significant is that each
of these liberation parties utilized the issue of decolonization and the right of
self-determination as the basis for and the foundation of their respective announced states. Consequently, with the liberation party's announcement of its
state, the focus shifts from a technical discussion of how and under what conditions a non-self-governing people will exercise their right of self-determination, to whether that people have in fact exercised that right. In short, the existence of the liberation party's state and its acceptance by members of the
international system force other states to view the conflict as proof that the indigenous people either were denied their right of self-determination by the em-

battled state[40] or are exercising their right of self-determination through the creation of their state.[41] Naturally, the advancement of either perception among states erodes the legitimacy of the embattled state's position and increases the pressure on that state to seek a termination of the conflict. Thus, in the context of liberation parties that internationalize the conflict, the discussion on decolonization accelerates and becomes dynamic rather than mired in details and obstructions.

## INTERNAL MOBILIZATION

The new state, however, as a representative of its peole, can only be credible if the liberation party has first achieved a unity of purpose and support. These goals are accomplished through subordinating internal fractionalizing forces. Thus, to gain legitimacy and support, those liberation parties which seek to internationalize the conflict reorganize their society within the indigenous culture. An example of a cultural framework used as a unifying factor in the formation and maintenance of statehood is religion. Israel, Algeria, and the Saharan Arab Democratic Republic are prime examples. Yet, in each of these cases, the liberation party subordinated or destroyed societal barriers based upon gender, class, or tribal affiliation. Consequently, the liberation party gained support from previously repressed segments of the society and the diminished viability of competing allegiances.

Common societal barriers subordinated by liberation parties seeking to internationalize the conflict are those based upon gender. Out of military necessity, the domestic role of women is superseded by the war effort. Women are given military training and used in military support roles. During the Algerian revolution, according to statistics from the Ministry of Former Moujahidines, there were 10,949 active women participants.[42] In the Western Sahara, women are responsible for the maintenance and defense of the refugee camps.[43] Placed in positions of importance, women are given access and allowed input in the decision-making process of the liberation party. Thus the party modifies the traditional role of women and portrays itself as more egalitarian than the government it is attempting to replace. The National Liberation Front's goal of power sharing with all the Algerian people[44] and the Polisario Front's goal of social justice with all citizens equal before the law[45] are examples of this policy. In each case, the liberation party sought to have women view the conflict as one in which they have a real stake in the outcome and give primary allegiance to the party over family and tribal allegiances.

Other barriers, such as class or tribal affiliation, may also be neutralized or undermined. Private property is allowed in the Saharan Arab Democratic Republic so long as it is nonexploitative. However, national property belongs to the people.[46] Thus distinctions based upon wealth or ethnic origin,[47] such as status or privilege, are minimized while social services and resources are guaranteed to the people.[48] The degree and type of reorganization implemented is dependent upon the situation confronting the liberation party. While the Algerian Revolution commenced in 1954, it was not until 1958 that the National Liberation Front proclaimed the Algerian Republic. This long period indicates the difficulty the National Liberation Front had in subordinating competing factions and attaining sufficient support to be a credible representative of the Algerian people.

In the Western Sahara, the Constitution of the Saharan Arab Democratic Republic clearly reflects the Polisario Front's internal policy. A few excerpts should suffice:

*Article 3*. Islam, the State religion, is the source of laws. The Arabic language is the national and official language.

*Article 4*. . . . The achievement of socialism and the application of social justice are one of the objectives of the State.

*Article 5*. The family, the basis of society, is founded on morality and religion.

*Article 6*. All citizens are equal before the law. They have the same rights and duties.

*Article 7*. Liberty of expression is guaranteed within the limits of the law and the interests of the people. Education, health and social protection are rights guaranteed to all citizens.

*Article 8*. National property belongs to the people. Private property is guaranteed as long as it does not involve exploitation.

Readily apparent is the cultural framework of family, religion, language, and the reconsituted society of social justice and equality before the law. As to the ongoing process of securing allegiance and nation building, the state will achieve these goals through the administration of Koranic schools, the abandonment of Spanish as the official language, and the adoption of symbols such as the state flag and motto.[49] However, the reconstituted society of social justice and the indigenous culture are not totally complementary and, upon successful completion of the war, could be a source of friction.

As previously noted, the liberation party modified the traditional role of women while maintaining the family and religion as the source of morality and law. During the execution of the war an equilibrium must be maintained between adherents of the expended role of women and religious fundamentalists. However, upon completion of the war, strict enforcement of Koranic laws regulating women or pursuing social justice and equality for women could result in a backlash from the opposing faction. This dilemma was recently observed in Algeria with the adoption of the family code. Initially, women demonstrated against provisions of the code based upon a perceived curtailment of rights. Consequently, an amended code, more palatable to women, was adopted.[50] In short, divergent goals promoted by the liberation party so that different factions would support the creation of the new state now act as a limitation on how far any one faction's demands can be met. This is not to say that the limitations and balance maintained between various factions is of equal strength.

While the liberation party, for purposes of unity and support, stresses equality and removes overt signs of differentiation between sectors of the society, the actual policy pursued mandates a sharper differentiation between factions. In order to fulfill the functions of statehood and solicit recognition of its announced state, the liberation party creates a hierarchical political and military command. Thus, while women's traditional role in society may have been altered by their use in support roles or by the granting of autonomy in their own sphere, such as the maintenance and defense of the refugee camps, they are generally limited to the lower or middle administrative levels of the reconstituted society. This limitation has a twofold effect. Since future leaders will come from the higher military or political administrative levels of the society, there is an inclination to perpetuate women to the lower administrative levels of the society. More significantly, since women are not in the highest levels of government, when there is a clash between women and some other sector of the society, regardless of the rhetoric, the government usually retreats on women's rights. In Algeria, the adoption of the family code, even though amended, signifies a retreat from the professed goal of equality by the limitations imposed on females. Thus the need to gain unity and support from constituent elements of the society in order to pursue a policy of internationalization actually mitigates against the liberation party having a uniform commitment or execution of its professed goals.

## IMPLEMENTING THE STRATEGY

With regards to the actual process of internationalization, the mere announcement of a new state in and of itself is insufficient. The initial response of Morocco and Mauritania to the announcement of the Saharan Arab Democratic Republic was to "dismiss the declaration as a farce."[51] In order for the liberation party to achieve its desired goals, recognition of the new state is mandatory and is thus diligently sought. Due to the composition of the international system, there are only three ways in which the liberation party can achieve recognition for their state: (1) have their state recognized as such by other states; (2) have their state enter into treaties with other states; and (3) have their state accepted as a member of an international organization comprised of states.[52] Liberation parties that internationalize the conflict pursue all three avenues. Each of these approaches will be dealt with.

Michael Akehurst has noted that "outright victory for one side or the other will create a situation which international law cannot ignore, and no amount of recognition or non-recognition will alter the legal position; but in borderline cases . . . recognition or non-recognition by other states may have a decisive effect on the legal position."[53] Both the National Liberation Front in Algeria and the Polisario Front in Western Sahara sought to bring about this decisive effect by gaining recognition for their respective states. While it has been correctly noted that the Polisario Front "followed Algeria's lead in working to develop external support,"[54] misconceptions abound with regards to this process. Certain authors state that "Even those governments most sympathetic with the Polisario's objectives found it hard to take seriously 'ministers' from a vast ill-defined area composed of rock and sand which called itself the Sahraoui Arab Democratic Republic, and whose only settlements were simply camps made up of hundreds of tents pitched around water points."[55] This conclusion clearly indicates an unfamiliarity with both international law and the Western Sahara.

The assertion that the Western Sahara is "a vast ill-defined area" is erroneous. Since 1958, the former Spanish Sahara has had well-established boundaries. The southern and eastern boundaries are well demarcated. The frontier is definite and marked by pillars. To the west lies the Atlantic Ocean. The only boundary that is not demarcated is the northern one. However, Spain and Morocco concluded a treaty in April of 1958, in which the northern boundary was established at 27°40' north latitude and has since appeared on maps as such.[56] Moreover, even if the Western Sahara, and thus the Saharan Arab Democratic Republic, was comprised of territory that was "ill-defined," such a factor is irrelevant with regards to the extension of recognition. The following two examples should suffice to prove this point: (1) the state of Israel was recognized as such before its boundaries were even defined and (2) Saudi Arabia and Oman, who are both recognized as states, have a common undefined border.

Equally erroneous is the assertion that the Saharan Arab Democratic Republic is comprised of "only settlements" that are "simply camps made up of hundreds of tents pitched around water points." On October 31, 1975, even prior to the Madrid Accords, Morocco forcibly occupied the cities and towns of El Aioun, Smara, Bu Craa, Haouza, Jdiria, and Farsia.[57] The occupying forces of Morocco in the north and Mauritania in the south engaged in looting, rape, mutilation, internment, and napalming of civilians.[58] Saharans fled to the interior where the Polisario Front established refugee camps on the Algerian border.[59] Although these camps may be the tent settlements referred to, the very occupation of the cities and towns proves conclusively that there is more than desert, tents, and oases within the announced territory of the Saharan Arab Democratic Republic. Moreover, even if the Saharan Arab Democratic Republic was primarily comprised of "rock and sand" and "tents pitched around water points," such factors are irrelevant with regards to the extension of recognition. In fact, upon attainment of independence, several of the current states of North Africa and the Middle East were of similar composition.

The essential characteristics of a state are well settled. Article 1 of the Montevideo Convention of 1933 on the Rights and Duties of States is illustrative:

> The State as a person of international law should possess the following qualifications: (a) a permanent population; (b) a defined territory; (c) a Government; and (d) a capacity to enter into relations with other States.[60]

The former Spanish Sahara had a defined territory, a permanent population, and the colonial national council, the Djemaa, had transferred all authority over the population to the Polisario front.[61] Thus, upon the withdrawal of the Spanish and the announcement of the Saharan Arab Democratic Republic, all the necessary elements were present for recognition.[62] All that remained was for the states to acknowledge the existence of the new republic.

Commencing with the very announcement of the Saharan Arab Democratic Republic, the Polisario Front launched initiatives to gain recognition for their state. On February 27, 1976, the proclamation of the new state "was read before several thousand Saharans and some 40 foreign journalists at Bir Lahlou, 130 kilometers from the Algerian frontier which the Moroccans claimed to have captured on February 8."[63] Aside from reporting the proclamation, the presence of foreign journalists served two complementary purposes of the Polisario Front: (1) to attest to the fact that the Polisario Front has the support of the vast majority of the Saharans and is their rightful government and (2) to attest to the fact that that government controls the entire territory except for several fortified cities and towns.[64] In other words, the journalists were meant to spread word that the Moroccan and Mauritanian claims were false[65] and that the announced Saharan Arab Democratic Republic had the necessary elements of statehood: a territory, a population, and a government.

Within one day of the Polisario Front's announcement, Madagascar became the first state to extend recognition to the Saharan Arab Democratic Republic.[66] While the Polisario Front would continue to use journalists for the aforementioned reasons, they had not relied on them alone. Polisario Front officials had been meeting with officials of other governments; however, with the proclamation of the Saharan Arab Democratic Republic, the Polisario Front's diplomatic initiatives intensified. In March of 1976, Mohammed Lamine, the prime minister of the Saharan Arab Democratic Republic, met with Fidel Castro of Cuba.[67] At the same time, the Polisario front was either meeting with or sending information to the United Nations, the Organization of African Unity, and the Arab League.[68] As Mohammed Abdelaziz, secretary general of the Polisario Front, stated:

> We regularly dispatch information missions to African countries, and to other regions of the world. We are optimistic, and we expect new recognitions for our Republic.[69]

These initiatives reaped quick benefits. At the end of February 1976, an Organization of African Unity ministerial meeting voted seventeen to nine, with seventeen abstentions, to recognize the government of the Saharan Arab Democratic Republic.[70] Moreover, by April 1, 1976, ten states had extended recognition to the Saharan Arab Democratic Republic.[71] Thus governments had taken seriously ministers from an "area composed of rock and sand which called itself the Sahraoui Arab Democratic Republic."

The Polisario front had clearly followed the trail blazed by the National Liberation Front. When the Algerian Republic was proclaimed, the same phenomenon of a flurry of diplomatic initiatives was observable. As Eldon Greenberg, when discussing the laws of war and the Algerian Revolution, noted:

> The FLN, for its part, strived to gain international acknowledgment in both political and legal terms. It is notable, however, that until the formation of the GPRA the FLN was not sure what status to seek; only thereafter did it actively pursue international recognition of its belligerent status. . . . After the formation of the GPRA, the Algerians made a strenuous effort to appear to fulfill the qualifications of a belligerent power and thereby (they hoped) to acquire the right to be treated as such under the laws and customs of general war.[72]

These initiatives and their efforts were significant. In the 1959 Monrovia Conference of nine independent African states, the Algerian delegation was seated with full rights and their flag was flown over the Liberian Parliament.[73] By 1960, the Algerian Republic had become a member of the Arab League and had acceded to the four Geneva Conventions of 1949.[74] Upon conclusion of the conflict, some thirty states had extended recognition and the Algerian Republic had established permanent missions abroad, with additional offices in Geneva, Bonn, Rome, London, and New York. Accordingly, Greenberg concludes, "Although largely in concert with ideologically, racially, and strategically sympathetic powers, the series of recognitions and the flurry of diplomatic activity were relevant to, if not really conclusive of, the juridicial position of the GPRA. . . ."[75] In short, the Algerian Republic had achieved that decisive effect to which Michael Akehurst had referred.

Simultaneously, the virulence of the embattled state's response to these initiatives is in direct proportion to the progress of the liberation party in internationalizing the conflict. As previously stated, the embattled state seeks to maintain control over the conflict by asserting that it is solely a domestic issue.

In order to maintain this defensive posture in the light of recognition of the newly proclaimed state, the embattled state attempts to undermine the basis of the liberation party's state. Thus the embattled state disseminates assertions antithetical to the liberation party's claim to the attributes of sovereignty: a population, a territory, and a government. The French asserted "that the FLN had never succeeded in exclusively controlling a single portion of the country and therefore had never fulfilled an essential condition for belligerence,"[76] that the National Liberation Army was only an army on paper, and that the National Liberation Front did not have the support of the Algerian population.[77] These assertions were obviously not in accord with the reality of the situation.[78] As Eldon Greenberg noted:

> The purpose of the debate, rather, was psychological and political and involved the very tenability of the continued claim put forward by the French government to any degree of authority exercisable over Algeria. Recognition of FLN or GPRA belligerency would have meant acknowledging—in effect, if not under traditional legal notions—that another state, with an effective government, was the adversary; and this would have foreclosed, or at least drastically limited [the justification for continued French prosecution of the conflict].[79]

For the exact same reason, Morocco and Mauritania sought to undermine the basis of the Saharan Arab Democratic Republic.

Initially, Morocco and Mauritania asserted that the Saharans were their brothers who welcomed the annexations.[80] As attacks on Moroccan and Mauritanian positions continued and states recognized the Saharan Arab Democratic Republic, Morocco asserted that the Polisario Front was a foreign-policy arm of Algeria and Algerian army regulars dressed as Saharan guerrillas to raid Moroccan territory.[81] Thus, not only did the Polisario Front lack a territory, a population, and a government, there was no Polisario Front, only Algerians. As in the case of France, these assertions were not based on reality. Yet to insure that these assertions were not given credence and thus derogate the Polisario Front's effort to gain recognition for the Saharan Arab Democratic Republic, the Polisario Front took journalists and various interested people on tours through the Western Sahara.

In late december 1976, London's *Sunday Times* reporter Sadie Wykeham told the BBC that the Polisario Front controlled the Sahara, except for heavily fortified towns held by Morocco and Mauritania. Wykeham stated that on a week-long tour with the guerrillas she traveled more than 800 miles and watched the bombardment of Moroccan garrisons.[82] In 1977, Tami Hultman, editor of *Africa News,* toured the Western Sahara and was surprised that the Polisario Front did not conform to the accepted image of guerrillas who come from Algeria, make hit-and-run raids, and flee back across the border. Hultman states:

> I remember the surprise of coming upon a base camp with a fence around it and a sign saying in Arabic (I was told), 'Do Not Enter.' It was the central military region headquarters.[83]

Tony Hodges, who toured the Western Sahara in March of 1979, expressed similar surprise and related being driven through the territory on tarmac highways with headlights being used.[84] In June and July of 1979, this author toured the Western Sahara from Algeria to the Atlantic Ocean and saw military staging areas, liberated towns, and military commanders responsible for different regions of the territory. Thus, when questioned about Morocco's continued insistence that it was being attacked by Algerian guerrillas, a Polisario Front representative stated: "So many journalists have seen our true situation, that we don't have to respond to that lie any more."[85]

Nevertheless, by dispelling these assertions, the liberation party removes impediments to recognition of its republic. Moreover, as recognition is extended, the divergence between these assertions and reality widens, international support for the embattled state decreases, and that state's position becomes increasingly untenable. France characterized the Algerian Revolution as rebellion and liberation fighters as criminals.[86] Yet the National Liberation Front both physically and administratively controlled vast stretches of Algeria.[87] Moreover, by December 1959, sixteen states had recognized the Algerian Republic.[88] Thus when this issue was discussed at the United Nations, despite protestations that such discussions intervened in France's internal affairs, the representative of Haiti stated quite bluntly:

> I do not see, legally speaking, how one can dispute the status of insurgency created by the fact of war and the circumstances surrounding it, and which presages the birth of the future State. . . . The Algerian question has passed the state of discussion or vain silence. The time has come to force or to ease the impending birth, and we must show ourselves to be skillful midwives.[89]

This statement, by a state which had not recognized the Algerian Republic and was friendly with France, was not atypical. As the liberation party's state gains recognition and stature, the embattled state becomes increasingly isolated, and thus forced to modify its position. As Mohammed Bedjaoui noted, "The sustained upward trend of the Algerian Revolution has compelled France . . . to recognize belligerency in Algeria in spite of itself."[90]

On April 11, 1960, the Algerian Republic officially announced its intention to accede to the Geneva Conventions of 1949 which ameliorate unnecessary suffering during hostilities.[91] The effects of this accession were profound. If France, who was a party to these Conventions, recognized a state of belligerency, such recognition would destroy its basis for fighting. Conversely, not applying the Conventions would destroy France's credibility as a responsible member of the international community. This latter point was forcibly brought home. The Algerian Republic published a white paper which showed that the conventions were applicable, that France was continuing to violate them, and urged all other parties to the Conventions to persuade France to obey her treaty obligations.[92] France finally had to yield in that its characterization of the conflict and justification for fighting were no longer credible. Initially, liberation fighters were characterized as criminals who were tried and executed for treason.[93] At the May 1961 peace conference, Louis Joxe, chief French negotiator, stated that "we recognized in them, the quality of combatants. We see in them the delegates of a political organization who present themselves as candidates for power."[94] Since 1958, and the initiation of the process of internationalization, as Eldon Greenberg noted, "the prior political insistence on the integrated relationship of France and Algeria gradually yielded to notions of limited Algerian sovereignty, then to various degrees of 'interdependence,' and finally to complete sovereignty."[95] This same phenomenon is currently occurring in the Western Sahara.

Aside from using journalists and other people to prove that it had the attributes of sovereignty, the Polisario Front attempted to have the conflict viewed in the context most favorable for gaining recognition of the Saharan Arab Democratic Republic. In November 1976, the United Nations Committee on Decolonization passed a resolution reaffirming the right of the people of Western Sahara to self-determination. In a speech to the committee, Salim Mansur, spokesman for the Polisario Front, had stated: "Everyone knows that our religion is undergoing a war situation following the illegal occupation of our territory by the Moroccan-Mauritanian forces of aggression—a war of colonial conquest."[96] Thus Morocco and Mauritania had not only committed aggression and an illegal occupation, they had commenced a war of colonial conquest. To the Third World, due to their recent history, a war of colonial conquest is anathema.

As Mohammed Abdelaziz, secretary general of the Polisario Front, had intimated, the Polisario Front gave priority to gaining recognition for their republic from African countries.[97] In Africa, the boundaries were drawn by colonial powers without regard for ethnic groups. Consequently, any assertion of historical ties to territory or attempt to rectify past wrongs through force is viewed as a way of ushering in an era of instability, bloodshed, or war with no guarantee that the resultant frontiers will be a substantial improvement over the previous ones. These dangers devolve from the imprecision of the concept of a people: is a people defined by linguistic, religious, cultural, geographical or other criteria? Conflict over criteria leads to war as it did in Alsace-Lorraine. Thus the Organization of African Unity has continually asserted that decolonization and the inviolability of colonial boundaries are necessary for peace in Africa.[98] The occupation of the Western Sahara is a direct threat to these values and consequently Africa is the main battleground for the Polisario Front's diplomatic initiatives.

Despite threats from Morocco and Mauritania that they would withdraw from the Organization of African Unity if it grants recognition to the Polisario Front, an Organization of African Unity ministerial meeting voted at the end of February 1976 to recognize the government of the Saharan Arab Democratic Republic.[99] By the Mauritius summit conference in July 1976, nine of the states that had recognized the Saharan Arab Democratic Republic were African.[100] Thus, even though the Saharan Arab Democratic Republic was not allowed to attend that conference, its interests were represented. Although Morocco and Mauritania claimed that the Saharan issue was closed and that any discussion by the Organization of African Unity would be interference in their internal affairs, the heads of state approved a special summit to deal with the Saharan issue.[101]

By August of 1976, the Polisario Front had adopted a constitution for the Saharan Arab Democratic Republic. Coming six months after the Polisario Front commenced seeking recognition for their state, the constitution is a product of this process and clearly reflects this policy. A few excerpts should suffice:

PREAMBLE

The Saharan Arab Democratic Republic is the fruit of the . . . historic struggle of the Saharawi people to safeguard its national independence and territorial integrity . . . in accordance with international authorities which recognize its inalienable right to self-determination and to independence. . . .

The Saharan people are an Arab, African and Muslim people. They choose a policy of non-alignment; they struggle for the unity of the peoples of the Arab nation and of the African continent . . . and equitable world order . . . where nations are united in equality and mutual respect. . . .

*Article 2.* The SADR is part of the Arab nation, the African family and the community of peoples of the Third World. . . .

*Article 4.* The search for the unity of the peoples of the Arab Maghreb is a step towards Arab and African unity. . . .

In short, the document is specifically oriented towards Africa and the Third World. The appeal is to ideologically, racially, and strategically sympathetic powers. This is evidenced by the express language of the constitution and the Polisario Front's diplomatic initiatives.

On January 5, 1977, Hakim Ibrahim, foreign minister of the Saharan Arab Democratic Republic, met with Organization of African Unity Secretary General William Eteki to discuss the special summit and when it might be scheduled.[102] During this period, both Prime Minister Mohammed Lamine and Secretary General Mohammed Abdelaziz of the Saharan Arab Democratic Republic issued public statements calling on the Organization of African Unity to schedule the special summit on the Saharan war.[103] These exhortations and the responses of the embattled states clearly delineate the diplomatic struggle.

Ironically, the threats of embattled states, in this instance to withdraw from the Organization of African Unity, while understandable, are nevertheless counterproductive. Through repetition the threats lose their efficacy and alienate other states by frustrating discussion of the issue. Thus intransigence by the embattled states, instead of aiding their position, actually causes a coalescence and hardening of states in opposition, even of states who do not accept the full position of the liberation party. In March 1977, at an Organization of African Unity ministerial meeting, Morocco walked out of the opening ceremonies to protest the presence of a delegation from the Saharan Arab Democratic Republic.[104] Again Morocco and Mauritania threatened withdrawal.[105] The Togolese government, who was hosting the conference and had also recognized the Saharan Arab Democratic Republic, stated that it had invited the Saharans and Morocco's gesture was inappropriate since the Saharans did not attend the sessions.[106] By June 1977, the Polisario front had converted the embattled states' intransigence into further political gain. Colonel Seyni Kountche, head of state of Niger, announced that his country would defend the right of the Saharan people to self-determination within existing colonial boundaries at the upcoming summit of the Organization of African Unity. The colonel said that if Morocco's argument, that it was entitled to a portion of Western Sahara because of precolonial ethnic ties, was accepted, then Algeria could claim parts of northern Niger and Nigeria could claim areas of southern Niger. He called the Moroccan/Mauritanian attempt to annex Western Sahara a "Pandora's box."[107] According to *Le Monde,* during this period, similar statements were voiced by leaders of Cameroun, Mali, and other French-speaking West African States.[108] These statements, by states which had not recognized the Saharan Arab Democratic Republic and had been previously sympathetic to the Moroccan and Mauritanian position,[109] clearly demonstrate the escalating lack of support for the embattled states.

Simultaneously, since the embattled states were militarily and politically stronger than the liberation party, many military actions were initiated by the Polisario Front not for military advantage, but for aiding the diplomatic struggle. That these engagements were coordinated with the diplomatic struggle is evident by the location and time of the attacks. While the heads of state of the Organization of African Unity were meeting in July 1977, the Polisario Front attacked the Mauritanian capital of Nouakchott.[110] This attack was obviously political, since the Polisario Front was incapable of either occupying or even maintaining a heavy concentrated attack capable of inflicting extensive damage throughout the city. The Polisario Front also attacked the Atlantic coastal town of Aargub[111] and the far southern area of Mauritania.[112] Again the intent was not for military advantage, since the Polisario front retreated when reinforcements arrived at Aargub.[113] Aargub is 500 inhospitable desert miles from the Algerian border, and Mauritania claimed to control all the territory in between. Thus these attacks were meant to destroy the tenability of the Mauritanian position that the "POLISARIO is only a small group of malcontents who raid from bases in neighboring Algeria."[114] These attacks proved conclusively that the Polisario Front was able to launch major attacks and that it had to be operating out of bases within the Western Sahara. Moreover, these attacks were timed to the Organization of African Unity meeting to show that body that the war in Western Sahara was not an issue that could be continued to be ignored or avoided despite the threats from Morocco and Mauritania. The result was that the Organization of African Unity finally scheduled the special summit on the war in the Western Sahara for October in Lusaka, Zambia.[115] That this was a significant achievement for the Polisario Front is evidenced by the fact that this was only the second time in the history of that organization that a special summit had been scheduled.[116]

Although the special summit of the Organization of African Unity was cancelled due to several problems,[117] the Polisario Front continued to seek acceptance of the Saharan Arab Democratic Republic. By 1978, the Polisario Front had succeeded in getting Spain to acknowledge that Morocco and Mauritania had failed to abide by their promise in the Madrid Accords to consult the Saharan population with regards to decolonizing the territory.[118] This admission clearly undermined the positions of the embattled states, who had cited the Madrid Accords as justification for the partitionment and annexation of the territory. Simultaneously, the Polisario Front utilized military attacks in conjunction with tours by journalists to prove that they were in actual control of the territory except for a few fortified strongholds. Moreover, military attacks were concentrated against Mauritania, the weaker of the occupying powers.

On July 10, 1978, Mauritania experienced a coup caused by the war. Two days after the coup, the Polisario Front announced a unilateral cease-fire as a "goodwill gesture."[119] Mauritania then commenced negotiations with the Polisario Front, partially withdrew from the southern sector of the Western Sahara, and exchanged prisoners.[120] This change of position constituted de facto recognition of the Saharan Arab Democratic Republic. As President Khrushchev of the Soviet Union stated during the Algerian Revolution:

> It may be taken that our meetings and conversations with the representatives of the Algerian Provisional government indicate *de facto* recognition of the Government. I would like to add that it is not we alone who give *de facto* recognition to the Algerian Provisional Government, but the whole world, beginning with the President

of the French Republic, General de Gaulle, because he has begun negotiations with that Government.[121]

In short, in order to negotiate, the embattled state has had to accept the liberation party as an equal. Consequently, in the Western Sahara as in Algeria, after the commencement of negotiations other states extended recognition. By July 1979, the number of states that had recognized the Saharan Arab Democratic Republic had grown to twenty-two.[122]

While negotiating with Mauritania, the Polisario Front continued the diplomatic struggle. In December a Polisario Front–endorsed resolution passed the General Assembly of the United Nations which reaffirmed the right of Western Sahara to self-determination, called on the United Nations to follow "actively" the Saharan dispute, and for the first time mentioned the Polisario Front by name in commending them for their cease-fire.[123] A counterresolution, sponsored by Morocco and Mauritania, also was passed which said that the Saharan issue is a question most properly addressed by the Organization of African Unity.[124] Morocco and Mauritania obviously wished to have the issue referred to a forum in which they believed they could exert greater pressure. However, the Polisario Front had also chosen the Organization of African Unity as the primary body for their diplomatic initiatives. Consequently, with regards to the second resolution, a Polisario Front official stated: "We have welcomed this resolution. It's not antagonistic. It's complementary. You could include it inside our own."[125] Moreover, in 1978, the Organization of African Unity had formed an ad hoc committee to investigate the Saharan conflict.[126]

Through the first half of 1979, the Polisario Front continued to commence diplomatic overtures and seek support. At the end of February, a delegation was dispatched to Iran to persuade the new government there to recognize the Saharan Arab Democratic Republic.[127] In March, at the ministerial meeting of the Organization of African Unity, Algeria sponsored a resoultion supporting the Polisario Front. The measure, though, was tabled until July, when the ad hoc committee investigating the matter would present its report.[128] Finally, on July 12, 1979, six days into the foreign ministers' meeting of the Organization of African Unity, the Polisario Front ended its one-year cease-fire and attacked the town of Tichla in the Mauritanian zone of the Western Sahara. The ad hoc committee investigating the conflict quickly met with representatives of the Polisario Front to discuss the attack and seek the release of Mauritanian prisoners.[129]

The attack on Tichla was meant to accomplish two goals. First, the attack was timed to coincide with the Organization of African Unity meeting. Thus the attack was a signal to that body that the Saharan conflict was an issue of importance demanding attention. Second, the attack was on a Mauritanian-held town on the anniversary of the Polisario Front's unilateral cease-fire. Thus the message to Mauritania was that unless there was movement in the negotiations, the Polisario Front was prepared to continue the war. The Polisario Front even issued a communiqué which pointed out that Mauritania had never formally reciprocated on the cease-fire and had stalled on its promise to turn the southern zone over to the Saharans. The communiqué bluntly stated: "We are tired of talk which isn't followed by action."[130] Subsequently, the Polisario Front achieved both goals: movement in the Organization of African Unity and movement by Mauritania.

At the heads-of-state summit meeting of the Organization of African Unity of July 17–20, 1979, the report of the ad hoc committee was accepted and a resolution adopted by a vote of thirty-three to two with eight abstentions. The resolution called for a cease-fire in the Western Sahara and a general and free referendum in the territory to allow the inhabitants to exercise their right of self-determination. The referendum would consist of the choice of either total independence or maintenance of the status quo.[131] Morocco's King Hassan rejected the call for a referendum, stating: "It's impossible to ask Moroccan citizens if they wish to be Moroccan."[132] Liberain President Tolbert, chairman of the Organization of African Unity, stated that the vote indicated "a clear consensus in Africa for self-determination in the Western Sahara."[133]

On August 5, 1979, Mauritania signed a peace treaty with the Polisario Front and surrendered her claims to the southern sector of the Western Sahara.[134] This treaty put to rest any question about the Saharan Arab Democratic Republic lacking territory or any of the necessary attributes of statehood. By October, an additional eleven states had extended recognition, bringing to thirty-three the number of states that recognized the Saharan Arab Democratic Republic.[135] In September 1979, the Conference of Non-Aligned Countries passed a declaration supporting the call for a referendum in the territory and deplored the Moroccan occupation of the former Mauritanian zone of the Western Sahara.[136] On November 21, 1979, the U.N. General Assembly passed a similar resolution.[137] By the 1981 heads-of-state summit of the Organization of African Unity, forty-five states had recognized the Saharan Arab Democratic Republic.[138] Of these, twenty-six were African and constituted a majority of the members of the Organization of African Unity. With the Polisario Front seeking membership in that body, in order to forestall what appeared imminent,[139] Morocco finally agreed to a referendum in the Western Sahara.[140]

Although Morocco's announcement was a temporizing measure, the change from not asking "Moroccan citizens if they wish to be Moroccan" only came about because of pressure exerted by the liberation party's use of the institutions and norms of the international system. Moreover, Morocco had been forced to adopt a position favorable for additional concessions to the liberation party. King Hassan stated that Morocco had "decided to envisage a procedure of controlled referendum, whose message will comply with the recommendations of the Ad Hoc Committee of Wise Men, as well as with the conviction Morocco has of its legitimate rights."[141] However, the Ad Hoc Committee had urged all parties to the conflict to effect a cease-fire,[142] and the Organization of African Unity, in adopting the recommendation, had called for the convening of a meeting of the parties concerned, including the representative of Western Sahara.[143] Thus the stage was set for a meeting between representatives of Morocco and the Polisario Front. If Morocco refused to meet with the Polisario Front and the referendum could not be implemented, the Saharan Arab Democratic Republic would be admitted to the Organization of African Unity. Conversely, if Morocco did meet with the Polisario Front, then the liberation party had achieved de facto recognition.

On August 19, 1981, an Organization of African Unity committee of seven African heads of state met with the parties on implementing the proposed cease-fire.[144] Moroccan Foreign Minister Muhammed Boucetta stated that one of Morocco's "fundamental points" was "no negotiation with POLISARIO."[145] This position of the embattled state, while necessary for maintaining that the liberation party is not an equal member of the international system, guarantees an equally firm response. For if the liberation party alleges to be an independent sovereign state, then it cannot let another state negotiate in its place without giving credence to the embattled state's position. Understandably, the Polisario Front's position, as stated by Mahmoud Abdel Fatah on behalf of Foreign Minister Hakim Ibrahim, was that "the OAU cannot act until POLISARIO and Morocco begin negotiation."[146] The meeting, therefore, concluded without any procedure for achieving a cease-fire.

On October 13, 1981, the Polisario Front launched a three-prong attack on the Moroccan garrison of Guelta Zemmour.[147] Upon conclusion of the battle, the Polisario front claimed 1100 Moroccan casualties, five aircraft destroyed, and eighty-eight vehicles captured.[148] The significance of this attack was two-fold. First, the Polisario Front demonstrated it could launch major engagements, and thus no cease-fire could be achieved without its participation in negotiations. Second, since Guelta Zemmour is over 350 kilometers from Algeria, the logistics and coordination for such a battle destroyed the usual Moroccan characterization of attacks as raids from Algeria. Faced with this repudiation, Morocco proffered its own explanation for the debacle. Instead of acknowledging that the Polisario Front had military staging areas in the Western Sahara, as was observed by this author two years earlier, Morocco claimed the attack came from Mauritania, that Mauritanian soldiers participated, and that sophisticated Soviet weaponry was deployed.[149] These allegations, despite a retaliatory bombing of Mauritania on October 21, 1981, [150] were quickly discredited.[151]

Although untenable, Morocco's allegations were not without purpose. By asserting "no African state" had soldiers trained to use SAM-6 missiles, and intimating Cuban or East German advisers were responsible,[152] Morocco was in essence alleging Soviet intervention. The Soviet specter was meant to facilitate military assistance from the United States.[153] By February 1982, Secretary of State Alexander Haig was in Morocco discussing arms sales to counter the Soviet missiles.[154] Haig's visit closely followed visits by Secretary of Defense Caspar Weinberger, Ambassador at Large Vernon Walters, Chairman of the U.S. Foreign Relations Committee Charles Percy, and a top-level military mission headed by Francis West,[155] all of which highlighted America's commitment to Morocco. Unfortunately, there is an inherent incongruity between expanded military operations and a cease-fire.

On February 5, 1982, just prior to the Organization of African Unity mini-summit on implementing the proposed cease-fire and referendum, the Polisario front charged Morocco with using American military advisers in the occupied towns of Smara and El Aaiun.[156] While Morocco could not substantiate the deployoment of SAM-6 missiles and T-55 tanks, the increasing American involvement was apparent. At the same time, the twenty-six African states that recognized the Saharan Arab Democratic Republic informed the Organization of African Unity secretary general of their desire to have that state admitted as a member.[157] Thus, when the mini-summit convened in Nairobi, unless progress could be made in negotiations, the prospect was one of imminent admission of the Saharan Arab Democratic Republic and a military escalation. Morocco's claim that negotiations should be with Algeria[158] was clearly rejected. The mini-summit called upon "the two parties to the controversy, Morocco and the Polisario Front, to observe a cease-fire" and urged said parties to begin negotiations to that effect.[159]

Morocco rejected the call for direct negotiations,[160] and within a week established a joint military commission with the United States.[161] Thus, on February 23, 1982, at the ministerial meeting of the Organization of African Unity, the Saharan Arab Democratic Republic became the fifty-first member of that body.[162] Morocco protested the admission again, asserting that the new member was neither independent nor sovereign, but controlled by Algeria.[163] Such an admission, however, was not unprecedented. Morocco has supported the admission of Algeria to the Arab League prior to its independence from France and with a provisional government operating amost exclusively from Tunisia. Additionally, Guinea-Bissau had been admitted to the Organization of African Unity prior to its independence from Portugal. Other members felt that the admission inappropriately superseded the Implementation Committee's peace efforts.[164] Consequently, nineteen states walked out of the meeting.[165]

The boycott highlighted the refutation of Morocco's position. All Morocco had left was obstructionist tactics. Since five states, other than the twenty-six which had sought the admission, had refused to join the boycott, [166] such tactics could only be counterproductive. Thus, as Morocco sought to disrupt the functioning of the Organization of African Unity,[167] the Saharan Arab Democratic Republic gained recognition from Upper Volta and Mauritius,[168] states which had initially opposed the admission, from Nigeria,[169] and from Mauritania, which changed its recognition from de facto to de jure.[170] Finally, on November 12, 1984, Morocco withdrew from the Organization of African Unity.[171] The next day, the Organization of African Unity adopted the Implementation Committee's report which stressed that Morocco had frustrated all attempts at resolving the conflict.[172]

## CONCLUSION

As Japan, a founding member of the League of Nations, withdrew from that body because of its occupation of Manchuria, so too Morocco, a founding member of the Organization of African Unity, was forced to withdraw from that body. Both withdrawals demonstrated the lack of support for the occupying power. Conversely, the Polisario Front has grown in stature and, as the current vice president of the Organization of African Unity,[173] has additional access to institutions and states for exerting pressure to achieve a termination of the hostilities. Moreover, the growing number of recognitions demonstrate not only an adherence to legal norms, but an acceptance of the Polisario Front as the true representative of a unified society.

# PART II

# The Consolidation of Power:
# The Fall of Monarchy,
# The Rise of Absolutism,
# and the Definition
# of the Political Arena

The consolidation of power is never a simple process. Historically, almost every country has gone through more than one framework of government. How many Americans today know that the first colonial effort to establish a new set of institutions for self-rule after the Revolution of 1776 resulted in "failure"? The Constitution replaced the Articles of Confederation only after a period of prolonged domestic strife, intense class conflict, and rising animosities. Yet the American experience was a political picnic in comparison to the centuries-long development that Western European nations required to reach their present forms.

Thomas Callaghy, in his "Absolutism, Bonapartism, and the Formation of Ruling Classes: Zaire in Comparative Perspective," compares contemporary African states with European states from the sixteenth century, and with Latin American countries from the time of their colonial breakaways to the present. He enables us to delineate more sharply differences between Latin American and African Third World countries and to see similar forces in play across the globe and over time. Callaghy also illuminates the interplay of class, state, and administrative structures. He defines state formation as sets of complementary and competing processes, as the creation of organizations of domination, as the projection of new definitions of authority, and as struggles for dominance between interests and classes in which external and internal forces seek the fulfillment of their own ideal and material interests. Deftly, in a few broad strokes, Callaghy allows us to see contrasting profiles of these societies—the shape of their states, of their administrative structures, and of their social classes—and how they change over time.

The original frontispiece of Thomas Hobbes's *Leviathan* pictures the state as a noble kingly figure holding the sword of justice. Callaghy depicts for us a political aristocracy as maggots feeding on carrion. Political theorists might talk about grand ideas such as the "search for sovereignty," the seeking after "final and absolute political authority in the political community," the "diminished dependence vis-à-vis internal societal groups." We can generalize about how the Zairian absolutist regime has created an administrative monarchy which has recentralized power. What we are really talking about, however, is how Mobutu and his gangsters strip the carcasses of the poor.

Callaghy reminds us that current Marxist theory has rebelled against "making the state a dependent variable," against denying the possibility of political autonomy, and against viewing the state merely as an instrument of "the ruling class." He further reminds us that, even according to Marx and Engels, the "dominant class" does not necessarily always control the state. What for Engels were "exceptional" periods of history, Callaghy points out, in fact consisted of substantial portions of the seventeenth, eighteenth and nineteenth centuries—from the absolute monarchies of the seventeenth and eighteenth centuries to the Bonapartism of the First and Second empires. During these periods of absolutism and Bonapartism, the state balanced and accommodated conflicting groups and classes and accumulated power at the expense of competing interests.

Contrary to common impressions, the state had less power under absolutism than under Bonapartism, because the structures of sustained systematic control were less developed. Class development was also less advanced than under Bonapartism, and personal leadership skills were more important. As Callaghy puts it, "the class situation is simply more fluid, more in flux, under absolutism" than under Bonapartism. A rising bourgeoisie during the period of European absolutism sought the protection of the state, was in turn subject to its control, but did not have to fear a still very small proletariat. By the time of European Bonapartism, a much more advanced bourgeoisie nestled even more willingly into the embrace of the state because the proletariat had become a stronger entity, a more threatening antagonist.

These straightforward and apparently simple contentions then enable Callaghy to argue that the class-based politics of Latin America has given rise to bureaucratic and military authoritarian rule more comparable to Bonapartism than to the authoritarianism of contemporary African states. This absolutist state, which Callaghy analyzes, can be brutal yet surprisingly weak. It can instill passivity but not necessarily the acceptance of its authority. It can maintain basic order but be threatened not merely by periodic eruptions, but with fear for its very existence. A new state must still cater to ancient powers which it finds hostile but cannot destroy. Under absolutism, territorial integrity, administrative unity, and political centralization are all problematical: both the state and society are in the process of being created. Under Bonapartism, the framework of government already exists, and the crucial issue is who will control it.

Callaghy is convincing in depicting a *noblesse d'État,* a political aristocracy consisting of royal servants and the king's men, his chosen patrimonial instruments. Yet some will object that Callaghy goes too far in depicting this "state nobility" as simply the creatures of the king. These officials occupy offices and organizational positions. By the time Callaghy finishes enumerating the various categories ("all top-level administrative, political, and military officials," the "middle-level administrative and military officers in Kinshasa," the territorial prefects and military officers in the regions), it would appear that he is well on his way to describing key elements of an "organizational bourgeoisie." Although "loyalty to Mobutu is allegedly the "ultimate requirement" for membership in this aristocracy, the attachments of civil servants can change as quickly as the official portrait of Reagan can replace that of Carter, or DeGaulle that of Pétain.

Callaghy also points out how the absolutist state attempts to prevent the development of an industrial or commercial bourgeoisie with an independent economic base. Here is another reason why absolutism results in a lack of economic development. This is shrewd insight. Failure of France to develop economically as rapidly as did Britain owed much to the success of Louis XIV in centralizing his power at the expense of the lesser nobility and in his emasculating the business bourgeoisie. Nevertheless, we must note that state political leaders in regimes as different as the Ivory Coast and Kenya, Ghana under Nkrumah and Asante under the Prempehs, tried to stunt the growth of entrepreneurial activities because of the threat of interests founded on powerful new economic forces. However, they did not always succeed.

From the absolutism of Louis XIV to the absolutism of Zaire's Mobutu, there are limits on the power of great personal leaders. More is involved than *la faveur royale*. As Callaghy himself points out, "the political aristocracy is consolidating itself as a class . . . the political aristocracy is a class in reality, and it is becoming increasingly conscious of its existence as a class and therefore of the existence of generalized class interests." This would seem to indicate something more than a group of individuals solely dependent upon the whim of one man. Nevertheless, Callaghy goes on to claim that "this political class" is still more of a "political aristocracy," rather than "a national bourgeoisie," because it so frequently merely assumes "the status elements of positions," rather than actually fulfilling "many of their real functions": that they merely enjoy the trappings of office and milk whatever benefits they can from their positions without doing any real work. Even the more indolent officials, however, operate within the framework of a capitalist system, and, as Callaghy points out elsewhere in his study, external connections with multinational corporations and banks make for major differences from the early absolutism of sixteenth-century France. The cynical among us who believe that no ruling group is altruistic will hardly be surprised that members of the Zairian "kleptocracy" don't have much of a sense of a "public purpose," or of the "collective good," or that they have demonstrated only a feeble commitment to bettering the conditions of the lives of those over whom they rule. Rulers, even absolutists, worry about "the public good" because their own safety is at stake. There are *reasons* why absolutist states did not make it into the modern age. Failure, among other things, to produce a rational administration and higher standard of living for the masses on the part of the absolutists was punishable by revolution. Callaghy's provocative study goads us to additional questions about whether the decline of Mobutu's absolutism, as well as its rise, will parallel that of previous regimes.

We may find possible answers to these questions in a study of Africa's longest-lived absolutist state, Ethiopia.

Even regimes of long duration can suddenly be overthrown. Ethiopia existed as a feudal variant of absolutism for hundreds of years. Robert Grey, in "The Petite Bourgeoisie in the Ethiopian Revolution," analyzes the development, within the heart of an absolutist state, of what became a powerful force in its overthrow. Grey's study shows that the consolidation of power is not something permanent. It is not a stage of development fixed once and for all, but rather part of the continuous process of political development.

The terrible famine of 1973–1974 and the additional damage to the economy from the rise in oil prices jarred Ethiopia's dominant class. The old regime had withstood worse shocks in the past, including the Italian conquest. This time, however, changes in the fundamental social structure paved the way for the political revolution which, no matter what its immediate causes, rested upon newly self-conscious social classes.

The power of the petite bourgeoisie came from political skills and attitudes honed by growing awareness of the objective precariousness and danger of its economic position in society. Grey's key point is that "it was the combination of this vulnerability and its political skills and attitudes, which triggered by the facilitating circumstances of 1974, brought the petite bourgeoisie into national politics, and undermined the imperial regime of Haile Selassie." At the same time, Grey recognizes that the petite bourgeoisie could not by itself overthrow the imperial government. This, he maintains, was accomplished by "an organized subset" of the petite bourgeoisie, "its military component."

Grey does enable us to appreciate the precariously balanced position of the military, as he does with the petite bourgeoisie in general. However, his major insights in this article deal with education and the process of politicization. He contributes to the analyses of political participation by analyzing the mechanisms that link education to politics. Thus he argues that although the schools did not explicitly teach the value of political participation, education expanded people's interests and equipped them with a sense of their own confidence. Students became active participants in a variety of areas which ultimately extended to politics.

Grey does not ignore the material aspects of education. The costs and pain of acquiring an education in Ethiopia were enormous. To leave home and to assume the role of an adult at a young age took a psychic toll. The price of room, board, books, and supplies, the inability to earn an income while studying, and the financial support demanded from parents and friends were all enormously burdensome. As an investment for potential earning power and social status, the expenses undoubtedly were well worth their risk. However, every student knew the risks were enormous. Most of those who began never finished. Objectively, the chances of succeeding were in fact low. As Grey puts it, the student had to "try to maximize his possibilities of success." Turning to politics came naturally. "Conditions of severe vulnerability" forced students to see their situation as a political one "in which power might fruitfully be brought to bear to enhance their chances for educational success, as well as to improve their living conditions as students."

Grey expands the definition of "political" to include decision making and allocating resources within the schools themselves. Boycotting a particular teacher or classes or headmasters or protesting policies by the Ministry of Education were all political acts. Strikes against poor food, inadequate scholarships, and raises in tuition all became major issues of the day. In a sense, intra- and interschool activities provided practice for confrontations with the state. Students carried their sense of shared risk, shared economic deprivation, intense communications, and sense of group cohesion into the political arena. Students had found that strikes and other political action could be effective; they turned with increasing confidence to confront the emperor himself.

Grey has elaborated these insights into a general study of the petite bourgeoisie. In so doing he has provided us with an enormously valuable study of the details and mechanics of rising class formation and class consciousness.

# CHAPTER 4

# Absolutism, Bonapartism, and the Formation of Ruling Classes: Zaire in Comparative Perspective

## Thomas M. Callaghy

### MOBUTU SESE SEKO, THE ZAIRIAN STATE, AND ITS POLITICAL ARISTOCRACY

This chapter conceptualizes the state of Mobutu Sese Seko as an African variant of early modern European absolutism. Responding to a severe crisis of order and authority in Zaire in the early 1960s, Mobutu seized power in a military coup d'état in November 1965. Over time his regime evolved from a relatively typical military autocracy into an African version of an absolutist state with key elements of single-party authoritarianism and military despotism. This evolution took place haltingly and unevenly, but surely, and was greatly facilitated by considerable external assistance.[1]

Historically, absolutism has been intimately associated with attempts at the formation of stronger states. The state is an organization of domination, controlled with varying degrees of effectiveness by a ruling group or class which seeks to control a population in a given territory using an administrative apparatus backed by a coercive capability and various legitimating ideas. State formation is a struggle for dominance by a ruling group or class with internal societal groups and classes, and a struggle with external groups, organizations, and forces for compliance, resources, and the fulfillment of the rulers' ideal and material interests. State formation entails the initiation and projection of a new definition of authority in opposition to those that already exist; it is a struggle for internal control, political unification, and external security. One can view the process of state formation as a *search* for sovereignty—"the idea that there is a final and absolute political authority in the political community and no final and absolute authority exists elsewhere."[2] The search for sovereignty by the ruler and a ruling class is a quest for separation, autonomy, and diminished dependence vis-à-vis internal societal groups and classes and external groups in the world political and economic environment.

The Zairian absolutist state is an authoritarian early modern state organized around a presidential monarch who adopted the Belgian colonial state structure and patrimonialized it. He created an administrative monarchy and then used it to recentralize power. In this state form, patriarchal patrimonialism and emergent bureaucratic forms of administration are both salient characteristics.[3] As with all absolutist states, Mobutu's kingdom has distinctly limited capabilities. Old forms and structures of authority continue to operate. Mobutu has increased his personal discretion beyond the confines of both traditional (precolonial) restraints and modern, legal ones, but he has used elements of both for legitimation purposes. He has appropriated the coercive, administrative, and financial means to increase his patriarchal patrimonial power. He has used early modern police and military forces and a cadre of territorial administrators or prefects—the king's men—to control all key societal groups via the corporatist elements of the single party, the Popular Movement of the Revolution (MPR), and to emasculate the power of all traditional and quasi-traditional intermediary authorities. With these coercive and administrative instruments, Mobutu has sought to "whittle away traditional rules and practices"[4] and limit the power of workers, students, churches, etc. This has been an uneven and halting process, but the distinction between state and subject has become increasingly sharp. Like its early modern European predecessors, Zairian absolutism "c'est tout d'abord l'expression d'une *volonté* de puissance qui s'est exercée dans tous les domaines."[5] It is a will to dominate, desire for unification, obedience, and glory. But because the reality is often so hollow, the authoritarian structures of absolutism are grandiosely promulgated in an effort to overwhelm any doubt about the strength of the state.

Success has been both remarkable and limited. Basic order has been maintained, but with periodic and sometimes significant external assistance. This might be considered an achievement, although a brutal one, given the country's history, but the authority of the Zairian absolutist state often appears like a "sort of authoritarian bragging which drowns in an often mocking passivity."[6] In the depths of the regions, the norm is disobedience tempered by absolutism. Centralized administrative control has increased since the early 1960s, but it is still far from being unlimited. It is just unsupervised. Authority relations are still mediated to a significant degree. De Tocqueville's statement holds true for the Zairian absolutist state: "Centralized administration was established *among* the ancient powers, which it supplanted, without, however, destroying them."[7] The Zairian absolutist state is an emerging organization of domination seeking to expand its domain in a very hostile and uncertain environment, both internally and externally. The survival of this early modern state never appears assured; uncertainty remains a pervasive fact for the ruler and his political aristocracy.

The Mobutu strategy of state formation is highly organic-statist in orientation, that is, entailing a vision of politics which stresses the organic harmony and order of the political community as guaranteed and structured by a relatively autonomous state. This orientation rejects individualistic, autonomous-group, and class-based forms of conflict in favor of state-structured and controlled interaction. The state is seen as necessary to regulate conflict, and this regulation is achieved in large part by the "architectonic action" of the ruler and a political ruling class and by the control efforts of a territorial administrative apparatus and the army and police forces which support it. Mobutu's strategy entails: (1) the consolidation and use of coercive force (with considerable external assistance) to reestablish general political order and prevent or contain overt political unrest; (2) an intense personalization (patrimonialization) of power; (3) a recentralization of power along the lines of the authoritarian colonial state using a territorial administrative apparatus to dominate the population, especially to control ethnic, regional, religious, and linguistic particularisms as they merge in complex ways with emerging class factors and the uneven effects of modest levels of socioeconomic modernization; (4) the emasculation or elimination of all alternative sources of autonomous authority, traditional or modern; (5) the maintenance of severely constricted and channeled political participation (departicipation) in which a highly corporatist single state party is recognized as the only legitimate political arena; (6) the establishment of an "ideology" (Mobutuism) which consists of an eclectic blend of legitimating doctrines, a set of expectations of what the state requires of its "citizens" (subjects, actually), and a political religion built around the presidential monarch; and (7) neomercantilist economic policies designed to increase the economic and political power of the state, its ruler, and his political aristocracy. In the process of carrying out this strategy of state formation, a ruling class, here characterized as a political aristocracy, has emerged which is both the child of the state and its principal internal support. These elements are held together and guided by highly personalistic rulership and politics, resulting in a patrimonial administrative state controlled by a presidential monarch and a political aristocracy and using a very eclectic blend of legitimating doctrines.

## ABSOLUTISM AND BONAPARTISM
## IN COMPARATIVE PERSPECTIVE

Absolutism is an early modern form of organic-statist authoritarianism, and Mobutu's Zaire is a contemporary form of absolutism which has the "modern" corporatist overlay of the single-party apparatus. In its legitimating rhetoric, the European absolutist state stressed the necessity for and legitimacy of order and unity in its search for sovereignty and autonomy in order to control and balance societal forces in the interest of the common good of all. It was a heavily authoritarian and statist view of governance in which the state closely controlled, but did not abolish, all intermediary authorities—particularistic, functional, and class. Absolutism was above all attempted state formation, a much more patrimonial form of domination in a society significantly less developed socially, economically, and administratively than exists in the current corporatist, bureaucratic-authoritarian states of Latin America.

The absolutist state more closely resembles earlier colonial and postcolonial periods of Latin American history that constituted what Richard Morse calls a "model of the patrimonial state," the two principal elements of which were organicism and patriarchalism.[8] In fact, the most crucial structural administrative element of European absolutism—the *intendant* system of field administration—was transferred directly to the New World in the eighteenth century by French advisers to the Spanish monarchy, and, as a result, it became a major element of the authoritarian centralist tradition in Latin America.[9] A more developed and bureaucratized version of this European absolutist legacy was transferred by Belgium to what is now Zaire. Also central to the Belgian colonial enterprise in Zaire was the organic-statist legacy of the administrative law tradition of chartered associations, the roots of which go back through seventeenth-century absolutism via Roman and Church law to the Roman Empire.

Alfred Stepan considers absolutism to be part of the organic-statist tradition and notes that in the Roman Empire, seventeenth-century absolutism, and the two Napoleonic regimes "there was a major accumulation of power by the state at the expense of interest groups."[10] In these cases, the state played, in Marxist terminology, a "nonhegemonic" or balancing role between societal groups and classes because of the state's position of theoretical and substantive relative autonomy—a notion central to the organic-statist model of governance. The major Marxist "exceptions" are absolutism, Bonapartism, and the Asiatic mode of production.[11] Only absolutism and Bonapartism will be treated here.

Marxist analysis of the state has long suffered from what Nicos Poulantzas has called "economism,"[12] that is, from downplaying or even eliminating political factors and making the state a dependent variable, thereby denying any *possible autonomy* for it.[13] According to Engels, however, there are periods of history in which the dominant class does not control the state; these are "nonhegemonic" periods. For France he lists "the absolute monarchy of the seventeenth and eighteenth centuries" and "the Bonapartism of the First and still more of the Second Empire."[14] These "exceptions" thus account for a substantial portion of the seventeenth, eighteenth, and nineteenth centuries. It is imperative to assert theoretically the possibility of the relative autonomy of the state and then to investigate it in each empirical case and over time since ruling classes *and* the interests they protect may shift, often dramatically, over time. John Lonsdale makes a similar point:

> If European history over the last two or three centuries shows two abstract types of state, absolutist and bourgeois, at war with each other within actual states from above and below, then the state at any one moment can scarcely be reduced to a necessary managerial level of its characteristic mode of production. The same must be all the more true of modern Africa in the past century. Past relations of power continue everywhere as ideological shadows over the present, fetters on new opportunities for expanding productive forces.[15]

Absolutism, then, is the primary *early modern* Marxist, nonhegemonic exception, and it fits the conditions of Mobutu's Zaire more closely than Bonapartism primarily because socioeconomic and class development are much less advanced and patrimonial forms of politics, leadership, and administration are more important than in Bonapartism.[16] Above all, the class situation is simply more fluid, more in flux, under absolutism, particularly the seventeenth-century French absolutism used as the referent here, than it is under the Bonapartism of Louis Napoleon. In fact, the important classes are different in each case. In European absolutism there was a rising and consolidating, but not yet dominant, bourgeoisie which was both protected *and* closely controlled by the state and a very small, emerging proletariat; whereas in Bonapartism, as Engels indicates, the bourgeoisie is well consolidated and the proletariat has developed into the other economically and politically important class. In this sense Bonapartism is more comparable to contemporary bureaucratic, military, and corporatist authoritarian rule in Latin America, where developed class-based politics is much more central than it is to the authoritarianism of most African states. In fact, Philippe Schmitter, Guillermo O'Donnell, and others have suggested that the notion of Bonapartism is useful within the Latin American and broader corporatist contexts, especially to stress the relative autonomy of the state and the role of class-based, particularly working-class, factors.[17]

This is not to say that Zairian absolutism has no Bonapartist elements. It *does,* particularly in regard to Louis Napoleon—his rise to power via a military coup (that is, the usurpation of power rather than its traditional inheritance), the early presidentialism, and consolidation of power using plebiscites and other trappings of democracy, his personal despotism as emperor, and the political importance of the military, although I argue that Zaire is not a military regime per se.[18] Despite these clear Bonapartist elements, Mobutu's regime is most accurately characterized as an absolutist regime, that is, a patrimonial monarchy in the context of *early modern* state *formation.*

Thus there is an additional central difference between absolutism and Bonapartism in that the very nature of the state–society struggle is different. Political, territorial, and, above all, administrative unity and centralization are still being struggled for, are still problematic, under absolutism while they are assured and assumed characteristics under Bonapartism. As Poulantzas puts it, absolutism is concerned with "the *birth* of bureaucracy," not its achievement.[19] The state is still an early modern agent of unification, struggling for sovereignty in a context of relative autonomy. Poulantzas stresses this search for sovereignty by the absolutist state, connecting it with an organic-statist orientation:

> The sovereignty of the state . . . appears to be linked to the problem of the unity of "strictly political" power: a power which is seen as representing the unity of the subjects of the state in the public sphere. The state is held to embody the general public interest—a new theme on the agenda: this is the essential principle of the concept of *reason of state.* This concept covers precisely the independence of a state power, unconstrained by any extra-political limit, *inasmuch* as it is the power which represents the general interest.[20]

He also underscores the fact that the absolutist state is a "transitional state" linked to *emerging* capitalism, which it both fosters and controls via mercantilist policies. The absolutist state "functions in favor" of capitalism, which "is not yet dominant" or fully developed as it becomes under Bonapartism. In this respect, "the bourgeoisie is not the politically dominant class" under absolutism "and often not even the economically dominant class."[21]

An effective way to specify the essential characteristics of a given regime is to compare it to situations which at first appear similar but upon further examination tend more to highlight differences. Such is the case with a comparison of Mobutu's authoritarian regime in Zaire with bureaucratic-authoritarian corporatist states in contemporary Latin America. The literature on these phenomena is particularly useful and welcome because of its renewed concern with the state as an important concept and the state–society struggle as a worthy focus of analytic attention.[22]

The major differences from the situation in Zaire stem from the fact that the authoritarian Latin American states in question (primarily Argentina, Brazil, Mexico, Peru, Chile, and, to a lesser extent, Uruguay) are not early modern states. In early modern states a single "national" political structure does not hold sway in a direct and unmediated way via a relatively bureaucratized administration, unified legal system, and coercive apparatus over all people in all localities. In the typical situation, local, decentralized, usually patrimonial forms of rule compete with central authorities for compliance, legitimacy, and resources from the same set of people. Intermediary authorities of various types thus prevent the maintenance of a direct state–subject or "citizen" relationship.[23] With independent political histories dating back to the early nineteenth century, these Latin American states are significantly more developed than Zaire. As "late developing industrial states" in the throes of the third, that is, capital industrialization, stage of the delayed-dependent development syndrome, their orientations and problems, and tools and structures for coping with them, are significantly different than in Zaire.[24] While specific comparisons are made here with the Mobutu regime, the differences hold broadly for much of black Africa. A list of the more important differences would include the following:

1. Zaire is still in the primary product, outward-oriented export stage of development; it does not have the important industrial sector of "deepening" capitalism which aims at advanced industrialization. One result of this is that the political economy of Zaire is more akin to early modern neomercantilism than to the more advanced and effective state capitalism of these Latin American states.

2. Well-developed class-based politics within a widely recognized national arena does not exist in Zaire. As a result, the internal class structure that the ruling class confronts is not as complex and various forms of particularism are politically more a concern than in Latin America.

3. Zaire, as a result of its lower level of development, is not as integrated into the international capitalist economy, and, partially as a result of this, its bourgeoisie is not anywhere near as large, developed, cosmopolitan, or internationalized.[25]

4. Zaire has not experienced a previous populist regime which significantly activated and mobilized a complex but limited pluralism leading to a socioeconomic crisis of political authority. The emergence of an authoritarian regime in Zaire was the result of a crisis that was much more exclusively political (i.e., order oriented) and particularistic in nature.

5. Zaire does not have a significant, much less well-organized working class which has been previously mobilized by a populist regime.

6. The ruling group in Zaire is not a multiclass coalition and is much less modernizing and developmentally oriented than in Latin America.

7. Zaire is not a case of military domination by a highly professionalized, bureaucratized, and developmentally oriented military. This partially accounts for the less well-developed repressive capabilities of the Zairian regime.

8. The administrative state and its political aristocracy in Zaire are not anywhere nearly as bureaucratized, functionally differentiated, technically oriented, or effective as in those Latin American cases. Patrimonial characteristics are more dominant in Zaire, although they are clearly still important in Latin America. Again, as a result, repressive and policy implementation capabilities are much less developed.

9. Sizable and professionalized technocratic groups, both civilian and military, do not exist in Zaire. This in large part accounts for the much less well-developed social and economic planning and implementation capabilities in Zaire and for a more personalistic approach to politics and policy-making.

In many ways Zaire is more comparable to the early postcolonial period of Latin American history. This results from the combined effects of: (1) a centralist and organic-statist colonial legacy; (2) patrimonial forms of rulership and politics overlaid by pseudoconstitutional forms of government; (3) an early modern context of political breakdown, territorial fragmentation, and strong particularism; and (4) low levels of socioeconomic development in a primary product export economy. The Latin American experience is particularly useful here because of the much longer political histories and experience with socioeconomic development and its consequences that these countries have.

## THE RISE OF A ZAIRIAN POLITICAL ARISTOCRACY

As in seventeenth-century Frances, the Zairian absolutist state has created its own political aristocracy—a *noblesse d'État*—which in turn supports its creator. The absolutist monarch rules through this political nobility which is "the nucleus of decision and impetus in all the affairs of the kingdom."[26] The members of this new official realm are above all "royal" servants, the king's men, his chosen patrimonial instruments, "ses créatures." One Zairian observer describes it as "a ruling elite perceived by the mass as foreign and better considered."[27] It is a consolidating but still relatively fluid class, one firmly rooted in the organization structures of the state and held together by complex, yet partially shifting patron-client networks and factions as it was in seventeenth-century France. There are variable relational, ethnic, regional, patron-client, educational, and political criteria for entry. Loyalty to Mobutu, the patron of patrons, is, however, the ultimate requirement for entry and continued membership.

This state class consists of several groups: (1) all top-level administrative, political, and military officials, sometimes called the "presidential family" (an appropriately patrimonial term)—close presidential advisers, all members of the "royal" councils (Political Bureau and Executive Council), state commissioners (ministers), field-grade military officers, regional commissioners, key officials in the parastatal sector, and most of the people's commisioners (members of the Legislative Council) and Central Committee members—and also includes relatives of Mobutu who hold pseudopolitico-administrative positions;[28] (2) middle-level administrative and military officers in Kinshasa; and (3) the rest of the territorial prefects and military officers in the regions and middle- and high-level officials in the mostly moribund regional state services.

One European observer calls it a "bourgeoisie d'État," "une classe dirigeante," and notes the

> intention of the President to prevent the development of a bourgeoisie with an economic base which could escape his control. The high bourgeoisie is therfore exclusively a bourgeoisie of the State.[29]

This analyst divides the state bourgeoisie into three groups: (1) *la clique présidentielle*—most family members and close Zairian and foreign advisers; these several dozen people have almost unlimited license to plunder; some of them hold sensitive politico-administrative or military positions, but Mobutu rotates them to new posts from time to time; (2) *la confrérie régnante*—these several hundred people "occupy almost all of the important political, administrative and economic positions"; here uncertainty is greater, rotation is more frequent, and the possibilities of the "politics of appropriation" are wide open; the material perquisites, formal and informal, are enormous; each *confrère* creates his own patron-client network; ethnic and regional criteria may be important, but they are not necessarily dominant; loyalty and some competence are also important; and (3) *la grand bourgeoisie potentielle*—middle- and lower-level state officials and military officers who aspire to membership in the *confrérie régnante;* they are usually clients in the networks of the *confrères* or the presidential clique and also partake in the "politics of appropriation," but to somewhat a lesser degree.[30]

The members of the political aristocracy serve "the policies, designs, ambitions and weaknesses of the king"; they serve "the wishes of princes by conviction, servility and career interest at the same time."[31] The status of these political nobles is not a traditional one, but rather one that comes from being an official of the new absolutist state. Such was the case in seventeenth-century France as well. Neither are these state agents modern civil servants; rather, they are early modern state officials—regime, not public, servants. Finally, the political nobility is composed of sets of partially interlocking, partially competitive patron-client networks.

The political aristocracy is the major avenue of upward mobility in the Zairian absolutist state. Power, wealth, and prestige are obtained through these royal offices. Mobutu heaps rewards, honors, and riches on "ses créatures" *as long as* they remain loyal to and dependent on him. They are patrimonial servants, and the foundation of the whole system is *la faveur royale*. Without it, they have nothing.

As in absolutist France, the politics of appropriation appears almost normal; it shocks only when it becomes too exaggerated. The line between private and state property is almost nonexistent. Embezzlement, fraud, theft, illicit economic ventures of all kinds, including widespread smuggling and export-import swindles, are all common:

> Entry into the *confrérie* is validated by the granting of some spectacular presidential gifts (Mercedes cars, luxurious houses . . .) which are the visible signs of membership; but the non-visible advantages are more considerable: any new high official can upon installation freely embezzle massive sums. This tapping is so important and so ritual that the President cannot not know about it. Without a doubt it is part of a presidential control system for political personnel.[32]

One estimate puts the amount of revenue lost or diverted at roughly 60 percent of each annual operating budget. In 1975 the Shaba regional commissioner was reportedly grossing $100,000 a month, of which only 2 percent was his salary. Also in 1975 a prominent general reputedly had a monthly salary of 45,000 Zaires plus numerous informal payments, including 8000 Zaires a month paid to him out of a special account in the Banque de Kinshasa. An important member of the Political Bureau was receiving a monthly salary of 17,000 Zaires for that position alone, and he held numerous others as well. Each newly appointed member of the Political Bureau or the Executive Council would receive a 17,000-Zaire "settling-in allowance" to allow him to purchase some of the "essentials" needed to maintain the lifestyle expected of a high member of the political aristocracy. In 1977, the volcano of Nyrangongo near Goma at the northern end of beautiful Kivu erupted, doing substantial damage to the surrounding area. Mobutu, as the concerned patriarchal ruler, donated 20,000 Zaires of his "personal" funds to the victims of Goma. The people never saw the funds; they simply disappeared. Mobutu was forced to give another 20,000 Zaires.[33]

As in seventeenth-century France, the political aristocracy in Zaire does not invest its ill-gotten gains in productive ways. The European observer who uses the term *bourgeoisie d'État* admits that this group is not an emerging *"bourgeoisie économique:"*

> The ruling class, which with the benediction and complicity of the President of the Republic takes an important part of the national revenue, does not invest its funds in manufacturing enterprises. The money not consumed by luxury products and services or distributed among kinsmen or clients is invested in real estate, commercial enterprises or transport or placed overseas in the case of hard currency.[34]

And as one economist put it, "In this country the notion of long-term investment is practically unheard of."[35]

Mobutu is clearly aware of these processes, which he termed *"le mal zairois"* in a November 1977 speech:

> To sum it up, everything is for sale, everything is bought in our country. And in this traffic, holding any slice of public power constitutes a veritable exchange instrument, convertible into illicit acquisition of money or other goods, or the evasion of all sorts of obligations.
>
> Worse, even the use, by an individual, of his most legitimate right is subjected to an invisible tax, openly pocketed by individuals.
>
> Thus, an audience with an official, enrolling children in school, obtaining school certificates, access to medical care, a seat on a plane, an import license, a diploma, among other things, are all subject to this tax which is invisible, yet known to the whole world.[36]

*But* since this almost prebendal form of remuneration is politically crucial, he privately condones it, practices it himself on a massive scale, and encourages it in others, and, as a result, it goes on and on . . . just as it did in seventeenth-century absolutist France. Patrimonial forms of administration and extraction are clearly dominant.

The November 30, 1973, Zairianization measures are one of the most remarkable indications of the patrimonial relationship between the Zairian presidential monarch, foreign capital, and the political aristocracy as well as of the power of this consolidating ruling class. Mobutu called for efforts to achieve total economic independence (basically mercantilist goals) and announced that most foreign-owned small and medium-size enterprises would be taken over—wholesale and retail shops, farms, plantations, ranches, and small factories. Rather than being taken over by the state, however, they were given to individuals as *private* property. Roughly 1500 to 2000 enterprises were taken from their non-Zairian owners, and members of the political aristocracy (or their "stand-in" relatives and friends)—from state commisioners to prefects at all levels—acquired most of them. It is a remarkable example of patrimonial prebendal administration, the emerging power of the political nobility, and "the conversion of political power and position into economic wealth for the benefit of the few, at the expense of the many."[37] The attribution process was a purely political one, and, as one *acquéreur* put it, "Unbelievable things happened at the practical level."[38] Mobutu himself and other members of the top levels of the political aristocracy acquired huge holdings.

Because of the disastrous economic consequences of this fantastic takeover, Mobutu had to retreat somewhat by late 1974. The state was to take over the businesses from the individual members of the political nobility. The president appointed roughly 100 "delegates-general" to supervise state control of these businesses, but few of them were actually turned over to the state. Thus the same purposes and interests were still served. But the economic chaos continued, and Mobutu was forced to invite some of the foreign owners back in 1975. In most cases, however, the new owners were to take Zairian partners, frequently the former *acquéreurs*. In fact, this solution is probably the most beneficial one for all concerned, for what good is a disintegrated business to a member of the political aristocracy? This is the ultimate solution for members of the political aristocracy because this way they can appropriate wealth due to their political position without having to take much of a hand in producing it, that is, without having to perform true bourgeois functions.[39]

As noted earlier, Poulantzas believed that European absolutism was linked to emerging capitalism. It was, however, capitalism of a particular type. The performance of an African patrimonial state such as Zaire clearly highlights what Weber called "the negative anticapitalist effect of patrimonial arbitrariness":

> The patrimonial state lacks the political and procedural *predictability,* indispensible for capitalist *development,* which is provided by the rational rules of modern bureaucratic administration. Instead we find unpredictability and inconsistency on the part of court and local officials, and variously benevolence and disfavor on the part of the ruler and his servants.[40]

As Weber pointed out, however, patrimonialism is differentially amenable to various types of capitalism: "Under the dominance of a patrimonial regime only certain types of capitalism are able to develop fully . . . the individual variants of capitalism have a differential sensitivity toward such predictable factors." For Weber, the opportunities of expansion are limited for "production-oriented modern capitalism, based on the rational enterprise, the division of labor and fixed capital, whereas politically oriented capitalism, just as capitalist wholesale trade, is very much compatible with patrimonialism." Patrimonial rulers need the "treasure" from trade "above all for the maintenance of their following, the body-guards, patrimonial armies, mercenaries and especially officials." The result is what Weber called "patrimonial capitalism,"[41] and Zaire's political aristocracy is clearly reflective of this type of capitalism.

Centralizing patrimonial states, then, are best linked to emerging capitalism of a political character, historically the type associated with "the age of mercantilism, when the incipient capitalist organization of trades, the bureaucratic rationalization of patrimonial rulership and the growing financial needs of the military, external [foreign affairs] and internal administration revolutionized the financial techniques of the European states." Weber cautioned, however, that the "bureaucracy" of such states "was still as patrimonial as was the basic conception of the 'state' on which it rested."[42] I believe that this holds true for Africa today as well. The apparent economic nationalism of the early Mobutu period, for example, turned out to be heavily patrimonial and statecraft centered rather than a manifestation of a bureaucratic statist developmentalism. When the rational imperatives of bureaucratic statist development came into conflict with the patrimonial core of the administrative state and its consolidating political class, the former gave way to the latter.[43]

To say that a Zairian political aristocracy exists is not to say that it is a completely coherent and unified class. Transethnic in character, it is usually fragmented into various competing factions, or "fractions" as some Marxist writers call them. Existence in the political aristocracy is often precarious, and individuals hedge against this uncertainty by maintaining clientalist ties with internal *and* external groups upon which they might be able to fall back and by the politics of appropriation. Because the benefits of membership are so great, factional disputes within the ruling class revolve more around a secure place in the state than around ideological or policy positions. Despite these internal divisions, the political aristocracy is consolidating itself as a class. It does so primarily by establishing patron-client ties and alliances within itself. Class closure mechanisms are also becoming of much greater importance, especially in education and career opportunities. The political aristocracy is a class in reality, and it is becoming increasingly conscious of its existence as a class and therefore of the existence of generalized class interests. In fact, the officials of the political nobility have developed an absolutist subculture which greatly aids the consolidation of the administrative state.

This political class inherited the colonial administrative state but often assumed the status elements of these positions and neglected to fulfill many of their role functions.[44] This is one of the reasons for calling this class a political aristocracy rather than a "national bourgeoisie" and for referring to the "patrimonialization" of the colonial state. The capability of the state to do more than maintain basic order and extract resources is often crippled because role performance becomes ritualistic. A general insouciance permeates the administrative life of the state, and such a situation is not conducive to the formulation and implementation of state policies. This is a crucial characteristic of early modern states generally. The Zairian political aristocracy manifests a weak sense of public purpose and collective or societal good. It has demonstrated a notably feeble commitment to increasing the standard of living of the masses over whom it rules. This can be demonstrated by an analysis of the policies for which it actually allocates resources and for which it shows a real commitment to implementation. This problem is compounded by the venality of the political aristocracy. As a result, "development" programs usually get only what is left over after the political aristocracy has achieved its interests.

Most of the new African ruling classes have a "project"—what Frederick Cooper calls "the ruling class's project of self-aggrandizement combined with enough redistribution to maintain its tenuous and vital hold on the state."[45] This project cuts across a wide range of resources, internal and external, and leads to both collaboration and competition with internal and external groups. The degree to which this class will develop genuine bourgeois characteristics will vary greatly from state to state. To say that African ruling classes have such a project is not to say it is an easy or inevitably successful one:

> But it is not a project that has been altogether successful, and the very difficulties
> of transforming privileged access to resources into accumulation of productive cap-

ital have often fostered the tendency of this class project to take the easier forms of urban real estate speculation and compradorism. The class basic of state action has been compromised by the particularistic power base of its members and the high stakes of state control.[46]

Given political classes can follow different routes in pursuit of their projects, resulting in different relationships to external actors and varying mixes of collaboration and competition and of capitalist and noncapitalist characteristics. Leys correctly notes, for example, that Zaire does not have a "politically cohesive production-oriented class of capital," and Cooper points out that "if the Zairois political class owes its existence to outside forces, it has taken off on its own internal mission"—what others have called "parasitic capitalism."[47]

Zaire is clearly not in a "bourgeois" phase at all. As only a very nascent domestic bourgeoisie exists, domestic capitalism is still in the earliest stages of development. In large part, this is due to the "blockage" nature of Belgian colonial policy. There is now some evidence that an incipient domestic bourgeoisie may be forming in Zaire. Using data gathered in Kisangani, Janet MacGaffey posits "the *emergence* of a *small* commercial middle class that is *relatively* independent of political ties, and the *beginnings* of local capitalist development."[48] Most of this activity takes place outside the political field of Kinshasa, in the "informal sector," in the "irregular," or *magendo,* economy.

To evaluate the importance of the findings about the new commercial middle class, its size and weight *relative to* other groups need to be assessed. Zaire is light-years behind Kenya or Nigeria in the development of an indigenous capitalist class with true bourgeois characteristics.[49] MacGaffey's findings are important because they indicate the beginnings of such a development in Zaire. I would argue that as such a group becomes more important, President Mobutu and his political aristocracy will seek energetically to control its development and collect state and personal "rents" from it, at least in urban centers such as Kisangani. Their capacity to do so fully, however, remains a very open question, one with important implications for the development of commercial and production capitalism in this patrimonial state.

Last, although other classes and protoclasses exist in Zaire, the political aristocracy does not have any serious *internal class competitors* for control of the state. Coalition conflict does occur, however. Rather, it faces a multiplicity of societal groups and emerging classes which pose problems and difficulties for it. In this absolutist state there are peasants, workers, petit bourgeois clerks, traders, and businessmen, etc., but for lack of size, social weight, and/or organization they do not constitute class competitors for power, for control of the state apparatus. Class conflict between and within elements of emerging classes does take place, but nonclass forms of conflict are still of equal or greater importance. Viable radical revolutionary movements representing peasants and workers also do not as yet exist. The political aristocracy struggles with societal groups, organizations, and classes by consolidating its position in the state, by using it to control them, and by calling on external help when it has trouble doing so. Thus the political aristocracy maintains relative autonomy from other internal groups and classes, and class consolidation and state formation become mutually reinforcing processes for it.

## EXTERNAL CHALLENGES AND THE RELATIVE AUTONOMY OF THE POLITICAL ARISTOCRACY

Various external actors have tried to alter the nature of the Zairian absolutist state and the actions of its ruler and his political aristocracy. Zaire was born in the international arena, and it has remained there. International assistance has been a continuous and pervasive factor supporting the emergence, consolidation, and survival of the absolutist state in Zaire and its ruling class. Such support was crucial to Mobutu's control of the armed forces from the earliest days, crucial to his first "coup" in September 1960, crucial to his seizure of full power in 1965 as an African *caudillo,* crucial to the emergence and consolidation of the political aristocracy, and crucial to an ability to survive a severe debt crisis and two external invasions in 1977 and 1978. A word of caution is necessary, however, for although external assistance has been essential, it has not been all determining. Mobutu and his ruling class have maintained a significant degree of relative autonomy; external influence does have its limits:

> Although outside powers may reckon on the possibility of achieving their interests in Africa by affecting governmental change or by affecting the outcome of territorial struggles, they are as impotent as are other actors, including the military, to alter fundamental processes of African political life. It would require massive intervention, comparable in intensity and duration to the colonial period, to influence patterns of political development.[50]

The Mobutu regime would not exist today without external support, past and present, but its ruler and his political aristocracy have successfully fought off challenges to their relative autonomy.

Since his earliest days in the turbulent crucible of Zairian politics, Mobutu has shown a Machiavellian flare for establishing and manipulating shifting coalitions of support, both internally and externally. Other states, international organizations, transnational corporations, and external groups such as the Catholic church have complex, shifting, and often competing sets of economic, politico-strategic, and normative interests to pursue in the Zairian arena. The interstices created by these multiple sets of interests often permit some room for maneuver, some autonomy for the absolutist ruler and his political aristocracy.

Economic and fiscal reform, military reorganization, and political liberalization efforts have all been initiated in Zaire as a result of direct pressure by external actors following internal crises caused to a substantial degree by the nature of the regime. The intent of the external actors was to alter certain characteristics of the absolutist state, but the reform efforts have had only marginal effect. The core of the absolutist state—Mobutu's personal discretion and the power of the political aristocracy—remain, in large part thanks to the assistance of external supporters, but despite their efforts to induce some change in the nature and structure of this early modern state. In this context, Zaire's long-standing debt crisis and the politico-military reforms undertaken in the aftermath of the two invasions of Shaba Region from Angola in 1977 and 1978 will be discussed briefly.

The Achilles' heel of Mobutu's Zaire may well be its financial condition.

This issue is directly linked to the nature of this highly personalized, author-itarian but insecure, conservative, and corrupt regime. The current financial chaos highlights the distinct limits, precarious nature, and intensely patrimonial character of this absolutist state. It also reveals a good deal about the way external actors relate to it. The Zairian financial system is the weakest point of the regime. In fact, "system" is too strong a word because Zairian finances have nothing that could be called order or clarity, even approximate. "System-atic disorder" is more the norm. Zaire is potentially a wealthy country, one of the most well endowed in Africa, but it is now on the verge of financial and economic collapse. The Zairian absolutist state has a large revenue by African standards, but it also has a weak, inefficient, and massively corrupt financial structure. Zaire's rulers cannot understand how they can be in such desperate financial straits when such large sums of money pass through their hands.

Mobutu Sese Seko, as a presidential monarch, and his political aristocracy have an insatiable desire for more revenue. It is central to the political logic of both regime maintenance and class consolidation. But they also have a basic ambivalence toward this crucial resource. The revenue of the state belongs to them, and they should spend it as they see it. There is no distinction between the finances of the state and personal finances. Mobutu and his political aris-tocracy are political, not economic, animals. They know that power and glory, two of their chief interests, depend on money, but they do not want to be overly concerned with the "details" and consequences of producing and managing it. This ambivalence toward the economic realities of finance is a core character-istic of the absolutist state and in large part accounts for its shakiness.

Two major things result from this situation: (1) reliance on "extraordinary" financial measures, especially the corruption which is the glue holding much of the system together, along with rash and uncontrolled expenditures; and (2) extensive and unwise borrowing, leading to huge debts and near bankruptcy. In fact, the extraordinary measures are almost "normal" practice. In this re-gard, Weber noted:

> The patrimonial state offers the whole realm of the ruler's discretion as a hunting ground for accumulating wealth. Wherever traditional or stereotyped prescription does not impose strict limitations, patrimonialism gives free reign to the enrichment of the ruler himself, the court officials, favorites, governors, mandarins, tax col-lectors, influence peddlers, and the great merchants and financiers who function as tax farmers, purveyors and creditors.[51]

The result of such activities in Zaire, especially in conjunction with structural economic difficulties brought on by neglect and the effects of a world reces-sion, has been financial and economic crisis. The financial condition of Zaire was excellent in the late 1960s and early 1970s, particularly because of the high price of copper, which accounted for about two-thirds of Zaire's foreign exchange earnings. By the late 1970s, however, Zaire was nearly $5 billion in debt and on the verge of economic collapse.

There are multiple causes of this crisis: the dramatic fall in the price of copper, the closure of the Benguela railroad since the Angolan civil war in 1975–1976, the disastrous economic effects of the Zairianization moves be-tween 1973 and 1975, rising oil costs, and a world recession. The situation was compounded by the Shaba invasions in 1977 and 1978. As serious as these factors were, however, they are far from the whole story. All of these conditions were made far worse by other factors. Political factors are very important, and they relate directly to the nature of the ruler and his political aristocracy—massive and rash spending and borrowing when revenues were high, rampant corruption and fiscal mismanagement, and lack of understanding and concern about the rapidly deteriorating situation. And, of course, the effects of the Zairianization measures can also be considered political and class factors.

Mobutu and the political aristocracy know that lending is a two-way street, and they have shrewdly played the debt repayment game by attempting to manipulate slightly shifting coalitions of external actors and the financial, economic, *and* politico-strategic interests they seek to protect or expand. They are managing their dependence for survival, however, not for development or the welfare of the mass of Zairians. Given the severity of Zaire's situation, Mobutu and his political aristocracy have done amazingly well so far in this game of brinkmanship. They may not understand the finer technicalities of the international financial system, but they do understand the politics of international finance:

> The very bonds of economic dependency have been used with virtuosity. The regime adroitly trades on the premise that its creditors cannot afford either to see it fall, or to see Mobutu fall. Bankruptcy would be as inconvenient for the banks as for Zaire; at each negotiating brink, a temporizing formula is found, the debt rolled over one more time, while all await the millennium of higher copper prices.[52]

What are the chances of major reform or change? Because of the nature of the political aristocracy and its leader, the chances are very slim indeed; the record on this point is very clear.

Under International Monetary Fund (IMF) and other external pressure and guidance, Mobutu and his government put together six stabilization plans (in 1976, 1977, 1979, 1981, 1983, and 1985). In each case, the IMF extended substantial standby credit (SDR912 million, about $1.2 billion, for the fourth stabilization plan). The plans aimed to cut corruption, rationalize expenditures, increase tax revenues, limit imports, boost production in all sectors, improve the transportation infrastructure, eliminate arrears on interest payments, make principal payments on time, and generally improve financial management and economic planning. Zaire's public and publicly insured debt has also been rescheduled by the Paris Club countries six times (in 1976, 1977, 1979, 1981, 1983, and 1985)—a world record. Zaire's private creditors rescheduled their part of the debt in April 1980 and again in May 1985, and nine World Bank and Western country aid consortia meetings have been held to generate larger official assistance (one in 1977, two in 1978, and one each in 1979, 1980, 1981, 1982, 1983, and 1985). The World Bank has supported these efforts directly via structural adjustment loans and technical assistance.

The results of the first two stabilization plans were so meager that the IMF and the World Bank decided in 1978 to send their own teams of experts to Zaire directly to take over key financial positions in the Bank of Zaire, the Finance Ministry, and the Customs Office. In December 1978, the head of the Bank of Zaire team, Erwin Blumenthal, a retired German central banker, took dramatic measures which struck at the heart of the power of the political aristocracy. He cut off credit and exchange facilities to firms of key members of the political nobility, including several of Mobutu's closest collaborators, and imposed very strict foreign exchange quotas. Efforts to impose budgetary control over the presidency and the military have been for the most part delayed or circumvented, however, and ways were usually found around the foreign exchange controls. In addition, Nguza Karl-i-Bond, a former foreign and prime minister, charged from exile in June 1981 that Mobutu himself had siphoned off substantial amounts of IMF and World Bank assistance.[53]

In August 1979, Zaire hired a multinational "triumvirate" of investment banking firms—Lazard Frères, Lehman Brothers, and Warburg. For very high fees, they performed the following tasks: assessed the actual size and structure of Zaire's debt (the World Bank had already tried to do this once); compiled a series of useful information memoranda; assisted Zaire in two Paris Club reschedulings (1979 and 1981) and in several donor club meetings; advised on and helped to guide the complex negotiations for the London Club private bank rescheduling in 1980; and dealt with the IMF, the World Bank, Western governments, and private banks in an ongoing way. In October 1982, the "triumvirate" severed its contract with Zaire, in large part because of the intransigence of its ruler and key elements of the political aristocracy. It can be argued that Mobutu and the political aristocracy used the "triumvirate" quite consciously to provide international "management" cover or legitimacy behind which they could continue to pursue their own narrow personal and class interests.

The valiant efforts of the various internationally sponsored teams at the Bank of Zaire, the Office of Debt Managment, Customs, Finance, and Planning have been limited in their impact. The maneuvers of the political aristocracy to detour the controls have been creative, persistent, and, to a substantial degree, successful. The political aristocracy has both systematically harassed and "worn down" the teams over time; the teams change composition frequently and are often difficult to recruit, and the personnel are few in number. They are not substitutes for domestic political will and administrative capability. At best they are supplements. Erwin Blumenthal, in a 1982 report on his year in Zaire in 1978–1979, stated that it is

> alarmingly clear that the corruptive system in Zaire with all its wicked and ugly manifestations, its mismanagement and fraud will destroy all endeavors of international institutions, of friendly governments, and of the commercial banks towards recovery and rehabilitation of Zaire's economy. Sure, there will be new promises by Mobutu, by members of his government, rescheduling and rescheduling again of a growing external public debt, but no (repeat: no) prospect for Zaire's creditors to get their money back in any foreseeable future.[54]

By late 1985 Zaire was still over $4 billion in debt, and the economy continued to disintegrate. The decline in the level of agricultural production continued in most sectors as did the disintegration of the country's transport and communications infrastructure. The impact of this dismal fiscal and economic situation on the welfare of the population has been severe, although so far it has not been manifested in major outbreaks of political unrest. The formal or expressed willingness of the political aristocracy to take effective measures comes and goes. It comes only under substantial and coordinated external pressure and the perception of regime officials that, for the moment at least, they have no other alternatives. It ebbs dramatically when external pressure eases, slows down or is worn down, when disputes between external actors can be manipulated, or when a crisis of a politico-strategic or military nature can be used to "delay" reforms.

To carry out effectively and consistently the external demand reforms would undermine the very core of the absolutist state—the personal discretion of its ruler and the fiscal largess and corruption which constitute the glue holding the system together. Such reforms are a direct threat to the political aristocracy. Here the imperatives of calculability, of rationality, come into direct conflict with the personal. The bureaucratic clashes with the patrimonial, and the latter will most likely win out. The absolutist state will try to extract more resources from internal groups through higher taxes, new taxes, and more effective tax collection, but only from some of the "citizens," not all. The degree of external acquiescence is critical. In this case, who is dependent on whom? Externally, Mobutu and his political aristocracy will continue their attempts to reschedule the debt, extract additional resources from friendly Western powers and international organizations, and hope that the prices of copper, cobalt, diamonds, etc., will rise dramatically.

Western actors have periodically tried to "get tough" with Zaire, with only modest results. In 1982, for example, the IMF terminated Zaire's 1981 three-year extended fund facility for noncompliance. At the time there were those within the highest reaches of the political aristocracy who counseled that Zaire need not make any serious efforts to service the debt or institute reforms because its external "patrons" or "kin" in the international "extended family" or "lineage group" would have to bail them out. This is truly patrimonial imagery. In one sense this argument is a new and rather different version of the concept of the "neocolonial state"—that is, that Western actors are responsible for bailing out regimes that they support irregardless of their performance. It is almost a form of "reverse neocolonialism." On the other side there were those in Western circles who argued that Mobutu and his political aristocracy should be allowed to stew in their own juices. After a brief lapse, however, the logic of the interests (political, strategic, and economic) on both sides and a joint fear of the politics of brinkmanship and collapse dictated that the ritual dances of the debt game begin again.[55] The fifth IMF facility did come, but only after Zaire had managed to abide relatively well with most of the performance criteria of an informal or trial "shadow program" in late 1982 and early 1983.

There was some apparent short-term change, which generated a wave of quite extraordinary optimism by Western actors. There have been previous waves of optimism, such as with the externally induced political "liberalization" after the 1977 invasion of Shaba Region and the vigor with which Erwin Blumenthal had attacked his job at the Bank of Zaire in 1978. These waves have always come crashing down, however. This latest one most likely will as well, but the charade of coping with the debt continues, as witnessed by the IMF, Paris Club, and London Club agreements with Zaire in the spring of 1985. The ultimate issue is, of course, the productive capacity of the economy as a whole and the viability of its infrastructure, both of which are still disintegrating. In this regard, it should be noted that the 1984 investment budget was only $35 million. This figure constituted just the counterpart funds on *existing* external donor projects. This leaves aside the question of implementation. Given this climate, one might wonder how many foreign firms or investors are going to be willing to make major new investments in Zaire.

There may well be a real economic marginalization of Africa under way, a "de-linking" and a steady withdrawal of Western interest. As Cooper has nicely phrased it, "Capital has not invariably won the battles it fought in the first and second occupations of Africa—to make production predictable and orderly throughout the continent . . . the march of Africa into the world economy does not appear to follow a straight line."[56] The argument above about the differential sensitivity of various forms of capitalism is not meant to be a deterministic one. Surely capitalist development in Africa is not out of the question; it is just difficult and takes place slowly, incrementally, and unevenly. This is reinforced by the fact that external corporations and investors have a choice where they go in the ongoing changes in the international division of labor, especially in the context of world recession, protectionism, and comparative advantage calculations which tend to favor Africa the least:

> Multinational corporations have considerable power, above all, to choose the kind of state [and class] they need to cooperate with . . . they do exercise some choice over the battleground. Africa's guerrilla army of the underemployed may well appear less attractive than the more disciplined batallions of South Korea, Taiwan, and Hong Kong, or even the foot soldiers of Brazil. . . . Whether Africa plays a significant role in the shift in manufacturing markets in Europe and North America is doubtful, and within Africa concentration is likely in a very limited number of places, such as Zimbabwe and South Africa, where effective state services and a labor force that is well socialized and dependable as well as cheap are available.[57]

This argument holds equally well for the commercial banks or "finance capital" as it does for "industrial capital."

As Richard Higgott notes, "Africa may well be more peripheral, dependent and in greater economic crisis by the end of the current decade than it was in the 1960s."[58] It is a potential peripheralization rather different from the one the world system theoreticians have had in mind, and one that is in large part due to the nature of African ruling classes and the problems they confront rather than to the iron laws of international capitalism. Instead of maintaining or increasing the level of integration into the world capitalist economy, the reverse may be taking place for a sizable number of countries. Most African countries with debt problems will find it difficult to export themselves into a stable and manageable debt situation, much less out of debt.

In addition, because of the current economic and fiscal crisis and the nature of the state and its ruling class, local capital, where it exists, will not be inclined to make important medium- and long-term investment in new productive capacity for eventual profit. There are even indications that the money economy is shrinking in a number of countries and/or that *magendo* economic activity is becoming significantly more important. The availability of an "exit option" varies considerably from country to country, but, unlike most of the major Latin American countries with debt problems, it is a viable if not preferred option for African rural populations. It may also play an important role in reducing the tensions created by recession, austerity measures, infrastructure decline, and domestic political repression and economic extraction, both formal and informal. In the case of Zaire, the shrinking of the money economy, the rise of *magendo* activity, and the exit option are all present to varying degrees in many parts of the country. These processes are accompanied and in large part caused by a progressive patrimonialization and functional contraction of the inherited colonial state structure and are linked directly or indirectly to the unproductive nature of the Zairian political aristocracy.[59]

The two invasions of Shaba Region from Angola in 1977 and 1978 had major external and internal repercussions. In particular, they engendered military reorganization efforts, a reconciliation with Angola, and a series of political "liberalization" measures—all of which were to a large extent the direct result of pressure and influence by Zaire's international friends and supporters. These changes were aimed at controlling, moderating, or co-opting internal oppositon and dissent while giving the regime more legitimacy in the international arena, thereby facilitating external support efforts.[60]

Military reorganization and retraining efforts were undertaken by Belgian, French, Chinese, and American advisors, all to little avail. Mobutu's military remained more a gendarmery performing "occupation" functions than a force capable of dealing with serious military threats. After all, Mobutu does not want a military capable of effectively replacing him.

Starting after Shaba I in 1977, Mobutu announced a series of power-sharing measures designed to increase popular participation. For the Political Bureau, eighteen of its thirty members were henceforth to be elected, and elections for the Legislative Council were to be reformed by allowing more than one candidate for each seat. Those who were allowed to run, however, were carefully scrutinized, and almost all of them came from the political aristocracy. After early indications that Mobutu might allow other candidates for president, he was the only candidate when the elections were held in October 1977. In early 1978 Mobutu allowed members of the Legislative Council to question regime officials about governmental matters, and he also removed several high regime officials who had been critized by internal and external actors. Some discussion about the formation of a second political party was also permitted. Quite unexpectedly this "liberalization" allowed a courageous but small and harassed internal opposition to manifest itself and become quite feisty, particularly by embarrassing key members of the political aristocracy in Legislative Council hearings and by calling for free elections and more political parties. As a result, Mobutu struck back.

In a major speech to the Legislative Council on February 5, 1980, Mobutu, as presidential monarch of the absolutist state, dramatically announced, "As long as I live, I will never tolerate the creation of another party." In another comment, revealing for its clearly organic-statist thrust, Mobutu insisted that "There can be no negotiations about the peace and unity the country found after the chaos of 1960–65."[61] He scolded the Legislative Council for the excesses of its hearings and announced that henceforth they could only be held with his express permission. In addition, the election of some members of the Political Bureau would not be repeated, and after its current term was up in 1982, he would again appoint all its members. He had earlier expanded the size of the Political Bureau to thirty-seven, so that the eighteen elected members became a minority. The absolutist core of the state was reasserting itself.

These acts of retrenchment were typically "balanced" by measures to attack corruption, including prohibiting state commissioners (but not Political Bureau members) from engaging in business activities, reform education curricula, reorganize parastatal marketing activities, and restructure the secret police. But in this early modern authoritarian state, the likelihood that these reforms would ever be effectively implemented for any length of time was minimal.

These actions were directly responsible for a major strike and violent demonstrations by university students at all three campuses of the national university in April 1980. In addition to university-related demands, the students called for the removal of the entire Political Bureau and the establishment of a multiparty system. The demonstrations were stopped and the campuses closed by army troops, the students evacuated to the interior, and the university shut down. There were also large-scale illegal strikes by primary school teachers between March and June.

In August 1980 Mobutu took another step to emasculate the few remaining powers of the Legislative Council by creating a new institution, a 121-member party Central Committee whose functions would be only advisory. In short, it was meant to eclipse an already badly weakened Legislative Council. Shortly after the defeat of the Carter administration in the 1980 elections in the United States, Mobutu's government arrested key leaders of the internal opposition, all of whom were members of the Legislative Council.

Then, in early 1982, renewed student protest demonstrations and more wildcat strikes erupted, accompanied by increased agitation for a second legal political party. Mobutu found it necessary to reiterate emphatically his decision against any second party. He rejected this major threat to his personal domination that of his political aristocracy in language that stressed unity, order, discipline, and personal loyalty. In a major speech to the fourth meeting of the party Central Committee on March 15, he declared:

> Unfortunately, those embittered persons full of hatred and resentment toward the head of state personally, possessed with deepseated tribalism that has become second nature and trampling under feet the Constitution and the laws of our country, those embittered persons have agreed to set up a tribalist and ethnic cartel aimed at creating restlessness. . . . I have said on several occasions and I want to repeat it today— loudly, publicly, plainly and emphatically—Zaire is a unitary state and will remain unitary. Our national party is the MPR and it is the only one. As long as I am alive, this will always remain so. This is clear and distinct and cannot be questioned.

He also felt it necessary to deny that "Western circles—American in particular—have put pressure on me, imposed conditions and issued orders to me so that a second hypothetical party will be allowed in Zaire. This is a tasteless legend. Let's be serious."[62]

Thus the presidential monarch and his political aristocracy effectively turned away or seriously blunted externally demanded reform efforts designed to cope with the economic and fiscal crises and to liberalize the regime politically. In short, they demonstrated considerable relative autonomy from both external and internal actors by neutralizing direct threats to their power and interests, and without destroying the external assistance they do need to survive.

## CONCLUDING REMARKS

Three of the most important processes in Africa today are attempted state formation, the emergence of ruling classes, and the development of particular forms of capitalism, and they are closely intertwined phenomena. This chapter has stressed the complex interrelationship between state formation, patrimonial forms of power, class formation, and economic activity; and while external actors and influences are important in shaping them, internal processes do indeed have lives of their own. The ability of external actors to structure African regimes is limited.

Much of the writing on Africa in the postcolonial period suffered from both voluntarist and ahistorical views of the state and class. The state was perceived to be strong, or strong enough at least to put into action the desires of those who controlled it. On the side of liberal or "bourgeois" social science, the state, under the wise and legitimate leadership of modernizing elites, was to serve the new nation by pursuing policies of development and democracy. On the Marxist side, radical leadership groups were to combat neocolonialism and underdevelopment by constructing socialist states in the interests of the oppressed masses, or comprador elites served the interests of international capitalism and/ or fostered the development of capitalism in the periphery.

Both views have proved to be inaccurate. Now analysts of all varieties write about state decay, state decline, the withering away of the state which has been run into the ground by external actors and forces and/or local ruling classes, or even assert that a real state no longer exists. The state is "overdeveloped," "underdeveloped," or both at the same time; ruling classes are weak and unproductive, populations remain "uncaptured," and *magendo* economies spring up out of the ground. I suspect, however, that reality has not changed as much as our views and conceptualizations of it. Many of the processes that now attract attention have been under way since the day of independence, if not before. Certainly expectations by actors and analysts alike have been way too high. The African state is a feeble, blunt instrument of domination in the hands of whichever actor or class perceived to be in control—the IMF and monopoly and finance capital, a modernizing elite, radical populists, African socialists, Afrocommunists, a comprador ruling class, a state bourgeoisie, absolutist presidential monarchs and their political aristocracies, or an emerging capitalist bourgeoisie.

Unlike the case in most of Latin America today, the consolidation of viable state structures is still uncertain in much of black Africa, patrimonial forms of rulership, administration, and capitalism are still dominant, and class structures are still very much in flux. Politically conscious and organized peasant and working classes are still in a nascent stage of development, and true bourgeoisies remain very fragile creatures. Multiclass-based national politics is still in its infancy in Zaire and in much of the rest of black Africa. Despite the impact of the dependency and world system literatures on African studies, capitalism is still emerging in most of black Africa. In this sense, the best part of the Marxist literature on Africa today is that which focuses on the articulation of modes of production, that is, emphasizes social formations rather than Africa's full-fledged incorporation into a world capitalist system. In fact, that incorporation, although important, is only partial. In this context, the notion of Bonapartism is not at all appropriate to much of black Africa today; the state, class, and economic variables simply do not fit. More attention needs to be paid now to the links between social formations, the state, and particular forms of politics and administration.

Weber stressed that "in the interest of his domination, the patrimonial ruler must oppose . . . the economic independence of the bourgeoisie." This did not mean that the ruler succeeded, as the result emerged "everywhere according to the outcome of the resultant historical struggles."[63] In other words, different countries followed different paths as the result of concrete conflicts between real actors, the outcomes of which could not be fully predicted. There is thus nothing mechanistic or deterministic about Weber's views on state formation or the development of capitalism. The same holds for Africa today. The paths that different countries take are determined by the presence and balance of facilitating factors and by struggles between rulers, emerging classes, status groups, organizations, and particularistic forces, both internally and externally. Cooper quite rightly points out that "Africa itself is heading in different directions."[64] Whichever direction it is, a Colin Leys emphasizes, "like early capitalism everywhere, [it] is painful, wasteful, and ruthless." His final assessment rings true: "It would be as mistaken to think that capitalism is in the process of developing all the countries of Africa as it is to suppose that it has not developed, and cannot develop, any of it."[65]

As a presidential monarch, Mobutu does not want an autonomous bourgeoisie and has worked to stunt the growth of one. Absolutist monarchs in early modern Euorpe also feared rising bourgeoisies, but in the end they were unable to prevent their development into powerful and partially autonomous socio-economic and political forces. Although monarchs come and go, classes are much more tenacious. The Zairian political aristocracy, in all its unproductive glory or infamy, will most likely outlive its creator-monarch in one form or another, and, depending on the skill of future rulers, it may move in the direction of developing autonomous socioeconomic and political power, hopefully of a more productive nature.

One of the benefits of the broad comparative framework used here, however, is that it reminds us that such changes take a very long time and are greatly influenced by both external and internal, political and economic factors and struggles. One thing that we must be aware of is what I might call the "Fault of Analytic Hurry"—the desire to rush things along, whatever the path, to see things as real before they actually are, to read substantive weight into social processes, institutions, and actors that do not possess them. This has been one of the major problems with the analysis of class factors in Africa for quite some time now. It could apply just as easily to bureaucratization, the development of capitalism, or any of the other factors discussed here. Analysts cannot rush or control social processes; change is slow, incremental, uneven, often contradictory from a given analytic point of view, and dependent on the outcome of unpredictable socioeconomic and political struggles. At the same time, we cannot afford not to look for changes. As John Iliffe's favorite African proverb says, "He who waits for the whole animal to appear, spears the tail."[66]

The likelihood of major, guided or unguided, socioeconomic or political structural change in the medium run in Africa is not high, but, as the historical record of seventeenth- and eighteenth-century Europe and nineteenth-century Latin America suggests, changes do take place, albeit very slowly, very unevenly, and in ways that do not at first appear to go in any given direction. Our task is to look closely at current reality and then try to sort out the up and down cycles of surface change from the longer-run changes that appear quietly, but which, cumulatively and eventually, do gather social, economic, and political weight and alter the basic design of the underlying structure of domination and socioeconomic reality.

Finally, this chapter posits the need for more systematic efforts to merge

Weberian notions of political authority, domination, administration, and economics with much of the recent excellent material on class and the structural bases of power and authority in Africa and the need for broader comparison of the African experience with situations in other areas, both historical and contemporary.

# CHAPTER 5

# The Petite Bourgeoisie
# in the Ethiopian Revolution

## Robert D. Grey

Initial scholarly assessments of the causes of the Ethiopian revolution of 1974 focused heavily on facilitating circumstances, especially the famine of 1973–1974, desolating much of the country, and the rise in world oil prices following the Arab oil boycott.[1] In reaction to this literature, there emerged a number of scholarly pieces emphasizing prerevolutionary changes in Ethiopian society, changes which, it was argued, shaped the character of the Ethiopian response to these circumstances. Marina Ottaway, Bereket Habte Selassie, and others discussed the centralization and bureaucratization of the Ethiopian state, the development of commercial agriculture, the birth of a limited industrialization with its accompanying urban work force, and the growth of education.[2] These political, economic, and social changes were accompanied by the development of new "groups" in the society. Ottaway identifies new classes, the entrepreneurial and bureaucratic bourgeoisie and the urban proletariat, and old classes, the aristocracy and the peasantry. She also identifies groups not "class(es) in the Marxist sense of the term": the educated and those in government service, students, military elites, civilian elites, a "labour aristocracy," and other "corporate interests." Bereket takes an equally diffuse view of the forces created by these changes, emphasizing "nations," or ethnic groups as well, as important new political actors. In discussing those whose protests and demonstrations undermined the imperial regime in the winter and spring of 1974, and those who removed and replaced that regime in the fall, neither author characterizes them as classes. They were students, teachers, taxicab drivers, discontented soldiers, etc.

More recent scholarship[3] continues to emphasize these new forces and also manifests the same ambivalence as did Ottaway and Bereket about the adequacy of class analysis to explain the revolutionary mobilization. Thus Addis Hiwet talks about mass participation in the events of 1974 and C. Mahrdel, too, focuses on the masses. Negussay Ayele discusses both masses and classes, as does Azinna Nwafor. Such language implies a role for both the peasants and a (substantial) urban working class in the revolutionary unrest of 1974.

However, there is little empirical evidence of the former's involvement, and the latter, while active, did not constitute a numerically substantial force. "Mass analysis," moreover, allows these analysts to discuss the political role of the petite bourgeoisie as if that group was merely a part of this mass and, thus, tends to downplay the need for careful analysis of the petite bourgeoisie. In this analysis, I shall emphasize the revolutionary role of that class. Moreover, I will spell out *why* this new class in Ethiopian society was especially likely to respond to the conditions of 1974 in a revolutionary fashion, a task none of the existing literature has really undertaken.

A second area of dispute among analysts concerns the appropriate "class" designation (or, for the matter, revolutionary character) of the military personnel who took power at the end of 1974. My position is that those mobilized during 1974, both civilian and military, shared certain characteristics which identified them as parts of a single class, the petite bourgeoisie. However, I will also detail the particular characteristics of this subset of the petite bourgeoisie, and the revolutionary relevance of these characteristics.

My central argument, then, is that the nature of the process which led to the development of the petite bourgeoisie both alienated that class from the imperial regime and, at the same time, gave it certain political skills that made it both receptive to mobilization and, if mobilized, an effective political force. I shall further argue that the economic position of this class made both its relatively high standard of living and its economic security highly precarious. It was the combination of this vulnerability and its political alienation and skills which, triggered by the facilitating circumstances of 1974, brought the petite bourgeoisie into national politics and undermined the imperial regime of Haile Selassie.

While the activism of the petite bourgeoisie made continued imperial rule impossible, in itself the class could neither deal the death blow to the imperial government nor replace it. It was an organized subset of the class, its military component, which, because of its control of arms and its organizational and communication skills, could move the revolution these further steps. This argument, as I develop it, will both clarify how and why the petite bourgeoisie became a crucial element of the Ethiopian revolutionary process and illuminate the limits of such class analysis in explaining Ethiopian developments.

## THE NEW PETITE BOURGEOISIE

The early development of education (see below) in Ethiopia was designed to fulfill important needs that Haile Selassie had identified, both that of developing a political resource of use in averting European conquest of Ethiopia and that of developing a new governmental administrative structure which would help him in his pursuit of centralized political power.[4] Both promoted the growth of the government bureaucracy, and it was the bureaucracy which absorbed most of the newly educated Ethiopians. Thus, for instance, in 1965, the central government employed in administrative offices in Addis Ababa somewhere between 16,000 and 25,000 people.[5] In 1963, the equivalent administrators in the manufacturing sector, for the whole country, numbered 1400.[6] At that point, then, some 95 percent of the educated employed were employed by government. It was this salariat which formed the corps of the new petite bourgeoisie.

There were, however, other elements of the petite bourgeoisie. A number of those who had received some formal education joined the Ethiopian military, a force with approximately 40,000 men in the prerevolutionary army and much smaller numbers in the navy, air force, and police. Most of these individuals had received at least an elementary education, while many junior officers had undertaken postsecondary study.[7] Given the limited numbers of Ethiopians who had received any formal education, military personnel were thus part of a small elite. Employed, as was the civilian salariat, by government and, like them, dependent on their salaries for a living, they, too, should be considered a part of the petite bourgeoisie. Of course, the military personnel differed from their civilian counterparts in a number of respects, some of which became crucial during the revolution of 1974, as I shall argue below.

A final component of the petite bourgeoisie was a very different group made up of the small shopkeepers, individual petits entrepreneurs who, like their fellows in the salariat, "owned" little and were dependent for their livelihood on what they could get from the money economy. This group constituted a small part of the total group, however, and I shall essentially ignore them in the following analysis.

Thus the new petite bourgeoisie consisted largely of people (mostly males) who had received some formal schooling and, as a consequence, a salaried position either in the government's civilian bureaucracy or in its military ones. They were a class in the sense that they were economically dependent neither on what they directly produced from the land, nor on what they were paid for their labor as a factor of industrial production, nor, finally, on what they expropriated from such direct producers. They lived, instead, on salaries they were paid as government employees or income they earned as small businessmen.

## ORIGINS OF THE ETHIOPIAN PETITE BOURGEOISIE

The Ethiopian petite bourgeoisie is a relatively new class. The traditional social structure of the society was dominated by a landowning aristocracy and largely consisted of exploited peasantries.[8] Into this essentially feudal, and rural, structure, Haile Selassie, upon assuming substantial national power in the 1920s, began to introduce new elements. Thus, in 1925, he started a school in Addis Ababa, which introduced some 250 boys to foreign languages and other subjects of formal "Western" education.[9] Although not the first school in the empire, it represented the first sustained commitment to the production of a new "class." By the Italian invasion of 1935, perhaps 4000 students had received some education in this and other schools founded by the imperial family.

With minor exceptions, the preinvasion school system was an elementary system. Those completing the education available to them there and wishing more had to be sent abroad. Some 250 students received college degrees prior to World War II. A small number of these were slaughtered by the Italians during their occupation of Ethiopia.

Upon the liberation of Ethiopia in 1941, imperial support for formal education was resumed. By academic year 1944–1945, there were some 20,000 students, and this continued to increase every year, reaching some 150,000 pupils by 1959–1960, and over half a million by 1969–1970.[10]

This expansion of the educational system nevertheless left the vast majority of the young people of the country outside of the system. Even the last figure represents less than 10 percent of the school-age population. While this is relatively insignificant in terms of a goal of fully educating the Ethiopian population, these numbers nevertheless represented a sizable group which had undergone experiences new in Ethiopian history, experiences which gave them both attitudes and skills necessary to political activism.

## STUDENTS AND SUPPORT FOR THE IMPERIAL SYSTEM

There is some, albeit weak, evidence that, by the 1960s, students had become alienated from and antagonistic towards the imperial regime. The most direct evidence for the early development of such feelings was support by university students for the abortive coup of 1960.[11] Studies of student attitudes also found that in the mid-1960s students in the secondary school systems no longer regarded their governmental system as legitimate.[12] In a political system in which censorship was virtually total and students assumed the presence of police spies, however, such attitudes were seldom openly articulated.

## EDUCATION AND POLITICIZATION

Students of political participation in the Western world have found a very strong link between social class and participation. The more intense the level of involvement, the more likely the upper classes are to be overrepresented and the lower classes underrepresented. Efforts to assess the relative weight of the component parts of socioeconomic status (SES)—income, the prestige of one's occupation, and education—in increasing participation have suggested that education is the most important factor. Thus Almond and Verba found that the relatively highly educated were "more aware of the impact of the government on the individual . . . more likely to report that he follows politics and pays attention to election campaigns . . . has more political information . . . more likely to consider himself capable of influencing the government."[13]

This analysis, and other participation analyses, emphasize the greater insight the educated have into the potential opportunities or threats politics has for their values. It also suggests that the educated are more likely to feel that they have resources appropriate to influencing politics and can afford to spend these resources to maximize their well-being. Another participation advantage the educated would appear to have is skills—for example, articulateness—appropriate to the successful influencing of politics.

From this perspective, it is not any explicit teaching of the value of participation in the schools which leads to the education–participation link. Rather it is the development through education of wide interests, generally useful skills, and a sense of one's own competence which increase not only one's tendency to participate in politics but one's tendency to be an active participant in various spheres of life. There are other studies, however, which suggest that the schools do convey attitudes more directly linked to political participation, attitudes such as a sense of civic obligation or a sense of high political efficacy.[14]

Education was of crucial importance for the Ethiopian student. Unlike many students in the developed countries, Ethiopian students were not in school because they had to be. Not only was education not mandatory, it was costly for the student in a number of basic ways. It removed him/her from home and it required the expenditure of very scarce funds for room and board, books and supplies, uniforms, etc.; it required the investment of a substantial quantity of energy, and it delayed the assuming of an adult role, with its financial rewards.

These costs are acceptable, of course, in a context in which the perceived gains are very high. As the perception was strong that there was a direct and close link between one's educational attainments and one's future economic well-being and social status, the costs undoubtedly seemed a reasonable investment.[15]

At the same time, they were a risky investment. Few of those who began school completed it. Attrition tended to be high at every transition point in the school system.

If both costs and possible gains were high, and if the probabilities of success were low, the student had to try to maximize his possibilities of success. One strategy was to "learn" what he was taught. Another strategy was to develop personal relationships with those teachers and administrative personnel whose friendship might compensate for any inadequacies in academic achievement.

Finally, the students, under conditions of severe vulnerability, redefined their situation as a political one, in which power might fruitfully be brought to bear to enhance their chances for educational success, as well as to improve their living conditions as students. They become political actors within the schools themselves. From the middle 1950s on, this tendency became more and more characteristic of students in the secondary schools of Ethiopia, as well as those in the university, whom I will analyze later.

During the decade 1955–1965, there were major student "actions" in more than twenty out of fifty-eight secondary schools in the Ethiopian Empire.[16] In the subsequent decade, virtually all schools had such actions, with repeated actions in each school becoming more and more common.[17]

Some "actions" were on a relatively small scale, for example, a boycott of a particular teacher. More typical was a boycott by students of all classes, sometimes accompanied by attacks on teachers and headmasters. These were not trivial incidents. The Ministry of Education frequently had to settle the strikes. There were occasional clashes with the police. Finally the army had to be called in to settle one strike in 1965.

The ostensible provocations for these strikes varied widely. Some were strictly academic: overly harsh grading, too high a rate of student failure, or a sadistic disciplinarian. In the days when secondary students were boarders, receiving room, board, and tuition from the government, there were living-standard complaints: poor food or inadequate stipends. When these "welfare schools" were closed down in 1961–1962, there were strong student protests.

Neither the frequency of strikes nor the range of catalytic events which seemed to provoke them is, in itself, significant. Both acquired significance inasmuch as they indicated that students were prepared to turn to political action to transform situations which distressed them. That readiness reflected a number of psychic orientations produced by the educational experience and productive of political participation.

The students were undoubtedly motivated to act by their sense of high stakes, stakes which they all shared. This sense of shared risk (and of shared economic deprivation, since the life of a student is an economically impoverished one) helped to produce a sense of group cohesion, of group consciousness. This development was furthered, of course, by the intense communications which occurred among students.

Before group consciousness is likely to turn into political action, students must also believe that the conditions to which they object can be altered, that political authorities have the power to do so, that student actions can force such authorities to make the desired changes, and that there are relatively low (or relatively unlikely) costs associated with action.

The students learned that strikes can be an effective tactic. Teachers were relieved of responsibilities; headmasters were transferred. However, some students were expelled, others arrested. They also learned, then, that political action can be costly.

If critical attitudes toward authority, whether that of the schools or that of the government, increase with education, and if willingness to act to promote one's interests also increases with education, both tendencies should be most striking among university students. In coming pages I will discuss the political attitudes and activities of the university students, those most thoroughly exposed to the educational system whose impact I have been examining.

## THE POLITICAL WORLD OF THE UNIVERSITY STUDENTS

An extremely small percentage of students completed twelve years of elementary and secondary school, passed the twelfth-grade-leaving examination, and entered the university.[18] The political environment they entered was a unique one. Most attended the branches of Haile Selassie 1 University, where they were exposed in detail to the politics of the country. One campus was two blocks from Parliament, while the main campus was less than a mile from there. Both campuses were within easy marching distance of the emperor's palace. Many students in this environment became highly politicized, strongly concerned with their nation, their political system, and their political leaders, and highly committed to political action.

The students articulated some of their political concerns. Student newspapers—*News and Views, Struggle,* and *Message*—were forceful in defense of student interests, from discussions of the inadequacies of the cafeteria and student housing to an attack upon the editor of the major English-language newspaper, the *Ethiopian Herald* for his blanket condemnation of student demonstrators.

These newspapers also commented on political matters. Usually they restricted themselves to analysis and criticism of international politics: Rhodesia, South Africa, Vietnam, Czechoslovakia, military coups in other African countries, etc. They did, however, implicitly criticize the government through attacks on foreign involvement in Ethiopia, for example, the presence and activities of the Peace Corps. The students dared not say it was their government which invited, and could remove, the Peace Corps. At times, however, they openly criticized Parliament, though not the emperor. In addition, students wrote abstract articles on revolution and evolution, never discussing, of course, Ethiopia.[19]

These newspapers were put out by and were largely appendages to the student organizations of the university system. In addition to the National, Addis Ababa, and Main Campus student unions, there were organizations for each constituent college of the university. The existence and activities of such organizations made it clear that, at least for some students, such reported psychological traits as overwhelming distrust of others,[20] which crippled their ability to operate in groups, had been overcome. On the other hand, these groups met infrequently and did little. This inactivity was certainly in part due to mutual suspicion and distrust preventing group cooperation. Another contributing factor was the very real danger students faced if they got involved in political activities. Finally, the groups were handicapped by overly rigid rules and a formalistic adherence to these rules. In the spring of 1966, for instance, the Main Campus Student Union tried to pass a resolution against U.S. involvement in Vietnam, only to fail in a series of meetings because they could never get their quorum, one-half of the entire student body of the main campus.

Despite their usual ineffectiveness, these organizations did lead major student political actions. There were university demonstrations in Addis Ababa every spring except 1967 during the five-year period of 1965–1969. In 1965, the students marched in support of a land reform bill before Parliament, and in 1966 they protested to close a "concentration camp" for indigents the government had established outside Addis Ababa. In 1968, they attacked American influence at the university, and in 1969 demonstrated against, among other things, the inadequacies of the educational system. Similar student activities continued every year until the revolution.

As the list of student concerns demonstrates, these were not revolutionary students. They attacked government policies, but not the government. They marched to Parliament, knowing Parliament was ineffectual. They appealed to, rather than attacked, the emperor. Even the most radical students were, in the context of world student movements, a moderate group.

University students realized, to a greater extent, tendencies whose development I have traced among less educated students. They were a highly self-conscious group:

> We University students are being looked at by our countrymen with awe and respect. We are considered to be perhaps the only sector of the population which can come up with new, practical devices to lead to prosperity our society which is beset with numerous obstacles and challenges. What we University students have to ask ourselves sometime is whether we are really living up to what is expected of us and the respect accorded us.[21]

They were a critical group:

> We insisted on marching to Parliament to arouse the conscience of the peoples' representatives. That the Senate President implies in his reply to our petition that there are neither rich nor poor among Ethiopians, and that they, as law makers, have nothing to do with the matter, has forced us to have second thoughts about our representatives in the Parliament. We definitely did not expect such a singularly simplistic reply, because we believe that the Parliament should have some form of control over administrative agencies of the government.[22]

They felt an obligation to act in the political sphere: "Although our primary duty as university students is to attend classes, none of us can remain indifferent to, and oblivious of, any social injustice done to our fellow Ethiopians."[23]

## THE POLITICAL WEIGHT OF THE PETITE BOURGEOISIE

As a percentage of the total population, the petite bourgeoisie was relatively small. However, such people were not randomly distributed either geographically or occupationally. Although primary schools were somewhat widely distributed throughout the empire, secondary schools were found only in the larger cities [see Table 5.1] and postsecondary education was concentrated, for the most part, in Addis Ababa. Students had to leave the villages to attend school, and it is clear that they did not, upon leaving school, return to the villages. Thus, although the educated, broadly conceived, constituted a small part of the total population, they constituted a much more significant part of the urban population. This concentration further increased their probable political impact.

While their education had politicized them and their geographic concentration heightened both the likelihood that there would be a "group" response to any significant stimulus and that this response would be politically weighty, it was their common vulnerability which gave them a shared interest and made them intensely sensitive to the economic developments of 1974.

Members of the petite bourgeoisie, civilian and military, were vulnerable in a number of senses. The vast majority were employed by government, the only significant employer of this group. Their continued employment and their standard of living were dependent upon the whims of a not very bureaucratized system, of a system where the protection of highly placed patrons offered the only security against being reduced to poverty. While such protection might preserve their individual positions, it offered no security against threats to the well-being of the class. As I shall demonstrate, just such a threat arose during 1974 and led to the class-based rejection of the imperial system that then occurred.

## THE IMPERIAL REGIME UNDER ATTACK

In late 1973 and early 1974, two crucial phenomena coincided. A severe drought in several provinces devastated the peasants, reduced urban food supplies, and raised urban food prices.[24] The substantial increase in world oil prices following the Arab-Israeli War of 1973 fueled price increases, as well.[25] The resulting

**Table 5.1**  Geographical Concentration of Ethiopian Secondary Students, 1963–1964

| | | |
|---|---|---|
| Addis Ababa | 4,933 | 41.4% |
| Shoa Province[a] | 1,543 | 12.9 |
| Eritrea[b] | 1,666 | 14.0 |
| Remainder of the Empire[c] | 3,785 | 31.7 |
| Total | 11,927 | |

[a]Province whose capital is Addis Ababa.

[b]Province whose capital is the second-largest city in the country, Asmara.

[c]Remaining twelve provinces.

*Source:*  Derived from the *Ethiopia Statistical Abstract, 1965,* Central Statistical Office, Imperial Ethiopian Government, 1966.

inflation hit hard a relatively small percentage of the Ethiopian population outside of drought areas. Peasants elsewhere were relatively unaffected, and there was little rural unrest during the revolutionary year.

For those in the urban areas, and those on salary elsewhere, the situation was very different. Their standard of living was rapidly eroded. Both the proletariat and the petite bourgeoisie were extremely vulnerable to inflation and only government action could somehow ease their plight.[26]

Beginning in January 1974, various groups began to protest their living conditions. Initially, a small army unit stationed in the south objected to its lack of food and drinking water. By the end of February, not only had other military units begun to demand improvements in their living conditions, but civilian activism began to surpass that of the military. Students, teachers and taxi drivers all mobilized to protest not only their immediate economic deprivations, but other aspects of their situations, including policies that might affect their long-term security.[27] By the beginning of March, the Confederation of Ethiopian Labor Unions, the national union of the small number of organized workers,[28] had joined the spreading protest movement, issuing an extensive list of demands and holding a reasonably successful general strike when these were not initially met. Joining the movement over the next several months were a wide range of diverse groups including such unusual protesters as the priests of the Ethiopian Coptic Church, the Muslims of Addis Ababa, and the prostitutes of the capital as well.

Most of these groups, at least in the beginning, limited their demands to economic and/or corporate issues. Yet given the Ethiopian context, where little private enterprise existed, the government automatically became the focus of their attention. Only it could possibly satisfy their demands.

This narrow perspective was not shared by all. The highly educated, especially the students, doubted the government's willingness or ability to undertake the basic reforms this segment of the petite bourgeoisie felt was necessary. Moreover, unlike the proletariat or other segments of the petite bourgeoisie, the highly educated had, over a number of years, come to question the very legitimacy of the political system. Thus this "intelligentsia" articulated, earlier than others, demands for sweeping political, social, and economic gains far transcending their immediate economic and/or corporate interests.[29]

The response of the imperial government was, at first, to try to satisfy the narrow economic and corporate demands with which it was confronted. Thus, for example, military salaries were raised, as were those of other bureaucratic employees. A proposed educational reform which angered teachers and students was withdrawn. Soon, however, the government reacted to the pressures upon it in a different way. On February 27, the prime minister and his cabinet resigned, an act unprecedented in Ethiopian politics, where these officials were responsible neither to the public nor to Parliament, but to the emperor alone. Never had such officials previously resigned; they had been removed at the desire of the emperor. This changing of top officials was to occur twice more before the removal of the emperor and his replacement by a military council, the Dergue, in September.

Beyond a change of personnel, moreover, other, more basic changes were promised. In late March, the emperor established a constitutional commission which he said would create a truly parliamentary system. Investigations into possible crimes by government officials were initiated. Such changes, moving far beyond the limited economic issues, seemed the act of a government whose resources for coping with the demands upon it were rapidly running out.

The political activism just described took place essentially between January and April of 1974. The most active element of this "popular movement"[30] was the educated segment of the petite bourgeoisie. They were also virtually the only group calling, at that time, for truly sweeping political, social, and economic change. Nevertheless, as the year continued, other urban groups became both more militant and more revolutionary in their thoughts and actions.[31] These activities severely strained the resources and legitimacy of the imperial regime of Haile Selassie.

The Ethiopian imperial system had lasted, in one form or another, for hundreds of years. During the fifty-year reign of Haile Selassie,[32] wealth and power remained in the hands of an exceedingly narrow imperial elite and its aristocratic entourage. At the same time, however, that elite's predominance had come to rest increasingly on the support of a bureaucratic base, developed by Haile Selassie as a resource against both his foreign and domestic opponents.

That bureaucracy was staffed by a new class, the petite bourgeoisie. Educated in the new schools of the empire, they had been provided the knowledge necessary to the management of modern bureaucracies. At the same time, they had been "taught" both anti-imperial sentiments and the skills of political activism. As the base of the new imperial structure, their continued support was necessary to its stability. For a long time, that support was provided, however reluctantly, in return for financial well-being. When the government, its resources severely strained by both the drought and the oil price increase, no longer could buy off the petite bourgeoisie, they withdrew that support and expressed their opposition more intensively than any group had previously done, manifesting their political attitudes and using their skills.

But that is all that the petite bourgeoisie could achieve. On its own it could neither deliver the death blow to the old regime nor, as a group, replace it. The military bourgeoisie, however, could achieve both.

## THE REPLACEMENT OF THE IMPERIAL REGIME

Military personnel were part of that small minority of Ethiopians who had received formal education.[33] Junior officers tended to have at least some college, while NCOs and enlisted men, for the most part, had at least a few years of elementary school. They presumably shared with their civilian counterparts not only the experience of formal education, but the attitudinal and skill consequences alluded to above. Finally, as salaried employees of the government, they, too, were economically vulnerable.

It was that vulnerability which led to initial military involvement in the protests of early 1974.[34] The government, for obvious reasons, proved even more responsive to military demands than to civilian ones, for example, raising military salaries three times during the year and removing officers who had indulged in particularly egregious behavior. To some extent, these concessions demobilized, or appeared to demobilize, the military as a significant part of the protest movement. Yet, by June, an organization emerging from the military had become a major force in the Ethiopian government, and by September it had become the government. How and why did this happen?

Although there had been an unsuccessful coup attempt in 1960, there were no subsequent attempts, nor did the military seem to promote its corporate interests.[35] In the spring of 1974, however, the imperial government, in attempting to defuse both urban unrest and that of the military, not only made economic and political concessions to both civilians and soldiers, but decided on a policy of selective repression of its opponents. The army, along with police units, had to be the instruments of that repression. Rather than relying on standing lines of command, lines which had been seriously compromised by the firing of some officers and the presumed attachments of others to descredited political leaders, the new prime minister, Endelkatchew Makonnen, established a new military committee. From late March into May, special military units under its control put down both civilian strikes and isolated actions of more radical military units.[36] Inasmuch as the members of this committee came from various units and various ranks, a new principle of military organization, a far more political one, a conciliar one, was introduced. This new committee, in return for utilizing its influence with the army to put down popular resistance, extracted from the government political concessions, most basic of which was the arrest of the former prime minister and other high-ranking officials. I would argue that with this initial involvement in politics of a military committee, two important new elements entered Ethiopian politics: conciliar rule within the military and political involvement by the military.

During the next several months, these principles were further developed. Although the original military committee faded from the scene, a new one replaced it.[37] In late June, a small group of officers and NCOs from the Fourth Division in Addis Ababa issued an invitation to all of the military and police units in the country to send as many as three representatives each to Addis Ababa to form a committee. The resulting body of 120 representatives proceeded to declare itself the Armed Forces Coordinating Committee, or *Dergue*. From that time on, until it deposed the emperor on September 12 and declared itself the Provisional Military Government, the Dergue became increasingly the effective decision maker in the Ethiopian government. Step by step, during the next several months, it took over the government. It dictated the identity of cabinet members, the creation of a constitutional revision committee, the arrest of former high officials, the release of the press from censorship, and numerous other measures. Finally, it deposed the emperor and itself assumed full governmental power.

Thus, unlike those civilians with whom it shared both economic vulnerability and the skills to engage in political activity, the petite bourgeoisie of the military was able both to remove the imperial government and to replace it. It was able to accomplish these further steps because it possessed not only the motivation to carry them out, but the resources necessary to do so.

Three types of resources seemed central to the seizure of power. At least initially the Dergue had substantial legitimacy among all the units of the army and police, a legitimacy based on its representative character, alluded to above.[38] Thus these units did not bring their resources into action against the Dergue. This acceptance of the Dergue was crucial to its initial, and continuing, success.

With that acceptance, the Dergue could bring to bear against the government, or any other group in society, overwhelming coercive power. Although in Ethiopia, as in the United States, a substantial part of the male population owned firearms, military and police units monopolized modern armaments and effective concentrations of firepower.

Finally, the Dergue possessed organizational skills lacking to the civilian petite bourgeoisie.[39] Although the organizations created by the military during 1974 differed substantially in form from the standard military hierarchy, they nevertheless utilized the organizational skills created within that hierarchy. In a society in which such skills were in short supply, military personnel were the most effective organizers around.

I do not wish to exaggerate the resources of the military. There was, for instance, opposition within military ranks, both in 1974 and later, to the Dergue's coming to power and to its policies. Such opposition, however, was limited, scattered, and easily repressed.[40] Among supporters of the Ancien Regime, civilian opponents of the military regime, and external enemies, there arose armed opposition to the Dergue, put down only with great difficulty and at great cost.[41] Finally, the organizational coherence of the Dergue was clearly limited. The gradual character of its assumption of power, its subsequent severe internal conflicts,[42] and its difficulty in achieving a stable institutional structure[43] all reveal the difficulties the military had in utilizing its organizational skills. Nevertheless, in the revolutionary politics of 1974, where the desertion of the petite bourgeoisie had undermined the imperial regime, the military's resources were more extensive than anyone else's and adequate to the tasks of overthrowing and replacing that government.

In this essay I have tried to outline why, in the Ethiopian revolution of 1974, the petite bourgeoisie, civilian and military, was the decisive political actor. Although small in number, members of this class were concentrated in the cities, the present focus of Ethiopian politics. Their shared educational experiences had both promoted their political disaffection from the regime of Haile Selassie and provided them with political skills. As, for the most part, government employees they shared a potential economic vulnerability, a potential realized in 1974.

The resulting disaffection of the civilian segment of this class, concentrated in and dominating the central government bureaucracy, severely weakened the regime. The military component of the class had to join the struggle to make it fully effective, however. Military resources—legitimacy among military units, high coercive capacity, and organizational skills—were adequate to bring down and replace a weakened government, introducing, albeit in uniform, the political era of the petite bourgeoisie.

# PART III

# The Consolidation of Power: Schisms, Fractions, Coalitions, and Contradictions in Postindependence Dominant Classes

Part III continues the analysis of the consolidation of power on a national level in Cameroon and in a small ethnic enclave in northern Zambia.

Ndiva Kofele-Kale, in his "Class, Status, and Power in Postreunification Cameroon," clarifies political developments in one of the most difficult-to-understand countries of Africa. Cameroon endured many changes in forms of government from 1961 to the present, passing from a federal system to a unitary form of government, from a vast variety of political parties to a one-party dictatorship. Ethnic groups have combated each other across regional lines, Muslim-Christian differences have further exacerbated tensions, and these conflicts have taken place within a country united only after long divisions between separate English and French colonial rule.

Kofele-Kale makes sense out of all of these divisions, confronting and categorizing all the major interpretations of Cameroonian politics. He bases his analysis on a massive collection of empirical data about the ethnic, religious, and linguistic background of the present Cameroonian leadership. This yields a remarkable picture of who Cameroon's leaders are and of what they do. Reading his analysis of the anglophone bourgeoisie carefully, one finds an almost Stendhal-like portrait of social and political striving, in which the English-speaking Cameroonians "cross over" to the dominant Francophone camp. These members of the Cameroon organizational bourgeoisie changed their names, they strived for the right accent in their exclusive use of the French language, they married properly, and they encouraged the "francophonication" of their children in a desperate bid for power.

However, Kofele-Kale uses not the tools of the novelist but those of the social scientist. His tables analyze the regional structures of Cameroon, the distribution of deputies in the National Assembly as well as of seats in the Central Committee of the political party and the National Political Bureau; he studies the distribution of ministers, vice ministers, prefects, and subprefects and he analyzes their religious, ethnic, and language background. With these tools, he challenges the three prevailing images of Cameroonian society. The first image shows a society divided along ethnic-regional lines, especially the well-known division between the north and the south. The second image is of religious confrontation, the Muslim north clashing with the Christian south. The third image is of the unique effort to unify the once separate countries of English and French Cameroons into a single African nation.

Kofele-Kale admits the significance of these divisions but finds them of particular vehemence when manipulated by "unscrupulous political leaders" in order to "promote their selfish class interests." Indeed, the fundamental contradiction in postreunification Cameroon, he maintains, is "class rooted." He argues that a "small dominant class," the national organizational bourgeoisie, dominates Cameroonian society and disproportionately enjoys whatever benefits are available. This dominant class cuts across ethnic, religious, and regional differences. It is an organizational bourgeoisie which dominates, manipulates, and exploits the mass of Cameroonian workers and peasants. The study focuses on the Anglophone bourgeoisie as a branch of the national dominant class, but one with its own ideology and consciousness. Part of the fascination of this study is how Kofele-Kale examines the three major constitutional changes since 1961—federation, formation of a national party, and inauguration of the unitary form of government—in terms of the efforts on the part of this bourgeoisie to protect its class interests. He argues, for example, that the Anglophone bourgeoisie had long opposed a unitary state, allegedly on principle. However, once the spoils of prestige, power, and wealth began to shrink, the bourgeoisie became increasingly disenchanted with the federal arrangement. Similarly, once the material interests of the Anglophone political leaders coincided with the proponents of a single party, they dropped their once inviolate commitment to a democratic organized opposition.

Through painstaking analyses of the personal backgrounds of a wide range of prominent Cameroon figures (which he bases upon a massive accumulation of data as well as extensive personal knowledge), Kofele-Kale disproves a number of current commonly accepted theories about the nature of Cameroonian political rule. He shows, for example, how it was not true that a "small inner circle of northern Muslim Fulani" party leaders ran the country. He clearly demonstrates that southerners as much as northerners were members of the dominant class and part of the governing structure, that religious commitment did not produce the type of collective action observable, for example, in the Islamic brotherhoods of Senegal.

Rather than a crude analytic division between two regions, north and south, Kofele-Kale's more subtle analysis breaks the country down into six distinct regions or areas. He challenges the usual picture of a contrasting developed Francophone Cameroon and an *underdeveloped* Anglophone Cameroon. In this new analysis, the Anglophone region, in comparison to the north, comes out considerably better off than previously thought.

Kofele-Kale's work establishes the strong Anglophone component of all branches of the government and the party. This "tiny minority of Anglophones" has gained these positions of power and prestige and access to great wealth, he argues, through its effective exploitation of mass discontent. It has advanced its own narrow corporate interests at the expense of its deprived followers. Kofele-Kale has succeeded in identifying an organizational bourgeoisie in Cameroon, in breaking it down into its various components, including bureaucratic political and business elements, and in then demonstrating its role in the construction of the national Cameroonian state.

George C. Bond, in his "Religion, Ideology, and Property in Northern Zambia," also shows how an emerging new class ensconced itself in power, even though, in the instance which he describes, the scale of the entrepreneurial efforts was much smaller. The activity which he describes centers on the ability of this new class to adapt prevailing traditional religious beliefs to legitimate its very modern and quite exploitative economic activity. Bond develops his analysis almost like a storyteller, with an eye for the significant detail and unexpected turn in his analysis. His case studies catch one off guard and add convincingly to the impact of the truth that he presents.

He begins his study by recounting how a group of leading Yombe citizens in northern Zambia described "their kind of people" as members of a cooperating society where everybody helped one another and respected each other's claims as kin, neighbors, or friends. The Yombe contrasted their society with that of Westerners, whom they saw as isolated competitive individuals, indifferent to the needs of their relatives and neighbors. Bond first surprises us by showing how these idyllic images are in fact self-serving—not merely self-congratulatory, but images contradicted by the growing inequalities produced by the spread of capitalist entrepreneurial activities, commercial farmers, wealthy traders, and chary politicians who knew how to use their offices to turn a profit.

Bond's ultimate concern is with "the manner in which culture and ideology, and consciousness and religious beliefs, are generated and affected by fundamental changes in the process of production and appropriation." He contributes an understanding of how the persistence of existing religious forms can obscure changes in the productive base of a society which, in turn, have changed the personal and social relationships of production. Bond paints a picture of an ideology so deeply embedded that people accept as "natural" and essential that which is in fact created and promulgated to serve particular class interests. Yombe beliefs about ancestors and witchcraft, he argues, enhance entrepreneurial activity and the rise of individualism.

Yombe men have migrated to the mines of the copper belt and, in one of the most urbanized and industralized regions of Africa, have become part of an African proletariat that is part of an individualized free wage-labor force. In the countryside, Bond tells us, the same people who are miners are also peasants. The prevailing ideology in the countryside had been that of kinship. The chief beneficiaries of this system were the senior men who could demand help from other members of their descent group for the cultivation of their farms. With the spread of capitalism, the ideology of kinship enables senior men to appropriate the labor of their juniors. An ideology which once served the community—for example, as the basis for sharing during times of food shortages—has become, with the increasing commercialization of the country-side, an ideology which serves as the basis for capital accumulation.

Where individual demands for goods and service conflict with those of the community, Bond demonstrates, the ideological dimensions sometimes take the form of a conflict between witchcraft and ancestor worship. Ancestor worship emphasizes collective relationships, whereas witchcraft consists of individual acts against collective interests.

Some individuals can be coerced into sharing goods—such as in Bond's example of a dispute over a bicycle—by appealing to the sanctions of ancestors in order to reinforce lineage solidarity. The "community" can also threaten individuals intent on personal self-advancement with accusations of witchcraft. Although, on the basis of Bond's first examples, one might infer that the Yombe's ideology of ancestor worship and witchcraft would hinder the development of capitalist entrepreneurial activities, the "community" did not charge the most commercially successful men in the village either with practicing witchcraft or with displeasing the ancestors. In analyzing how the richest man in the village succeeded in accumulating large fields and developing enormously profitable business activities, Bond shows us how Yombe's religious beliefs "served as screens behind which certain men appropriate labor and transform their and other relationships to property and persons."

Finally, Bond tells us that the beliefs of the Yombe were themselves part of the process of production, that the ideology of communitarianism does not necessarily hinder capitalist development but, indeed, can be accepted by the most humble classes, even though it facilitates their control from above. Ideology functions in complicated ways. His sophisticated analysis, however, leaves no doubt as to whose interests are served.

# CHAPTER 6

# Class, Status, and Power in Postreunification Cameroon: The Rise of an Anglophone Bourgeoisie, 1961–1980

**Ndiva Kofele-Kale**

Few African states have succeeded to the degree that Cameroon has in maintaining the stability and continuity of its polity for a protracted period after constitutional independence was granted. And fewer still have been successful in experimenting with various forms of political arrangements without upsetting the delicate patchwork of national unity. Yet Cameroon has in the last twenty-three years gone from a federal system (1961–1972) to a unitary form of government (post-1972– ), and from multiparty politics (1960–1966) to a one-party dictatorship (1966– ). And until the abortive coup d'état of April 6–8, 1984, these major changes to the basic structures of the system were effected without, as Professor Le Vine reminds us, the polity getting scarred "by the all too common traumas afflicting its neighbors" (Le Vine, 1980: 1).

Indeed, the words "peace" and "stability" have become the central pillars of a state ideology in Cameroon. This was attested to in an interview with the government-owned *Cameroon Tribune* (February 23, 1980: 32), by S. T. Muna, speaker of the National Assembly, who, when asked to comment on the country's greatest achievement since reunification, responded this way: "I would say right off—the formation of the CNU [Cameroon National Union] party in September 1966. . . . Because *the CNU has enabled us to build our country in unity, peace and political stability*" (my emphasis). This same theme was articulated by the former president of the CNU, Mr. Ahmadou Ahidjo,[1] in a General Policy Speech to the CNU Third Ordinary Congress in Bafoussam in 1980: "Judging from our achievement whose stock we will take, our progress as a whole speaks for itself. It is also indicative of encouraging perspectives and reflects the image we want to present to Africa and the World; *an image of a young nation assured of security and stability*. . . ." (my emphasis).

To a certain extent the Ahidjo regime was successful in promoting its version of Cameroonian reality both at home and abroad (see *West Africa*, April 14,

1980: 665–666; *West Africa,* May 5, 1980: 786–787).[2] Yet the rosy picture of uninterrupted postcolonial history characterized by political stability and peaceful change which it presented not only concealed significant discontinuities and contradictions within the Cameroonian polity but also glossed over tensions of a potentially disruptive nature. More important, the obsession with "peace" and "stability" left unanswered the all-important questions: stability for whom, at what price, and for whose benefit (cf. Markovitz, 1977)? A major objective of this inquiry is to identify the major contradictions in postreunification Cameroon and to show how these contradictions have influenced the distribution of wealth, status, and power in the society. While the focus is on Cameroon under Ahidjo's leadership, my comments apply with equal force to the post-Ahidjo era. Even though some welcome changes have taken place since Biya succeeded Ahidjo in 1982, he has yet to dismantle the structures and institutions bequeathed him by his predecessor. For the purposes of this discussion, suffice it to say that the socioeconomic cleavages that plagued Ahidjo's Cameroon continue to dog the successor regime.

## The Problem

Current orthodoxy attempts to explain disparities in wealth, status, and power as rooted in primordial factors. Out of this thesis has emerged three images of Cameroonian society. One image shows a society cleaved along *ethnic/regional lines* whose most prominent manifestation is the dichotomy between the north of Cameroon and the south (Azarya, 1976; Beti, 1972; Nelson et al., 1974; Prouzet, 1974). A second image is that of a society divided along *religious lines* with a predominantly Muslim north opposed by a heavily dominated Christian south (Azarya, 1976; Nelson et al., 1974; Prouzet, 1974). In both of these images, the Muslim north, although fearful of the Christian south, is able to dominate the latter through the advantage it enjoys in numbers and its monopoly of the levers of power. The third image of Cameroonian reality is set against the backdrop of the *different colonial experiences* sectors of Cameroon underwent; the result, a Francophone-Anglophone contradiction so explosive that it threatens to destroy twenty years of national unity (Benjamin, 1972; Buo, 1976; Kofele-Kale, 1983; Nelson et al., 1974).[3] In fact, for some writers, the postreunification marriage between ex–British Cameroons and the former Cameroon Republic was a union of unequals with the seeds of its own eventual destruction embedded into it from the moment of its birth (Benjamin, 1972; Stark, 1980). At issue is the widespread perception by Anglophones that the more dominant French-speaking sector wants to erase all remaining vestiges of the English-speaking "personality." Anglophones resent the hubris implied in the "Frenchification" of Cameroon and are rankled by Francophone domination in every sphere of Cameroonian life.

While conceding the potency of these cleavages, particularly when exploited by unscrupulous political leaders to promote their selfish class interests, I intend to argue that their disruptive nature has been somewhat overstated (Kofele-Kale, 1980a, 1981). And, as a counter to this current orthodoxy, I shall instead argue that the fundamental contradiction in postreunification Cameroon is class rooted. By focusing attention on economic disparities within the society, one hopes to demonstrate that class divisions and concomitant class interests are a compelling reality and, furthermore that power, prestige, and wealth are enjoyed by a small dominant class—the national bourgeoisie, whose composition cuts across the aforementioned cleavages traditionally cited as forces which undermine the basis for unity and political stability. The point I seek to emphasize here is that the mass of Cameroonian workers and peasants are subordinate to, and exploited by, this national bourgeoisie.

Second, it will be my contention in this analysis that an Anglophone bourgeoisie, understood as a tributary of the national mainstream bourgeoisie, with its own ideology and consciousness, began to crystallize in the period leading to and shortly after reunification in 1961. This group constitutes the dominant class in Anglophone Cameroon and as a class it has been the immediate beneficiary of the fruits of reunification. A critical examination of the three major constitutional changes Cameroon has experienced since 1961—federation, formation of a national party, and inauguration of the unitary form of government—will show that for each of these changes the Anglophone bourgeoisie had definite class interests it wanted to protect, and it therefore shifted ground either in support of or in opposition to these changes only when it was felt that: (1) the new arrangement would provide the best protection for gains already made and/or (2) it would be suicidal to hold on to the old arrangement from the point of view of its collectively perceived political and economic interests.

This thesis will be presented in three steps. First, with respect to the eleven-year federation, it will be shown that of preeminent interest to the Anglophone bourgeoisie, which negotiated its terms on behalf of the Anglophone masses, was *control* over a West Cameroon state and the spoils—in terms of prestige, power, and wealth—that came with regional autonomy. Federation was good and desirable only when the Anglophone bourgeoisie was allowed to preside over an autonomous Anglophone state. As soon as this autonomy began to be whittled down and the spoils started shrinking, the Anglophone bourgeoisie became increasingly disenchanted with the federal arrangement. When the end came, it was met with a collective sigh of relief because at that point the federal system was no longer able to improve on the accrued psychic and material gains made by the Anglophone bourgeoisie.

Second, the speed with which the principal Anglophone political leaders—men who had a long history of opposition to the very concept of a single party—climbed onto the one-party bandwagon would suggest that their intentions were not entirely motivated by pristine ideological considerations. Individual greed, ambition, and personal aggrandizement as well as the corporate interests of their class were equally significant motivating factors. As Professor Le Vine has pointed out, the years 1962–1966, which were a prelude to the formation of the national party, "witnessed a complex political ballet in which the principal parties and politicians simultaneously strove to retain their influence in the West and maneuvered to put themselves in the best possible position for the merger of all parties at the national level . . ." (Le Vine, 1971: 96). The futility of hanging on to the multiparty system was clear to most of these politicians. The system therefore had to be abandoned. Having reached this judgment, the Anglophone bourgeoisie wasted no time in inserting its representatives right into the cockpit of the new political arrangement, that is, the decision-making bodies of the new single national party. Third, these carefully calculated moves to remain at the controls were very much in evidence when the unitary system was introduced. The decision to go ahead with it met no organized opposition from the Anglophone bourgeoisie, who in fact welcomed it as a framework within which gains made in the old federal system and privileges garnered following the formation of the national party could be preserved and protected.

The remainder of this essay will be devoted to marshaling evidence to sustain the preceding observations. But first it is worthwhile recapitulating the basic outlines of my argument. These are that (1) class, not regionalism or ethnicity, remains the most fundamental contradiction in the postreunification Cameroon state and (2) the Francophone-Anglophone contradiction is superficial in the sense that it masks the sense of solidarity and unity of interests existing between the Anglophone and Francophone ruling classes, both of whom constitute a national bourgeoisie.

## CLEAVAGES IN CAMEROONIAN SOCIETY

### The North-South Split

Many students of contemporary Cameroon have fallen into the habit of bifurcating the country into two hostile geographical camps: a north fearful of southern infiltration and domination and a south resentful of northern privileges and political hegemony (Azarya, 1976; Bayart, 1978: 51; Nelson et al., 1974; Prouzet, 1974). According to one group of authors, this feeling of mutual distrust and antagonism between the north and south is deep-seated: "Traditionally the Fulani have been almost universally resented by the southern groups, except perhaps for the Bamoun. The reasons for this animosity include a history of conflicts as well as religious and cultural differences. In recent years a major factor has been the belief among the southerners that Fulani leaders, by their control over their society, can produce monolithic support for political objectives" (Nelson et al., 1974: 159; see also Azarya, 1976: 40–44, 64–65). Following Nelson and Azarya, it is possible to identify three possible factors which have helped in reinforcing the prevalent view of a north-south cleavage in Cameroon. These are the view of the north as (1) an ethnic/cultural and religious monolith, (2) the dominant political group, and (3) the group with privileged access to and control over a disproportionate share of the economic and political spoils.

*Ethnic Homogeneity Factor.*   Cameroon is noted for its bewildering cultural and ethnic heterogeneity. However, the north presents a contrasting view to this general pattern of ethnic diversity. Unlike the south, where ethnic multiplicity is at its highest, the north appears, on the surface at least, to be an unusually homogeneous society, united under one dominant ethnic congeries, the Fulbe. The truth of the matter is that the majority of northern peoples are *not* Fulbe but the so-called pagan groups, like the Kirdi, who make up roughly 75 percent of the total population of North Cameroon. This notwithstanding, the fact that these groups have been under Fulbe subjugation for over a century has led some writers to suggest that these dominated groups usually go along with their Fulbe overlords in their opposition to and fear of southern groups. (Nelson et al., 1974: 159; Azarya, 1976: 64–65). In this respect the north is treated as one huge, undifferentiated ethnic leviathan held together by collective distrust of the south.

But the north is far from being a homogeneous society. Its population is cleaved into a dominant Islamized Fulbe, who number less than one-third of the total population, and the dominated Kirdi peoples, by far the majority in this region. This is a most significant division despite the tendency among some observers to underplay it. However, Professor Willard Johnson, a keen observer of Cameroon politics, succeeds in driving home this point. In his estimation, "The cleavage in the northern society most threatening to the political stability of the state and most difficult to overcome is that which distinguishes the immigrant Fulbe and the mostly pagan (called 'Kirdi' by the Fulbe) communities which originally occupied the northern plains" (Johnson, 1970: 65). This cleavage aside, we also find that even among the Kirdi peoples great diversity exists—Mundang, Tupuri, Guisiga, Massa, Mbum, Duru, etc.—which belies the popular view of an ethnically homogeneous north.

*Northern Political Hegemony.* The north accounts for approximately 30 percent of the Cameroon population and covers roughly one-third of the land space. It therefore enjoys an advantage in size which could easily be mistaken for political hegemony. But the case for northern political control goes beyond the issue of population size and area. Cameroon achieved independence in 1960 (and reunification in 1961) under the leadership of a northerner, Ahmadou Ahidjo, and a northern-based party, the *Union Camerounaise* (UC). Of equal significance in coming to grips with this issue of northern hegemony is that fact that (1) the man Ahidjo replaced as prime minister on the eve of independence, Andre-Marie Mbida, was a southerner, and (2) the radical nationalist party— the *Union des Populations du Cameroun* (UPC)—which led the struggle for freedom and reunification and which was subsequently destroyed under Mr. Ahidjo's early rule, was predominantly a southern movement (Chaffard, 1967: 397–410). The UPC's top leadership—Um Nyobe, Moumie, Ouandie, Mayi Matip, Osende Afana—was in the main southern, and the party drew its strongest support from the southern region (Joseph, 1977).

Although Mr. Ahidjo's UC was later to broaden its regional base and become the nucleus for the national party, the Cameroon National Union which was to emerge later, the view has continued to persist that the Cameroon government during the Ahidjo years was dominated by a northern/Fulbe-based political party. Azarya (1976: 50) observes:

> When the UC became a national party, the Northern monopoly over top party positions was broken and some southerners were given important positions in the party and government. However, the real influence of southerners on central decision-making did not match their high official position. *The inner clique around Ahidjo, where the real political power was located, remained exclusively composed of old-time friends of Ahidjo and founders of the UC in the North. These people were Muslim and most of them were Fulbe.* (my emphasis)

Writing in a similar vein, Professor Le Vine talks of a small inner circle of northern Muslim Fulani party leaders, like Moussa Yaya, Mohaman Lamine, Sanda Oumarou, and Sadou Daoudou, who ran the country. They were all, in Le Vine's view, "Ahidjo's men, they owed their positions to him and were schooled under his auspices in politics and in the uses of power. Of the group, probably the most important until recently was Moussa Yaya, whose rise in the party suggested to some observers that he was being groomed for one of the top government positions" (Le Vine, 1971: 118).

The problem with this notion of an "inner circle" of northerners which ran the country is the failure to delimit the boundaries of this clique. Was it made up, for instance, of the members of the party's Central Committee or the Political Bureau? Did it include the senior government ministers (*ministres d'état*)? What about the longest-surviving members of Ahidjo's cabinet—were they also included? The lack of consensus as to the criteria for inclusion into the "inner circle" means that determination of its composition will vary with the observer. Frequently mentioned as members of this "inner circle" are cabinet ministers who had served in one position or another without interruption since the early 1960s; those occupants of strategic ministries like the armed forces, territorial administration, education, and foreign affairs; the senior ministers (*ministres d'état*); and the top leaders of the national party. But can an identifiable "*north-ern* clique" emerge from these various levels of decision making? Not quite. In what amounts to a major reversal of his earlier position, Professor Le Vine has recently pointed out that although Ahidjo "may in fact [have controlled] the system through some sort of 'northern mafia' . . . *the composition of his governments and party central committees belied that charge*" (Le Vine, 1980: 3; my emphasis). The evidence to back up Professor Le Vine's position is quite convincing. I have examined the composition of President Ahidjo's cabinet on the eve of the unitary state and the one appointed shortly after May 1972. Of the nineteen-member "preunitary" cabinet, only three were northerners, and in the immediate "postunitary" cabinet of twenty-nine ministers and vice-minis-ters, six, or 20 percent, of the cabinet positions were held by people from the north. Northerners were by far a minority in the preunitary federal cabinet, outnumbered by the south-central region with seven cabinet positions and the west with four. Only the littoral, with two posts, and east, with no represen-tative, held fewer cabinet positions in 1969 than the north. The same pattern of distribution was carried over into the 1973 cabinet: north and west each held six portfolios, east one, littoral one, while Anglophone Cameroon claimed seven and the south-central region eight positions; the last two regions accounting for almost one-half the entire cabinet.

An examination of the regional origin of the thirty-one-member cabinet ap-pointed in 1975 showed that of the nine ministers who had been in the cabinet eight or more years, only one was from the north (Sadou Daoudou) while five came from the south (Biya, Ayissi Mvodo, Tsanga, Kamga, and Onana Awana). Of the five who had been cabinet ministers sixteen years or more, again only one was a northerner. It is true that the key ministry of Armed Forces, which had always been held by a northerner (Sadou Daoudou, 1960–1979, and Mai-kano Abdoulaye, 1979–1983), did not change hands, but the equally important portfolio of Territorial Administration has remained in southern hands since 1960 (first Enoch Kwayeb, then Ayissi Mvodo, and now Fouman Akame). The four *senior* ministers in the 1978 cabinet, all of whom had held office for at least a decade, included one northerner. Turning attention to the key deci-sion-making organs of the Cameroon National Union, the Central Committee and the National Political Bureau, their composition belied the charge of north-ern dominance. Of the forty-two elected members (1973–1980) only ten (24 percent) were from the north. If representation was based in proportion of pop-ulation, then the north would have been entitled to twelve members in the Central Committee. In the National Political Bureau the combined southern representation was 75 percent of the total membership. In addition, the second-most-influential leadership position after that of national president (Ahidjo), that of political secretary was held by a southerner (Ayissi Mvodo and, subsequently, Sabal Lecco), and so too were the four vice presidents (in 1980 Foncha, Biya, Tchoungui, and Kwayeb).

It is obvious from the preceding discussion that the charge against a northern mafia/clique which dominated the political life of Cameroon during the first republic has been slightly overdrawn. Southerners as much as northerners were intimately involved in the running of the system.

*The Privileged Northern Population.* Other factors that have reinforced the north-south cleavage are widespread perceptions held by southerners that northerners are unfairly favored in terms of access to positions of prestige and power. Usually cited are the advantages northerners enjoy in terms of recruitment into the senior cadres of the civil service, the granting of scholarships for secondary and university studies, and access to bank loans on very liberal credit terms (Schissel, 1983). For example, decree No. 66-436 of December 20, 1966, which outlines the criteria for recruitment into the public service, differentiates two lists of candidates who are successful in the examinations for entry into civil service categories B, C, and D. Candidates from list A are those from educationally backward regions—"originaries des régions insuffisamment scolarisées"—while list B is comprised of candidates from the rest of the country. In practice this distinction, as Prouzet points out, tends to favor candidates from the north, who are recruited under less stringent conditions and criteria in contrast to their colleagues from the south (Prouzet 1974: 120). A similar policy obtains with the granting of scholarships for study at the University of Yaounde and recruitment into the Joint Forces Military Academy (EMIAC) and into the National School of Administration and Magistracy (ENAM), training ground for the nation's beureaucratic bourgeoisie and popularly referred to as *l'école du Nord* to indicate northern domination:

> In the first place, a special preparatory cycle for the entrance examination is set up only for candidates "coming from insufficiently educated regions." In addition, although a secondary school degree [baccalaureate] is required in principle for admission to this school, candidates from these regions can enter on the basis of [lower degrees]: the BEPC, the elementary school certificate, or the *capacité en droit*, according to their geographic origins. policies governing the distribution of fellowships are also based on the same considerations. In the educated regions of the country, a student will receive a full scholarship only if the secondary school degree was received before age 18, whereas students from undereducated regions have till age 23 to pass the baccalaureat in order to obtain the same financial aid. (Prouzet, 1974: 120–121; my translation)

The admirable objective behind this policy of affirmative action which was to close the chasm separating north and south in terms of socioeconomic development should be noted. However, this factor does not appear to have struck a sympathetic chord among the equally deprived southern masses who are equally in need of these opportunities as their northern compatriots.

The fact of the matter is that the northern population has always lagged behind the south in the acquisition of education and professional skills. In 1970, for instance, school enrollments averaged 64 percent nationwide, 94 percent for the south-central, 83 percent for the littoral, 80 percent for the west, and only 22 percent for the north (Clignet, 1976: 31). Six years later, the relative position of the north in the area of school enrollment had hardly changed. The 1976 census reports a 9 percent increase in school enrollment for 6–14-year-olds in the north, up from 22 to 30.9 percent. And although the north comprises 29 percent of the population, only 4 percent of all secondary school pupils were from this region (Azarya, 1976: 52). The gross disparities in educational benefits between the north and south aside, the north has also trailed the south in terms of representation among the higher- and middle-ranking administrative personnel where recruitment has always depended on the possession of superior educational or technical and professional skills. These positions were usually monopolized by the better-educated southerners. In 1961 only 3 percent of these positions were occupied by nationals from the north (Binet, 1961: 23; Azarya, 1976: 51). Azarya found not a single judge nor a secondary school principal of northern origin in 1971 (p. 519). Not much has changed since then. Of the nine titular and substitute judges of the Supreme Court in 1978, not one was from the north. And of the entire phalanx of top judicial officers in the country (titular and substitute judges of the Supreme Court, High Court judges, chief magistrates, and the various *procureurs generaux* and their deputies), only two were of northern origin (Ediafric, 1976: xxiii–xxvii). To bridge the gap between the north and south, the former was "systematically advantaged in the allocation of financial resources by the government; *this was openly admitted and justified as giving priority to the development of the least developed parts of the country*" (Azarya, 1976: 51; emphasis added).

## The Christian-Muslim Division

Another variant of the north-south contradiction is expressed in the form of a so-called religious division between a predominantly Christian south and an Islamized north. One writer claims that "A certain amount of unease existed in the early 1970s between the Muslim President and the Roman Catholic Church, in part because of different concepts of the duty and powers of the state over the individual but *primarily because of the coincidental association of Christianity with the Southern peoples. Southern Roman Catholics were particularly strong among the ethnic groups most hostile to northerners*" (Nelson et al., 1974: 164, emphasis added). Much has been made of the fact that it was a Muslim leader and a northern-based party that replaced Mbida (who was a staunch Catholic and an ex-seminarian) in 1959; and that this same leadership was responsible for the brutal suppression of the radical nationalist movement whose preeminent leader, Um Nyobe, was a southerner and a Christian to boot (Prouzet, 1974: 109; Bayart, 1978: 54–55). Additional evidence to support the Christian-Muslim division thesis consists of an ad nauseam recitation of instances where the Christian church has clashed with the state, for example, the deportation in 1962 of the editor of the Catholic newspaper *La Semaine Camerounaise* for publishing a story which the government found particularly offensive (Prouzet, 1974: 107–108; Bayart, 1978: 63; Le Vine, 1971: 129–130), and the "Ndongmo affair" (Le Vine, 1971: 130–132; Beti, 1972), where the Catholic bishop of Nkongsomba was tried and sentenced to life imprisonment (later commuted) for subversive activities.

Historically, Christian missionary penetration was confined to the southern regions of Cameroon while Muslim influences swept most of the north (Horner,

1956). This in part explains why, numerically, more Christians are found in the south and, conversely, more Moslems are in the north. But despite the fact that both Islamic and Christian proselytization has been going on for over a century, the Cameroonian population is still overwhelmingly animist. Most estimates put the number of Christians at around 2 million and Muslims anywhere from 700,000 to 1 million[4] in a total population of over 7 million. When appropriate allowance is made for nominal as opposed to practicing converts, the number of Christians and Moslems is likely to drop appreciably. Given the fact that about 65 percent of the population propitiates with their deity outside the framework of the main religious denominations, it would seem that the Christian-Muslim division is overdrawn, to say the least.

What we find instead is that Cameroon is neither a religiously homogeneous society nor, for that matter, a highly fragmented one. But of the several religions practiced, no one appears to dominate. Furthermore, the membership of the major foreign religions cuts across several ethnic lines. Thus it is safe to conclude that religion in Cameroon is not, in Crawford Young's (1976: 21) words, a "primary basis of politically relevant collective identity." Religion has yet to produce the phenomenon of Islamic brotherhoods, that one finds in Senegal (Behrman, 1970; O'Brien, 1971) and Nigeria (Cohen, 1969; Paden, 1973). Nor has it provoked the kind of intense political rivalry among political groups that one finds, say, in India (Young, 1976) or Lebanon (Hudson, 1968; Binder, 1966) or Uganda (Lockard, 1980; Young, 1976).

An examination of the religious affiliation of key members of the party and government will indicate a reasonable balance between Christians and Muslims. Ahidjo is a Muslim while his prime minister, Biya, who would later succeed him as president in 1982, is a Catholic. Roughly 75 percent of the members of the CNU Political Bureau are Christians and only 25 percent of the Central Committee members are Muslims. All the party vice presidents are Christians. As Prouzet points out (1974: 106, my translation)

> . . . certain politicians never hid their Christian origins. A case in point is André Fouda, mayor of Yaounde, former minister, and member of the UNC Political Bureau, who is a practicing Catholic. Another case is Eteki Mboumoua, national education minister from 1961 to 1968, [former] secretary general of the OAU, considered to have been too favorable toward religious schools; another is Public Health Minister Bernard Fonlon, also criticized for taking lenient positions toward health institutions of the churches.

Not only was the government and party heavily saturated with Christians, but they were the type who made no pretense about their faith. Yet they were able to interact and work closely with their Muslim colleagues without any overt signs of hostility.

It is true that the church establishment, especially the very powerful Catholic hierarchy, and the central government have had a number of clashes over the years, provoked in part by the regime's view of the church establishment as a potential opposition capable of attracting a sizable following. In a country where one party dominates, such opposition can hardly be looked upon too kindly by party leaders, be they Muslims or Christians. Again, tensions between the church and state have erupted over differing interpretations of the central government's role in the promotion and protection of the fundamental human rights of the Cameroonian citizens guaranteed in the Constitution. The Ahidjo regime was notorious for its disregard for these basic rights (Prouzet, 1974: 142–146, 260–262, 270–271, and 278–299; U.S. State Department, 1981: 36–41; Derrick, 1983: 2273–2274; Bayart, 1978: 63). These institutional conflicts have, however, not risen to the level of violent and protracted church-state confrontations such as we have witnessed in Poland and Iran under the Shah.

## The Francophone-Anglophone Contradiction

Cameroon entered its postcolonial phase with the distinction of being the first African state to have included within its borders two territories that had undergone different colonial experiences. But what was to become the country's best-known characteristic turned out, some would argue, to be its most enduring contradiction. I am referring here to the post–World War I partition of the German colony of Kamerun into British and French mandates under the League of Nations, and then, after World War II as part of the U.N. trusteeship system. The legacy of this split is found contemporaneously in the persistence of the French language in one sector of Cameroon and English in another. History aside, the Anglophone-Francophone dichotomy has been reinforced by several other factors. The first is size. A quick glance at a map will reveal that the two sectors are unevenly balanced; the Anglophone sector covers only 9 percent of the total area and supports about 21 percent of the total population (see Table 6.1). By way of contrast, Francophone Cameroon enjoys a four to one population advantage and a ten to one advantage in size over the Anglophone sector. The differences in size offer only partial explanation for the Francophone-Anglophone dichotomy and the popular view of Francophone hegemony.

The origins of this perception go back to the very nature of reunification itself, that is, the negotiations leading to it and the eventual outcome. To begin with, when the two Cameroons reunited in October 1961, one of the contracting parties, the Cameroon Republic, was already an independent sovereign state. On the other hand, the British Trust Territory of Southern Cameroons was, by the terms of the U.N. plebiscite, to have achieved its independence by *joining* the sovereign Cameroon Republic. The following statement by the leader of the Francophone delegation, Mr. Ahidjo, is quite revealing: "The Cameroon Republic and the territory previously under British trusteeship constituted a single historic unit. . . . But on the other hand, they were two distinct political entities: on one side, an *independent sovereign state possessing an interna-*

**TABLE 6.1** Population Breakdown by Region

| Region | Population | Percentage | Area (sq. km.) | Percentage |
|--------|-----------|------------|----------------|------------|
| West Cameroon | 1,495,272 | 21 | 42,210 | 9 |
| North | 2,089,791 | 29 | 164,050 | 35 |
| South-Central | 1,393,608 | 20 | 115,940 | 25 |
| West | 968,856 | 13.5 | 13,890 | 3 |
| Littoral | 841,456 | 12 | 20,220 | 4 |
| East | 342,850 | 5 | 108,900 | 23 |
| Total | 7,131,833 | | 465,210 | |

*Source:* Ministry of Economic Affairs and Planning, *1976 Census.*

*tional legal personality;* on the other, a territory *without a political interna-tional status"* (Ahidjo, 1964: 23; my emphasis). In the negotiations for union the representatives of the Cameroon Republic were to capitalize on this tech-nicality, insisting all along that due recognition be given to their status as senior partners (Stark, 1980). They did succeed in forcing through this point, with the result that the Francophones were able to dictate the terms for federation which proved to be quite advantageous to them (Benjamin, 1972). One of the consequences of the apparent inequality in bargaining power was the fact that the Francophone sector made fewer institutional adjustments in entering the federation. For instance, throughout the federalist phase, 1961–1972, a low degree of differentiation was evident between the federal and east (Franco-phone) state organs. The federal and eastern capital was one and the same—Yaounde—and their respective institutions were essentially one "in origin as well as in function" (Ardener, 1967: 289–290). It was often difficult to tell in many instances where the eastern state jurisdiction left off and where that of the federal government began. The lines were quite blurred, and this only rein-forced Anglophone perception of Francophone domination.

Reunification, for the Anglophone sector, has remained a dominant fact of life requiring greater adjustments (Ardener, 1967: 290; Ndongko, 1975: 98; *West Africa,* 1966: 371). Edwin Ardener, who has monitored the political pulse of Anglophone Cameroon longer than most, has correctly observed that the story of the first few years of reunification was "one of various attempts to link West Cameroon in some effective way to its partner, and of the gradual discovery of new ways of doing this by the East" (Ardener, 1967: 20). This was not a particularly smooth transition and there were quite a few bumps on the way. Under the best of conditions the process of consolidating national boundaries and state power is frequently accompanied by tensions. In Camer-oon, where forty years of different colonial experiences had to be taken into the calculus for change, these routine tensions that are a necessary part of na-tion-building were magnified several-fold. We can begin to trace the origins of the widespread perception of a postreunification Cameroon under Franco-phone hegemony to this period of adjustment and acquaintanceship. Writing in 1967, *West Africa*'s itinerant correspondent for Francophone Africa made the following observations about Anglophone attitudes toward the Federation:

> Though in the long run the advantages could well outweigh the disadvantages, right now West Cameroonians tend to feel they are getting a raw deal. The influence of the French-speaking East is now, for the first time, really being felt: not only are Yaounde's powers considerable, but prices have risen considerably; French and Common Market goods are replacing the familiar British or Nigerian goods; the power of East Cameroon is being felt. Good or bad, *if West Cameroonians were today given the choice, they might well choose independence—from Nigeria and the French-speaking east."* (*West Africa,* July 8, 1967: 880, in Le Vine, 1971: 102; emphasis added)

What could have caused Anglophones, who so enthusiastically and overwhelm-ingly elected to rejoin their Francophone kith and kin, to begin to entertain grave doubts about the federation barely six years after it was consummated?

Anglophone complaints about the federation as well as other postreunifi-cation arrangements can be broken down into three areas. The first is *economic.* Anglophones point to the economic underdevelopment of their region and argue that it has become relatively more backward than when it first joined the federation in 1961. This view is properly captured in the following statement, made in 1976 by an Anglophone Cameroonian. According to him, the region is

". . . worse today than it was before reunification in 1961 or even during the federal period. Economic and political programs have been transferred from the regions to Yaounde, the political capital, and Douala, the economic capital . . . [the] once bustling and prosperous Anglophone cities such as Tiko, Victoria, Buea, and Kumba have virtually become ghost towns, while the Francophone areas such as Douala, Yaounde, and the Northern region, particularly the President's hometown of Garoua, are booming." (Buo, 1976: 18)

Eight years later, a nonpartisan observer would echo this refrain. Writing recently for the London publication *West Africa,* which enjoys a wide readership in Cameroon, Joseph Komla Naweri observed:

Whilst it is conceded that the last 25 years have seen some noteworthy development projects in Cameroon, it is altogether another question as to whether such development as has taken place is balanced in any sense. Everyone knows, for example, that certain areas of North Cameroon have excellent roads but without the motor vehicle traffic that would justify those roads, whereas certain areas of South Cameroon with very dense motor vehicle traffic have had to make do with very bad roads. Ironically, certain areas are actually less developed today, 25 years after independence, than they were at the close of the colonial period. Nowhere is this more glaring than in the anglophone South-West Province; in 1960 for example, certain stretches of roads in and around the main towns of Victoria, Buea, Tiko Kumba and Mamfe were tarred, all of these towns had credible water supply systems, Buea with a sparkling golf course and Victoria with impeccable Botanical Gardens. (1983: 2558)

Indeed, the relative underdevelopment of Anglophone Cameroon is a reality few people have bothered to contest. It is worth noting, however, as the Cameroonian economist Ndongko (1980) has ably demonstrated, that the problem of economic deprivation is not unique to this region. It is one shared by several other regions in the country. Table 6.2, which summarizes the most pertinent economic data for the former six regions of the republic, shows that two regions, north and east, join Anglophone Cameroon in forming a triad of the most economically underdeveloped regions in the country. Having said this, it is again worth pointing out that in comparison to the north, the Anglophone region comes out considerably more advanced economically. This is not to suggest that Anglophone complaints about the relative backwardness of their region should be brushed aside, especially when we take into account the fact that this region is the nation's breadbasket and the source of its considerable oil wealth. I only wish to signal the fact that this problem cannot be explained in isolation, but can be better understood when viewed within the context of inequalities *among* and *within* the six regions in the country;[5] not in Manichean terms as a distinction between a developed Francophone and an underdeveloped Anglophone Cameroon.

The fear of "Gallicizing" everything that has gone into the molding of a separate and distinct Anglophone personna constitutes the second set of complaints leveled by this group against an insensitive Francophone-dominated (so it is perceived) regime. Having agreed to join in a *bilingual* union in which

TABLE 6.2 The Regional Structure of Cameroon, 1970

| Sq. Km. | East | West | North | Littoral | South-Central | Former West Cameroon |
|---|---|---|---|---|---|---|
| A. AREA | 109,000 | 14,000 | 153,589 | 21,000 | 118,000 | 42,400 |
| B. POPULATION (1969) | 288,000 | 800,000 | 1,400,000 | 680,000 | 1,170,000 | 1,250,000 |
| Rural Population (%) | 90% | 80% | 92% | 32% | 70% | 90% |
| Population Growth Rate | 2.0% | 1.5% | 1.3% | 4.5% | 2.0% | 2.3% |
| Population Density | 2.6 km² | 56 km² | 9.7 km² | 30 km² | 23 km² | 28 km² |
| C. EDUCATION—Primary School Attendance | 63% | 80% | 27% | 81.2% | 88.8% | 57% |
| % of Population in School | n.a. | 45% | 20% | n.a. | n.a. | 14% |
| The Labor Force | n.a. | 310,000 | n.a. | 300,000 | 632,000 | 600,000 |
| No. of Wage Earners | n.a. | 16,000 | n.a. | 60,000 | 73,000 | 33,000 |
| D. HEALTH—No. of Persons per Dr. | 28,000 | 29,000 | 83,000 | n.a. | 14,500 | 40,000 |
| E. MAIN PRODUCT | | | | | | |
| Coffee (tons) | 6,297 | 32,600 | 260 | 27,380 | 5,406 | 11,430 |
| Cocoa (tons) | 7,500 | n.a. | n.a. | 3,368 | 94,200 | 8,000 |
| Cotton (tons) | — | — | 68,000 | — | — | — |
| Bananas (tons) | — | — | — | 28,000 | 350 | 61,036 |
| Groundnuts (tons) | 7,200 | 16,000 | 53,000 | — | 19,988 | — |
| Maize (tons) | 18,000 | 112,000 | 26,000 | — | 28,000 | — |
| Plantain (tons) | 153,000 | 73,000 | — | 200,000 | 273,000 | — |
| Manioc (tons) | 111,700 | — | 119,000 | 92,000 | 180,390 | n.a. |
| Yams (tons) | — | 18,000 | — | 26,000 | 12,000 | — |
| Sweet Potatoes (tons) | 560 | 47,000 | 35,000 | — | 5,000 | 20,000 |
| Palm Oil (tons) | — | n.a. | — | 9,700 | 10,000 | 17,215 |

*Source:* Data compiled from *Cameroon*, Ministry of Information and Tourism, Yaounde, 1970; *Elaboration de IIIe Plan Quinquennal 1971–76*, Regional Synthesis, November 1960; and *Third Five Year Economics & Social Development Plan: 1971/72–1975/76—The Regions*, Yaounde, June 1972. Adapted from Wilfred A. Ndongko, "The Political Economy of Regional Economic Development in Cameroon," in Ndiva Kofele-Kale, ed., *An African Experiment in Nation Building: The Bilingual Cameroon Republic Since Reunification*, Boulder, Col.: Westview Press, 1980, pp. 227–250.

inherited colonial differences in language and institutions were to be respected and creatively integrated into a new collective national experience, Anglophones instead found themselves buried under the weight of the dominant French way of life. To them the reality of two decades of reunification has been the marked preference for French-style institutions—administration, police, army, university, etc.—over their British-style equivalents. Such was the case under the federal system and this has continued to be the case in the subsequent unitary phase of postreunification history (Chumbow, 1980: 298). They have watched with consternation the decline of the use of English in a country where English and French are the *constitutionally* designated official languages. Yet, for many Anglophones this very organic document only paid lip service to the concept of bilingualism. For instance, during the first decade of reunification, the constitution contained a glaring contradiction; on the one hand, it prescribed French and English as the country's official languages (Article 1:4) only to allow, on the other hand, until the provision was eventually dropped, that the French text was the authentic one (Article 44 of the 1972 constitution).

This perceived deliberate reduction of the importance of English cut deeply into the collective Anglophone ego. For to them language loyalty, as Beban Chumbow (1980: 299) points out, has taken on the same significance as nationalism does for nationality, that is, a state of mind, following Weinreich (1953: 99, in Chumbow, 1980: 299), in "which language (like nationality) assumes a high position in a scale of values, a position in need of being defended." Although French and English *theoretically* enjoy co-equal status as official languages in Cameroon, Chumbow has persuasively argued that with only one-fourth of the country's population, the Anglophone sector entered the union "from the onset [with] the scales naturally tilted in favour of French ascendancy" (p. 298). As a result, the trend towards bilingualism has tended to be

> unidirectional in that, by far more anglophone . . . efforts effectively achieved a respectable degree of bilingualism than francophone. This obviously retrogressive ascendancy of French over English as a result of the population factor . . . and in part to the "frenchification" effect of the French colonial policy which presented the French language to all its colonies as the language of civilization "par excellence." Since French has a *de facto* popularity and superiority (despite a *de jure* equality with English), francophones have a less natural urge or stimulus towards acquiring English. (Chumbow, 1980: 298)

Strong support for Chumbow's argument comes from one who can hardly be accused of antigovernment bias, Dr. Solomon Nfor Gwei, who had served briefly as secretary-general in the Faculty of Arts & Letters of the University of Yaounde and who since 1978 has been the vice-minister of agriculture. His 1974 study, based on extensive personal interviews with administrators, faculty (mostly Cameroonians, some of whom were products of the University of Yaounde), and students who were then enrolled at the university, conclusively demonstrated the inherent asymmetry in Cameroon's bilingual policy with respect to the University of Yaounde (Gwei, 1975: 435–447). Gwei found that in this citadel of higher education, Anglophone students averaged a pitiful 6 percent of the total student population over a ten-year period, 1964–1974 (p. 444). Anglophone students were not only outnumbered by their Francophone cohorts in the university as a whole, but in some faculties and specialized institutes, for example, the *grandes écoles,* there were hardly any Anglophone students matriculating (p. 446). The problem of Anglophone student underenrollment was paralleled in the teaching and administrative staff (p. 436). Anglophone faculty personnel were then, and continue now to be, grossly outnumbered by Francophones while the administrative support services (clerical and secretarial staff) have always been inadequate. Gwei's study points:

> Because the English-speaking students form a tiny minority, the language of instruction, the teaching methods, the educational programmes, the examination system and the social atmosphere at the University do not tend to favor them but rather the French-speaking majority. That they are often ignored is obvious from the fact that the University calendar, publications, notices, etc. hardly ever appear in English. (p. 447)

And, with prophetic vision, Gwei warned that "unless steps are taken to protect the interest of the minority, the tendency is often to ignore them and their own interests and aspirations. The reaction of members of the minority groups to problems which weigh heavily on them would be either one of submission or protest" (p. 446–447). Over the years Anglophone students at the University of Yaounde have steadfastly refused to submit to the status quo. They have instead dared to express their dissatisfaction with the monolingual trend in the country as a whole in several celebrated bloody skirmishes with government forces, one of which we witnessed when Anglophone students took to the streets to protest the former minister of national education's ill-advised and poorly thought-out move to force-feed them French. The *casus belli*—if one may so call it—was a series of recently instituted reforms in the Cameroon General Certificate of Education, one of which required French as a compulsory subject even though English was not required as a compulsory subject for the baccalaureate for Francophone students (*Cameroon Tribune,* English ed., November 16, 23, and 30, 1983). "The publication of this Order," according to one observer, "sparked off an anglophone students' boycott of classes and demonstrations repressed by police brutality at Yaounde University and throughout the anglophone provinces of Buea, Kumba and Bamenda. The situation did not calm down until 11 days later when President Biya issued a statement calling on the students to return to classes and announcing the setting up of a Commission of qualified and experienced persons of both anglophone and francophone backgrounds to go into the students' grievances" (Naweri, 1984: 202; see also *Cameroon Tribune,* English ed., December 7, 1983, p. 3, and *Cameroon Post,* December 1, 1983, pp. 3–4).

The third set of complaints voiced by Anglophone Cameroonians is political in nature. This is usually presented in two forms: (1) the loss of regional autonomy and hence control over their own state followed by the relegation of Anglophone leaders to inferior roles in the national decision-making councils, and (2) their numerical underrepresentation in the two branches of government concerned with policy-making (the Party and the Executive) as well as in the higher echelons of the bureaucracy. Sammy Kum Buo put forward the case for Anglophone Cameroon quite forcefully: ". . . since reunification . . . Anglophones have never constituted more than one-fourth of the cabinet and no Anglophone has ever held the powerful portfolios of defense, finance, foreign affairs, territorial administration or education. And of the country's eighteen ambassadors serving abroad, only two, Ambassadors Epie and Kisob in Canada and Liberia, respectively, are English-speakers" (Buo, 1976: 18; see also Ko-fele-Kale, 1983: 2871–2872). During the federalist phase, when the country was divided into six administrative regions each under a federal inspector of administration, at no time was any one of these proconsuls an Anglophone. Following the dismantling of the federal inspectorate system and the introduction of provinces headed by governors, only one of the two provinces in the Anglophone sector was headed by a governor native to the region. He was also the only indigene governor out of a total of seven.[6] During the early years of reunification, all the secretaries-general (i.e., permanent secretaries) in the ministries were Francophone. Only in the last eight years have Anglophones been appointed to these positions—and the number has never been greater than two, less than 10 percent out of a total of twenty-four as of 1978.

To take another example, of the ten major financial institutions, that is, six commercial banks[7] and four development banks (in which the Cameroon government held shares as of 1980),[8] only one, Cameroon Bank Ltd., was headed by an Anglophone; and of the country's fourteen principal development organizations,[9] only the Cameroon Development Corporation (CDC), principally located in Anglophone Cameroon since 1948, is headed by an indigene. Clearly, the case for Anglophone underrepresentation in the middle- and higher-ranking levels of the administration as well as in the important party and executive policy-making bodies is strong—that is, if we persist in treating the Francophone sector as a monolith. As we have already indicated, for the purposes of this analysis the country will be viewed as consisting of six regions whose boundaries coincide with those of the former federal inspectorates. This approach forces us to avoid the parochialism implicit in Anglophone insistence on seeing their region as special and their problems as unique only to them. By adopting the comparative regional approach, we are able to situate the Anglophone predicament in its national context while allowing for comparisons to be made not between Anglophones and Francophones but among the six regions. The portrait that emerges from this exercise shows a significant Anglophone representation, relatively speaking, in all levels of policy-making and execution, that is, in positions of real power as well as in those with high visibility and prestige but of little political consequence.

*Deputies in the National Assembly.*    These are positions with more prestige than political power (Etonga, 1980; Bayart, 1980; Le Vine, 1980). Anglophone representation in the 120-member (enlarged to 150 in 1983) Assembly has always been 24 or 20 percent, roughly the proportion of Anglophones in the total population (21 percent). As Table 6.3 shows, of the six regions only the littoral was underrepresented relative to its share of the total population. Among the chairmanships of the five parliamentary committees where most work on legislation takes place, at no time was at least one committee not chaired by an Anglophone. Between 1973 and 1980, the Committee on Production, Urbanization, Construction and Rural Exchange was under the chairmanship of Dr. E. M. L. Endeley while two other Anglophones served as vice-chairpersons, respectively, of the Committee on Constitutional Laws (Foretia) and the Committee on Education and Social Affairs (Gwen Burnley). Other committees and their respective chairmen in 1980 were: Foreign Affairs—André Fouda (south-central); Finance, Economic Affairs, Planning and Infrastructure—Malouma Raymond (east); Education, Information, Cultural and Social Affairs—Naoue

**TABLE 6.3** Distribution of Deputies in the National Assembly by Region, 1973–1980

| Region | No. of Deputies | Percentage | As a Proportion of Total Population |
|---|---|---|---|
| North | 36 | 30 | 35 |
| West Cameroon | 24 | 20 | 25 |
| South-Central | 23 | 19 | 24 |
| West | 21 | 17.5 | 16 |
| Littoral | 10 | 8.5 | 14 |
| East | 6 | 5 | 6 |
| Total | 120 | 100.0 | 120 |

1973–1978, Poufong 1978– (west); and Constitutional Laws, Justice, Legislation, Rules and Armed Forces—Moussa Yaya (north). And, of course, the speaker of the house, Solomon Tandeng Muna, was and still is an Anglophone.

*Policy-Making Bodies of the National Party.* This refers to the Central Committee and the National Political Bureau. Cameroon being a one-party state, these party councils play a crucial role in the formulation of national policy (see *CNU Militants Guide,* 1976: 17–23). Membership in either or both of these organs could be viewed as an index of the politically powerful personalities in the country. Anglophone representation in both the Central Committee and National Political Bureau remained quite strong under Ahidjo, as Tables 6.4 and 6.5 indicate. In the former body, Anglophones held eight of the forty-two elected positions and were tied with the north in having the largest number of representatives—three each—in the twelve-member National Political Bureau.

*The Powerful and Prestigious Positions in the Executive Branch of Government Where a Good Deal of Policy-Making and Execution Take Place.* Here we are speaking, first, of the national executive, that is, ministers and vice-ministers. The 1968 cabinet contained two Anglophone full ministers and one vice-minister for a total representation of roughly 16 percent. The north had three (15.8 percent) representatives in this cabinet, the west four (21 percent), seven (thirty-seven percent) for the south-central, two (10.5 percent) for the littoral, with no representation from the east (note that the speaker of the Fed-

**Table 6.4** Distribution of Seats in the Central Committee of the CNU by Regions (Elected Members), 1973–1980

| Region | No. of Members | Percentage |
|---|---|---|
| North | 10 | 23.8 |
| West Cameroon | 8 | 19.0 |
| South-Central | 10 | 23.8 |
| West | 8 | 19.0 |
| Littoral | 3 | 7.0 |
| East | 3 | 7.0 |
| Total | 42 | 100.0 |

**TABLE 6.5**　Distribution of Members of the
National Political Bureau of the CNU by
Regions, 1973–1978

| Region | No. of Members | Percentage |
|---|---|---|
| North | 3 | 25 |
| West Cameroon | 3 | 25 |
| South-Central | 2 | 16.5 |
| West | 2 | 16.5 |
| Littoral | 1 | 8.5 |
| East | 1 | 8.5 |
| Total | 12 | 100.0 |

eral House, Marigoh Mboua, and the secretary-general, Doumba, were both
from the east). In the enlarged twenty-nine-member cabinet appointed shortly
after the unitary state was declared in 1972, Anglophone representation improved from 16 percent to 24 percent (i.e., from three to seven cabinet members). The percentage of northern representation also increased, to 20.7 percent
(six members). Although the south-central continued to enjoy a lead in absolute
numbers (eight), its proportion of cabinet posts dropped from a 1968 high of
37 percent to 27.6 percent; such, too, was the case with the west, which increased its absolute share in numbers from four to six but held on to the same
proportion of cabinet positions. The obvious loser was the littoral, whose share
dropped from 10.5 percent (two) to 3.4 percent (one) between 1968 and 1972.
The biggest improvement was in the east, which for the first time received one
cabinet position. In the 1975–1980 cabinet, which was now headed by a prime
minister, Anglophone representation was the *second* highest, outnumbered only
by the share of portfolios held by representatives from the south-central region
(see Tables 6.6 and 6.7). Of thirty-one ministers and vice-ministers, the Anglophones held seven, or 22.5 percent, of the total. Among the four senior
ministers (*ministres d'État*), one was an Anglophone—E.T. Egbe, minister of
state for posts and telecommunications—who, until he was cashiered from the
cabinet in 1984, had the distinction of being one of the very few ministers to
have held on to a cabinet position without interruption for over twenty years!
　　Less powerful and prestigious positions include the regional executives, that
is, provincial and divisional service heads (governors, prefects and subpre-

**TABLE 6.6**　Distribution of Ministers and Vice-Ministers by Region in the 1968
and 1972 Cabinets

| Region | 1968 Cabinet No. of Ministers | Percentage | 1972 Cabinet No. of Ministers | Percentage |
|---|---|---|---|---|
| North | 3 | 15.8 | 6 | 20.7 |
| West Cameroon | 3 | 15.8 | 7 | 24.2 |
| South-Central | 7 | 37.0 | 8 | 27.6 |
| West | 4 | 21.0 | 6 | 20.7 |
| Littoral | 2 | 10.5 | 1 | 3.4 |
| East | 0 | 0.0 | 1 | 3.4 |
| Total | 19 | 100.0 | 29 | 100.0 |

**TABLE 6.7**  Distribution by Region of
Ministers and Vice-Ministers in the 1975 Cabinet

| Region | No. of Ministers | Percentage |
|--------|------------------|------------|
| North | 6 | 19.5 |
| West Cameroon | 7 | 22.5 |
| South-Central | 8 | 25.8 |
| West | 5 | 16.2 |
| Littoral | 3 | 9.6 |
| East | 2 | 6.4 |
| Total | 31 | 100.0 |

fects).[10] In the higher ranks (governors and prefects) Anglophone representation was 28 percent compared to 35 percent for south-central and 15 percent for the north, 9 percent each for the west and the littoral, respectively, and only 4 percent for the east. When all ranks are combined (governors, prefects, and subprefects), the proportion of Anglophone, north, and east representation dropped to 17.6 percent, 13 percent, and 3 percent, respectively. The south-central still maintained its lead with 32.5 percent, followed by the west with 20 percent representation in the politically powerful regional executive positions. The greatest gain in this combined category was posted by the west, whose share of regional positions increased from 8.7 percent at the higher ranks (governors and prefects) to 20 percent of all ranks.

Finally, in the judiciary, the third branch of government, among the top judicial officials in the nation (titular and substitute judges of the Supreme Court, High Court judges, and magistrates and the *procureurs-généraux* and their deputies) Anglophone representation was roughly 17 percent compared to 3.8 percent for the north. In addition, *all* the top law officers serving in Anglophone Cameroon were native to this region.

The preceding analysis has attempted to establish the strong Anglophone presence in all branches of government and party: in the National Assembly, where the positions are sought more for their prestige and status than power; in the principal policy-making organs of the national party; and within the national and regional executives which confer both power and prestige to their

**TABLE 6.8**  Distribution of Administrative Departments (Headed by Prefects) by Regions, 1973–1978

| Region | No. of Departments | Percentage | No. of Prefects by Region of Origin | Percentage |
|--------|--------------------|------------|-------------------------------------|------------|
| North | 6 | 15 | 6 | 15.3 |
| West Cameroon | 9 | 23 | 12 | 30.7 |
| South-Central | 9 | 23 | 14 | 35.9 |
| West | 6 | 15 | 3 | 7.7 |
| Littoral | 5 | 12.8 | 2 | 5 |
| East | 4 | 10.2 | 2 | 5 |
| Total | 39 | 100 | 39 | 100 |

**TABLE 6.9**  Distribution of Administrative Subdistricts (Headed by Subprefects) by Region, 1973–1978

| Region | No. of Subdistricts | Percentage | No. of Subprefects by Region of Origin | Percentage |
|---|---|---|---|---|
| North | 20 | 15 | 18 | 13 |
| West Cameroon | 22 | 16 | 20 | 15 |
| South-Central | 47 | 35 | 45 | 33.3 |
| West | 17 | 12.5 | 33 | 24.5 |
| Littoral | 18 | 13 | 14 | 10.5 |
| East | 11 | 8 | 5 | 3.7 |
| Total | 135 | 100 | 135 | 100 |

members. By way of contrast and for the sake of perspective, the analysis shows that the north, with close to one-third of the total population, was, relatively speaking, underrepresented in the Central Committee of the CNU and within *all* ranks of the national and regional executives. How, then, can one reconcile this apparent ubiquity of Anglophones in the higher councils of state with the persistent claims that their region has been treated as the orphan of the republic?

A possible approach, and the one favored by this author, is to distinguish between the Anglophone masses and their privileged ruling class. The complaints legitimately speak to the deprivation of the masses, as it were, the group that has yet to enjoy the fruits of two decades of postreunification progress. In contrast, a tiny minority of Anglophones, which since reunification has had access to the national corridors of power, wealth, and prestige, has effectively exploited mass discontent in order to advance its own narrow corporate interests. This group, together with an equally privileged Francophone minority, constitutes the dominant class, that is, the national bourgeoisie, in postreunification Cameroon. The Anglophone bourgeoisie has in the last twenty years kept its narrow class interests at the forefront while paying no heed to those of the majority population. Its support for or opposition to the major political changes the country has experienced during this period was predicated on calculations of the advantages to be gained from these arrangements and not out of any deep ideological commitment to ease the plight of the Anglophone majority. What the composition of this bourgeoisie is and its *modus operandi* will be taken up in the next and final part of this essay.

## THE ANGLOPHONE BOURGEOISIE IN FOCUS

In his path-breaking study *Power and Class in Africa* (1977), Professor Irving Leonard Markovitz identified an organizational bourgeoisie which he defined as " . . . a combined ruling group consisting of the top political leaders and bureaucrats, the traditional rulers and their descendants, and the leading members of the liberal professions and the rising business bourgeoisie. Top members of the military and police forces are also part of this bureaucratic bourgeoisie" (p. 208). The members of this organizational bourgeoisie are distinguishable by their strategic locations in society, from which they make major decisions that affect the life chances of thousands of their compatriots; they are located in the agencies that enable them to derive their livelihood from the "national income," from the productive efforts of others; they are distinguishable by their general health, height and weight, the chances of survival of their children, their manner of speech, their leisure activities, their eating habits—the food they consume as well as the manner of its consumption—their means of transportation, the games they play, the conversation of their wives, the work habits and values the attempt to inculcate in their children—every aspect of their existence. (pp. 205–206)

We can extract from Markovitz's definition five essential features of the organizational bourgeoisie: (1) it is a small class of very privileged people; (2) it is parasitical, drawing its lifeblood from the national exchequer, as it were; (3) its members are the first beneficiaries of the fruits of economic growth because of their strategic location at the apex of society; (4) they are the major decision makers and the impact of their decisions reach far into the most obscure and the remote interstices of society; and (5) their decisions are invariably made to insure that corporate gains from economic growth are preserved.

What Markovitz has done *circum* Africa, few have attempted in Cameroon (Kom, 1971; Joseph, 1977).[11] This oversight is quite consistent with orthodoxy in certain sectors of Africanist scholarship which continues to promote the myth of a classless African society long after it has been exploded (Lewis, 1966; Lloyd, 1966, 1967, 1971; Kimble, 1963; Zolberg, 1969). The focus of this study is on the Anglophone bourgeoisie, a fraction of the national bourgeoisie with its own ideology and consciousness, which began to show its corporate face shortly after reunification in 1961. This group constitutes the "ruling class" in Anglophone Cameroon and, as a class exhibits all the essential features of Markovitz's organizational bourgeoisie. Of particular interest for this analysis are the decisions this class has made over the last two decades and their cumulative impact on the lives of the Anglophone population. This class—then in its embryonic stage—played a leading role in the negotiations which led to the birth of the Federal Republic of Cameroon in 1961; as a midwife, it helped in the delivery of the single party in 1966; and when the decision was made to replace the federal system with a unitary form of government in 1972, its collective voice could be heard above the din proclaiming this event to the populace. It will be shown that, whereas each of these major decisions were to prove unpopular, the Anglophone bourgeoisie supported them precisely because they worked to their advantage.

But who belongs to this class? The Anglophone bourgeoisie is comprised of (1) a bureaucratic elite of governors, secretaries-general, prefects, subprefects, and directors, people who hold key administrative positions in the national center or at the provincial level; (2) a political elite of top party leaders, ministers and vice-ministers, deputies in the National Assembly, and leading traditional rulers; and (3) a business elite consisting of a tiny stratum of entrepreneurs engaged in retail trade, transportation, and construction, landowners and landlords with extensive real estate holdings, and wealthy farmers.

## The Bureaucratic Elite

The bureaucratic elite is an extremely small class nationwide, numbering no more than a few hundred, to at most several thousand people, according to some estimates (Gonidec, 1969: 16–18; Prouzet, 1974: 85). Prouzet offers the following description of the bureaucratic bourgeoisie: "Les cadres des administrateurs civiles forment en premier lieu un groupe social privilegié par rapport aux autres couchés de la population. Là, où le paysan de la brousse utilise, comme unité monetaire dans ses transactions, la pièce de 25F CFA, le citadin issue de la classe administrative emploiera le billet de 5,000F CFA" (p. 117). As a rule, members of the bureaucratic bourgeoisie enjoy extremely high incomes. It is estimated that those at the top of the pyramid, about 2.1 percent of the total population in active employment, consume one-third of the national revenue compared to 40 percent of national income shared by 89.4 percent of the labor force (Prouzet, 1974: 81). The range of salaries between the highest-paid laborer and the highest-paid civil servant is in the order of 1:30 (Prouzet, 1974: 80). This bureaucratic elite, of which the Anglophones are a part, is an extremely privileged class; its children attend the best secondary schools in the country (a few are sent abroad) and usually on government bursaries; their wives are chauffeured around in "Kitchen cars" supplied by the state; their retinue of servants—houseboys, nurse-babies, gardeners, nightwatchmen, chauffeurs, and so on—are all on the state payroll. As individuals they have access to all kinds of loans from the various banks in which the government has a controlling interest, not to talk of the unlimited opportunities open to them for appropriating state funds for personal use.

The older Anglophone bureaucrats in this stratum were trained in Nigeria and Britain and served in the old Nigerian, and subsequently West Cameroon, public service. Many were members of the Kamerun Society—an organization of English-speaking Cameroonian intellectuals—who were called upon for advice by the politicians during the negotiations leading to reunification. However, the younger generation of top-level Anglophone bureaucrats are in the main bilingual in French and English, products of local institutions of higher learning and in particular the *grandes écoles* such as the National School of Administration and Magistracy (ENAM), the National School of Journalism (ESIJY), the Institute for International Relations (IRIC), the Combined Military Academy (EMIAC), and so on.

## The Political Elite

The remarkable thing about this stratum is its longevity in office, though not necessarily in the same posts. I found, for instance, that 75 percent of the members of the 1973–1978 National Assembly were carry-overs from the defunct state legislatures or the former Federal House. Sixty-three percent of the Anglophone deputies in this same parliament were also carryovers from the West Cameroon House of Assembly (Kofele-Kale, 1980a: 79). Among them are men like Endeley, Muna, and Foncha, whose political careers span over *thirty* years, or E. T. Egbe, who has held one national post or another since 1961. In Cameroon, political leaders who have been cast out, as Professor Le Vine notes, are usually brought back to the inner circle—"en reserve pour la Republique"—and offered "continued high salary but no official position, rustication to some local administrative position, [or] a prebend in the Party. Unless they have done something truly offensive, those whom [Ahidjo] does not eventually recall have generally been permitted to enter or resume profitable civilian callings" (Le Vine, 1980: Appendix B). The composition of the Anglophone political elite has changed very little since reunification; the same names appear again and again with a bewildering consistency on the rosters of the various councils of state: Endeley, Foncha, Muna, Fonlon, Elangwe, Ekangaki, Effiom, Angwafor III, Egbe, Foretia, and Burnley, to name only a few.

## The Business Elite

Markovitz has correctly pointed out that not every businessman qualifies for inclusion among the organizational bourgeoisie, only those whose impact is nationwide (Markovitz, 1977: p. 210). This holds true for Anglophone entrepreneurs, a minority of whom can truly be considered a business bourgeoisie in the above sense. Two things must be noted with respect to the Anglophone business bourgeoisie. The first is that it neither controls nor owns the means of production, distribution, and exchange. It is essentially a parasitical class, able to survive precisely because of its proximity to those who control the state budget. The leading Anglophone businessmen owe their wealth to generous government loan policies and lucrative government contracts where competitive bidding is a smoke screen designed to deceive the outsider, since most decisions are made a priori. A second characteristic of the Anglophone business bourgeoisie is the prominent role it plays in national politics. Nangah, reputedly the most successful of the lot, participated in the preunification discussions, and since then he has held a number of party offices at the local level. The same was true of Kilo, while others, like Paul Bamileke, Fojungoh, Fomenky, Che, and Paul Sinju, are invisible or anonymous power brokers in their respective communities. But, as our review of the three major constitutional changes since reunification—federalism, single-party system, and unitary government—will show, the Anglophone bourgeoisie as a whole shed its anonymity as it went in feverish pursuit of its class interests.

## Federation

The Anglophone bourgeoisie entered into negotiations that led to the creation of the federal system with well-defined class interests in sight. Their objectives were threefold: "(1) to create a set of federal institutions and delimit federal and state jurisdictions; (2) to preserve virtually intact the local autonomy hitherto enjoyed by the two states; and (3) to maintain as long as possible the political status quo in both Cameroons" (Le Vine, 1971: 81–82; also Le Vine, 1961a: 7, 8, 10; 1961b: 774–775; Gonidec, 1961: 370–395; 1962: 13–26; Johnson, 1970: 200–232; Enonchong, 1967). Although federalism was an agreement between the Francophone and Anglophone bourgeoisies, the argument has been advanced that because the Anglophone negotiators were no match for the sophisticated Francophones, they were outmaneuvered into accepting an arrangement that worked to their disadvantage (Stark, 1980: 109). I do not find this position particularly persuasive. The Anglophones were represented in these negotiations by a core of intellectuals (Fonlon and Ekangaki) and legal experts (barristers Sam Endeley and Egbe) as well as a cast of veteran politicians like Muna, Jua, Foncha, and Mukete—men who had honed their political skills in the rough and tumble of preindependent Nigerian politics. These were no neophytes on the negotiating table, but seasoned politicians with many battle scars. That the federal system turned out to be less than what the Anglophone masses had been led to expect by their leaders had very little to do with the political naiveté of this leadership class.

I shall venture to argue here that the federal system failed to live up to the expectations of the Anglophone masses precisely because it was never constructed for them. Rather it was a system designed to promote and protect the class interests of the Anglophone bourgeoisie. To carry through this argument, two points will be established in this section: (1) that in their eagerness to consummate the federal union, the Anglophone bourgeoisie not only failed to inform its followers about the weak bargaining position Anglophone Cameroon was in, but in fact misled them into believing that *maximum local autonomy* for their state would be one of the irrevocable guarantees of the federation; and (2) that though the fragility of the Anglophone economy was well documented and known to the politicians who negotiated the terms of federation, this less than sanguine economic portrait was blithely ignored by the bourgeoisie in its quixotic pursuit for political power. But the lack of viability of the Anglophone economy made a mockery of claims to Anglophone autonomy, since it was clear to all but the most unreconstructed believers that the region could not survive by itself without massive external assistance. In other words, later complaints by the Anglophone bourgeoisie that their region was the victim of Francophone-caused underdevelopment were chimerical and should be properly viewed as a disingenuous attempt by this class to deflect public blame from their misleadership.

Three factors are of crucial importance in any attempt at understanding the pre- and postreunification Anglophone political economy. The first is that the territory remained persistently plagued by budgetary deficits which provoked the need for extensive and continuous subsidies from the British colonial administration, the Nigerian government, and later the federal Cameroon government. A second prominent feature of its political economy is the dominant role of the Cameroon Development Corporation (CDC), a semipublic corporation established in 1946 to take over and administer most of the former German plantations confiscated at the beginning of the World War II (Ardener et al., 1960; Bederman, 1968; Bederman and DeLancey, 1980). And a third feature was the inability of the Anglophone bourgeoisie to develop *independent* and *dependable* sources for capital accumulation. Let us briefly review each of these points.

The problem of recurrent budgetary deficits was merely a reflection of the more fundamental problem of the general fragility of the Anglophone economy. Its solution was to come through profits realized by the CDC. But this was not to happen. Between 1922 and the eve of World War II, the British-dominated Nigerian government claimed to have spent more on Southern Cameroons than it received in revenues from the territory. And in the years 1943–1949, the trust territory received subsidies from Nigeria to the tune of 1 million pounds sterling. The first and perhaps only time the Southern Cameroons had a surplus of revenues over expenditures was when the CDC plantations began to register a profit. But from 1945 to 1959, according to Johnson, the pattern of budget deficits and external subsidies was again repeated: "recurring deficits, periodic revision of the scheme of revenue allocations and repeated disappointments over the level of revenue from the CDC profits and from customs and other taxes contributed to the constant worry among Southern Cameroons officials about the financial stability of the Territory" (Johnson, 1970: 104; see also Ndongko, 1975: 78–79). The expectation that the CDC would be a major source of revenue was never borne out. The corporation's net profits declined from an all-time high of 60,285 pounds in 1953 to nil in 1955. On the eve of reunification, profits stood at 47,620 pounds, a 20 percent drop from the 1953 level (Johnson, 1970: 102).

When the Anglophones joined the federation in 1961, the economy continued to suffer from what a correspondent of *West Africa* (July 7, 1962: 745) referred to as "chronic insolvency." Benjamin, whose sympathetic treatment of the Anglophone predicament was banned in Cameroon when Ahidjo was in power, noted that "as early as 1961, the federal government had . . . paid out grants-in-aid which represented two-thirds of West Cameroon's budget" (Benjamin, 1980: 199). The federal government continued to subsidize West Cameroon's budget, right up to the eve of the switch to a unitary form of government, much like Nigeria had done prior to reunification. To reduce further the expenses of the state, certain areas which were under the jurisdiction of the federated states (for example, the West Cameroon police force, were brought under federal government control. In the meanwhile, the Anglophone bourgeoisie devised ways to reduce its dependence on the federal government. Attempts to set up several self-financing schemes— such as the Cameroon Commercial Corporation, United Cameroon Trading Company, Cameroon Bank Ltd.—to provide this much-needed independent financial base all met with limited success. Under the KNDP government these enterprises were transformed into patronage structures run by individuals whose only qualification was their party loyalty. The Cameroon Bank Ltd., the first indigenous bank in Anglophone Cameroon, almost went bankrupt but for the timely intervention of the federal government. The bank was run as the personal property of the party in power and on the principle that loans were to be given as rewards to the party faithful under the most generous terms. Loans were canceled as bad debts at the first sign of insolvency, while other portfolios were repayable in ninety years in a country where the average life expectancy did not exceed half that figure.

The Anglophone bourgeoisie was forewarned of the weak economic base of their state even before negotiations for reunification commenced. Three studies commissioned between 1959 and 1961—the Phillipson Report of 1959, the 1960 Berrill Report, and the Anderson Report of 1961—all contained this message. The Phillipson Report, which was commissioned by the Foncha administration, was never made public by the KNDP leadership. Foncha and his associates, in suppressing the findings of this study, *intentionally misled* the Anglophone population about the nature of the territory's financial viability, falsely raising popular expectations of a "considerably *autonomous* state in a Cameroon Federation" (Johnson, 1970: 107). The fluctuation in the margin of profits posted by the CDC was nothing new. It had bedeviled not only the Foncha administration (1957–1961) but also the Endeley one which preceded it. And when the east-west customs barrier was lifted, the Anglophone bourgeoisie feigned surprise and complained bitterly about the loss of revenue from this source. There was no reason for this reaction. Harmonization of customs borders should have been anticipated as a matter of course; after all, the continued existence of this customs wall was contrary to the spirit and practice of federalism. Finally, having failed to develop alternative sources for raising revenue, the Anglophone bourgeoisie was in no position to complain about federal

government subventions which were, in the words of the West Cameroon secretary of state of finance, P. M. Kemcha, "thoroughly unsatisfactory" (*Estimates of West Cameroon, 1966–1967,* in Benjamin, 1980: 216). Nor should
Prime Minister Jua have expressed surprise at the fact that he was presiding
over a shell of a state whose claim to sovereignty was more fiction than fact
(Benjamin, 1980: 199).

In conclusion, we can either agree with Johnson (1970: 110–111) that the
Anglophone bourgeoisie did not really understand the financial implications of
reunification or, consistent with the view being advanced here, conclude that
secure in the belief that its corporate interests were intact, the Anglophone
bourgeoisie did not therefore bother to scrutinize the long-term impact on the
Anglophone masses of the system they had helped erect. That the latter belief
turned out to be illusory, eventually forcing the Anglophone bourgeoisie to
abandon the federal system in favor of a unitary form of government, will be
taken up below.

## The Single-Party State

The single party emerged in 1966 following the dissolution of all political parties in the country. As a concept, the one-party system had limited appeal in
Anglophone Cameroon (Rubin, 1971: 150). Johnson, who has given us the
fullest account of the rise of the national party, informs us:

> For most West Cameroonians, however, the thought of a single-party was disturb-
> ing. The *Cameroon Times,* normally biased toward the KNDP, carried editorials
> and private letters decrying any interpretation of the agreement [between Ahidjo's
> UC, the party in power in East Cameroon, and Foncha's KNDP, the governing party
> in the West, to form a parliamentary union in the federal Assembly] as an endorse-
> ment of or attempt to create a single party system, which they thought would lead
> invariably to dictatorship and a denial of free speech. Spokesmen for the KNDP
> stated privately that they feared the single party idea itself more than the rise of now
> diminished opposition leaders. Instead, their propaganda stressed their desire simply
> to build a "national party." (Johnson, 1970: 264)

A study on national political orientations conducted by this author found that
the single-party political culture had still not taken firm hold in the Anglophone
sector of the country even after seven years of its introduction (Kofele-Kale,
1980a: 79). The mass of Anglophones remained alienated from the national
party and expressed this alienation through their low level of political knowledge. Few could correctly identify their national party leaders, and most surprising of all was the inability of the mass public to identify even *local* CNU
leaders, with whom presumably they are most likely to come into frequent
contact (p. 76).

Having been schooled in the tradition of multiparty politics, the Anglophone
political leadership was equally hostile to the idea of a single-party state. Almost a year before the CNU was inaugurated, Anglophone leaders of the two
principal political parties in the state legislature—the KNDP and the CPNC—
issued a joint communiqúe from Yaounde on August 19, 1965, in which they
pledged "to work for the preservation of [their] existing parliamentary system
and political institutions in West Cameroon" (Fonlon, 1966: 7). Dr. Bernard
Fonlon, a prominent KNDP official, argued against the installation of the single

party in Cameroon: ". . . everywhere in Africa, people are being told that in order to speed up the economic and social development of the continent, the one party state has become a must. But *almost everywhere where this system is being implemented, we witness the suppression of liberty, the elimination of debate, the imposition of silence and the rise of despotism"* (Fonlon, 1966: 7–8; my emphasis). Yet, having registered in such strong language his distaste for the single party, Fonlon was later to serve on the twelve-member working committee—which also included E. T. Egbe in the chair, S. M. Endeley (brother of Dr. Endeley, leader of the CPNC), and Nzo Ekangaki—which drafted the CNU's statutes.[12] And when the first CNU provisional committee was established, the Anglophones were again represented by none other than Dr. Fonlon, Messrs. Egbe, Ekangaki, Foncha, Elangwe, Jua, and Dr. Endeley. In the space of one year, Fonlon and the other principal Anglophone politicians were to abandon their public stance vis-à-vis the single-party state, to become grey eminences in the new party hierarchy, a party which has in many ways confirmed Fonlon's worst fears about the single-party leviathan (Fonlon, 1966; see also Bayart, 1980; Etonga, 1980; Eyinga, 1978; Kofele-Kale, 1978, 1980a, 1981).

The shift from opposition to courtship and support for the single party was a tactical maneuver on the part of the Anglophone bourgeoisie. This apparent change of heart had much to do with the bourgeoisie's perceptions of changing power relationships and forces in the nation and the extent to which these could be profitably exploited to serve their narrow class interests. The Anglophone bourgeoisie was able to read the handwriting on the wall, and the message which it carried was unmistakably clear: the days of multiparty politics in their state were drawing to a close and the new game in town now was the single party (Johnson, 1970: 278–285). The process began with the consolidation of all political parties under the benign canopy of Ahidjo's UC, which had already been accomplished in the Francophone sector. In the Anglophone sector, the party in power, the KNDP, had long entered into a *mariage de convenance* with the UC in the federal Assembly. All that remained was for the rest of the Anglophone political parties to dissolve into the KNDP/UC grand alliance so as to clear the way for the arrival of the national party. The maneuverings that went on before the CNU was ushered into the political daylight have been captured in the following observation by Victor Le Vine: "Between 1962 and 1966 West Cameroon witnessed a complex political ballet in which the principal parties and politicians simultaneously strove to retain their influence in the West and maneuvered to put themselves in the best possible position for the merger of all parties at the national level . . ." (Le Vine, 1971: 96). A few examples of this jockeying for advantageous position by this fragment of the Anglophone bourgeoisie will suffice.

Foncha, life president of the KNDP, who had retained the post of prime minister of West Cameroon along with that of vice president of the federal republic, was required by the constitution to relinquish one of the offices. He chose to give up the former. In the ensuing intraparty fight over the vacated premiership, the victor, Augustin Ngom Jua, suspended his rival, S. T. Muna and his associates, from the KNDP (Ardener, 1967: 332–333; Johnson, 1970: 267–276). The expelled KNDP members then quickly formed a new party, the Cameroon United Congress (CUC), "with policies and initials aimed at reflecting Ahidjo's ideas and obtaining his favour" (Stark, 1980: 118; Johnson,

1970: 274). In the case of the CUC leadership, the jockeying for position so as to be more proximate to the national power center than the other rival parties was artfully attempted through the choice of a name for their party. However, Muna's parliamentary clique was not the only Anglophone party which sought to place itself strategically close to the UC. Foncha, whose KNDP already enjoyed a head start as the parliamentary ally of the UC in the federal House, at first refused to give his assent to the formation of a national party, on the grounds that the opposition CPNC would be gaining ground at the KNDP's expense (Stark, 1980: 118). But even more agonizing for Mr. Foncha was the fear of losing his position as *life* president of the KNDP in the event that a national party came to being (Stark, 1980: 118; Nelson et al., 1974: 148). He was prepared, however, to join a national party only after a single party had been established in West Cameroon. Foncha's proposal was to have all dissident political parties dissolve and declare membership in the KNDP. Only after this had been achieved could one then start talking about forming a national, as distinct from a regional, party (Johnson, 1970: 265).

The CPNC opposition also had definite views on the subject of a single party; in fact, the CPNC did appear *plus royaliste que le roi* on this issue. A series of election reversals and defections of its parliamentary members (three prominent CPNC parliamentarians, E. E. Ngone, F. N. Ajebe-Sone, and S. N. Tamfu had "crossed the carpet" to join the government party) saw the CPNC's political strength and influence reduced dramatically (Rubin, 1971: 150–151). Having taken inventory of its political assets and recognizing that as far as regional politics went its influence would continue to wane rather than improve, the CPNC leadership quickly jumped onto the one-party bandwagon, becoming, in Rubin's words, "the principal advocate in West Cameroon of the idea of a single party for the nation" (Rubin, 1971: 150; see also Stark, 1980: 117; Johnson, 1970: 265–267, 276).

This brief review of the role played by various Anglophone parties and politicians reveals that their support for the single party was not predicated on ideology but more upon a careful calculation of the profits to be derived from it. The views of the Anglophone masses whom these politicians purportedly represented were ignored. Despite the fact that the single-party idea had limited appeal among the populace, this factor was ignored by the Anglophone leadership, who, it would appear, were more concerned about protecting their corporate interests and less about the long-term effects of its decision on the electorate.

### The Unitary State

A country's constitution, in the normal course of its political history, is altered only under the most exceptional circumstances, and even then never by one person. In any free society, attempts at major alterations of its organic document involve, as a matter of course, the active participation and advice of the governed. A careful reconstruction of the sequence of events that led to the abolishment of the federal system in 1972 would suggest that this decision was entirely Ahidjo's (Stark, 1980). Briefly recalled, on May 7, 1972, in a meeting of the CNU Political Bureau, Mr. Ahidjo announced *his* intentions to end the federation. Two days later, a draft constitution for a unitary state was announced, and on May 20 the Cameroonian people were asked to ratify that document in a referendum. On June 2, the *United* Republic of Cameroon received its official birth certificate in the form of *presidential* decree No. 72-270. The whole exercise took *less than two weeks*—to be exact, thirteen days from the time the referendum was announced before the National Assembly on May 8 to when it actually took place on May 20. There were no public debates either at the elite or the grass roots levels. In Anglophone Cameroon, according to Stark, there was little opposition to the event among the political leadership, and even relief among many of them (Stark, 1980: 101). For example, the Fako CNU section under the leadership of Dr. E. M. L. Endeley adopted a resolution congratulating the president for declaring a unitary state (see *"Rapport de la Section Departmentale du Fako"* presente par Dr. E. M. L. Endeley au *Deuxième Congrès UNC à Douala,* 1975: 335). In his report to the Second Congress of the CNU, held in Douala in 1975, the CNU section president for Mezam, Angwafor III, was undeniably hyperbolic in the effusive praises he heaped on Mr. Ahidjo for his decision to terminate the federalist phase: "The glorious revolution of May 20, 1972, is the result of a wave of change which began in 1966," he declared. "This peaceful revolution," he continued, "is the first stage toward pan-African unity." (*Deuxième Congrès UNC à Douala,* 1975: 397).

Why was there no opposition within the party? Why did the Anglophone leaders, especially those who were members of the Party Political Bureau,[13] not oppose it? Why did they not mobilize the Anglophone masses against this affront to their state rights? After all, it is generally conceded that only the Anglophones had a vested interest in retaining the federal system, since under it their political leaders were able to retain some control over their internal affairs, while for the masses federalism was the lesser of two evils because they "feared the changes that would be brought about by the incorporation in a French-oriented society—not only linguistic and cultural changes but also such matters as a diminished attention to civil rights" (Nelson et al., 1974: 151). Indeed, for most Anglophones, the Cameroon Federation (1961–1972) was the institutional expression of the highest ideals of the reunification movement. This most profound and powerful statement of Cameroon nationalism was the essence of a forty-year struggle for which so many gave up their lives (Kofele-Kale, 1980b). The dismantling of the federal framework meant not only the death of a dream, but it signaled to most Anglophones the ultimate retreat by their national leaders from a commitment to the Cameroon people to create for them a sociopolitical system capable of balancing the entrenched differences resulting from the country's dual colonial heritage. The lurch toward the unitary and stiflingly centralized state should have been cause for concern to the Anglophone leadership. Yet this was not the case. Why?

Cameroon federalism, as Stark points out in his excellent review of its life and death, was an agreement between the elites from both sectors. It was primarily an "elite symbol and concept" (Stark, 1980: 109, 127). And as a political accommodation between the two ruling groups its continued survival was predicated on the advantages both sides derived from the arrangement. Apparently, the Anglophones felt they were getting less and less from the federal system. As Stark called it, Anglophone leaders had given up hope of any political or economic powers for their region. This point has been amply commented on by leading students of this period of Cameroon's political history (Le Vine, 1971: Chapter 3; Johnson, 1970; Rubin, 1971: esp. Chapter 7). The period from independence to 1966, according to one commentator, "saw a gradual erosion of the power of regional interest [read West/Anglophone Cameroon] and the growth of the forces of national unity" (Nelson et al., 1974: 148). This was manifested in a number of areas, in particular, those in which state and federal jurisdictions overlapped, such as education, administration, local government, and internal security. The federal government gradually took over the West Cameroon educational system, creating an administrative system which paralleled that at the state level. In the ensuing jurisdictional conflict between the two systems, the federal government always triumphed. The state public service was merged into the federal one, the police and the prisons were also federalized. With the whittling down of its local autonomy, the Anglophone bourgeoisie realized, in Dr. Stark's words, that "there was nothing to be gained by clinging to the old boundaries, old parties, and old views of federalism" (Stark, 1980: 122). It was time to move on to a new arrangement without great loss to previously made gains. So it was that 63 percent of the Anglophone deputies in the postunitary National Assembly were former parliamentarians in the former West Cameroon House of Assembly (Kofele-Kale, 1980a: 78, 93). In the new cabinet announced shortly after the unitary state was approved in a national referendum, Anglophones held seven portfolios and were led by Mr. S. T. Muna—the last prime minister of West Cameroon—who was named minister of state. Muna was subsequently elected speaker of the National Assembly, remaining second in command to the president until the constitution was amended in 1975. Of the seven Anglophone cabinet members only three (Awunti, Bongwa, and Achu) had not held previous political office. Of the remaining four, Egbe had been in the federal cabinet since 1961, while Luma and Elangwe were secretaries of state in the former West Cameroon. These and other segments of the Anglophone bourgeoisie were the immediate beneficiaries of the new unitary arrangement.

We close this section by raising the question of how it has been possible for the Anglophone bourgeoisie to maintain its hold over Anglophone society for this long. How could it have fooled the populace for so long and with such consistency? It has achieved this feat through its artful ability to shift gears at the appropriate time. The Anglophone bourgeoisie has succeeded in maintaining its dominant place in society in two ways: (1) through appeals to ethnicity, that is, by presenting themselves as the *interlocuteurs valables* of their respective ethnic groups; and (2) by use of a process I wish to call "crossing over," that is, the tendency to pass off as Francophones, to cross over to the camp considered to be the most powerful and influential in the country.

In Cameroon, direct appeal to ethnic affiliation is generally considered contrary to national unity and is *theoretically* frowned upon. A law passed in June 1967 placed a ban on any associations whose members were recruited on the basis of primordial ties. Yet, as Bayart (1980) and this author (1981: 23–26) have pointed out, ethnic origin remains an important, if muted, criterion for determining who gets what in the country. In most appointments to high office, an ethnic arithmetic formula is used, and in the case of the cabinet each of the major ethnic congeries in the country is represented. For example, the two vice-ministers of education since 1972 have both been Anglophones and from the *same* ethnic group, Vakpe. When the Meme representative on the cabinet, Henry Namata Elangwe, was relieved of his ministerial post in 1980, he was immediately replaced by another Meme indigene, Albert Kome Ngome.

This has been the pattern throughout the two decades of reunification and the examples above can be multiplied many times over in other governmental institutions (Decraene, 1979: 5; Le Vine, 1980: 3). Recognizing the fact that power, status, and prestige are determined by some ill-defined "ethnic arithmetic criteria," the Anglophone bourgeoisie has sought to have its role as ethnic brokers legitimized (Kofele-Kale, 1981: 25–26). So, we find certain fragments among them who were previously ethnically neutral, such as the so called Creoles of Victoria, now finding it necessary and expedient to reestablish some kind of ethnic authenticity. Many now openly claim to be Vakpe or Isu, these being the two groups indigenous to Victoria which for long were not considered as civilized as the Creoles.

The second method used by the Anglophone bourgeoisie in consolidating its position consists of "crossing over" to the Francophone camp. This is accomplished in several ways: through marriage; exclusive use of the French language even when conversing with fellow Anglophones; change of name, so John becomes Jean, for instance; and so on. This process of "Francophonization" is predicated on two (mis)perceptions of Cameroonian reality: (1) that power and privilege are monopolized by the Francophones and (2) therefore that Francophones are the "in crowd" while Anglophones are the "outsiders." To profit then from the system, one who is not an "authentic" Francophone can at least masquerade as one. Interestingly enough, the phenomenon of crossing over is generally associated with those migrants from former French Cameroon who settled in the British Trust territory and never returned to their home areas (Ardener et al., 1960: 196–197); Ardener, 1967: 296–298; Le Vine, 1964: 196; Chem-Langhee and Njeuma, 1980: 27 ff.). Although this group of "French" Cameroonians has lived in the Anglophone sector for up to fifty years, many now, for expediential reasons, choose to reaffirm links with their ethnic brethren across the once Anglo-French divide.

This process in and of itself is one that should merit encouragement; after all, it was the frustrations and anger at the artificiality of the Anglo-French boundary—which split ethnic groups, clans, families, etc.—that sparked the reunification struggle. (Chem-Langhee and Njeuma, 1980: 27). Rather, it is the Machiavellian twist given by the Anglophone bourgeoisie to this genuinely expressed need to reidentify with "lost" brothers that is of paramount interest in this analysis. It is the manner in which top-level Anglophone bureaucrats, politicians, and businessmen who were originally from these emigrant/ethnic groups play up this heritage in order to partake in the ethnic arithmetic game.

## SUMMARY

In its first two decades of postcolonial history, Cameroon remained an island of stability in a violence-prone and unstable African continent. Having succeeded where most have failed, the Cameroonian recipe for survival deserves both lay and expert attention. But as often happens with these elixirs of life, the specific ingredients that go into making them so potent are not easily discernible to the uninitiated eye. The significance of Cameroon's achievement in maintaining a peaceful and stable polity over the years is not as self-evident as many of its admirers would have liked. Various interpretations are possible as the following questions indicate. Does this achievement reveal anything about who in Cameroon profit(s) from stability? Does it reflect the material and psychic contentment of the Cameroonian masses? If not, could it possibly be masking some deep-seated tensions in the society? And, were this to be the case, through what medium would these subterranean tensions choose to express themselves?

The first task of this paper, then, was to isolate and review critically the oft-cited cleavages of tribe, region, and religion which, taken singly or in one of several combinations thereof, constitute the orthodox view of Cameroon's most fundamental contradictions. In opposition to this orthodoxy, a class analysis was offered. This approach sought to demonstrate that economic divisions and conflicting class interests are present in Cameroon and are fundamental to any understanding of its postcolonial politics. Within this context an attempt was made to reassess the Anglophone-Francophone division which for many remains perhaps the most explosive of all the contradictions and the most ominous of all the banked tensions in Cameroon. Consistent with the class analysis adopted, an Anglophone bourgeoisie was identified as the class that has consistently and systematically exploited the Anglophone-Francophone cleavage, as well as others, to advance its narrow corporate interests. Given its strategic location at the summit of society, this class was able to profit from the three major constitutional changes Cameroon has experienced since reunification in 1961.

## REFERENCES

Ahidjo, Ahmadou (1964). *Contribution to National Construction*. Paris: Editions Presence Africaine.

Ardener, Edwin (1967). "The Nature of the Reunification of Cameroon," in Arthur Hazlewood (Ed.), *African Integration and Disintegration*. London: Oxford University Press.

Ardener, Shirley, E. W. Ardener, and W. A. Warmington (1960). *Plantation and Village in the Cameroons*. London: Oxford University Press.

Azarya, Victor (1976). "Dominance and Change in North Cameroon: The Fulbe Aristocracy." Sage Research Papers in the Social Sciences (Studies in Comparative Modernization Series, No. 90-030). Beverly Hills and London: Sage Publications.

Bayart, J. F. (1978). "The Political System," in Richard Joseph (Ed.), *Gaullist Africa: Cameroun Under Ahmadu Ahidjo*. Enugu, Nigeria: Fourth Dimension Press.

———. (1980). "One-Party Government and Political Development in Cameroon," in Ndiva Kofele-Kale (Ed.), *An African Experiment in Nation Building: The Bilingual Cameroon Republic Since Reunification*. Boulder, Col: Westview.

Bederman, Sanford H. (1968). *The Cameroons Development Corporation: Partners in National Growth*. Bota: Cameroons Development Corporation.

——— and Mark W. DeLancey (1980). "The Cameroon Development Corporation 1947–1977: Cameroonization and Growth," in Ndiva Kofele-Kale (Ed.), *An African Experiment in Nation Building*.

Behrman, Lucy (1970). *Muslim Brotherhoods and Politics in Senegal*. Cambridge, Mass.: Harvard University Press, 1970.

——— (1972). *Les Camerounais occidentaux: La minorite dans un Etat bicommunautaire*. Montreal: Les Presses de l'Universite de Montreal.

Benjamin, Jacques (1980). "The Impact of Federal Institutions on West Cameroon's Economic Activity," in Ndiva Kofele-Kale (Ed.) *An African Experiment in Nation Building*.

Beti, Mongo (1972). *Main basse sur Le Cameroun: Autopsie d'une decolonisation*. Paris: Editions Maspero.

Binder, Leonard, (Ed.) (1966). *Politics in Lebanon.* New York: Wiley.

Binet, J. (1961). "Les cadres au Cameroun." *Civilisations* 12: 21–38.

Buo, Sammy Kum (1976). "How United is Cameroon?" *Africa Report* (November–December): 17–20.

Chaffard, Georges (1967). *Les carnets secrets de la decolonisation,* Tome I. Paris: Calmann-Levy.

Chem-Langhee and Martin Z. Njeuma (1980). "The Pan-Kamerun Movement, 1949–1961," in Ndiva Kofele-Kale (Ed.), *An African Experiment in Nation Building.*

Chumbow, Sammy Beban (1980). "Language and Language Policy in Cameroon," in Ndiva Kofele-Kale (Ed.), *An African Experiment in Nation Buiding.*

Clignet, Remi (1976). *The Africanization of the Labor Market: Educational and Occupational Segmentation in Cameroun.* Berkeley and Los Angeles: University of California.

Cohen, Abner (1969). *Custom and Politics in Urban Africa: A Study of Hausa Migrants in Yoruba Towns.* Berkeley and Los Angeles: University of California Press.

Decraene, Phillipe (1979). "Cameroon: Ahidjo's Quest for Unity." *The Guardian* (February 25): 12.

Derrick, Jonathan (1983). "Things Fall Apart." *West Africa,* October 3.

Ediafric (1976). *Les Elites Camerounaises: Qui est qui au Cameroun.* Paris: Ediafric La documentation africaine.

Enonchong, H. N. A. (1967). *Cameroon Constitutional Law.* Yaounde: Centre d'Edition et de Production de Manuels et d'Auxiliaires de L'Enseignement.

Etonga, Mbu (1980). "An Imperial Presidency: A Study of Presidential Power in Cameroon," in Ndiva Kofele-Kale, (Ed.), *An African Experiment in Nation Building.*

Eyinga, Abel (1978). *Mandat d' Arret pour cause d' elections: De la democratie au Cameroun.* Paris: Editions l' Harmattan.

Fonlon, Bernard (1966). *The Task of Today.* Victoria: Cameroon Printing and Publishing Company, Ltd.

Gonidec, P. F. (1961). "Les institutions politiques de la Republique Federale du Cameroun." *Civilisations* 11, 4: 370–395.

——— (1962). "Les institutions politiques de la Republique Federale du Cameroun," *Civilisations,* 12, 1: 13–26.

——— (1969). *La Republique Federale du Cameroun.* Paris: Berger-Levrault.

Gwei, Solomon Nfor (1975). "Education in Cameroon: Western Pre-colonial and Colonial Antecedents and the Development of Higher Education." Unpublished Ph.D. dissertation, Department of Education, the University of Michigan.

Horner, N. A. (1956). "Protestant and Roman Catholic Missions Among the Bantus of Cameroun." Unpublished Ph.D. thesis, The Hartford Seminary Foundation.

Hudson, Michael (1968). *The Precarious Republic: Political Modernization in Lebanon.* New York: Random House.

Hugon, P. (1968). *Analyse du sous developpement en Afrique noire: l'exemple de l' economie du Cameroun.* Paris: Presses Universitaires de France.

Johnson, Willard (1970). *The Cameroon Federation: Political Integration in a Fragmentary Society.* Princeton, N.J.: Princeton University Press.

Joseph, Richard A. (1977). *Radical Nationalism in Cameroun.* London: Oxford University Press.

Kale, P. M. (1967). *Political Evolution in the Cameroons.* Buea: Government Printer.

Kimble, David (1963). *A Political History of Ghana: The Rise of Gold Coast Nationalism.* Oxford: Clarendon Press.

Kofele-Kale, Ndiva (1978). "Patterns of Political Orientations Toward the Nation: A Comparison of Rural and Urban Residents in Anglophone Cameroon." *African Social Research* (December) 26: 469–488.

————— (1980a). "The Political Culture of Anglophone Cameroon: Contrasts in Rural-Urban Orientations Toward the Nation," in Ndiva Kofele-Kale (Ed.), *An African Experiment in Nation Building.*

————— (1980b). "Reconciling the Dual Heritage: Reflections on the 'Kamerun Idea,'" in Ndiva Kofele-Kale (Ed.), *An African Experiment in Nation Building.*

————— (1981) *Tribesmen and Patriots: Political Culture in a Polyethnic African State.* Washington, D.C.: University Press of America.

————— (1983) "Cameroon: Checks and Balances." *West Africa* (Dec. 13): 2871–2872.

Kom, David (1971). *Le Cameroun: Essai d'analyse economique et politique.* Paris: Editions Sociales.

Laye, Camara (1968). *A Dream of Africa* (Dramouss), trans. James Kirkup. London: Collins.

Le Vine, Victor T. (1961a). "The New Cameroon Federation." *Africa Report* 6, 2: 7, 8, 10.

————— (1961b). "Unifying the Cameroons." *West Africa* (July 15): 774–775.

————— (1964). *The Cameroons From Mandate to Independence.* Berkeley and Los Angeles: University of California Press.

————— (1971). *The Cameroon Federal Republic.* Ithaca, NY: Cornell University Press.

————— (1980). "Perspectives on Contemporary Politics in Cameroon." Department of State, Washington, D.C. (unpublished).

Lewis, W. A. (1966). *Politics in West Africa.* New York: Oxford University Press.

Lloyd, P. C. (1966). *The New Elites of Tropical Africa.* London: Oxford University Press.

————— (1967). *Africa in Social Change.* Baltimore: Penguin.

————— (1971). *Classes, Crises and Coups.* London: MacGibbon and Company.

Lockard, Kathleen G. (1980). "Religion and Politics in Independent Uganda: Movement Toward Secularization," in James R. Scanitt (Ed.), *Analyzing Political Change in Africa: Applications of a New Multidimentional Framework.* Boulder, Colo.: Westview Press.

Markovitz, Irving Leonard (1977). *Power and Class in Africa.* Englewood Cliffs, Prentice-Hall.

Merton, Robert K. (1973). *The Sociology of Science.* Chicago: University of Chicago Press.

Naweri, Joseph Komla (1983). "The Beginnings of Freedom," *West Africa,* November 7.
————— (1984). "Restless Anglophones." *West Africa,* January 30.

Ndongko, Wilfred A. (1975). *Planning for Economic Development in a Federal State: The Case of Cameroon, 1960–1971.* Munich: Weltforum Verlag.

————— (1980). "The Political Economy of Regional Economic Development in Cameroon," in Ndiva Kofele-Kale (Ed.), *An African Experiment in Nation Building.*

Nelson, Harold D., Margarita Robert, Gordon C. McDonald, James McLaughlin, Barbara Marvin, and Philip W. Moeller (1974). *Handbook for the United Republic of Cameroon.* Washington, D.C.: U.S. Government Printing Office.

O'Brien, D. B. Cruise (1971). *The Mourides of Senegal.* Oxford: Clarendon Press.

Paden, John N. (1973) *Religion and Political Culture in Kano.* Berkeley and Los Angeles: University of California Press.

Prouzet, Michel (1974). *Le Cameroun.* Paris: Librairie Generale de Droit et de Jurisprudence.

Rubin, Neville N. (1971). *Cameroun: An African Federation*. New York: Praeger.

Schissel, Howard (1983). "Cameroon's Economy: Myth or Reality?" *West Africa* (Sept. 12): 2107–2108.

Sklar, Richard L. (1963). *Nigerian Political Parties: Power in an Emergent African Nation*. Princeton, NJ: Princeton University Press.

——— (1975). *Corporate Power in an African State: The Political Impact of Multinational Mining Companies in Zambia*. Berkeley and Los Angeles: University of California Press.

Soyinka, Wole (1973). *Collected Plays I*. London: Oxford University Press.

Stark, Frank M. (1980). "Federalism in Cameroon: The Shadow and the Reality," in Ndiva Kofele-Kale (Ed.), *An African Experiment in Nation Building*.

U.S. State Department (1981). *Country Reports on Human Rights Practices*. Washington, D.C.: Government Printing Office.

Weinreich, U. (1953). *Languages in Contact: Findings and Problems*. The Hague: Mouton.

Young, Crawford (1976). *The Political of Cultural Pluralism*. Madison, WI: University of Wisconsin Press.

Zolberg, Aristide (1969). *One-party Government in the Ivory Coast*, rev. ed. Princeton, NJ: Princeton University Press.

# CHAPTER 7

# Religion, Ideology, and Property in Northern Zambia

## George C. Bond

This article explores some cultural formulations of the Yombe, a *Bantu*-speaking population of northern Zambia. My interpretation developed over a period of time in response to a conversation I had in Muyombe, in which a group of leading Yombe citizens compared Western society and kinship with their own. These men began their discussion by characterizing themselves and their kind as people, *Bantu,* and me and my kind as chickens, *Nkuku.* They considered themselves as belonging to a well-ordered society in which everyone knew his place and respected the rights, privileges, and claims of others as kin, neighbors, or friends. Theirs was a society based on cooperation and mutual assistance, one in which the individual was part of and subordinate to the collective will of the agnatic group and the community. (What struck me at the time, and does still, is that they were presenting me with a classic Durkheimian view of society.)

In contrast to their view of themselves as *Bantu,* they viewed Westerners as *Nkuku,* solitary figures pecking in the dust for their own gain, regardless of the needs of others. Western kinship and society were seen to be based on a collectivity of related but competing individuals who attached little value to sharing or to mutual assistance, and who were indifferent to the needs and demands of their kinsfolk and neighbors. Assistance was rendered only for money, and men worked only for wages. Western society was one based upon the individual, but theirs upon the collectivity, the corporate group. In Maine's terms (1946: 259), these Yombe men viewed their social system as one based on status, and the Western system as one rooted in contract (Johnson and Bond, 1974: 57). By making the distinction between *Nkuku* and *Bantu,* they were able to reduce their experiences of capitalism to a succinct and manageable contrast. They had penetrated an ideological premise deeply embedded within Western culture, and by rejecting its validity for their own society they obscured the growing inequalities that their actions as commercial farmers, politicians, and entrepreneurs were producing within their own corner of northern Zambia. These men showed such astuteness in their understanding of the "inherent" ideological forms of Western society, that I now wish to try my hand at unraveling these particular metaphors and exploring the implication of their ideological premises.

The general purpose of this paper, then, is to delve into Yombe culture in order to illuminate a particular ideational construction pertaining to inequality that shapes and mediates individual and collective consciousness. I am assuming that this ideological field is based in the material conditions of living, and may thus experience change. The more specific purpose of the paper is to explore the role of religious ideology within the context of changing property relationships within the community of Muyombe.

In its simplest form, I take ideology to be a construction of ideas about the world and, in this situation, a construction of ideas relating to social inequality. The notion of ideological field refers to the range of ideologies within a society, to that domain in which paradigms are formulated, established, and contend, lending some degree of credence to human affairs. There is often a situational dimension to the ideological field, with praxis constantly shaping the parameters of the field.[1] There is thus the application of theoretical understandings in practical situations, leading to exploration as individuals redefine themselves and their relations to rights in labor and property. Labor was being redefined as something other than personal and inalienable and property as something other than collective, reducible to joint rights.

Any attempt to explore the manner in which Yombe customary religious beliefs—beliefs in God (*Leza*), ancestors (*Viwanda*), and witches (*Ufwiti*)—mediate and shape consciousness as well as social relationships relating to property may well be viewed within the larger context of a rising debate between those who adhere to the neointellectualist tradition of Frazer and Tylor, reinforced by Weberian sociology, and those materialsts who stand within the Marxist tradition.[2]

Within the neointellectualist school there appears to be a swing away from concern with the sociology of religion, toward an exploration of political history, bringing to bear the full weight of the Weberian formulations. In his paper "Inequality and Action: the Forms of Ijesha Social Conflict," Peel argues "the inadequacy of an influential prevailing approach to the analysis of class formation in Africa, that which posits a transition from a state of classlessness . . . to the inevitable predominance of class over all other bases of action" (1980: 474). Peel considers that "non-class modes of consciousness and action" have been of great importance in contemporary Africa, and he rejects the use of the concept "false consciousness" to explain away the existence of nonclass modes. Religious beliefs, for example, are as important for understanding action as is one's position in an economic or productive process.

While in general sympathetic to Peel's position, I cannot agree with his assumption that most forms of consciousness are grounded in a "rationality of the present." Different forms of social consciousness are neither simply nor solely grounded in "a rationality of the present" (Peel, 1980: 475) but in the conditions of history, cultural notions of the social person, and changing social relations of production and property, a point that I have explored in a previous paper (Bond, 1978). Scholars such as Van Binsbergen have explored the ideological components of social classes in the making, and I share their preoccupation with both intra- and interclass ideologies. Yet the concreteness of proximate classes is debatable in Central Africa; the class structure is tenuous and elusive, affecting both the separation and distinctiveness of peasantries and proletariats and the understanding of class consciousness and ideological constructions and mediations (Bond, 1979). Van Binsbergen is also concerned, as I am, with the manner in which culture, ideology, consciousness, and religious beliefs are all generated and affected by fundamental changes in the process of production and appropriation. In his article "Religious Innovation and Political Conflict in Northern Zambia" (1976), Van Binsbergen provides an interesting exposition of the nature of religious innovation in Zambia. His theoretical position assigns primacy, however, to production over ideology, at the same time recognizing the dialectical nature of their interpenetration.[3] He sees the penetration of capitalism in Zambia as producing major infrastructural changes in both urban and rural areas, which, in turn, set into motion the processes of peasantization and proletarianization, thus formulating new superstructures (1976: 107–108).

As part of his formulation, Van Binsbergen assumes that a separation exists between the proletariat and peasantry. Yet, in many of the rural areas of northern Zambia, and probably elsewhere in rural Africa, the peasant and the proletarian are often one and the same person at different phases in his life career. This is not a matter of gender, and it is profoundly misleading to argue, as Lionel Cliffe has done, that "in a sense, the man is worker and the woman is the peasant in this kind of situation" (1978: 328). Furthermore, the penetration of capitalism may be uneven even within a single local area, so that changes in the superstructure cannot necessarily be expected to be uniform. My own research indicates that even those people whose lives have been most changed by advancing capitalism do not *necessarily* generate or seek new superstructural forms. On the contrary, my case material demonstrates that existing forms may obscure the manner in which the "infrastructure" is being affected by new choices and decisions, leading toward changes in the relationships of man to his labor and his product. Van Binsbergen asserts that "under capitalism free autonomous farmers" become a "peasant class" in a worldwide society (1976: 112). This situation, according to his formulation, should lead to the dissolution of "traditional" religious beliefs and the fabrication of new ones to suit the new productive modes. But it may well be that "old" forms such as ancestor worship and its innovative companion, witchcraft, are eminently compatible with peasantization and proletarianization. Among other reasons, they provide individualized explanations for economic failure. The causes of failure are not seen to lie within the economic arrangements of society and its system of social inequalities, but may be attributed to spiritual beings and personal shortcomings.

From my perspective, ideology may be so deeply embedded an aspect of culture that the members of a society take it as a natural and an essential part of ordinary affairs. At this point that which is "natural" is no more than a moment of culture. It is this "inherent ideology," what Rude has termed "a sort of mother's milk ideology," which I now intend to explore (Rude, 1980: 28).

## II

I have elsewhere described the basic features of Yombe society (Bond, 1976). Here I present a brief overview of Yombe social arrangements as a general background for a discussion of the beliefs and practices of the ancestor cult and witchcraft and of the manner in which they provide an ideological framework that enhances entrepreneurial activity and the rise of individualism within the wider context of modern capitalism.

The Yombe are sparsely distributed over an area of some 625 square miles in Isoka District in the Northern Province of Zambia. A small branch of the Tumbuka peoples, most of whom are concentrated in the Northern Province of Malawi, the Yombe number about 15,000. Land within the chiefdom of Uyombe is fertile, and has been more than plentiful for the cultivation of the three main crops, maize, millet and beans, although it is conceivable that with enclosure and changing farming methods there might be increasing pressure upon the land. Land has traditionally not been subject to rent, sale, or individual inheritance, but, as Ken Post points out, in such a situation "land *use* rights must be treated as more important than property rights" (1972: 228), particularly with increasing commercialization of the countryside. Historically, residence was frequently shifted and access to land was acquired by applying to the village headman, who controlled land but did not own it, the right to ownership being vested in the chief and his royal agnates.

In 1965 the principle agricultural implements used by the Yombe were hoes and axes, and there were no local industries or home crafts. The main source of cash was the sale of crops, maize, beans, and some millet. By 1981 fundamental changes were under way that might well alter economic arrangements within Uyombe and neighboring areas. New crops such as hybrid maize, rice, and a variety of vegetables had been introduced. Sheep and goats had been added to the inventory of livestock which in 1965 had included only cattle. A few men living in Muyombe, the chiefdom capital, were plowing large farms, using plows and tractors hired from the District Headquarters. Both men and women were being hired to work in the fields. But fundamental changes are contingent upon more inclusive economic forces such as Zambia's foreign debt and, thus, changes in the social and economic order must yet be viewed as tenuous and contingent.

Dramatic though these economic changes appeared to be, they did not seem to have had any appreciable effect on a pattern of labor migration which has been a feature of Yombe life for over sixty years. Through the constant movement of its men, the rural community of Uyombe has been locked into the demands of an urban industrial complex based upon African labor. As labor migrants, the Yombe have become part of the growing African proletariat whose employment is based on individual contracts with employers and whose human worth is measured in monetary terms. The individual's social persona, a cultural amalgam and synthesis of a highly integrated matrix of personalized relationships, has been fractured and reconstituted primarily as a unit of labor, the product of a system of production that subjects the individual to the dictates of contractual relationships involving the state as well as the employer. The same men who form the proletariat in the urban, industrial areas are also the peasants of the countryside. The Yombe peasant is as much a part of the Copper Belt, one of the most urbanized and industrialized regions in all of Africa, as he is of what colonial government reports described as the "dead north," because of its lack of economic development, even when compared with other parts of rural Zambia. Both urban and rural Zambia are shaped by the same economic forces. The rural areas are, however, the dependent and subordinate partner in their relationship.

### III

Agnatic kinship remains important both as a principle of social organization and for the transmission of property rights. The Yombe are still organized into dispersed, exogamous, corporate descent groups with a depth of four to six generations. The shallow depth and the resulting narrowness of span are probably a consequence of the meager and nondurable nature of the property transmitted within the descent groups of the common folk. In the precolonial period the more durable items of value included objects such as hoes, axes, and spears; cattle and muzzle-loading guns were also owned, but were few in number. The Yombe traditionally practiced slash and burn (swidden) millet cultivation; according to my informants, maize and *dambo* cultivation (cultivation along the banks of rivers and streams) were introduced by missionaries in the late nineteenth century and led to a more settled pattern of village life.

Kuper argues that the "lineage model" has no value for anthropological analysis for two reasons. The first reason is that the lineage model fails to represent the folk models of the actors and, second, that "there do not appear to be any societies in which vital political or economic activities are organized by a repetitive series of descent groups" (Kuper, 1982: 92). There is some merit in Kuper's overall argument, but I have never been aware that the analytic constructs of the social sciences must conform to or be on the same scale as that of the folk ones. In his intellectual enthusiasm to discard "lineage theory," Kuper tosses the baby out with the bathwater. The entirety of Yombe society is not based on agnatic principles. But vital political and economic activities do occur within the context of groups whose membership is based upon agnatic descent. Important rights in property, status, and women are contained in these groups, rights that are backed by jural sanctions and a body of local court decisions. Agnatic descent groups are not merely normative constructs; they provide the context in which important economic activities occur related to property, labor, and status. The Yombe have their own understanding of rights and of the items to which these rights refer. For example, an axe is not merely a material object but an extension of self, of a social persona. There is within Yombe notions of property a tension between the rights of the collectivity and that of the individual. The individual, to be recognized as a social person, is part of an agnatic collectivity and, thus, the property he acquires has claims made upon it by his agnatic group. Costly items such as grinding mills are often the focus of unresolved struggles between the agnatic collectivity and the individual.

The agnatic descent groups are divided into segments which are theoretically arranged in a hierarchy according to the relative seniority of the lineage founder and his wives. The descendants of an elder brother are senior to those of a junior one, the descendants from a first wife are senior to those from a second wife, and so on. In practice, disputes over seniority occur frequently. Most disputes are concerned with the control and distribution of lineage property or with attempts to transform individual property rights into collective ones. These disputes are often expressed in the cultural idiom of ancestor worship and witchcraft accusations. Any individual who is anxious to assert his claim to property must endeavor to avoid either the supposed intervention of the ancestors on behalf of his agnatic kin or being charged with the practice of witchcraft.

Although all lineage property is under the lineage head, the basic property-holding units are the generational councils. These councils consist of sibling groups; younger brothers and sisters (real or classificatory) look to the eldest brother to represent their interests and claims within the lineage. There is a marked cleavage between adjacent generations and a correspondingly strong permissive familiarity between alternate generations; men and their grandsons are thought to be "brothers" who must stand together against the avarice and neglect of the intervening generation. The cleavage between proximate generations is formalized in rules relating to the acquisition, control, and distribution of bridewealth. In theory, men are entitled to the bridewealth of their sisters and they are expected to make the marriage payments of their "sons," but they are not entitled to the bridewealth of their "daughters." The actual practice does not, however, always conform to the theory.[4]

Generational councils may control a considerable portion of lineage wealth; they receive the bridewealth of their "sisters" and their members are entitled to inherit one another's property and wives. They are the primary units in which rights in property and persons are held and transferred. Members of the councils are known as *Banangwa* (free people) because they are supposed to be free with their goods and services, to help and care for each other and to honor the claims made upon their labor and property. The councils are bound by their ties in property, but should these ties bind too tightly, the Yombe believe that witchcraft may render them asunder, even though the ancestors may be able to reintegrate the fibers. The head of the council is entrusted with its portion of the lineage's wealth, and it is he who is primarily responsible for the distribution of wealth and the welfare of his brothers and sisters. As the eldest son, he inherits from the council above his, once the last man in his father's generation has died.[5]

Seniority within the agnatic descent group is demonstrated during the times of planting and harvesting millet and maize. According to the ideology of kinship, members of an agnatic descent group are supposed to help cultivate one another's farms in order of seniority. The group first works a day in the fields of the lineage head, then in the fields of the next senior agnate, and so on down the line. At each stage, however, the man whose land has been worked on leaves the group, in order to complete the tasks of planting and harvesting on his own land. When the turn of the most junior agnate comes, no one but he and his wife and children remain in the group. Those who benefit most from the system are the senior men of the descent group, in particular the head and his apparent heirs, who are usually the heads of generational councils. In this way the kinship ideology serves as a basis for capital accumulation. It also provides for the potential redistribution of food in times of shortages. With the increasing commercialization of the countryside, however, such surplus as may be accumulated by senior men tend to be sold on the market for cash and the money spent on personal items or investments.

The Yombe are not a wealthy people, and their possessions are still few and humble. Their very poverty has been a primary factor in labor migration. Men leave to earn money and to acquire objects such as shotguns, blankets, bicycles, and grinding mills. One should not underestimate the social and practical value Yombe attach to such objects. Shotguns are expensive items and only men of wealth and standing own them. They are used for hunting game for meat. Blankets are used not only as cover against the chilly nights but as valued

items of bridewealth. Bicycles are the main means of rapid and efficient transport throughout the countryside; the Yombe use them to carry heavy loads such
as bags of maize and millet and they often compare them to motorcars. Grinding mills provide a housewife with an easy and quick means of having flour
at a not too burdensome cost and the mill owner with a local source of cash
income.

The goods which an individual buys with his own money or enterprises,
such as shops and bottle stores, which he finances with money he has earned
himself are not considered lineage property. In Yombe theory an individual is
free to dispose of them as he pleases. Nevertheless, in a society with so few
material goods a struggle frequently occurs in which a man's agnates attempt
to redefine his rights over his own personally acquired property. The agnates
want to share the property while he is still alive. If they are successful in subordinating his rights to those of the agnatic group, the item becomes lineage
property.

An illustration of the process whereby an individual's property is transferred
to his lineage is provided by the case of Kafura Enda's shotgun. I shall describe
Kafura's social background in some detail, since I shall also be discussing him
later in the paper.

### Case 1

**Background.**    Kafura Enda, a man in his early fifties in 1964, was a successful and relatively prosperous businessman. He was one of my tutors in
Uyombe and one of the men who told me that Westerners were *Nkuku,* an
observation that he repeats each time I see him.

Kafura is well educated, having completed Standard VI at the Livingstonia
Mission in northern Malawi. After completing his studies he returned home,
where he quarreled with his father over the treatment of his mother. He then
left for the Copper Belt, without his father's permission or blessing. He stayed
on the Copper Belt for more than a year without finding a job. When he became
seriously ill and returned to Muyombe begging his father's forgiveness, his
father gave him medicine and made an offering on behalf of his son to the
ancestors. Kafura recovered rapidly and decided to return to the Copper Belt.
This time he asked his father's permission, which he received, along with a
coin containing the spirit of his paternal grandfather. Kafura found a well-
paying job as a clerk on the Copper Belt and sent his first wage packet home
to his father. He continued to send money home, and also saved as much as
possible. After several years he came home, married his first wife, worked as
a teacher, and opened a small store using his meager savings. By 1964 he
owned two general stores, a bottle store, and a petrol pump and was also engaged in a number of other commercial schemes. He had three wives, a large
brick house, and a pickup truck. As his father's "eldest" son he was his apparent heir and the head of his generation council. During the 1970s he went
into commercial farming, bought a tractor, and became a major producer of
hybrid maize. By 1981 his fortunes had been seriously affected by the decline
in the Zambian economy.

**The Case of Kafura's Shotgun.**    In 1963 Kafura applied for and received a
license to purchase an expensive shotgun. He bought the gun using his own

money and thus it was his personal property to dispose of as he pleased. The years 1963 and 1964 were very busy for him, and he found that he did not use the gun. He decided to sell it, and because he had not consulted his *Banangwa* (his agnates) when he bought the gun, he saw no reason to discuss the sale of it.

Dedzu, Kafura's younger brother, hearing of the impending sale, discussed the matter with his brothers (real and classificatory), who decided that the gun belonged to all of them. Dedzu told Kam, his FFBSS (father's father's brother's son's son), to borrow the gun while they approached the prospective buyer. Their argument that the sale of the gun would lead to serious conflict amongst brothers was sufficient to dissuade the buyer, who reported the conversation to Kafura. Kafura, without openly acknowledging the fact, relinquished control of the gun to Dedzu, who kept it in his house. The agnates were satisfied with the outcome and had only the highest praise for Kafura. The shotgun now belonged to the lineage.

Kafura was one of the wealthiest entrepreneurs in the chiefdom of Uyombe and a powerful political figure. Part of his power stemmed from his united agnatic base; his younger brothers (real and classificatory) were active in the local United National Independence Party (UNIP) and customary chiefdom politics. He valued and relied upon the support of his agnates and saw no reason for antagonizing them over a shotgun. He lost very little from accepting their claims and indeed enhanced his reputation as a wise and generous kinsman and community leader. For all prominent entrepreneurs like Kafura, a reputation for being generous, wise, and honest was in no way detrimental to business, which relied on the goodwill of the community.

This case illustrates the manner in which personal property is directly transferred into lineage property. The whole event was handled smoothly, without recourse to ancestors or accusations of witchcraft. Kafura had no real need for the gun or for the proceeds of its sale, and hence there was no real conflict of interests. In cases where an individual owner is more resistant, the techniques used by the agnates are more complex, and both the ancestor cult and witchcraft may be involved.

## IV

There has been a tendency within British African anthropology for two sociologies of belief to develop, one concerned with religion and the other with witchcraft (and sorcery). The separation is especially pronounced in the works of the late E. E. Evans-Pritchard. In the preface of MacFarlane's book *Witchcraft in Tudor and Stuart England,* Evans-Pritchard makes the observation that "anthropology has shown that when religious beliefs, whether those of spiritual cults or ancestor cults, are strong, witchcraft beliefs are relatively weak" (1970: XVI). This statement illustrates the dichotomous way in which religion and witchcraft have been implicitly treated. (There are, however, marked exceptions, such as S. F. Nadel's discussion of Nupe religion and Victor Turner's view of the Ndembu.) My intention here is to view Yombe indigenous religious beliefs as including both ancestor worship and witchcraft. Both form part of that ideological field relating to notions of property, and both are deeply embedded in Yombe culture. Both are important parts of the explanatory system of Yombe culture, providing explanations of misfortunes. While witchcraft offers an explanation for personal misfortunes, the ancestor cult may be used to explain the misfortunes of both individuals and collectivities. Belief in ancestors and witchcraft are two sides of the same ideological coin in that they propound the same values, though one stresses the solidarity of the social group and the other the possibility of its subversion. Witchcraft contains the notion of the primacy of the individual over the collectivity.

Yombe belief in ancestors provides an ideological framework for relationships based on status. It reinforces the collective nature of Yombe society since it relates to kinship, community, and property. It provides for relationships of inequality suited to a confined local community primarily dependent upon hoe cultivation. More significantly, as I will emphasize later, it is also suited to the obfuscation of changing labor and property relationships. While ancestor worship emphasizes collective relationships, beliefs in witchcraft emphasize the acts of the individual, although assigning to them a negative value. Witchcraft is seen to consist of the acts of individuals against the collective interests of an organized body such as the agnatic descent group or community. Witches are believed to operate always alone: there are no beliefs in covens of witches. I was often told by the Yombe that if only witches would cooperate and use their powers constructively, they could easily outstrip the achievements of Western technology; however, the destructive nature of witches' behavior prevents the harnessing of their powers for useful ends. Witches are concerned primarily with their own gains and aggrandizement, at the expense of others.

The misfortunes of individuals and kin groups are mainly attributed either to the work of a witch or to the actions of the ancestors. In order to determine which agency is involved, the afflicted seeks the advice of ritual practitioners, diviners (*Ng'anga*) or prophets (*Ncimi*). Through the manipulation of mechanical devices the diviners claim to be able to contact their own ancestors, who in their turn will discover the cause of the misfortune from the ancestors of the afflicted. Prophets claim that Christian spirits help them to identify the cause of the misfortune as well as the remedy for it. In some African societies, such as the Tallensi (Fortes, 1949: 329), the power of the ancestors is thought to be greater than the harmful force of witches; this is not the case in Uyombe. If a misfortune is thought to be caused by witchcraft, the Yombe regard the matter as outside the ancestors' control. For them, ancestors and witches are two equal and opposing forces in society. Belief in the ancestors emphasized the collectivity and concerned the effect of the dead upon the living; witchcraft stressed the powers of the individual, and involved the living affecting the living. Of course, from another perspective, both ancestors and witches may be viewed as part of the same ideological field, defining and reinforcing the same appropriate human behavior. If misfortune is attributed to an ancestor, the afflicted person requests his descent group head (or the head of his mother's descent group if the ancestors are thought to be from her side) to make an offering to the ancestor. The structure of the ascriptive basis of kinship is thus reflected in the access of individuals to spiritual authorities and powers, since it is believed that the ancestors will accept prayers and offerings only from the proper persons. This belief provides descent group heads with ritual power which they can use to reinforce collective claims over individual interests.

Numerous types of misfortunes are thought to stem from the ancestors. They are also believed to intervene whenever there has been a breakdown in social relationships, especially amongst agnates (Bond, 1978). Yombe believe that ancestors can make their presence known in small ways, particularly to the heads of descent groups when their authority and claims are disputed. This is often the case in disputes over property. To illustrate the point I take the example of Patson's bicycle.

## Case 2: Patson's Bicycle

Matson and Patson Nyem are full brothers. Matson, a man of about forty in 1964, is the head of his descent group, and Patson is next in line. After spending ten years working on the Copper Belt as a cook and bricklayer, Matson returned to Uyombe in 1956 to help his aging parents. When his father died in 1963, he assumed full responsibility for his descent group. That same year his brother Patson decided to come home after working as a pump-boy in the mines. Patson brought home with him money and goods, which he distributed generously. The only item which he seemed to prize and wished to keep for himself was his bicycle. He did not use it often, however, because he suffered from *cimbusa,* an illness usually attributed to possession by an alien, unclean spirit (Bond, 1975). In 1965 Matson's wife died and he began using Patson's bicycle to visit a prospective bride. One day Patson himself decided to use the bicycle but to his chagrin found his elder brother about to take it. The two men argued and the elder surrendered the bicycle. Subsequently, Patson suffered a relapse of his illness, which confirmed Matson's suspicion that the ancestors were troubled. He consulted his agnates. They agreed with him and beer was prepared in order to validate or refute their suspicions. They also consulted a diviner, who condemned Patson for regarding the bicycle as his own personal property but who also confirmed their suspicions that the ancestors were angry with Matson for fighting with his younger brother. Other members of the descent group pointed out that the bicycle was as much theirs as Patson's, since they had replaced parts for it. The beer to the ancestors confirmed all this, and a ritual meal was held to heal the breach in the relationship. Although Patson was allowed to keep the bicycle, both he and his agnates recognized that it was no longer his personal property.

This example illustrates the role of the ancestors in disputes over property. As the head of the descent group, Matson was able to gain the cooperation of his fellow agnates. He could himself initiate contact with the ancestors, supposedly on Patson's behalf, by making the ritual offering of millet beer, *finga.* Matson took the further step of consulting a supposedly impartial diviner, and both he and his agnates were satisfied when his suspicions of the causes of Patson's relapse were confirmed. Patson had little choice other than to comply with the will of his agnates, since he had little cash and recognized that he would have difficulty in maintaining his family and his bicycle if he were to alienate his kinsfolk, a point which they were not reluctant to make. Patson's bicycle therefore became lineage property, though left in his care.

This case illustrates the way in which appeals to the ancestors may be used to reinforce lineage solidarity. In other cases witchcraft accusations may also be brought against an individual who is appearing to threaten the lineage by his attempts at personal advancement. The Yombe believe in witchcraft as an active force which may affect them as individuals, as members of kin groups, and as whole communities. It is viewed as a constant threat from which no Yombe is entirely immune. Even the chief, the head of the chiefdom ancestor cult, who is thought to be able to know witches and to possess powerful medicines against them, is not immune to witchcraft, and he and his chiefdom may be harmed by it.

The region of northern Zambia and Malawi has a long record of antiwitchcraft movements. The major movements have occurred during periods of increasing economic and political uncertainty in the mining industry. During the early 1930s, for example, a period of devastating economic depression in the Copper Belt, a group of witchfinders known as *Bacapi* swept throught he countryside attempting to cleanse it of witches (Richards, 1935). The tapering off of the boom in the mining industries in the early 1950s coincided with the rise of two noted prophets, Lenshina in northern Zambia and Chikanga in Mawi (Bond, 1979). Both offered protection from witchcraft. During these periods of economic depression the employment opportunities for Africans were limited, and many sought the relative security of rural life.

In the late 1950s there was a new force within the countryside; the United National Independence Party (UNIP), which rapidly spread through the Northern Province of Zambia. The colonial policy of returning unemployed Africans and political agitators to their chiefdoms of origin helped spread the politics of the towns to the countryside and to make the rural social matrix, itself experiencing changes, more conducive to the rise of political protest against agents of the colonial state such as chiefs. Several alternatives were open to chiefs. They could join the protest and thereby jeopardize their colonial posts, as did Nsokolo, the Mambwe chief, in 1953 (Watson, 1958: 186); they could oppose the politics of protest directly on its own terms; or they could redirect protest from the domain of politics into that of religion through the pervasive cultural idiom of witchcraft beliefs in the malevolence of the individual against the collective good of the community. The latter was the course taken by the Yombe chief (Bond, 1976) and other Isoka chiefs before him (Fields, 1982a, 1982b). In Weberian terms, traditional authority based upon the sanctity of the order embodied in chieftainship was experiencing a profound disruption that constituted a threat to precedent (Weber, 1947: 341–358); thus order could be restored only by renewing the sanctity of the ruler and his estate. An affinity obtained between political protest, no matter how diffuse, against the "traditional" order (and the colonial state that encapsulated and preserved it) and the necessity for periodic ritual cleansings involving witchfinders. It would, however, be incorrect to say that economic depressions and political protests were the causes of witchcraft or witchfinders, though these conditions were certainly conducive to an increase in the scale of the ritual activities of witchfinders. The reaction of the Uyombe chief to the founding of UNIP branches was to call in the prophet Chikanga to ferret out and neutralize all the witches in the chiefdom. Though all activities associated with witchcraft were illegal, colonial agents in the field turned a blind eye to this event. Not surprisingly, many of those who were discovered to be witches were young party leaders and rivals of the chief.

None of the major antiwitchcraft movements of the 1930s, 1940s, and 1960s were able to eradicate witchcraft. On the contrary, their effect was to make the belief in witchcraft even stronger. The belief framed (or delineated) the individual as such and, although of the "traditional" or customary domain, was relevant to the complex progression of the capitalist order. Witchcraft enunciated the isolated and potentially detrimental individual, an individual who was thought to be dangerous to the integrity of the corporate group and the norms it expressed. It was an ingredient of the customary order and yet part of the process transforming relations of status and use-value to those of contract and exchange-value.

In contrast, ancestor worship framed the collectivity and provided the context for reabsorption through relationships of use-value. It preserved the mask of the "traditional" order, assuming the substitutability of commodities. For an entrepreneur to obscure the changes brought about by his activities in relation to property and labor, however, it was best to align himself with the ideology of ancestor worship rather than of witchcraft.

The Yombe view witchcraft as a pervasive force. They believe that to become a witch one must actively desire to become one and must seek training in the use of medicines. The medicines are not in themselves harmful; it is the interaction of the witch with the medicines which produces the effect. Most Yombe agree that a witch must have a reason for acting, whether it be jealousy, avarice, or thirst for status and power. But the most common causes stated for witchcraft is the desire to gain or to protect property. Most Yombe agree that there would be little reason to bewitch a person from whom nothing could be gained in the way of property or status. The hope of acquiring valued property is thought to be the primary reason for bewitchment. An example is provided by the case of Shappy's grinding mill.

In 1965 there were six mills in Muyombe. They experienced frequent mechanical problems, so that at any one time no more than two or three were in working condition, and one or more of these might be tied up in disputes and, thus, not in use. By 1981 there were only three mills, the principal one being owned and operated by the cooperative; it was removed from the usual personal relationships that affect maize mills.[6]

## Case 3: Shappy's Grinding Mill

In 1962 Shappy Mugha, a man in his forties, returned to Muyombe from the Copper Belt, where he had been employed in the mines. During his long absence he had earned a reputation among the townspeople for his generosity, having sent money home to his agnates and made contributions toward self-help schemes.

Shappy had saved money, and in 1962 he bought a large maize and millet grinding machine for £500 and installed it next to his new brick house. He considered that he had provided well for his retirement in Muyombe. He shared the income derived from the mill with his four half brothers, who were the children of Shappy's mother and her second husband, Shappy's father's elder brother. Because Shappy was the eldest, he had always acted as though he were the head of his generational council, taking on the responsibility of caring for his half siblings when their father died.

In 1963, however, the half brothers, under the leadership of the eldest, Esan, claimed that they were senior to Shappy and were thus entitled to the grinding mill. Shappy refused to relinquish his claim to seniority and to surrender his property, but, since he feared witchcraft, he bought his half brother Esan a grinding machine for £300. The half brothers persisted in their claims nevertheless.

Shappy became ill and left for a hospital in the Copper Belt. His half brothers claimed that the ancestors were punishing him; he maintained that he was being bewitched. He stayed away for a year and during his absence he placed Esan in charge of both mills, still maintaining that the larger mill was his own personal property. When he recovered, he returned to Muyombe and found to his dismay that both mills were broken and that Esan had squandered the income. To add insult to injury, his half brothers asked him to repair the mills. Shappy refused to so do, padlocked his own mill, and moved to his maize farm.

The merits of the claims involved in this case were complicated, first, by the ambiguity of the kinship relationship and, second, by the use by both parties in the dispute of both the ancestors and witchcraft accusations to advance their rights in property. Esan and his brothers invoked the ancestors in their attempt to transform Shappy's property into lineage property, while he, in his turn, fended off their efforts by accusing them of witchcraft. The dispute could not be settled, and the community leaders refused to intervene on one side or the other, claiming that the case belonged to the *Mugha*. In this case the supposed will of the ancestors was not sufficient to persuade Shappy to relinquish his personal property. It remained his, but could not be used.

A further aspect of this case is that Shappy had only recently returned to Muyombe after a long sojourn abroad. One may argue that he did not fully grasp the subtle complexities of the ideological field and was thereby upstaged. His half brothers enunciated the principles of the ancestor cult, of relations of status, and of use-value. Shapy removed the illusion, revealing that the growing basis of inequality stemmed from property and individual ownership. The norms of the agnatic group were placed against those of the rights of the individual and his commercial activities. An impasse had been reached and, thus, the property itself was taken entirely out of use, for the moment restoring the illusion of the integrity and endurance of the "traditional" order.

There is a larger point. Grinding mills and similar valued productive objects are integrated into and become part of human social relationships. Because they do not remain external to the social relations of their owners, their mechanical operation and their use become subject to social and ideological conditions and constraints. The Yombe clearly understand that machines break and fall into disrepair and need to be repaired, but they also look for the social reasons for the mechanical failure. Reasons are not difficult to find. Grinding mills, and items like them, are thus part of Yombe society and culture and, conversely, they affect Yombe notions of property and productive relationships. The social and cultural integration is not without its consequences.

The cases that I have discussed thus far appear to demonstrate the strength of the collectivity, the agnatic descent group, at the expense of individual ownership of property. One might assume, therefore, that the ideology of ancestor worship and of witchcraft buttresses the preeminence of descent groups as the primary feature on the social landscape—a classic type of social anthropological analysis, and one which prominent Yombe citizens would themselves applaud. Ideology militates against individual ownership and entrepreneurial activity. I wish to argue, however, that the whole social landscape may be viewed quite differently. The most successful men in Uyombe are involved in individual commercial activities, own property, and yet manage to avoid being accused of witchcraft or of displeasing the ancestors. Yet few of them are members of the Free Church of Scotland—most have been suspended for marrying more than one wife. Moreover, they are the most vocal defenders of traditional customs and practices, of the ancestor cult and of lineage solidarity, even while they work to advance their individual gains. These men use ideology to manipulate others, and the ancestor cult, instead of being a hindrance to commercial and agricultural development, in fact serves to promote it.

Within Muyombe, if not all of Uyombe, there are only a handful of successful entrepreneurs. These men are powerful and influential, and it is they who shape the economic arrangements of the chiefdom. Blue Lembo may be taken as an example of a successful entrepreneur. I think it would not be incorrect to say that he and Kafura Enda (who was discussed earlier in connection with the shotgun) are among the most prosperous men in the chiefdom, and yet both might be considered among the most vocal supporters and adherents of the customary order.

## Case 4: Blue Lembo

Blue Lembo, a man of forty-eight in 1973, was among those men who told me that I and my kind were *Nkuku*. He was the head of a descent group and his generational council. In 1972–1973 the average annual household income in rural Zambia was $487 and only 7.8 percent of rural households had an average income of $1915. In 1972 Blue earned a total of $4500 from his lumber business ($2448), his salary as a court judge ($812), and his farm ($1240). His business and farm costs amounted to $1500.

Blue had returned to Muyombe in 1956, after spending several years on the Copper Belt. That year he went into the lumber business and three years later opened a small store. In 1963 his father retired as the chiefdom court assessor, and he was appointed to the post. Blue is highly knowledgeable of Yombe customary law: he supports it and the rituals related to the chiefdom ancestor cult. Moreover, he may be called upon by the chief to attend witchcraft disputes in the privacy of the chief's compound; all activities surrounding witchcraft, after all, are illegal. Blue fully understands Yombe customary beliefs and practices. He has never, as far as I know, been involved in a witchcraft dispute, and his brothers have never used belief in ancestors to convert his property into lineage property. Rather, it is he who uses customary notions to advance his economic enterprises.

Blue has carved out a farm of more than thirty acres in a region where the average farm size is less than five acres. His farm straddles the boundaries of two villages, an unusual accomplishment since most headmen are possessive of their land. His farm follows the course of a stream; it is fertile and easily irrigated. The manner in which he acquired the use of so much land was to claim that his father had built a settlement there after performing the appropriate rituals. Blue has now claimed the land as part of the right of his descent group, and though he does not own it, in 1973 he had begun to enclose it in order to protect the crops from wild animals.

A man and his family would find it very difficult to cultivate thirty acres using only hoes, and since 1968 Blue has acquired four plows and two trained oxen. In 1973 he had six men working for him on a permanent basis, and he paid them by the month. Blue and other entrepreneurs consider their enterprises to be theirs alone, since they are the ones who dispose of the products and use the cash as they please.

This case illustrates the manner in which customary rituals and rights may be called upon to enforce "old laws" to establish new practices. At the most Matt, Blue's father, had been the head of a small hamlet and not a village headman entitled to allocate land and perform territorial rites. Matt had cultivated a garden of less than an acre, but neither he nor his sons had lived there nor had they cultivated extensively in the area for at least thirty-five years. Instead of conforming to the usual practice of requesting land from the two headmen, Blue had successfully asserted a claim or right prior to theirs. He knew the law, customary procedure, and how to use them. He was also a highly respected member of the community and well connected in regional and national political structures. From one perspective the issue appeared to be and was viewed by Yombe as a small one. From another, Blue's interest in establishing a large, productive farm was shared by a growing number of hybrid-maize farmers. The number of hybrid-maize growers increased from 16 percent of the total Muyombe household heads in 1972, to 47 percent in 1976, to 73 percent in 1981. The years 1972 and 1973 appear to have been a critical transitional period. A gradual but marked shift was occurring in the agricultural technology and market value of crops, reflecting a change in national Zambian policy.

The social field of Yombe society was gradually being expanded and portions of it changed by the activities of Blue and others like him. They operated effectively within at least two spheres, the customary one based on agnatic kinship and ancestor worship and the one that they themselves, the colonial and Zambian governments, and the market economy have been creating. They accepted the ascriptive and particularistic principles of the customary order, those principles and beliefs that emphasized relationships of status, the collectivity over the individual. They did not attempt to position themselves outside their society and culture, but accepted their own religious ideology, gave it prominence, and used it to shield their interests. They too, just like the common folk, belonged to corporate groups and honored their obligations while actively pursuing the success of their own personal enterprises. They provided for the wives and children of brothers working abroad, represented the interests of these brothers within the kin group and the community, and expected these dependents to cultivate their fields. But they did not expect their brothers to interfere in their commercial activities.

They were authorities on Yombe history and customs. They preserved them, molded them, and interpreted them in just the right manner to make them convincing and, of course, to support their interests. They were men who had been or were members of the Free Church. They usually attended church every Sunday; they also participated in ancestor rites. They knew the two ritual domains and could speak with authority about them.

Through their commercial activities they were generating a situation of growing inequality based upon the individual ownership of property and the payment of wages. By 1981 farmers were even hiring distant agnates as farm workers; within this particular commercial sphere, relations of kinship were being transformed into those of individual contract requiring the exchange of money for labor. However, within the customary domain of kinship and ancestor worship, employer and laborer might meet as equals or as junior and senior, sharing rights in lineage property, as the bridewealth of their "sisters" and the inheritance of a "father."

I think it is not incorrect to say that individualism was as much a part of the social field of Yombe society as was corporateness. The religious ideology of the customary order was pervasive, however; men worked for themselves and also worshipped their ancestors, enabling two domains to coexist and allowing for ethical and moral pluralism. Neither I nor my Yombe tutors are entirely *Bantu* or *Nkuku;* our societies possess elements of both.

## VI

This paper is a preliminary excursion into the domain of Yombe culture. In it I have attempted to explore Yombe culture to discover the properties of their embedded ideology, those cultural forms that the Yombe accept as an integral part of their ordinary lives but which serve as screens behind which certain men appropriate labor and transform their and others' relationships to property and persons. I take the terms in which my Yombe tutors characterized Yombe society and kinship to be essentially statements of ideology. As statements of ideology they may be neither true nor false, the only measure being their appropriateness to emerging patterns of social differentiation and inequality. The observations, the contrasts which they made between themselves as *Bantu,* men, and Westerners as *Nkuku,* chickens, may be treated as metaphors, and my task was to understand them and not accept them unquestioningly as accurate appraisals of the social reality.

The ancestor cult and witchcraft beliefs provided a convincing explanation for the prosperity of some and the economic failure of others. Failure was externalized and implanted in the supernatural, or else attributed to the agency of a malevolent, active human force. The ideology of collectivism was reaffirmed with each successful transformation of individual into collective property rights, as described in my first three cases. But, in fact, the affirmation of the reality of the ideology was mediating awareness of the developing disparities in wealth and property. That Kafura surrendered his gun, Patson his bicycle, and Shappy the effective use of his grinding mill, all appeared to reaffirm a collective ideology. Yet, in fact, this affirmation was over minor issues, since these were the pragmatic struggles of individuals to gain access to what little property they could. During a man's lifetime his personal property was his own, and agnates could not claim it directly through the courts. Their sole recourse was to turn to the customary moral and religious order, the beliefs in the efficacy of ancestors and witches. In this way the customary religious ideology served the interests of the common folk.

The claims of agnates to an individual's personal property appear to be related to the type of property. It would seem that claims over less expensive movable items such as bicycles and shotguns are more easily resolved than are those made over costly items such as grinding mills. The expectations surrounding the two forms of property are different. A grinding mill is a costly investment from which the owner expects a regular cash income. It is a business and the owner an intrepreneur who may hire workers. Bicycles and shotguns are not of the same order of investment. They are more easily integrated into customary notions of property and, although they are the source of disputes, have less profound consequences for the social order. A business may have a more fundamental effect on the nature of social relationships and notions of property and labor than the ownership of a bicycle or a shotgun. Ancestor worship serves as an effective screen to obscure the changes produced by commercial activities.

The growing pattern of economic differentiation based upon the personal ownership of property and the payment of wages to persons treated as free labor was the main issue. The same religious ideology at the same time afforded major entrepreneurs the opportunity to pursue their commercial activities and to operate effectively as individuals. The rights of Kafura and Blue to their shops, bottle store, lumber business, petrol pump, and, after 1972, their commercial farms were never challenged by appeals to ancestors or by witchcraft accusation. Instead they were highly praised by kin, neighbors, and friends as upholding collective rights and conforming to "traditional" custom.

The late Professor Victor Turner observed for the Ndembu that "whenever our kind of western individualism crops up in Central Africa, the tribal religions wilt and perish in a surprising short time, and with them vanish the ritual systems" (Turner, 1968: 22). This was perhaps too hasty an assessment. Yombe customary religion is very much part of the ritual field, as are other religious forms. It is, however, the most pervasive, persuasive, and dominant. At times of crisis, both personal and public, Yombe turn to it. It has lost very few of its functions and it has also gained new ones. A wealthy man may hire a poor agnate and yet they stand as approximate equals within the ancestor cult.

In my opinion, based upon my interpretation of Yombe culture, Van Binsbergen has too easily reduced a complex and, for me, very messy world into a simple dichotomy, assigning primacy or determinancy to infrastructure. As the Yombe have defined themselves as "of culture," so they have made themselves and their ideas as of the impregnable and timeless order of things natural or given. In their technologically simple society, ideology is embedded in the very tools of everyday life. The axe, *mbavi,* for example, has appropriate uses in the domain of both swidden cultivation and commercial farming. The significance of the axe lies in the fact that it is used to domesticate nature, from clearing of land for habitation and cultivation to constructing houses for the living, ancestor shrines, and sealing of graves. The axe is of the man, his personal property, representing his rights in status, property, and women. It represents a man's social persona, and when he dies it is he who is buried. His body is left to rot in the ground and return to nature. His axe is carefully kept in the house and becomes lineage property with its own authority or powers. Once inherited, it is of the person and also of the collectivity, representing a cumulative intra- and intergeneration force. It is individual, yet corporate; it is material, yet of spirit; and it is autonomous, yet dependent. It is an expression of Yombe culture and ideology. Put simply, Yombe beliefs are themselves part of the process of production. From this perspective one may collapse the distinction between infrastructure and superstructure; ideas move men and men move ideas. They do so, however, within the context of history.

The Yombe religious ideology of the past may be suited to the uncertain social and economic conditions of the present. As part of one process of subsistence it may help to sustain it; the converse also applies, namely, that the subsistence process may help to sustain the religious ideology. The customary religious ideology, by obscuring the emergent properties and consequences of commercial hybrid-maize farming, may allow these properties to take root and expand. "Western individualism" may fluourish within the shadow of a corporate ideology. The line (or relationship) is a fine and precarious one, related to the state of the larger Zambian economic potential to maintain the requirements of small-scale farming of hybrid maize. The small farmer growing hybrid maize enters into a subordinate and dependent economic relationship with the state. The Yombe are aware of this and so they still very actively practice swidden millet cultivation and local maize *Dambo* cultivation. Each form of cultivation is part of a cultivator's agricultural strategy as he plays off the requirements of subsistence and social obligation against a cash income.

Yombe entrepreneurs did not have to use the ideology of a new religion to separate themselves from the claims of kin, neighbors, and friends, as was the case in the Zambian community studied by Norman Long. The most successful entrepreneurs and commercial farmers in Kapepa parish were the Jehovah's Witnesses who had removed themselves from the obligations to and the demands of their kin and relied upon each other (Long, 1968). The Yombe employed an alternative tactic of using the indigenous religious beliefs and practices; they were radical while appearing conservative.

Bates feels that a stratification model of rural politics applied to only a few areas in Zambia, since land is still abundant and in most cases has not been transformed into extensive commercial farms. It appears, however, that the Yombe are witnessing the beginning of this process of stratification, with a few men claiming more and more land and employing wage labor at an increasing rate. The development is only in a rudimentary stage, and certainly the prevailing ideology in the chiefdom is still one which emphasizes what Bates calls "communitarianism" (Bates, 1976: 275). He maintains that "communitarianism" is incongruent with rapid economic growth, and I admit that this would probably be the case if the principle were rigidly adhered to by everyone in the society. But no matter whether I agree, there has been a marked change in the overall agricultural production in Muyombe over the past twenty years. In 1961, sixty-four households sold 173 bags of local maize to the government cooperative. In 1981, seventy-nine households sold 1874 bags of hybrid maize and kept 1058 bags of local maize for domestic uses. The Yombe case illustrates that "communitarianism" need not be a hindrance to economic change, as long as it is an ideology accepted by the common folk, which permits their manipulation from above. This ideology of collectivism is inextricably intertwined with Yombe customary religious beliefs; universal fears of misfortune are in this case bound up with beliefs in witchcraft and the power of the ancestors, producing a conformity to an ideology which mediates the consciousness of the common folk of their position in the overall economic system by emphasizing conformity to the group.

It is important that I stress that the situation I have outlined here is not necessarily true for more than a moment in time, but I think that any understanding of the complex relationships between economy and ideology must begin with a close examination of small-scale societies such as this one, where change is in the making.

## REFERENCES

Barnett, Steve (1977). "Identity Choice and Caste Ideology in Contemporary South India," in Janet Dolgin, D. Kemnitz, and D. Schneider (Eds.), *Symbolic Anthropology*. New York: Columbia University Press.

Bates, Robert (1976). *Rural Responses to Industrialization*. New Haven: Yale University Press.

Bond, George (1972). "Kinship and Conflict in a Yombe Village." *Africa* 42, 4.

———— (1975). "Minor Prophets and Yombe Cultural Dynamics," in M. Owusu (Ed.), *Colonialism and Change,* The Hague: Mouton.

———— (1976). *The Politics of Change in a Zambian Community.* Chicago: Chicago University Press.

———— (1978). "Religious Co-existence in Northern Zambia: Intellectualism and Materialism in Yombe Belief." *New York Academy of Sciences,* 318.

———— (1979). "A Prophecy that Failed: The Lumpa Church of Uyombe," in G. Bond, W. Johnson, and S. Walker (Eds.), *African Christianity,* New York: Academic Press.

Cliffe, L. (1978). "Labour Migration and Peasant Differentiation: Zambia Experiences." *Journal of Peasant Studies* 5, 3.

Evans-Pritchard, E. E. (1970). Preface, in A. D. J. MacFarlane, *Witchcraft in Tudor and Stuart England.* New York: Harper Torch Book.

Fernandez, J. (1978). "African Religious Movements," in B. Siegel (Ed.), *Annual Review of Anthropology,* Vol. 7. Palto Alto: Annual Reviews Inc.

Fields, Karen (1982a). "Charismatic Religion as Popular Protest." *Theory and Society* 11, 3.

———— (1982b). "Political Contingencies of Witchcraft in Colonial Central Africa." *Revue Canadienne des Etudes Africaines.* 16, 3.

Fortes, M. (1949). *The Web of Kinship Among the Tallensi.* London: Oxford University Press.

Johnson, A., and G. Bond, (1974). "Kinship, Friendship and Exchange in Two Communities: A Comparative Analysis of Norms and Behavior." *Journal of Anthropological Research,* 30, 1.

Kuper, A. (1982). "Lineage Theory: A Critical Retrospective." *Annual Review of Anthropology,* Vol. 11. Palo Alto: Annual Reviews Inc., pp. 71–95.

Long, N. (1968). *Social Change and the Individual.* New York: Humanities Press.

Maine, Henry, (1946). *Ancient Law.* London: Oxford University Press.

Nadel, S. F. (1954). *Nupe Religion.* London: Routledge and Kegan Paul Ltd.

Peel, J. D. Y. (1980). "Inequality and Action: The Forms of Ijesha Social Conflict. *Canadian Journal of African Studies* 14, 3.

Post, Ken (1972). "Peasantization and Rural Political Movements in Western Africa. *Archives Europeanes de Sociologie* 13: 223–254.

Rappaport, R. A. (1967). *Pigs for the Ancestors.* New Haven: Yale University Press.

Richards, A. I. (1935). "A Modern Movement of Witch Finders." *Africa* 8.

Rude, George (1980). *Ideology and Popular Protest.* New York: Pantheon.

Turner, Victor (1968). *The Drums of Affliction.* Oxford: Oxford University Press.

———— (1974). *Dramas, Fields, and Metaphors.* Ithaca: Cornell University Press.

Van Binsbergen, W. (1976). "Religious Innovation and Political Conflict in Northern Zambia: A Contribution to the Interpretation of the Lumpa Rising," in *African Perspectives 1976/2.* Religious Innovation in Modern African Society, ed. S. Van Binsbergen and R. Buitenhuis. Leiden: Africa Studies Centrum.

———— (1981). *Religious Change in Zambia.* London: Kegan Paul International.

Vayda, P. (1967). "Foreword," in R. Rappaport, *Pigs for the Ancestors.* New Haven: Yale University Press.

Watson, W. (1958). *Tribal Cohesion in a Money Economy.* Manchester: Manchester University Press.

Weber, Max. (1947). *The Theory of Social and Economic Organization.* Glencoe, Ill.: The Free Press.

# PART IV

# The Consolidation of Power: Woman's Role in Political and Economic Transformations

Studies on the origin and development of "the state" have in recent years spawned a new growth industry, with students of the subjects as diverse as Theda Skocpol and Pierre Birnbaum producing works of exceptional insight. Kathleen Staudt joins their company with her "Women's Politics, the State, and Capitalist Transformation in Africa." Staudt brings the category of gender to bear on an understanding of the consolidation of power of African states and the development of capitalism. Although her focus is on Africa, her contentions, like those of the other studies in this volume, have broader theoretical significance. Her work helps specify the exact nature of the relationship between the political development of the state and the emergence of capitalism out of African material life.

She begins with a key fact: in precolonial, precapitalist Africa women were often full participants in an economy beyond the household and played significant roles in the political decision-making process. Although the position of women differed depending upon the exact nature of diverse traditional political systems, Staudt maintains that the significance of African women in general was so important that we cannot ignore it. However, that condition changed. Now we see African women dependent and subservient in every aspect of their existence, in secondary or insignificant economic roles, without political clout, in every way dominated by men, an "unnatural condition."

Staudt's explanation of the change is that the modern state has artificially divided society into public and private spheres, synonymous with separate worlds of men and women, extrahousehold and internal household matters. There is the world of those who control or protect property and are active participants in the modern state, and those whose domain is confined to "simple" household concerns. As men have gradually gained the right of political participation,

189

Staudt maintains, "women have become property, controlled and protected by men." She analyzes the moral and legal foundations of these developments, as well as the role of churches and schools in fostering a supporting ideology.

Staudt argues a subtle point. The colonial state in Africa, as elsewhere, did more than serve the interests of a newly emerging bourgeoisie; it was more than an instrument of the colonial ruling class, "more important, it created the very conditions necessary for capitalist transformation." Staudt reinforces the argument that when women's work was confined to the household, it was no longer defined as labor; it was considered without cost and, therefore, left unpaid. Women's labor thus served to subsidize men and capital. Women's labor literally created men and their ability to participate with their labor in the cash economy. At one time able to work in their own traditionally defined sphere of economic activities, increasingly women became reliant on men. The compensation of women at the lowest subsistance levels boosted the ability of early capitalism to engage in primitive surplus accumulation. Men, women, and children were organized into the family unit analyzed long ago by Engels, to create and sustain cheaply a male wage earner. Staudt shows how "gender ideology" honored men as "family breadwinners," and otherwise acknowledged their male authority over women as compensation.

Once begun, the gender distinction undercuts women's economic basis for self-sufficiency. This, in turn, makes it more difficult for women to gain the political power necessary to protect their economic interests, and the circle closes more tightly. When, at a later date, some women begin to reassert demands for greater rights, these demands generally take the form of what Staudt calls "domestic feminism," an effort to alleviate women's status within the home. She maintains that this type of demand merely reinforces the gender division and therefore perpetuates the gender gap because it does not directly address the underlying source of women's inequality. So deeply embedded in the fabric of the state are these discriminatory gender distinctions that the efforts of even the most committed socialist leaders in declared socialist states come to naught. Too frequently they amount to merely forensic appeals or are confounded by deeply rooted realities over which they have no control.

The studies by Anne Lippert on Algeria and Sonia Kruks on Mozambique back up Staudt's propositions. Staudt, like Lippert, acknowledges the obvious differences among women based on class position. She considers the interaction of sex and class in politics and maintains, nevertheless, that "women's politics are another dimension of class politics, wherein the political process is used to advance the interests of those already privileged." The "women's movement" must pay for its narrow focus on legal issues such as marriage, divorce, and family law, even though women view these issues with great concern.

During the Algerian struggle for independence, nationalist leaders had proudly proclaimed that women would occupy key positions in the new social structures, that Algerians would participate as equals in institutions designed for universal mass membership, and that both men's and women's consciousness would change to welcome these innovations. In her "Algerian Women's Access to Power: 1962–1084," Anne Lippert advises us that she understands perfectly well that women's access to education, wealth, economic position, political power, professional training, etc., will vary with social background and other positional aspects of class membership. Yet, like Kathleen Staudt, Ester Boseurp, and many others before her, she points out that gender is an independent variable in the sense that women, as a category, together suffer common impediments in postindependence Algerian society.

"Some Algerians, both men and women," have resisted progressive changes in the status of Algerian women since independence. They have feared major changes in the traditional family structure, infringement of traditional Islamic beliefs, and the diminution of religious commitments. The growing strength of the Islamic reformist renewal movement in Algeria today, part of a worldwide return to fundamentalist religious beliefs, obviously has affected original declarations of commitment to feminine equality. Large-scale unemployment, severe budgetary constraints, and the crippled economy caused by international recession have added pressure to maintain the traditional position of women in the home. The prospective return of a large male immigrant population from abroad, where they have been unable to find work and where they are increasingly resented by Europeans beset by their own problems of economic decline, further complicates the economic difficulties in Algeria. This, in turn, exacerbates the integration of women as full members of society.

What then has happened to the original commitment of that new Algerian state, which in 1962 so proudly declared that it would share power with all of the Algerian people, including the most wretched of the earth, women?

Almost a quarter of a century after that original commitment, Anne Lippert presents us with a balance sheet. Without either apology or animus, she attempts to assess what has happened to advance women's political and economic share in the "nation-building process." She documents progress in the advancement of women in many spheres, but she also shows how this "progress" was both slow and limited to only part of the population. "The dependency of the power structure" on an increasing conservative Islam is only part of the reason. From the beginning, she finds, significant Algerian male leaders were ambivalent towards the position of women in society even as, in the midst of the bloody struggle for independence, they called for the devoted commitment of all Algerians, men and women, to the battle against the French. They voiced their unease with the revolutionary role of women despite the publicity which, they admitted, helped gain international recognition for the legitimacy of the cause of Algerian independence. Lippert quotes Mohamed Khiter's retort that after independence the Algerian woman would return to her couscous.

She provides data for the hitherto unanswered questions about to what extent, and in what roles, women were actually involved in the Algerian Revolution. She informs us about the overall percentage of persons reporting involvement in revolutionary activities, and then subdivides those activities into clandestine and legal activities as well as into rural and urban areas. She tells us something about who provided support services and which women were involved in the decision-making structures of the revolution in Algeria and abroad. She lets us know something about the women who were killed and those who were imprisoned, as well as something of the power base of those few women who held high positions.

In this study Lippert analyses the long-awaited Family Code, finally approved by the National Assembly and promulgated on June 9, 1984. The government originally introduced the Family Code in 1981, but could not proceed with its formal adoption because of widespread opposition. She finds the declaration of the Family Code, which places the woman "in an obedient position to the husband," difficult to reconcile with Algerian ideological commitments to feminine equality. She is, however, much more sanguine that the right of every citizen to an education has been substantially implemented. She shows that the history of women's access to education is one of gradual but major improvement. The increases from 1954 to 1984 in the number of women students, she maintains, is nothing short of "phenomenal." The situation is less encouraging when it comes to Algerian women's access to work. Lippert demonstrates a growing acceptance by the Algerian population of the role of women in significant positions in teaching, health services, law, and the social sciences. Nevertheless, the commitment to equal pay regardless of sex has not been achieved, and the number of women in significant policy roles within the economy remains minor or nonexistent. Her final assessment is that women have enjoyed qualitative and quantitive improvements in status and their enjoyment of political rights since 1962, "although that progress can be qualified as minimal." She finds, however, that a basis now exists for greater expectations of improvement in the future. Whether or not we share Lippert's judgments, she has provided us the evidence to draw our own, perhaps less optimistic, conclusions. Her work, like that of Staudt, illuminates added difficulties new states have in the consolidation of power.

# CHAPTER 8

# Women's Politics, the State, and Capitalist Transformation in Africa

## Kathleen Staudt

[Regarding politics] "As for me, I am a woman, so I have 'no mouth' in it."

"From ancient time women have borne men, without women men are nowhere . . . You know too well that we, the women, shoulder the greater part of the problems in the community."

These two seemingly different comments from Ghanaian women[1] allow some basic questions to be raised about politics and the state. What is politics? Who defines what issues are on the political agenda? And how does the nature of the state expand or contract that agenda?

Africa is a world region in which women, whether producing and processing food, trading on both large and small scales, or carrying water and gathering firewood, visibly participate in a wider economy, beyond that of domestic household units. Moreover, Africa stands out above other world regions with its widespread female-solidarity organizations, suggesting women's vital and collective voice in the polity. However, the modern state has diminished women's voice and power.

The modern state artificially divides society into public and private spheres. The public sphere consists of extrahousehold affairs; the private sphere, internal household matters. This division of reality into public and private comes to parallel the male and female worlds, even though the indigenous precolonial reality did not always conform to that division.[2] Over time, the state, through its policies and systems of participation, *creates* that reality.

Historically, those who control or protect property and capital have comprised the modern state's active participants and decision makers. With the gradual extension of political participation to men or through male authorities, women have come under the control and protection of men. The moral and legal foundations of this state define men as authorities over and representatives of women and children. This penetrates the private sphere and profoundly affects male-female power relations within it.

At the turn of the century, the colonial state in Africa aimed to forge a new society, laying a moral and legal foundation for women to be part of a private sphere, controlled and protected by men. This foundation did more than simply serve a budding bourgeois class in the colony or the colonizer government; more important, it created the conditions deemed necessary for capitalist transformation. Women's labor, no longer defined as work, began to subsidize men and capital. Both to foster and enable men's participation in a cash economy, this transformation required that women work in the home, become economically dependent on men, and articulate consumer demands to stimulate the economy. Women's or gender issues, once part of the indigenous political agenda, were depoliticized and women as public actors disappeared. Early capitalism, initiating conditions whereby money attaches to valuation, cannot sustain widespread individual compensation at subsistence levels along with all the inequalities it generates. Instead, it requires one adult (a woman, and often her children) to provide the unpaid labor and income-substituting activities which maintain cheap wages for one family member, usually the man.

To give added thrust to these harsh economic realities was a gender ideology which portrayed men as "family breadwinners," whose responsibilities were to earn wages to support a family and pay the family or hut tax. As a further ideological incentive, men were symbolically compensated with authority over women for the loss of autonomy their incorporation into the state implied.[3] In a colonial context with its superiority-inferiority complex based on conformance to modern "civilization," the domestication of women became a "mark of civilization" for people to strive for.

The economic and ideological components of state-created public and private spheres meant that no policy and program supports were relevant, or even justified, for women, whatever their breadwinner or economic activities, because they were the responsibility of male breadwinners. State decision makers formulate policies and conduct politics with men in mind, or with the picture of reality in which men control and represent women. Once in place, the gender distinction undermines women's economic base and the political means to protect that base, thereby generating and perpetuating gender inequality.

Not surprising, women lack much interest in "official" politics and policies, which are seemingly irrelevant to them. A partial extension of the political agenda and of participation rights offsets this tendency somewhat. Women, as the last category to be incorporated into the chain of participants in the modern state, compete with the well endowed, politically experienced, and other late entrants. Moreover, the few women activists, often *among* the well endowed, voice concerns compatible with the modern state. Almost invariably, those activities reinforce and reproduce the power relations that the state protects. Even under socialism, the state has so deeply embedded public and private spheres which correspond with gender that real transformation of male-female reality is unlikely.

To support these arguments and illustrate their dynamics, I first characterize the political economy of women in indigenous sub-Saharan African societies and then examine more specifically how the colonial state molded a new reality of public-private dimensions. In particular, I analyze both British and mission education and training programs for women. Following that, I review how people responded to the state, focusing on women's politics in the nationalist and postindependence eras.

## THE INDIGENOUS POLITICAL ECONOMY OF WOMEN

Sub-Saharan African societies were in the past characterized by loose (if any) boundaries between public and private as the "modern" world now knows them. The domestic sphere covered more than single conjugal units and incorporated multigenerational compounds and lineages. Besides being active in household, food collection/production, crafts, and trade, women publicly participated in the political collectivity of prestate and non-Islamic societies. Women used their work and reproductive capacities to create public valuation of women. As an Asante proverb describes: "It's a woman who gave birth to a man; it's a woman who gave birth to a chief."[4] Women's many obligations gave them a certain autonomy, a pattern which lingers today with polygyny, large numbers of female-headed households, and spouses maintaining separate incomes.

Prestate West African societies had no public-private dichotomy which corresponded to gender. Since the domestic or private sphere was an integral part of the public sphere, "power, authority, and influence within the 'domestic sphere' was *de facto* power, authority and influence at certain levels within the public sphere."[5] Economic activities were as much a part of domestic as occupational roles. Kamene Okonjo discusses what she calls "dual-sex" political systems, which are defined as assigning specific roles to men and to women and granting women's full participation by right.[6] Still, political institutions could be segregated by sex. In her analyses of precolonial southern Nigeria, Nina Mba, for example, documents separate women's institutions among the Ibo and Igbo peoples and women's integration (albeit in minor proportional terms) into general councils among the Yoruba.[7] Either way, women's issues were profoundly politicized and central to the interests of the collectivity.

Women's political functions in prestate and community politics were rich in variety and broadly representative of all sub-Saharan Africa. In southeastern Nigeria, women's authority structures paralleled men's to function as women's courts, market authorities, and overseers of village welfare. Women managed their own affairs in kinship institutions, age grades, secret and title societies. In markets, women fixed prices, settled quarrels among traders, and imposed fines to enforce their will.[8] Ibo villages had women's councils at various territorial levels.[9] Among the Mende in Sierra Leone, women's secret societies, called *Bundu,* protected women's rights and served as political support bases and training grounds for women chiefs, such as for Madam Yoko of the Kpa Mende Confederacy.[10] In Cameroon, Bamileke female farmers belonged to the *Mensu,* a women's society composed of the best cultivators. The *Mandjon* was a group of important women who administered village work done by women, such as clearing paths.[11] Among the Kikuyu in Kenya, women's age-segmented organizations matched those of men's and performed a wide variety of functions, including judgment, mutual aid, initiation into womanhood, cooperative farm labor, religious ceremonies, and disciplinary action among women.[12]

The kingdoms of the central lakes region, southeastern Africa, and West Africa had formally defined female authorities such as Queen Mother, Queen, or other royal positions, some of which still continue today.[13] The *Ohemaa,* or female ruler, among the Akan in Ghana occupied the senior of two stools, a visible repository of political authority. She advised the chief and had jurisdiction over domestic matters and those of the royal family.[14] Elsewhere, women represented women's interests in the political system. Among the Yoruba, the *Iyalode*, a woman chief selected on the basis of her achievements (rather than birth), served as spokesperson for women and represented their interests in opening new markets and judging infractions. Disruption and interference with her trade were reasons why Efunsetan, a powerful *Iyalode* in Ibadin, was spokeswoman for the chiefs who opposed Latosa, an aggressive war chief.[15] The *Iyalode*, like the *Omu* among the Igbo, presided over a council and counselors whom she elected.[16] The Bamileke Fong's mother, regarded as the equivalent of a chief, presided over women's secret societies.[17] Still common in contemporary times are women's rotating credit societies, agricultural communal labor groups, and church and cultural associations.[18]

However prevalent women's participation, African societies were not unstratified by gender, class, or status.[19] Not all societies had women's associations or authority structures, and in rigidly stratified societies with titled female leaders, ordinary women were often excluded from politics. In the rich variety of African precolonial state societies, such as the Baganda, rulers recruited men to participate in large-scale social labor, such as corvée public works, conscription, or collective labor, in order to accumulate surpluses to maintain their states. Karen Sacks argues that such labor made men "adults" in society's eyes, thereby denying adulthood to women and defining them as wards of men.[20] Regardless of stratification patterns, the material accumulation of most African societies prior to colonialism limited the scope of existing resources, which were distributed unevenly (or evenly) by gender, class, and status. The colonial state hastened and aggravated this stratification, setting the stage for an expansion in the totality of resources to distribute unevenly, with men accumulating a disproportionate share of opportunities, wage employment, mobility, and credit.

## THE COLONIAL STATE: AN IMPOSITION OF PUBLIC-PRIVATE DISTINCTIONS

With the imposition of European colonialism in Africa, groundwork was laid to conceive of work, its value and reward in ways already present in the highly differentiated and sex-segregated industrializing world. The best and the brightest of administrators selected for the colonial service were products of late-Victorian middle-class society in which women preserved the home refuge for men, who in turn insulated women from the pressures of public life.[21] In this ideological model, men are the family breadwinners and men's work in the wage economy or in commercializing agriculture is viewed as necessary for "modernization."[22] Policies were thereby established to pressure men to enter the wage economy through taxation, to train men for a commercial economy and civil service, to put property in men's names through land reform, and to subsidize men's farming through credit and extension.

While women remained active participants in economic production, that production was not valued with rewards in the same way as other (wage) work. With the spread of market economic systems, labor was redefined "so as to make it virtually synonymous with work for which cash or other forms of remuneration were paid."[23] Other productive activities, once recognized as work, eventually were regarded as not quite "economic."

A general obliviousness to women's indigenous political authority eliminated women's political agenda and women as political actors. Old Ashanti men and women in Ghana responded to an historian's query about women in the formal state hierarchy as follows:

> The white man never asked us this; you have dealings with and recognize only men, we supposed the Europeans considered women of no account and we know you do not recognize them as we have always done.[24]

Once a moral and legal foundation of male authority was established, women were defined out of policy and political reality. State formation had high costs,[25] among which was included women's loss of rights in nonstate spheres. Former female-managed political responsibilities (such as judicial functions) were removed from their hands to be replaced with the now male-controlled administration, male-run Native Courts, or the private market, in which women participated but in increasingly marginal ways. Moreover, as Achola Pala points out, the imposition of a head or hut tax under colonialism established wives as financial liabilities of husbands.[26] The colonial state laid the foundation for societies to conform with its cultural notions of appropriate gender relations in industrializing class society, in which women enable and stimulate male work force productivity through home labor (which in Africa includes food production and water and fuel collection) and consumer demand as well as serve as a low-skill reserve labor force. In this conception, women are also politically conservative and thus help maintain a given political order.

## "Civilizing" Home Labor

The state delegated some of this newly conceptualized private sphere to the Christian missionaries, whose ideology and activities also prescribed an extreme dichotomization of gender along the lines of antiquated Victorian norms. While in theory British indirect-rule philosophy had "no intention of using public authority to impose standards of European society," its deferral of education to the missions had very profound impacts on families and private lives.[27] Early colonial governments put little or no energy into public education, especially for girls, but they did support and cooperate with mission education. As late as the 1950s, mission stations still controlled 80 to 90 percent of schools, with supplementary government grants-in-aid provided.[28] Christian missions, as custodians of morality extending into all areas of life, considered family life the legitimate object of social intervention, given its role in inculcating values, socializing children, and the like. The missions established home and marriage training programs for African women, which provided resilient models for later governmental "development" efforts. "Modern" standards were set, which men and women used to evaluate themselves and each other. Those among the earliest exposed to education, missions, and social policy augmented a privileged class which emulated and internalized these standards. In this standard, women are helpmates, appendages, and financial dependents on men as well as moral guardians of the home, family, and children.

Early female education was justified on the grounds of providing "special education in various forms of domestic life" and "civilized homes and helpmates" for educated Chrisitan men.[29] The initial volumes of the *International Review of Missions,* a quarterly journal begun in 1912, contained descriptions of special work among women and a regular section which was called "The Ideal of Womanhood as a Factor in Missionary Work." An example among the Kongo spells out the gender-distinct forms of education:

> Our youths [men?] are being trained in industrial arts and our girls to use their hands, make their own clothes and above all to be purer wives and better mothers.[30]

The British colonial historian Lord Hailey stated that there were "few mission stations where some girls or women are not receiving a valuable if limited training in the domestic sciences."[31]

The lasting effects of the male-head/female-helpmate model turn into a "community property" ideology. Whatever the good intentions of the philosophy that family life is corporate, harmonious, and without separate economic interests, when implanted upon a society that respected separate female property, "various categories of property are merged" and "the husband assumes the dominant role in controlling everything." Young Westernized Christian Nandi take this position.[32]

Also promoting gender-distinct education was the Phelps-Stokes Fund, which sponsored two commissions to African countries to introduce the experience of practical industrial education for blacks in the American South. A central notion of industrial education was that it be adapted to what became educator-defined "needs of the people." A commission report recommended more schools for girls, including instruction

> for the special needs of the young women. These schools will necessarily be concerned first of all with the preparation of food; second, with household comforts; third, with the care and feeding of children, and the occupations that are suited to the interests and ability of women.[33]

While technical education was promoted for all, women's technical education was a special type: "The chemistry of cooking or the art of needlework afford efficient media for education."[34] An aftermath of the commissions, the Jeanes Schools, established in various colonies during the 1920s and 1930s, saw the ennoblement of home and motherhood as key components in elevating women's status and civilization itself; "home development" was the "mark of civilization," and woman "personifies home influence as no other member of society can."[35]

Women's work in agriculture was recognized in the works of colonial historians, outside education commissions, and mission journals. Yet officials persistently refused to recognize the reality or legitimacy of alternative women's activities and then to provide policy and program support to farmers who were women. Rather, the ever-present sewing, needlework, and cooking programs institutionalized household tasks as women's responsibilities and thereby extended domesticity without providing women with support to transform their subsistence farm work in the commercialized economic context. Lord Hailey remarked on the difficulty "converting people to agricultural practices where established custom regards it as proper for women."[36] Women, evidently, were not people. Meanwhile, the church and state sometimes worked together to subsidize men's commercial farming, such as in Northern Rhodesia.[37]

Beginning in the early 1940s, the colonial state increased attention to social policy as a result of changes in the international arena, the growth of African nationalism, and Colonial Development and Welfare Act funding. "Mass education" and "community development" became the buzzwords of the time, and new journals with this developmental ideology disseminated social program models. A focus both on the "masses" and on "communities" necessarily integrated women more fully into administrative activity, on somewhat different but still familiar domestic terms.

Various articles and conference reports commented on the "neglected" but "vital role of women" in community development.[38] Still, training programs of the early 1950s gave priority to domesticity for women. Missionaries described a rigidly disciplined girls' boarding school which adopted girls to "a more highly developed life, more closely conformed to modern ways" in three training stages. In stage one, girls live in dwellings which resemble those of the village; in the next, they go into more modern buildings where "they learn to cook on a stove and to keep the house clean and pleasant"; and in the last years,

> which are devoted entirely to domestic training and child welfare, the senior girls live in approximately the same conditions as students in a European domestic-economy school. The principle adopted in this boarding school, a principle, none the less, which has been much debated, is *to take the little girls between six and eight years of age and to keep them, without ever letting them go home, until they marry.*[39] (emphasis added)

Supplementing the individualistic approach to increase women's domestic skills were group strategies which, besides reflecting a community development mass approach, were administratively cost-effective, given the volunteering upon which implementation was based. In the homecraft movement, women were trained to set up clubs to teach cooking, child care, hygiene, sewing, and mending. In a Ugandan school, girls were also taught English besides cooking, sewing, and needlework.

> They need to know enough [English] to be able to follow printed instructions in books on domestic subjects: to use a recipe, to act on instructions about laundry, to make cushions, curtain covers, etc., to use paper patterns and to understand simple books in the simple level of domestic interests with English women whom they meet.[40]

Secondary schools even today contain a "hidden curriculum" to prepare girls primarily for marriage with classes in housecraft.[41]

Although shrouded by domesticity, some programs addressed women farmers. Belated as it was, colonial officials must have recognized that women's food production enabled widespread male out-migration for wage employment and eliminated the need for a "family wage" to be paid to men (however much this contradicted the ideology promulgated). Moreover, mission schools, Jeanes Schools, and nongovernmental organizations like Girl Guides and the YWCA trained women in leadership and social work and provided arenas in which women could interact and share experiences. In Kenya, these experiences produced the first generation of national women's leaders whose ideology, however, was formed by the gender confines pervading education.[42]

## Female Consumerism

The public-private distinction conceptualizes women as consumers who moti-
vate men. A colonial official in Kenya described a deliberate policy "to create
competition and jealousy," to spur men's productivity:

> She must be educated to want a better home, better furnishings, better food, better
> water supplies, etc. and if she wants them she will want them for her children. In
> short, the sustained effort from the male will only come when the woman is educated
> to the stage when her wants are never satisfied.[43]

Occupational training matched not only the sex-segregation of the industrialized world, but also the conception of women as secondary compared to
men primary earners. A proposal in Northern Rhodesia (now Zambia) called
for females to be educated as "children's nurses" and "girl domestic servants."
The "Chambers of Mines and Commerce have already forseen the latter as a
means of releasing further supplies of African male labor to industry."[44] (In
contrast to other world regions, men often work as domestic servants in Africa.)

## Women as Political Stabilizers

In a public-private world, women maintain the established political order. Here,
the colonial model collided with women's indigenous political institutions and
authority, invisible except in periods of crisis.

Among famous incidents associated with colonial misperceptions about
women's power were what women called the Women's War in Aba of depres-
sion-era Nigeria. In response to rumors that Native Authorities would impose
new taxes, women utilized their traditional political institutions, *mikiri* (meeting), to mobilize women. *Mikiri* had always provided a forum for women to
discuss their interests as traders, farmers, wives, and mothers; their most important functions involved promoting and regulating women's major activity,
trading. Women's main weapons included "sitting on a man" (or a woman),
boycotts, and strikes; "to sit on" meant gathering at a compound, dancing, and
singing scurrilous songs detailing grievances. In 1929, women used these
mechanisms against Native Authorities and demonstrated in what official documents termed "mobs," "operating in a state of frenzy," stamping, making
noise, and destroying offenders' huts.[45] In Pare District, Tanzania, during the
1940s, women participated in tax riots against Native Authorities. Following
men's inability to influence the situation, women mobilized themselves to stone
officials, after which authorities perceived the situation as taking on "new and
uncontrollable dimensions." The graduated-tax idea was dropped the following
year.[46] The most thorough study of women's political history in southern Nigeria documents constant and continuing protest activity among women against
fixed produce prices, water fees, produce inspection, taxes on women, and the
loss of communal land.[47]

During the nationalist-inspired guerrilla movement (labeled Mau Mau) in
Kenya, outreach to women (due to what was termed "the innate conservatism
of the female sex") was advocated to put a brake on "extremist" husbands.
The government-initiated Maendeleo ya Wanawake women's group was associated with government rehabilitation efforts, and at a 1955 conference en-

titled "African Women in the Development of Kenya," the commissioner for community development and rehabilitation, T. G. Ashwith, stated that

> . . . this movement is doing a tremendous amount to overcome Mau Mau. The clubs in the Emergency areas are providing rallying points for women who are opposed to Mau Mau. . . . This is not just tea and buns. We are doing something of great practical value.[48]

Remarkable about this effort, however, was colonial officials' clinging to their gender ideology, however much at odds it was with indigenous reality:

> I cannot resist the idea that if the Kikuyu wives had really been in the know and consulted from the beginning on the Mau Mau movement (*I know this is speculation and that there are many women now in the movement*) there would have been no Mau Mau.[49] (emphasis added)

A wide variety of mission and development programs laid the foundation for a society that was divided into public and private, at one and the same with men and women. The private world was penetrated in ways which institutionalized household tasks as women's responsibilities and all else as men's, thereby justifying and perpetuating the neglect of women in other public policies.

Attention to the overarching conception of the state, particularly the colonial state, diffused as it was by force, should not divert analysts from attempting to understand the ways in which indigenous peoples received, maneuvered, and accommodated themselves to the new institutions in which they were ensnared. Intricate patterns of domination and subordination fed into colonial state formation.

## Reaction and Consolidation

Recent studies of African law have analyzed the creation and transformation of "customary law," a "blend of tradition and wishful thinking," that occurred as those consulted, male elders, responded to the contemporary threats posed by temporarily loosened control over women.[50] Martin Chanock, writing on then Northern Rhodesian, now Zambian, case law, shows how customary law— the most effective means by which men exerted power in Native Courts under colonialism—was contrived and used to reestablish control over women in what he calls an alliance between African men and colonial rulers.[51] Marcia Wright, too, analyzing cases in a magistrate's court in a nearby area around the turn of the century, found "no issue more sensitive than the control of women," as changed economic opportunities opened new alternatives and demand for women.[52] Women could play one legal system off the other, which historians have periodized as what occurred under state *formation*.[53] As state control was *consolidated* in the 1930s, a period analyzed in western Kenya, societies in which neither men nor women "owned" land were transformed into societies in which landownership became a male right. Jean Hay, with Gordon Wilson, attributes this to "conservative backlash from Luo men, and from male elders in particular, and their desires to re-establish control over women." Before 1945, a combination of land surplus and labor shortage eased women's ability to negotiate for themselves, to evade lineage controls over how they disposed of their goods, and to return to their homesteads of birth if marriages proved unsatisfactory.[54] The nationalist period signaled another shift.

## WOMEN'S POLITICS: NATIONALIST AND POSTINDEPENDENCE ERAS

Nationalist movements, by their very nature, focus on the struggle for independence, rather than on class or gender interests. Women participated in nationalist movements, the outcomes of which, however, were grounded in a continuation of the modern state with its now established public-private distinctions. Women, differentially incorporated into the state and divided among themselves, begin to articulate very different kinds of demands. Many are alienated from politics and withdraw from or reject this redefined political order to the greatest extent possible. The rest perpetuate a public-private distinction, either as members of a privileged class articulating interests that benefit that class, or as those controlled or co-opted in authoritarian politics.

### Nationalism and Depoliticized Women's Issues

Nationalist movements drew initially from the educated, urbanized World War II veterans and from the wage-earning populace, most of whom were men. As mobilization extended in the 1950s, women became active participants, both in protest activity and in guerrilla movements. African nationalist leaders such as Modiko Keita (Mali) and Sekou Touré (Guinea) publicly praised women's participation in militant action. Touré even exhorted women to deny sex to husbands unless they joined the party. Women collaborated in the famous Guinea 1953 strike which weakened the French colonial government. Women traders refused to sell chickens, eggs, and milk to the French; they, and peasant women, collected rice for the strikers. Ghanaian women were actively involved in the nationalist struggle, providing financial support and organizing trade boycotts. Madame Quezzin Coulibay (Ivory Coast) mobilized Abidjan women to invade prisons where party members were jailed at 3 A.M., surprising guards; a jolted government released party leaders two days later.[55] Women also were active in guerrilla movements in both support and military functions from Algeria, Guinea-Bissau, Mozambique, Zimbabwe, and Angola to Kenya.

The Sudanese women's movement of 1946–1974 started simultaneously with the nationalist movement and Communist Party. The Sudanese Women's Union, successor to the earlier Women's League, published a magazine and articulated goals which could be accommodated by the state, such as equal pay for equal work, extended maternity leaves, and secular as opposed to Islamic divorce laws. Called "prostitutes" by conservative forces after independence, the Women's Union faced a rival group of "reactionary women, hastily organized," and soon experienced demise. Growing once again after the 1964 revolution, the Union saw government responsiveness to measures for which they had pressed. When the Communist Party fell out of favor with the Nimieri regime, however, the Union was abolished. Thereafter, the Sudanese Socialist Union established a Women's Affairs Committee.[56]

Who benefits from the kinds of measures women advocated? Equal pay and maternity leave for work in *wage* labor exclude the overwhelming majority of ordinary women workers. Elsewhere on the continent there is a dismal regularity to this cycle of narrow goals that serve select interests and that result in political vulnerability and the replacement of leadership.

The implantation of male government under colonialism, its continuation, and the simultaneous depoliticization of most women's issues to the private sphere became institutionalized at independence and thereafter. Former women's issues disappeared from the public or political agenda. Women's agricultural and trade activities where neither viewed as economic nor measured in national statistics, the indicators for which were developed in states with longstanding gender dichotomies.

Deprived of public resources to build on and extend their economic base in this commercialized economy, or deprived of even the "need" for those resources given the prevailing gender ideology, the resource gaps between men and women became aggravated. Any and all studies which examine the comparative male-female distribution of agricultural services, from Ghana and Senegal to Tanzania, Kenya, and Botswana, find that women get less extension, training, and credit than men. Such distribution patterns are bound to reduce women's comparative productivity.[57] Yet these phenomena are not viewed as "political."

## Women's Politics as Class Politics

While women share commonalities from their reproductive capacities, the overall sexual division of labor, and the state conception of women, there are obvious differences among women based on their class position and resulting differences in opportunities and lifestyles.[58] Women have not been universally disadvantaged, thus suggesting the importance of sex and class interaction in politics. Given the near universal advantage of those with more education, money, and land in politics, women with those resources are politically advantaged and can acquire skills appropriate in given regimes along with a sense of "winnable" political goals. That very winnability narrows the political agenda to demands compatible with the conception of women that the regime can accommodate. Moreover, very rarely do women activists in conventional politics articulate genuinely redistributive issues. Rather, their issues benefit themselves in a particular class. Thus, despite the appearance of pluralism, women's politics is another dimension of class politics, wherein the political process is used to advance the interests of those already privileged.

A narrow focus on legal issues, specifically marriage and divorce law reform, has taken up much of women's political energy. And again, questions must be raised about who would use and benefit from those reforms. The National Council of Ghanaian women focused consistently on marriage law reform, but after years of parliamentary debate, bills were finally tabled.[59] The Ugandan Council of Women also dwelt on marriage and divorce laws.[60] While the Kenya (now independent) Maendeleo ya Wanawake national women's organization expressed public concerns over a wide range of issues such as female deference to men, male authority, and rural women's extensive labor burdens, group political activities addressed marriage and divorce law reform and the Affiliation Act, which, before being abolished by an all-male assembly, offered unmarried mothers and offspring financial support. The wider issues and concerns, however, were tinged with the gender ideology of colonialism and built on an idealized conception of womanhood:

European women had for years condemned the everyday drudgery they saw locally. . . . It is not the onus of physical labour that evokes the greatest outcry but the norms of deference. Much of the criticism of work was made not on medical grounds but for its symbolic importance—women being treated as 'beasts of burden.' . . . The Swahili term of respect for a European woman, 'memsahib,' should be extended in its use [to] African women.[61]

Women's persistent, if ineffective, demands for legal change in family law were consistent with the conception of the state. While not denying the fundamental importance of equitable legal foundations, such goals would neither transform gender realities nor affect the mass of ordinary women.

The spokeswomen who represent organizations in conventional politics absorbed an ideology of public-private that reinforced values associated with capitalist transformation. The president of Maendeleo ya Wanawake stated during International Women's Year that a "woman's place is in the home" and that a woman "should lay more stress on her domestic role." Like the individualism and symbolic affirmations of equality expressed in the Kenyan media, she lays responsibility for sex disparities in individual women's hands, who by "working harder" and proving they "can work as hard as men" can "go forward."[62]

Besides reinforcing the public-private distinctions, women activists who ostensibly represent women's interests may pursue policies that benefit their own class. Local elite women in western Kenyan community politics requested a women's center during an electoral campaign. In the past, women's centers were associated with sewing clubs, in which those elite women participated at five times the rate of ordinary women and absorbed therefrom the associated gender ideology. The ensuing sewing and knitting programs were both irrelevant and time-consuming for the majority of women farmers. A special marketing arrangement for selling vegetables to the distant township through the externally funded cooperative was known only to the elite women. In the distribution of agricultural extension training and credit, wealthy women farm managers benefited in ways similar to corresponding men farm managers, thus obscuring the uneven gender distribution issues among the rest. Should the wealthier women take up this redistributive issue in Kenya's zero-sum politics, more for other women would mean less for themselves. Their economic stakes lie more in their households than in solidarity with other women.[63]

Elsewhere, the promotion of nursery schools has been called "prestige politics." These usually fee-based nursery schools, although subsidized by the government, are only affordable to the already well-off.[64]

## State Construction of Demands

The now established state and the economy it has nurtured either cannot or refuses to cope with comprehensive gender issues. As everywhere, the state itself plays a vital role in structuring people's demands in ways that benefit the power relations on which it is based. Even if women do not actively seek to focus on family law and welfare issues, the institutions with which they interact virtually compel them to do so. In program terms, home economics and community development activities such as handicraft training dominate government orientations toward women. Home economics, part and parcel of ministries of agriculture, is a separatist approach to women and ordinarily considered a "social" policy outside economic and development priorities.

Contemporary states have established women's bureaus and women's ministries in government to initiate special programs for women and/or to monitor existing programs. The United Nations has long advocated the creation of what it terms "women's machinery," a practice which expanded after the U.N. International Women's Year Conference in 1975. While these kinds of changes coincide with a gender ideology which focuses more on women's wage labor and political participation and thus holds the promise for more comprehensive women's issues, governments respond largely in terms of welfare, now nearly etched in stone with decades of policy and program precedents, or let programs shrivel for lack of budgetary commitment. Bureau advocates face a bureaucratic elite which absorbed and internalized the notion of women as domestic helpmates and guardians of the home. As James Brain concludes in an analysis of women in seemingly progressive Ujamaa villages of Tanzania:

> the sentiments of relatively uneducated and unsophisticated men settlers were far more in accord with the views of President Nyerere regarding justice for women than were those of the ruling elite, who in rejecting colonial rule have nevertheless retained attitudes about appropriate sex roles not very different from those found in bourgeois Victorian England.[65]

And meanwhile, governments have contained within manageable terms energized political women who are seeking to expand the political agenda.

Structurally, most women's bureaus, women's ministries, and advisory committees are attached to social or welfare ministries of low priority and low budgetary resources. Oki Ooko-Ombaka concludes, in a U.N. study which analyzes the effectiveness of this "national machinery" for women based on questionnaires responses from seventy-nine countries (including Africa), that women are "still a marginal consideration in development strategies."[66]

## Political Marginality and Women's Political Withdrawal

On the whole, women face a political system whose agenda they neither control nor influence systematically. With the historical legacies of their issues (becoming nonissues) and their minute representation in the largely male activist pool, women's politics is fairly ineffectual. Women activists play pluralist politics but often lose pluralist political games, being late joiners, voicing social issues not seen as economic, or threatening male interests. Women's political marginality in various kinds of regimes is illustrated in the following examples.

Abidjan women traders unsuccessfully utilized various strategies to reduce market rental fees, including delegations and fund-raising to facilitate entree with officials. Past support women gave to the mayor, party, and president was forgotten.[67] Women beer brewers in Nairobi, while successful in securing some household units for women in a relocation project, piped water for their community, and delays in slum unit demolishment, have no access to formal jobs and education and face constant police harassment and consequent insecurity at the margin of survival.[68] Still, there is some evidence of women voting the interests of their specific occupations interests, such as women traders, breadbakers, butchers, and fishmongers in Ghana.[69] However important franchise rights, voting does little to expand political agendas or control officials in between elections or when there are no elections.

Women fare no better in corporatist or authoritarian regimes, which absorb women (and sometimes dismiss them at whim) or accommodate them in minimal ways. To centralize voluntary associations and subordinate them to the ruling party, Nkrumah replaced the Federation of Ghana Women (thought to support the opposition) with the National Council of Ghana Women. Political parties following Nkrumah have also had women's party wings, but they are little more than paper organizations during elections.[70] In Zambia, the urban party's Women's Brigade polices markets in order to end "profiteering" among petty traders.[71] The women's party wing in Mali cannot support a women's issue that the party does not support, according to women's party officials.[72] The National Congress of Sierra Leone Women, the women's wing of the All Peoples Congress, supposedly links women's issues to party policy formation. Women members recruit others and serve general party needs. During an attempted coup, women challenged soldiers; they also created a women's militia to protect the prime minister after an attempted assassination. The mostly middle- and low-income petty trader members receive questionable returns, although they pay entry and monthly fees. Filomina Chioma Steady says the following vegetable seller's account is typical.

> She feels that she has to appear in favor of the government and join Congress or else they would be thrown out of their one-room apartment and her husband would be thrown out of his job. . . . She finds being a member financially impoverishing. . . . She is a member of Congress because all the people in her yard are APC supporters.[73]

Still, women are, on occasion, partially victorious. Women cassava traders in eastern Zaire acted on their strong feelings of exploitation when they successfully protested no less than three separate tolls that local authorities required they pay for apparent private gain. Women's actions were quite extraordinary, considering the absence of indigenous female authority. Terms of trade continue to marginalize women, however.[74]

While socialist regimes expand the public agenda somewhat to involve women by including women's issues, much of the private sphere remains ignored, cost-effective as that still is for a fledgling economy. Moreover, women's labor obligations in the public sphere appear to increase. Under the collectivization policy in Mozambique, for example, about 10 percent of the population worked in communal villages and producer cooperatives. Women were encouraged to participate in production, and in villages with what have been termed "correct political orientations," they were remunerated directly for their labor. (Presumably, husbands appropriate the value of their wives' labor in villages with "incorrect political orientations.") But domestic work and food production remained unremunerated. Although the government party promotes women's political participation and reserves one of seven leadership positions for a woman, she represents the women's party wing and is thereby relegated to party-defined women's issues such as mobilizing women and fund-raising for crèches and orphanages.[75] Still, a partial extension of public into private spheres exists in party aims to socialize child care.

However limited or ineffectual women's politics, women's more common response is to withdraw from conventional politics into more autonomous management of their own affairs to the extent this is still possible with an ever expanding state. In Ghana, women are largely indifferent to conventional politics, while active in their own economic associations. When queried, women claim no concern with politics, as revealed in the opening quote for this article:

"As for me, I am a woman, so I have 'no mouth' in it." In exchange, women want no interference from men or government.[76] Elsewhere, the elaborately organized market women of Lagos exert little pressure on government outside of protests against blatant corruption and political incompetence, even for better market services.[77] Enormous gaps between men and women in voting participation, and considerable gaps in organizational participation researchers deemed "political," have been discovered in Nigeria.[78]

How is this great divergence between elaborate female-solidarity organizations in indigenous polities and limited participation in official politics explained? To paraphrase Jane Jaquette, women may find conventional politics for negotiable women's issues to be irrelevant to their needs. Women are alienated from the process and, to a lesser degree, from the goals of politics.[79]

With the prevailing public-private distinctions, women's issues are not conceptualized as political, thus rendering politics of little use to them. As the following example reveals, the Tanzanian national women's organization is unable or unwilling to articulate the real politics of gender in conventional politics. The party women's wing is involved primarily in day care, maternal and child health issues, and, more minimally, in economic activities such as cooperatives. In contrast to these priorities, women analyzed their situation in a participatory project, using Freire-like consciousness-raising techniques, as follows:

> Women do not work as hard as the men. They work harder. When we go to the field, he sits under a tree telling me where to cultivate and then complains when the work is not done quickly enough.

> Why is it that men leave us to carry all the baggage? I go to the field with a hoe on my shoulder and a child on my back. He carries nothing. Then I return with the hoe, the child and a huge container of water on my head. Still he carries no part of the load.

> The money is spent on drinking, not on us or on the children. We share the work, or do more of it, but he takes all the money telling us it is his—that he earned it. It is a joke.

Here, colonialism, capitalism, and the state have aggravated indigenous gender subordination. Neither the women's wing nor women in development activities support programs to question or transform a "gender system in which men control the lives of wives and children but are not economically responsible for them."[80]

With both their marginality in conventional politics and the depoliticization of their issues, it is not surprising that many women withdraw or are alienated from contemporary politics, preferring instead to manage what is left of their own affairs autonomously. While the ability to remain autonomous suggests the still limited power of the state, women's autonomy also magnifies gender participation gaps in conventional politics and thus women's continued marginality in those politics.

## CONCLUSIONS AND IMPLICATIONS

Public-private distinctions are social creations which seemingly create the proper setting for capitalist transformation and the long-term interests it serves. Much of precolonial Africa, while gender stratified, had no such distinctions. As such, gender issues were political issues, reflected in organizations and authority structures, and both relevant and central to society. The colonial state actively created gender distinctions, however much they diverged from indigenous reality. In so doing, men became the public actors, both economic and political, and women, the private, apolitical guardians of the household. The dichotomy was a hierarchical one, allocating to men greater social valuation, and to women, subordination.

After decades, this ideology gradually penetrated educational institutions, law, policies, and government programs, thus making its way into people's consciousness and political participants' agendas. While the notion of public itself extended somewhat into the private sphere through social policy, both the state and politically active women negotiated demands compatible with the public-private distinction, thus reinforcing that distinction. As one of many competitors in the political process now, women face overwhelming odds against further extending the political agenda and women within it. Besides, women's politics, like other politics, is dominated by class interests which perpetuate a political agenda inimical to comprehensive gender redistribution. Periodically, however, women rise to assaults against their interests and reveal either visions of indigenous female institutions or the severe affronts to their sense of justice. Such activities prompt curiosity, too, about just how deeply the public-private ideology has penetrated or how long it will take to incorporate all women.

In this article, the state is viewed as a relatively autonomous actor, forging gender identities and institutionalizing them in law and policy. The processes synthesized here raise questions about whether the state can ever accommodate women's comprehensive gender concerns, or whether women can transform this edifice responsible for undermining their economic and political activities. Reformers seek redress from the state, but can the contemporary state, which undermined women's centrality to politics, be part of the solution for women? Many women remain aloof from politics, preferring autonomy or resisting incorporation, however much the state envelops them ultimately.

States, however, may be forever with us. While superficially beneficial to men's or capital's interests on a short-term basis, policies which buttress male authority for ideological reasons, relieve the state of distributing resources to women, or use women's backs to supply cheap food, water, and fuel collection create long-term outcomes that are ominous for development transformation, whatever the economic system. Once recognized, perhaps state foundations will shift away from their gender distinctions and the power relations they protect. What emerges as the new subordinate category in this inherently hierarchical edifice, nonetheless, remains an open question.

# CHAPTER 9

# Algerian Women's Access to Power: 1962–1985

## Anne Lippert

One of the basic promises of the new Algerian state was its commitment to share power with all segments of the Algerian people. Twenty-three years after independence this goal has not been fully realized due to the interaction between the state and its constituent elements. At independence, Algeria inherited a society of conflicting allegiances based upon ethnic and familial affiliations, alliances formed during the struggle for independence, class, and gender distinctions. Although a tenuous unity had been achieved by the FLN (the Front de Libération Nationale) through the course of fighting the French, culminating in a generalized desire of most of the Algerian people for independence from France, this was a fragile unity wherein competing factions had been either neutralized or subordinated, but not exterminated.[1] Thus postindependence Algerian society has been one in which segments of the society have counterbalanced, or been used to counterbalance, conflicting forces for state unity. One segment which has received particular attention in this regard has been that of Algerian women.

Since 1962, the date of independence, there has been increased prominence of Algerian women in the structures of the state (schools; party, through UNFA; industry), but despite periodic efforts of Algerian state leaders to forward women's political and economic share of the nation-building process, real advances by women in many sectors have been largely minimal. The slowness of progress can be attributed in part to the dependency of the power structure on religion (Islam) as a unifying and necessary prop for its legitimacy and the growing conservative nature of Islam in Algeria today as elsewhere in the Moslem world. It can also be attributed to an ambivalent commitment to this goal by some Algerian male leaders and by the slowness of the society to change certain values. This paper will be an examination of these phenomena.

In discussing the role of women in Algeria, that is, the development of their status, rights, and political participation since 1962, it is necessary to emphasize that women as such do not constitute a "class" in Algeria. Further, officially, classes do not exist in Algeria. Yet to the outside observer there are indeed classes, including the ruling bourgeoisie, the petite bourgeoisie (including intellectuals and professionals), and the working class (both urban working class and rural agricultural workers).[2] Women belong to classes. For example, it is likely that more daughters of the ruling bourgeoisie and the petite bourgeoisie will go to school and remain there for a longer period of time than the daughters of the rural working class. However, the problems of women's status, rights, and political participation go beyond class boundaries. This analysis will focus on the problems of women as women and will analyze some of the political, religious, economic, and historical factors which have inhibited the full acceptance of women into society as equal members.

The resistance of some Algerians, both men and women, to a change in status for the Algerian woman, which would in turn mean major changes in the traditional family structure of Algeria, is responsible in part for the slowness in implementing programs to incorporate women into the power structure. (What is meant by "the power structure" are those positions in the state where actual power is wielded, that is, where goals for the society are established and the attainment of those goals monitored.) Aside from Algerian Islamic family traditions, resistance to changes in the status and roles of women derives from a variety of factors, French use of the issue of women's emancipation as a propaganda device during the war for independence and growth in the strength of the Islamic reformist renewal movement in Algeria today being two of these. The issue is further complicated by the problem of unemployment in a society that has a large male immigrant population abroad because of lack of work in Algeria itself, and which may soon see a reintegration of part of this overseas population due to economic problems in France.

## ALGERIAN WOMEN, THE WAR FOR INDEPENDENCE AND EXPECTATIONS OF POWER SHARING

The first question that must be asked in looking at the anticipation of increased power sharing for women in the Algerian state following independence is where this expectation originated. In answer, one can say that state documents from the Charter of Tripoli, 1962, to the Charter of Algiers, 1965, to the National Charter, 1976, all included as a major goal of the state, women's necessary and full participation in that state. Whether this goal was more rhetorical than attainable, some women who actively participated in the war for independence had hoped to take part in nation building as they had in the struggle, and the postindependence state documents promised this participation.[3]

These women had the support of persons like Frantz Fanon, who claimed that due to the revolution, the condition of women in Algeria was undergoing a "revolutionary mutation." Regardless of whether Fanon was saying these words for the French, for Algerian male leaders, or for certain Algerian women, it is clear that the revolutionary mutation of which he was speaking took place in a small group of women whom Fanon knew because of his own work in the revolution. Some of Fanon's critics, like Juliette Minces, seem to take his words at face value. They believe that the psychiatrist did not really take into account the "motivations and modalities of women's participation in the struggle."[4] That is, they believe that the majority of women militants played traditional, supporting (feminine) roles in the struggle for independence and of these women, many were pleased to take up their traditional peacetime roles again after the war.

Certainly there were Algerian women active in the revolution who were satisfied to return to customary familial roles after independence. One example of this phenomenon, Ouardia Haroun, is lauded in a recent issue of *Révolution Africaine,* the FLN party publication. An article commemorating the anniversary of the Congress of the Soummam, August 20, 1956, makes special mention of this woman from Ifri in whose home the Congress was held. Haroun fed and sheltered the leaders of the revolution for the fifteen days of the meeting and coordinated village support for the meeting. Following the Congress she continued to be involved in support activities for the militants. Today, however, Madame Haroun lives with her only son in Ifri, in his home since her own home is an historical monument and her husband, a guerrilla, died in the war. Madame Haroun is proud of her past, but she expresses contentment at filling the traditional and dependent role of widow and grandmother.[5]

Another example is Djamila Bouhired, an Algerian woman tortured by the French who became the focus of international support for the Algerian cause. In interviews in 1971 with Walid Awad and Khawlah Qalaji she spoke of her satisfaction in her role as mother and wife. In the 1970s Bouhired was also involved in an Algiers neighborhood group to improve social conditions, but, according to the interviews, her primary interests were family commitments.[6]

The cause of raised expectations for power sharing by some women militants is not completely clear. It is true that as early as 1957 the FLN talked about the role of the Algerian woman in the struggle, noting that "Algerian society is not one without women," and that "Algerian women are at the heart of the combat."[7] These early statements are hardly revolutionary, so that it is no surprise that none of the leaders of the revolution from the time of the Committee of Twenty-Two, including the nine historical leaders, to the leaders of the revolution in the final days of the struggle were women. Women became associated with the revolution and were active in both rural and urban areas of Algeria in part because the FLN needed them to perform certain tasks and they could more easily escape detection than Algerian men. The literature indicates that there was an uneasy acceptance of the revolutionary role of the more daring Algerian women by Algerian male leaders, despite the fact that the FLN use of women in the revolution was important for gaining international support of their conflict.[8] For example, as noted earlier, the torture of Djamila Bouhired, publicized by French and other European supporters of the Algerian cause, was helpful in gaining recognition of the cause outside Algeria.[9]

Despite the active commitment of women like Bouhired, no woman was named to the National Council of the Algerian Republic, 1956; no woman became a member of the provisional governments of the Algerian Republic, 1958, 1960, 1961; no woman assisted in writing the Charter of Tripoli or the Charter of Algiers. This may seem to be belaboring the point, but if in Algeria today there is ambivalence about expanded roles for women in the state, the ambivalence has its roots in the period of the revolution itself. Gisèle Halimi notes that during a meeting she arranged with Ben Bella and Mohamed Khider with Djamila Boupacha on behalf of the Algerian women imprisoned by the French, when Djamila mentioned a change in women's roles after independence, Khider retorted that after independence the Algerian woman could return to her couscous.[10]

One question that has not been clearly answered in most discussions of women's involvement in the revolution is to what extent women were actually in-

volved, in what numbers and of what age group. Some records of the numbers
and nature of women's participation in the revolution can be found in the Ministry of Former Moudjahidines. According to statistics from this office, some
10,949 women were active in the struggle for independence. To give an idea
of the proportion of women involved in the struggle, only 3.25 percent of all
persons reporting involvement in revolutionary activities during the struggle
for independence in Algeria were women.[11]

Twenty-two percent of these women were involved in clandestine activities
in the cities while 78 percent were involved in rural areas. In a study of this
data and these women, Djamila Amrane shows that of this very possibly incomplete total, only 3271 women reported clearly defined roles that they had
played in the revolution. Those women involved in civilian roles in the struggle
exercised the following functions: providers of food and shelter, guides, liaison
agents with the guerrillas, collectors of funds, munitions and medicines, nurses,
terrorists, seamstresses, and secretaries. Those women who served with the
military were nurses, secretaries, cooks, and washerwomen.[12]

What Amrane's study substantiates is that most women militants, except for
the few women involved in terrorist acts, provided support services to the male
militants. The male leaders viewed those support services as appropriate activity for women. What is also clear from the data from the ministry is that
the women militants, even the best-known like Djamila Bouhired and Djamila
Boupacha, were not involved in the decision-making structures of the revolution either in Algeria itself or abroad. No moudjahida has reported to the
Office of Former Moudjahidines that she held a major decision-making post.
To reiterate, the roles of women in the revolution paralleled their activities prior
to the armed struggle, that is, they were, for the most part, nurturing, feminine
types of roles.[13]

Not only were most Algerian women in the revolution filling traditional
female roles, but most of these women were providing support to husbands
and relatives. Of those women reporting militant activities, 52 percent were
over thirty years of age and more than 28 percent were between the ages of
twenty-one and thirty at the time of their involvement. Thus about 80 percent
of the Algerian women actively engaged in militancy were married, and reports
reveal that most of these women's husbands were in the Liberation Army.[14]
One might say that the women complemented the roles of their husbands in
the struggle.

The activities of these women certainly matched those of Algerian males in
risk. Amrane shows in her study that 8.5 percent of the women engaged in
militant activities were killed and another 11.5 percent were imprisoned. Thus
one woman in five actively involved in the revolution was detained or killed.[15]
The numbers of these women, of course, are small when compared with the
total feminine population of Algeria, but so are the numbers of male militants
when compared with the total male population of the country. What the statistics show, however, is that there was significant participation by women in
the struggle, but that this participation was chiefly in supporting roles to the
male militants.[16]

Despite the commitment and involvement of Algerian women in the struggle, at the time of independence, and in the first years of independence, it
appears that a woman's appointment to and, consequently, long tenure in a
position of power was frequently dependent upon the power base she wielded

through a marital relationship.[17] Ben Bella certainly did appoint a number of women to official positions, at least in the latter days of his presidency, and a number of women were elected to the First National Assembly. Nonetheless, it is clear that there was bitter disillusionment on the part of a few women militants due to their failure to achieve an expectation of shared power and to the slowness of the state to make meaningful changes in the status of women.[18] Fadela Merabet's books, *La femme algérienne* and *Les Algériennes*,[19] are permeated with the angry frustration of a woman who had hoped for major changes in women's status and roles in the new society and who had been completely disappointed. Both Merabet and Germaine Tillion (*Le harem et les cousins*)[20] attribute much of that failure to achieve progress in women's status, rights, and participation in the political process to Algerian family law and customs and to the tendency of male Algerian leaders to equate an "authentic Algerian mode of life" with Koranic traditions.

## THE STATUS OF ALGERIAN WOMEN AS DESCRIBED IN STATE DOCUMENTS

Concepts about women as revolutionaries, enunciated in some early FLN publications, were followed by clear statements of principle on equal rights for women in the first document of independent Algeria, the Charter of Tripoli, 1962, and in the first national constitution, 1963, which noted that Algerian women were to share legal rights as citizens equally with Algerian men. Again, in 1976, as the National Charter was written, debated, revised, and approved and a new constitution promulgated, prolonged attention was given to the status of Algerian women in the society and to the promise of equal rights for women.[21]

The new constitution[22] has a number of articles that speak to women's rights. Fundamental liberties and the rights of women as citizens are guaranteed in Article 39 of the constitution: "All citizens have equal rights and duties." That article also states that all discrimination based on prejudice due to sex, race, work, or trade is forbidden. Article 41 notes that the state assumes the equality of all its citizens by suppressing obstacles to that equality whether those obstacles be economic, social, or cultural. This is, perhaps, an attempt to assure women that cultural patterns will not delay forever their access to full equality before the law. The idea is reinforced in Article 42, which says that "all the political, economic, social and cultural rights of the Algerian women are guaranteed by the Constitution." Article 44 and Article 59 speak to economic rights. Article 44 guarantees access to employment without discrimination and Article 59 guarantees a right to work and equal pay. Article 67 says that all citizens (women included, of course) have the right to health services. Finally, Article 81 declares that the Algerian woman must fully participate in building a socialist state and in the development of the nation. All of these articles speak in one way or another of modernism, of woman's role in that new society, and make explicit references to kinds of equality.[23]

At the same time, Article 65 of the constitution states that the family is the foundation of society, its primary unit, and benefits from the protection of the state and society.[24] The article itself appears to be a truism; still, one should include this article in the listing of those that protect the rights of women. Certainly the majority of Algerian women marry and establish families, and state protection of that institution means, of necessity, protection of women.

Nevertheless, the implementation of this article through the establishment of a Family Code that maintains traditional Algerian family dynamics seems to war with the very ideas of economic, social, and cultural equality detailed in other articles of the constitution. This particular problem will be described in detail in the discussion of the Family Code, "that body of domestic law whose purpose is to protect the family as the integral social unit and to guarantee an authentic Algerian character to an Algerian Islamic society."[25]

To argue that these articles of the constitution are rhetoric and do not articulate real national goals in Algeria is to imply that no articles of the constitution have any weight. There is no way to accept any one part of the constitution at face value and arbitrarily to reject other parts. Either the constitution enunciates real goals for the nation or it is a sham. Efforts by Houari Boumédiène, the second president of the Republic, and by Chadli Bendjedid, the third president, to incorporate women into the political process is some evidence that these goals, imperfectly achieved or remote in implementation, are still real goals.

Just as the constitution delineates women's status and rights, so does the Family Code describe women's rights and duties in marriage. A reading of the recently promulgated Family Code would lead one to conclude that the thrust of the code is to maintain a number of traditional family values, tied to Koranic law. Given that the Koran's statements about women at the time of its writing were revolutionary and liberating for women, *sura* such as "Men have authority over women by virtue of the preference God has accorded men over them and because of the financial responsibilities they bear for their maintenance"[26] would seem to relegate women to a totally dependent position. Further, Koranic and *Shari'a* rulings on marriage, divorce, and inheritance, although advances in Mohammed's day, appear restricting in the twentieth century. It is for this reason, perhaps, that while trying to remain faithful to the spirit of the Koran, those Algerian leaders responsible for the writing of the new Family Code have attempted to take into consideration contemporary Algerian society. The result has been a compromise.

If there has been one issue that has caused enormous reaction in Algeria over the past twenty years, it has been the updating and enaction into law of a Family Code. Since the early 1960s the Family Code has been a matter of concern and discussion by women, a matter of national debate, demonstrations, and general irritation. Within the party it has remained a point of divergence for men and women, with many women expressing the hope that a Family Code would take into consideration the realities of Algerian family life and the expectations of women.[27] At its last work session in February 21, 1980, the Fourth National Council of UNFA (Union Nationale des Femmes Algériennes) stressed the necessity of "an authentic, progressive and revolutionary Family Code."[28]

After periodic announcements from 1966 on that the Family Code was to be revised and published, it was finally announced in 1981 that the code would be promulgated at the end of December 1981. In the Algerian capital, on December 23 of that year, a group of one hundred Algerian women protested the secrecy surrounding the discussion of the Family Code in the National Assembly. *Le Monde* reported that the women had chanted "Down with the Family Code!" and had sung the hymn of the women FLN combatants. This was the fourth demonstration in four months according to news reports.[29] Whether or not the Algerian government saw these reactions to the proposed Family Code as significant, the Code was not approved or published in a final form as had been foreseen. Women members of the National Assembly and the newly appointed Madame Z'hor Ounissi, secretary of state for social affairs in the Ministry of Health (later named minister for social protection), were appointed to serve on the committee from the National Assembly, which with other groups reviewed the proposed Family Code and recommended changes in it.[30] Following discussions in 1982, 1983, and 1984, in committee, and in debates and discussions via television, the newspapers, and the National Assembly, a new Family Code was finally approved by the National Assembly in May 1984 and promulgated on June 9. What is significant in the remarks by Algerian leaders about the Code is their insistence that the Code does not deal with the status of women, only with the status of the family.[31] Thus the earlier proposed document on personal status was withdrawn, a partial victory for women opponents.

Major changes have occurred in the document from the proposed version of 1981 and the Code of 1984. In the approved Code, earlier explicit references to adult women as minors have been eliminated. (In the 1981 version of the Family Code, no woman could leave the country without the written permission of a male relative. And, indeed, in 1976, the rector of the University of Oran required that all Algerian women teachers accepting summer scholarships for study abroad have the written permission of their husbands or fathers.)[32]

The Family Code,[33] a body of law, defines the family as the primary unit of the society and notes that it is made up of persons joined by ties of marriage and birth. It further states that the family is based upon the union of its members, the good understanding among family members, and is marked by healthy education of the members, good morals, and the elimination of social evils. (One of the social evils that the state decries is divorce. In Algeria one marriage in six currently ends in divorce. Although this is a generally low rate for divorce among developed nations, there has been a rise in divorce in Algeria and the state is concerned with the effects of this rise.)[34] The document is divided into three main topics: marriage and the dissolution of marriage, legal representation, and inheritance.

Marriage, according to the Code, is a contract between a man and a woman undertaken in due legal form. Its purposes, among others, are the establishment of the family based on affection, concern, and mutual assistance, the moral protection of the two spouses, and the preservation of family ties. Free consent to the marriage by both parties is required, as is a dowry. A marriage "guardian" (father, relative, or the judge if there is no one else) is still required for the woman, but the functions of that guardian are restricted to representing the bride in the marriage. The two parties to the marriage can include in the marriage contract anything not forbidden by the Family Code. Thus a woman might elect to have as part of the contract that she have the right to exercise her profession after marriage.

The question of polygamy, a very sensitive issue during the debates, has been resolved by permitting more than one wife "IF THE REASON FOR THIS IS JUSTIFIABLE" (the words are in caps in the actual document).[35] The document does not go into the possible reasons for electing to take more than one wife, but the inability of a wife to have children or an incurable illness are some of the reasons frequently cited. The Code is emphatic, however, that if a man is to have more than one wife, equal support and attention must be provided all wives, and that marrying more than one woman can only be done after informing the present wives and the fiancée of his intentions. Those women who do not consent to the proposal are entitled to sue for their dowry (the fiancée) or to ask for divorce. In recent years the number of polygamous marriages has been fairly small. The requirement of equal support for all wives is a difficult standard to achieve. Nonetheless, for those women who would have liked to have polygamy outlawed, the Code seems to come down on the side of the Koranic traditionalists.

The dowry remains part of the marriage contract and the Code states clearly that this sum (property) belongs totally to the wife once the marriage has been consummated or the husband dies. The dowry is important in that it provides some financial security to the woman, provided that her husband and his family have been able to provide more than a token dowry.

The Code notes in Article 36 that the marriage partners share mutual responsibility to maintain the marriage. The obligations of the two spouses are the following: "to safeguard conjugal ties and the duties of a common life; to jointly contribute to safeguarding the interests of the family, the protection of the children and a healthy education for them; to safeguard family ties and good relations with parents and close relatives." The description of these obligations, as well as the description of marriage itself, seems fairly progressive as husband and wife share equally in these duties. There are distinctions raised between husband and wife, however, in describing the specific responsibilities of each.

The husband (Article 37) is required to provide for the support of his wife within his ability to do so (unless she has left the family home) and to treat all wives equally if he has more than one. (This latter requirement appears in several places in the document.) The wife has the right to visit her relatives and to entertain them in her home. She also has full control of her own property. But the Code also says that she must obey her husband and defer to him as head of the family, nurse his children if she is able to do so, and be responsible for their upbringing. She is to respect the parents of her husband and his close relatives. In the description of duties and responsibilities, the Code again returns to the traditional view of the husband as head of the family and provider and the wife as obedient partner. The document goes from insistence on the equality of the relationship and duties to enforcing a family hierarchy and requiring specific kinds of duties from the wife that are not required from the husband, but that have been traditional expectations in Algerian society.

Little in the document restricts the husband from divorcing his wife except Article 52, which describes the redress for the wife in the event her husband abuses this right to divorce. Article 53, however, outlines in great detail those reasons for permitting divorce by the wife: the inability of the man to have children, refusal of the husband to share the marriage bed for a period over four months, failure of the husband to maintain his wife, long imprisonment of the husband, an absence by the husband that lasts over one year, during which time he ceases to support the family, and so on.

A recognition, by those writing the Code, of the current state of the family in Algeria is obvious. For example, one section of the Code provides that if the father abandons his family or disappears, the judge can authorize the wife to sign all documents for the children (school, etc.). This provision, however, again recalls the very traditional role of the father as head of the family. The mother cannot sign these documents unless the father is not present in the home and she has been legally authorized to do so.

In the case of divorce, the wife has custody of the children, girls until they reach the age of eighteen (legal age to be married), boys until the age of ten or, if it seems in the best interest of the boy, sixteen, provided that the wife has not remarried. While the father is regarded as head of the family, the mother is considered to be the one best suited for raising the children, and her rights to the children are not ignored.

One other article of the Code that was hotly debated during the years the Code was being revised was marriage with Non-Algerians. Article 31 provides that Moslem women can only marry Moslem men. Undoubtedly this is due to the fact that juridically the children belong to the father and are Moslem through him. Here, again, distinctions between men and women follow traditional lines in the code. Some acknowledgment of the difficulty some women have with this provision is recognized, however, for marriage with foreigners is permitted to both Algerian men and women provided that the marriages occur in conformity with state statues.[36] Bitterness over the issue stems from the fact that many Algerian leaders married non-Moslem, non-Algerian women. Those women like Djamila Bouhired who married Christian, non-Algerian men would be in jeopardy.[37]

The importance of maintaining the line of the father is so great that adoption is forbidden in the code as it is in traditional Koranic law. Nonetheless, relatives and others, if they are Moslem, can assume the guardianship and care of children not their own. Family rights prevail, however, and at any time a father or mother or both may request the return of the child to their home. If the child has reached the age of reason, he/she can elect to return or not to return to the parent(s). This insertion of children's wishes reflects attention to contemporary social thought.

In the section on inheritance the Code preserves the rights of all parties, including wives, daughters, aunts, sisters, and mothers, to family goods and property. It is to be noted that an individual cannot will away his total fortune without the consent of those who by law should inherit. Thus an individual has the freedom to dispose of one-third of his property, but the remaining two-thirds remain for traditional distribution unless the prospective heirs decide otherwise.

This brief description of some aspects of the new Family Code demonstrates the attempt on the part of Algerian authorities to make the Code and its interpretations of Koranic law sensitive to some of the issues of the family as it exists in Algeria today.[38] At the same time, the Code remains traditional in its description of the father as head of the family and in retaining for the male the right to take up to four wives. The new Family Code, then, is a compromise between those state elements wanting to eliminate from it all vestiges of reference to women as subordinate to men in marriage (the fully equal couple) and those state elements desiring to maintain the male as head of his family and enjoying all the rights permitted by the Koran and long-standing practice in Algerian life. What is noteworthy in this compromise is the insistence by the state that it has the right to write, approve, and promulgate the Family Code against the opposition of conservative religious leaders who would take a Family Code as their *prerogative*.[39]

To summarize, all references offensive to some Algerian women have not been removed from the Code, but repeated statements by the minister of justice, Boualem Baki, that the document is not one describing and legislating the status of women indicate the government is sensitive to those very delicate issues.[40] It appears that the new Family Code is an attempt by the Algerian state leaders to balance opposing segments of the society and to achieve a temporary (fragile?) peace on the issue of the family while providing protection to the Algerian family, notably the wives and children. Still it is difficult to reconcile statements in the constitution about equality of Algerian men and women before the law when the Family Code still places the wife in an obedient position to the husband.

## IMPLEMENTATION OF RIGHTS: WOMEN'S ACCESS TO EDUCATION

The Algerian constitution provides that every citizen has the right to education and that the state is to assure equal opportunity of education for all (men and women regardless of stratum).[41] Education is to be free and attendance at elementary school (ages six to fourteen)[42] is obligatory. Certainly from the earliest days of the Republic, this commitment to education for all is one of the least contested goals of the state. One reason for this is that several segments of the population, from the Ulemas to the Communist Party to male militants in the struggle, believed that education for all, and particularly for women, was essential to build a modern Algeria.[43] Some of this belief stemmed from the traditional view of women as educators of the children. Uneducated wives could very well disadvantage one's children. At the same time, a number of Algerian male and female leaders believed that full participation by women in the development of the state could only come about through education. If women were to share in all levels of participation in nation building, that is, in the social services, in education, in medical services, as members of the National Assembly and of local assemblies, they required the same educational opportunities as men. Thus for years one of the primary goals of UNFA has been to enlarge the access of women to education.

The government's commitment of its resources to education, and thus to education for women, is easy to document as budget reports over the years reveal that at least one-fourth of the yearly national budget has gone for educational purposes.[44] The numbers of elementary, secondary, and technical schools and universities have multiplied.[45] In describing goals for the next five-year plan (1985–1989), the Council of Ministers in June 1984 reiterated this commitment of the nation's resources to education. In a summary of their discussion they noted that education remains a major priority of the state and that in the new plan, major building, staffing, and programmatic support would go to education. Since in the past few years special focus has been placed on providing personnel to work with new technologies, funds for technical training are to be expanded.[46]

The history of women's access to education is one of gradual improvement in postindependence Algeria. In 1954, at the start of the Algerian Revolution, over 95 percent of Algeria's Moslem women were illiterate. In fact, according to Robert Aron, 90 percent of the total Algerian population was illiterate.[47] Only 14.6 percent (302,000) of all Algerian primary-school-age students were in primary schools in 1954 and a total of 4260 Algerians were in secondary schools. During the course of the revolution the French accelerated the rate of access to education for both Algerian girls and boys. Nevertheless, in 1954, a total of only 53,120 girls were enrolled in elementary schools and 952 girls in secondary schools.[48] In 1958, four years after the start of the revolution, this number had grown to 118,000 girls in both elementary and secondary schools. By 1963–1964, however, the year following independence, 472,373 girls atteded elementary schools and 30,218 girls were in secondary schools. Despite the remarkable increase in women students in the high schools, still only 31 percent of the total students in those schools were women.[49]

The history of women students at the university is parallel. In 1954 only 22 Algerian women were university students. This number grew to 374 women by 1963–1964, 18 percent of the total number of Algerian students at the university. The largest percentage of these women (138, 37 percent) were enrolled at the Faculty of Letters. Other major fields of interest for women were sciences, 53 (14 percent); medicine, 81 (22 percent); law, 52 (14 percent).[50]

In 1963–1964, 47 percent of the girls in schools, as opposed to 62 percent of the boys, were from the rural areas of the nation. Almost 39 percent of the girls who attended school had fathers who were administrators of government employees.[51] Thus it appears that impetus for education of girls came from those homes where the fathers themselves were educated and where the father was from the bourgeoisie or petite bourgeoisie rather than from the rural agricultural working class.

One factor that may very well have influenced the access of women to education right after independence was the successful attempt by Fatima Khemisti, herself a member of the National Assembly, to get a law passed by the Assembly setting the minimum age for marriage for a girl at sixteen (now eighteen).[52] This provision tended to prolong the time of schooling for girls and may thus account for some increases realized over the past several years in primary and secondary education of women. A further impetus to education for women was the perceived desirability of having a wife (or daughter-in-law) who had had primary, and perhaps secondary, school training.[53]

In 1967–1968, of a total of 1,462,776 Algerian students in elementary schools, 544,776 (37 percent) were girls. In the same year, of 148,754 students in secondary schools, 39,201 (26 percent) were girls. At the universities in that year there were 2220 women students among a student population of 9720; that is, 23 percent of the college student population was female.[54] Although the total numbers of female students increased overall and at all levels of schooling, percentage increases of women students were generally slight.

Figures available for the 1978–1979 academic year indicate continued slow advances in this sector. In that year, 72 percent of all children of elementary-school age were enrolled in classes. Of the total of 2,972,242 children, 1,226,932 (41 percent) were girls. That same year, of the 844,291 students in the secondary schools, 312,075 (37 percent) were women students. Of the 53,841 students enrolled in the universities, 12,677 (24 percent) were women.[55]

By 1983, according to statistics available from the Algerian government in October 1984, three girls to four boys were receiving an education in the elementary schools, two girls to three boys were in the middle and secondary schools, and one women to three men was attending the university.[56] Obviously there continues to be a tendency of families to educate male offspring over female offspring, but the gap between the numbers of girls and boys being educated continues to be reduced.

The increases from 1954 to 1985 in actual numbers of girl and women students in Algeria is phenomenal, of course, but it is a phenomenon related to the astronomical increases in educational opportunities for all the youth. Nevertheless, even if one focuses on the percentage increases of girl and women students enrolled in Algerian schools, it is evident that gradual advances are being made in women's education, particularly on the elementary and secondary levels. It is possible to argue that this phenomenon is a natural evolutionary occurrence, unrelated to the educational rights for women finally articulated in the constitution of 1976. However, it appears to this analyst that the impetus given to education and the willingness of the government to encourage, legislate for, and devote major resources to universal education (that is, including women) indicate that it is a primary national goal and that achievement of that goal is a planned process. It also appears that the gradual increases in the percentages of girls and women having access to education derive from the state's commitment to education of women.

To understand other educational changes occurring for women in Algeria, it is useful to examine the changes in professional choices made by women students at the universities. In 1978–1979, of 12,677 women students at the universities, 3159 (24.5 percent) were in medicine. Other fields showed the following enrollments: exact and technical sciences, 1919 (15 percent); biological sciences, 1479 (12 percent); agricultural sciences, 834 (6.5 percent); economics, 984 (7.5 percent); law and political science, 1406 (11 percent); social sciences and arts, 3000 (23.5 percent).[57] In the 1982–1983 academic year over 60 percent of the women enrolled at the university chose sciences as their fields of study while 40 percent elected letters and humanities. (Twenty-five percent of these women were in medical fields, but only 2 percent were in the exact sciences.)[58] It is clear from the above that more women are gradually electing scientific and technical training. While there are some marked changes in women's selections of areas of study, most of the new areas chosen are those which still provide access to feminine sorts of professions: medicine and nursing, social service work, teaching, legal services.

In recent years a number of technical schools also have accepted women students. Three of the oldest programs for women, Birkhadem (600 women interns receiving profesional training in 1975), Oran (130 women interns in 1975), and Skikda (100 women interns in 1975), have the largest numbers of women students.[59] Birkhadem, the first of these training centers, was created in 1969 by President Boumédiène to provide skilled women workers for the Algerian labor force.[60] Birkhadem has served as a pilot model for other such schools. In 1980, of 55,737 trainees in technical institutes (other than training institutes for teachers), 7202 (13 percent) were women. Of this number, 1277 were receiving training as typists, secretaries, seamstresses, and domestic helpers; 1215 were being trained as administrative clerks; and 2872 were receiving paramedical training. The other women were receiving training in a variety of fields, including some specialized industrial training.[61] The technological institutes also provide training for primary and middle school teachers. Of the total of 12,041 teachers in training in these institutes in 1977, 4325 (36 percent) were young women.[62] As with the university courses selected by Algerian women, it is apparent that most of the technical training for women is for so-called feminine kinds of occupations.

Besides the kinds of technical training described above, short-term training courses have been instituted for women workers. One of the most frequently cited example is the training program at the Sonelec plastics assembly plant in Sidi Bel Abbès. At the start of this program in 1978, 250 women were employed at Sonelec after a two-week training period. In 1980, 1320 women were factory assembly line workers at the plant and earned about 1024 dinars a month. In 1985 almost 2000 women were employed at the plant, which meant that women held almost 46 percent of the total number of industrial jobs there.[63] Brief technical training programs like the one at Sonelec have been set up elsewhere as new industry is developed in some of the industrially underdeveloped areas of Algeria. This short-term training, however, leads to specific jobs and, generally, to those kinds of jobs (low pay and requiring precise manipulation, small hand movements) that are being relegated to a feminine work force throughout the developing world.[64]

In summary, since 1962 there has been decided progress in Algerian women's access to education. Much of this progress is due to government support of women's education. Each year larger numbers and a greater percentage of school-age girls and women are attending elementary and secondary schools, the universities, and technical training institutes. In addition, some women are now also receiving short-term technical training, which makes it possible for them to find employment in the industrial sector. At the same time, however, although there have been shifts in the fields chosen by women for study, most Algerian women (like their sisters abroad) are choosing "feminine" fields of study, that is, health services, teaching, social services, and administrative support areas.

## IMPLEMENTATION OF RIGHTS: WOMEN'S ACCESS TO WORK

One of the Algerian state's purposes in providing education for women is to enable that segment of the Algerian poulation to help in the process of nation building. As the state attempts to deal with increasing demands for health care, schooling, and social services, the need for women to work in these fields increases. A large proportion of these services are provided to women who make up over half the Algerian population. The state's interest in providing work opportunities for women also stems from national needs for labor in those fields that men tend to reject and from state advantage in making a population as self-sufficient as is possible.[65] Finally, rhetoric or not, a great deal of attention is given in party publications to the need for full participation by women in all sectors of life, including work, in the development of the socialist state.

Women in contemporary Algeria need to work for a variety of reasons. Despite the requirements of the Family Code that fathers support the children of a divorced wife, many Algerian women are the sole support of their children. They work to provide their children with a home, food, clothing, and school supplies. For some Algerian women, the inability of a husband to find work or to be employed because of disability forces them to seek employment. For other Algerian women, their work augments a family budget. With two salaries a family may have the financial freedom to start savings to purchase an apartment or home, buy a car, provide for relatives, go to Mecca, take a family vacation at one of the Algerian resorts, provide more educational and recreational opportunities for children. A single salary will take care of the primary needs of the family, that is, rent, food, clothing, utilities. The second salary means that the family can enjoy some luxuries.

Other reasons for women working include family needs (for example, agricultural labor on family property), a desire to use one's education, the wish to have an existence and an identity outside family responsibilities, and so on. In short, most of the reasons for women working in countries like the United States can also be found for women working or seeking work in Algeria.[66]

What Algeria has experienced in the past twenty years, like most other developing nations, is an accelerated move from rural to urban living. In 1966, 32 percent of the Algerian population lived in cities; by 1977, that percentage had increased to 40 percent. Over 72 percent of the population now living in the cities was not born there. What the percentage change in persons migrating to the cities means in total numbers of people actually living in the cities is even more striking. Algeria has one of the highest birthrates in the world. In 1966 there were about 12 million Algerians, in 1977 that number was about 18 million. Thus the total population increase in Algeria over a ten-year period was about 50 percent.[67] In examining the access of women to paid employment in Algeria it is necessary to look at those increases in women's employment in relation to changes in residence patterns and total increases in the female population and the female active population.

In 1966 about 99,830 women were working outside the home; in 1977 the number had grown to 143,050.[68] Although this growth represents a real increase in numbers, there was only a small increase during that time span in the actual percentage of women working. According to census figures, the percentage increase of women having paid employment in urban and rural areas together grew from 1.82 percent in 1966 to 2.61 percent in 1977.[69] What is to be expected, however, is that in that period of time, while urban migration increased, there was a decrease in the percentage of women employed in the rural sector, from 1.12 to .083 percent, and an increase in urban employment, from 2.92 to 5.12 percent.[70]

A factor that must not be ignored in looking at these figures is that there is a great body of working women in Algeria who do not receive salaries, that is, those women who work as mothers and homemakers, rural women who are unpaid assistants in agricultural work, female relatives who assist with children and household chores in families. It may be that much more refinement is necessary in compiling the statistical data that will give a clearer view of what percentage of women is actually working and the relationship of unpaid to paid employment.

Of the total working (salaried) population in Algeria today, about 94 percent are men and 6 percent are women. As Fatiha Hakiki notes in her study on "Salaried Work and Domestic Work," 80 percent of the salaried women are to be found in urban areas. Using official Algerian census documents she demonstrates that the kinds of work done by these women changed in the years 1966–1977, even if the percentages of women working did not increase remarkably. Of the 99,830 women working in 1966, 18,568 (18.6 percent) were involved in scientific or liberal professions. This number rose to 43,630 women in those professions in 1977, or 30.5 percent. The increase demonstrates, perhaps, a growing acceptance by the Algerian population of women's participation in teaching, health services, law, and social science fields.[71]

In 1966, 1248 women were directors or top-echelon managers. In 1977, that number had increased to 1731 women in these positions, but the actual percentage of women in these posts had declined.[72] Apparently, access to these positions has become even more difficult for women as more and more men compete for them. Of the salaried women employees in 1966, 10,482 (10.5 percent) were in administrative work (secretaries, assistants, etc.). By 1977 women in administrative work numbered 31,371, or 21.9 percent of the female work force. This sector, like that of the liberal and scientific professions, showed a healthy increase both in actual numbers and in percentages in the ten-year period. Women agricultural workers, however, numbered 22,731 (22.77 percent) in 1966 and 7437 (5.2 percent), an overall numerical decrease of 15,292 in that ten-year period as well as a hefty total percentage decrease of 17.57 percent.[73]

State emphasis on industrial development to the detriment of agricultural development could partly explain the decline in agricultural work for women. It can also be explained by the exodus of young women between fifteen and twenty-five years of age from the countryside to the cities to marry poor city dwellers dependent upon family still residing in the countryside to find them wives because of their disadvantaged economic position.[74] Another factor, of course, is the urbanization process occurring in Algeria, the impetus of rural occupants to move to urban centers to find work. One caveat about the figures for agricultural workers is that the figures given for 1966 appear to include 3304 nonsalaried women workers, that is, women farming their own land. It is not clear that this is the case for the 1977 figures. Thus both the numerical and percentage decreases might be less in those ten years, since the manner of collecting and reporting data may not be uniform.[75]

Another sector in which there was a percentage decrease in women workers from 1966 to 1977 was, surprisingly perhaps, the industrial sector. In 1966, 14,645 women worked in industry, that is, 14.67 percent of the total female work force. In 1977, 14,391 women (10.06 percent) did so.[76] What these figures may reflect is a reluctance by the Algerian population to accept women working in factories. The reluctance of families to this work might be due in part to a greater difficulty in arranging for marriages for these women because of popular prejudice against it.[77] In addition, the urban working class wants its daughters as well as its sons to advance beyond the economic and social level of the parents. White-collar positions such as teaching or nursing, not incidentally closely related to the traditional role of the mother in the home, are means of changing economic and social status, while factory work is not. This tendency to elect education as a means of changing social status is not a new phenomenon in Algeria, but existed in preindependence Algeria as well.[78]

An article on women factory workers in *Algérie Actualité,* a national weekly in French, discusses the problems of women factory workers in the Sonelec plastics assembly plant at Sidi Bel Abbès.[79] The article indicates that there is resistance, both in the general population in Algeria and in the families of those women employed in the plant, to women doing that work. Nevertheless, despite the reluctance of the families (notably the fathers and brothers of the women) and contrary public opinion in Sidi Bel Abbès, 1920 women continue to work at Sonelec. That they do so stems from the extreme poverty of their families which necessitates their working; the death of a father or his abandonment of the family, which also makes their salaried work necessary; the lack of status of these women in their homes (unmarried), which can be altered somewhat by their working and having a wage.[80] The fact that the Algerian government has found it necessary to use the Algerian press to praise women workers at Sonelec indicates the extent of the reluctance of Algerian society to accept women in these kinds of professional activity for women where it serves state purposes.[81]

In 1985, despite societal difficulties and pressures, the Algerian state had not abandoned its efforts to provide additional employment for women. The new five-year plan (1985–1989) has as a goal the creation of 200,000 new jobs for women, an annual average increase of about 70 percent according to some sources.[82] What must be noted is that the 200,000 jobs for women are 21 percent of the total of new jobs planned for the period. In addition, the press has stepped up its coverage of women as role models in less traditionally feminine occupations: policewomen, artists, judges, writers, lawyers.[83]

An additional factor leading to women's employment in the cities has been the rising divorce rate in Algeria. In the case of women who have come to the city from the countryside, those divorced rarely return home.[84] Further, given that the mother is generally the parent charged with the care of the children and that frequently the divorced husband does not provide the financial assistance required by law, it becomes the responsibility of the mother to find employment to support her children.[85] Boukhabza notes that in 1970, 20.1 percent of the women twenty years of age were heads of families. This percentage decreased to 18.5 percent for those twenty-one to twenty-four years of age and 13.7 percent for those twenty-five to thirty years of age; it then rose to 14.6 percent for those between thirty-one and thirty-four and continued to rise to 15.7 percent, thirty-five to thirty-nine; 17.5 percent, forty to forty-four; 15.8 percent, forty-five to forty-nine; 20.5 percent, fifty to fifty-four; 18.7 percent, fifty-five to fifty-nine; 19.7 percent, sixty to sixty-four; 24.8 percent, sixty-five.[86] Although these high percentages of women heads of family stem in part from divorce, it must be cautioned that the deaths that occurred in the male population during the revolution are also responsible for some of the figures. Another factor contributing to the number of women heads of families is the number of Algerian migrant workers in France and other countries of Europe who leave their wives and children in Algeria. Even if the woman receives assistance from her husband working abroad, she is the titular head of house.

In reviewing the facts available concerning women's access to paid employment in Algeria, it seems clear that there has been some increase in work opportunities for women in contemporary Algeria, but that the advances in paid employment for women are primarily in urban centers and most opportunities for work are in what most societies regard as appropriate, "feminine" work, that is, teaching, health care occupations, service occupations, family service (cleaning and child care), secretarial and clerical work, crafts. Women in the countryside appear to be losing ground. There are, however, some women (689, or 0.6 percent of all workers in the domains) working in the self-managed domains. In 1976, 1004 women were members of the cooperatives (1.3 women for each 100 men).[87] The proportion of women working in these areas, of course, continues to remain small. Seasonal labor is more likely to be feminine than year-round participants in cooperatives or in self-managed domains.

A study in 1982 by the National Office of Statistics of 10,000 Algerian households (a microcosm suggesting the macrocosm) estimates that in 1982 about 245,000 women were actually in the paid work force. Two-thirds of these women (as opposed to one-half in 1977) were working in administration and public service (the government, teaching, the health professions). The study showed, of course, that there was a marked relationship of educational level to employment possibility for these women. Two-thirds of the women surveyed who had completed secondary school had paid employment, and three-fourths of the women who had completed postsecondary studies were gainfully employed.[88]

Although the constitution stipulates that there should be equal pay regardless of sex, it appears that there are differences in salaries for men and women workers in the same categories of work in both public and private industry. Certainly the difference is far greater in the private sector. In a brief exposé published in *Algérie Actualité* in 1981, Abdelkader Hammouche noted disparities in salaries for men and women in the government figures on salaries from 1974 to 1977.[89] In all cases, he stated, women earned less than men in similar positions, but in the private sector the difference was sometimes almost equal to the women's wage. In categories of public employment such as teaching, nursing, medical technology, and so on, salaries for men and women are identical in principle. Actual differences for men and women occur because it is more likely that lower job classifications are assigned to women and because fewer women have access to administrative posts.[90] Insufficient data exists at the present time in Algeria to clearly demonstrate the extent of differences in women's and men's salaries for identical work. However, UNFA and officials in the Ministry of Work both claim that women are seriously discriminated against in the matter of salary in the private sector.[91]

Despite wage discrimination in the private sector, attempts have been made by the Algerian government to ensure equal pay for equal work by men and women in all sectors. The Statut Général du Travail (SGT), the new code governing pay for workers put into effect in January 1985, attributes pay according to job classification, experience, education, length of service, and so on. All of these factors have a percentage value. The SGT also states fixed social security contributions for the employer and employee. No distinctions are made by sex, although certain technical jobs are most probably going to be held by men rather than by women.[92]

In summary, education plays an important role in the access of women to paid employment, whether that education be an advanced degree or a short-term training course. Government policy, defined in the constitution, is that all citizens should have access to work. The state is giving some attention to women in the labor force, and, despite high unemployment, there has been no state policy that women should be held back in their efforts to find work until work is available for all males. The most recent five-year plan (1985–1989) calls for almost doubling the number of women currently estimated to be in the work force. Equality in access to work and in pay, however, still has not been achieved despite governmental verbal assent to these goals. Nonetheless, the SGT addresses the issue. In certain professions such as teaching there is no salary discrimination, although more men than women will be appointed to administrative posts. Finally, despite positive encouragement by the government of salaried work for women, the total number of paid women remains small and the number of women in important decision-making positions in the economy is minor, if it exists at all.

## IMPLEMENTATION OF RIGHTS: WOMEN'S ACCESS TO PARTICIPATION IN THE POLITICAL PROCESS

The Algerian National Charter stated "that it is still the woman herself who remains the best defender of her own rights and dignity, as much by her behavior and qualities as by her untiring struggle against prejudice, injustice and humiliations."[93] Thus, while the charter and the national constitution guarantee women full participation as citizens of the state, there is an implicit understanding by the state that there are impediments to that full participation that lie within the society itself. The state of necessity has set up and continues to perfect institutions to educate its citizens for the kind of state it purports to be: a democratic republic that is Islamic, Arabic-speaking, and socialist.[94]

Among those institutions established by the state wherein this education occurs are five Algerian bodies, notably the UNJA (l'Union Nationale de la Jeunesse Algérienne), the UNPA (l'Union Nationale des Paysans Algériens), the ONM (l'Organisation Nationale des Moudjahidines), the UGTA (l'Union Générale des Travailleurs Algériens), and the UNFA (l'Union Nationale des Femmes Algériennes). These organizations are nationwide associations to which Algerian women belong and by means of which they can and do have some access to state power structures, since the five bodies are that group of "organizations of the masses" which, for the most part and in some form, have been part of the national organizational structure since 1963. In recent years FLN control of these organizations has been greatly increased. Leadership in the organizations currently implies membership in the party, although this was not always true in the past.[95] The constitution considers that these five organizations are those to be charged with recruiting the masses to the programs of the state and educating those fractions of the society with their responsibilities and the roles they must play in the development of the nation.[96] Although, as noted above, these organizations are closely tied to the FLN, each body also has its own structural autonomy.[97]

The most important of these organizations from the point of view of the Algerian women is undoubtedly the UNFA. Established in 1962, the UNFA held its First National Congress in November 1966,[98] about one year after Boumédiène seized power from Ben Bella. The party, the FLN, and the Algerian government all viewed the UNFA as a means of inserting women into the political and economic life of the nation.[99] To what degree the UNFA has successfully done this is frequently debated.

Writing in the UNFA official magazine, *El Djazaïria* in 1973, Fatiha Hadri noted that there were only 50,000 UNFA members in Algeria at that time. Recalling to her readers that the feminine population of the country numbered over 7 million persons, Hadri asked, "Where are the other women?"[100] It appears that UNFA membership has been avoided by large numbers of women for a variety of reasons. Some women can see no need to participate in the UNFA. Their activities are confined to their families, and husbands or fathers might not encourage this sort of participation since they in turn are not members of the party. Other women believe that the UNFA leadership is controlled by former militants for FLN party purposes. Still others think that they can be more effective in union or worker activities.[101]

Whatever the reality, official government policy has been that UNFA should serve as a conduit for the election of women to decision-making groups in the nation. The Second National Congress of UNFA in 1969 fixed as one of its specific goals to increase the number of women serving in the APCs (Assemblées populaires communales) and APWs (Assemblées populaires de wilaya) as well as in the APN (Assemblée populaire nationale).[102] UNFAs success rate in this endeavor is apparently not very good. According to Tabrizi Bensalah, the UNFA proposed five candidates for the National Assembly in 1977, one of which was elected. A total of ten women, however, were elected to the National Assembly that year. (A UNFA publication, however, listed all women Assembly members along with the list of women directors of UNFA.)[103]

As most Algerian women believe, the UNFA's goals do reflect FLN party goals. The desire to increase women elected to assemblies in 1969 was a party directive. The Third National Congress of the UNFA in 1974 ended at about the same time as party texts on the Agrarian Reform came out. The UNFA was called on to assist in promulgating these texts and the organization actively began its work with rural women in that year.[104] The Fourth Congress in 1978 was used by the FLN to mobilize women's support of the National Charter and of the constitution, realizing, of course, the interest of the UNFA in Algerian women fully participating in nation building, as articulated by the charter.[105] The Fifth National Congress, in 1983, noted that fewer women, in comparison with the total population, were actually involved in the political life of Algeria than at an earlier time in the state. Congress delegates, with FLN complicity, called for an increase in women in all spheres of Algerian life.[106] The actual language quoted in the official FLN publication referred to "social, demographic, cultural and economic constraints that up to now shackle efforts to assure women's presence in all sectors of work."[107] That congress also called for a national policy to control the birthrate in Algeria, an idea that would have been rejected by President Boumédiène in 1967,[108] but which has been receiving a great deal of emphasis from the party since 1982 and since 1983 is actively promulgated by party publications.[109] At the same congress delegates approved an amendment to their bylaws that would provide that all officers of the UNFA be members of the FLN.[110]

Part of the purpose of the UNFA, of course, has been to involve women in grass roots organization. In this effort it appears that they have been somewhat successful. Through UNFA efforts, about 130 centers to teach illiterate women and to provide some training for trades have been set up in both rural and urban areas. UNFA meetings and *El Djazairia* have been used to explain certain "revolutionary" governmental decisions to the membership and to others. For example, UNFA membership has been used as "outreach" to explain and promote the national reforestation project, the Agrarian Reform, liberation struggles of other nations and Algeria's support of these, national campaigns for vaccination of children, sanitation, and against illiteracy.[111]

It is through the UNFA also that delegates to a number of international women's meetings are selected, including UNESCO and other U.N. sponsored meetings, those of the Arab League, and other groups. The UNFA has regularly sponsored international women's conferences, in particular Pan-African and Third World Nation conferences. UNFA members have served as secretary-generals of several of these groups.[112]

The UNFA has been involved in a number of local and national projects besides those mentioned earlier. It has helped to set up craft groups in the government-sponsored Agricultural Villages. Since 1971 it has been involved in establishing home-work cooperatives throughout the nation. In 1976 there were over a thousand women in these cooperatives in Algiers alone.[113] In 1983, as in several years previously, the UNFA sponsored a number of "volontariats," similar to those sponsored by the students' organization in rural areas. The volunteer teams of women from the UNFA are generally composed of women schoolteachers, children's care experts, doctors, midwives, and other professionals. Medical personnel generally provide medical services in the areas they visit, caring in particular for women and children. Other members of the team discuss appropriate topics with the inhabitants of the area they visit (in 1983 the Family Code) and assist in agricultural and industrial projects.[114]

There is a reluctance on the part of UNFA leadership to use the term "feminism" in their discussions of women's issues, fearing apparently that it has a pejoratively "Western" connotation or that it might appear divisive to male FLN leaders. In a report about the Fourth National Congress, September 30–October 3, 1978, it was noted that "concerns about health and education, rather than specifically feminist issues, dominated the debates."[115] Regardless of terminology used, one could argue that the concerns of the UNFA in the areas of health, work, and education are very clearly feminist issues. Certainly the final statement of the UNFA Council in 1980, stressing the necessity of an authentic, progressive, and revolutionary Family Code, were feminist statements, as were the calls by the Fifth Congress for insertion of women in "areas of real power."[116]

Women are members of other "organizations of the masses," in particular the UGTA and the UNJA, but most of the leaders of these organizations tend to be men and national heads are all men. Two women, however, are members of the Central Committee of the FLN and several women have been elected to the party's Council of the National Committees. The two women members of the Central Committee (1984) are Z'hor Ounissi, minister for social protection, and Fatima-Zohra Djeghroud, secretary-general of the UNFA.[117] Newly named to the ministerial level in February 1984 was Leila Ettayeb, vice-minister of education in charge of secondary and technical education.[118] She, however, does not sit on the Central Committee.

Whatever one might say of the weaknesses of the FLN and these "organizations of the masses," the fact that these groups have been established and have provided a number of women with practical political experience on the communal, wilaya, and national levels (along with benefiting women through a number of their programs) is tangible evidence of some improvements in women's access to power structures in Algeria since 1962. Until independence, Algerian women were generally excluded from any form of political participation in the nation.

To judge to what extent Algerian women have been fully integrated into the political process, it is necessary to look beyond the voting rights given to Algerian women (some of whom still let husbands or sons exercise these rights for them, according to Algerian news reports) and laws protecting women, and examine the extent to which women are represented in the governing bodies, both local and national, of the state. In studying the few statistics available, which, admittedly, are incomplete, it appears that there has been some forward and backward movement in the number of women elected to these posts, as has occurred elsewhere, including the United States. There are three kinds of general assemblies in Algeria to which women candidates have been elected: the APC (Assemblies of the Communes, small local assemblies now called *mouhafadhas*), the APW (Assemblies of the Wilaya, larger regional assemblies), and the APN (National Assembly).

In the 1975 elections for the APCs there was a total of 11,520 seats available. Of these, 160 were won by women. In 1977, for APW elections, there were 1233 available seats; thirty-seven went to women. In that same year, for the APN elections, women won 10 seats out of 261.[119] In March 1982, however, although a total of forty-two women presented themselves for election to the National Assembly, only four women were actually elected to the 281-member assembly; thus both the number and percentage of women elected to the APN declined.[120] (This, of course, is why the UNFA is calling for FLN support of women candidates for the assemblies.)

The failure of women to be elected to regional and national office may stem from a variety of reasons: a cultural belief on the part of many Algerians that women should not be elected to office, absence of better-known women's names on the ballot, a constituency containing persons from conservative areas of the nation, lack of knowledge about the women running for office and their capabilities, failure of the FLN and UNFA effectively to muster support. There appears to be some correlation between the number of women elected to office and a concerted effort by government and party officials to have women elected to office. In 1966 a joint directive from the coordinator of the FLN Executive Committee and the minister of the interior urged that women candidates be presented every time an election was to be held.[121] Prior to the APC elections in 1967, President Boumédiène made a television appearance requesting the Algerian population to elect women to these communal committees. That year 260 women presented themselves for election and 208 women were elected (out of 10,239 seats).[122] The results are not always so dramatic, but there is some success from this kind of official reinforcement of the idea that women are to be elected to office.

For the December 13, 1984, elections for the APC and APW bodies, FLN directives repeated the call for greater representation of women in these governing bodies. Three hundred eighty-eight women were candidates for the 27,075 APC seats (1.4 percent) and eighty-eight women were candidates for 1840 APW seats (4.8 percent). Certainly the number of women candidates presenting themselves for election had doubled since 1967, but because of the total increase in the APCs and APWs, there was little or no increase in the percentage of women candidates. Most of these women candidates were from larger urban centers.[123] The program for action of the Fifth Congress of the UNFA does continue to put pressure on FLN leaders to assure more representation by women in the next APN elections.

Since 1967, Algerian women have been elected to the presidencies or to the executive committees of the APC. In 1975, for example, women were elected presidents of the communes of Dar Beida (Wilaya of Algiers) and Hammadia (Wilaya of Tiaret). That same year three women held seats on the Executive

Committee of the city of Constantine (three seats out of a total of eight). In Oran in 1975, one woman was elected to the Executive Committee (one seat out of eleven).[124] The total number of women who have held these positions since 1967 is unknow, however, because statistics have not been kept. Data on the class and social strata of the women elected is also not available for the same reason and because the data currently being kept does not divide class/strata data into male/female. It was reported that in the 1982 National Assembly elections, 80 percent of the APN deputies were classified as workers (including agricultural workers).[125] In the 1984 APC and APW elections, 20 percent of the candidates for the APC and 30 percent of the candidates for the APW were teachers. Seventy percent of the candidates for both the APC and APW were between the ages of twenty-five (age required) and forty.[126]

To summarize, women in Algeria take part in a number of national organizations which provide them with training for future responsibilities in the state and which give them access to state power structures. (Madame Ounissi is, perhaps, the best example at the present time. A former member of the National Assembly and active in the UNFA, she has assumed a major ministerial position and is highly regarded for her competent work in the Ministry of Social Protection.) A number of women serve as elected members of the National Assembly, of the wilaya assemblies and councils, and of local assemblies and councils. There are now two women ministers and two women members of the Central Council of the FLN. At the same time there is inadequate representation of women in these assemblies and in the government. It appears that the UNFA will continue to put pressure on the FLN leadership to change this.

## CONCLUSIONS

It appears that there have been both qualitative and quantitative improvements in the status of women and women's enjoyment of political rights in Algeria since independence in 1962, although that progress can be qualified as minimal. Women, like men, are citizens with the right to vote and are guaranteed equal protection under the law. They have made remarkable strides in the battle against illiteracy and for education, but this has had its greatest effect on younger generations, who have had access to more schooling and more of whom live in urban areas. Access to paid employment and to administrative positions for women in some sectors of the economy is growing. Women are represented, in small numbers to be sure, in a number of national governing bodies. They participate in the national organizations of the FLN and hold executive responsibility in some of these. There is one woman minister and one vice-minister in two areas of "women's" concern: education and social services. A growing number of women hold important administrative posts in both education (directors of schools, high schools, universities)[127] and health services (directors of pediatric services, directors of nursing). If the Algerian woman still seems at the periphery of the power structure of the Algerian state, it is because the number of women so involved still is small, because no woman is yet a member of the Political Bureau of the FLN, and because no woman manages one of the important state industries.

This statement, however, must be placed against the context of Algerian society in 1962. Given that comparison, one can assert that there has been immense progress for women in Algeria since independence. It must be noted that even in developed societies such as the United States, major growth in women's participation in political life is a fairly recent phenomenon and access to positions of power was slow until the 1960s.

Perhaps the strongest case for arguing that women are effectively making impacts on Algerian society is that of the Family Code. Granted that although in writing the Code state leaders were balancing ideas from all segments of the state, including fundamentalist Islamic leaders, it appears that women were successful in keeping the Code from being approved and published in its worst (least progressive) forms. Even as late as early November 1983, party publications were talking about a "Personal Status Code," not about a family law code, with all the possible ramifications of women as unequal to men because of Koranic law.[128] In spring 1984, after women National Assembly members, women FLN Central Committee members, and other women had participated in discussions on it, the Code was drastically changed. Boualem Baki (minister of justice) noted in June 1984 that following the study of the National Assembly, thirty articles of the Code were amended, twenty-one articles were adopted, and twenty-two articles were dropped.[129] Even if Algerian women concerned about the Code did not succeed in getting as progressive a document as they had hoped for, enormous gains were made in the final product over earlier reported drafts.

The rhetoric of full participation for the Algerian women in the building of the nation is not just rhetoric. Continued discussion of women's issues in *El Moudjahid* (Algiers' daily newspaper), *Algérie Actualité, Révolution Africaine,* and *El Djazaïria* does not let the Algerian citizen lose sight of the need to improve woman's status in that nation and to allow her full enjoyment of the rights the constitution gives her. Television documentaries and feature films dealing with women's issues (among others, education, *Le Vent du Sud,* by Benhedouga; the problems of the Algerian woman factory worker, *Leila et les autres,* by Sid Ali Mazif; participation by educated women in life in Algeria, *Nouba des Femmes de Chenoua,* by Assia Djebar) continue to evoke debate.[130]

Whether improvement in women's status is equal in all classes/strata of the society is a question that is unanswerable for lack of sufficient and appropriate data. It does appear that those women benefiting from educational and work opportunities and living in more urban centers (women from the bourgeoisie and the elite) have greater advantages than those women who are deprived of education for whatever reasons and who live in rural areas. This, however, is not particularly surprising. A fifty-year-old woman in 1984, for example, with the position of rector of a university will have to have been educated in part prior to the end of the war for independence, and this fact alone would argue that she belonged and belongs to an upper middle "class."

Algerian university women scholars have begun to research the status of Algerian women and to publish empirical studies encompassing women's issues from incidence of cancer to contraception, from women in the workplace to the dowry.[131] In 1980 two four-day Study Days on Algerian women were held at the University of Algiers and later at the University of Oran. Held under the auspices of the communal and wilaya assemblies, the UGTA, the UNFA, and university rectors, these Study Days demonstrated a new trend in efforts to gain full participation for women, that is a movement from emotional claims to fact-finding that will enable women to develop strategies for the full implementation of the constitution.[132] A number of these studies and the published documents from the Study Days are now available to Algerian leaders, to the UNFA and other organizations, and to those departments of the state involved in developing programs for women. Some of these studies have been used by sections of the Ministry of Social Protection and have been expanded by the ministry in its work to serve the needs of women.[133] The mere presence of these studies assures that party leaders and government ministers cannot ignore women's issues and problems.

In summary, if progress for Algerian women is not as clear and as pronounced as many would like it to be, there is now a basis for expectation, that another twenty years will show significant improvement in women's status and rights in Algeria.

# PART V

# The *Encadrement* of the Population: The Social Basis of Ideology and Planning

"*Encadrement* of the population" means creating frameworks for development. First used by the French after the Second World War, the phrase refers to a process attempting to facilitate the efficient organization of both the human and material resources of the society. These French planners were in the forefront of the type of planning that involved both the organization of production and also—along with facilitating the spread of scientific knowledge and technical assistance—changes in attitudes of peasant producers towards their physical and social environment.

In *Power and Class in Africa* I argued:

> For development to occur, certain material and psychological requisites must be instituted. Economic growth requires not only tractors, improved seed, and technical know-how, but a willingness on the part of the population to utilize the fruits of Newtonian science. The organizational capability of integrating the exchange of goods, services, and information on a nation-wide basis is also necessary. These needs and goals necessitate bureaucracy and an expanded state apparatus as well as new types of membership associations. In traveling through rural areas, the presence or absence of the regional and local branches of various departments and corporations differentiates African countries. Returning to the same village over a number of years, one notes in the build-up of the *fonctionnaires* some of the most visible physical changes. What is needed, therefore, is a "web of activity" linking together diverse people in multiple activities and reinforcing networks of interaction. "Encadrement" conveys the sense of this activity strikingly, for it connotes the reorganization of the population into a *cadre*, a framework for development.[1]

*Encadrement* of the population therefore has always involved (1) the creation of new organizational forms, including administrative structures directed to advancing the task of economic development, as well as that of the political

233

unity which is its universal prerequisite; and (2) creating new ways of thinking, new mental frameworks for development.

In "From Nationalism to Marxism: The Ideological History of Frelimo, 1962–1977," Sonia Kruks demonstrates the changing significance of ideology in the encadrement of a population. She shows how official thought in Mozambique resulted from a process of conflict and struggle. She argues that the adoption of Marxism by the major political movement in Mozambique, FRELIMO, resulted from *internal* development. FRELIMO's Marxism was the outcome of domestic class conflicts within the framework of the struggle against Portuguese colonialism in a country characterized by both great poverty and a developing indigenous capitalism with all of its promise and difficulties.

Kruks raises, and then contests, alternative interpretations of the introduction of Marxism in Mozambique. She rejects the contentions that FRELIMO adopted Marxism because it was simply a "puppet" of the Soviet Union or China, or that Marxism was simply a rhetorical device used in a struggle between "elites" coming from different ethnic groups. On the contrary, Kruks argues, FRELIMO succeeded remarkably in overcoming ethnic diversity and, furthermore, changes in the dominant ideology had all the "marks" of an "*internally* developed doctrine." Kruks shows how the process of political and economic development in Mozambique went through a series of stages. FRELIMO passed from nationalism to a Marxist analysis of the nature of the struggle with the Portuguese, to the establishment of a Marxist-Leninist party, to the present framework of state and society. FRELIMO moved ideologically from nationalism to Marxism, according to Kruks, because of its entire course of historical internal development—not simply because of immediate problems of the post-independence situation or because of any desire to solicit Soviet aid. Above all, what happened, she maintains, was that the leaders of the political movement had to confront some bitter fruits of their own success. Successful in wrestling territory from the Portuguese, the new African administrators realized that they had to confront the outbreak of a class conflict within its own ranks. Originally FRELIMO, like most African nationalist movements, consisted of broad alliances of a variety of groups, some of them inherently in conflict but temporarily united in their opposition to Portuguese colonialism. Because of their success in liberating significant areas of territory from the Portuguese, FRELIMO, sooner than most nationalist movements, had to face the problems of its "internal contradictions." These included class antagonisms which emerged within the heart of the movement, as "the old feudal chiefs and the new embryo capitalist class" aligned themselves together against the populist majority of the FRELIMO leadership.

Although Kruks does not provide the detailed evidence to document or illustrate the nature of the class conflict, she shows how the conflict was, on the one hand, rooted in the development of an agricultural surplus and the organization of an internal and external commerce and, on the other hand, determined by the necessity of maintaining the support of the mass of the peasantry, without whose aid the war against the Portuguese could not be won.

As the Portuguese pulled out of Mozambique, the transfer of power threatened economic crisis and the collapse of basic institutions of government. Kruks analyzes how the necessity of preventing a total economic and social collapse opened the way to state control over key elements within the economy and facilitated the transition towards a noncapitalist society. As part of a process of encadrement, FRELIMO turned not only to state intervention but also to mass political mobilization through what it called "dynamizing groups," local organizations of citizens meant to educate the population, maintain production, and "guard the revolution."

The founders of *Animation Rurale* in Senegal, the Ujaama villages in Tanzania, and "community development" in Ghana had in mind objectives similar to these. Kruks sees the creation of the dynamizing groups as an extension of the policies of "people's power" originally developed in the liberated zones in the struggle against Portuguese colonialism. The most recent development in Mozambique centers around the creation of a "vanguard party." Kruks sees an inherent conflict between the principles of increased democratization and the growing centralization of power as a basis of growing tension in the future evolution of politics in Mozambique. On the one hand she quotes Machal to show how, without a vanguard party, the danger arises of the army developing as the most dynamic and self-conscious political element in society—a lesson well learned in the experience of so many other African states. On the other hand she argues the great importance of a stage between capitalism and socialism, which FRELIMO calls popular democracy: a set of institutions which enables the development of "a multiplicity of nongovernment structures through which the masses can participate in the making of decisions which affect their lives." Kruks goes on to raise the possible tensions between FRELIMO's "vanguardism" and their commitment to popular participation.

Richard W. Franke, in his "Power, Class, and Traditional Knowledge in Sahel Food Production," deals with the social basis of planning in the *encadrement* of the population. Franke uses class analysis to understand four different systems of capabilities to increase food production and at the same time protect a fragile environment. He presents us with an extraordinarily sophisticated account of the relationship between a society and its environment. His understanding of the interrelationships between political power, class, and traditional knowledge enables him to propose a series of measures for more socially beneficial structures for development.

In his analysis of the economic development of the Sahel, Franke contends that the French colonizers had no regard for the land or for the laborers. Peanut production in Senegal and Niger and cotton production in Mali and Chad exploited and harmed the land. However, Franke maintains, the "most positive environmental developments were maintained in societies where the producing classes had the greatest power and the ruling classes were either absent (Douzou, Dogon) or had their power checked (Serer) or where their power was in the process of disintegration (Dina)." On the other hand, powerful ruling classes among the Hausa, Bambara, and Wolof sacrificed ecological upkeep through their policies of voracious consumption and exploitation.

After the great devastation and famine which left tens of thousands of people dead, Franke asked, "What can be done to develop the Sahel and make it drought-proof?" As in the remarkable study he did with Barbara J. Chasin, *Seeds of Famine: Ecological Destruction and the Development Dilemma in the West African Sahel*,[2] Franke argues that more is involved than simply the forces of nature, that, indeed, the basic causes of the vast human toll of suffering came from man-made forces of political domination and class exploitation.

Thus he maintains that even an aid program in the billions will not meet the real needs of the mass of the population unless the *encadrement* processes incorporate the best features of complementary traditional modes of production.

The drought by itself did not result in widespread misery. Over the centuries the people of the Sahel developed ways of confronting their always precarious environment. Franke argues that a sophisticated combination of caravan trading, fishing, animal herding, and agriculture resulted from many centuries of experimentation and today contains the best elements for the reconstructing and new *encadrement* of the Sahel.

The central hypothesis of Franke's paper, based on the best available historical and anthropological evidence, maintains that the most ecologically productive systems of production in the Sahel have occurred under two conditions: (1) agriculturalists and pastoralists intensively interacted and exchanged information about plants and animals and (2) "producing classes have had substantial power vis-à-vis the dominating classes or, conversely, where ruling classes have had the least power and privilege relative to the producing classes." In highly stratified societies, ruling classes not only maintained themselves in luxury but also consumed capital resources to support their repressive apparatus and defense networks. Societies with the least powerful ruling classes, Franke contends, are much more likely "to develop and implement practices that maintain fixed capital such as land and its associate improvements such as trees, animals, etc." In great detail, he spells out the nature of herding and farming symbiosis. He also shows how the expansion of commercial agriculture has worked against the traditional patterns of cooperation and how governments have supported the interests of the politically more important farmers. He urges that the people of the Sahel develop their own traditional knowledge and material resources rather than risk increasing dependency on imported fertilizer with its wild fluctuations of price and supply. A more secure "important element" in a strategy of greater African independence would be "the creation of a people's science with an emphasis on developing local knowledge and techniques."

Franke proposes a creative mixture of traditional knowledge and modern science. He does not suggest a return to the isolation of a more egalitarian past, but he does declare that there are ways to recreate modern versions of the nonexploitative character of some of the more ancient societies. In *Seeds of Famine,* Franke discussed a variety of small-scale production experiments in the Sahel where all those which were successful "emphasized the management and control of the means of production—land, labor, technology—by the producers themselves." In the present study, the final results of Franke's analysis also leave us with a sense of the feasibility of creating structures for development which are not only more productive but also more humane than has widely been thought possible.

# CHAPTER 10

# From Nationalism to Marxism: The Ideological History of FRELIMO, 1962–1977

## Sonia Kruks

When Mozambique became independent in June 1975, power was handed over by Portugal to the national liberation movement, FRELIMO.[1] FRELIMO had been constituted in 1962 as a broad nationalist movement or "front." Its aim was to end Portuguese colonial rule in Mozambique, and it had been engaged in a guerilla war against the colonial regime for a period of ten years, from 1964 to 1974. Some twenty months after independence, in February 1977, FRELIMO declared itself to be no longer a popular "front" organization but a Marxist-Leninist vanguard party, engaged in the tasks of constructing "the political, ideological, technical and material base" for the development of a socialist society in Mozambique.[2] The construction of a socialist society, guided by the "science" of Marxism-Leninism, was declared to be the only way forward for Mozambique.

In the decade since it achieved independence, Mozambique's project of developing a socialist society has been increasingly threatened by a mutually reinforcing set of difficulties. These include, most centrally, South African hostility, leading to, among other things, the devastation of Mozambique's infrastructure by the South African–backed Movimento Da Resistência Nacional (MNR).[3] The MNR damage has been compounded by a prolonged sequence of floods and droughts, resulting in serious localized famines. The situation has been yet worsened by the increasingly adverse terms on which Mozambique—like so many Third World countries—has had to export its primary products and to purchase on the world market such items as fuel, machine parts, and drugs. Additionally, as FRELIMO itself admitted in 1983, overemphasis on high-technology agriculture and large industrial projects has frequently involved a wasteful allocation of precious resources, while problems of bureaucratization, formalism, and poor communication with the mass of the population have also taken their toll on the revolutionary project.

It is against the backdrop of this litany of woes that Mozambique took two significant steps in 1984: signing the Nkomati Accords with South Africa and entering the World Bank and the IMF. The Nkomati Accords, a mutual non-aggression pact, required FRELIMO radically to reduce its long-standing support for South Africa's African National Congress (ANC), expelling most ANC personnel from Mozambique. In exchange, South Africa agreed—a promise as yet unfulfilled—to bring about the end of MNR terrorism within Mozambique.[4] Entry into the World Bank and IMF was indicative of a more general turning to the West, seeking aid and investment to help get the Mozambican economy out of its present disastrous nosedive. This has been paralleled by an internal encouragement of the private sector and more emphasis on market mechanisms as instruments of economic policy. These events have led some observers recently to ask how much of the original socialist project remains in Mozambique. As one long-term and sympathetic observer, John Saul, has recently put it:

> . . . there can be no escaping the hard fact that Mozambique has been literally bludgeoned into "compromise." To the extent that this is the case, the fundamental question becomes one of whether, under such testing circumstances, Mozambique has made the best of the limited room for maneuver it has been able to find—and whether it has been left with enough such room to revitalize its socialist project.[5]

My intention is not to attempt to answer Saul's question—at least, not directly. The main focus of this paper is not on the future of the revolutionary project in Mozambique, but on its past. Yet, since this past does of course have a bearing on the future, my discussion also will have a certain indirect bearing on his question, for what I examine below is what I call the "ideological history" of FRELIMO. That is, I examine the history of FRELIMO's shift from a conscious identification of itself, when it was founded, as a broadly based nationalist movement to its identification of itself as a Marxist-Leninist vanguard party after independence. The question which prompts such an historical examination concerns the depth of the rooting of Marxism in FRELIMO. It is important to know whether or not Marxism is simply an intellectual trapping, added at one time to attract Eastern Bloc support but as easily dropped at another to attract Western assistance for an ailing economy. Our assessment of the present and future must take the answer to this question, concerning the past, into account.

In 1977 FRELIMO gave its own interpretation of its ideological development, contained in the report that the Central Committee made to the Third Congress.[6] The essence of this account was that, starting as a broadly based nationalist movement, FRELIMO's development towards Marxism was fueled by its own experiences and difficulties during the war of liberation. In particular, it was fueled by the realization that what was essentially a *class* conflict had developed within its own ranks, as the movement wrested territory from the Portuguese and had to confront a range of day-to-day social and economic issues in the "liberated zones."

What is at issue, and what I examine below, is *not* specifically whether FRELIMO was correct in this interpretation of its own history. I do not set out to answer the question: What evidence is there that a class conflict developed within FRELIMO? My questions concern the accuracy of FRELIMO's later analysis of itself: Is it true, as FRELIMO said in 1977, that the leadership had started to move towards Marxism many years earlier? Has Marxism provided a framework of analysis, a set of tools for orienting strategies and developing work methods, for many years? In short, has Marxism become part of what we might call the "lived experience" of FRELIMO cadres? Or, conversely, is it just an ideological package, handily picked up for some purposes, but as easily shed for others?

The method I use to answer such questions is, primarily, a close analysis of FRELIMO's own documents, from its inception in 1962 until 1977. Carefully cross-checking what we may regard as FRELIMO's "official" 1977 account of its own ideological development against numerous earlier documents, I examine whether a study of this earlier material does or does not justify FRELIMO's later interpretation of its own ideological development. The writings I draw on are of two kinds. First, I will use material written initially for internal use but which has since been made available, including speeches made by the leadership to FRELIMO cadres, conference and committee meeting documents, and articles from FRELIMO's internal journal, *Voz da Revolução*. Second, I draw on material written or translated explicitly for a Western audience, such as in FRELIMO's English-language journal, *Mozambique Revolution,* interviews given to Western journalists, and Eduardo Mondlane's book, *The Struggle for Mozambique.*[7]

## THE BIRTH OF A NATIONAL LIBERATION MOVEMENT

At its inception, FRELIMO was a broad and heterogeneous alliance of groups and individuals, united only in their opposition to Portuguese colonialism. As the first president of FRELIMO, Eduardo Mondlane, wrote, "Like all African nationalism, the Mozambican form was born out of the experience of European colonialism."[8] During the late 1950s, when agitation for independence was rife in colonial Africa, Mozambican exiles resident in nearby British colonies established the first Mozambican nationalist organizations. Those in Kenya and Tanganyika merged in early 1961 to form the Mozambican African National Union (MANU), modeled mainly after its Tanganyikan counterpart, TANU, even down to the adoption of an English name. Organizations were also formed in Southern Rhodesia (UDENAMO) and Malawi (UMANI).[9] They attempted to follow the model of the organizations in the British colonies, using peaceful means such as petitions and protest letters to forward their cause. However, the very fact that they existed only outside the borders of the Portuguese colony indicates clearly that Portuguese colonialism at the end of the 1950s was significantly different from its British and French counterparts. At a time when both Britain and France were preparing and performing careful programs of decolonization and mass African political parties were being recognized, Salazar's regime was in no condition[10] or mood to follow their example; and the degree of repression inside Mozambique made an organized internal movement of any scale impossible.[11]

Although all three of the foreign-based nationalist organizations were demanding Mozambican independence, they remained divided by their different ethnic bases.[12] Even when, in 1961, following Tanganyikan independence, all three moved their offices to Dar-es-Salaam at the invitation of Nyerere, they were unable to agree on a common platform and merge. However, they were rapidly joined in Dar by a new wave of more militant exiles, who were coming to independent Tanganyika not to look for work but to escape the increasing political repression inside Mozambique. It appears to have been this group which

provided the main impetus for unification,[13] along with pressure from established African leaders such as Nyerere and Nkrumah. Thus it came about that
FRELIMO was born as an uneasy alliance of the older exile-based nationalist
groupings and more recently arrived, and often more militant, refugees, the
latter representing the growing internal resistance to the Portuguese.

The program the movement established at its First Congress, in September
1962, was a minimal platform, clearly designed to be acceptable to all the
diverse elements it contained. The Resolutions proclaimed:

> . . . the union of all Mozambicans regardless of ethnic origin, financial means,
> religious and philosophical beliefs, or sex, in the struggle using every available means
> for the immediate and complete liquidation of Portuguese colonialism and for the
> winning of national independence."[14]

At one level, then, "unity" implied simply overcoming tribal divisions. But,
perhaps more significantly, it also implied accepting into the movement Mozambicans of different "financial means," thus embracing not only peasants
and urban workers but also, for example, traditional chiefs, traders, and small
artisans—as long as they supported the common cause of liberation from Portuguese colonialism. All "Mozambican patriots" could unite against the enemy.
Thus, in this first stage, FRELIMO did not define its struggle in class or even
economic terms. It was a classical nationalist movement, uniting groups on the
basis of patriotism and the struggle to end foreign domination. As Marcelino
dos Santos was later to write, FRELIMO was a "front," "not because it is a
federation or something like that, but because in FRELIMO all the social groups
are represented."[15] How was it then that this broad nationalist movement was
to become transformed within fifteen years into a Marxist-Leninist vanguard
party?

## THE PROCESS OF RADICALIZATION

Although FRELIMO was founded as a nationalist front, it appears to have
contained a more radical element from the very beginning. It was not, however,
a foregone conclusion in 1962 (even though it perhaps appears as one in the
1977 account) that the radical element would emerge as the final leadership;
nor is it clear that most of the more radical members of FRELIMO actually
considered themselves to be Marxists.

Statements linking FRELIMO's struggle to the world struggle against imperialism are to be found very early on in its history. Indeed, one of the resolutions of the First Congress states that FRELIMO "Affirms its solidarity with
the peoples who are waging the struggle against all forms of colonialism and
imperialism."[16] There are also, as Alpers has well documented, some public
affirmations of the socialist nature of the struggle in Mozambique to be found
in documents as early as the end of 1965.[17] However, anti-imperialism and
affirmations of socialism as one's goal are not to be confused with Marxism—
indeed, they are compatible with an explicitly *anti*-Marxist position, as in Nyerere's theory of African Socialism.[18] It is thus important to note that in an
interview given in 1967 Mondlane explicitly identified the Tanzanian model of
socialism as also being FRELIMO's.[19] He argued for the necessity of a socialist
state in Mozambique not on the basis of the Marxist criteria of class structure

and class struggle, but on the grounds of the *lack* of private ownership or wealth (and thus lack of class divisions) among Mozambicans. Thus:

> We have no chance to inherit anything from Portugal, or to accumulate wealth on our own. So what do we do? We have to start with whatever is available. And what is available is the state. The state will have control of all natural resources, and the people will invest their energies in the activities of the state.[20]

Did Mondlane, its president, represent the most radical position in FRELIMO? Probably not. It seems likely that a few of the intellectuals in the leadership, men such as Dos Santos and Rebelo who had studied in Europe, were already acquainted with and sympathetic to Marxism in 1962. As Dos Santos obliquely put it:

> A study of the experience of other countries and the general knowledge acquired by humanity in its struggle against oppression penetrated the minds of quite a few in the leadership. So right from the start, in 1962, different ideologies were reflected at the top.[21]

In the early days these differences of ideology do not appear to have presented a great problem for FRELIMO. The nationalist struggle was primary and all, from simple patriots to near Marxists, could unite in the common cause. Although there were widespread early defections from the movement over the question of using armed struggle as the main tactic, this conflict does not appear to have been interpreted in class terms or in terms of nationalists versus socialists.[22] However, following the launching of the armed struggle in 1964,[23] the ideological rifts were to open, with a growing radicalization of that element in FRELIMO which was already disposed to see the struggle as more than one for simple political independence.

According to the 1977 account, it was the dynamic of the liberation struggle itself which produced the radicalization. It was not a question of theory or book learning primarily (though, as the above quote from Dos Santos suggests, these were also present), but of the *practical* consequences of the success of the armed struggle. By the end of 1965, the Portuguese were withdrawing their administration from large areas in the northern provinces, leaving FRELIMO with the tasks of day-to-day government. Once FRELIMO had responsibility for running these "liberated and semi-liberated zones," the platform of anti-colonialism ceased to offer a sufficient basis for unity and a divergence began to develop within the movement. Although this divergence was expressed in opposing views over a variety of issues, from military tactics to the role of women in the war, it was essentially, so the 1977 account argues, a divergence of *class* interest. For once FRELIMO controlled its own areas, the question arose as to whether or not various forms of oppression and exploitation of Mozambicans by Mozambicans were permissible in what was the embryo of the forthcoming independent state.

There are indeed some mentions of the divergence in statements made during the years when it was taking place, but these are of a vague and rather general nature. For example, Samora Machel (at that time secretary of the Department of Defense), in a speech to the armed forces on September 25, 1967 (the anniversary of the launching of the "armed struggle"), talked of "insufficiencies on our part, which have created contradictions in our midst." These, he said, had manifested themselves in contradictions between the armed forces and the population in certain areas, due primarily to "lack of respect for the popular masses" on the part of some "comrades." These had also been conflicts within the military command in some areas, "the fruit of ambition and personal interest in certain of our comrades."[24] Similar statements were also made in his speech on September 25 of the following year.[25]

It does not appear to have been until after the assassination of Mondlane, in February 1969, that these contradictions were first identified, at least in print, as the manifestations of two distinct "lines," one popular and revolutionary, the other that of people who "wanted . . . to substitute themselves for the Portuguese colonists in exploiting our people."[26] And it is only in yet later works, notably the 1977 *Report,* that the struggle of the "two lines" is primarily interpreted as a *class* struggle rather than as a struggle against a few misguided and corrupt individuals. In the *Report,* two sources of oppression and exploitation are said to have existed once the Portuguese had withdrawn:

> The economic and administrative presence of colonialism having vanished from these zones there remained on one side feudal structures and with these the anti-democratic authority of the landchiefs [*regulos*], the oppression of women and youth and tribal division. On the other side there developed new exploiters, elements who began to show signs of substituting themselves for the colonialists in exploiting the people.[27]

In a series of conflicts the old feudal chiefs and the new embryo capitalist class are said to have aligned themselves together against the populist and democratic positions of the majority of the FRELIMO leadership. "Class antagonism"[28] emerged within the very heart of the movement. The period of open class antagonism, of the "two lines," as it was called, lasted until 1969. I do not intend to summarize all aspects of FRELIMO's account of the conflict, nor will I relate all the complex and sometimes nasty events, including expulsions and assassinations, associated with its history.[29] Instead, I will focus on those aspects which FRELIMO has identified as being most important in the gradual development of a Marxist perspective of the struggle among a wide section of the leadership. These are, first, the economic or class aspects; second, the question of race, or what is called "the definition of the enemy; and, third, the question of political power.

With the establishment of the "liberated zones" by 1965, opportunities for exploitation of the local peasantry by FRELIMO members emerged. Cooperative production was encouraged and its success in many localities led to the need also to establish marketing and even exporting organizations to handle the surplus. It was above all the development of agricultural surplus and the need to organize internal and external commerce which "gave rise to the objective conditions for the emergence of new exploiters."[30]

Especially in Cabo Delgado, the cooperatives were "infiltrated" by individuals who used the rhetoric of collective production but were interested only in personal gain. They represented the embryo of a new capitalist class, trying to control cooperative organizations in order to siphon off profits to their personal foreign bank accounts,[31] speculating in products in short supply, such as soap and salt, and even employing labor in their private fields in exhange for these prized commodities.[32] The accounts given are not clear as to the full extent or the exact mechanisms of these forms of exploitation,[33] but they are linked with the activities of a group headed by Nkavandame, a traditional Makonde "chair-man," or land-chief, in Cabo Delgado, who was not only FRELIMO's sec-retary in that province (the highest provincial-level post) but also the director of FRELIMO's Department of Commerce. The fact that Nkavandame was not removed from his position as provincial secretary until January 1969 suggests that he and his group held considerable power within FRELIMO for several years.

The essential antagonism, then, according to the *Report,* was seen as one of class, in an orthodox Marxist sense. However, it was said to have been manifested not only in direct relations of exploitation but also through diver-gences over a whole range of issues. Of these, the question of the "definition of the enemy" is said to have been central, with the "reactionaries" taking a racist position, arguing "that only the white was an exploiter" while blacks never exploited their fellows.[34] This definition of the enemy, based on skin color, served as a mask to hide the exploiter's real action. It also led to ar-guments over the treatment of captured Portuguese soldiers, the "reactionaries" arguing that they should always be killed, all whites being the enemy, while the more radical section of the leadership argued for a policy of clemency, since many of the soldiers were poor whites, "sons of the Portuguese People."[35] Another vexing issue was the role of whites and "mixtos" in FRELIMO. Sym-pathetic whites were welcomed into the front, but the "reactionaries" objected to them and they became the targets of vicious attacks, some of them public.[36] In having to clarify their own definition of the "enemy" against that of the racists, the radical wing of the FRELIMO leadership would appear to have moved increasingly away from simple nationalism and towards an analysis of their struggle in terms of economic and social relationships.

Closely linked to the economic and racial issues was the question of political power. When FRELIMO moved into the "liberated zones," they did not move into a total political vacuum. Although the main power—both economic and political—had been that of the colonialists, there also still existed in many areas forms of precolonial political organization. Land-chiefs, usually known as *regulos* or by the English word "chairmen," had often been sustained in the trappings of power by the Portuguese, to be used in a weak form of indirect rule, as tax collectors and enforcers of order and obedience. New *regulos* had even been appointed by the Portuguese in some cases to fill this role.[37]

In the early stages of the struggle, some of these *regulos* had rallied to FRELIMO and were even within the leadership. But as the Portuguese with-drew, many of them sought simply to substitute their own rule for that of the colonialists. Some simply wished to rule as traditional feudal chiefs, exacting tribute from local subjects. Others, as in the case of Nkavandame, wished to use the traditional political forms as a means of consolidating more modern ways of accumulating. Faced with these tendencies, the problem facing the rest of the FRELIMO leadership was "To know whether we should establish a pop-ular administration, a People's Power, or simply maintain the old system of administration, Africanizing it."[38]

The decision was made to attempt the former; to "Africanize" alone could be no safeguard against exploitation. Furthermore—as FRELIMO had realized soon after the war started—without the ever increasing support and partici-pation of the mass of the peasantry it would be impossible to extend their military successes against the Portuguese. Thus a piece of FRELIMO's internal journal in 1965 quoted Mao's famous dictum: "The people is to the guerilla as water is to the fish." Directives were issued to "respect, aid and defend the people," never taking anything, "not even a needle or a piece of bread."[39]

In the "liberated zones," FRELIMO thus decided to come into the open and court mass participation. With "membership open to every adult Mozambican," it attempted to provide "a coherent structure for mass representation."[40] The movement in many areas effectively *was* the administration, with elected committees at various levels—province, district, locality—both making and implementing decisions on matters as diverse as production, health, and education. In a country with no recent tradition of democratic participation, it was not an easy system to operate. As Mondlane himself observed in 1968:

> . . . the achievement of independence in itself does not change overnight the attitudes of the people, and colonial rule essentially discourages all the qualities which make for successful democracy. Among the uneducated, authoritarian rule discourages initiative, a sense of personal responsibility, and breeds instead an attitude of non-cooperation with government."[41]

It was necessary continually to struggle against the passivity and evasion of responsibility of the mass of the peasants and, Mondlane adds, also against its opposite, "elitism" on the part of those few who did have education and who had worked for the colonial government. Breaking now clearly with Nyerere's conception of socialism based on African traditions, Mondlane stressed by 1968 that FRELIMO was attempting to introduce forms of government, and of social and economic organization, which were "essentially new, owing their origin only marginally to African traditional life and not at all to the colonial system."[42] These new forms, summarized in the phrase "People's Power," were intended to be the basis for victory not only over colonialism but also over the internal enemy, the Mozambican exploiters.

## THE SECOND CONGRESS: TACIT MARXISM

By 1968, when the Second Congress was held, this shift in perspective became quite explicitly articulated, although not formulated in Marxist terminology. The First Congress had simply called for unity against the colonial oppressor. By 1968 the goals were stated very differently. No longer is the struggle simply for "national independence," but also "for the establishment of a social and democratic order in Mozambique" and the struggle in Mozambique is seen to be an integral part of a world anti-imperialist movement.[43]

The Second Congress adopted two main "theses" for the successful continuation of the struggle in Mozambique. These were "Prolonged People's War" and "People's Power." With regard to the first thesis, the stress on "prolonged" war implied not only a recognition that the military struggle was going to have to be a long one to tip the balance against the Portuguese, but that a long struggle would be necessary also to permit the development of political consciousness among the mass of the population.[44] The idea of a "people's" war implied the necessity for mass mobilization and participation in the war: only if the masses actively supported FRELIMO, only if the *political* battle to win mass support was won, could FRELIMO hope to win the long-term military battle. "Our war," said the Second Congress's "Resolutions on the Armed Struggle," is "essentially a political war."[45]

The thesis of "People's Power" was closely linked with that of "Prolonged People's War." Thus:

> The administration of the liberated zones aims at establishing the people's power. Only through an adequate administration will it be possible to consolidate the defence of the liberated zones, to promote its growth and the economic and social progress of the people, and thus to lay the basis for a victorious development of the revolutionary armed struggle for national liberation."[46]

Among steps necessary to establish the "People's Power" were the direction of administration in the "liberated zones" by FRELIMO committees at all levels and the establishment of People's Management Committees to supervise "general tasks" whenever possible. The Congress also stressed the need to raise the economic and social well-being of the masses, since this would help to "raise their revolutionary spirit."[47] Raising production through the introduction of cooperative organization, better techniques, and more implements, developing commercial networks for producers, and health and education programs were advocated in the Resolutions[48] as *essential* accompaniments to "People's Power."

Although the language used in the Resolutions of the Second Congress was not yet that of Marxism, it is clear that the perspective had shifted from that of a nationalist to that of a class struggle. The "masses" were not yet analyzed into their component classes; nor, in fact, was the transition to "socialism" explicitly mentioned as a goal. But the manner of situating FRELIMO's struggle in the wider context of the world struggle for "liberation,"[49] the stress on popular mobilization and participation, and, perhaps more than anything, the recognition of the need to construct a *material* basis for revolutionary consciousness of the masses all point to the existence of a tacit Marxist analysis of the struggle. At this stage, as Aquino de Bragança, a longtime participant observer, has remarked, "FRELIMO was essentially a peasant movement directed . . . by a Marxian core."[50] According to de Bragança, who knew him well, Mondlane was already describing FRELIMO's ideology as "a Marxist-Leninist type doctrine" in the months before his death in early 1969. In an interview with de Bragança, given in late 1968, Mondlane said:

> There is an evolution of [our] thought which has taken place during the last six years . . . FRELIMO is now, truly, much more socialist, revolutionary and progressive than ever and the present tendency is increasingly in the direction of the Marxist-Leninist type of socialism.[51]

Why, then, did FRELIMO not declare itself to be a Marxist-Leninist party in 1968? One tactical reason would appear to have been that Mondlane and the other radical leaders were reluctant to produce an open split with the "reactionary" elements still in the front, lead by Nkavandame and others. According to de Bragança, Mondlane was "obsessed with the desire to maintain the unity of the movement"[52] and still hoped to convince Nkavandame of the correctness of the majority position. Another reason, later given by Machel, was that the bulk of the membership was not yet ready: revolutionary ideology had to mature among the masses, to grow out of their experience, and FRELIMO had to remain a broad front until such time as the masses were ready for a "vanguard"—that is, a Marxist-Leninist party.[53]

## THE PERIOD OF CONSOLIDATION AND EXPANSION

The Second Congress did not end the struggle within FRELIMO. At the end of 1968, apparently with the support of the Portuguese, Nkavandame attempted to declare the province of Cabo Delgado autonomous. In January of 1969 he and his allies were finally expelled.[54] A month later Mondlane was assassinated by a letter bomb in Dar-es-Salaam. Mondlane's death sparked yet more contention. Simango, then vice president, was suspected of having links with Nkavandame, himself thought to be implicated in Mondlane's assassination. Rather than appoint him president, an eleven-day meeting of the Central Committee, held in Tanzania in April, appointed a three-man "Presidential Council" consisting of Simango, Dos Santos, and Machel. Simango retaliated by making a public attack on the Central Committee, in which some of the issues FRELIMO had described in 1977 as being central to the "two lines" emerged very clearly. He attacked both the multiracialism of FRELIMO and its growing emphasis on internal class issues. "If there is an indigenous bourgeois class at the moment," he wrote, "and if it is willing to contribute . . . we must accept its co-operation."[55] By May of 1970, Simango and several others had been expelled from FRELIMO and Machel was elected president by the Central Committee.[56]

The emergence of Machel as president would appear to have represented the consolidation of the "Marxian core" of FRELIMO. This process of consolidation is also apparent in the Central Committee's own reflections on the events as they took place. In a document produced in April 1969, when the Presidential Council was established, the Central Committee clearly recognized the economic basis of the conflict, defining FRELIMO's struggle as both a nationalist and an anticapitalist struggle. As they put it:

> . . . our struggle is, in the last analysis, a struggle between the interests of the oppressed working classes of Mozambique and the oppressor class, *foreign or domestic.* . . . The CC reaffirms that FRELIMO, vanguard of the Mozambican people, will prosecute without difficulty the armed revolutionary struggle of National Liberation against Portuguese colonialism and imperialism *as well as against the exploitative capitalist and reactionary forces that exist among the Mozambican population.*"[57]

In Machel's numerous speeches and writings of the early 1970s, Marxism is never *explicitly* mentioned, yet his method of analysis and policies are firmly rooted in Marxism. To illustrate this, I will consider the example of his analysis of the situation of women in Mozambique.[58] His analysis is clearly related to the standard Marxist-Leninist analysis of the "woman question"[59] and locates the oppression of women within the context of their economic exploitation in a society based on private property. It was, he argues, only when society started to produce a surplus that "the material bases were created which permitted the development of a strata in the heart of society which would appropriate the fruits of the labor of the majority."[60] In this context women, as sources of labor and future labor, also became objects of private appropriation. Bride-price, or *lobolo,* which was general in Mozambique, expressed this reality.

To explain how the exploitation of women is perpetuated, Machel uses an orthodox "base and super-structure" model: "ideology and culture" are the "mechanisms" through which private property relations are sustained.[61] Above all, they are used to inculcate passivity and resignation in women.[62] In combating the exploitation and oppression of women, it is thus necessary to incorporate women into the general political and military fight against oppression[63] and to involve them further in the work of production. It is also necessary to fight at the ideological level against their oppression. The struggle for women's emancipation is vital in Machel's view, but it is vital as part of the *wider* struggle for liberation. Taking a concept of Mao's, he argues that "the *antagonistic contradiction* is not between men and women but, rather, between women and the social order, between all the exploited, women and men, and the social order," while the other contradictions between men and women are of a "*secondary* character."[64] Machel's discussion of the position of women demonstrates not only a thorough knowledge of the main concepts of Marxism, but also an ability to apply them to develop analyses of Mozambican realities. Many of his other speeches demonstrate the same ability.[65]

The early 1970s were a period of consolidation and expansion for FRELIMO. The internal conflicts were apparently essentially over and military advances against the Portuguese continued. In the summer of 1970 a major Portuguese military offensive, Operation "Gordian Knot," designed to drive FRELIMO out of the "liberated zones" of Cabo Delgado, was stalemated and FRELIMO started a major counteroffensive in the area of the Cabora Bassa dam in Tete Province. In July 1972 a new front was also opened in the central province of Manica and Sofala.[66]

Simultaneously, the "revolution" in the "liberated zones" was being consolidated. The "mass line" and the political nature of health and education were stressed. Hospitals, for example, were supposed to provide not only health care and health education, but also literacy classes and political education for their patients. A stay in hospital, said Machel, should be a revolutionizing experience.[67]

The consolidation of the "mass line" in such areas as education and health was paralleled by a growing emphasis on the class issues underpinning such policies. Particularly important was the Central Committee session of December 1972 (the Fifth Session). This was later said to have analyzed the period of the "two lines" in explicitly class terms for the first time. It identified FRELIMO's political line with what was described as "the scientific ideology of the working classes." The Central Committee also decided to "qualify" the principle that FRELIMO was a "front." Since, they said, attempts had been made by people within FRELIMO to use the "front" to "take power to continue to oppress and exploit the people," it was decided to emphasize the point that FRELIMO was a "front" which "has as its point of departure the negation of the exploitation of man by man."[68]

In 1973 the first step was taken towards the creation of a party—the establishment of "committees of the party" within the armed forces. These brought together the "most conscious, most dedicated, most disciplined" elements of the military wing of FRELIMO.[69] Another important step was the founding of a Party School in early 1974. Addressing its first group of students, Machel talked openly in the language of Marxism:

Science, and the objective understanding of our country and of the world acquired through the practice of class struggle and production, are the basis of our thinking.[70]

The aim of the course was to prepare "cadres" who would have the task throughout the country "of instilling the new consciousness and organizing the vanguard." Through study at the school, Machel said, they would raise the consciousness they had all already developed in the struggle, in "practice." The task would be "to synthesize this practice, free it from subjectivism and empiricism, raise it to the level of revolutionary theory, so that we can enrich practice."[71] Thus, on the eve of the transition to independence, FRELIMO was conceiving itself increasingly as a proto-Marxist party, although its public stance was still that of a broad popular "front."

## THE FIRST YEARS OF INDEPENDENCE

Obviously, with the April 1974 coup in Portugal and the coming of independence in June 1975, after a nine-month period of transitional government, FRELIMO's earliest goal—the end of direct foreign domination—had been achieved. But the broader goals of the Second Congress were far from being realized. "People's Power" in the "liberated zones" was one thing, creating equivalent political and economic forms for the entire nation another. The national bases of support for FRELIMO and its policies were ambiguous. While there is evidence that there had been significant clandestine political work and recruitment of members, as well as military activity, in the southern three-quarters of the country,[72] still much of the population must almost certainly have had little direct contact with FRELIMO prior to late 1974.

If enthusiasm for the movement of national liberation ran high, knowledge of what it stood for—beyond the end of Portuguese rule—must surely have been slight. A population over 90 percent illiterate,[73] controlled for decades by colonial fascism, and totally lacking therefore in any experience of democratic political participation and which had *not* gone through the learning process of the war and the "liberated zones," could hardly have been expected to provide a fertile ground for the development of a socialist society.[74] On the other hand, with the control of the main cities, FRELIMO had, for the first time, access to the traditional constituency of Marxist movements: the proletariat.

The Mozambican proletariat is small, and it is hard to characterize it within a classical Marxist framework. Calculating from the 1980 census, one arrives at a figure of only 3 percent of the economically active population as being both urban in residence and employed in one of the categories of work commonly designated as "proletarian": industry, construction, or transport and communications.[75] A far greater percentage of so-called industrial workers in Mozambique are employed in small-scale industry in *rural* areas (packing on tea estates, for example), while many urban employees are to be found in domestic service—and we may assume that many more were found there before independence. To make the picture yet more complex, a large proportion of those who had considerable experience of wage work before independence obtained it as migrant workers, "semiproletarians," going from rural households to work as temporary mine labor in South Africa,[76] or as seasonal laborers on the big plantations. Given this ambiguous composition, and given also the ferocity of Portuguese controls over labor and the ubiquity also of forced labor,[77] it is hardly surprising that levels of political and trade union organization among the Mozambican "proletariat" were generally low. There were, however, exceptions—most notably the dock workers in Lourenço Marques—who had a long tradition of militancy[78] and who perhaps provided some grounds for optimism concerning the future role of the proletariat in a transition to socialism in Mozambique. But FRELIMO remained cautious. The Eighth Session of the Central Committee, meeting in February 1976, concluded that the industrial proletariat had not yet reached the level of political consciousness necessary for it to fulfill its vanguard role: it had been weakened through repression and the dominance of "bourgeois ideology" and sections of it had even been deliberately "bought off" by the colonial regime in order to divide the class.[79]

Even so, at the Third Congress, in February 1977, the proletariat was to be designated as the "leading force" of the Mozambican revolution,[80] in "alliance" with the broad peasant masses who, dispersed and yet more backward, could not qualify for this position. It was also to be stated that although socialism was the *long-term* goal, the conditions did not yet exist for its development because of the political and economic backwardness of Mozambique. The initial tasks of FRELIMO as a Marxist-Leninist party were to be to establish an intermediate phase, "popular democracy," and not socialism.

The period beginning with the "transitional government" was one of considerable economic and political difficulties, and these were also undoubtedly a factor in the decision to transform FRELIMO into a vanguard party. As FRELIMO interpreted it, capitalism, having been militarily defeated in Mozambique, began a new offensive by attempting to undermine the new political forces and the economy. As Machel summed it up in his speech to the Eighth Session, "revolutionary armed struggle" was being replaced with "class struggle" as the principal agent of social transformation.[81] There were, he said, systematic efforts being made to divide and demoralize FRELIMO and, in particular, to create new elites and thus a "bourgeois restoration."[82]

On the economic front, not only did the rapid exodus of Portuguese settlers[83] lead to the collapse of vital sectors of the economy, such as much commercial and cash crop production and the rural distribution network,[84] and not only was there a flight of capital, but what could be seen as conscious and deliberate sabotage took place. Farm and irrigation machinery was deliberately destroyed,[85] cattle slaughtered, and available foodstuffs withheld from the market to create artificial shortages.[86] Factory owners forged their accounts in their attempts to export more capital before leaving, left taking repair manuals and plant designs with them,[87] even broke their own machines before departing.

In the face of the ensuing economic crisis and threatened collapse, FRELIMO initiated a series of measures, including the "state intervention" of abandoned enterprises,[88] a state farm program, and the encouragement of cooperative production on abandoned land. There was also a program of nationalizations.[89] Shortly after independence, land, health and education services, undertaking, insurance, and banking were taken under public control. In early 1976, rental housing was also nationalized. While some of these measures— such as the nationalization (and subsequent great expansion) of education, nationalization of undertaking and rental housing—were clearly designed to give the mass of the population some immediate benefits from independence, other measures, such as the nationalization of land and banking, are best explained as primarily defensive measures. Their main aim would appear to have been to prevent a total economic and social collapse in the face of the Portuguese exodus. The effect of the various measures introduced was, however, to do far more than that. They opened the way to quite wide, though by no means total, state control over key areas of the economy and created the possibility of at least rudimentary planning for the transition to a noncapitalist society.

Even more important for a comprehension of the decisions of the Third Congress, it was decided already during the period of the "transitional government" to attempt to contain the crisis not by state intervention alone, but also through mass political mobilization. Between the autumn of 1974 and the Congress, "dynamizing groups" were established in virtually all places of formal employment—factories, schools, hospitals, government departments, etc.—and on the basis of residency areas in the countryside.[90] Members of "dynamizing groups" were not necessarily FRELIMO members and were elected by mass meetings of workers or residents. However, structurally, the "dynamizing groups" were conceived as an extension of FRELIMO organization,[91] as a way of opening formal channels through which FRELIMO could contact and mobilize the mass of the population.

The functions of the "dynamizing groups," well summed up in their slogan, "unity, vigilance, work," were manifold.[92] Apart from general education, mobilization, and support functions, arguably they had in this period two main functions: first, to help keep minimal production going in situations where managers and technical personnel were leaving and to encourage and organize higher levels of production, by dealing with such questions as work discipline and workplace hygiene, urging peasants to resume and increase cash crop production, etc.; and, second, they were the cornerstone of a policy of "popular vigilance," designed to limit sabotage and corruption. Especially in factories that continued to be privately owned, the "dynamizing groups" were supposed to exercise a watchdog function. In government offices, "intervened" firms, hospitals, and the like, they were supposed to watch out for petty corruption or theft and to provide a channel for criticism of people in positions of responsibility.

In the creation of the "dynamizing groups" one can see the attempt to extend the policies of "People's Power," developed in the "liberated zones," to the rest of the country. The earlier insistence that policies must have the active support and involvement of the masses to succeed is repeated. Furthermore, with the creation of the "dynamizing groups" a network was created which was able to provide the organizational basis for party cells when FRELIMO became a vanguard party; and a process of political education and formation was initiated which could later provide recruits to the party who would already have had some experience of political work. Thus, by early 1977, the basic institutional forms were already in existence for the transition to a Marxist-Leninist vanguard party.

## THE THIRD CONGRESS: MARXISM-LENINISM

As I have previously pointed out, the terms "Marxism" and "Marxism-Leninism" are not to found in documents or in speeches by FRELIMO leaders prior to the Third Congress, even though they were evidently thinking within a Marxist framework. However, in the main policy document of the Third Congress, the *Report of the Central Committee*,[93] "socialism" is declared to be the long-term goal in Mozambique and "Marxism-Leninism," the "scientific tool" of the masses led by a "vanguard party," the means to its attainment. Marxism-Leninism, says the *Report*, constitutes the theoretical synthesis of the rich experience of the oppressed classes and peoples of the World. . . . Creatively applied and developed in the process of our struggle, it is a powerful light which illuminates the path for the working classes to follow in the process of building the new society.[94]

However, the new society, in the form of socialism, cannot be built at once. Rather, the present phase is described as "popular democracy," a "long historical epoch" during which "profound transformations" of society will have to take place prior to attaining the era of socialism. Before examining FRELIMO's conception of "popular democracy," however, I will consider FRELIMO's decision to transform itself from a "front" to a vanguard party.

## Creation of a Vanguard Party

The attempt to create the basis for a transition to socialism need not *necessarily* imply the creation of a vanguard party. It could well be argued, as it was in Tanzania, that what is needed is a *mass* party[95] in which the majority of the people can be incorporated and mobilized. In Mozambique, however, such a view was not adopted. With the Third Congress, FRELIMO ceased to be a broad "front" organization—even though it retained its name—and became a vanguard party in the classical Leninist sense. That is to say, it became a cadre party, with membership only open to selected militants who successfully fulfilled a period of candidacy and with a "democratic centralist" structure in which decisions of superior levels are held to be always binding upon the lower levels of the party.[96] The broad masses of the population, it was decided, should be organized not in the party but in the "mass democratic organizations," such as the women's and youth movements, under the control and tutelage of the party.

The reasons given for this decision are various. Although they relate mainly to conditions in Mozambique following independence, it is clear that the concept of vanguardism was already prominent, at least in Machel's thinking, prior to independence. In early 1974, discussing the problem of drawing increasingly wide strata of the population into FRELIMO, yet still managing to elevate its "ideological rigor," he talked of the development of an "organized revolutionary vanguard" within the "heart of the front."[97] It was, he argued, above all the armed section of FRELIMO, the FPLM,[98] which served the function of a vanguard:

> In the context of a broad front without a vanguard party, which is our situation, the army develops as the most dynamic and conscious sector of the front, the sector which produces proven cadres, not only for combat tasks, but for all other tasks.[99]

The *Report* echoes this view in 1977, stating that, although the revolutionary process was started in Mozambique without a vanguard party, the leadership "had a vanguard character" and "the FPLM, in practice, constituted an organized vanguard of the people."[100] This was especially so, it is claimed, following the period of the "two lines," when it was realized that the battle was against "national" as well as "foreign" class enemies.[101]

With independence, the *Report* argues, the situation changed yet further and the formal establishment of a vanguard party became necessary. First, the "intensification of class struggle" required a more organized leadership of the working classes: only with a disciplined and ideologically advanced vanguard at their head could the working classes hope to win the battles against the reactionary forces at work.[102] Second, the tasks of "popular democracy," of building the bases for the transition to socialism, required the leadership of a vanguard, a vanguard capable of grasping the principles of Marxism-Leninism and applying them to the Mozambican situation,[103] capable of mobilizing and organizing the masses for their numerous tasks.

The argument for a vanguard party was not made, I would argue, solely at the level of political organization and tactics. Nor was it made simply because vanguardism is a routine part of Marxist-Leninist doctrine. It grew out of FRELIMO's analysis of the role of different classes in Mozambique. Although the war had been fought primarily with the support and participation of the peasantry, it was argued that the peasantry cannot play the leading role in the new phase, the struggle to create the "bases" for the transition to socialism. The peasantry, the Eighth Session argued, had shown, even in the "nonliberated zones," a strong nationalist sentiment and a resistance to colonialism. However, certain rural elements, their basis in traditional "feudalism," had been encouraged by the Portuguese to develop forms of capitalist organization. "This situation," the Central Committee concluded, "creates the objective base which favors the development of an agrarian bourgeoisie,[104] animated by the desire to substitute itself for the displaced colonial bourgeoisie. For this reason and because of the generally low ideological level of the peasantry, steeped in "obscurantism" and the traditional oppression of youth and women,[105] it must fall to the proletariat to be the "leading class" in the "worker-peasant alliance."

However, the proletariat in Mozambique is, as we have seen, both numerically small and lacking in political experience. It must play the leading role in the broad alliance of the working masses characterized as a "worker-peasant alliance," but it is ill-equipped to do so. The proletariat is destined to grow into the "leading class," but is not yet so:

> Fighting for the social control of its own production, the working class . . . thus gradually incorporates the conditions which turn it into the leading force of the process of liberation.[106]

In the meanwhile, and as an aid to the development of the proletariat, revolutionary leadership must remain with the vanguard party, whose members may be of any class origin, but whose proven revolutionary practice and grasp of revolutionary theory should enable them to unite and lead the masses.

> The historic mission of the Party is to lead, organize, orient and educate the masses, thus transforming the popular mass movement into a powerful instrument for the destruction of capitalism and the building of socialism.[107]

It was stressed in 1977 that it is ultimately the "masses" and not the party who make the revolution.[108] The party does not substitute itself as the agent of revolution—at least in theory. But with the Stalinist experience in mind and with FRELIMO's own stress on the *lack* of development of the revolutionary class, one is bound to raise the question: What prevents the party from acting "on behalf of" the masses, imposing policies which in reality oppress or even exploit the masses?

FRELIMO's answer would be that there are two kinds of safeguards. One would be their methods of work. In the long years of the liberation struggle, moving experimentally towards new forms of social organization in the "liberated zones," FRELIMO developed work methods incorporating a process of "criticism and self-criticism" in which collective evaluation of action became the norm. "Criticism and self-criticism," the careful scrutiny of each cadre's actions by the cadre and his or her comrades, continues to be advocated,[109] and should be a check on tendencies to elitism, corruption, or insensitivity to the masses.

If one looks at what has happened since 1977, it would appear that these methods are deeply ingrained within the party. Indeed, it is striking, in comparison with other vanguard parties, how willing the FRELIMO leadership has been—albeit in a carefully controlled way—to invite criticism, and also to criticize itself in public. This was seen particularly clearly in the case of the Fourth Congress, in 1983. Mass discussion of a set of "theses" prepared prior to the Congress produced widespread debate and criticisms of both local officials and policy matters. At the Congress itself, the Central Committee's report, *Out of Underdevelopment to Socialism*,[110] criticized previous social and economic policy, including the stress on "big projects" and the failure to support family agriculture and have sufficiently involved the masses in the planning process. Many of the delegates to the Congress, some of whom were fairly uneducated peasants, added their own vigorous criticisms to those of the leadership.[111]

However, this having been said, such "criticism and self-criticism," although vital, comes always, by definition, too late. It is only after mistakes have been made, abuses of power committed, that an attempt to correct the situation is made through this process. Thus a second kind of safeguard has also been deemed necessary—a say for the mass of the population in making the decisions that affect their lives. To this end, numerous institutions of "popular democracy" have been established in Mozambique. But FRELIMO's very real commitment to fostering grass-roots participation has uneasily coexisted in tension with their vanguardist and centralist tendencies, and has too often been subordinated to the latter.

## Popular Democracy

Already prior to independence, Machel had talked of "the process of popular democratic revolution"[112] in relation to FRELIMO's policies in the "liberated zones." At the time of independence, in June 1975, the Seventh Session of the Central Committee had defined the postindependence phase for the whole country as "popular democracy" and in 1977 the concept was fleshed out into a series of concrete political, economic, and social policies.

The concept of "popular democracy" in fact appears to have two distinct, though closely connected, meanings: it refers, as suggested above, to the development of a political system designed to enable the masses to participate in the making of decisions which affect their lives; it also, as we have seen, refers to a general phase of social development, intermediate between colonial capitalism and socialism, in which levels of production and the socialization of production are supposed to increase hand in hand and the political consciousness of the masses to mature.

As a political system, "popular democracy" implies two processes. The first involves the development of a multiplicity of nongovernment structures though which the masses can participate in decision making. These included not only extending the party, with cells being established in as many workplaces as possible, but also the continuation of less ideologically selective organs, such as the "dynamizing groups" in residential areas, establishing "production councils" and then trade unions in places of employment, and consumer cooperatives. The proliferation of "mass democratic organizations," under the guidance of the party and in which it was planned to organize large sections of people according to particular interests, was also seen as vital. These organizations were described as "the contact point between the Party and the People,"[113] through which it would be possible for FRELIMO cadres "to know and feel, at every moment, the problems, the needs, the opinions, the criticisms, and suggestions of diverse sections of the population."[114] The womens' movement (OMM) and the youth movement (OJM) are presently the most developed of the "mass democratic organizations," but others—for example, organizations of journalists and artists—do already exist, as do the beginnings of trade unions.

The second process involves the development of a new range of democratic state institutions, necessary if "the colonial-capitalist state apparatus" is to be destroyed.[115] In particular, a whole range of "popular assemblies," ranging from a national assembly down to the basic administrative unit, the locality, were called for by the Third Congress. Those at the lower levels were to provide organs for the masses to participate directly "in resolving their immediate problems and in orienting and controlling government action at various levels."[116] The first assembly elections were held in late 1977. The election process consisted of public meetings to discuss and evaluate candidates, followed by a vote by show of hands. The initial process elected members of 814 Locality Assemblies. Although candidates had to be approved by the local "dynamizing group" and were often local notables, many were rejected—sometimes in rather heated meetings—because of allegations that they had, for example, collaborated with the colonial secret police.[117] Higher-level assemblies, culminating in the national-level Popular Assembly, whose task it was to approve all new laws, were indirectly elected from and by the lower assemblies.[118]

However, in practice the role of the Locality Assemblies, the grass-roots organs, appears to have been minimal with regard to decision making. Although the number of such assemblies was to be increased to 1322 in the 1980 elections, in 1983 the Central Committee was to conclude:

> Their impact on society, however, does not match up to their numbers, ability and influence. . . . They operate formally but the practical effect of their leadership is not felt.[119]

A firm commitment was made to the goal of making Locality Assemblies organs of local decision making and even implementation:

> They must be given, by juridical right, precise powers over sectors that are important for the people, such as planning and distribution of the means of production necessary for the family sector, control over supplies and, in the urban areas, control over management of state housing.[120]

Just how this local power is to be preserved within the framework of overall state planning is not, however, an issue that has yet been clearly addressed. As a political system, "popular democracy" can be seen as an attempt to extend the institutions of "People's Power" from the "liberated zones" to the country as a whole. However, as has been shown in the discussion of FRELIMO's vanguardism, the masses are not considered wholly trustworthy. There is, clearly, a tension between FRELIMO's vanguardism and their advocacy of democracy.

At this point, of course, we need to return to some of the broader issues concerning the Mozambique's place in southern Africa. If forms of external pressure and the ensuing economic disintegration continue after "Nkomati" to be as intense as before, one might reasonably predict that "popular democracy" will wither under the exigencies of military mobilization and a war economy. If, on the contrary, Mozambique is able to pursue its internal development plans within a more favorable international framework, there is at least the possibility that "popular democracy" will become something considerably more than formal rhetoric.

## CONCLUSIONS

The essence of FRELIMO's own account of its ideological history is the assertion that the adoption of Marxism is an *internal* development, a result of FRELIMO's own process of learning. My reading of the material available from the period 1962–1977 suggests that FRELIMO's own interpretation does seem broadly justified. The leadership that took power in 1975 and declared FRELIMO to be a Marxist-Leninist party in 1977, did indeed have a long apprenticeship in Marxism. They had internalized it, as their own tool of analysis and policy formation, long before 1977. What I have called a tacit Marxism would appear to have been developed by 1968 at the latest. Furthermore, it is clear that what was developed was not simply a rhetoric, or a prepackaged "canon" supplied from without. For, as I have shown, there are numerous instances of the leadership using a Marxist framework in order to examine specifically Mozambican realities, such as bride-price or the problems of mobilizing the peasants in the "liberated zones." FRELIMO's decision in 1977 to declare itself a Marxist-Leninist party while retaining its own name, and not renaming itself a Communist party, well symbolizes its relationship to the Communist states.

Naive anti-Communism—such as the Portuguese indulged in[121]—apart, the main way of attempting to dismiss FRELIMO's adoption of Marxism has been to describe the conflicts within FRELIMO as simple power conflicts between "elites" coming from different ethnic groups. According to this interpretation—put forward most forcefully by Opello[122]—the period of the "two lines" was not a period of growing class conflict within FRELIMO, but simply a period of competition for "the highest power and status roles," conducted along ethnically divided lines. It is undoubtedly true, as Opello well documents, that many of the would-be leaders who were expelled from FRELIMO used tribal and racial arguments to stake their claims. However, as Opello himself points out, these leaders failed to bring about significant defections from the rank and file. This lack of defection suggests that FRELIMO had in fact been remarkably *successful* in overcoming tribal disunity. Furthermore, the fact that tribal and racial arguments were used against it does not imply that the radical leadership was also "really" fighting either a tribal battle or a "power and status" battle, just choosing to camouflage it in what Opello calls "Marxist rhetoric." Nor does it imply that their "two lines" analysis was necessarily wrong. The problem with Opello's argument is that it too simply assumes Marxism to be a foreign and extraneous doctrine, handily and superficially introduced to meet the ideological needs of one faction, and does not look at the gradual *internal* evolution towards Marxism which I have documented.

Similarly, the more general formulations of Jowitt concerning the "integrating" and "differentiating" functions of Marxism-Leninism in African movements have to be rejected, at least for the Mozambican case.[123] What is at issue here, as in Opello's argument, is a kind of reductionism. Both authors simply rule out the possibility that Marxism could be adopted for its own political and analytical strengths, and instead look "behind" it for other motives. But it is not tenable to argue in the case of FRELIMO that Marxism was adopted to "differentiate" the new "elite" from the colonial power it was fighting against. Given the fascist characteristics of the colonial power in the case of Mozambique, "differentiation" could as well have been served by the mildest of liberal programs—as indeed it was in 1962. Nor is it helpful to say, with regard to FRELIMO, that Marxism was adopted because of its "integrating" potential. On the contrary, it proved to be divisive to the leadership, and a simple nationalist program with strong racist overtones would surely have proven a far more effective ideology of "integration."

Had Marxism been adopted by FRELIMO only because of foreign pressure or because it appeared to be a useful facade for an elite to hide its "real" interests behind, one could expect it to be easily abandoned. Indeed, such a reading would invite one to interpret "Nkomati" and the current turning to the West for economic succor as an opportunistic abandonment of the project of socialist transformation by a leadership who was never serious about it and whose overriding goal is to maintain its personal power. My reading of the history of FRELIMO's ideological development suggests we must have another interpretation. Whether or not FRELIMO does in fact turn out still to have, in Saul's words, "room to revitalize its socialist project," we may be sure that a serious attempt to revitalize that project will be made.

# CHAPTER 11

# Power, Class, and Traditional Knowledge in Sahel Food Production

## Richard W. Franke

The great Sahel drought and famine of 1968–1974 left dead from one hundred thousand to a quarter of a million people. Precipitation failures in 1977, 1978, and 1980 occurred over large areas of the Sahel, again bringing on localized famines; and in 1984–1985 the region joined east and southern Africa in a famine that has received widespread media attention.

What can be done to develop the Sahel and make it drought proof? The aftermath of the Sahel drought and famine has been the organization of one of the most extensive development programs in modern times. In 1977 the Western powers agreed at an Ottawa, Canada, meeting on a $10 billion program for food self-sufficiency and self-sustaining development in the region by the year 2000. When one considers the fact that the Sahel contains less than 50 million people, the $10 billion aid commitments amounts to one of the highest per capita contributions in the history of Western aid to any poor region, sur- passed perhaps only by the Marshall Plan for post–World War II Europe and the large U.S. aid packages to Israel and Egypt.

The postdrought problems in the Sahel are pressing, indeed. The region has suffered many centuries of intensive abuse of its environmental resource base. In some areas, desertification may be permanently removing land from culti- vation. The urgency of protecting and reclaiming the Sahel is thus great. On the other hand, most Western "donor" nations have little scientific and histor- ical background upon which to design and implement the vast development program envisioned in the Ottawa document. Indeed, as we have shown else- where (Franke and Chasin, 1979, 1980), the historical record so far suggests strongly that Western policies have been major contributors to the current de- graded state of the Sahel that renders its food production systems so vulnerable to shifts in the weather.

At the same time, the Sahel *is* a delicate region, bordering the desert, with unreliable rainfall, and in many areas thin or otherwise difficult soils. It thus

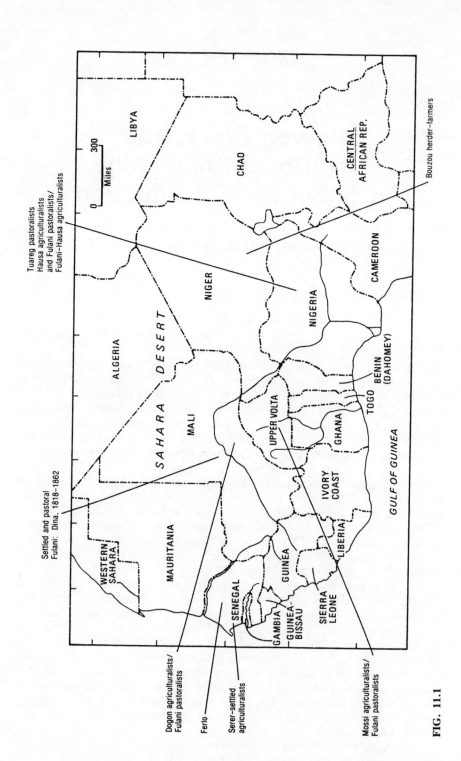

**FIG. 11.1**

poses serious problems to the development experts, who often seek quick and spectacular solutions.

Over many centuries, the indigenous peoples of the Sahel, despite raids, wars, the rise of slave-based empires, and other human catastrophes, hammered out a series of adaptations to their problematical environment. From the delicate pastures of the desert fringe to the more lush high savannas that grade into the tropical rain forest of the Atlantic coast, Sahelians have developed a wide range of combinations of caravan trading, fishing, animal herding, mixed animal herding—agriculture, and agriculture.

It is one of the major hypotheses of this essay that these adaptations, deriving from many centuries of experimentation with the land and other resources, represent valuable potential elements for any reconstruction of the Sahelian environment. Research into these production systems, however, suggests further that power and class factors have played and continue to play important roles in influencing the course of environmental adaptation. More specifically, the evidence reveals that the most ecologically sound Sahelian production systems have arisen where: (1) farmers and herders have been in intensive contact, exchanging knowledge about plants, animals, and their interrelations; and (2) producing classes have had substantial power vis-à-vis the dominating classes or, conversely, where ruling classes have had the least power and privilege relative to the producing classes.

Why should positive developments in Sahelian food production systems arise in regions with intense herder–farmer interaction? This correlation seems relatively easy to explain. Where two different but related productions systems are in lengthy contact, it would seem likely that experimentation over time would produce mixtures of the systems that would have high survival value.

But why should the power and class factors outlined in hypothesis (2), above, obtain? The key to understanding this feature of Sahelian food production systems and the development and maintenance of traditional knowledge would seem to lie in the nature of the traditional knowledge itself, for, as we shall see, the common feature of the systems to be examined is a positive effect on maintaining the main fixed capital asset for the production system: soil fertility.

This maintenance feature can be best understood by looking first at its opposite. It is difficult to maintain fixed capital resources in stratified societies, and this is most easily seen in the extreme case where a nonproductive but self-aggrandizing class has taken control of the society, become a ruling class. The ruling class needs to expand production to satisfy its needs for luxury, simply to maintain itself as a nonproductive class, to support its repressive apparatus (police and military, who are also mostly nonproductive), and to support its international trade and defense networks. The ruling classes that arose in the precolonial Sahel had all these needs, and in areas where their control and penetration into the villages was most extreme, resource-maintaining practices had to be sacrificed to increased output. This could require excessive use of the soils, as happened in some areas, or it could take the form of intensified exploitation of local labor: farmers and herders responding to the demand for surplus production for their rulers would not have the time or initiative to engage in proper composting, production of high-quality fertilizer, acacia–cattle seed cycles, and the like. The spread of modern power and class relations was thus most likely correlated with the decline of indigenous resource protection practices except in those cases where producers escaped to the fringes of the empires and could maintain control over their own labor and reap its benefits themselves; or, as in one case to be explained, where an organized movement for redistribution and a lessening of the demands of the rulers could make use of a similar strategy.

Those societies with the least powerful ruling classes, because they produce primarily for needs of the producers, are not as susceptible to pressure to skew the distribution of fixed capital and labor time solely towards increasing the amount of the final product. In agriculture, this means that they can devote substantial amounts of labor time to maintaining their fixed capital resources, much as an artisan spends time maintaining tools and equipment that the factory worker has little concern for.

Societies in which there is little exploitation of labor by a nonproductive ruling class thus correlate positively with a capacity to develop and implement practices that maintain fixed capital such as land and its associated improvements: trees, animals, etc.

The plan of this essay is first to outline several important features of Sahelian farming and animal herding system in order to establish hypothesis one, above, that traditional Sahelian farmer–herder interaction led to ecologically sound productive systems; then to examine in detail for such systems, in order of increasing degrees of stratification, which further verify hypothesis two, namely, that class inequality undermines these fruitful farmer–herder systems. A final section of the essay will be devoted to consideration of possible development implications of the findings.

## SAHELIAN FOOD PRODUCTION SYSTEMS

West Africa south of the Sahara can be pictured as a great flat pan tilted slightly towards the south. From the south towards the north are a series of ecological zones running from east to west, each drier than the last until the desert is reached. As the tropical rain forest shades into dense grasslands, shifting cultivation techniques change with longer fallow periods in the savanna areas. The true Sahel is a region with 300–600 millimeters (12–25 inches) annual rainfall and is characterized by thin, sandy soils and a "parkland" savanna with medium to short grasses and widely dispersed shrubs. The Sahel is a transition zone where agriculture gives way to animal herding.

It is precisely this transitional character of the Sahel that has led to some of the most important human production innovations in integrating plants, animals, and human energy. Because both agriculture and pastoralism are found in close proximity, there have developed a series of exchanges of products, personnel, and knowledge that have co-enriched both food production systems.

### Agriculture

From the tropical rain forest through the entire savanna grassland zone and into much of the Sahel, agriculture has become the major food-producing system. Using the widely accepted practice of shifting or "slash and burn" cultivation, Sahelian farmers cut the trees and bushes, allowing them to dry out on the fields during the long dry season. Just before the rains, the fields are fired, allowing the accumulated minerals to be released from the debris in a way that favors their reabsorption into food plants (Russell, 1973; Geertz, 1963). Burning seems to speed up the natural decomposition process without causing major environmental damage (Lamotte, 1975; Moran, 1979: 219–221).

Millet and sorghum are the principle grain crops, being well suited to the brief, intense rains and long periods of hot dry weather that characterize the region. Along with grains, cotton, sesame, sweet potatoes, manioc, eggplant, peppers, and shea butter are grown, and mango as well in the wetter parts of the savanna. Several types of beans, cucumbers, and corn are also produced. West Africa is the scene of an apparently independent development of both dry and wet rice cultivation and, in some areas, of irrigation systems (Portères, 1970: 47; Forde, 1960: 126).

## Animal Herding

North of twelve to fourteen degrees north latitude, the absence of the tsetse fly combines with the dry grasslands ecology to favor the herding of animals over agriculture as a major food-producing system. Animal herding makes possible the use of lands that are difficult or impossible to develop for agriculture. Animals can be moved with the shifting rains to make use of the best pasture conditions throughout the year. Diversity of animals—camels, cattle, sheep, goats—and social institutions such as lending of animals to other groups helps herders hedge against the possibility of losing too many of their animals to either drought or epidemics (Smith, 1978; Swift, 1973, 1977). Herders also display substantial medical skills with their animals and ecological knowledge of the pastures (de St. Croix, 1944; Veyret, 1952; van Raay and de Leeuw, 1974).

## Herding and Farming Integration

Perhaps of greatest significance in assessing the potential of traditional Sahelian food production systems are the various forms of integration of animal herding and crop cultivation systems that have developed in the region over many centuries.

Herder–farmer symbiosis involves exchanges at two levels. During the dry season, herders camp with their animals on the edge of a farming village. They exchange meat and milk for the grain of the farmers, thus improving the diets of both groups. But another series of exchanges occurs as well. Cattle graze on the harvested fields, gaining dry-season food that helps reduce their weight loss during this period. Simultaneously, the cattle provide several services to the farmers' land: they strip the millet or sorghum stalks and break up ridges with their hooves, thus simplifying the future use of the land for grain production. In addition, the cattle droppings provide manure fertilizer that improves soil fertility and leads to higher grain output.

Social relations between herders and farmers include a mixture of hostility, alliance, tension, amicability, and sometimes violence. Among the major zones of herder–farmer interaction is the region of Maradi in southern Niger. Here Bouzou herders will spend part of the dry season on the fields of Hausa or Bouzou cultivators. Herders develop more or less permanent alliances with farmers, returning year after year to the same fields, the same owner. Part of the millet received by the herders is in payment for the cattle manuring the fields. If the payment is judged insufficient, the herding family may choose to ally itself in the future with a different cultivator (Mainet, 1965: 51). In addition, some farmers may own animals which they lend out to herders who take them to the northern pastures and the salt cure during the rainy season months (ibid.: 54; Nicolas, 1963c: 6).

A problem with the system, however, is that animals often damage the farmers' crops, causing the relations to degrade into violence (Nicolas, 1963c: 1). One of the most tension-ridden areas where farmer–herder interaction occurs is the Zgaret region in western Niger. In 1916 Bella and Tuareg herders burned the granaries of the Kado agriculturalists, and in 1964 another period of tension resulted in the Bella herders paying fines of 10,000 francs and afterwards refusing the Kado the right to farm lands under Bella control (Sidikou, 1974: 199, 203–205, 209). Nonetheless, the same herders and farmers who are at each others' throats during the early rainy season, when the animals may wreck the crop, have quite a different view of each other in the dry season, when symbiotic needs become paramount:

> This is the time of true peace between the two communities. Bringing a bit of millet or some small gifts, the Bella are allowed to camp on the farmers' fields and install their animals which fertilize the fields. . . . The Bella who visits the village is received with open arms. . . . the somber times of tension are forgotten. (Sidikou, 1974: 209)

Several hundred kilometers west of Niger another pattern obtains. In Senegal's Ferlo, Wolof peanut farmers are pushing onto Fulani pastures, driving the latter closer to the fringe of the Sahara. Despite the social tensions and environmental strain brought on by expansionist commercial agriculture (Franke and Chasin, 1980: 104–106; Klein, 1979: 80–89; Sall, 1978) and despite tensions and complaints over use of water in some cases, cooperative exchanges could still be reported in the 1970s for the Diourbel area just west of the Ferlo:

> The farmer . . . views the arrival of the herdsmen during the dry season quite positively. Cattle are allowed to graze crop residues which provide the farmer the chance for soil enrichment without the problem of transport of organic fertilizer to the fields. There is also the ready supply of milk and butter . . . [for which] the farmer allows the herdsman access to the well or wells in the area. (Ware, 1979: 163–164; cf. Grenier, 1960: 54)

Indeed, Ferlo-area Fulani have proved useful in agricultural development: local farmers were found to have difficulty in training and using animal-drawn farm implements while herders could make this adjustment with relative ease (Ware, 1979: 172). The possibility thus exists for a new set of cooperative relationships based on herders' skills in animal tending, if the competition for land and other resources could be worked out. Throughout the Sahel, with present policies, however, the expansion of commercial agriculture seems destined to work *against* the establishment of new patterns of cooperation and exchange as governments tend to support the interests of the politically more important farmers and the expansion of cash crops, whatever the long-term detriment (Gallais, 1972: 305; McCown et al., 1979; Barral, 1974).

Despite its many imperfections, then, including in particular the problem of violence between the major parties and the difficulties the system has had in surviving the effects of cash crop agricultural expansion, the establishment of herder–farmer integrated production relations nevertheless allowed for the development and maintenance of several highly important adaptations preserving the fragile ecology of the Sahel:

1. It allows the cattle to stay on the northern pastures during the rainy season, helping to maintain plant species variety that inhibits ecological degradation.
2. It allows the cattle to move over large distances, thus spreading the seeds of acacia species, reinforcing plant species variety.
3. It allows the animals a dry-season resting place free of the tsetse but also with grain stalks for food and water resources nearby.
4. It allows for use of the animal dung and other services during the dry season to improve the soils of the grain producers' fields, thus increasing overall output of food.
5. It generally keeps the animals away from the farms during the cultivation season when they can damage the crops and allows the herds to graze a few months in pastures where they do not compete for resources with grain producers.

In addition to these overall features of herder–farmer integration, there are several specific adaptations involving potentially important scientific discoveries that might provide useful starting points for current research into ways to protect the Sahel, stop desertification, and develop the region. It is to these specific adaptations, and the conditions in which they seem to have arisen, that we now turn our attention.

## TRADITIONAL KNOWLEDGE AND ENVIRONMENTAL PROTECTION: FOUR CASE STUDIES

Along the several thousands of kilometers of contact between herders and farmers, Sahelians have exchanged milk, butter, grain, manure, animals, and the like for many centuries. Out of this intensive contact between two different adaptations to the environment and two different but mutually interdependent food production systems, Sahelians have developed at least four apparently significant additional mechanisms for maintaining the environment:

1. A highly developed land use rotation among the Bouzou of Niger.
2. A complex system of fertilizer composting among the Dogon of Mali.
3. The intensive use of *Acacia albida* trees among the Serer of Senegal.
4. An innovative set of land use regulations among the nineteenth-century Fulani of the Niger River Inland Delta or Mali.

In each of these cases, the agricultural resource base has benefited from association with the knowledge passed on from the herder–farmer interactions. In each case, further, it has been the more egalitarian farming group that has adopted and maintained the improved practice, rather than a more stratified neighbor that presumably had similar opportunities.

### A Bouzou Village: Farming with a Herders' Land Use System

Located seventy kilometers west of Zinder, Niger, the village of Zengo Iletafane is composed of former Tuareg vassals who may have originated in the

Aïr region far to the north, but who migrated about 120 years ago into the Zinder region. Here they were given protection and partially absorbed by the highly stratified Hausa agriculturalists (Nicolas, 1962: 155–156).

Despite their cultural and technical similarities with the Hausa—they use the same basic farming implements and cultivate the same crops—the Bouzou of Zengo Iletafane have apparently invented a possibly model system of land use that combines elements of their herder past with those of their farming present.

The essence of their innovation is the creation of parallel land strips, separated by thin rows of tall grasses to mark the extended family property lines. Crosscutting these east–west strips are the temporary compounds of the Bouzou, all of which run along a north–south axis, protected on one side by a fence of thorny bush material which also keeps the animals away from the fields. The system is organized on a total area of 1300 meters wide and 1800 to 2400 meters in length (ibid.: 139).

At any given time about two-thirds of the fields are planted, one-third is fallow. The house and compound row moves each year about one hundred meters east until a certain point is reached. Then the entire village moves back to the western edge and begins moving east again. The entire cycle takes twelve years from west to east (ibid.: 141–143).

What are the advantages of this highly structured land use system? First, it allows for an organized rotation of crop and fallow, thus preventing any particular parcel of land from deteriorating more rapidly than any other. Second, the Bouzou have several animals which are corralled at night along the residential strip so that they fertilize intensively the north–south section that is to be opened for planting the following year (ibid.: 149). Supplemented by human food wastes, ashes from burnt underbrush, and weeds that are pulled twice during the growing season, but left loose on the ground as a mulch (ibid.: 148), the Bouzou fields maintain a high degree of fertility and, by 1962 at least, had not suffered the decline brought on by peanut monocropping that afflicted some of the nearby Hausa farmers who worked essentially the same kinds of soils (ibid.: 160; cf. Franke and Chasin, 1979). In summarizing the novelty and the sophistication of the Bouzou village land pattern, a French observer wrote:

> The entire territory is thus periodically passed over, lived upon, fertilized, cultivated, then left to fallow by a sequence of herds, cultivations, compounds, and people. At the head of this sequence come the animals, followed immediately by the house-compounds; immediately thereafter come the agricultural fields, protected from the animals by a thorny bush barrier. (Nicolas, 1962: 144)

Several aspects of this system of production should be noted. First, the Bouzou come from a herding background and, indeed, their mobile village adaptation to farming suggests an application of herding concepts of land use to farming. Unlike the Hausa, who separate the two enterprises, the Bouzou keep them integrated much of the year, although the herds must be taken fifteen kilometers north to a forest area for late dry-season grazing (ibid.: 150–151). Second, the Bouzou of the village of Zengo Iletafane have resisted—at least until quite recently—the imposition of (Hausa) hierarchy, having maintained instead a basically egalitarian structure. The "chief," recognized by the Hausa, has little authority among the Bouzou and no power to interfere in land exchanges, inheritance, or the like (ibid.: 157). The egalitarian and collective orientation of the Bouzou—a high level of cooperation is required to maintain the organized passage of the herds, houses, and people—also contrasts with the individualistic and politically more "ambitious" Fulani herders nearby (ibid.: 159). Thus we see an ecologically sound food production system developing out of the matrix of herding and farming and integrated mixtures of both and being maintained in an egalitarian social structure that has resisted pressures from above the village level by more hierarchical neighbors.

The Bouzou crop and fertilizing rotation system is not without its difficulties, however. When studied around 1960, the system was showing early signs of disintegration from a series of related factors. Among these were land fragmentation resulting from population growth, the influence of Islam, the spread of Hausa lifestyle resulting in more polygamy, the investment in textiles rather than in cattle, and the possible development of unmovable houses. All these factors were compounded by the spread of peanut monocropping outside the village that was reducing fallow areas and forests nearby and also spreading consumer and taxation pressures (ibid.: 161). A cattle epidemic in 1958 exacerbated these tendencies, as some extended families were hit harder than others. In the newly expanding commercial environment, this could result in the rise of permanent inequalities and a breakdown of the collective egalitarian structure that was maintaining the cyclical land use pattern (ibid.: 162).

Nonetheless, the village of Zengo Iletafane is of potential scientific interest, a source of experimentation in a rational use of land. It is unfortunate that recent analyses of the Sahel or proposals for reducing its drought vulnerability or developing and maintaining its resources have not made reference to Zengo Iletafane.

## Household Composting: The Dogon of Mali

Several hundred kilometers west of Zengo Iletafane live the Dogon of Mali. The Dogon are well known to ethnographers because of their elaborate religious art and rituals (Griaule, 1965). An as yet little researched aspect of Dogon culture, however, is the intricate agricultural adaptation to one of the most varied environments in the Sahel zone and the development of a potentially important form of composting and other methods of maintaining soil fertility.

The Dogon population of about 250,000 in the early 1960s was distributed along an escarpment southeast of Timbuktu. The people inhabit the ridges of the escarpment, where they apparently sought refuge in earlier centuries from Fulani attempts to convert them to Islam. In addition to the fortresslike villages along the ridges, the Dogon now also inhabit the plateau to the northwest and parts of the Seno Valley that lies to the southeast of the escarpment.

In a region where 60 percent of the 500–700-millimeter rainfall (just at and above the Sahel parameters of 300–600 millimeters) falls in July and August (Gallais, 1965: 124), the Dogon make use of valley, plateau, riverbanks, and hillsides to produce staple millet and a variety of dry-season vegetables both for local consumption and for the market.

Dogon rainy-season crops and techniques are similar to those found in other parts of the Sahel. The Dogon, however, are especially expert at associating *Acacia albida* with their millet fields, particularly on the Seno Plain where some of the trees appear to be two to three centuries old and are fairly evenly distributed at about forty to fifty per hectare (ibid.: 126). The trees are protected in some fields by rings of thorny branches. Burning of these fields is either very rapidly ended or not done at all where the trees are younger and perhaps could be harmed by the fire (Mounier, 1981). Distinctions regarding the length of establishment of the *Acacia albida* lead to different patterns of rotation, length of fallow, and length of cropping (Gallais, 1965: 126, 131). Fulani cattle graze harvested millet stalks and provide a light manuring to these fields.

The originality of Dogon farming practices, however, concerns the use to which the majority portion of the animal dung is put: into an intense composting process. During the dry season, much of the animal dung is collected and placed in a shallow hole in the center of the compound courtyard. Here it is further enriched with millet stalks, peelings from the kitchen, ashes from the fires, baobab fruit and/or peelings, and human wastes. In addition, small animals or even a horse will be tethered on this compost heap at night, adding more dung and, equally important, mixing and breaking up the materials with their stamping and walking about (ibid.: 128). Unfortunately, the precise organic and chemical content of this material may not yet have been subjected to modern analysis, but it is likely of value in enriching the local soils.

Indeed, the Dogon, because they live in a part of the Sahel with steep slopes, and because some river water is available nearby, have focused their agricultural creativity on preserving and enriching the soil rather than on improving water use techniques. During the rainy season, for example, some of the compost will be spread by youth work groups on certain of the millet fields, usually those with the youngest or sparsest distributions of *Acacia albida* (ibid.: 127–128).

During the long dry season, however, the compost is added to another of the remarkable features of traditional Dogon agriculture: dry-season vegetable gardens. These gardens produce peppers, onions, Guinea corn, potatoes, manioc, and tobacco (ibid.: 132, 136). So important is soil preservation to the Dogon that in some places they have created small rock-walled water catchments, in others raised soil dikes, and in others dry-season reservoirs where small wells are dug down to six meters deep and where small terraces are filled with sand and compost to a depth of thirty to forty centimeters. In a few privileged locations, irrigation canals are possible behind cement dams, and banana trees—imported from wetter regions to the south—grow right in the canals (ibid.: 134). For the most part, however, the Dogon irrigate these fields with the laborious technique of splashing the water over the dike in a calabash. This time-consuming practice may allow for closer monitoring of soil and growing conditions than would more technically advanced processes, but it lessens labor productivity. Finally, the soil in these small rockbound catchments is itself transported by youth work groups in ten-kilogram basket loads to the sites where water is easiest to procure (ibid.: 136; Paulme, 1940: 150–153). One might say that Dogon irrigation is half bringing water to the soil and half bringing soil to the water.

A drawback to Dogon agriculture is that the system leaves the Dogon underemployed in general, but they are more productively active in the dry season—the time of the vegetable plots—than are other, comparable African farmers in similar environments (Gallais, 1965: 139–141).

Despite its low labor use capacity, the Dogon food production system demonstrates great appreciation of the properties of soil, the *Acacia albida,* crop rotation, the uses of cattle, and the possibilities of making use of ecological zones with steep inclines and high erosion danger. The need for further research into Dogon techniques—if examined and improved upon via modern scientific methods—is implicit in the summary of their achievements: "The courtyard compost is exceptional for Subsaharan Africa" (ibid.: 37) and, "In a severe environment of chaotic rock piles blackish hardened stone, and sandstone slabs, Dogon farmers have triumphed over the challenge of nature's austere conditions" (ibid.: 126).

But what kind of society has made these accomplishments? How well do the Dogon fit the hypotheses suggested earlier in this essay and illustrated in the case of the Bouzou?

In terms of the close relations between herders and farmers, the Dogon present a slight variation which nonetheless seems to correspond to the hypothesis that animal herding and farming are mutually enriching production systems. While they resisted absorption into or conquest by the Fulani, the Dogon maintained close contact with Fulani herders whose animals leave behind the droppings that form the basis for the courtyard compost mixture. The Dogon gardens, however, do not coordinate well with the herders' passage through the region in the dry season: the animals often damage the carefully prepared gardens, and conflict ensues between the owners of the land and owners of the beasts (ibid.: 133).[1]

Historically, the Dogon have parallels to the Bouzou. They appear to be made up of refugees from an ancient drought and, more recently, have resisted the imposition of Islam and hierarchical structures and control by installing themselves in the rugged cliffs that provide military protection from otherwise more numerous and powerful neighbors including the Fulani (N'Diayé, 1970a: 246–247; Paulme, 1940: 21–23). By controlling a region that had important productive resources, especially during the dry season, however, the Dogon apparently found it necessary to develop a degree of political integration for defense. This led to the formation of a confederation of four large patrilocal and patrilineal family groupings unified somewhat around a central "chief," the *Hogon* (Griaule and Dieterlen, 1954: 89–90).

The *Hogon,* however, is not a chief with special forces under his control (Palau Marti, 1957: 50). Elected from a council of elder men, the *Hogons* from each of the four family groupings are more representatives of their families. The highest-ranking *Hogon* seems to have mainly ritual duties in the elaborate Dogon cosmological observances that have been the central focus of anthropological studies. Indeed, while one author types the Dogon political system an "elective theocracy" (N'Diayé, 1970a: 249), another considers the term "anarchy" more appropriate (Palau Marti, 1957: 50). The term *Hogon* itself seems to derive from a Dogon word meaning "wealthy one," suggesting a close relationship between economic and political power (Paulme, 1940: 182), but the *Hogon's* actual political and economic privileges are limited to passing out judgment on criminals—done only with the assistance and approval of the council of elders—and, theoretically, controlling the markets. But the control of the markets appears to be limited to announcing their occurrence with a drum signal.

Aside from the *Hogon* and the council of elders, the Dogon have little other social stratification and no class divisions. Among the peoples of modern Mali, the Dogon are considered to be those with the *least* developed castes (N'Diayé, 1970a: 253), though ironworkers, woodworkers, leatherworkers, and griots are kept apart and do not marry with the farming people who make up the majority of the Dogon (Palau Marti, 1957: 48–49; Paulme, 1940: 48–50, 288).[2]

In addition to the limited development of castes, Dogon society has minor inequalities between men and women and an elaborate system of age groups around which much of the social and economic life of the people is organized. While not presenting as dramatic an example of egalitarianism as the Bouzou, the Dogon indicate a cultural amalgam that grew out of contacts between farmers and animal herders and that maintained a high degree of egalitarianism by fleeing the powerful empires around them and establishing themselves in a remote and defensible area, where they could prevent the rise of a ruling class. The Dogon thus conform to the power and class hypothesis advanced at the beginning of this essay.

### The Serer and the *Acacia Albida:* Maintaining the Soil

The Bouzou are nearly perfectly egalitarian, and the Dogon represent a case of minimal development of castes. The third and fourth examples of traditional knowledge in Sahel food production, however, represent cases where substantial inequality has taken hold. Indeed, in both cases, the Serer of Senegal and the nineteenth-century Fulani empire of Macina, ruling classes have crystallized. In these cases we find that the maintenance of beneficial forms of traditional knowledge occurs where the ruling class's power is checked either by relative power on the part of the producers (Serer) or is in the process of being reversed as part of a political revolution (Macina). In both bases as well, we find the operation of the herder–farmer exchange as a major element in the historical development of the society which has maintained a beneficial practice. Let us look first at the Serer of Senegal who have made use, par excellence, of one of the Sahel's most valuable resources, the *Acacia albida*.

*Agriculture and the* **Acacia Albida.**   One of the most important potential production resources in the Sahel is the *Acacia albida*. This tree has the quality of shedding its leaves during the rainy season so that they do not block out the sunlight during the agricultural growth period and drop at the right time for the rains to speed the rotting process which transfers nutrients to the soil (Pélissier, 1966: 270). It gets its leaves during the long dry season, providing shade for animals and possibly aiding in water retention of the soil during the times when evaporation is most likely. The *Acacia albida* thus acts as a kind of counterbalance to the depletion which intensive agriculture might bring to a fragile environment. It also helps to maintain even temperatures and, perhaps most important, returns soil nutrients such as nitrogen, calcium, potassium, and phosphate through its leaf droppings, thus improving the agricultural potential of the soil (Pélissier, 1966: 265–271; Giffard, 1971: 20; Giffard, 1964; Charrau and Vidal, 1965).[3] While the effects of the *Acacia albida* can be reduced through trampling of the soil by too many animals and by failure to hoe the soil to maximize its potential by mixing the deposited mineral materials, harvest gains of 37 percent with peanuts and 104 percent with millet have nonetheless, been achieved in the absence of additional fertilizer when the *Acacia albida* is present on the fields (Giffard, 1971: 9–10; Charreau and Vidal, 1965: 625). Thus the *Acacia albida* can be said to provide a major alternative to the (increasingly expensive) commercial fertilizers which seem to add very little beyond what the debris from the tree is able to put into the soil. The large numbers of birds attracted to the tree's leafy branches in the dry season also leave their droppings around the base of the tree (Nicolas, 1960: 426).

In addition, the effects of the tree in maintaining soil humidity during the dry season are a brake on erosion, so much so that one scientist has claimed that planting of the *Acacia albida,* when combined with grazing of as few as eighteen cattle per 250 acres during the dry season for additional fertilizing, "practically allow[s] for a continuous exploitation of the soil" (Portères, 1952: 147, 149). The presence of sufficient numbers of *Acacia albida* dispersed on an agricultural field may thus vitiate the need for fallow periods (Pélissier, 1966: 272), supporting the development of high population densities and permanent food supplies without environmental degradation.

*Animal Herding and the* **Acacia Albida.**   The *Acacia albida* has another significant feature: its seed pods are deposited at the end of the dry period and must pass through the digestive tract of a ruminant, apparently cattle or camel, to be able to germinate effectively. The most concentrated sites of the tree are in selected agricultural zones of the Sahel, including parts of Niger, the Dogon area of Mali (Gallais, 1965), and, in particular, the Serer area of Sine in Senegal. A 1952 distribution map of *Acacia albida* in Senegal indicates that the tree is present in its highest densities—ten per hectare—in a region corresponding closely with the Serer ethnic zone of the country. It has relatively little presence outside that zone (Giffard, 1964: 29). The correlation of the high density of *Acacia albida* and the Serer farmers is not an accident of nature. Although *Acacia albida* seeds may require the stomach of a ruminant for germination, the young trees are highly susceptible to destruction by those very animals' grazing activities. They thus require well-planned *human* protection including the resetting of fallen trunks, pruning of the trunk up to certain heights, and keeping grazing animals away from the leaves. So much care and devotion is required that the Serer speak of "raising" a tree with the same expression they use for bringing up a child (Pélissier, 1966: 269; Giffard, 1971: 16).

*The Serer and the* **Acacia Albida.**   The development and use of *Acacia albida* in agriculture stands out as a striking feature of Serer food production. Indeed, the Wolof, agricultural neighbors of the Serer, make little use of the acacia park with its complex interplay of tree, cultivated crop, animal germinator, and human caretaker. Why should this be so? The rapid twentieth-century spread of the peanut, the expanding monocrop pushing impoverished Wolof farmers off their impoverished soils, seems to contrast sharply with the Serer and their more sound use of resources. As a French geographer noted for the Wolof not long before the 1968–1974 drought hit the entire zone:

> Too many examples, especially from the surrounding areas of the largest villages, have already offered the heartbreaking scene of large areas where shifting sands, pushed by the wind, have replaced formerly cultivable soils on which a complete removal of the trees and cultivation without fallow deprived those soils of their structure and their fertility. (Pélissier, 1966: 169)

One reason that such scenes did not occur among the Serer is that the Serer integrated peanut production into their traditional crop cycles and preserved much of their soil with the *Acacia albida* (ibid.: 237). But other reasons go perhaps deeper into the history and social structure of the Serer.

First, the Serer, while currently agriculturalists, seem to have their origins far to the north of the Sine. They share linguistic and cultural affinities with Fulani herders of the Middle Senegal River Valley, where an archaeological site locates an early Serer village between Matam and Podor (ibid.: 192–193).

The Serer may thus have lived in symbiotic relationship with Fulani herders (ibid.: 194). The Serer and their appreciation of the relations between cattle, crops, and *Acacia albida* could have originated in the herder–farmer exchange system described earlier in this paper. As summarized by one of their major European students:

> For these ancient Sahelians, longtime associates of the Fulani, if agriculture is a necessary vocation, herding is a passion. . . . Animal herds . . . are . . . the means of producing a resource much appreciated—milk—and they are especially an instrument for maintaining the fertility of the soils and the permanent capacity of the fields for cultivation. (ibid.: 236)

The Serer are believed to have left the Senegal River Valley in the eleventh or twelfth centuries and moved into the Sine sometime thereafter. At that time, the Serer brought with them an egalitarian social structure and established dispersed communities in which extended family and compound groupings, under the leadership of a group of elders, controlled their production resources for their own consumption and for exchange under their own auspices. Much of the millet was produced on collective fields (ibid.: 225–234).

The level of caste and class stratification that arose more recently among the Serer is a topic of some complexity. According to French geographer Paul Pélissier, the Serer developed little stratification over the several centuries from their migration into Sine and Saloum. Indeed, Pélissier argues that even the imposition of the *guellewar* warrior caste in the fourteenth century had little impact on the Serer, with the *guellewar* never able to dominate a "passive, controlled, frustrated peasantry" as happened among the more hierarchical Wolof neighbors (Pélissier, 1966: 108–109). Even the artisan castes and the *tyeddo,* or more recent warrior replacements of the *guellewar,* who became powerful in Senegal with the rise of the European slave trade (Diop, 1972: 23; Barry, 1972: 90; Franke and Chasin, 1980: 60–61) were a thin Wolof overlay. The artisan castes were absorbed into the Serer farming economy, where they practice their specialties only during the dry season (Pélissier, 1966: 208).

On the other hand, Martin Klein, who has written a detailed history of one period of Serer social development, offers substantial evidence to indicate that the Serer *did* produce caste and class stratification, even to the rise of a ruling class or nobility that lived off taxation of one-tenth of the produce of the farmers and who had direct control over bodies of armed warriors, the *tyeddo,* who made up part of the entourage of the court. In addition, precolonial Serer society also had village chiefs who were representatives of the royal family and nobility (Klein, 1968: 1–17).

At the same time, the producing class appears to have maintained a *relatively* powerful position in Serer society compared to their Wolof neighbors. Klein notes that "there was a constant tension between tyeddo and peasants" (ibid.: 19). In response to taxes and tribute—signs of exploitation and of great power on the part of the nobility—Serer farmers could offer two important forms of resistance. First, they might migrate to the fringe areas of the immense forests of their region where warrior and court control over them was minimal (ibid; Pélissier, 1966: 197–203). Indeed, some Serer, called Serer-N'Diéghem, have managed to maintain egalitarian social structures, avoiding the rise of a ruling class, and in some "fringe areas of Sine, there are no *tyeddo,* and local people can date within the last century or two the arrivals of members of different caste groups" (Klein, 1968: 5, 11).

Another option for Serer peasants was to fight. If they chose to fight rather than migrate, Serer peasants were armed and on occasions could force the *tyeddo* warriors out of their villages if impositions of the nobility were deemed too severe (ibid.: 19). It appears that the tenuous balance between peasants and warriors/nobility was upset in the late nineteenth century when a French military force was put to the service of *merchants,* a class which then rose to greater importance than ever before (ibid.: 44).

The complexities of Serer political and social structural history are thus great, but for purposes of this essay, it is the contrast with the neighboring Wolof that is most striking and of greatest importance. Ruled by powerful chiefs who may have once used a monopoly on animals as a source of their power (Pélissier, 1966: 151), the Wolof have little institutionalized exchange relations with herders except in a few areas such as Diourbel (ibid.: 152; Ware, 1979). The Wolof traditionally make little use of animal manure, and they have leveled much of the forest where animals could be kept during the rainy season (Pélissier 1966: 152).

The Serer, thus, while far more stratified than the Bouzou or the Dogon, and while having an incipient ruling class, are nontheless consistent with our general hypothesis: the precolonial Serer ruling class was checked in extending its powers over the producers by the possibilities of migration to fringe areas in the forests and by the fact that the peasants carried arms and could resist the warrior caste in carrying out what the peasants considered excessive levels of exploitation by the nobility. In contrast to the Wolof, whose agricultural practices and political organization led them, under French domination, to develop the ecologically destructive "Mouride" movement (Franke and Chasin, 1980: 78–82), the Serer producing class held onto enough power to maintain the ecologically viable grain–acacia–cattle cycle.

In each of the three otherwise different instances looked at so far, then, we have seen a positive correlation between the degree of power held by the producing class and the ability of the producers to maintain their fixed capital assets. The fourth and final example to be surveyed provides evidence of yet another type of power and class effect on the maintenance of traditional knowledge. In the early nineteenth century, a vast political movement among Fulani herders of the Niger River Inland Delta produced a series of reforms that included the preservation *and* some innovations of traditional knowledge. This was the Dina, the Fulani empire of Macina.

### The Fulani Empire of Macina: Regulated Herder–Farmer Land Use

In central Mali, just before the Niger River reaches its northernmost point near Timbuktu and turns south towards the Atlantic Ocean, there lies one of Africa's

most important potential food-producing regions. Beginning in August and lasting for three to five months, the Inland Delta of the Niger River floods an area
as extensive as England and Wales (Church, 1968: 18–19). Today, the region
of which the delta is the major economic component contains 20 percent of
Mali's people and 25 percent of its animal herds (Gallais, 1975: 354–355).
The Niger Inland Delta has been a major site for the development of West
African empires and their capital cities, including Jenné, Mopti, Segou, Timbuktu, and, east of the bend, Gao, capital of Songhay. These empires include
that of Mali (1400–1494), Songhay (1494–1591), Moroccan conquest (1591–
1670), several Bambara kingdoms (1670–1810), and Tukulor rule (1861–1893)
just preceding the French colonial takeover (Monteil, 1932: 94–120; Gallais,
1967, vol. I: 82–93).

In the midst of these empires, however, there arose one political system that
encompassed major reforms in land use between farmers and herders. Much
of the spirit of these reforms is still in place in the region today. This was the
Fulani Dina, or empire of Macina, which was founded in 1818 and lasted until
overrun in 1862.

The Dina is of interest in the history of Sahelian indigenous food production
knowledge because of its apparent positive accomplishments. These include
increasing the capacity of the system to feed a large population, the parallel
expansion of agriculture and pastoralism, each system providing inputs to the
other, and the avoidance of famines that hit nearby areas (Gallais, 1975: 359–
360).

How were these accomplishments made? The most important feature of the
Dina's food production system lay in regulating the interactions between farmers and herders. This was achieved through a six-part program (Gallais, 1967,
vol. I: 94–95; vol. II: 362–365)

1. Fishing areas were marked off and protected.
2. Animal trek routes were marked off and protected.
3. Herding officials had fixed payment scales for hired herders and for dam-
   ages caused by animals to crops.
4. Standard weights and measures were introduced.
5. Markets were controlled by the central government.
6. Market officials, appointed by the government council, were responsible to
   higher government authority.

Underneath these general organizational features, the Dina carefully organized and monitored the herding economy so that it would interact in a positive
way with the farming base of the empire. In 1821, the third year of the Dina,
all government officers were called to the capital city of Hamdallay (near Jenné).
There they made an inventory of pastoral camps, trek routes, and pasturing
areas (Ba and Daget, 1955: 81). Herds were divided into three types: those
kept for reproduction, those kept for milking—and allowed the longest time
in the flood recession pastures of the Niger Inland Delta—and a small number
of animals kept in the villages year round.

The empire was controlled by a grand council of forty *marabouts* (Islamic
clergy) who supervised the district heads of the five provinces. Each province
had subdistrict heads who supervised seven head herders each. These head

herders were in charge of three main herders who took care of 300 head of cattle, so that each head herder was responsible to the subdistrict officer for a total of 2100 animals and twenty-one main herders (ibid.: 82).

Returns to herding were carefully regulated. For example, animals returning from the rainy-season trek north would be put on farmers' fields for a fee of forty cowries paid by the landowner. Twenty of these cowries went to the herders and twenty to the government escort unit. Milk from the milking herd would be divided as follows: one-third to the owner, one-third to the herder, and one-third to the government for distribution to needy people in the villages (ibid.: 83).

The Dina thus made possible an organized and peaceful movement of cattle from the flood recession pastures of November to April to the Sahelian pastures in July to September (Gallais, 1975: 355).

The nineteenth- and early twentieth-century expansion of agricultural and animal production rendered possible by the Dina innovations make it a case of some importance. Indeed, evidence suggests that recently local officials and some Malian herders and farmers in the area of the former empire have attempted to reconstitute the code of farmer–herder relations of the Dina, albeit with changes in the exact locations of routes, measurement of fees, etc. (Gallais, 1975: 365–366; 1979: 135). Reinstituting the Dina code, however, is a task of major proportions, for during the colonial period many changes were brought about, including changes in land use rights, expansion of chiefly lands, increases in taxes, and allowing Tuareg and other herders from farther away to pasture in the area. These processes were compounded by the independent Malian government's decision in the early 1960s to open the pastures of the Macina area to all herders who wanted access, and yet again by the drought of 1968–1974, which drove many herders from more northerly zones into the Niger River pastures in a desperate attempt to save their animals (Gallais, 1975: 361–362). What was once done by an independent empire is also more difficult to accomplish in local and regional councils unless there is firm backing from the central government and at least an absence of interference from outside projects.

How does the empire of Macina fit with the hypotheses presented earlier? The rise of the Dina at a point of contact with herders and farmers fits easily into our hypothesis that the zone of contact is the zone in which the most valuable innovations would occur. But how is the fact that the Dina was a tightly organized *empire* with a clear ruling class of privileged officials to be reconciled with the correlation noted in the three previous cases? This question is of significance because the Dina bears some resemblances to modern revolutionary societies.

Most knowledge about the Dina comes from oral accounts handed down by local residents of the Macina region (Ba and Daget, 1955: 25, 253). There is thus some chance of romanticization, but the data nonetheless all point in the same direction: the Dina was an attempted social revolution *against* the excesses of authoritarian Bambara rulers and *towards* a greater degree of social and economic quality.

Much of the evidence concerns Cheikou Amadou, the founder and first leader of the Dina. A *marabout* of humble origins, according to the stories passed down about him, Amadou organized the Dina in part to spread Islam to animist Fulani groups. But in part, also, the legends about Cheikou Amadou center on his nonacquisitive, nonauthoritarian behavior, including his taking and enforcing a personal vow of poverty (ibid.: 44) by living partly from his own labor such as the making of rope, the fibers of which he turned himself, and by selling Korans copied by his hand (ibid.: 53). Although he took one-fifth of various fines and taxes in the empire for himself and the grand council (Monteil, 1932: 106–110, 113), he lived in simple quarters and even had the grand mosque of the capital city built in a simple style without minarets or ornamentation (Ba and Daget, 1955: 47).

Furthermore, Amadou is known in stories for overturning the abuses of middle- and even high-ranking officers of the empire and for favoring the cause of the oppressed and downtrodden (e.g., ibid.: 46, 59). The picture of a political leader of a large region with ample resources engaging in production and renouncing the wealth and privilege that might accompany his power contrasts sharply with the historical evidence concerning the nearby Bambara ruling groups who were expelled by Amadou and his followers from much of the Niger Delta. The most important case in point is the Bambara king of Segou from 1808 to 1827, Da Monson. Da was allegedly a haughty, vain, and tyrannical ruler, full of vindictiveness (Monteil, 1924: 90–97; Ba and Daget, 1955: 59). He looked down on the Fulani herders as inferiors[4] and, after being defeated by Amadou in 1818, continued harassing the Dina, in one case sending a raiding party that stole 5000 heads of cattle and forced the empire to send armed cavalry detachments along with herders and animals during the trek season (Ba and Daget, 1955: 91).[5] It seems almost certain that these raids, which also came from Tuareg herders on the northern edges of the empire, compelled the Dina to strengthen its military rule, tighten its security forces, and probably to increase taxes or tribute to the central treasury.

Although recognized by the great Nigerian political leader Osman dan Fodio and having loose diplomatic relations with leaders as far away as Constantinople (Ba and Daget, 1955: 59; Monteil, 1924: 114), the embattled Dina never achieved peace with its surrounding enemies and, finally, eighteen years after the death of Cheikou Amadou in 1844, Tukulor invaders dismantled the formal political organization that had been established by herders resisting the autocratic domination from Segou. Nonetheless, in this brief period of striving for an Islamic-based just society, Amadou and his followers established a pastoral code that:

> was based upon awareness of the constraints of the natural environment and . . . was inspired by a concern for equity and justice and peace among the peoples of the Delta, [and was] a veritable social and economic revolution that has not ceased to bring benefits and to be adaptable to new conditions for more than a century afterwards. (Gallais, 1975: 359)

The empire of Macina thus corresponds generally to the hypothesis that ecology-maintaining food production practices correlate positively with those societies having the least powerful and exploitative ruling classes: the Dina was a partially successful attempt to oppose inequality and institute less hierarchical relations between herders and farmers while reducing inequality generally. Harassed and attacked from the outside, and lacking a fully developed egalitarian ideology, the empire was compelled to institute militarization of the pastoral economy for protection and had to continue depending on appropriation of surplus from the producers in the form of taxation, tribute, and the reward for its troops through the capture of war booty. What remained of the power and privilege of the rulers of Segou and their vassals intermixed with the less hierarchical structures of the Fulani herders and the impulse of a radical Islamic movement—all in the setting of a rich environment that would yield direct and immediate benefits if more rationally managed.

## POWER, CLASS, AND TRADITIONAL KNOWLEDGE

From this survey of four different types of Sahelian societies, it seems that the general two-part hypothesis outlined at the beginning of this essay has been confirmed. Those peoples with experience in both animal raising and farming were likely to create food production practices in which the animal and plant exchanges inherent in the herder–farmer interactions were improved upon or were able to create land use systems that drew on the elements of both systems to minimize ecological harm while maintaining a reasonable output. Furthermore, in each of the four cases representing increasing levels of stratification, the most positive environmental developments were maintained in societies where the producing classes had the greatest power and the ruling classes were either absent (Bouzou, Dogon) or had their power checked (Serer) or where their power was in process of disintegration (Dina). By contrast, among those Sahelian societies where powerful ruling classes *did* emerge, such as the Hausa, Bambara, and Wolof, the maintenance of fixed capital assets was sacrificed to the needs of the nonproductive exploiting classes.

The history of the Sahel did not end with the rise of African rulers, however. From the late nineteenth century up to the 1960s, new and more powerful ruling classes imposed their exploitative powers on the region. The most important of these came from France, which dominated most of the Sahel, pushing peanut production with its severe harm to the land in Senegal and Niger and pushing cotton production in Mali and Chad. For decades a nearly total disregard for the land and for the laborers characterized French colonial rule.[6] Only those groups that lived in regions somewhat marginal to colonial interests or who were difficult to reach because of their location could evade or resist the colonial impositions. The Dogon were not really brought under French domination until the 1930s, for example, while nearby, in the former Dina region, massive changes were wrought in the "Office du Niger" scheme to produce cotton and rice for export. The Bouzou seem to have been left untouched while Hausa farmers nearby became subject to a massive peanut cash-cropping program from 1930 to 1965. The Serer survived on the edges of a major peanut expansion in the Sine Saloum partly because they inhabited some of the least accessible parts of the basin, but perhaps also because the more stratified Wolof responded more easily to commercial exploitation, their own local rulers and religious leaders attaching themselves for gain to the expanding colonial economy and to the great detriment of the ecology of Senegal (Pélissier, 1966; Franke and Chasin, 1980: 63–83; Klein, 1979).

Those Sahelian societies that had the most powerful producing classes and the least exploitative and least powerful ruling classes and that represented an intermingling of herding and farming production systems thus developed and preserved a set of ecologically promising practices for maintaining the principal fixed capital asset in farming: the land. They also left a record of correlations that has potential implications for our understanding of the relations between social structures and production systems.

And, finally, both the techniques and the correlations may contain elements that could be utilized in the Sahel's search for development without desertification and famine vulnerability. How can the points raised in this essay be integrated into Sahel development, and how do they compare with the Sahel Development Program as it is currently unfolding?

## TRADITIONAL KNOWLEDGE AND SAHELIAN DEVELOPMENT

Perhaps the most obvious way in which the evidence and analysis from this study could be brought to bear on Sahelian development would be through what one could call the modern scientific use of traditional knowledge. In our view, this would entail three major efforts:

1. Further research and evaluation of traditional knowledge.
2. Dissemination of findings to other Sahelian peoples than the one producing an innovation.
3. Creative intermixing of modern science with the findings from traditional knowledge.

In each of these areas there has been some development in recent years, but there is much left to be done, and serious questions must be raised about the overall direction of current development policies in this field.

### Research into Traditional Knowledge

Most of the information from earlier sections of this study has been derived from other research in the Sahel. That there is awareness of traditional knowledge in the Sahel at some level is thus apparent, but it is also apparent that most of the data had to be culled from two sources: (1) widely scattered comments usually not part of a major investigation or (2) the work of a small group of French geographers and plant scientists who were able to conduct initial studies of some traditional food production systems, especially during the 1950s and 1960s. Thus a very limited amount of evidence exists on a subject which might well yield much more information if priority were given it. Indeed, British geographer Paul Richards has called for just such studies of "folk ecology" as part of the construction of alternative strategies for environmental maintenance in the Sahel and had conducted some research into this area (Richards, 1975).

However, other studies, for the most part, nearly totally neglect the possibilities of learning from traditional systems and presume the expansion of modern imported methods of production with virtually no role for locally developed techniques. In a recent study of the possibilities for increasing irrigated rice production in the Sahel, for example, two specialists survey a wide range of factors including world prices for inputs and shadow prices for numerous variables. Significantly, one of the main areas treated in their essay, which was financed by USAID and is probably a major policy paper for the region, is the Niger Inland Delta. The essay offers not a word on the Dina, herder–farmer relationships, or, indeed, the existence of animal herding alongside rice cultivation (Humphreys and Pearson, 1979/1980). The monocrop spread of modern irrigated rice, however, may well endanger the remaining elements of the old Dina system and could well lead to unintended soil erosion of the areas outside the irrigated zones as the nomads could lose their dry-season pastures and be forced to overconcentrate their animals on the fringes of the delta.[7] Similarly, a detailed study of the Niger Inland Delta, also commissioned by USAID, ignores the relations between herders and farmers. Ironically, this second study, while more in depth than the rice analysis just mentioned, makes use of Gaillais's history of the delta (Gallais, 1967) but neglects entirely the history of the Dina and its implications, which Gallais himself made one of the cardinal points of the history (McC. Netting et al., 1980). A related study of Fulani herders in the same volume ignores with only minor exceptions the importance in many parts of the Sahel of the herder–farmer relationship (Reisman, 1980). Even a special review of the state of knowledge concerning the *Acacia albida,* commissioned by USAID in the late 1970s, limits itself to questions concerning agricultural yields, soil effects, general botanical properties, and pod nutritive potential, neglecting the herder–farmer and cattle–tree–land interractions (Felker, 1978).

Work by researchers outside the United States appears to reflect similar bias. An FAO-sponsored "Expert Consultation" held in 1977 on the topic of "Organic Recycling in Africa" concluded in part with the recommendation that "technicians and scientists need to study more closely the basic practices of the small farmers," but the scientific papers presented were based almost entirely on the supposition that outside research and techniques are to be imposed. Indeed, even in the recommendation, the only reason is "so that proposals for the introduction of new systems could be easily understood, integrated, and accepted by these farmers" (FAO, 1980: 1).

And at a 1978 Sahel Symposium in London, two well-known British experts discussed the Sahel's future problems and potential without a mention of the folk ecology that had been called for by Paul Richards only three years earlier (Grove, 1978; Cloudsley-Thompson, 1978). Finally, in one of the very few scientific studies to focus on the herder–farmer relationship, the authors conclude, after a superficial survey of some types of linkages between the production systems, that "adaptation to former conditions are proving nonadaptive to new conditions and new adaptations are slow in developing" (McCown et al., 1979: 330). The authors, however, do not investigate the specific ecology-maintaining techniques that have been discussed in this study.[8]

The importance of this neglect both general and specific should be evident. If the research on the *Acacia albida,* its effects, and possible similar phenomena is not made prominent, it is easy to advocate the settling of herders on the one hand or the expansion of irrigated cropping on the other. Both these projects threaten to sever or further erode the integrated herder–farmer systems presently existing in the Sahel. Ranching schemes in particular may break up the farmer–herder integration unless that integration is worked into the design of the ranch—a difficult task if the ranch is primarily established to produce large numbers of animals for the market.[9] One or the other of these policies might indeed be appealing for reasons of expanding the supply of grain or meat, but what will happen to the overall environment, especially on the desert fringe? If the cattle are important in spreading *Acacia albida,* are they also important in spreading *Acacia raddiana, Acacia seyal,* and other varieties (cf. Monnier, 1981: 187)? And if cattle are removed from the ranges or if their trek routes are drastically interfered with, what alternative methods are being investigated to maintain the tree distribution when the cattle—perhaps their main vector for spreading the trees—no longer appear as they once did on the ranges or, indeed, are forced to overgraze and trample them? A more serious appreciation of this potential problem would derive, it seems to us, from a more serious appreciation of traditional adaptations by Sahelian herders and farmers.

Another area where traditional knowledge is not being applied is with fertilizer. The Dogon composting technique provides a dramatic contrast with current policy. Rather than seek to elaborate, improve, and disseminate this practical and possibly effective composting system, which might be adapted to other Sahelian cultures and might be relatively inexpensive, many of the Sahel development projects utilize or project the use of commercial imported fertilizers. Commercial fertilizers greatly simplify matters for the outside agencies that already know where to order them and are already familiar with the kinds of scientific tests needed for their application. Development of the Dogon system or a related system would be far more difficult for outside agencies to effect.

But whose development is it, after all? If the Sahel trades immediate production gains for a new form of dependency, this time on outside fertilizer, mechanical equipment, and the like, how and when will it be able to develop its own resources in a way that will allow it to control those resources? In the long run, it may be more advantageous for the Sahelian countries to have the resources and knowledge to develop Dogon composting, which can be done mostly with their own materials, rather than risk falling victim to a sudden massive increase in the world price of fertilizer or even sudden shortages. The many recent economic crises among the wealthy nations ought to provide a rationale for not tying oneself too closely to the economies of those nations. The creation of a people's science with an emphasis on developing local knowledge and techniques would be an important element in such a strategy of independence.

## Dissemination of Scientific Knowledge in the Sahel

Whatever its achievements and potential, traditional knowledge in the Sahel has been severely limited by its isolation, with a small number of societies relatively cut off from the main interchanges of ideas and experience. This is precisely an arena in which modern science could compensate for a weakness inherent in traditional knowledge. In the case of the Dogon, for example, would it not be possible to conduct modern experiments on their composting practices and, if these indeed turn out to be beneficial, to disseminate them to other parts of the region where they might also be of use? The recent establishment of a Sahel Institute in Bamako, Mali, would bode well for such a possibility, but only if the institute receives funds and other assistance for this kind of endeavor. At present, however, it appears more likely that the Sahel Institute will be a clearinghouse and repository for more of the kinds of research that brings a modern agricultural agenda with no concern for or interest in the findings that could derive from a serious study of traditional knowledge and its implications. Fortunately, many Sahelian scholars are intensely nationalistic and interested in what can be learned from their own cultures; but, unfortunately, most of the financial resources for scientific research come from organizations such as USAID, the World Bank, and French Overseas Aid, which do not as yet seem to have a commitment to the kinds of studies that would be required.

## Creative Mixing of Traditional Knowledge and Modern Science

In addition to discovery through more research and dissemination through modern communications, the application of modern scientific research techniques could result in new, creative syntheses. Earlier French studies in the 1950s and 1960s verified the value of the *Acacia albida* and made possible proposals for its use in reestablishing soil fertility in Senegal. Some scientists who studied the *Acacia albida* in detail also made use of their knowledge of other experiments in other parts of the world, noting the possibility of creating bands of trees interspersed with fields as has been developed in arid zones of China and the Soviet Union (Charrau and Vidal, 1965: 623; Giffard, 1964: 32). It appears that small-scale experiments were carried out but did not sufficiently interest either the colonial government at the time or the independent state of Senegal in more recent years.

But the example remains, and a few others have followed. One of the most persistent proponents of an amalgam of traditional knowledge and modern scientific creativity is French geographer Jean Gallais. Gallais, who has attempted to draw attention to the importance of the land use system of the nineteenth-century Dina, has also advocated its modification to modern conditions, including smaller units of territory to correspond with the greater population density, a new classification of land types with regulations for their use, and new controls over the use of different types of pasture, with local councils to supervise these controls and relate the different regions to each other (Gallais, 1975: 365–366; cf. Barral, 1974). This process has led to a proposal in 1979 that Mali become the first of the Sahelian countries to develop and implement a pastoral land use code (Gallais, 1979: 135).

Finally, a most intriguing proposal has been made by R. H. MacLeod of the Earth Resources Development Research Institute in Washington, D.C. MacLeod specializes in the interpretation of satellite photographs of the Sahel—certainly one of the most modern of scientific advances—but he also has an interest in and respect for the traditional production systems of the regions. Studying both the traditional and the modern has led MacLeod to propose a system of food production for the Sahel which he calls "climax agriculture." MacLeod defines climax agriculture as a system of production which "recreates the characteristic conditions of the original ecosystem, but does so through use of crop, forage, and timber plants in a carefully managed fashion" (MacLeod, 1976: 3–4). The variety that would be produced by nature, left alone by humans, is thus simulated with its many advantages in water retention and wind protection, thus lessening the changes of desertification as well as preventing outbreaks of pest damage by not allowing individual species to be concentrated over one large area. The proposal leads to alternatives to many current ranching schemes in the region. The current schemes emphasize the use of single species of grasses as cattle feed. "But," as MacLeod notes, "in the Sahel, shrubs can provide dry season feed while grasses cannot" (1975: 7). If MacLeod is correct in his observation, shrubs of a variety of species, including perhaps some acacias in the desert fringe areas, would contribute towards this modified recreation of some of the most primitive production systems of the Sahel. With the tools and techniques of modern science, MacLeod's proposal points in the same direction as does a remark by Gallais, summarizing the approach he has attempted to develop:

> . . . so much remains to be discovered, to be subjected to experimentation. The most immediate goal is to convince the technocrats that a modern undertaking can rest upon sociological knowledge of tradition. (Gallais, 1977: 280)

## Power, Class, and Development in the Sahel

Finally, what is the development implication of a positive correlation between ecologically beneficial practices and those social structures with the *least* powerful and exploitative ruling classes? The implication, in our view, is clear: nonexploitative modern forms of society have the best chance of maintaining their fixed capital resources. Producing primarily for local needs, the Bouzou and Dogan were able to maintain their environments relatively well because they were not subject to the expansionary production schemes of nonproductive ruling classes. In the present-day Sahel, however, with higher population densities, the rise in urban centers, the spread of industrial commodities, and the like, it is surely not reasonable to propose a return to the isolated, self-sufficient, more egalitarian past. Is there a way, however, to recreate a modern version of the nonexploitative character of these more ancient societies?

The full answer to this question will only be given by developments among Sahelian social groups and nations, but there are some intermediate signs of the potential. On a small scale, local governmental bodies and democratic herder and farmer groups have joined with some development projects in the creation of nonexploitative production experiments in the Sahel (Franke and Chasin, 1980: 228–239). These projects, while not the final word in offering what may be needed, do have one common feature to which we can point: they all emphasize the management and control of the means of production—land, labor, technology—by the producers themselves, that is, those people closest to and with the greatest interest in protecting their resources.

Similarly, but on a larger scale, the temporary creation of a society moving towards greater equality by the nineteenth-century Dina is one example of an experiment that might be attempted in a twentieth-century form. The Dina was cut off by intrigues and attacks from other Africans, and eventually by French colonial expansion. Later, during the anticolonial movements, many African nationalist leaders espoused radical egalitarian—usually socialist—ideas, but these ideas often did not come to fruition because the class base of the leadership of the nationalist movements was usually from one of the exploiting classes themselves (Markovitz, 1977: Chapters IV–VIII). The modern social structure of the Sahelian countries includes powerful exploiting classes with a strong interest in increasing production and controlling the labor of the farmers and herders no matter what the cost to the fixed capital of their countries. These classes include merchants, landowners, and, perhaps most important in the Sahelian countries, government bureaucrats, all of whom together constitute an "organizational bourgeoisie" (ibid.). This organizational bourgeoisie is a nonproducing class that derives its wealth and power from two very different sources in the current development situation. On the one hand, it must exploit the land and labor of the producers—mainly farmers and herders in the Sahel—to maintain its privileges. At the same time, it is offered various opportunities for self-aggrandizement by participating in the administration of the massive Sahel Development Program that itself will bring some $10 billion into the region between the years 1975 and 2000.

In its relations both with the producers to whom it looks down and the foreign aid establishment to whom it must look up, the Sahelian organizational bourgeoisie is pressured, and has as its own self-interest, to expand production and follow the advice of experts of the "donor" nations. Expansion of production is dictated locally because the organizational bourgeoisie stands to benefit by the high prices for cereals and the possible opportunities for cattle sales in the rich markets of the heavily populated coastal countries to the south. Expansion of production is dictated internationally because the Sahel Development Program has been devised with the counsel of Western experts, who see food self-sufficiency or its near equivalent as a way to stabilize the region politically and help to halt the spread of revolutions generally in Africa.[10]

Perhaps they have other goals as well, but the outside experts do not have an immediate material interest in fashioning a slow, careful, producer-oriented strategy of development with environmental maintenance. Their entree into the region is, after all, not by means of their connections with the producing classes, but via the class that makes international contacts—the organizational bourgeoisie.

This set of power and class relations may well explain the reluctance of practitioners or theorists of Sahel development to devote time or resources to serious evaluation of the potential of traditional knowledge. The Western experts have an internationally approved agenda. The local organizational bourgeoisies have an interest in getting "development" as fast as possible, so why offer major criticisms of the program when there is grain to be marketed and meat to be sold?

Careful studies and evaluations of the possible development implications of the herder–farmer integrated food production system and of the effects of non-exploitative forms of society are both likely to be of little interest to the majority of current Sahelian developers. Such studies may be of great interest, however, to Sahelian farmers and herders and their friends and allies in other parts of the world. In our view, this study has demonstrated the need for future research in this field. Despite powerful social forces inhibiting it, perhaps there will be those who do such work in the interest of the producers, the land, the animals, and, ultimately, of the entire people of the Sahel.

# REFERENCES

Ba, A. H., and J. Daget (1955). *L'Empire peul du Macina, I (1818–1853)*. Institut Français d'Afrique Noire. Centre du Soudan. Etudes Soudanaises, no. 3.

Barral, H. (1974). "Mobilité et cloisonnement chez les éleveurs du nord de la Haute-Volta: les zones dites 'd'endrodomie pastorale.'" *Cahiers ORSTOM*, Série Sciences Humaines 2 (1974): 127–135.

Barry, Boubacar (1972). *Le royaume du Waalo: le Sénégal avant la conquête*. Paris: François Maspero.

Beauvilain, Alain (1977). "Les peul de Dallol Bosso et la sécheresse 1969–1973, Niger," in Jean Gallais (Ed.), *Stratégies pastorales et agricoles des Sahéliens durant la sécheresse 1969–1974.* Bordeaux: Centre d'Etudes de Géographie Tropicale, no. 30.

Bernus, Edmond (1966). "Les Tuareg du Sahel nigérien." *Les Cahiers d'Outre-Mer* 19, 73: 5–34.

———— (1979). "Le contrôle du milieu naturel et du troupeau par les éleveurs touaregs sahéliens, in *Pastoral Production and Society: Proceedings of the International Meeting on Nomadic Pastoralism, Paris, 1–3 December, 1976,* pp. 67–74. London: Cambridge University Press.

Charrau, C., and P. Vidal (1965). "Influence de l'*Acacia albida* sur le sol, la nutrition minerale, et les rendements des mil *Pennisetum* au Sénégal. *L'Agronomie Tropicale* 20, 6–7: 600–626.

Church, R. J. Harrison (1968). *West Africa: A Study of the Environment and of Man's Use of It.* London: Longman's, Green, and Co.

Cloudsley-Thompson, J. L. (1978). "Human Activities and Desert Expansion." *The Geographical Journal* 144, 3: 416–423.

de St. Croix, F. W. (1944). *The Fulani of Northern Nigeria.* Lagos: Government Printer.

Diop, Majhemot (1971). *Histoire des classes sociales dans l'Afrique de l'ouest: le Mali.* Paris: François Maspero.

———— (1972). *Histoire des classes sociales dans l'Afrique de l'ouest: le Sénégel.* Paris: François Maspero.

Dunbar, G. S. (1970). "Africa Ranches Ltd., 1914–1931: An ill-fated stock raising enterprise in Northern Nigeria. *Annals of the Association of American Geographers* 60, 1: 102–123.

Dupire, Marguerite (1963). "Les facteurs humaines de l'économie pastorale." *Etudes nigériennes* 6.

Dyson-Hudson, Rada, and Neville Dyson-Hudson (1980). "Nomadic Pastoralism," in Bernard Siegel et al. (Eds.), *Annual Review of Anthropology,* vol. 9, pp. 15–61.

Felker, Peter (1978). *State of the art: Acacia albida as a complementary intercrop with annual crops.* University of California at Riverside. Department of Soil and Environmental Science. USAID Grant no. AID/afr-C-1361.

Food and Agricultural Organization of the United Nations (FAO) (1980). *Organic Recycling in Africa.* FAO Soils Bulletin, no. 43.

Forde, Daryll (1960). "The Cultural Map of West Africa: Successive Adaptations to Tropical Forests and Grasslands," in Simon Ottenberg and Phoebe Ottenberg (Eds.), *Cultures and Societies of Africa,* pp. 116–138. New York: Random House.

Franke, Richard W., and Barbara H. Chasin (1979). "Peanuts, Peasants, Profits, and Pastoralists: The Social and Economic Background to Ecological Deterioration in Niger." *Peasant Studies* 8, 3: 1–30.

———— (1980). *Seeds of Famine: Ecological Destruction and the Development Dilemma in the West African Sahel.* Montclair, N.J.: Allanheld, Osmun, and Co.

Gallais, Jean (1965). "Le paysan Dogon." *Les Cahiers d'Outre-Mer* 18, 70: 123–143.

———— (1967). "Le Delta Intériur du Niger." Institut Fondamental de l'Afrique Noir. *Mémoires,* no. 79. 2 vols.

———— (1972). "Essai sur la situation actuelle des relations entre pasteurs et paysans dans le Sahel Ouest-Africain," in *Etudes de Géographie Tropical Offertes a'Pierre Gourou.* Paris: Mouton.

———— (1975). "Traditions pastorales et développement: problèmes actuels dans la région de Mopti (Mali)," in T. Monod (Ed.), *Pastoralism in Tropical Africa,* pp. 354–366. London: International African Institute.

———— (1977). *Stratégies pastorales et agricoles des Sahéliens durant la sécheresse*

*1969–1974.* Bordeaux: Centre d'Etudes de Géographie Tropicale. Travaux et Documents de Géographie Tropicale, no. 30.

——— (1979). "La situation de l'élevage bovin et le problème des éleveurs en Afrique occidentale et centrale." *Les Cahiers d'Outre-Mer* 32, 126: 113–144.

Geertz, Clifford (1963). *Agricultural Involution: The Processes of Ecological Change in Indonesia.* Berkeley: University of California Press.

Giffard, Pierre-Louis (1964). "Les possibilitiés de reboisement en *Acacia albida* au Sénégal." *Bois et Forêts des Tropiques* 95: 21–33.

——— (1971). "Recherches complémentaires sur *Acacia albida* (Del.)." *Bois et Forêts des Tropiques* 135: 3–20.

Gillet, H. (n.d.). "Plant Cover and Pastures of the Sahel," in *Man and the Biosphere,* pp. 21–27. Technical Notes, no. 1. UNESCO.

Grenier, P. (1960). "Les Peul du Ferlo." *Les Cahiers d'Outre-Mer* 13, 49: 28–59.

Griaule, Marcel (1965). *Conversations with Ogotemmeli: An Introduction to Dogon Religious Ideas.* London: Oxford University Press.

——— and Germaine Dieterlen (1954). "The Dogon of the French Sudan," in Daryll Ford (Ed.), *African Worlds: Studies in the Cosmological Ideas and Social Values of African Peoples.* pp. 83–110. London: Oxford University Press.

Grove, A. T. (1978). "Geographical Introduction to the Sahel." *The Geographical Journal* 144, 3: 407–415.

Humphreys, Charles P., and Scott R. Pearson (1979/80). "Choice of Technique in Sahelian Rice Production." *Food Research Institute Studies* 17, 3: 235–277.

Klein, Martin (1968). *Islam and Imperialism in Senegal: Sine-Saloum, 1847–1914.* Stanford, Cal.: Stanford University Press.

——— (1979). "Colonial Rule and Structural Change: The Case of Sine Saloum," in Rita Cruise O'Brien (Ed.), *The Political Economy or Underdevelopment: Dependence in Senegal,* pp. 64–99. Beverly Hills: Sage Publications.

Lamotte, Maxime (1975). "The Structure and Function of a Tropical Savannah Ecosystem," in Frank B. Golley and Ernesto Medina (Eds.), *Tropical Ecological Systems.* pp. 179–222. New York: Springer-Verlag.

Leupen, A. H. A. (1978). *Bibliographie des Populations Touarègues.* Leiden: Afrikastudiecentrum.

McC. Netting, Robert, David Cleveland, and Frances Stier (1980). "The Conditions of Agricultural Intensification in the West African Savannah," in Stephen P. Reyna (Ed.), *Sahelian Social Development,* pp. 187–505. Abidjan: U.S. Agency for International Development. Regional Economic Development and Services Office, West Africa.

McCown, R. L., G. Haaland, and G. de Haan (1979). "The Interaction Between Cultivation and Livestock Production in Semi-Arid Africa," in A. E. Hall, et al. (Eds.), *Agriculture in Semi-Arid Environments,* pp. 297–332. New York: Springer-Verlag.

MacLeod, N. H. (1975). *Food Production in Deserts,* Washington, D.C.: Earth Resources Development Research Institute.

——— (1976). *Climax Agriculture Plus an Analysis of the Process and Stages of Desertification/Aridification and Rehabilitation in the Arrondissement of Filingue, Niger.* Washington, D.C.: Earth Resources Development Research Institute.

Mainet, Guy (1965). "L'élevage dans la région de Maradi." *Les Cahiers d'Outre-Mer* 18, 69: 32–72.

Markovitz, Irving Leonard (1977). *Power and Class in Africa.* Englewood Cliffs, N.J.: Prentice-Hall.

Monnier, Yves (1981). *La poussière et al cendre: paysages, dynamique des formations végétales et stratégies des sociétés en Afrique de l'Ouest*. Paris: Agence de Coopération Culturelle et Technique.

Monteil, Charles (1924). *Les Bambara du Ségou et du Kaarta*. Paris: Gouvernement Général de l'Afrique Occidentale Française, Publications de Comité d'Etudes Historiques et Scientifiques.

———— (1932). *Une Cité Soudanaise: Djénné, Métropole du Delta Central du Niger*. Paris: Société d'Editions Géographpiques, Maritimes et Coloniales.

Moran, Emilio (1979). *Human Adaptability: An Introduction to Ecological Anthropology*. North Scituate, Mass.: Duxbury Press.

N'Diayé, Bokar (1970a). "Les Dogon," in *Groupes Ethniques au Mali*, pp. 244–275. Bamako: Editions Populaires.

———— (1970b). *Les Castes au Mali*. Bamako: Editions Populaires.

Nicolas, Guy (1960). "Un village haoussa de la République du Niger, Tassao Haoussa." *Les Cahiers d'Outre-Mer* 13, 52: 421–450.

———— (1962). "Un village bouzou du Niger: Etude d'un terroir." *Les Cahiers d'Outre-Mer* 15, 58: 138–165.

———— (1963a). "Notes ethnographiques sur les structures du terroir dans la vallée de Maradi, République du Niger, Missions 1961–1962." *Etudes nigériennes* 8.

———— (1963b). "Notes ethnographiques sur les techniques agricoles dans la vallée de Maradi, République du Niger, Missions 1961–1962." *Etudes nigériennes* 8.

———— (1963c). "Notes ethnographiques sur l'élevage dans la vallée de Maradi, République du Niger, Missions 1961–1962." *Etudes nigériennes* 8.

Ormerod, W. E. (1978). "The Relationship between Economic Development and Ecological Degradation: How Degradation has Occurred in West Africa and how its Progress Might be Halted." *Journal of Arid Environments* 1, 4: 357–379.

Owen, John (1973). "A Contribution to the Ecology of the African Baobab." *Savanna* 2, 3: 1–12.

Oxby, Clare (1975). *Pastoral Nomads and Development: A select Annotated Bibliography with Special Reference to the Sahel with an Analytical Introduction in English and French*. London: International African Institute.

Palau Marti, Montserrat (1957). *Les Dogon*. Paris: Monographies Ethnologiques Africaines, Press Universitaires de France.

Paulme, Denise (1940). *Organisation social des Dogon (Soudan français)*. Paris: Les éditions Domat-Montchrestien.

Pélissier, Paul (1966). *Les Paysans du Sénégal*. Saint-Yrieix (Haute-Vienne): Imprimerie Fabrègue.

Phillips, Ralph (1958). "Cattle." *Scientific American* (June 1958).

Portères, Roland (1952). "Linear Cultural Sequences in Primitive Systems of Agriculture and their Significance." *African Soils* 2, 2: 133–149.

———— (1970). "Primary Cradles of Agriculture in the African Continent," in J. D. Fage, and Roland Oliver (Eds.), *Papers in African Pranis* pp. 43–58. [orig. in *Journal of African History* 3 (1962)].

Reisman, Paul (1980). "The Fulani in a Development Context," in Stephen P. Reyna (Ed.), *Sahelian Social Development*. pp. 71–186. Abidjan: U.S. Agency for International Development, Regional Economic Development and Services Office, West Africa.

Richards, Paul (1975). "Alternative Strategies for the Africa Environment: 'Folk Ecology' as a Basis for Community Orientated Agricultural Development," in Paul Richards (Ed.), *African Environment: Problems and Perspectives*. African Environment Special Report No. 1. London: International African Institute.

Roberts, Richard (1981). "Fishing for the State: The Political Economy of the Middle Niger Valley," in Donald Crummey and C. C. Stewart (Eds.), *Modes of Production in Africa—The Precolonial Era*, pp. 175–204. Beverly Hils: Sage Publications.

Russell, W. M. S. (1973). "The Slash-and-Burn Technique," in Richard Gould (Ed.), *Man's Many Ways*, pp. 86–101. New York: Harper and Row.

Sall, Alioune (1978). "Quel aménagement pastoral pour le Sahel?" *Revue Tiers Monde* 73: 161–170.

Sidikou, Arouna Hamidou (1974). "Sédentarité et mobilité entre Niger et Zgaret." *Etudes nigériennes* 34.

Smith, Susan E. (1978). "The Environmental Adaptation of Nomads in the West African Sahel: A Key to Understanding Prehistoric Pastoralists," in Wolfgang Weissleder (Ed.), *The Nomadic Alternative: Modes and Models of Interaction in the African-Asian Deserts and Steppes*, pp. 75–96. The Hague: Mouton.

Swift, Jeremy (1973). "Disaster and a Sahelian Nomad Economy," in David Dalby and R. J. Harrison Church (Eds.), *Report of the 1973 Symposium on Drought in Africa*, pp. 71–78. London: School of Oriental and African Studies.

———— (1977). "Sahelian Pastoralists: Underdevelopment, Desertification, and Famine." *Annual Review of Anthropology* 6: 457–478.

van Raay, Hans G. T. (1974). *Fulani Pastoralists and Cattle*. Occasional Paper No. 44. The Hague: Institute of Social Studies.

———— and Peter N. de Leeuw (1974). *Fodder Resources and Grazing Management in a Savanna Environment: An Ecosystem Approach*. Occasional Paper No. 45. The Hague: Institute of Social Studies.

Veyret, P. (1952). "L'élevage dans la zone tropical." *Les Cahiers d'Outre-Mer* 5, 17: 70–83.

Ware, Theresa Anne (1979). *Wolof Farmers and Fulani Herders: A Case Study of Drought Adaptation in the Diourbel Region of Senegal*. Ph.D. Dissertation. The University of Michigan.

# PART VI

# The *Encadrement* of the Population: The Bureaucratic Development and Restructuring of Labor and Business in South Africa

These studies of South Africa demonstrate a relationship between the changing forces of production, the emergence of new bureaucratic structures, and class divisions and antagonisms. They clearly illustrate problems and social trends which are relevant for the entire continent. Ronald T. Libby analyzes the interrelationships between both regional and international external forces in the development of South Africa's national bourgeoisie, and the impact of these factors on party realignments in South Africa. Stanley B. Greenberg and Hermann Giliomee deal with class divisions within black South Africa's labor force and the South African state's role in fomenting class fragmentation. Both studies emerge out of a need to confront the problems of changing social relations and new class realities arising from changes in the nature of production in South Africa.

The basic reality underlying the new bureaucratic and political structures, and the class divisions, analyzed by Greenberg and Giliomee is a qualitatively higher rate of unemployment of black workers than South Africa has ever known. Where once recruiters from the mines had to address meetings, advertise, provide inducement of all sorts to attract African workers, now tens of thousands of applicants mill about the recruiting office desperate for work. The attitude of the administrative board officials is that there is an unlimited supply of labor. Greenberg and Giliomee argue that the purpose of the Bantustans *currently* is not to provide cheap African labor or to ease "the process of capitalistic accumulation" by allowing subsistence families to cheaply produce workers who could migrate to the mines and afford to work for extremely low wages. They also reject the popular argument that the creation of the Bantustans was meant to preserve "traditional tribal structures" in order to create indigenous allies who would legitimate a repressive social order. Rather, they have found that agricultural production has declined to the point that the Bantustans cannot provide even the barest subsistence to a vastly overgrown population.

Money sent from the wage earners in South Africa supports the huge African rural populations, instead of the other way around—that is, subsistence agriculture creating wage workers. Equally striking, this study reports that the Bantustan bureaucracies, once thought essential to labor control and vital as an ideological prop of the puppet governments, have virtually disintegrated and are easily bypassed by Africans seeking wage employment. Because the Bantustan officials are no longer capable of providing essential services for the welfare of the peoples under their control, they are in no position to legitimate anything.

Even though the Bantustans are no longer capable of fulfilling their "historic functions," Greenberg and Giliomee argue that they are more than "dumping grounds for the redundant and functionally superfluous." "The Bantustans," they maintain, "are the institutional underbelly of an emerging racial and class order that fosters areas of privilege and, dialectically, areas of exclusion." The South African state has used the Bantustans to divide the African majority by creating "areas of privilege and rights," thus fostering collaboration with a well-placed, increasingly well-off African minority. This study points to a growing gulf between official ideological declarations that the South African state's role in the affairs of the market has declined and the rural reality. The bureaucratic structures of the Bantustan authorities disintegrate; the administrative boards of the South African state grow ever stronger. This study underlines the hollowness of the South African rhetoric.

Greenberg and Giliomee demonstrate how the new bureaucratic institutions of the South African state, backed up by its full legal and coercive sanctions, have fragmented the South African population into legal and illegal workers, and into those employed by large corporations and manufacturers and those who have access to only the smaller, lower-paying firms. Some African workers can live legally in the cities and have access to education and training which will provide for upward mobility. Still other Africans become "commuters" who travel far distances and are second-rate members of the labor force in comparison to the permanent urban residents, but who are still socially and economically ahead of the "illegals." The "illegals," in turn, are still better advantaged than those left without resources in the distant rural areas. To "struggle" comes to mean gaining access to "open" labor markets; to become "legal," to gain permission to become part of the legitimate system.

South Africa's manufacturing sector does not need labor from the Bantustans. The state sector draws upon impoverished male labor for the cheapest-paying jobs on the state railways and in rubbish removal. Rural women from the Bantustans are almost never employed and are the ones who are the most desperate. This is why Greenberg and Giliomee contend that "It is upon such distinctions and such hierarchies of privilege that the state has sought to construct a strategy of control and collaboration." Greenberg and Giliomee have revealed to us a most sophisticated schema of divide and rule which pits one religion, ethnic group, and region against another and also creates additional divisions within the division of labor. The South African state has apparently succeeded in creating administrative structures to foster class divisions and to direct those antagonisms inwardly among blacks and away from itself.

The greatest stimulus for change in South Africa, some analysts have maintained, will come from external forces, especially from the intervention of black African states. The South African government has itself feared the possibility of encirclement by unfriendly regimes. Through arms and trade it has reached out to bribe and to coerce potential enemies. To those who predicted bitter confrontation with increasingly resentful and antagonistic African governments, South Africa can point to a long list of recent successful diplomatic and trade victories, ranging from international meetings with leading officials of the Ivory Coast, Senegal, Ghana, Nigeria, and Kenya, to the establishment of treaties with Angola and Mozambique.

Where, then, are the external pressures on South Africa? Ronald Libby suggests some interesting possibilities in his study "Transnational Corporations and the National Bourgeoisie: Regional Expansion and Party Realignment in South Africa." Libby demonstrates the impact of regional trade upon both the class structure of South Africa and on political alliances threatened by divisions within the dominant bourgeoisie. Patterns of trade, he maintains, have affected the framework of both political and economic conflict in the Republic of South Africa, and have created new structures of industry and government. They have touched not only foreign policy, but domestic matters ranging from petty apartheid to the recognition of trade unions and black representation in national parliaments.

Libby challenges the assumption of most experts that the African states in the region cannot affect the political outcome of the conflict in South Africa. In this study he lays the groundwork for a reconceptualization of the nature of dependency relationships among the eleven states in the southern African regional economy. He shows that the Republic of South Africa has demonstrated an ambivalence in its foreign policy towards ideologically hostile states in the area. This ambiguity is rooted in economic conflict between what he calls "regionally oriented" and "nonregionally oriented" social groups in the republic. Thus he points out that even though the Republic of South Africa repeatedly crossed the borders of its neighbors and engaged in other acts of aggression, it did not interfere with a growing network of commercial and economic ties with those same governments. Libby argues that within South Africa, transnational corporations must manufacture and make decisions based upon a wider regional orientation, and they have therefore come into conflict with other, smaller national manufacturers. The capital-intensive, regionally oriented manufacturers depend upon skilled white labor; in contrast, the labor-intensive, national manufacturers rely upon unskilled and semiskilled nonwhite labor. Willing supporters of black commercial and industrial firms, the regionally oriented manufacturers also favor the elimination of the racial discrimination of petty apartheid; and, above all, they seek government policies strengthening relations with other black African governments in the region. They are concerned to promote the expansion of their markets beyond the boundaries of the Republic of South Africa. They must expand because their productive capacity requires that they operate according to regional economies of scale for maximum profitability.

In opposition to these economic interests and political policies, smaller members of the commercial and industrial bourgeoisie have allied themselves with the white labor unions to combat the development of black business and the imminent rise of increasingly skilled segments of the black labor force. Libby goes beyond the pioneering work of Heribert Adam and Stanley Trapido to show how the ruling National Party has gone beyond its humble beginnings as a party of Boer farmers, aligning itself with the regional manufacturing segment of the national bourgeoisie to further a policy of normalizing relations with black African states in the region. Both the regional manufacturing segment of the dominant bourgeoisie and a major wing within the National Party have attempted to broaden the base of their rule by winning over significant numbers of English-speaking whites—the former basis of the organized opposition party. These policies have in turn fomented the splitting off in 1982 of the first Afrikaner opposition party in South Africa's history, the Conservative Party.

Libby documents in great detail the reliance of the regional manufacturing interests on a transcontinental market. By the year 2000, trade to African countries will amount to as much as one-third of the total value of South Africa's manufactured exports. Already the oil, computer, and automobile industries in South Africa are overbuilt for the existing domestic market. Without the expansion of regional markets other firms could not survive.

The regional manufacturers which now depend primarily on a skilled white labor force would willingly substitute appropriately trained black workers who, although educated, would still be cheaper than Europeans. To this end, the regionalists would be willing to accommodate a permanent settled black urban labor force. They have strongly endorsed programs of organized housing for blacks. They welcome a more affluent segment of black workers as a growing consumer market for their products. They approve of the rise of black urban businesses both as a potential market for their products and as allies in reaching a greater black mass clientele, and also because a growing black bourgeoisie would provide a growing stake for a *minority of the African majority* in the continuance of a stable society. However, the other segment of the white bourgeoisie, the nationalists, already serves the same market of black consumers and in every way fears the rise of a competitive black petite bourgeoisie as competitors in the same commercial areas.

Libby and Greenberg and Giliomee thus help us better to understand some of the cross-pressures that underlie contemporary conflicts in South Africa.

# CHAPTER 12

# Transnational Corporations and the National Bourgeoisie: Regional Expansion and Party Realignment in South Africa

## Ronald T. Libby

The existing literature assumes that, as the economic core of southern Africa, the Republic of South Africa has political leverage over the poorer, nonindustrial black African states in the region without, however, incurring any political costs to itself.[1] Most "area experts" also tend to exclude or at least minimize the possibility that the so-called peripheral states in the region are capable of effecting a political outcome of the conflict in South Africa.

This study argues that black African states in the region are not any more "dependent" upon the regional economy than is South Africa. To the contrary, as the center of the regional economy, South Africa is more sensitive to changes in it than are other African states whose regionally oriented economic interests are relatively less important.

Economic conflict between regionally oriented and nationally oriented social groups in the Republic of South Africa explains much of the ambivalence in its foreign policy toward ideologically and politically "hostile" states in the region. An understanding of this conflict in these terms will help explain, for example, the ostensible incongruence of South Africa's armed attacks against insurgents in bordering countries while at the same time South Africa has not disturbed the extensive commercial and economic ties, including aid programs.

In what follows we focus upon South Africa's manufacturing and commercial sectors. We shall seek to explain the political significance of South Africa's regionally oriented manufacturing and commercial corporations for the South African state. We argue that a major division has emerged within the country's business community between a *regionally oriented* manufacturing and commercial segment represented by large-scale firms (i.e., South African and foreign) and a segment of smaller, *nationally oriented* industrial and commercial businesses. The regionally oriented corporations strongly favor governmental

291

policies which promote dialogue between South Africa and African governments. They also favor state support for black commercial and small-scale industrialists, the elimination of job discrimination, influx control, and universal
enfranchisement (albeit not in a unitary, majority-ruled state). Their policies
are designed to create a political environment which facilitates the expansion
of the markets of regional corporations, lowers their costs of labor, and increases levels of profitability.

The majority of small white owner-operated commercial and industrial
businesses together with white workers represented by politically powerful trade
unions oppose these policies. The white petite bourgeoisie regards the emergence of black industrial and commercial businesses in the urban areas of South
Africa as a threat to its access to a large and growing black consumer market.
And white workers regard governmental policies which are designed to eliminate job discrimination as a threat to their privileged labor position. They also
regard governmental overtures to "hostile" black African states on South Africa's borders, such as declarations promising to dismantle apartheid in order
to normalize relations with these states, as a threat.[2] For example, white trade
unions regard the recognition of black trade unions as a threat to their labor
power and the white petite bourgeoisie regards the elimination of legal barriers
to the entry of black entrepreneurs into urban areas as a competitive threat.

To cope with increasing internal and external threats to white political hegemony in South Africa, the ruling National Party (NP) aligned itself with
large-scale, regionally oriented corporate interests in order to normalize relations with "hostile" black African states and to attract the votes of English-
speaking whites and thereby broaden the NP's base of political support.[3] However, this contributed to the most serious political split in the history of the
ruling NP.[4] The ex-leader of the powerful Transvaal NP, Dr. A. P. Treurnicht,
and seventeen other MPs broke with the National Party in 1982 over the leadership's decision to implement a multiracial constitution, which symbolized to
them the elimination of Separate Development.

Under Treurnicht's leadership, the first Afrikaner opposition party in the
Parliament since 1948 was formed—the Conservative Party (CP).[5]

There are historical parallels between the political realignment which is currently under way within the ruling NP and a major political realignment which
occurred in 1924. Comparable with the successful efforts of the Afrikaner Nationalist Party of General Hertzog, which formed an electoral alliance with the
Labour Party in 1924, the CP of Treurnicht (along with the Herstigte Nasionale
Party [HNP] of Jaap Marais) is seeking to attract the political support of white
miners, industrial workers, and state employees along with the petite bourgeoisie in opposition to the NP under Botha's leadership.[6] Also comparable with
Prime Minister J. C. Smuts, who was forced to form a political alliance with
"big capital" (primarily mining) through an electoral alliance with the South
African Party and the Unionist Party in 1920, P. W. Botha is attempting to
form an alliance with large-scale corporate interests represented by the Urban
Foundation (UF).[7] And comparable with the political realignment which occurred in 1924 in which Smuts's South Africa Party was defeated, the success
which the CP under Treurnicht has in winning the electoral support of white
labor and the white petite bourgeoisie will determine the speed with which the
NP will implement its reforms, and its ultimate success, and perhaps going

beyond them to incorporate urban and "homelands" blacks into its multiracial constitutional plan.

## STATE SUPPORT FOR TRANSNATIONAL CORPORATIONS[8]

At a very early stage in the development of manufacturing industry in South Africa, industrialists recognized that it was necessary to find markets outside of South Africa for their output. After 1925, they received support from the new Pact government, which established trade commissioners in several African countries. The obvious candidate for market penetration was Rhodesia, since it had the largest consumer market in Africa next to South Africa itself. And, in fact, by the 1930s South African's manufacturing industry dominated the Rhodesian economy. However, market opportunities were also identified in the Congo, Nyasaland, Angola, Tanganyika, Kenya, and countries farther to the north (Bozzoli, 1981: 192).

South African governments have continued to emphasize the importance to the country of expanding manufactured exports to African countries in the region albeit for different reasons. For example, General Smuts referred to South Africa's "rightful place as leader in pan-African development" (Williams, 1948: 164). This theme was adumbrated by Eric Louw, South Africa's foreign minister in 1957, and by Dr. Diederichs, the state president in 1974. Speaking in response to the government's detente initiative toward African countries, Diederichs said that a common market for southern Africa was an attainable ideal (Leistner, 1976: 26). The most recent expression of this state ideology was the so-called Constellation of Southern African States (CONSAS) announced in 1979.[9]

The government's "outward-looking policy" of the 1960s, détente in the 1970s, and the CONSAS concept of the 1980s were all designed primarily to mitigate the "hostility" of black African countries to South Africa's policy of Separate Development and to disarm the antiapartheid movement in Western countries. The centerpiece of this strategy was the tactical use of South African–based transnational corporations to expand alliances of important social groups within southern Africa who benefit from the maintenance of these regional economic ties. South Africa's initiatives to reduce political tension with African countries in the region depend upon the continued operation of South African–based transnational corporations in these countires.

While there was nothing new in Botha's constellation-of-states proposal (which was originally proposed by Hendrik Verwoerd in the late 1950s), what is new is the explicit linkage in the strategy of dismantling apartheid as a *sine qua non* for gaining the cooperation of African states in the region. Hence, the elimination of apartheid which includes the accommodation of urban blacks, coloreds, and Indians in South Africa's multiracial structure is regarded by the South Africans as the minimum which potential black "allies" in the region will accept. Thus, in order to "normalize" or stabilize relations with black African governments in the region and thereby secure South Africa's borders against attacks by liberation movements, there must be clear signs of eliminating Separate Development at home. And, of course, if South Africa can normalize its interstate relations in the region, that would, potentially at least, counter some of the antiapartheid presure upon South Africa's Western trading and investment partners to apply economic sanctions against it.

It is probably because a new constitutional dispensation (involving coloreds and Indians but excluding blacks) would be highly visible to the outside world and yet would not in itself threaten white political hegemony that they received the highest priority in Vorster and Botha's agenda to deal with the "total onslaught."

From the point of view of transnational corporations, state support is necessary for them to operate in large markets according to economies of scale. This requires unified markets which are regional in scope.[10] Marais (1981: 42–43) notes, for example, that for reasons of economy of scale, large, capital-intensive industries in South Africa require government assistance in the form of tariff protection to take control of the entire domestic market. To that end, large firms have received subsidies in the form of below-market prices for their industrial inputs. For example, between 1952 and 1970, ISCOR, the huge state iron and steel corporation, did not raise the price of its steel. This had the effect of lowering the costs of production for manufacturers in South Africa, which enabled them to maintain their comparative economic advantage in regional markets. The huge Sasol state corporation has also subsidized the South African chemical industry, which has likewise given them a comparative advantage in southern African markets.

In effect, large corporations cannot operate profitably unless they are able to function without political interference not only in the Bantustans and the "white (urban) areas" of South Africa, but also in African countries, particularly in the southern region. For this reason, large-scale corporate interests have tended to oppose economic policies which are designed to implement Separate Development.[11]

Supporting the operations of South African–based transnational corporations in the southern African region helps to resolve acute problems facing both the government and large corporate interests. The maintenance of regional export markets contributes to the economic viability of transnational corporations. It facilitates the transfer of technology by transnational corporations with headquarters in metropolitan countries and guarantees the financing of these industries from abroad. This increases the economic stake of Western countries in South Africa, thus partially offsetting antiapartheid pressure on Western governments.

## TRANSNATIONAL CORPORATIONS AND REGIONAL MARKETS

From the perspective of South African–based transnational corporations, southern Africa as a market is important, and its potential is even more important. For example, southern Africa has a total geographical land area of 8.1 million square kilometers, or about one-fourth of the entire African continent. In 1982, it was inhabited by an estimated 118.7 million people, with more than one-fourth of them in urban areas and with a combined gross national product of US$101.2 billion at 1982 market prices.

As a percentage of South Africa's exports, exports to Africa outside of the Customs Union area (i.e., excluding Namibia, Botswana, Lesotho, and Swaziland) was estimated to be approximately 14 percent of the total in 1975.[12] When this figure is added to that of Custom Union countries and taking into account the increase in South Africa's exports to African countries from 1975 to 1982, the exports to African countries could be as high as 25 percent of the total value of South Africa's merchandise exports.[13]

Moreover, what is particularly significant about South Africa's penetration of regional markets (in addition to offsetting partially its trade deficits with Western countries) is that for important manufacturing industries, southern Africa is the only major external market. Table 12.1 contains data on South Africa's exports to African countries outside of the Customs Union (i.e., excluding trade with Botswana, Lesotho, Swaziland, and Namibia) in 1983. These data indicate that 45 percent or more of plastics, resins and rubber products, footwear, and millinery as well as 39 percent of chemicals and chemical products and 21 percent of miscellaneous manufactured goods were marketed in African countries, primarily in southern Africa.

Therefore, from the standpoint of these industries, at least, the maintenance and expansion of regional markets is integral to their continued growth and prosperity. One explanation for the fact that South Africa (like Israel at present and Japan during the 1950s) tends to export capital-intensive goods to nearby countries, whereas its more labor-intensive goods such as ore and unprocessed primary products are exported to major metropolitan export markets, is what is termed a "two-tailed" comparative advantage.

The economies of scale required by the high-growth or leading industries in South Africa such as petroleum, chemicals, machinery, electrical products, computers, and vehicles makes it imperative for these industries to expand their markets in order to reduce the costs of their operations and thus to ensure their profitability. These industries are overbuilt for the existing South African market.[14] In fact, many of them were originally designed to serve regional markets as well as the South African market.[15]

For example, the automobile industry has practically saturated existing markets. In the October 1977 issue of *Management* magazine, Tony Koenderman observed that economies of scale in the industry are normally dependent upon sales per model of 100,000 a year. However, in South Africa, in 1978 an estimated three-fourths of the models were sold at below the breakeven point. This has produced a situation of vicious price-cutting and has led industry analysts to conclude that, given the difficulties in exporting to Western industrial countries, the only solution is to expand car sales to blacks in South Africa.[16]

In the case of the oil transnationals, there are eight firms which are not only competing among themselves for a small, stagnant market but they have had to contend with competition from government-sponsored Sasol coal-to-oil conversion plants, nuclear power stations, and natural gas projects (*Management,* March 1985).

Much of South Africa's rapid industrial growth has been based upon these capital-intensive, high-technology sectors. For example, South Africa's manufacturing sector as a percentage of GDP rose from 3.8 percent in 1911 to 25.7 percent in 1982, while agriculture, forestry, and fishing declined from 21.1 percent of GDP in 1911 to 7.9 percent in 1982, and mining declined from 27.6 percent of GDP in 1911 to 10.7 percent in 1982. While the GDP increased at an annual rate of 4.5 percent in real terms, the average annual growth rate of manufacturing output during this period was 6.9 percent. The growth rates for agriculture and mining during this period were only 2.8 percent and 3.0 percent, respectively.

The rapid rise of industries producing intermediate products and processed raw materials is evident in their high average annual growth rate of 8.6 percent. The producers of metals, metal products, electrical machinery, paper and paper products, and rubber goods also experienced a high average growth rate of 9.0 percent. Processed raw material outputs such as iron and steel, basic chemicals, and oil and petrol had an average growth rate of 8.6 percent and motor vehicles grew at a rate of 9.9 percent a year. From his survey of South African industrial performance between 1916 and 1975, Marais (1981: 30) concludes that there has occurred a spectacular long-run expansion of the manufacturing sector relative to other sectors of the economy. Concomitant with this rapid rise in the growth of manufacturing generally, there was a significant trend toward accelerated growth in the science-based, capital-intensive industries whose continued growth and prosperity depends upon expanding markets—both to blacks in South Africa and to African states in the region.

Marais (1981: 40) argues that the growth in these capital-intensive industries between 1956 and 1975 played an important part in South Africa's overall export performance. While this stimulated growth in the economy and increased export earnings, it also resulted in a situation of surplus production which makes it necessary to export even at a loss.[17]

## TRANSNATIONAL VERSUS NATIONAL COMMERCIAL AND MANUFACTURING INTERESTS

We can distinguish a structural division within South Africa's white business community between large-scale, regionally oriented transnational firms and small-scale, local or nationally oriented firms. South Africa's commercial and manufacturing sectors are characterized by an overwhelming number of small firms. However, the economic power in these sectors is concentrated in the hands of the state and the twelve largest corporations.

In 1982, there were estimated to be approximately 75,000 small business firms in South Africa.[18] In the commercial sector, about 90 percent of all firms are small and roughly 80 percent of all industrial firms are small. Small firms are responsible for about 60 percent of total retail business, whereas they contribute only 20 percent of the total gross manufactured output. Small firms tend to supply small markets that would be uneconomical for larger firms. Small firms are relatively labor intensive, less efficient in their use of labor, and they tend to employ excessive numbers of people out of proportion to their size of operation. These firms are also less mechanized and have lower overheads.[19]

Small firms have had to compensate for this inefficiency by paying lower wages than larger firms. Bradley (1982: 38) notes in this regard that small businesses have come to rely upon blacks and white women because they cannot afford the luxury of discrimination and because blacks and white women are often willing to work for lower salaries than white men without guarantees of job security and other benefits which employees of large firms expect.

By contrast, business power in South Africa is concentrated in a handful of large corporations. Lombard (1984: 3) notes, for example, that only twelve groups of companies control 80 percent of gross assets of all companies listed on the Johannesburg stock exchange.[20] Tregenna-Piggott (1980: 194–195) estimates that only 2.7 percent of all firms control 50 percent of the total turnover and the largest ten public corporations control 40 percent of the total assets quoted by industrial companies. Only 3.5 percent of all manufacturing firms employ over 50 percent of all labor in that sector (du Plessis, 1978: 14).

An important structural difference between large and small firms in South Africa is the racial composition of their labor force. Small retail businesses and industrial firms tend to be labor intensive, they produce almost entirely for the domestic market, and they rely heavily upon black skilled labor (substituting for white labor wherever possible). By contrast, large commercial and industrial firms tend to be capital intensive, they depend upon large, regional markets, and they require a skilled labor force which to date is largely white. While there is no data available on the racial composition of the work force of large and small firms in South Africa, there is data to suggest that blacks predominate in the more labor-intensive industries such as clothing, textiles, and food. By contrast, whites are more prominent in the capital-intensive iron and steel, engineering, and metallurgical industries, and in chemicals, banking, and finance.[21]

It is in the large, capital-intensive, high-technology firms where there has been the least substitution of blacks for whites. This is due largely to strong white trade union pressure on the government to restrict apprenticeship training opportunities for blacks and to limit their professional training opportunities. By contrast, the small, labor-intensive firms (where white trade unions are not powerful) have shifted away from white labor to blacks and white women for the bulk of their work force.

The political significance of the structural differences between large, capital-intensive, regionally oriented corporations and small, labor-intensive, nationally oriented firms is that these groups of firms have conflicting economic interests.

## CONFLICTING INTERESTS OF LARGE AND SMALL FIRMS

In the aftermath of the 1976 black urban unrest and accelerated by the resurgence in unrest beginning in late 1984, large-scale corporate interests represented by the Urban Foundation adopted a strategy for coping with black urban unrest which potentially threatens small white businesses.[22] The principal architects of the UF were Harry Oppenheimer (its first chairman) and Anton Rupert of Rembrandt with Sam Motsuenyane, the president of the National African Federated Chambers of Commerce (Nafcoc).[23] Nafcoc is an umbrella organization of 14,000 members in 1984 with over a hundred chapters throughout South Africa.

The significance of the UF's informal association with Nafcoc for present purposes is that by 1977 their economic interests overlapped sufficiently for them to informally affiliate under the umbrella of the UF. We shall briefly discuss the nature of their overlapping interests and the implications of this for other major economic groups—specifically, small-scale white, commercial, and industrial businesses.

The economic interests of large-scale corporations would be well served by state intervention on behalf of urban Africans. While the collective size of the black consumer market is growing, to date it has not been tapped by the large, capital-intensive corporations. The reason is that although the black industrial

**TABLE 12.1**  South African Merchandise Trade with Africa, 1983 (Excluding Botswana, Lesotho, Swaziland and Namibia)

| Commodity Group | Exports to Africa, R'000 | Exports to Africa as a % of Total Exports per Group | Imports from Africa R'000 | Imports from Africa as a % of Total Imports per Group |
|---|---|---|---|---|
| 1 Animal and animal products | 39,396 | 18.3 | 5,023 | 6.3 |
| 2 Vegetable products | 67,783 | 11.0 | 44,488 | 8.7 |
| 3 Animal and vegetable fats and oils | 9,843 | 27.8 | 1,648 | 1.2 |
| 4 Prepared foodstuffs | 53,845 | 11.2 | 53,539 | 13.7 |
| 5 Mineral products | 39,788 | 1.9 | 17,140 | 7.4 |
| 6 Chemicals and chemical products | 168,291 | 39.0 | 3,511 | 0.3 |
| 7 Plastics, resins, and rubber products | 37,181 | 45.9 | 1,742 | 0.3 |
| 8 Hides, skins, and leather | 1,518 | 1.2 | 4,074 | 7.4 |
| 9 Wood and wood products | 6,056 | 10.8 | 15,618 | 13.1 |
| 10 Pulp, paper, and paperboard | 31,288 | 11.7 | 1,996 | 0.4 |
| 11 Textiles | 26,371 | 5.0 | 54,100 | 7.7 |
| 12 Footwear and millinery | 2,745 | 42.3 | 3,895 | 4.4 |
| 13 Nonmetallic miner products | 16,915 | 46.1 | 642 | 0.4 |
| 14 Gems and jewelry | 1,162 | — | 46,228 | 45.6 |
| 15 Base metals and metal products | 138,157 | 7.3 | 43,758 | 5.7 |
| 16 Machinery | 105,684 | 46.9 | 15,145 | 0.3 |
| 17 Vehicles and transport equipment | 34,439 | 19.1 | 7,508 | 0.4 |
| 18 Optical and other instruments | 7,240 | 21.8 | 1,454 | 0.2 |
| 19 Musical instruments | — | — | — | — |
| 20 Misc. manufactured articles | 4,486 | 21.4 | 3,678 | 2.3 |
| 21 Works of art, collectors' pieces | 59 | 1.7 | 281 | 1.3 |
| 22 Unclassified | 4,841 | — | 369 | — |
| TOTAL | 797,091 | 3.9 | 325,658 | 2.0 |

*Source:* Monthly Abstract of Trade Statistics, January–December 1983, Tables 2 and 3, Pretoria, Government Printer.

labor force has undergone substantial expansion during the past twenty years, their wages are too low to constitute a market for the durable consumer goods and intermediate products in which large firms specialize. Most African workers, for example, cannot afford to purchase a television or automobile or own a home (even under the concessionary terms of the ninety-nine year leaseholds which were recently inaugurated by the government). And even if black workers could afford household appliances, most urban townships do not have electrification. Therefore, if the UF and other representatives of large corporate interests such as the Federated Chamber of Industries (FCI) were able to activate state intervention into black urban areas to build housing, provide electrification, and improve public services plus increase the wages of black workers, it would expand markets for their output.

It is estimated that the blacks' share of South Africa's purchasing power was R1.9 billion in 1971, which constituted 22.4 percent of the total. The figure for 1975 was R3.75 billion, which was 25.7 percent of total private consumption expenditure.[24] The National Productivity Institute has estimated that, based upon a growth rate of 5 1/2 percent in GDP between 1973 and the year 2000, black purchasing power would increase to R19, billion or an estimated 32 percent of the total. Hence it is clear that the black industrial labor force constitutes a consumer market of growing importance.

However, the growing size of the black consumer market conceals the very low individual or household income of the majority of urban blacks. The executive director of the FCI has estimated, for example, that in 1975 the per capita annual income of urban blacks was R176, projected to rise to only R538 by the year 2000 (Reynders, 1977: 234). In 1977, it was estimated that 55.3 percent of all African households in Soweto were below poverty datum levels. The significance of this is that the black consumer market is largely restricted to the purchase of nondurable and semidurable consumer goods—that is, goods in which the small, labor-intensive industries and businesses specialize. For example, Reynders estimates that 45 percent of the income of black urban workers is spent on food, beverages, and tobacco and an additional 16 percent on clothing and footwear (Reynders, 1977: 234). Hence, even with the projected increase in the proportion of black workers in supervisory and skilled job categories by 1990, the vast majority of black workers will remain in the unskilled and semiskilled job categories, which means that their individual and household income will remain low. In terms of the structure of the black urban market, it will mean that without massive governmental intervention into black urban areas to provide public infrastructure along with housing and without further amendments to the Group Areas Acts and the elimination of barriers to black skilled wage equality which block the formation of a permanent black urban labor force and middle class, the market for durable consumer goods will remain small.[25]

However, the owners and operators of small white industrial and commercial firms (i.e., the national bourgeoisie) do not share the large corporations' interest in supporting the formation of a black urban bourgeoisie. In fact, the white petite bourgeoisie regards state support for black urban businesses as a potential threat to them. Black businesses are concentrated primarily in the commercial and service sectors (i.e., general trading stores, garages, and transport) largely because they require small capital outlays and low technology.[26] At present, blacks purchase most of their necessity or convenience goods from black businesses (formal and informal) in the black residential areas but they buy most of their durable goods from white-owned shops in the "white (urban) areas." The absence of a retail infrastructure in the black urban areas as well as the high prices of products available in black residential areas has forced blacks to patronize white businesses in the Central Business Districts (CBDs).

Studies suggest that black consumers would prefer to do most of their purchasing at shops in the black residential areas if goods of the same variety, price and other factors were the same as they are in the CBDs. However, there is an absence of supermarkets, butcheries, liquor stores, cafés, restaurants, and pharmacies in the black residential areas to satisfy this need. It is this economic vacuum which the large corporations in alliance with small black entrepreneurs are proposing to fill that threatens small white businesses.[27]

The UF is seeking to mobilize the resources of the state to foster the formation of urban infrastructure for small black businesses including financial support and management and advisory services. This is part of the UF's strategy to forge "reform alliances" by using the private sector to accommodate blacks in the political reform process (*Financial Mail,* August 2, 1985). A major thrust of the UF's initiative is the removal of "institutional discrimination" against black urban entrepreneurs.

However, the removal of the mass of bureaucratic regulations that act as barriers to black entrepreneurs in black urban areas and in "white" CBDs threatens the entrenched advantages which the white petite bourgeoisie enjoys in South Africa. There exists a plethora of rules, acts, and licensing regulations such as the Machinery and Occupational Safety Act, as well as administration boards which control zoning practices, which act as barriers to potential black entrepreneurs.[28] For example, under the terms of the Machinery and Occupational Safety Act, there are "thermal" and "ventilation" requirements which the facilities in most black urban townships cannot meet. Another example of legal discrimination against black entrepreneurs is the Bantu Urban Areas Act, which limits commercial development in black townships to daily basic necessities, thereby forcing blacks to shop in white areas for their basic needs. Any attempt to remove the legal barriers to the entry of black entrepreneurs into black urban areas and into the CBDs will undoubtedly be opposed by the small white firms.[29]

Large-scale corporations are therefore seeking to form an alliance with an emergent black petite bourgeoisie based upon a mutuality of economic interests which are not shared by the white petite bourgeoisie or white workers. Large corporations wish to have a permanent, skilled and semiskilled black labor pool in the urban areas and wish to encourage state intervention in black townships for the purpose of "managing the reform process" and creating markets for their output. The black petite bourgeoisie is principally interested in gaining state support to enable them to operate in black urban areas free of restrictions and protected against competition from white commercial interests. They would also like to be able to operate businesses in the CBDs.[30]

The major objectives of the black entrepreneur is to remove the obstacles to their economic expansion and growth. In addition to licensing restrictions, the principal obstacle to back capitalism at present is the lack of freehold rights for blacks in urban areas. Without ownership rights, black businesses do not have the security necessary to negotiate major business loans.

In the aftermath of the upheavals of the late 1970s, the state has made concessions to urban African businessmen, and the large corporations were instrumental in gaining governmental approval of these concessions.[31] A potentially important breakthrough occurred in 1978 with the passage of the Bantu (Urban Areas) Amendment Act (No. 97), which authorized ninety-nine-year leaseholds for urban Africans who are outside of the "homelands" (i.e., in "white [urban] areas"). While few Africans have to date been granted the leases (in 1983, only 57,200 houses were available for purchase under the ninety-nine-year scheme), ostensibly due to civil service "obstructionism," it nevertheless does minimize the economic insecurity of urban blacks.[32]

Through the agency of the UF, large corporations were instrumental in securing this legal modification of Separate Development. Without the lobbying of the UF in Parliament and the lobbying of cabinet members and top civil servants by major Afrikaner industrialists on behalf of the UF, the leasehold legislation would never have been voted out of parliament (Myers, 1980: 73–74).

## EMERGENT CLASS CONFLICT IN WHITE POLITICS

White, conservative political opposition to the "reform strategy" pursued by the Botha government and the UF (on behalf of large corporations) has precipitated the most serious political challenge to the NP within the white electorate since the party came to power in 1948.[33] White trade union opposition to the NP's limited implementation of the Wiehahn and Riekert proposals has found a political outlet in their support of the conservative opposition Afrikaner Herstigte Nasionale Party (HNP).[34] The April 1981 (white) general election and the October 1985 by-elections in South Africa revealed the potential electoral threat to the NP from blue-collar support for the HNP. The white union support for the HNP and its leader, Jaap Marais, on the basis of "stopping the advance of blacks in industry" has produced an unprecedented degree of electoral support for the HNP. It was estimated, for example, that one-third of all Afrikaners (who comprise 60 percent of the white electorate) voted for the HNP in the general election of 1981.

While the HNP has only one seat in parliament, the other conservative Afrikaner party, the Conservative Party (CP), holds 18 seats, of which 16 representatives won as Nationalists prior to the split in the party in 1982.[35] Present projections expect the HNP/CP at this stage to win between 25 and 32 seats in a general election (a general election must take place before the end of 1989). At present, the NP holds an unassailable majority of 126 parliamentary seats out of 178. However, it faces the danger of serious inroads by the conservative Afrikaner parties on the right and by the official opposition party, the Progressive Federal Party (which has 27 seats), on the left. This could pose a threat to the NP's centrist position in the white electorate, which is the basis of its claim to be the only party capable of governing South Africa.

The second major source of opposition to the NP's alliance strategy with large commercial and industrial corporations are conservative Afrikaner civil servants and lower-income state employees whose economic security and social status are threatened by the dismantling of the state institutions responsible for administrating and maintaining Separate Development (Adam and Giliomee, 1979: 186). Opposition to the NP is strong within the middle and lower echelons of the state bureaucracy, especially in the departments of Defense, Law and Order, National Education, and Cooperation and Development. Officials in these ministries have a vested interest in administering the approximately 4000 laws and 6000 regulations affecting the private sector (Coker, 1981: 239). An example of their opposition to the NP's labor reform strategy was the government's withdrawal of its legislative proposal embodying the recommendations of the Riekert Commission when it was discovered that in the process of drafting the legislation (involving the repeal of sixty-two separate acts of Parliament), the civil service had completely subverted the intention of the legislation.

In the Transvaal, which is the seat of the state bureaucracy and where the leader of the CP, Andries Treurnicht, headed the Transvaal National Party before his defection in 1982, the CP has its stronghold of electoral support. For example, in national opinion surveys, the CP has consistently polled 19 percent of the white electorate, compared to as high as 40 percent in the Transvaal. However, following the CP's strong showing in the urban Primrose Parliamentary by-election of 1984, Treurnicht has claimed that the CP is a political power capable of defeating the NP in any seat in the country. He has asserted that the CP's political support is no longer restricted to the traditional strongholds of Afrikaner conservatism in the rural areas of the Orange Free State and the Transvaal. Treurnicht claims that the CP is now acceptable to Afrikaners and English-speakers in the urban areas.

While CP supporters are strongly opposed to any modification of Separate Development such as the government's De Lange Committee Report, which recommended the phasing out of discrimination in education[36] and the formation of a single education ministry for all racial groups, and the constitutional "power-sharing" reforms which include coloureds, Indians, and whites, opposition to the NP converges with the HNP in their opposition to the ruling party's alliance strategy with large corporations. For example, Paulus has attacked the Chamber of Mines (representing the major mining companies) for supporting the black National Union of Mineworkers' demand that job reservation be ended. And Treurnicht has attacked the relationship between "big business" and the government on grounds that it has placed the burden of financing "multiracialism" upon whites.[37] He argues that this has placed a massive burden on white taxpayers while the rate of taxation on big business has fallen during Botha's administration. Treurnicht has charged that under Botha's government, the building societies have been "bleeding the middle class dry." He has asserted out that the six largest banks have paid less than 1 percent of their profits in tax in 1983/84 while an estimated 20,000 farmers have been forced off their land for nonpayment of debt owed to the banks. The principal beneficiaries of the dramatic fall in the value of the land are said to be the gold-mining companies. With the deepening of the recession, it has enabled them to "buy up South Africa" (*The Star* [Johannesburg], September 9, 1985). Treurnicht has claimed, for example, that the Anglo-American Corporation alone controls 72 percent of the total listed companies on Johannesburg's stock exchange.

A major source of electoral support targeted by the CP is the small, commercial and industrial white business community. CP election campaign appeals have in fact promised to prevent black businessmen from entering the Central Business Districts and they have vowed to retain the Group Areas Act (*South African Observer,* September 1984: 10). The CP has promised to cut the general sales tax in half, reduce income tax by 10 percent, and abolish the estate duty which is designed to appeal to the commercially active white population, among others.

The extent to which the government supports the corporate strategy of allying with an emergent black petite bourgeoisie in urban areas by removing the legal barriers to black entrepreneurs will determine, at least in part, the CP's success in attracting election support from the white petite bourgeoisie. A major election shift of the small-scale white business community away from the NP has an added significance in terms of potential party realignment in South Africa. To compensate for the loss of conservative Afrikaner support for Botha's government, the NP has sought to attract the English-speaking segment of the white electorate.[38] If the CP is able to make serious inroads among English-speaking voters who tend to be concentrated in the business sector, it would undoubtedly tend to frustrate the NP's efforts to fashion a solid white voting coalition to support its reform policies.

## PARTY REALIGNMENT: AN HISTORICAL ANALOGY

The current crisis within the ruling NP appears to have parallels with the political crisis of 1920, which resulted in a major realignment in South African politics. For the purpose of drawing out the parallels between these two periods we shall briefly outline the circumstances leading to the party realignment of 1924.

In 1910, the ruling party of South Africa was the South Africa Party (SAP), which was led by two ex-generals in the Anglo-Boer war, Louis Botha and J. C. Smuts. The SAP was dedicated to reconciling the bitterness between the Dutch and English which was an aftermath of the Anglo-Boer war (1899–1902). When General Botha died in 1919, Smuts formed a new government. However, since important political constituencies remained outside of the SAP, the government's base of support was tenuous. One important group which formed an opposition party was comprised of Afrikaner nationalists who supported a "South Africa first" policy independent of the British Empire and who wanted their Afrikaner identity protected. This group of Afrikaner nationalists was led by General J. B. M. Hertzog, who organized the National Party in 1914 (the forerunner of the second National Party under D. F. Malan, which became South Africa's ruling party in 1948). This party was committed to the so-called two streams policy in which the Dutch and English nationalities were to flow separately but in principle be accorded equal importance. In practice, however, Afrikaner national sentiment was supreme.

A second important political group which was outside of the SAP were English voters who were drawn primarily from the commercial and mining industries. They did not trust the SAP's commitment to maintain South Africa's ties with the British Empire. English voters were represented by the Unionist Party, which was led by the infamous (at least from the standpoint of Afrikaner nationalists) L. S. Jameson, who led the abortive Jameson Raid. The raid was largely carried out at the instigation of Cecil Rhodes to undermine the Afrikaner-controlled Transvaal Republic. The third major political group outside of the SAP was the Labour Party, whose following was largely comprised of English-speaking white workers who were primarily miners. The Labour Party was led by Colonel F. H. Creswell, whose following was violently anti-Smuts and motivated, incongruously, by European socialist doctrine and the fear of being replaced by a cheaper, nonwhite labor force.

Without a firm and distinctive voting constituency, the SAP found itself in the position of suffering an eroding electoral position. The Afrikaner nationalists were growing in their support of the National Party of Hertzog, and English business and labor interests withheld their support for the SAP. In these circumstances, General Smuts's base of political power was shrinking. This forced him to seek a political alliance with an opposition party in order to remain a power.

Since the SAP had committed itself to maintaining South Africa in the British Empire and since the Unionist Party was alarmed by the Upsurge in Afrikaner nationalism which posed a threat to South Africa's involvement in the empire, a SAP–Unionist Party alliance was a natural development. Therefore, in 1920, when the SAP failed to gain a majority in the Parliament, it was forced to form a coalition government with the Unionist Party (which was completely absorbed) in order to retain control of the government.

This set the stage for an alliance between the two opposition parties—the National Party and the Labour Party. This party alliance was ultimately successful in unseating the SAP, resulting in a coalition government in 1924 called the Pact government. The cementing of a political alliance between an Afrikaner nationalist party and white workers (Afrikaners predominated in the white labor force after the depression of the 1930s) proved to be an enduring electoral alliance that has been the basis of the National Party's political support since 1948.

Events leading to the electoral realignments of 1924 suggest parallels with the current crisis facing the NP. Comparable with the SAP's eroding electoral position, the NP of P. W. Botha has sought to ally with large corporate interests in order to compensate for the loss of conservative Afrikaner–working-class political support.[39] And comparable with the strategy of the National Party of Hertzog and the Labour Party in forming an alliance to defeat the SAP, the CP and the HNP are beginning to coordinate their election campaigns in order to defeat Botha's National party. The success of the CP and the HNP in putting together an election coalition comprised of white workers, the white petite bourgeoisie, as well as lower-income state employees will undoubtedly affect the NP's ability to implement its reform strategy.

## CONCLUSION

A major conflict of economic interest has arisen within South Africa's white business community between a handful of large, transnational commercial, industrial, and financial corporations and numerous small, national commercial and industrial firms. The transnational corporations require large, unified markets in southern Africa to operate profitably while the small firms depend upon local, national markets in South Africa. The transnational corporations carry on an active trade with African states in the region as well as having substantial investments and retail outlets there.

In order to cope with the growing political tension in the region between neighboring African states and South Africa and to cope with black urban unrest, the transnational corporations have embarked upon a "reform strategy" of dismantling the economic structures of apartheid. However, the removal of legal barriers against black urban entrepreneurs (which is central to the reform strategy) threatens the interests of small white businesses.

The Urban Foundation, which represents the interests of large corporations, has embarked upon a strategy of "reform alliances" with black urban entrepreneurs. The UF is seeking to mobilize the resources of the large corporations as well as securing massive state financing to establish an urban infrastructure for small black businesses. The removal of legal and economic barriers to black entrepreneurs in urban areas threatens to undermine the entrenched advantages which the small white businesses enjoy.

Conservative Afrikaner political parties—the Conservative Party and the Herstigte Nasionale Party—are seeking to win the electoral support of the owners of the small white firms (i.e., the white petite bourgeoisie). The CP in particular has appealed to them on the basis of a promise to oppose any attempt to remove economic barriers against black entrepreneurs in urban areas. The CP's and the HNP's political strategies converge in their attacks against the ruling National Party's support for large corporations at the expense of the small white business community, white workers, and lower-income state employees. Their success in coalescing this white voting bloc will determine the ability of the National Party to carry out the reforms necessary to cope with the political crisis confronting it. There are historical parallels between the current position of the National Party and a major party realignment which occurred in South Africa in 1924.

# REFERENCES

Adam, Heribert (1978). "Interests Behind Afrikaner Power." *Social Dynamics* 4, 2.

———— and Hermann Giliomee (1979). *Ethnic Power Mobilized: Can South Africa Change?* New Haven and London: Yale University Press.

*African Business* (London) (September 1984). "SA's Black Middle Class: Traitors or Saviors?"

Botha, P. W. (1979). Opening Address in "Towards a Constellation of Southern African States." Meetings between the Prime Minister and Business Leaders, Carlton Centre, Johannesburg, November 22, 1979. Pretoria: Information Service of South Africa.

Bozzoli, Belinda (1981). *The Political Nature of a Ruling Class*. London: Routledge & Kegan Paul.

Bradley, Elisabeth (1982). "Small Business—Views, Opportunities and Challenges." *S.-Afr. Tydskr. Bedryfsl.* [*South African Journal of Business Management*] (Pretoria) 13, 1.

*Chicago Tribune*, October 25, 1985.

Coker, Christopher (1981). "The South African Elections and Neo-Apartheid." *The World Today* (June).

Davies, Robert, and Dan O'Meara (1985). "Total Strategy in Southern Africa: An Analysis of South African Regional Policy Since 1978." *Journal of Southern African Studies* 11, 2 (April).

du Plessis, R. G. (1978). "Concentration of Economic Power in the South African Manufacturing Industry." *The South African Journal of Economics* 46, 3.

*Finance Week* (Johannesburg), August 22–28, 1985.

*Financial Mail* (Johannesburg), August 2, 1985.

*Financial Mail* (Johannesburg), August 16, 1985.

*Financial Mail* (Johannesburg), August 23, 1985.

Glendenhuys, Deon (1982). *What Do We Think? A Survey of White Opinion on Foreign Policy Issues*. Braamfontein: The South African Institute of International Affairs.

———— (1984a). *The Diplomacy of Isolation: South African Foreign Policy Making*. New York: St. Martin's Press.

———— (Ed.) (1984b). "South Africa's Regional Policy." *Regional Co-operation: The Record and Outlook*. Braamfontein: The South African Institute of International Affairs.

Giliomee, Hermann, 1983. "The Disintegration of the Nationalist Movement, c. 1965–1983." Unpublished manuscript.

———— (March 12, 1985). Private communication.

Hackland, Brian (1980). "The Economic and Political Context of the Growth of the Progressive Federal Party in South Africa, 1959–1978." *Journal of Southern African Studies* 7, 1.

Houghton, D. Hobart (1976). *The South African Economy*, 4th ed. Cape Town: Oxford University Press.

Innes, Duncan (1983). "Monopoly Capitalism in South Africa," in the South African's Research Service's *South African Review* No. 1. Johannesburg: Raven Press.

Kroon, J. (1984). "'n Struktuuranalise van Swart Sakeondernemings in die Republiek van Suid-Afrika." *S.-Afr. Tydskr. Bedryfsl* 15.

Leistner, G. M. E. (1976). "Southern African Community of Interests—A South African Viewpoint." *South African Journal of African Affairs* 1 and 2.

———— (1981). "Towards a Regional Development Strategy for South Africa." *The South African Journal of Economics* 49, 4.

Libby, Ronald T. (1987). *The Politics of Economic Power in Southern Africa: The Limits of Economic Coercion*. Princeton, N.J.: Princeton University Press.

Lombard, J. (1984). "Power in the Market Economy." *Focus on Key Economic Issues* 34. Johannesburg: Mercabank.

*Management* (Johannesburg), March 1985.

Marais, G. (1981). "Structural Changes in Manufacturing Industry 1916 to 1975." *The South African Journal of Economics* 49, 1.

Myers, Desaix, III, *et al.* (1980). *U.S. Business in South Africa*. Bloomington and London: Indiana University Press.

Nattrass, Jill (1981). *The South African Economy*. Cape Town: Oxford University Press.

Nedbank Group Limited (1983). *South Africa: An Appraisal*. Johannesburg: Nedbank Group Economic Unit.

*New York Times*, September 15, 1985.

*New York Times*, December 5, 1985.

O'Meara, Dan (1983). *Volks-Kapitalisme: Class, Capital and Ideology in the Development of Afrikaner Nationalism, 1934–1948*. Cambridge: Cambridge University Press.

Prinsloo, M. W. (1984). "Political Restructuring, Capital Accumulation and the 'Coming Corporatism,' in South Africa: Some Theoretical Considerations." *Politikon* 2, 1.

*Randy Daily Mail* (Johannesburg), March 19, 1985.

*Rand Daily Mail* (Johannesburg), June 29, 1982.

Reynders, H. J. J. (1977). "Black Industrial Entrepreneurship." *South African Journal of Economics* 45, 3.

Saul, John S., and Stephen Gelb (1981). *The Crisis in South Africa*. New York: Monthly Review Press.

Savage, M. (1984). "Ownership and Control in South Africa: Themes in Domination." Unpublished paper delivered at ASSA Conference in Johannesburg.

Schlemmer, Lawrence, and David Welsh (1982). "South Africa's Constitutional and Political Prospects." *Optima* 30, 4.

*SA Digest* (Pretoria), August 2, 1985.

South African Institute of Race Relations (SAIRR) (1984). *Survey of Race Relations in South Africa, 1983*. Johannesburg: Author.

——— (1985). *Survey of Race Relations in South Africa, 1984*. Johannesburg: Author.

*South African Observer* (Pretoria), 1984.

South Africa, Republic of (1983). *Monthly Abstract of Trade Statistics* (January–December). Pretoria: Government Printer.

Southern African Development Coordination Conference (SADCC), (1984). *SADCC Agriculture: Toward 2000*. Rome: Food and Agriculture Organization of the United Nations.

*The Star* (Johannesburg), July 8, 1985.

*The Star* (Johannesburg), July 15, 1985.

*The Star* (Johannesburg), July 29, 1985.

*The Star* (Johannesburg), August 26, 1985.

Tregenna-Piggott, J. V. (1980). "The Welfare Cost of Monopoly in South African Manufacturing Industry." *The South African Journal of Economics* 48, 2.

Williams, Basel A. F. (1948). *Botha, Smuts and South Africa*. London: Hodder and Stoughton Ltd.

Wolpe, Harold (1983). "Apartheid's Deepening Crisis." *Marxism Today* (January).

# CHAPTER 13

# Managing Class Structures in South Africa: Bantustans and the Underbelly of Privilege

**Stanley B. Greenberg**
**Hermann Giliomee**

The black rural areas of South Africa, the Bantustans, have for some time now been considered an integral part of South Africa's political economy. References to dual, separate economies—one white, capitalist, and progressive and the other black, subsistent, and stagnant—have passed from the scholarly discourse on South Africa, though some, like businessman Harry Oppenheimer, still speak of blacks leaving the "subsistence sector" for the glitter of the "cash economy."[1] Instead, authors of widely varied views now write of the Bantustans' historic and contemporary role and function within a larger South African economy.

Some, like Colin Bundy, Leonard Thompson, and Monica Wilson, depict viable African peasant communities in the late nineteenth century that adapted traditional methods and generated agricultural surpluses for sale to the developing urban markets: in the Ciskei, northeastern Cape, western Transkei, and Basutoland, there was a "virtual explosion of peasant economic activity."[2] More recently, research has focused on the Bantustans as dumping grounds for surplus peoples: redundant black farmers and farm laborers displaced by a consolidating white agriculture; the "unproductive, unemployed, disabled and youth" impoverished and excluded by a developing capitalist economy.[3]

The Bantustans in this century have served principally, it seems, to "cheapen" African labor and facilitate the process of capitalist accumulation. In the period before World War II, the Bantustans, by providing social security for the young and old and by providing sufficient land for a marginal subsistence, allowed migrant laborers to take up work at extremely low wages. The Bantustans, Harold Wolpe and now John Cell argue, were part of a precarious balancing act: a state-managed land shortage to encourage proletarianization, yet with sufficient land to support some African household members whose yield would supplement and suppress urban wages. As the balance has shifted away from economic viability, the Bantustans have been asked to play a yet larger role in managing and legitimating the repressive racial order. The preservation of "traditional tribal structures" has proved important to the ideologies of collaboration and the administration of labor control.[4]

In this essay, it will become apparent that the Bantustans, characterized by utter destitution and administrative disintegration, can no longer sustain the economic and political orders. With faltering agricultural production and massive overpopulation, the Bantustans provide meager security and virtually no sustenance; remittances from the wage economy, rather than marginal agricultural production, sustain these massive African rural populations. The Bantustan bureaucracies, administratively necessary to the labor control framework and integral to the ideology of these fictitious African states, have fallen into utter disrepair. They have been bypassed by the African laborers, desperate for wage employment, and by the South African state which has had to create alternative institutions of control.

This essay will illustrate the changing role and position of the Bantustans.[5] It will become apparent that the conventional portrayal of the Bantustans is no longer appropriate, as structured and massive labor surpluses preclude any subsistence functions; the Bantustans no longer "cheapen" labor, facilitate the extraction of surplus value, or further accumulation in this narrow sense. Later, the essay describes the disintegration of tribal structures and the expanding role of central state institutions in the labor process. Bantustan officials, unable to regulate the labor market or deliver essential labor services, are no longer in a position to enlist collaborators or legitimate any labor process.

If the Bantustans can no longer perform their historic functions, then what part do they play in South Africa's political economy? Are they simply dumping grounds for the redundant and functionally superfluous? Another part of the report will consider the elements of a new understanding of the Bantustans and their present functionality. They serve not as some residual setting for the excluded but as a necessary element in contemporary African class stratification. The Bantustans are the institutional support for an emerging racial and class order that fosters areas of privilege and, dialectically, areas of exclusion. It will become apparent, despite the preliminary aspects of this research, that the Bantustans are today a necessary part of a state strategy to segment the black majority, to create areas of privilege and rights, and to foster collaboration.

Black South Africans in the townships and cities, even those in the small rural towns, have challenged the institutions of this new order. They have attacked African collaborative councillors who would assume administrative control in this stratified labor framework. They have challenged the asumptions that would permit class stratification, privilege, and collaboration. Indeed, African uprisings through 1984 and 1985 have made the administration boards in the towns unworkable and called into question the government's ability to fashion any strategy for control.

Yet the Bantustans and their poverty remain—an imposing backdrop to the daily struggle that now characterizes the labor market and African townships. The survival and character of this racial and class order depends on this struggle, but also on the future of the Bantustans, in effect, the state strategy on the rural end. The Bantustans are the underbelly of privilege, the institutional accompaniment of state efforts to manage class structures in South Africa.

## RISING LABOR SURPLUSES AND DECLINING ECONOMIC FUNCTIONS

Today, outside virtually all the tribal bureaus, magistrate's and mine recruiting offices in the rural areas stand clusters of idle workseekers. At the Ngwelezana township, near the Richards Bay "growth point," up to 350 will wait by the magistrate's office looking for work. Last year, an official recalls, "I had a thousand people at my gate every day." Such queues of workseekers lead officials to extreme conclusions. The labor official for the Port Natal Administration Board observes, for example, that "at this point in time, there is an unlimited supply of labor." TEBA (mine recruiting) officials in the Transkei, KwaZulu, and Lebowa report that usually 300 to 500 workers stand at the doorstep every morning, with perhaps only fifty mine jobs available. TEBA officials everywhere believe that, in the absence of quotas, they could readily double their "labor output" without considerable effort and without labor agents. Some, like those in the Northern Transvaal, Bophuthatswana, and southern Natal, believe they could triple their output.[6]

For many Africans in the rural areas, there is no labor market. The Northern Transvaal Administration Board sends its mobile units into a portion of Lebowa but neglects most of it, while bypassing Gazankulu altogether. The board officer admits that "parts of Gazankulu are not being tapped." Large portions of the African rural areas receive virtually no requests for employment ("requisitions"). At Maluti in the Transkei, the tribal bureau receives no requisitions from Umtata for months at a time—the waiting hall with its rows of benches standing empty and silent, the columns for posting job notices unmarred by a single piece of paper. Other research has found a similar pattern at Sterkspruit and the tribal bureaus across all of the Transkei.[7] At Motetsi in Lebowa, just twenty-five kilometers from Pietersburg, some months pass without a single requisition; other months are better, perhaps 200 jobs, though usually from a few bulk requisitions for construction laborers. An official of the Lebowa Department of Interior observes that "very few employers come this time of year."

Across KwaZulu, even in the immediate vicinity of industrial areas, there are widespread reports of an ever-closing labor market. In recent years there has been virtually no labor recruiting in Umbumbulu south of Durban, Ingwavuma well north of Richard's Bay, Ongoye near Ladysmith, Okahlamba near Escourt, Inkanyesi near Eshowe, Mapumulo near Greytown, and Vulamehlo near Umzinto.[8]

The contraction of the labor market and growth of labor surpluses are evident in TEBA's abandonment of labor agents and runners. While previously TEBA and the mining industry relied upon them to seek out mine labor in the more remote rural areas, the ready supply of labor in recent years has made such a network superfluous: the demise of the agents, a Transvaal official observes, is "one of the penalties of the oversupply of labor." Officials of ACRO (the coal mine recruiting organization) near Pietersburg used to advertise vacancies, sending African runners on bicycles to advertise posts. Now, people come on their own, without notice, from as far away as Tzaneen. The TEBA networks have also been abandoned in KwaZulu and Transkei.[9]

Since mines "open" and "close" within a matter of days, TEBA offices conventionally take whatever labor is available on their "doorsteps." "There are sufficient numbers calling at our doors to fill our needs," a Transvaal officer observes. "It is very easy to go outside the door and pick up the five that fill the bill. The actual recruiting of labor has actually stopped." In Durban, a TEBA official states that "they're stacked up at our door." An official in the Pietersburg area describes the new mood:

> The TEBA recruiter has an easy time of it these days. He must just sit back and wait for them to come in. I remember when I had to address meetings, give all sorts of parties, drive all over. Those days are in the past.

The use of "valid-reengagement guarantees" (VRGs) has become so widespread that traditional mine recruiting areas are frequently "closed" to new applicants. In the Northern Transvaal and KwaZulu, including Maputoland, there is some recruitment of novice miners: 27 percent of those engaged in 1982 in KwaZulu were novices. (In 1980, 42 percent were novices.) But in the Transkei, TEBA officials indicate that novice recruitment from January to October never rises about 10 percent. As a consequence, the "mines are virtually closed until October. The orders are very sparse. Only a VRG can be offered work." In Lesotho, the percentage of reengaged experienced miners rose from 30 percent in 1976 to 60 percent in 1979; in the Transkei, the percentage of VRGs was already high in 1974, around 80 percent, but rose to nearly 90 percent by 1978.[10]

Under conditions of labor surplus, announcements of work opportunities often produce quite startling results. At Maluti in the Transkei, the arrival of an ISCOR recruiter in 1982 with a requisition for 300 experienced workers brought out over 1000 former ISCOR employees; an open request for 300 workers in 1978 brought out 4000 workseekers.[11] At Motetsi in Lebowa, the labor bureau clerk rings a bell to announce the arrival of a new job requisition. When he rings the bell on Monday, 200 to 300 people line up. In January, one officer observes, "there is a hell or a rush . . . if you ring that bell. They come out like moles out of their holes."

To protect against a rush of desperate job seekers, TEBA in Transkei has erected security fences around its offices—"not to guard against terrorism," an official notes, "but to keep the workers out, to keep them from tearing the place down." In King Williamstown, TEBA, which had for a number of years employed virtually no novice miners, received "a pretty considerable order" and announced it: "the blacks just flattened the fence."

There is widespread and corroborating evidence suggesting that the Bantustans are no longer vehicles for productive agriculture, that they can no longer provide basic subsistence—supplemental or otherwise. Charles Simkins estimates that since 1918 the African reserves have never supported more than a third of their inhabitants, and by 1970 they were supporting fewer than 20 percent. Since then, the dependence on the wage economy has grown more stark, with the percentage of Bantustan income derived from remittances and wages of migrants and commuters rising from 55 percent to 72 percent in 1976, with a corresponding drop in the percentage of income received from agriculture.[12]

Research in the Western Cape discovered that 40 percent of African migrant workers had no access to cultivatable land and 50 percent owned no cattle in the Bantustans; three-quarters of migrant families received less than R24 per month in 1976 from agricultural work.[13] In KwaZulu, earnings from labor exports increased from 54.3 percent of Bantustan GNP in 1960, to 70.4 percent in 1970, to 77.8 percent in 1976. By 1976, three-quarters of the income of Africans living in KwaZulu derived from remitted income of family members at work in the wage economy outside KwaZulu.[14]

The decline of subsistence production in the Bantustans and the growing dependence on the wage economy are evident in the firsthand impressions of labor control and recruiting officials. In Maluti (Transkei), one officer observes that "only the old people, the children and the useless still stay on farms." In light of mine officials' experiences with rainfall and drought conditions and labor recruiting, the observation seems increasingly plausible. In the past, when Africans still depended on income and food from their own plots, bad rains brought increased interest in wage work on the mines. But in 1982, the widespread drought brought almost no increase in the labor available to the mines. "With the population explosion," virtually all the African labor has been forced into the labor market, a TEBA official observes. "That chap has got to work: before, he might have had a piece of land, a few cattle, but now he has no choice but work." In KwaZulu, a TEBA official observes, "the question of seasonal rains and droughts has much less effect than it did ten years ago." The TEBA officer for the Matatiele district also confirms the pattern: the rains no longer have an impact on labor supplies in the Transkei.

South Africa's most prominent economists differ on the scale of South Africa's labor surplus problem. P. J. van der Merwe, an established economist and a high-level official in various state labor institutions, relies upon 1970 census data and unemployment increases in subsequent years to arrive at what he himself considers a "minimum" estimate. Unemployment and underemployment in the Bantustans rose precipitously during the early 1970s, from 32,000 in 1970 to 396,000 in 1976. Van der Merwe's estimates suggest that well over half of the new African entrants to the labor market in the early 1970s could not be accommodated in employment.[15] Other observers have supplemented census figures with employment surveys and estimates of underemployment in the Bantustans (based upon the numbers of workers who could be productively employed there).[16] These calculations, like van der Merwe's, suggest a rising tide of unemployment in the 1970s but, by contrast, place current unemployment levels at staggering heights and well above the census estimates. Simkins, incorporating measures of agricultural underemployment, places overall unemployment in South Africa at 22.4 percent in 1977—2.3 million people, almost all of whom were black.[17]

These quantitative studies and the personal impressions related earlier are apparently just snapshots of a gathering labor surplus problem. The numbers of unemployed likely doubled during the 1960s, a period of rapid economic growth, increased at a yet greater rate during the 1970s, when the pace of economic growth was a respectable 3 percent, and seemed almost certain to expand, perhaps even phenomenally, during the coming decades.[18] The prime minister's economic advisers project that with an annual growth rate of 3.6 percent (the actual figures for 1970–1977), unemployment would increase from 10.6 to 21.9 percent in 1987, from 903,000 to 2,406,000 persons. The African unemployment rate, even by these conservative government estimates, would likely exceed 26 percent.[19]

# DETERIORATING TRIBAL STRUCTURES AND EXPANDING STATE CONTROL

## Tribal Labor Bureaus: The Phantom Tribal Order

The tribal labor bureaus are virtually extinct in these rural districts. A few seem operative in KwaZulu near Pietermaritzburg and in the Bolobedu area northeast of Tzaneen, but virtually everywhere else—all of the Transkei, Bophuthatswana, and Gazankulu, nearly every place in KwaZulu and Lebowa—the tribal bureaus are inoperative. They sometimes receive communications about pending recruiting but not requisitions; instead, African workseekers must find their way to much more distant magistrate's offices.

In the Malumulele area in Gazankulu, an official observes that all fourteen tribal labor offices were closed in 1979, an observation confirmed for all of Gazankulu by an Interior Department official:

> People flock to the magistrate's office and do not ever touch the tribal offices. . . .
> These tribal offices are not functioning. They concentrate on the side of collecting taxes because requisitions come once in a blue moon.

A white official in KwaZulu observes that "in twenty years of service, I have never seen a tribal labor bureau operate properly"; he even laughs at the suggestion that a district labor bureau exists at the magistrate's office in Nongoma. An official at Ngwelezana near Empangeni also indicates that the tribal bureaus are ineffective. Workseekers travel to the magistrate's office instead: "People know this is the only place they can find work, except TEBA and farm labor." TEBA officials throughout KwaZulu note that Africans do not crowd around tribal bureaus, as there is no point; the jobs are elsewhere.

Current among both whites and blacks involved in labor recruitment is the belief that local tribal labor structures are corrupt and inefficient. TEBA officials in the Northern Transvaal claim that Africans must ordinarily pay two or three rand at the local tribal offices in Venda and Lebowa to get a workseeker's permit, even though there is no such requirement in law. "The minor official sitting in the sticks is the problem," one TEBA official observes. An official of the Northern Transvaal Administration Board confirms the impression, suggesting that in Lebowa, "money passes under the table." In Gazankulu, an interior official talks about corruption of the labor process at the local level: "Sometimes the fees must go under the table to get preference."

The functions of the tribal labor bureaus and, to some extent, the district bureaus at the magistrate's offices have passed to other organizations—the administration boards, employers, and the Chamber of Mines. Very little labor is in fact recruited by tribal bureaucratic organizations. The larger employers almost always send their own agents, who may advertise and who certainly do their own worker selection. An official at Malumulele (Gazankulu) indicates that 90 percent of the workers are hired directly by agents: ISCOR, for example, "might find them in the bush and bring them here for registration." An official of the Interior Department confirms that this pattern is nearly universal in Gazankulu. In Nongoma (KwaZulu), the magistrate indicates that ISCOR announces a date and time when it will show up at the magistrate's office to select new employees or the reemployment of experienced workers. The district labor bureau in fact has no capacity or system for recruiting or selecting labor. An official for the Matatiele district (Transkei) indicates that agents for the apple farmers, construction companies, railways, and ISCOR "come and fetch their own labor."

The tribal structures are left with paper responsibilities—placing their official stamps on labor requisitions, registering workseekers, and collecting attestations fees. But even these responsibilities have been stripped of their control or allocation functions. Most African workseekers in these districts apparently put off registering as official workseekers, avoiding the tribal officials until employment is actually offered. This practice was apparent in the Transkei district and the rural areas of Lebowa, Gazankulu, and KwaZulu.

Since employers almost always designate the magisterial districts or tribal areas in which they want to recruit labor, the central tribal authorities are left with no channeling responsibilities. Labor officials in Ulundi, Umtata, Sishego, and Giyani simply place their official stamps on requisitions. But even this role has been narrowed, as administration boards from Pretoria and the East Rand (via the Northern Transvaal board) increasingly go directly to the labor recruiting areas, bypassing the tribal bureaucratic structures altogether.

The payment of attestation fees, a final legal vehicle for associating the African worker with his or her tribal area, has in recent years been dispersed geographically and functionally. TEBA has for a long time conducted attestations at magistrate's offices in the white areas and sent checks to the magistrate's offices in the white areas and sent checks to the magistrates in the tribal areas who in turn distribute funds to the individual chiefs. Though the government has recently sent out a circular requiring that attestations take place in Bantustans, most TEBA offices seem to be successfully circumventing the regulations. In Vryheid, the magistrate has insisted that TEBA recruits from Nqutu be attested in KwaZulu but "the magistrate at Eshowe just threw it [the circular] in the trash," as apparently other magistrates have done in the Northern Transvaal. Administration boards have also taken on attestation responsibilities, further limiting the role of the tribal and district labor bureaus. The Pietersburg office of the Northern Transvaal Administration Board sends the fees to magistrates in Lebowa who place the funds in a trust account; similarly with Gazankulu, where the fees go into a general fund for tribal authority.

With the breakdown of tribal labor bureaus and TEBA's recruitment system, the labor market in these rural districts has become localized at nodes, leaving vast areas and populations virtually outside the legal labor market and leaving the rudimentary labor market in private hands. Information about employment opportunities, for example, is narrowly communicated. TEBA offices fill their job allocations "as fast as we can," frequently on the same day and usually from immediately available sources (TEBA official, KwaZulu). When the allocations cannot be filled off the "doorstep," TEBA will publicize somewhat more broadly that the mines are "open." The Nongoma TEBA representative on these occasions drives around the area in a sound truck. The Northern Transvaal district employs six "mobile runners" who travel by motorbike to "anywhere there is human population."

Sometimes labor agents will send out advance word that they will be hiring at a particular magistrate's office on certain dates; sometimes the magistrate's office, as in Maluti, will notify headmen and chiefs by mail and phone up traders in the area, though TEBA officials doubt the extent of such advertising.

Usually, the workseeker must be physically present at a labor office in order to take advantage of a job allocation or requisition. At Motetsi, the clerk rings a bell when a requisition or agent arrives. Only those who hear the bell, or word of it, have an opportunity for employment. Only those waiting outside the gate at Ngwelezana or those sitting on the rows of benches at the Umlazi labor office may respond to the announcement and the query, "Any takers?"

For those who do not live near these offices, this rudimentary labor market may impose unacceptable costs. The labor officer at the Northern Transvaal Administration Board describes the circuit:

> A person may live eighty kilometers from a tribal labor bureau and it recruits only on Wednesdays. When he goes there, he finds that they may not have a job. And then he must travel eighty kilometers back again.

In the Malumulele district, workers may have to travel as many as forty kilometers each way, just to see if work is available. At Nongoma, some workseekers will spend R2 in bus fare in order to wait at the magistrate's office; at Motetsi, they will spend R3.40. The former office had no job requisitions in April; the latter, only one—for workseekers previously employed at ISCOR. In the Northern Transvaal, TEBA has discontinued a policy, followed between 1975 and 1978, of refunding bus fares: "when the supply exceeded the demand, this refund, which amounted to a fair sum, was discontinued and the policy adopted that if a man wanted work he made his own way to the office and depending on whether there were mines open or not, he got a job or had to return home at his own expense."

## Administration Boards: The Central State Presence

Over the past decade, the official discussion of the black rural areas and black labor market has emphasized the growing role of Bantustan authorities in managing their own affairs and, at the same time, the declining role of the South African state in the affairs of the market. "The Republic of South Africa," wrote the Wiehahn Commission, "subscribes to the principles of a free market economy based on individual freedom in the market place." The Riekert Commission too asserted, as a goal, "the effective functioning of the free market mechanism." The rural reality in these areas, however, seems to contradict this official posture on two fronts: first, the Bantustan authorities exercise little control over labor matters—indeed, Bantustan bureaucratic structures seem to be disintegrating; and, second, the bureaucratic representatives of the South African state, particularly the administration boards, are clearly playing a growing role in the rural labor market.

In every area examined for this report, there was vivid evidence that administration boards are growing more and more involved in the regulation of African labor mobility. Administration boards have moved directly into the Bantustan districts where they were not previously active, and they have established a new bureaucratic presence. The most direct method has been the construction of new administrative board facilities in the Bantustans themselves. The Port Natal Administration Board now operates offices as part of a KwaZulu governmental complex in Umlazi and KwaMashu and plans to open new ones at Tzuma to service the rowing squatter areas around Inanda, a released area; it has opened up a labor office in a KwaZulu governmental complex in Ngwe-lezana just outside Empangeni and not far from Richards Bay. In each case, these offices register workseekers, post-job requisitions, and register contracts. For residents of the townships, these offices represent the final bureaucratic step toward legal employment.

The Northern Transvaal Administration Board is, through indirect and direct means, deeply involved in the labor market of Lebowa. For the commuter areas in Lebowa, proximate to white towns, the administration board circumvents tribal authorities and processes African labor directly. "But actually, in Pie-tersburg, our labor bureau acts as a tribal labor bureau," an official told us. "African labor comes here to us." But the board also moves more directly into the homeland labor market. In about one-third of Lebowa, the board operates a mobile van that travels a fixed route each week, stopping at various local tribal offices. The mobile unit carries three officials from the administration board and one from the tribal authority. Like the Port Natal offices, these pro-vide a final and necessary legal step to authorized employment outside the Bantustan. In the future, the board hopes to operate thirteen such vans, ex-panding the service to Gazankulu. In other areas of Lebowa, like Bolobedu, administration board officials sometimes accompany employers and set up shop at the magistrate's office. In Bophuthatswana, near Pretoria, the North Central Administration Board has established a border office at Hammerskraal which communicates just across the "border" by wireless radio to the magistrate's office serving as an "assembly center" for labor.

The growing presence of the administration boards in the Bantustan labor market is captured by a new concept in labor organization and control—"one-stop service"—which was touted at virtually every point in our field research. An official in Bolobedu describes this cooperation between the magistrate's office, the recruiting agent, and the administration board as a "one-stop" sys-tem: "They can go right to work." According to the labor officer at Durban, the establishment of an administrative board section in the KwaZulu govern-mental complex at Umlazi makes "this very much a one-stop service." How the introduction of the administration board into the Bantustan serves to further control is best described by an administration board official in the Northern Transvaal:

> The ideal is that his documentation should be ready when he leaves the homeland. That is why we are trying to get this one-stop system to work. This is a form of influx control. That is the ideal: before a person leaves the homeland, he must have a job and accommodation.

## MARKET HIERARCHIES

The Bantustan labor market operates on the fringes of the urban labor market, a repository for the functionless and spent to be sure, but much more. The Bantustans are part of a larger order that is increasingly stratified, increasingly chracterized by state-fostered hierarchies of privilege and disadvantage. The African world includes "legals" with access to the institutional labor market, larger employers and manufacturers and illegals with access to the informal sector, seasonal and day labor, and smaller, lower-paying firms; permanent (section 10) urban dwellers with opportunities for training and mobility and legal migrants with access to heavy and primary industry; "commuters" who stand behind the permanent urban residents in the labor queue but ahead of the illegals and those left behind in the more remote rural districts; it includes those in districts where labor markets are "open" and those in areas inaccessible to the labor recruitment system; those who have taken their chances in the illegal and legal urban labor market and those, like rural women and raw laborers, whose desperation makes possible low-wage recruitment for the farms, municipalities, and road construction. It is upon such distinctions and such hierarchies of "privilege" that the state has sought to construct a strategy of control and collaboration.

A precious few of these rural workers may come to sit atop the market hierarchy, as section 10(1), a, b, or c workers with permanent urban residence rights, but the government has severely narrowed the opportunity for such privilege. The Port Natal and Northern Transvaal boards have stopped building African accommodation in the "prescribed" areas and have begun in fact to constrict opportunities for "permanent" African residence in the white areas. For the Northern Transvaal, only 8 percent of the African labor force is considered "legal." "Our achievement," the board's labor officer declares,

> is to resettle all our townships in the white areas. In Louis Trichardt, we are in the midst of resettling all of the Venda. In the next five years, there will be no Venda in Louis Trichardt.

For the Port Natal board, only 5 percent of the employable Africans remain outside of the KwaZulu and African released areas; KwaMashu was incorporated into KwaZulu and there are evidently plans to incorporate the remaining African townships; the townships around the Empangeni and Richards Bay growth point were built originally in the KwaZulu Bantustan.

Other categories of "local" labor are emerging. These are somewhat less exclusive (and somewhat less privileged), though still outside the effective market space for most rural workers. The administration board at Durban considers longtime Umlazi and KwaMashu residents as "administrative section 10s"— in effect, locals with preferred access to housing and employment. The categories then encompass some Bantustan residents who might previously have been considered contract workers (section 10[1] d) and who now may gain access to more secure urban work. A form of "local" status has also been conferred on the townships around Empangeni and Richards Bay and on fixed radiuses around Pietersburg and Tzaneen, taking in Sishego in Lebowa and Nkowakowa in Ganzankulu. The workers in these "commuter" areas are given access to urban job opportunities before workers form more remote black districts. Administration board officials now speak of a special responsibility to protect such workers:

> It is in all fairness to the local people. Otherwise, you will have to cater to the influx. . . . All I say is that preference should be given to the local people. (Labor official, Ngwelezana.)

> I don't need to tell you that labor is a commodity. The employer will go for an illegal worker who will come cheaper. Our responsibility is to protect the permanent residents.

> There is exploitation. Of that you can be sure. In our own way we are trying to use the legal system to fight this exploitation. (Labor officer, Port Natal Administration Board.)

Because of this "preference," "local" workers can gain access to manufacturing employment and areas of commerce, to more skilled and better-paid positions, that never appear on a requisition at Nongoma, Maluti, Madjadji, or Motetsi.

The position of these "local commuter" workers is secured through restrictions on "legal accommodations"—a concept and practice that could not be adequately specified in this field research. In Ngwelezana near Empangeni, the power to grant clearance certificates for accommodation rests with a white magistrate who, together with the labor officials of the administration board, defines "local labor." While the system seems to limit access to "local status" in KwaZulu, both the magistrate and board officials deny complicity in influx control. The magistrate says:

> We are not refusing anybody employment. Influx control is being done by the administration board. They are the ones who insist that a man must have housing [to take up employment].

The administration board official, on the other hand, says:

> There is no influx control in KwaZulu. Anybody can come here for work, if they have "legal accommodation." If KwaZulu [that is, the magistrate] gives permission, then it's legal.

In Umlazi, clearance certificates for accommodation also remain under the control of a white magistrate, though there was some suggestion that there is a healthy trade in certificates—"one can get a good price for it."

Falling outside the concept of "local" labor are rural migrants (and likely some from the urban areas as well) who live illegally, without clearance certificates, in the townships or in emergent or established squatter communities. No doubt many who tire of waiting for the bell to ring at Motetsi or the posting of a requisition at Nongoma, and many of the women who reject farm labor and who cannot be requisitioned, "shoot straight," that is, circumvent the labor control regulations and make their way here—to the Wintervelds and Inandas of urban South Africa. In the latter case, the Port Natal Administration Board has defined some narrow areas—people born in Inanda, those residents there since 1968 and those living in "tent town" (a small Urban Foundation project)—where legal accommodation and, therefore, legal employment will be granted.

But for the rest of the some 600,000 people living there, the labor market remains a gray area. They may not register as workseekers and join the legal job market unless an employer will provide accommodation and send a specific requisition back through the bureaucratic channels, back to the magistrate's office somewhere in KwaZulu. These "illegals" operate outside the channels leading to the larger firms that use the statutory employment mechanisms. For the most part they are confined to casual and low-wage sectors that are willing to chance employing "illegals."

On the other hand, there are few effective state-imposed impediments to remaining in these squatter areas and taking up illegal or casual employment.

The seventy-two-hour provision for limiting African entry into "prescribed" areas has fallen into disuse in cities proximate to these Bantustans. Officials in Durban and Empangeni say they have abandoned the seventy-two-hour rule altogether. In the Durban area, the administration board has virtually given up the policing of "illegal" employment. The labor officer for Port Natal indicated that there were only seven inspectors "active in the field" for the entire Durban area. "To be honest about it," a board official concludes, "we are not very successful about following this up." The squatters, consequently, remain relatively free to find their niche on the margins of the legal labor market—casual jobs in construction, domestic service, smaller firms, sections of commerce, and, for many, prolonged or intermittent employment.

For those compelled to remain behind, there are only marginal opportunities for work and a livelihood. Large portions of the Bantustans, we discovered earlier, simply fall outside the institutional labor market, as there is no legal recruiting or requisitioning of labor. For those who can reach the rural labor market, there are sometimes opportunities for wage employment, but almost always within the lowest-paid, most unskilled and "undesirable" sectors of the economy. The rural African working population, as the most marginal, forms a "cheap" labor catchment for the mines, farms, and the state itself.

The manufacturing sector now shows little interest in the Bantustans as a source of labor. The requisitioning of labor in the African rural areas is confined to unskilled jobs (temporary laborers, night watchmen, and night soil removers), the "dirty" work (the foundries at ISCOR), "unpopular" sectors (seasonal work on the farms), and the "unpopular" firms. A labor official observes: "Most requisitions that come here people know are not good." In the Transkei, the recruiting of migrant workers for manufacturing has remained static since 1974, with virtually no increase since 1970.[20]

Only the state sector itself seems to value continued access to this impoverished labor pool. Requistions for the most part originate with civil engineering firms constructing large state-supported projects—also with the municipalities, the state railways, and parastatals. ISCOR plants at Newcastle, van der Bijl Park, and Pretoria were the most frequent recruiters of labor at Maluti (Transkei), Nongoma (KwaZulu), Modjadji (Lebowa), and in the eastern Transvaal. The South African Railways recruited large numbers of workers at Matatiele in the Transkei and Modjadji in Lebowa. The municipalities, particularly Johannesburg and Pretoria, recruit generally in the Northern Transvaal and in the Mount Frere area (Transkei) for rubbish removal workers.

Finally, the legal labor market, already contracted geographically and sectorally, has been narrowed further by gender segmentations and exclusions. Because of government regulations, the requisitioning of labor for urban areas has been confined almost exlusively to men. The magistrate at Malumulele (Gazankulu) can recall no requisitions for women; the Interior Department official in Lebowa notes that "99.99 percent of requisitions are for men." The Port Natal Administration Board requisitions women only for nursing jobs and for domestic service, but "only after local labor is exhausted and only in the immediate areas of KwaZulu." As a result, rural African women find themselves at the bottom of the hierarchy, seeking work in the least remunerative and stable areas—casual and daily farm work nearly everywhere, the sawmills in Lebowa, the roadworks in Maputoland and Venda, the very small firms in Gazankulu, and seasonally on the sugar estates in Natal.

## CONCLUDING NOTE

The South African government in recent years has fashioned new political institutions, grafted them onto the old, producing a fractured constitutional and political order. Whites remain in control of the central executive and parliamentary institutions, but coloureds and Asians have been granted separate representation in segregated parliamentary chambers; urban Africans have been excluded from the center stage of national politics but have been offered township councils with increased control of township affairs; the African migrants, commuters, and rural destitute have been offered yet more "independent" Bantustans and denationalization—the ultimate in constitutional exclusion.

Urban Africans have turned on such intitutions with a vengeance, leaving many of the state's contrivances in ruins. But the mass of Africans have yet to escape the institutional web that seeks to divide and ensnarl the African population.

In this essay, we have reviewed government efforts in the same period to lend a material reality to this political fracturing. The Bantustans, it appears, are part of an expanded state effort to manage class structures, to create areas of privilege and rights and areas of disadvantage and dire necessity. The Bantustans are the underbelly of this policy. They are the repository for the spent and redundant, but much more. The Bantustans accommodate the burgeoning surplus populations that take up the least stable and least remunerative work on the farms, mines, and state projects; they are the wellspring for the "illegals," the growing class of marginal workers who "shoot straight," entering the informal and illegal labor market on the fringes of the urban economy; they house the commuter populations who have been granted legal access to the industrial economy but who remain stuck in this political limbo. They are, perhaps above all, an awful contrast—a nightmare that gives concrete meaning to the "privileges" of those Africans who work and live legally in the white cities.


## APPENDIX: FIELD RESEARCH

During a two-week period in April 1982, the authors conducted a survey of labor conditions and labor control practices in selected parts of South Africa's African rural areas. The results were combined where appropriate with more extensive field research findings developed by Greenberg during the course of his research on the labor control framework in South Africa. That work spanned the period 1980 to 1984, and forms part of his forthcoming book, *Legitimating the Illegitimate*.

This survey, quite obviously, was not exhaustive. It focused on selective districts where one might explore the work on both the Employment Bureau of Africa (TEBA) and the various labor bureaus organized under tribal authorities. While travel time was a serious constraint, we were determined to look at districts remote from the urban ("prescribed") areas as well as ones more closely situated. And while our focus was on the African rural areas, the nature of the rural labor market necessitated an examination of the "commuter" areas just inside the Bantustans and of the appropriate administration boards.[21]

In Lebowa, we interviewed the labor officer for the district and tribal labor bureaus at Motetsi, just west of Sishego, and the magistrate at Madjadji who is responsible for the Bolobedu district labor bureau and the district's tribal labor bureaus on an agency basis. At Sishego, we held lengthy discussions with the secretary of interior, the assistant secretary, and labor officials, including the manager of the orientation center. In addition, we interviewed the assistant director of labor for the Northern Transvaal Administration Board at Pietersburg.

In Gazankulu, we interviewed the magistrate at Malumulele who administers the district labor bureau and met with the assistant secretary and secretary of the interior for Gazankulu, as well as with labor bureau officials at Giyani.

We had extensive talks with TEBA officials for this whole northern region, in particular, the district manager for the Northern Transvaal, but also his assistant and TEBA representatives at Tzaneen, Soekmekaar, Pietersburg, and Pafuri.

In KwaZulu, we interviewed the magistrates at Nongoma and at Ngwelezana near Empangeni and spoke to officials from the Port Natal Administration Board responsible for the labor bureaus at Umlazi and KwaMashu near Durban (but inside KwaZulu) and for the labor bureaus at Ngwelezana, Enseleni, and EsiKawini in the KwaZulu areas near Empangeni and Richards Bay. In addition, we held lengthy discussions with the chairman and director of employment services for the Port Natal Administration Board.

We conducted wide-ranging interviews with TEBA officials in the region, including the district managers for KwaZulu and Natal and TEBA representatives at Eshowe, Durban, Nongoma, and Ingwavuma. The latter two interviews included extensive travel in the Nongoma, Mkuze, and Maputoland areas, as far north as Kosi Bay.

Finally, our field research included a brief foray into the Transkei, traveling up through Kokstad and Matatiele, and interviewing the assistant commissioner and his labor officer at Maluti (for the Matatiele district of Transkei). We also interviewed TEBA's district manager for Transkei (previously, district manager for Bophuthatswana) and TEBA representatives for Kokstad and Matatiele.

# Notes

### Introduction: Continuities in the Study of Power and Class in Africa

1. The weekly news magazine *West Africa* has over the past several years continuously drawn attention to the seriousness of the drought. A recent editorial indicated both wonder and chagrin at the suddenness with which Western public attention was awakened to the famine. They trace "the trigger" to television reporting, and suggest the possibility that "the BBC team" was "routinely recycling its equipment from Johannesburg to London" and stumbled across the misery of Ethiopia along the way. The film of conditions in Korem, Ethiopia, immediately struck a chord of public sympathy. *West Africa* was chagrined because "what seems capricious is the way something like this becomes a press sensation, because of the chance of coverage." Outside of Ethiopia, the worst effects of the drought in Africa were in Chad, where thousands died from malnutrition, but *West Africa* points out that "there has been no TV coverage of Chad, so there has been no outcry." *West Africa,* November 5, 1984, pp. 2, 199. See also Peter W. Kaplan, "Grim Images: How Ethiopia Became News," *New York Times,* December 16, 1984, for a history and analysis of both television and newspaper coverage of the famine.

By the end of 1985, some African countries had enjoyed the best rains in ten years and total harvests rose by 76 percent. The situation, however, still remained critical in Burkina Faso, Cape Verde, Chad, Ethiopia, Mali, Mauritania, Niger, Somalia, and Sudan. In Ethiopia and Sudan alone, eight to ten million people existed on the edge of starvation. Cf. David K. Willis, "The African Famine," *The Christian Science Monitor,* December 6, 1985, p. 15; and especially *Food Situation in African Countries Affected by Emergencies, Special Report,* Food and Agriculture Organization of the United Nations, MR5805, September 2, 1985. The editors of *Africa News* in "UN Office: Famine Could Recur" (26,9) [May 5, 1986]: maintain that without an accelerated relief effort within the next few months, widespread famine will recur in 1986. See also publications by the United Nations Office for Emergency Operations in Africa, especially *African Emergency,* a periodic report on the crisis.

2. *New York Times,* November 29, 1984.

3. Ibid.

4. Ibid.

5. On a related matter, Gaim Kibreab in *African Refugees: Reflections on the African Refugee Problem* (Trenton, N.J.: Africa World Press, 1985), declares: "Present-day African societies are not only marked by international conflicts and by the presence of brutal and 'coercive power' but it can be argued that it is these conflicts and the violence unleashed to support them by the class that has the monopoly of state power that constitutes the main problem of refugeeism" (p. 36).

6. E. Wayne Nafziger, "Stagnation, Inequality, and Urban Discrepancies in Africa," a paper presented at the African Studies Association meeting, New Orleans, November 1985, summarizes the deplorable record of comparative economic growth and stagnation with a stress on "urban-rural inequalities." Cf. World Bank, *World Development Report, 1985* (New York: Oxford University Press, 1985); and Lloyd G. Reynolds, *Economic Growth in the Third World, 1850–1980* (New Haven: Yale University Press, 1985), especially Part III, "Recent Developers," pp. 268–386.

7. Cheryl Payer, in *The World Bank: A Critical Analysis* (New York: Monthly Review Press, 1982), contends that the World Bank's policies have intensified class division in the Third World. Robert L. Ayres, *Banking on the Poor: The World Bank and World Poverty* (Cambridge: The MIT Press, 1983), offers a much more sympathetic assessment.

8. Jean Mayer, president of Tufts University and vice-chairman of the Presidential Commission on World Hunger, wrote a letter dated soon after Cowell's article, but which did not appear in the *New York Times* until December 11, 1984, and which began:

> News stories and appraisals of the African famine may give the impression that nothing will solve the problem, so we should stop trying. That is not true. We can do something. *Not* acting will insure disaster.

For an exceptionally insightful account of the politics of agricultural policy, see Robert H. Bates, *Markets and States in Tropical Africa* (Berkeley: University of California Press, 1981); see also the collections edited by Bates and Michael F. Lofchie, *Agricultural Development in*

*Africa: Issues of Public Policy* (New York: Praeger, 1980); Jonathan Barker, ed., *The Politics of Agriculture in Tropical Africa* (Beverly Hills: Sage Publications, 1984); Carl K. Eicher and John M. Staatz, eds., *Agricultural Development in the Third World* (Baltimore: The Johns Hopkins University Press, 1984); and Fassil G. Kiros, ed., *Challenging Rural Poverty: Experiences in Institution Building and Popular Participation for Rural Development in Eastern Africa* (Trenton, N.J.: Africa World Press, 1985).

9. See also the study of Richard W. Franke and Barbara H. Chasin, *Seeds of Famine: Ecological Destruction and the Development Dilemma in the West African Sahel* (Montclair, N.J.: Allanheld, Osmun, 1980).

For a seminal study of the causes of famine, see Amartya Sen, *Poverty and Famines: An Essay on Entitlement and Deprivation* (Oxford: The Clarendon Press, 1981).

Susan George clearly and simply analyzes the political basis of hunger. See especially her *Feeding the Few: Corporate Control of Food* (Washington, D.C.: Institute for Policy Studies, 1979), and *Ill Fares the Land: Essays on Food, Hunger and Power* (Washington, D.C.: Institute for Policy Studies, 1984). Barbara Dinham and Colin Hines, in *Agribusiness in Africa* (Trenton, N.J.: Africa World Press, 1984), study the effect of big business, especially in East Africa.

Louise A. Tilly quotes a seventeenth-century statement before the Courts of Star Chamber— ". . . last year's famine was made by man and not by God"—to show the certainty of early English authorities that "death and famine" were caused and could be corrected by public intervention. "Food Entitlement, Famine, and Conflict," p. 135, in a collection edited by Robert I. Rotberg and Theodore K. Rabb, *Hunger and History: The Impact of Changing Food Production and Consumption Patterns in Society* (New York: Cambridge University Press, 1985).

Rene Dumont continues his acerbic and insightful essays, with Nicholas Cohen, *The Growth of Hunger: A New Politics of Agriculture* (London: Marion Boyars Publishers, 1980), and with Marie-France Mottin, *Stranglehold on Africa* (London: Andre Deutsch, 1983).

Funded by the Swedish International Development Authority, Earthscan, located in Washington and London, has published a series of important, clearly written small books on global development and environment issues, including Alan Grainger, *Desertification: How People Make Deserts, How People Can Stop and Why They Don't* (1982); Anders Wijkman and Lloyd Timberlake, *Natural Disasters, Acts of God or Acts of Man?* (1984); and Lloyd Timberlake, *Africa in Crisis: The Causes the Cures of Environmental Bankruptcy* (1985). See also the slickly produced but valuable *Ending Hunger: An Idea Whose Time Has Come,* The Hunger Project (New York: Praeger Publishers, 1985).

Michael Watts, in his mammoth study, *Silent Violence: Food, Famine and Peasantry in Northern Nigeria* (Berkeley: University of California Press, 1983), argues that a post–oil-boom expanding state and capitalism trapped peasants between precapitalist technology and market crisis and increased their vulnerability to drought-perpetuated disasters.

Mesfin Wolde Mariam offers a scholarly analysis of *Rural Vulnerability to Famine in Ethiopia: 1958–1977,* Sahibadad, India: Vikas House, 1984), with a particularly interesting assessment of the role of the state; a more current, journalistic account is Graham Hancock, *Ethiopia: The Challenge of Hunger* (London: Victor Gollancz Ltd. 1985); see also the report with annexes, *Famine in Africa,* Second Report From the Foreign Affairs Committee—Session 1984–85: HC56, House of Commons (London: Her Majesty's Stationary Office, 1985).

10. Douglas Rimmer assures us that "Certainly, the view that there is widespread antipathy to economic inequality in developing areas like West Africa should be questioned . . . gains in the incomes of some groups would not be regarded as seriously depreciated by an accompanying increase in the degree of inequality, so long as they did not imply absolute reductions in other incomes. For a time, at least, such unequally distributed gains might even be welcomed by those who were relatively disadvantaged by them, as holding out the promise that they too could benefit in the future." *The Economies of West Africa* (New York: St. Martins Press, 1984), pp. 48–49.

Crawford Young and Thomas Turner provide a less sanguine view of what they term "the colossal pauperization" of the lower classes and of a social consciousness expressed in terms of "distrust, cynicism, and despair," in *The Rise and Decline of the Zairian State* (Madison, Wisc.: University of Wisconsin Press, 1985).

For a throughful analysis of "the anatomy of the urban masses" and the distribution of income, see Richard Sandbrook, *The Politics of Basic Needs: Urban Aspects of Assaulting Poverty in Africa* (Toronto: University of Toronto Press, 1982).

Among those studies of the peasants which focus both on their plight and on the need for new organizational forms, see, for example, Torben Bager, *Marketing Cooperatives and Peasants in Kenya* (New York: Africana Publishing Co., 1980); Guy Belloncle, *La Question Paysanne en Afrique Noire* (Paris: Editions Karthala, 1982); Dessalegn Rahmato, *Agrarian Reform in Ethiopia*

(Uppsala: Scandinavian Institute of African Studies, 1984); Christoper Leo, *Land and Class in Kenya* (Toronto: University of Toronto Press, 1984); James Bingen, *Food Production and Rural Development in the Sahel: Lessons from Malis' Operation Riz-Segou* (Boulder, Colo.: Westview Press, 1985).

11. Irving Leonard Markovitz, *Power and Class in Africa* (Englewood Cliffs, N.J.: Prentice-Hall, 1977; 6th printing, 1984).

12. Cf. Irving Leonard Markovitz, *Léopold Sédar Senghor and the Politics of Négritude* (New York: Atheneum, 1969; London: Heinemann Educational Books, 1970).

13. Cf. Aristide Zolberg, *Creating Political Order* (Chicago: Rand McNally and Co., 1966).

14. The phrase comes from Frantz Fanon, *Wretched of the Earth* (New York: Grove Press, 1968).

15. For a discussion of the works of these and other modernization theorists, see my *Power and Class in Africa*, p. 290 and passim.

16. For a definition of these terms, see notes 38 and 39, below.

17. Robert H. Jackson and Carl G. Rosberg, *Personal Rule in Black Africa* (Berkeley, Calif.: University of California Press, 1982).

18. Samuel Huntington, *Political Order in Changing Societies* (New Haven: Yale University Press, 1968).

19. Cf. especially Thomas M. Callaghy, "Absolutism, Bonapartism, and the Formation of Ruling Classes: Zaire in Comparative Perspective," in this volume.

20. The studies in this volume by Grier, Kilson, Kofele-Kale, Bond, Kruks, and Greenberg and Giliomee are especially instructive on these points. Cf. *Power and Class in Africa*, Chapter IV, "Tribe, Tribalism and the Conditions for Social Development," pp. 98–172.

Cf. David Lan, *Guns and Rain: Guerrillas and Spirit Mediums in Zimbabwe* (London: James Currey Ltd., and Berkeley: University of California Press, 1985) for an analysis of how guerrillas in Zimbabwe won the support of the peasantry through the intervention of spirit mediums, the religious leaders of the Shona. See also Terence Ranger, *Peasant Consciousness and Guerrilla War in Zimbabwe: A Comparative Study* (London: James Currey Ltd., and Berkeley: University of California Press, 1985). Although based primarily upon fieldwork in Makoni district in Zimbabwe, Ranger, in his absolutely essential study enables us to understand the forces that produced a specific peasant consciousness in Zimbabwe which led to a different political outcome from that of either Kenya or Mozambique. A "Kenyan solution," according to Ranger, is based upon *Kulaks,* "rich" peasants, able, and willing "to turn the military harassment and displacement of poor peasants to their own advantage." A "Mozambican solution" presumes "a poor peasantry united in its determination not to allow the re-emergence of local 'exploiters'" (p. 15).

Intense peasant consciousness prevented both a Kenyan and a Mozambican solution after independence because "No matter how committed a politician might be to entrepreneurial capitalism, he could not possibly envisage clearing people off land in the communal areas in order to parcel it out to yeoman farmers"; nor could those more radically inclined "force the consciousness of a peasant class" readily to accept "collective agricultural production systems" (pp. 288, 289). Indeed, the Mugabe government declared that they would not coerce peasants into "collective or even cooperative patterns of settlement and production" (p. 289).

21. *Power and Class in Africa*, especially pp. 14–24 and passim.

22. P. T. Bauer, *Reality and Rhetoric: Studies in the Economics of Development* (Cambridge, Mass.: Harvard University Press, 1984), p. 90. Cf. Bauer, *Equality, the Third World, and Economic Delusion* (Cambridge, Mass.: Harvard University Press, 1981). In the later volume Bauer denounces theories of imperialism and dependency which allege that the West was responsible for the lack of development:

> The exponents of Western guilt further patronize the Third World by suggesting that its economic fortunes past, present and prospective, are determined by the West; that past exploitation by the West explains Third World backwardness; that manipulation of international trade by the West and other forms of Western misconduct account for persistent poverty; that the economic future of the Third World depends largely on Western donations. According to this set of ideas, whatever happens to the Third World is largely our doing. Such ideas makes us feel superior even while we beat our breasts. (p. 84)

Bauer maintains that contact with the West, rather than being the cause of proverty in Africa, was instead "the principal agent of material progress there." See also Melvyn B. Krauss, *Development Without Aid: Growth, Poverty and Government* (New York: McGraw-Hill, 1983), who argues that all forms of foreign assistance and "big government" are nothing but "welfare state" handouts which are the biggest obstacle to Third World economic development.

Nathan Rosenberg and L. E. Birdzell, Jr., in *How the West Grew Rich: The Economic Transformation of the Industrial World* (New York: Basic Books, 1986), an uneasy combination of shrewd insights and vulgar summaries of opposing theories, maintain that the breakup of centralized political and religious control gave the "economic sector" in the West the autonomy to experiment in the development of "new and diverse products, methods of manufacture, modes of enterprise organization, market relations, methods of transportation and communication, and relations between capital and labor" (p. 333).

23. Claus Offe, *Contradictions of the Welfare State* (Cambridge, Mass.: MIT Press, 1984), p. 119 and passim.

24. Why, furthermore, did foreign capitalism apparently seek to prevent the creation of an African permanently settled, free wage-labor working class in both "settler" and "peasant" Africa? This question in turn leads to others: Why is Africa poor? Why hasn't capitalism produced as much wealth in Africa as elsewhere? How were precapitalist and capitalist economies integrated into single social formations? What colonial policies produced "dangerous contradictions" that resulted in agricultural stagnation, migration to the cities, and intensified class conflict and which have continued to affect postcolonial African regimes?

Ruth First offers an interesting answer to some of these questions in her *Black Gold: The Mozambican Miner, Proletarian and Peasant* (New York: St. Martins Press, 1983).

For an interesting review essay on the changing position of the working class in Africa, see Bill Freund, "Labor and Labor History in Africa: A Review of the Literature," *The African Studies Review* (June 1984): 1–58. For a discussion of the emergence of employed labor and the changing size of the working class as well as extensive bibliographical references, see Chapter VIII, "The Consolidation of Power: African Labor, Peasants, and Farmers," in *Power and Class in Africa,* pp. 262–283.

See also, among others, Richard Jeffries, *Class, Ideology and Power in Africa: The Railwaymen of Sekondi* (Cambridge: Cambridge University Press, 1978); Bettie du Toit, *Ukubamba Amandolo: Worker's Struggles in the South African Textile Industry* (London: Onyx Press, 1978); Adrian J. Peace, *Choice, Class and Conflict: A study of Southern Nigerian Factory Workers* (Atlantic Highlands, N.J.: Humanities Press, 1979); Philip Daniel, *Africanization, Nationalization and Inequality: Mining, Labor and the Copperbelt in Zambian Development* (New York: Cambridge University Press, 1979); Bill Freund, *Capital and Labor in the Nigerian Tin Mines* (Harlow: Longman Group Ltd., 1981); Sharon Stichter, *Migrant Labor in Kenya: Capitalism and African Response 1895–1975* (New York: Longman, 1982); Charles Van Onselen, *Studies in the Social and Economic History of the Witswatersrand 1886–1914,* 2 vols. (Harlow: Longman Group Ltd., 1982); Shula Marks and Richard Rathbone, eds., *Industrialization and Social Change in South Africa: African Class Formation, Culture and Consciousness, 1870–1930* (Harlow: Longman Group Ltd., 1982); Peter Waterman, *Division and Unity Amongst Nigerian Workers: Lagos Port Unionism, 1940–60s* (The Hague: Institute of Social Studies, 1982); Jeff Crisp, *The Story of An African Working Class: Ghanaian Miner's Struggles, 1870–1980* (London: Zed Press, 1984); Denis MacShane, Martin Plaut, and David Ward, *Power! Black Workers, Their Unions and the Struggle for Freedom in South Africa* (Boston: South End Press, 1984); and Catherine Coquery-Vidrovitch and Paul E. Lovejoy, eds., *The Workers of African Trade* (Beverly Hills: Sage Publications, 1985), for a series of excellent studies that focus on labor in precolonial and especially nineteenth-century trade.

25. Cf. Joel Migdal, *Peasants, Politics and Revolution* (Princeton, N.J.: Princeton University Press, 1974); Allan and Barbara Isaacman, *Mozambique: From Colonialism to Revolution, 1900–1982* (Boulder: West View Press, 1983); Barry Munslow, *Mozambique: The Revolution and Its Origins* (New York: Longman, 1983); Patrick Chabal, Amilcar Cabral, *Revolutionary Leadership and Peoples' War* (New York: Cambridge University Press, 1983); James H. Mittleman, *Underdevelopment and the Transition to Socialism, Mozambique and Tanzania* (New York: Academic Press, 1981); Gillian Walt and Angela Melamed, eds., *Mozambique: Towards A Peoples Health Service* (London: Zed Press, 1983); John S. Saul, ed., *A Difficult Road: The Transition to Socialism in Mozambique* (New York: Monthly Review Press, 1985).

26. *Power and Class in Africa,* pp. 204–219. Richard Sandbrook (with Judith Barker), in *The Politics of Africa's Economic Stagnation* (New York: Cambridge University Press, 1985), denies that capitalism in any form has succeeded or is succeeding in Africa since 1960, that African states are "in any real sense" capitalist states, or that an independent national bourgeoisie, "in the classic western mold," either exists or is likely soon to appear (p. 155 and passim). Sandbrook sees change in the direction of "highly factionalized neo-patrimonial systems, not of class societies and modern-style class struggles" (p. 155). "In effect," Sandbrook declares, "we are designating as the dominant or ruling class a political elite which aspires to become a bourgeoi-

sie. But this aspiration itself connotes little more than an opportunistic exploitation of 'insider' privileges in many cases (e.g., Nigeria, Ghana, Uganda, Zaire), not the development of the classic risk-taking entrepreneurial behaviour" (p. 72). The indigenous bourgeoisie therefore is not a dominant class in Marxian terms, but "merely an embryonic class at most, dependent upon political power for its survivial and expansion" (p. 72).

I would agree with Sandbrook only that "class alone fails to explain African political life" (p. 63). He modifies his generalizations with qualifications ("Of course, the rate at which the bourgeoisie and proletariat form varies from country to country . . . " [p. 76]) that threaten to undermine his basic thesis. I would also disagree with his contentions that "extractions of economic surplus from peasants do not create the same tensions as in capitalist societies" (p. 65); that the "peculiar conditions" of postcolonial Africa threaten to break down African states into "an economically irrational form of 'personal' rule" (p. 12); or that one can assert the primary saliency of ethnicity or communalism without reference to class (p. 76).

Sandbrook lumps together the various components of the organizational bourgeoisie and thereby confuses the analysis of the nature of Africa's new dominant classes. This inhibits his ability to comprehend the productive potential of an expanding capitalism or the increasing *class* power of a continuously expanding bourgeoisie. Lower interest rates, lower oil prices (not excluding Nigeria), recovery from the drought, and a resurgent world economy will, even in classic trickle-down fashion, strongly spur Africa's developing capitalism and the business wing of the organizational bourgeoisie. (And already has. In Senegal, for example, GDP increased by 3.8 percent in 1985. President Diouf attributed the "return to growth" to lower oil prices and interest rates along with the "first good rainy season in 10 years" [*West Africa*, April 14, 1986, p. 791].)

27. What unites the organizational bourgeoisie and makes its component parts more than "a collection," but a "class," are its objective and intended exploitative relations of production and exchange. Top members of the liberal professions and the military do not by themselves necessarily determine the content of societal forms and objectives, but both reinforce and derive power from the other elements of the dominant ruling class. Again, the specific nature and content of the specific combination of elements vary over time.

For interesting studies which shed light on the nature of rule in Africa, see the collection edited by Nelson Kasfir, *State and Class in Africa* (London: Frank Cass, 1984). Kasfir feels that "those holding or benefiting from political power have not yet taken hold of the means of production" (p. 72). For interpretive overviews which deal with class but from contending perspectives, see: Claude Ake, *A Political Economy of Africa* (New York: Longman, 1981); S. Fogel, *Africa in Struggle: National Liberation and Proletarian Revolution* (Seattle: Ism Press, 1982); Bill Freund, *The Making of Contemporary Africa* (Bloomington: Indiana University Press, 1984); William Tordoff, *Government and Politics in Africa* (Bloomington: Indiana University Press, 1984); Roger Tangri, *Politics in Sub-Saharan Africa* (Portsmouth, N.H.: Heinemann Educational Books, 1985).

28. The work by Andrew Beveridge and Anthony Oberschall, *African Businessman and Development in Zambia* (Princeton: Princeton University Press, 1979), clearly shows the increasing involvement of African civil servants with business ventures. See also sources cited in note 44. See also the discussion in Chapter VII, "The Consolidation of Power: African Business," in *Power and Class in Africa*, pp. 231–261. A wealth of significant data is contained in Henry Bienen and V. P. Diejomaoh, eds., *The Political Economy of Income Distribution in Nigeria* (New York: Holmes and Meier, 1981); and I. William Zartman, ed., *The Political Economy of Nigeria* (New York: Praeger Publishers, 1983). Cf. Toyin Falola and Julius Ihonvbere, *The Rise and Fall of Nigeria's Second Republic, 1979–84* (London: Zed Books Ltd., 1985), who focus on the "class dimension of contradiction and competition between the bourgeoisie in the centre and in the states" in Nigeria's federal arrangement and who attack Bienen for alleging that most Nigerians aren't aware of the existence of a class structure or that conditions of inequality and poverty aren't worsening (pp. 8, 9, and 14).

29. Samuel P. Huntington, *Political Order in Changing Societies* (New Haven: Yale University Press, 1968), P. 60.

30. Cf. Ivan Szelenyi, "The Intelligentsia in the Class Structure of State-Socialist Societies," in Michael Burrawoy and Theda Skocpol, eds., *Marxist Inquiries: Studies of Labor, Class and States* (Chicago: The University of Chicago Press, 1982), pp. 287–326, for a reevaluation of Djilas and an exploration of the mechanisms of expropriation under state socialism.

31. This helps explain the rediscovery of the power of the state in recent years by a wide range of theoretical commentators, for example, Nicos Poulantzsas, *Political Power and Social Classes* (London: New Left Books, 1973); Claus Offe, *Contradictions of the Welfare State*, ed. John Keane (Cambridge, Mass.: The MIT Press, 1984); James O'Conner, *The Fiscal Crisis of*

*the State* (New York: St. Martins Press, 1973); Edward R. Tufte, *Political Control of the Economy* (Princeton: Princeton University Press, 1978); Erik Olin Wright, *Class, Crisis and the State* (London: New Left Books, 1978); Theda Skocpol, *States and Social Revolutions* (New York: Cambridge University Press, 1979); Bertrand Badie and Pierre Birnbaum, *The Sociology of the State* (Chicago: University of Chicago Press, 1983). For a series of case studies which raise interesting theoretical questions by focusing on class, state, and city, see Frederick Cooper, ed., *Struggle for the City: Migrant Labor, Capital and the State in Urban Africa* (Beverly Hills: Sage Publications 1984).

32. One of the strongest critiques of dependency and of world systems theories from the left came from Bill Warren in his suggestively titled *Imperialism: Pioneer of Capitalism* (London: New Left Books, 1980). Warren represents a school which we might call "neo-Marxist modernization" theory. Almost like the classical mainstream modernization theorists (e.g., Rupert Emerson, *From Empire to Nation* [Boston: Beacon Press, 1960], and W. W. Rostow., *The Stages of Economic Growth: A Non-Communist Manifesto* [New York: Cambridge University Press, 1971]), Warren argues that imperialism will be remembered in the long run not for the harm which it did but for the "progressive" forces which it set in motion. Unlike Emerson and Rostow, who emphasize "Newtonian" science and technology as the key to development, Warren argues that imperialism unleashed the productive forces of indigenous capitalism which, as in the history of the West, has revolutionized the forces of production, created higher standards of living, but also a wage-labor force which ultimately will revolt and create socialist societies. Albert Syzmanski offers a much more sophisticated Marxist perspective on international capitalism in his *The Logic of Imperialism* (New York: Praeger, 1981). In claiming his position in the Marxist mainstream and criticizing dependency and world systems analysis, Syzmanski agrees with Warren that the developed capitalist countries and their transnational corporations are now—not necessarily in the past—promoting industrialization in Third World, less developed countries. He particularly attacks what he calls the *Monthly Review* perspective of dependency theory, including the views of Baran, Sweezy, Amin, and Frank, and insists, among other points, that it is workers and not peasants who will be the carriers of socialist revolutions.

David G. Becker, in *The New Bourgeoisie and the Limits of Dependency: Mining, Class, and Power in "Revolutionary" Peru* (Princeton, N.J.: Princeton University Press, 1983), not only argues that strong indigenous bourgeoisies have developed and will develop in the Third World with the aid of strong states, but that through "democratic" process, subordinate classes can secure a "fairer share of developments' rewards." Therefore, "Deficient in explanatory power and unable to stand up to empirical tests, the 'theory' of dependency . . . no longer furthers, as it once did, the cause of general human liberation. It is time, therefore, for progressives to lay it to rest" (p. 342).

33. Timothy Shaw and Jane Parpart, in "Contradiction and Coalition: Class Fractions in Zambia, 1964–1984," *Africa Today* 30, 3 (1983): 23–50, provide evidence for the existence of division within the dominant bourgeoisie in Zambia. Steven W. Langdon, in *Multinational Corporations in the Political Economy of Kenya* (New York: St. Martins Press, 1981), also sees "an increasing potential in Kenya for tougher moves against the MNC [Multi-National Corporation] sector," with a social base in "a stratum of bureaucrats in the bureaucracy, independent of insider capitalists, and pushed by educational background and analytical tasks to skeptical perspectives on the MNC's [Multi-National Corporations]" (pp. 199–200). Langdon also argues that "in terms of a definition of development with equalitarian dimensions the MNC impact in Kenya was negative." Even though "MNC investment was important in financially assisting the bourgeoisies' emergence," it distorted growth in unproductive ways (pp. 186–189).

In contrast to Langdon (and in a direct attack on dependency theory—see below) Nicola Swainson, in a wonderfully detailed, provocative study, argues that an indigenous manufacturing bourgeoisie has come to exist in Kenya, that it is different from the indigenous commerical bourgeoisie, and that it has incrasingly succeeded in winning the support of the dominant faction within the Kenyan state in controlling foreign capital including the MNCs: (*The Development of Corporate Capitalism in Kenya, 1918–1977* [Berkeley: University of California Press, 1980]). Gavin Kitching, in his massively documented *Class and Economic Change in Kenya* (New Haven: Yale University Press, 1980), focuses on the rise of an African petite bourgeoisie and is reluctant to talk about the development of "class" politics because the people he describes play so many conflicting economic roles. Swainson does not share this reluctance. Nor do I.

On inter- and intraclass mobility, for example, the problem of "worker-peasants" who are not totally divorced from their rural "means of production," their land and farm tools, but who also need spells of wage work to afford to "reproduce" their farm households and agricultural plots, see Ruth First, who points out that mining capital accumulation advanced through labor extracted from external peasant economies, which in turn came to need and depend on the return of wages by the migrant miners reproduced in their continuing, successive generations: *Black Gold* p. 184. Victoria Bernal, "Peasant Production and Off-Farm Work in Household Economy at Hillat al Feki," in Jay O'Brien and Norman O'Neil, eds., *Economy and Class in Sudan* (New York: Ithaca Press, forthcoming), pp. 1–41, argues that we must examine the integration of households into regional economic systems if we are to understand how the decisions of peasants are affected by the commercial, wage-labor economy in which their households participate.

See especially the excellent study by Sharon Stichter, *Migrant Laborers* (New York: Cambridge University Press, 1985), who points out that migrancy was the predominant form of wage labor in Africa for the first half-century of capitalist development. She demonstrates that migrants were a unique class in both "the minimal sense" of occupying a definable place in the structure of production and also "in the larger sense" of engaging in individual and collective actions to further their class interests (p. 191).

Alexander Gerschenkorn's correlation between the degree of lateness of development and the role of the state is suggestive for understanding the role of the African state (*Economic Backwardness in Historical Perspective* [Cambridge, Mass.: Harvard University Press, 1962]). However, African states function differently than in the case of, for example, Japan's state-organized development. External involvements, especially colonialism, greater ethnic heterogeneity, a less developed productive base, and lack of precapitalist, centralized bureaucratic structures (in most cases) have diversely affected state-economy relations.

34. In some instances, the administrative capacity of the state has indeed declined to the point where, at least temporarily, it cannot effectively license imports, regulate exchange, control prices, operate market boards, or control labor. Western states also went through periods of backsliding and great distortion in the process of constructing the modern state. I do not underestimate these difficulties. I would, however, emphasize the enormity of the "bureaucratic phenomenon" in postcolonial Africa. Cf. *Power and Class in Africa,* pp. 199–209, 285–289.

On how the organizational bourgeoisie uses its office to determine the allocation of surpluses, see, for example, Joel D. Barkan, ed., *Politics and Public Policy in Kenya and Tanzania* (New York: Praeger, 1979; 2nd rev. ed., 1984). Uma Lele, in "Tanzania: Phoenix or Icarus," in Arnold C. Harberger, ed., *World Economic Growth* (San Francisco: Institute for Contemporary Studies, 1984), pp. 159–196, tells us that in Tanzania life expectancy has gone from forty-two at independence to fifty-two in 1980 (p. 171). However per capita income declined by nearly half from 1971 to 1981 (p. 159). Among other reasons, he points out that the high costs of marketing parastatals and their growing losses have made it difficult for the government to raise producer prices (p. 182). See also Robert Bideleux, *Communism and Development* (London: Methuen and Co., 1985), who also criticizes Tanzania for pursuing a large-scale town-based industrialization program (p. 57). Bideleux, who favors "the most cost-effective socialist alternatives to Stalinism," argues that increased peasant living standards, based on land and income redistribution, occurred under a wide variety of regimes including prerevolutionary Russia, post-1850s Ireland, modern Denmark, post-1905 Japan as well as Taiwan, South Korea, Yugoslavia, and Poland (p. 57).

35. Cf. *Power and Class in Africa,* pp. 209–210, for a discussion of Djilas' analysis of the "New Class" and Richard Sklar's idea of "the managerial bourgeoisie." See also by Sklar, "The Nature of Class Domination in Africa," *Journal of Modern African Studies* (1979): 536 and further.

36. See also Bates, *Markets and States in Tropical Africa,* as well as Thomas Callaghy's study in this volume. Callaghy argues strongly that the ruling class in Zaire has as a major feature its nonproductive economic role. To the extent this is true, Zaire would be at one end of a continuum.

37. Ernest Wilson, "Comparative Politics and Public Enterprises in Africa," unpublished paper.

38. "Dependency theory" was originated primarily in the 1950s by people associated with the United Nations Economic Commission for Latin America who sought a nationalist, not necessarily a socialist, solution for what they considered the "semicolonial" status of the region, and for the failure of traditional strategies of "modernization" to result in significant economic development. The "Marxian-dependency" school, including but not limited to Paul Baran, Andre Gunder Frank, and Samir Amin, argued—as one key idea—that imperialism resulted in the development only of underdevelopment in Third World countries. They argued contrary to Lenin's basic thesis that crisis of overproduction forced advanced capitalist countries to export surplus

capital to the Third World and thus reinforced those tendencies described and predicted by Marx for capitalism to reproduce itself in "barbarian" lands. Rather, dependency theory maintained, the capital flow *from* less developed countries intensified their poverty and provided the resources for the advance of the more industrialized nations. Celso Furtado represents the best example of a non-Marxist dependency theorist. See his *Development and Underdevelopment* (Berkeley: University of California Press, 1964); *Diagnosis of the Brazilian Crisis* (Berkeley: University of California Press, 1965; and *Economic Development of Latin America* (Cambridge, England: Cambridge University Press, 1976).

Paul Baran's pioneer essay, *The Political Economy of Growth* (New York: Monthly Review Press, 1957), can still be read with profit. Andre Gundar Frank's earliest books, *Latin America: Underdevelopment or Revolution* (New York: Monthly Review Press, 1969) and *Capitalism and Underdevelopment in Latin America* (New York: Monthly Review Press, 1967), represent the clearest and simplest expression of his "development of underdevelopment" thesis. In *World Accumulation, 1492–1789* (New York: Monthly Review Press, 1978), he attempts, like Wallerstein and Amin, to extend his studies to a global level. In *Lumpenbourgeoisie: Lumpendevelopment* (New York: Monthly Review Press, 1972) and *Dependent Accumulation and Underdevelopment* (New York: Monthly Review Press, 1978), he attempts to defend himself against the accusation of having neglected class struggles in both the developed and less developed countries. In his two volumes *Crisis: In the Third World* and *Crisis in the World Economy* (New York: Holmes and Meier Publishers, 1981), he backs off from what had sounded like an absolutist declaration that the less developed countries' condition would worsen and that no growth was possible. See Samir Amin's two-volume *Accumulation on a World Scale* (New York: Monthly Review Press, 1974); and *Unequal Development* (New York: Monthly Review Press, 1976).

39. World systems theorists see the development of an increasingly integrated world capitalist system which originated around the beginning of the sixteenth century, evolving through various stages eventually to include even the socialist countries. Capitalist market forces including trade and the flow of capital and labor integrate all countries in three interdependent, coexistent tiers which differ in their industrial and economic development, systems of labor relations, and state formations. In the wealthy industrial "core," wage-labor predominates; the poorest countries of the "periphery" export raw materials under a variety of labor-control mechanisms; the "semi-periphery" in numerous ways integrates the system and plays intermediary roles between the cores states and periphery.

Immanual Wallerstein's most important books include *The Modern World System* (New York: Academic Press, 1974) and *The Capitalist World Economy* (New York: Cambridge University Press, 1979).

Irene L. Gendzier, *Managing Political Change: Social Scientists and the Third World* (Boulder, Colo.: Westview Press, 1985), explains the continued "domination" of "modernization theory," since such concepts so "obviously distort rather than illuminate the analysis of political change" (p. 11) because of "their congruence with foreign policy" and as a conservative response to mass-based social and political movements (p. 4).

40. Rhoda Howard's *Colonialism and Underdevelopment in Ghana* (New York: Africana Publishing Co., 1978) represents an early example of the application of dependency theory to Africa. She argues that Ghana was integrated into the world economy as a "peripheral, primary export orientated economic unit" during the colonial period. See also W. Ibekwe Ofonagaro, *Trade and Imperialism in Southern Nigeria: 1881–1919* (New York: Nok Publishers, 1979); Yolamu Barongo, ed., *Political Science in Africa: A Critical Review* (London: Zed Press, 1983), especially the articles by Bjorn Beckman, "Political Science and Political Economy," pp. 101–112, Ikello Oculi, "Imperialism and the Politics of Area Studies," pp. 129–138, and Franz J. T. Lee, "Dependency and Revolutionary Theory in the African Situation," pp. 178–189; Bade Onimode, *Imperialism and Underdevelopment in Nigeria: The Dialectics of Mass Poverty* (London: Zed Press, 1982), especially Part Three, "Neo-Colonial Capitalism and Underdevelopment, 1960–1980," pp. 135–241; Rita Cruise O'Brien, ed., *The Political Economy of Underdevelopment: Dependence in Senegal* (Beverly Hills: Sage Publications, 1979); Okwudiba Nnoli, ed., *Path to Nigerian Development* (Dakar, Senegal: Codesria, 1981); Daniel A. Offiong, *Imperialism and Dependency: Obstacles to African Development* (Washington, D.C.: Howard University Press, 1982).

41. Two collections containing a wide range of critiques of dependency and world systems theory and which offer alternative theories based upon "class" and "modes of production" are Ronald H. Chilcote, ed., *Dependency and Marxism: Toward a Resolution of the Debate* (Boulder, Col.: Westview Press, 1982); and Ronald H. Chilcote and Dale L. Johnson, eds., *Theories of*

*Development: Mode of Production or Dependency* (Beverly Hills: Westview Press, 1983). Two other interesting critiques are by Ernst LaClau, *Politics and Ideology in Marxist Theory* (London: New Left Books, 1977), and James Petras, *Critical Perspectives on Imperialism and Social Class in the Third World* (New York: Monthly Review Press, 1970).

Ronald H. Chilcote, *Theories of Development and Underdevelopment* (Boulder, Colo.: Westview Press, 1984), offers the best set of summaries and description of the historical evolution of dependency and modes of production theory. Magnus Blomström and Bjorn Hettne, in *Development Theory in Transition. The Dependency Debate and Beyond: Third World Responses* (London: Zed Books Ltd., 1984), make much the same type of effort but less critically and less thoroughly. Stephen D. Krasner, *Structural Conflict: The Third World Against Global Liberalism* (Berkeley: University of California Press, 1985), focuses on the use that the politically weak Third World made of dependency theory as an ideology to challenge "vigorously, and with some success," the postwar international economic order (p. 42), especially through its "demands for movement from liberal to authoritative norms and rules over a wide range of issues" (p. 94).

For a provocative methodological critique of the "abstract schematisms" of mode-of-production analysis, see Peter T. Manicas, "Explanation, Generalisation and Marxist Theory vis-à-vis Third World Development," in D. Banerjee, ed., *Marxian Theory and the Third World* (New Delhi and Beverly Hills: Sage Publications, 1986), pp. 309–322.

Claire C. Robertson, in *Sharing the Same Bowl: A Socioeconomic History of Women and Class in Accra, Ghana* (Bloomington: Indiana University Press, 1984), the richly deserved winner of the African Studies Association's Herskovits prize, creatively employs mode-of-production analysis to focus on the evolution of male and female hierarchies. Robertson warns against assuming that Western social structures are universal or that one can automatically classify women's socioeconomic status with that of their husbands. She demonstrates how women can belong to separate classes or class fractions because their relationship to the means of production and their access to land, labor, and education differ substantially from those of men.

Ray A. Kea's *Settlements, Trade, and Politics in the Seventeenth-Century Gold Coast* (Baltimore: The John Hopkins University Press, 1982) also deserves special note as a richly detailed analysis of diverse modes of production and their evolution in the Gold Coast between the sixteenth and early eighteenth centuries. Kea shows how "roots of differentiation and conflict did not lie in the marketplace or in various forms of circulation (reciprocity, redistribution, and exchange)" but in "the class relations of production" (p. 289).

From a very different political perspective, see Miles Kahler, *Decolonization in Britain and France: The Domestic Consequences of International Relations* (Princeton, N.J.: Princeton University Press, 1984), who maintains that, contrary to the expectations of dependency theory, "the structures tying together center and periphery, so deeply rooted in the histories of those respective countries, crumbled very quickly" (p. 385).

42. Critics maintain that world systems theorists consider the world system a mode of production based on trade, not production, yet classes can exist only at the level of production. Fernand Braudel replies to this criticism: "But no historian would deny the effect of commercial expansion on the economy which it certainly helped to reach new heights. Many historians have chosen however to minimize that effect. The problem is fundamentally the same as the bitter dispute between those who attribute capitalist growth exclusively to the virtue of *internal* evolution and those who see it as being created from outside, by the systematic exploitation of the world—a debate which has little purpose since both explanations are perfectly acceptable": *Civilization and Capitalism, 15th–18th Century*, Volume III, *The Perspective of the World* (New York: Harper & Row, 1984), p. 579; first published in France under the title *Le Tempo du Monde* (Paris: Librarie Armend Colin, 1979).

Of the many countercritiques of Braudel and world systems theorists I would single out Elizabeth Fox-Genovese and Eugene D. Genovese, *Fruits of Merchant Capital: Slavery and Bourgeois Property in the Rise and Expansion of Capitalism* (New York: Oxford University Press, 1983). They maintain that the extension of commerce usually led to the "chaining down of labor and not at all to the separation of labor from the means of production which characterizes the capitalist mode of production" (p. 8). However, they do go on to say that if "the conservative function was the norm," the "progressive appeared only under highly special, if nevertheless epoch-making, conditions . . ." (Ibid).

For two very different assessments of the productive potential of merchant capital in Africa, see, for example, Fatima Babiker Mahmoud, *The Sudanese Bourgeoisie: Vanguard of Development?* (London: Zed Books Ltd., 1984), who clearly establishes the rise of a self-conscious bourgeoisie over three generations. She argues that it had "no major contradictions with the colonial system and continues to remain "truly dependent on international capital" (p. 145). She does show, however, that an indigenous "industrial bourgeoisie developed from the ranks of former commercial and agricultural capitalists" (p. 146).

Robert Shenton, in *The Development of Capitalism in Northern Nigeria* (Toronto: University of Toronto Press, 1986), maintains that although merchant capital—"parasitical in nature"— sought to preserve rather than transform the preexisting forces and social relations of production in northern Nigeria, it nevertheless acted as a powerful catalyst of social transformation. Shenton, like Michael Watt in *Silent Violence*, shows the intensification of northern Nigerian society's vulnerability to famine. He also shows that the intensification of agricultural labor through migration, mechanization, and settlement schemes can lead to the emergence of industrial capitalism.

43. Nevertheless, distinguishing between Marxist and non-Marxist theorists of dependency, it simply is not true that analysts such as Andre Gunder Frank and Immanuel Wallerstein have not considered that both "core and periphery" have a variety of class interests and conflict. More nuanced critiques like that of Douglas Friedman maintain that world systems and dependency analysis, even when they consider class struggle, always find that it is external forces which condition, focus, and ultimately determine the outcome of indigenous class struggles. Cf. Douglas Friedman, *The State and Underdevelopment in Spanish America: The Political Roots of Dependency in Peru and Argentina* (Boulder: Westview Press, 1984), especially Part I, "Dependency, Colonialism and Crisis," pp. 3–93.

44. See, further, Peter Evans, *Dependent Development: The Alliance of Multinational, State and Local Capital in Brazil* (Princeton, N.J.: Princeton University Press, 1979). See also Erik Davis, *Challenging Colonialism: Bank Misr and Egyptian Industrialization, 1920–1941* (Princeton, N.J.: Princeton University Press, 1983), who provides abundant empirical evidence to back up his contention that it was not true that Western imperialism actively sought to prevent Egyptian industrialization. Henrik Secher Marcussen and Jens Erik Torp, in *Internationalization of Capital: Prospects for the Third World* (London: Zed Press, 1982), provide an analysis of economic development in the Ivory Coast in which they confront both the empirical works and the theories of Samir Amin. For the range of Amin's work, see for example, *his Neo-Colonialism in West Africa* (New York: Monthly Review Press, 1973) and *Class and Nation* (New York: Monthly Review Press, 1980).

Colin Leys presents an honest, thoughtful reconsideration of his earlier work (especially his *Underdevelopment in Kenya: The Political Economy of Neo-Colonialism, 1964–1971* [London: Heinemann Educational Books, 1975]) and dependency theories in "Kenya: What Does Dependency Explain?" *Review of African Political Economy* (Jan–April 1980). This is part of a "Debate" on "Capitalist Accumulation in the Periphery—the Kenyan Case Re-examined," with contributions by Rafael Kaplinsky and J. S. Henley, pp. 83–113. The debate, and the rejection of dependency theory, continues in Bjorn Beckman "Neo-Colonialism, Capitalism, and the State in Nigeria," pp. 71–114 and Gavin Kitching, "Politics, Method, and Evidence in the 'Kenya Debate,'" pp. 115–152, in Henry Bernstein and Bonnie K. Campbell, eds., *Contradictions of Accumulation in Africa* (Beverly Hills: Sage Publications, 1985).

45. K. A. Owusu-Ansah, "Ghana," in Adebayo Adedej, ed., *Indigenization of African Economies* (New York: Africana Publishing Co., 1981), p. 133.

46. For an interesting, non-Marxist effort to come to grips with the existence of class in Africa, see Crawford Young and Thomas Turner, *The Rise and Decline of the Zairian State*, (Madison: University of Wisconsin Press, 1985), especially Chapter 4, "The Dynamics of Inequality: Class Formation," pp. 100–157. Their minimal conception is that "Class, however murky and controversial its definition may be, divides a civil society in structured patterns of inequality" (p. 18). They touch upon, if they do not always deal satisfactorily with, major issues of class theory including the structured basis of class divisions (the authors hedge by declaring that "These may be rooted in mode of production, status, or power"), class consciousness ("they may be expressed in varying degrees of class consciousness,"), and the relationships of class to political power and to the state ("the state is in part a reflection of class relationships within civil society, although not in so mechanical a fashion as classical Marxism would suggest") (pp. 18–19).

47. Ibid., pp. 343–344.

48. Ibid., p. 397.

49. Ibid., p. 79.

50. Ibid., pp. 78, 111.

51. Ibid., p. 79. Young and Turner's conception of a "politico-commercial class" poses difficulties, among other reasons, because (1) it seems to deemphasize the potential of this class for industrialization and (2), while they focus on state and political power, they don't take into ac-

count the special nature of African political power with its peculiar relations to the productive forces in society. Nevertheless, the term is revealing because it conveys the sense of a new grouping, a new type of phenomenon uniting elements of the state and of production. See also John D. Montgomery, "How African Managers Serve Developmental Goals," unpublished paper (Cambridge, Mass.: 1985), a 1984 study of 2000 "management events" described from their own experiences by managers from large public, private, and parastatal organizations in nine countries of southern Africa which found no basic differences in activities or attitudes of any of the African managers. Montgomery tells us that "the degree of attention African managers devote to their own affairs is perhaps not surprising . . . but the intensely internal preoccupation of these supposed entrepreneurs of development is not a good sign." Cf. Kenneth Paul Erickson, "State Entrepreneurship, Energy Policy, and the Political Order in Brazil," in Thomas C. Bruneau and Philippe Faucher, eds., *Authoritarian Capitalism: Brazil's Contemporary Economic and Political Development* (Boulder, Colo.: Westview Press, 1981), pp. 141–177, for a discussion of a Latin American example of entrepreneurship by the state, including control over powerful means of production. My impression is that the separation of state and economic interests and the demarcation of their respective roles is much more clearly defined in Latin America than in Africa. However, the subject cries out for more comparative work.

52. Fernand Braudel, op. cit., p. 623.

53. Fernand Braudel, *Civilization and Capitalism 15th–18th Century*, Volume II, *The Wheels of Commerce* (New York: Harper & Row, 1982), p. 460; first published in France as *Les Jeux de l'Exchange* (Paris: Librarie Armand Colin, 1979).

54. Cf. Michael G. Schatzberg, *Politics and Class in Zaire: Bureaucracy, Business and Beer in Lisala* (New York: Africana, 1980); Nzongola-Ntalaja, "Class Struggles and National Liberation in Africa," in Bernard Magabane and Nzongola-Ntalaja, eds., *Proletarianization and Class Struggle in Africa*, special issue of *Contemporary Marxism* 6 (Spring 1983): 57–94; Janet MacGaffey, "How to Survive and Become Rich Amidst Devastation: The Second Economy in Zaire," *African Affairs* 8 (1983): 351–366.

Kisombe Kiaku Miusi successfully ran for the Political Bureau in 1977. A successful businessman, he owned a furniture factory, a luxury department store, a national chain of stores, large cattle and poultry farms. He constructed schools, roads, and bridges; he employed over 1500 persons, including 20 university graduates and 30 foreigners. Young and Turner, op. cit., p. 119.

Young and Turner's account of the personal fortune of Mobutu is fascinating as an illustration of how political position enables the manipulation of key economic institutions (ibid., pp. 178–182).

55. Young and Turner, op. cit., pp. 117–119.

56. Samir Amin, "Senegal: The Development of the Senegalese Business Bourgeoisie," in Adebayo Adedej, ed., *Indigenization of African Economics*, (New York: Africana Publishing Co., 1981), pp. 309–321.

57. Hassatou Diallo, "The Economic Situation, Pre and Post-independence, and the Concept of Indigenization," in Adedej, op. cit., p. 326.

58. Amin, "Senegal," p. 318. Amin continues to maintain, in line with his previous theoretical contentions, that "the opportunities for accumulation within the reach of the Senegalese bourgeoisie are extremely limited." However, he does say that "some of the strongest commercial enterprises are contemplating some small and medium state industrial projects." And even though this is "a peripheral bourgeoisie, grafted on to the international market" with the concentration of peripheral capital towards the centre," there are "some obvious signs" that big modern landowners with large incomes from farming will invest in industry. But all of this will depend on government policy, (ibid., p. 320).

59. Ibid., p. 324.

60. Hassatou Diallo, op. cit., p. 323.

61. Cf. K. A. Owusu-Ansah's analysis of state legislative measures in Ghana during the 1970s which promoted the development of business and concentrated a large amount of Ghana's resources in the hands of a very few highly placed persons, in Adedej, op. cit., pp. 133–163.

See also Emeka Ezeife's discussion of the same process in Nigeria (in Adedej, op. cit., pp. 164–186). Ezeife claims that measures such as the Nigerian Enterprises Promotion Decree led to "the emergence of a few Nigerian capitalists and business tycoons at the expense of the masses" (p. 181). The Nigerian Enterprises Promotion Decree offered opportunities to acquire shares in business by the private placing of shares as well as by sale through the stock exchange. Those who benefited were "the elite who were already in business as proprietors and business executives, as well as civil servants, university staff members of the armed forces and other professionals" who had their own savings *or* "effective access to money from institutional lenders." Public sources, for example, the Nigerian Bank for Commerce and Industry as well as the major commercial banks in which the government had substantial or controlling shares, provided a substantial portion of the capital for the purchase of these shares. The mass of the farmers and urban brokers did not participate. The result was a further concentration of the nation's wealth in the hands of "the higher-income group" (p. 182).

Cf. Y. A. Faure and J.-F. Medard, *Etat et Bourgeoisie en Cote-D'Ivoire* (Paris: Editions Karathala, 1982). Mahmood Mamdani, in *Imperialism and Fascism in Uganda* (Trenton, N.J.: Africa World Press, 1984), argues that Idi Amin led a "neo-colonial" "fascist" regime founded on an expanding capitalism. Dianne Bolton, in *Nationalization: A Road to Socialism? The Lessons of Tanzania* (London: Zed Books Ltd., 1985), shows what happens to the distribution of income when a new state bourgeoisie controls the means of production.

62. Marvin Harris, *Cultural Materialism* (New York: Random House, 1980), p. 102. Howard Stein maintains that rather than contrast the colonial and postcolonial periods, the more fascinating comparison is *between* colonial experiences, especially the role of the colonial state in accumulation and class formation. He helps us understand how civil servants captured the state in Tanzania at independence, whereas "an incipient bourgeoisie" succeeded in Kenya. In Tanzania he worries that the "hegemonous group" will become a "non-productive tribute class" ("Theories of the State in Tanzania: A Critical Assessment," *The Journal of Modern African Studies* 23, 1 [1985]: 106).

63. On the remarkable political evolution of Animation Rurale and Community Development organization from popular-based movements to vehicles for professional advancement, see my *Organizing the Rural Poor: Self-Help and the Organizational Bourgeoisie,* forthcoming. Cf. Sheila Carapico, "Self-Help and Development Planning in the Yemen Arab Republic," in Jean-Claude Garcia-Zamor, ed., *Public Participation in Development Planning and Management: Cases from Africa and Asia* (Boulder, Colo.: Westview Press, 1985), pp. 203–234; and Barbara P. Thomas, *Politics, Participation and Poverty: Development Through Self-Help in Kenya* (Boulder, Colo.: Westview Press, 1985).

64. Crawford Young, in an important essay, *Ideology and Development in Africa* (New Haven: Yale University Press, 1982), breathes new life into the study of African ideology. Separating African states into "Afro-Marxist," "populist socialist," and "market-leaning capitalist" categories, Young evaluates their achievements according to six criteria, including economic growth, equality of distribution, and the preservation of human dignity.

65. Richard Jeffries, *Class, Power and Ideology in Ghana* (New York: Cambridge University Press, 1978). Jeffries analyzes the "radical populism" of the railwaymen of Sekondi in terms of processes of class formation.

66. W. G. Clarence-Smith, *Slaves, Peasants and Capitalists in Southern Angola, 1840–1926* (New York: Cambridge University Press, 1979). Clarence-Smith shows how the consolidation of the power of the colonial state created reserves of cheap migrant labor and a distanced ruling class.

67. Patrick Manning, in *Slavery, Colonialism and Economic Growth in Dahomey, 1640–1960* (Cambridge: Cambridge University Press, 1982), conveys a sense of the strong continuity of the dominant classes. The leading merchant and planter families of twentieth-century Dahomey were in large measure those of the nineteenth century, who had dominated Dahomey even before the French conquest. Despite their original dependence on slave labor, they very early turned "their commitment to a capitalist future." Manning also provides valuable data for the debate on "dependency" theory. See my review, "The Road to Economic Stagnation," *Africa Report,* July–August 1984, pp. 73 and 74. See also Bjorn Edsman, *Lawyers in Gold Coast Politics, 1900–1945* (Uppsala: Scandinavian Institute of African Studies, 1979); and Philip Bonner, *Kings, Commoners and Concessionaires: The Evolution and Dissolution of the Nineteenth-Century Swazi State* (Cambridge: Cambridge University Press, 1983).

Emile Vercruijsse, *The Penetration of Capitalism: A West African Case Study* (London: Zed Books Ltd., 1984), focuses on Ghanaian canoe fishing to analyze the transformation of production relations and "trace the process of articulation between the capitalist and the pre-capitalist modes of production in the fishery sector" (p. 130).

See also the valuable studies in Henry Bernstein and Bonnie K. Campbell, eds., *Contradictions of Accumulation in Africa* (Beverly Hills: Sage Publications, 1985). For example, Bonnie K. Campbell, "The Fiscal Crisis of the State: The Case of the Ivory Coast," pp. 267–310, tells us that at least two-thirds of Ivorian investors or promoters of small industries were members of the civil service or held political positions," and ". . . in at least one-third of the firms in which there are private Ivorian interests, there is also state participation" (p. 301).

68. Graham K. Wilson, *Business and Politics: A Comparative Introduction* (Chatham, N.J.: Chatham House Publishers, 1985), stresses how relations between government, business, and politics can vary both within the same country over time and between different capitalist countries at the same time. Andrew Beveridge and Anthony Oberschall, *African Businessmen and Development in Zambia* (Princeton: Princeton University Press, 1979). Other studies that help us better understand the range of the growing power of African business are: Sayre P. Schatz, *Nigerian Capitalism* (Berkeley: University of California Press, 1977); Jan S. Hogendorn, *Nigerian Groundnut Exports: Origins and Early Development* (New York: Oxford University Press, 1979); Stanley B. Greenberg, *Race and State in Capitalist Development* (New Haven: Yale University Press, 1980); Paul T. Kennedy, *Ghanaian Businessmen: From Artisan to Capitalist Entrepreneur in a Dependent Economy* (Munich: Weltforum Verlag, 1980); Nicola Swainson, *The Development of Corporate Capitalism in Kenya 1918–1977;* Steven Langdon, *Multinational Corporations in the Political Economy of Kenya;* R. Graham, *Monopoly Capital and African Development: The Political Economy of the World Aluminum Industry* (London: Zed Press, 1982); Thomas J. Biersteker, *Distortion or Development? Contending Perspectives on the Multinational Corporation* Cambridge: The MIT Press, 1981); Martin Fransman, ed., *Industry and Accumulation in Africa* (London: Heinemann Educational Books, 1982); E. Wayne Nafziger, *The Economics of Political Instability: The Nigerian Biafran War* (Boulder, Colo.: Westview Press, 1983); John Iliffe, *The Emergence of African Capitalism* (Minneapolis: University of Minnesota Press, 1983).

Goran Hyden has traveled a very rapid road from his reluctant, if unflinching, advocacy of a strong bureaucratic apparatus to capture the peasantry ("It is almost inevitable that the socialist modernizer will have to depend on such means as intimidation and coercion": *Beyond Ujaama in Tanzania: Underdevelopment and an Uncaptured Peasantry* [Berkeley: University of California Press, 1980], p. 224) to a new celebration of the freedom of the marketplace and "the need for a real bourgeoisie with roots in African society. . . . It paves the way for productivity gains and economic expansion by eliminating the constraining pre-capitalist structures": *No Shortcuts to Progress: African Development Management in Perspective* (Berkeley: University of California Press, 1983), p. 198.

## Part I  Revolution and the Struggle for Independence

1. See, for example, John Lonsdale, "States and Social Processes in Africa: A Historiographical Survey," *African Studies Review* 24, 2/3 (June/Sept. 1981): 139–225; Bruce J. Berman, "Clientism and Neocolonialism: Centre-Periphery Relations and Political Development in African States," *Studies in Contemporary International Development* 9 (1974): 3–25; and E. A. Brett, *Colonialism and Underdevelopment in East Africa: The Politics of Economic Change, 1919–1939* (London: Heinemann Educational Books, 1973).

2. Although capitalism has always involved exploitation, market forces ordinarily could not drive wages below their "natural" limits, namely, the literal cost of the reproduction of the worker at the prevailing standard of living. Future workers must be fed, sheltered, and protected before they become productive workers, and later, after their work, they must be provided for in their old age. Ordinarily, the cost of education, social security, medicine, health care, burial, and other basics are met by the state out of general revenues, or by taxing the business firms that hire the workers, or out of the workers' own income. In some way, the necessary resources come from within the normal confines of society. However, in Third World societies, these costs have been met by precapitalist or *non*wage rural and household sectors of the economy, which is primarily women's labor; see especially Claude Meillassoux, *Maidens, Meal and Money: Capitalism and the Domestic Community* (New York: Cambridge University Press, 1981). Wim von Binsbergen and Peter Geschire, eds., *Old Modes of Production and Capitalist Encroachment: Anthroplogical Explorations in Africa* (London: Routledge and Kegan Paul Ltd., 1985), offer a series of related case studies which grew out of the confrontation by a group attached to the Leiden African Studies Center with the work of the French Marxist anthropologists Claude Meillassoux, P. P. Rey, Maurice Godelier, and E. Terray.

3. Andre Gundar Frank, *Crisis: In the Third World* (New York: Holmes and Meier Publisher, 1981).

4. G. B. Kay, ed., *The Political Economy of Colonialism in Ghana* (Cambridge; Eng.: Cambridge University Press, 1972).

5. See, inter alia, Eugene Genovese, *The Political Economy of Slavery* (New York: Vintage, 1967).

## Chapter 1 Contradiction, Crisis and Class Conflict

1. See Bruce J. Berman and John M. Lonsdale, "Coping with the Contradictions: The Development of the Colonial State in Kenya, 1895–1914," *Journal of African History* 20 (1979): 487–505, and "Crisis of Accumulation, Coercion and the Colonial State: The Development of the Labor Control System in Kenya, 1919–1929," *Canadian Journal of African Studies* 14, (1980): 55–81; E. A. Brett, *Colonialism and Underdevelopment in East Africa: The Politics of Economic Change, 1919–1939* (New York: NOK, 1977); and the literature review by Simon Clarke, "Capital, Fractions of Capital and the State: 'Neo-Marxist' Analyses of the South African State," *Capital and Class* 5 (1978): 32–77. For initial and useful attempts at analysis in peasant Africa, see G. B. Kay, *The Political Economy of Underdevelopment in Ghana: A Collection of Documents and Statistics, 1900–1960* (London: Cambridge University Press, 1972), and Brett, "Relations of Production, the State and the Ugandan Crisis," *West African Journal of Sociology and Political Science* 1, (1978): 248–284. See also the present author's forthcoming *The State and Underdevelopment in Ghana: The Political Economy of Cocoa, 1900–1976*, and "Underdevelopment, Modes of Production and the State in Colonial Ghana," *African Studies Review* 24, 1 (1981): 21–47.

2. For an elaboration on the "materialist theory of the state," see John Holloway and Sol Picciotto, "Introduction: Towards a Materialist Theory of the State," in Holloway and Picciotto, eds., *State and Capital: A Marxist Debate* (Austin: University of Texas Press, 1978), pp. 1–31, and Berman and Lonsdale, "Crisis of Accumulation."

3. On the "slave mode of production" in Africa, see the contributions included in H. A. Gemery and J. S. Hogendorn, eds., *The Uncommon Market: Essays in the Economic History of the Atlantic Slave Trade* (New York: Academic Press, 1979), especially Martin Klein and Paul E. Lovejoy, "Slavery in West Africa," pp. 181–212.

4. See Ivor Wilks, "Land, Labour, Capital and the Forest Kingdom of Asante: A Model of Early Change," in J. Friedman and R. M. Rowlands, eds., *The Evolution of Social Systems* (London: Duckworth, 1977), pp. 487–534.

5. See John Mensah Sarbah, *Fanti Customary Law* (London: William Clowes and Sons Ltd., 1897), especially Chapter 6; Great Britain, Colonial Office, West African Lands Committee, *Minutes of Evidence* (London: H.M.S.O. [1917]), testimony by William Brandford Griffith, p. 496, and F. W. Crowther, p. 361. Griffith made reference to an article on the subject in the *Journal of the Society of Comparative Legislation* 7 (1906): 275.

6. See J. E. Casely Hayford, *Gold Coast Native Institutions* (London, Frank Cass, 1970; first published in 1903).

7. Wilks, *Asante in the Nineteenth Century: The Structure and Evolution of a Political Order* (London and New York: Cambridge University Press, 1975).

8. T. Edward Bowdich, *Mission From Cape Coast to Ashantee* (London: Frank Cass, 1966; first published in 1819), and Brodie Cruickshank, *Eighteen Years on the Gold Coast* (London: Frank Cass, 1967; first published in 1853).

9. See R. S. Rattray, *Ashanti Law and Constitution* (London: Oxford University Press, 1929), especially Chapters 4–6.

10. Marion Johnson, "Migrants Progress, Part I," "Part II," *Ghana Geographical Association Bulletin* 9, 2 (1964): 4–27, and 10, 1 (1965): 13–40. See also Polly Hill, *Migrant Cocoa-Farmers of Southern Ghana: A Study in Rural Capitalism* (New York: Cambridge University Press, 1963).

11. Johnson, "Migrants Progress, Part I" and "Part II."

12. Great Britain, Colonial Office, *Economic Agriculture on the Gold Coast, 1889* (London: H.M.S.O., 1890, C. 5897–40 [On cover, No. 110]), p. 11.

13. See Colin Newbury, "Prices and Profitability in Early Nineteenth Century West African Trade," in Claude Meillassoux, ed., *The Development of Indigenous Trade and Markets in West Africa* (London: Oxford University Press, 1971), pp. 92–94.

14. The Reverend E. Schrenk testified before the 1865 Select Committee of West Africa that while he welcomed the effect of trade in "enabling the native people to see different European articles which must enlarge their views," he lamented the fact that "cheap imported manufacturers tend to oust the products of native industry, remarking that no one along the coast would think of making iron and textiles any longer although six days' journey into the interior people were still doing so": quoted in David Kimble, *A Political History of Ghana: The Rise of Gold Coast Nationalism, 1850–1928* (London: The Clarendon Press for Oxford University Press, 1971), p. 7.

15. Anthony G. Hopkins, "Economic Imperialism in West Africa: Lagos, 1880–92," *Economic History Review* 21, 3 (1968): 587–573.

16. See Edward Reynolds, *Trade and Economic Change on the Gold Coast, 1807–1874* (Essex: Longman, 1974), and Klein and Lovejoy, "Slavery in West Africa."

17. See especially Sir Frederick D. Lugard (Lord Lugard), *The Dual Mandate in British Tropical Africa* (Edinburgh and London: William Blackwood and Sons, 1922), Chapter 18.

18. Quoted in Kimble, *A Political History*, p. 462.

19. Great Britain, Colonial Office, West African Lands Committee [WALC], *Draft Report* [1917], pp. 9–10.

20. Ibid., pp. 12–13.

21. See Reginald H. Green and Stephen Hymer, "Cocoa in the Gold Coast: A Study of Relations between African Farmers and Agricultural Experts," *Journal of Economic History* 26, 3 (1966): 299–319.

22. Kay, *The Political Economy of Colonialism in Ghana*, Part I, pp. 12 and 36.

23. Gold Coast, *The Gold Coast, 1931* [A. W. Cardinall, Census Officer] (Accra: Government Printer, 1932), p. 100.

24. Ibid., p. 201.

25. WALC, *Draft Report*, p. 34.

26. Ibid., p. 103. For a historical sketch of land law in Ghana, see S. K. B. Asante, "Interests in Land in Customary Law of Ghana—A New Appraisal," *Yale Law Journal* 74 (1965): 848–885, and *Property Law and Social Goals in Ghana, 1844–1966* (Accra: Ghana Universities Press, 1975).

27. WALC, *Minutes of Evidence*, p. 369. An indication of reliance upon certain imported foods comes from the list of items exempted from the items boycotted during the 1937–1938 holdup and boycott. See Rhoda Howard, "Differential Class Participation in an African Protest Movement: The Ghana Cocoa Boycott of 1937–38," *Canadian Journal of African Studies* 10, 3 (1976): 476–477.

28. Frederick Gordon Guggisberg, *The Gold Coast: A Review of the Events of 1920–1926 and the Prospects of 1927–1928* (Accra: Government Printer, 1927), p. 244.

29. Jarle Simensen, "Rural Mass Action in the Context of Anti-Colonial Protest: The Asafo Movement in Akim Abuakwa, Ghana," *Canadian Journal of African Studies* 8, 1 (1974): 29. See also his "Nationalism from Below—The Akyem Abuakwa Example," Historical Society of Ghana, *Akyem Abuakwa and the Politics of the Inter-War Period in Ghana* (Basel, Switzerland: Basle Afrika Bibliographien, 1975), pp. 31–60.

30. Simensen, "Rural Mass Action," p. 30.

31. See Guggisberg, *The Gold Coast*, pp. 23–24.

32. See P. T. Bauer, *West African Trade: A Study of Competition, Oligopoly and Monopoly in a Changing Economy* (New York: Augustus M. Kelley, 1967).

33. Howard, "Differential Class Participation."

34. Johnson, "Part II," p. 32.

35. C. Y. Shephard, *Report on the Economics of Peasant Agriculture in the Gold Coast* (Accra: Government Printer, 1936), p. 7.

36. Ibid., pp. 6–7.

37. See Hill, *Migrant Cocoa Farmers*.

38. Ibid., p. 1.

39. Major G. St. Orde-Browne, *Report on Labour Conditions in West Africa*, Cmd. 6277 (London: H.M.S.O., 1941), pp. 8–9.

40. Gold Coast, Department of Mines, *Reports, 1900–1939* (Accra: Government Printer).

41. Gold Coast, *Legislative Council Debates*, March 17, 1935 (Accra: Government Printer), p. 38.

42. Ibid., March 19, 1935, p. 9.

43. Ibid., February 20, 1941, p. 43.

44. Great Britain, Colonial Office, *Report of the Commission on the Marketing of West African Cocoa*, Cmd. 5845 (London: H.M.S.O., 1938 [The *Nowell Commission Report*]), Appendix F.

45. Gold Coast, Department of Agriculture, *Annual Reports, 1940–1947* (Accra: Government Printer).

46. Quoted in K. A. Busia, *The Position of the Chief in the Modern Political System of Ashanti* (London: Frank Cass, 1968), pp. 193–194.

47. *Legislative Council Debates*, February 25, 1942, p. 110.

48. Ibid., September 29, 1942, pp. 3–4.

49. See Lord Hailey, *Native Administration and Political Development in British Tropical Africa*, Confidential Report to the Colonial Office, 1940–1942 (Kraus Reprint, 1979) , Chapters One and Three.

50. Quoted in Busia, *The Position of the Chief*, p. 159.

51. Hailey, *Native Administration*, p. 133.

52. See Beverly Grier, "Cocoa, Class Formation and the State in Ghana," Ph.D. dissertation, Yale University, 1979, Chapter Three.

53. See Great Britain, Colonial Office, *Report on Cocoa Control in Africa, 1939–1943, and Statement on Future Policy*, Cmd. 6554 (London: H.M.S.O., September 1944), and *Statement on Future Marketing of West African Cocoa*, Cmd. 6950 (London: H.M.S.O., November 1946). See also Bauer, *West African Trade*.

54. For further discussion on the marketing board system and the controversy surrounding it, see Bauer, *West African Trade*, and Bob Fitch and Mary Oppenheimer, *Ghana: End of an Illusion* (New York and London: Monthly Review Press, 1966), pp. 40–47.

55. See Hailey, *Native Administration*, Chapter Three.

56. K. A. Busia, *Report on a Social Survey of Sekondi-Takoradi* (London: Crown Agents for the Colonies, 1950), p. 89.

57. See Great Britain, Colonial Office, Gold Coast, *Report to His Excellency the Governor by the Committee on Constitutional Reforms* [Chairman: J. Henley Coussey] (London: H.M.S.O., 1949), Colonial Number 248.

## Chapter 2   Anatomy of African Class Consciousness

1. J. S. Saul, "Africa," in G. Ionescu and Ernest Gellnor, eds., *Populism: Its Meanings and National Characteristics* (London: Weidenfeld & Nicolson, 1969), pp. 122–150.

2. Naomi Chazan, *An Anatomy of Ghanaian Politics: Managing Political Recession, 1969– 1982* (Boulder, Colo.: Westview Press, 1983), p. 143.

3. Cf. Peter Gutkind, "Reformism, Populism and Proletarianism in Urban Africa," *Ufahamu* 8, 3 (1978): 24–60.

4. Max Gluckman, *Rituals of Rebellion in South-East Africa* (Manchester: Manchester University Press, 1954), and Max Gluckman, *Order and Rebellion in Tribal Africa* (New York: Free Press, 1963). Gluckman's work helps to flesh out Shivji's analysis of "silent class struggle" in African systems. See I. G. Shivji, *Class Struggles in Tanzania* (London: Heinemann, 1976).

5. See Gutkind, op. cit., pp. 42–49.

6. Peter Lloyd, *A Third World Proletariat?* (London: Allen & Unwin, 1982).

7. *Kwahu District Record Book 1923–1928* (Accra: Ghana National Archives, Adm 92/1), p. 4.

8. Ibid., pp. 4–5.

9. *Census Report 1921*, pp. 49–66.

10. For examples of violence associated with such politics, see *Report on Ashanti for 1920*, (Accra: Government Printing Office, 1921), p. 22.

11. For the situation in Elmina, see *Winneba District Record Book 1910–1955* (Accra: Ghana National Archives, Adm 62/2), pp. 2–8.

12. The most authoritative study on *Asafo* is J. C. DeGraft Johnson, *The Asafo Organization of the Gold Coast: Sessional Paper No. XII of 1931–1932* (Accra, n.d.). See also Ibid., pp. 11, passim.

13. *Winneba Native Affairs* (Ghana National Archives, SNA11/1136); *Winneba District Record Book 1910–1955*, pp. 2–8, 19–27.

14. *See Report on the Police Department for the Year 1915* (Accra: 1916), p. 12.

15. *New Orders and Regulations Inaugurated by the Whole Kwahu Asafos at Abetifi* (Ghana National Archives, SNA 738, Adm 11/738).

16. *Asafo: Origin and the Powers of* (Ghana National Archives, SNA 738, Adm 11/738).

17. *Kwahu Native Affairs* (Ghana National Archives, Adm 11/1445).

18. *Asafo: Origins and the Powers of*.

19. Kwahu Native Affairs (Adm 11/1445).

20. Ibid.

21. *Kwahu District Record Book (1923–1928)* (Ghana National Archives, Adm 91/48), p. 4.

22. See Johnson, op. cit., pp. 54 ff.

23. *Kwahu Native Affairs* (Adm 11/1445).

24. *Kwahu District Record Book 1923–1928,* p. 64.

25. *Chiefs Record Book—Kwahu District* (Ghana National Archives, Adm 92/1), p. 101.

26. Ibid. The district commissioner recorded in 1932 a similar description of Kwahu chiefs which illustrates the dialectics of political development in Kwahu in the 1930s: "The great difficulty in the way of the successful working of the State Council is that the Chiefs are always at loggerheads among themselves. It is a great pity. I have personally never known a State in Ghana where the Chiefs are so constantly bickering. They also are continually interfering with each other's divisions and even with each other's tribunals. In fact if a man here gets a judgment given against him in one tribunal he has only to go to any other and the Chief there will help him to fight the judgment. I have tried to teach them that until they can get on well together and work for the good of the State instead of each for his own petty interests they will always be bound to have trouble from the *Asafo.* It is only natural that, when the latter see how disunited the Chiefs are, they should take advantage of it to try to get their own way" (ibid., p. 205).

27. See, for example, *Minutes of Emergency Session of the Central Provincial Council of Chiefs,* 26th–28th October, 1937 (Ghana National Archives).

28. *Kwahu District Record Book 1937–1952,* p. 11.

29. The best account of this policy is W. E. F. Ward, *A History of Ghana* (London: Allen and Unwin, Ltd., 1952), pp. 351–367. For an account of the modernizing outcomes of systematizing colonial administration in the Ahafo division of Ashanti, see John Dunn and A. F. Robertson, *Dependence and Opportunity: Political Change in Ahafo* (London: Cambridge University Press, 1973), p. 153–173.

30. *Kwahu District Record Book 1937–1952,* pp. 13–14, 162–163.

31. Ibid., p. 169.

32. *Kumasi District Record Book 1926–1951* (Ghana National Archives, Adm 176/9), p. 137.

33. Ibid., p. 400.

34. *Report on Ashanti for 1920* (Accra: 1920), p. 22 ff.

35. *Kumasi District Record Book 1918–1929* (Ghana National Archives, Adm 176/8), p. 101.

36. *Akim Abuakwa Native Affairs* (Ghana National Archives, Adm 11/1096), p. 21.

37. I first discovered this feature of agrarian populism during my research into Sierra Leone political development some two decades ago. See Martin Kilson, *Political Change in a West African State* (Cambridge, Mass.: Harvard University Press, 1966), passim.

38. *Report on Ashanti for the Period April 1926–March 1927* (Accra: 1927), p. 20.

39. *Report on Ashanti for 1920,* p. 4.

40. Cf. Chazan, op. cit., p. 144.

41. Cf. John Iliffe, *The Emergence of African Capitalism* (Minneapolis: University of Minnesota Press, 1983), pp. 40–42. Cf. also Robert Rotberg and Ali Mazrui, eds., *Protest and Power in Black Africa* (New York: Oxford University Press, 1970).

42. See *The Economist,* January 3, 1981, pp. 27–28. See also *The Washington Post,* May 12, 1982.

43. See George Balandier, *Afrique Ambigue* (Paris: Librarie Plan, 1957).

44. See Kilson, *Political Change in a West African State,* pp. 252–264.

45. See Martin Kilson, "African Autocracy," *Africa Today,* April 1966.

46. Joan Vincent, *African Elite: Big Men of a Small Town* (New York: University of Illinois Press, 1971), pp. 3 ff. See also Julian Steward, ed., *Contemporary Change in Traditional Societies: Three African Tribes in Transition* (Urbana: University of Illinois Press, 1967), and Thomas Callaghy's excellent analysis of the traditionalist cloaking of modern class and power patterns in Moboutu's Zaire, in *The State-Society Struggle: Zaire in Comparative Perspective* (New York: Columbia University Press, 1984), pp. 182–184, 352 ff.

47. Interestingly enough, both bourgeois and socialist theorists in the nineteenth century understood this aspect of democracy—theorists as diverse as Walter Bagheot and Karl Marx. Cf. W. W. Rostow, *The Stages of Economic Growth* (New York: Cambridge University Press, 1971), and especially Barrington Moore, *Social Origins of Dictatorship and Democracy: Lord and Peasant in the Making of the Modern World* (Boston: Beacon Press, 1966).

48. Karl Marx, *Capital* (New York: Scribner & Son, 1936), p. 813.

49. See Stanislave Andreski, *Parasitism and Subversion: The Case of Latin America* (New York: Pantheon Books, 1966). See also David Collier, ed., *The New Authoritarianism in Latin America* (Princeton, N.J.: Princeton University Press, 1979).

50. See, for example, David Gould, *Bureaucratic Corruption and Underdevelopment in the Third World: The Case of Zaire* (New York: Pergamon Press, 1980).

51. *The Wall Street Journal,* January 4, 1982, p. 28. See also Una Lele, "Rural Africa: Modernization, Equity, and Long-Term Development," *Science* February 6, 1981, pp. 547–553; and Rene Dumont, *False Start in Africa* (New York: Praeger Publishers, 1969).

52. Chris Allen and Gavin Williams, eds., *Sub-Saharan Africa* (New York: Monthly Review Press, 1982), pp. 82–83.

53. Victoria Brittain, "Ghana's Precarious Revolution," *New Left Review,* July–August 1983, pp. 50, 51. See also Emmanuel Hansen and Paul Collins, "The Army, the State, and the Rawlings Revolution in Ghana," *African Affairs,* January 1980, pp. 3–22.

54. Nii K. Bentsi-Enchill, "Ghana's Public Tribunals," *West Africa,* February 27, 1984, pp. 433–434. Further economic pressures finally ended the tribunals in 1985. Cf. KWESI Botchway, "Ghana: The Right Signals," *West Africa,* January 28, 1985, pp. 146–148.

55. Cf. Moore, *Social Origins of Dictatorship and Democracy.*

56. On the Ayatollah-controlled populist regime in post-Shah Iran, see Terrence Smith, "Iran: Five Years of Fanaticism," *The New York Times Magazine,* February 12, 1984. For African syncretistic religious leaders who might lead an Ayatollah-type rebellion in politically decaying African regimes, see Elizabeth Isichei, ed., *Varieties of Christian Experience in Nigeria* (London: Macmillan, 1982).

57. *West Africa,* May 6, 1985, p. 876.

58. See Gregory Jaynes, "At Least 1,000 People Killed as Nigeria Crushes Islamic Sect," *New York Times,* January 12, 1985.

59. For the range of restorationist sects and groups in African states, see James W. Fernandez, "The Ethnic Communion: Inter-Ethnic Recruitment in African Religious Movement," *Journal of African Studies,* Summer 1975, pp. 131–147. For a case study of a restorationst-type group in Senegal which, though now in intricate regime-sustaining ties with the ruling class, could under crisis situations play a major rebellious role, see Momar C. Diop, "L'état, la confrèrie mouride et les paysans Senégalais," *Travail Capital et Société,* April 1984, pp. 44–64.

60. See Martin Kilson, *Chiefs, Peasants and Politicians: Grass-Roots Politics in Ghana 1900–1980s* (in preparation).

61. Chazan, *An Anatomy of Ghanaian Politics,* p. 144.

62. Catherine Newberry, "The Tyranny of Cassava: A Women's Tax Revolt in Eastern Zaire," *Canadian Journal of African Studies* 18, 1 (1984): 39–43 ff.

## Chapter 3 Wars of Liberation and the International System

1. Joel S. Migdal, *Peasants, Politics, and Revolution: Pressures toward Political Change in the Third World* (Princeton, N.J.: Princeton University Press, 1974), p. 233.

2. David Ben-Gurion, *Israel: A Personal History* (New York: Funk & Wagnalls, Inc., 1971).

3. Ibid., p. 71.

4. As Ben-Gurion states (ibid., p. 67), the "Zionist General Council met at the beginning of April 1948, mainly to approve the decision made at the beginning of March by the Zionist Executive and the National Council to establish a Provisional Government and Parliament, even before the British departed." Thus the decision has been made not to seek U.N. aid in partitioning Palestine as that body had proposed.

5. Ibid., p. 79.

6. *Africa News,* July 29, 1976, p. 6.

7. United Nations, General Assembly, 31st Session, October 25, 1976, *Report of the Special Committe on the Situation with Regard to the Implementation of the Declaration on the Granting of Independence to Colonial Countries and Peoples* (A/31/23/Add. 5), pp. 17–18.

8. The Polisario Front stated that the declaration of the Saharan Arab Democratic Republic was necessary to prevent a juridical vacuum after Spain, the colonial ruler, stepped out. "Spain had the internationally recognized administration," said Mahmoud Abdel Fettah, "but it had no right to sell our sovereignty" (*Africa News,* February 21, 1977, p. 7).

9. See Ben-Gurion, op. cit., p. 65.

10. The Accords were a facade through which Morocco and Mauritania sought to gain control over the territory. Prior to the Accords, Morocco and Mauritania had already agreed to partition the territory. Moreover, Morocco promised Spain 35 percent of future phosphate production from the territory. It is clear that the inhabitants were not meant to exercise their right of self-determination. For a complete discussion of the illegality of the Accords, see U.S. Congress, House, Committee on Foreign Affairs, *U.S. Policy and the Conflict in the Western Sahara: Hearings Before the Subcommittees on Africa and on International Organizations,* 96th Cong., 1st sess. 1979, app. 1 (hereinafter cited as *Hearings*).

11. France had claimed Algeria as an integral part of Franch since the nineteenth century. At the time of the announcement of the Algerian Republic, France was firmly entrenched in metropolitan Algeria.

12. Mohammed Bedjaoui, *Law and the Algerian Revolution* (Brussels: International Association of Democratic Lawyers, 1961), p. 122.

13. According to Philippe Herreman ("Nous sommes condamnés à réussir dit-on dans les milieux algériens de Tunis," *Le Monde,* March 17, 1961, p. 2, July 5, 1961, p. 1), the Provisional Government of the Algerian Republic rejected suggestions from certain French quarters that northern Algeria might be given independence while France retained control of the Algerian Sahara with its petroleum and natural gas resources.

14. Morocco and Mauritania had already announced the partition and annexation of the territory.

15. Virginia Thompson and Richard Adloff, *The Western Saharans: Background to Conflict* (Totowa, N.J.: Barnes & Noble Books, 1980 , p. 257.

16. Ibid., p. 268, n. 31.

17. For the text, see *International Legal Materials* 2 (1963): 773.

18. *Africa News,* March 22, 1982, p. 6.

19. Thompson and Adloff, op. cit., p. 257.

20. Ibid.

21. Ibid.

22. On September 23, 1974, Morocco sent a letter to Spain requesting that Spain consent to having their claim to the Western Sahara adjudicated by the International Court of Justice (U.N. Doc. A/9771 (1974), Annex).

23. Mauritania also claimed the Western Sahara, and thus, on December 13, 1974, when the General Assembly of the United Nations requested an advisory opinion on the territory from the International Court of Justice, included was a request for an examination of Mauritania's claim (United Nations, General Assembly, 29th Session, 1974, G.A. Res. 3292, *Official Records* [A/ 9631], Supp. 31, pp. 103–104 .

24. In August 1974 the first goal adopted as part of a National Action Program by the Second Popular Congress of the Polisario Front was national liberation and complete independence of the Western Sahara; see *Africa News,* July 29, 1976, p. 6.

25. Bedjaoui, op. cit., p. 126.

26. An example would be the continued threats by Morocco, and initially Mauritania, to withdraw from the Organization of African Unity should that body grant recognition to the Polisario Front; see *Middle East Research & Information Project* 45 (1976): 6 (hereinafter cited as MERIP).

27. See U.N. Charter, art. 2, para. 1, in *Statutes at Large* 59:1031, or *United Nations Treaty Series* No. 993.

28. See ibid., para. 7.

29. Bedjaoui, op. cit, p. 126.

30. *Africa News,* July 29, 1976, p. 12.

31. Ibid., November 15, 1976, p. 11.

32. Ibid., September 4, 1978, p. 11.

33. See U.S. Congress, House, Committee on Foreign Affairs, *Arms for Morocco? U. S. Policy Toward the Conflict in the Western Sahara: Report of a Study Mission to Morocco, the Western Sahara, Mauritania, Algeria, Liberia, Spain, and France, August 5–18, 1979,* 96th Cong., 1st sess., 1980, app. 3 and 6 (hereinafter cited as *Report*).

34. See Khalfa Mameri, *Les Nations Unies face à la "Question algérienne" (1954–1962)* (Algiers: Société Nationale d'Edition et de Diffusion, 1969).

35. Flora Lewis, *New York Times,* August 7, 1981, sec. A, p. 23.

36. *Toledo Blade,* November 15, 1981, sec. D, p. 3.

37. Ben-Gurion, op. cit, p. 80.

38. Bedjaoui, op. cit, p. 85.

39. *Africa News,* July 29, 1976, p. 6.

40. This is evidenced by the resolutions adopted by international organizations which call for the exercise of the right of self-determination in the disputed territory. These resolutions are invariably adopted by numbers in excess of the number of states in that body that recognize the liberation party's proclaimed state. An example would be the Organization of African Unity resolution calling for a referendum in the Western Sahara which was adopted by thirty-three votes when only twenty-six states in that body recognized the Saharan Arab Democratic Republic; see *Report,* app. 3. Conversely, if there were no or very few states that recognized the liberation

party's proclaimed state, such a resolution would have been much harder to pass, let alone be brought to the floor for a vote.

41. The continually escalating number of states that recognize the Saharan Arab Democratic Republic clearly demonstrates this.

42. Djamila Amrane, "La Femme algérienne et la guerre de libèration nationale: 1954–1962," in Université d'Oran, *Cahiers du C.D.S.H.: Acts des journées d'étude et de réflexion sur les femmes algériennes* (Oran: Centre de Documentation des Sciences Humaines, 1980 , p. 204.

43. See Tony Hodges, *Historical Dictionary of Western Sahara,* African Historical Dictionaries No. 35 (Metuchen, N.J.: The Scarecrow Press, Inc., 1982), pp. 360–361. See also Anne Lippert, *The Saharawi Refugees: Origins and Organization, 1975–1985* (Ada, Ohio: SPSC Letter, 1985).

44. This goal is clearly codified in the Algerian constitution of 1976 wherein all barriers based upon sexual discrimination are suppressed by the state, with all citizens equal before the law and eligible for the National Assembly. For the full text, see Tabrizi Bensalah, *La République algérienne,* "Comment ils sont gouvernés" collection (Paris: Librairie Générale de Droit et de Jurisprudence, 1979), annexe 2.

45. As has the National Liberation Front in Algeria, the Polisario Front has codified this goal in the Constitution of the Saharan Arab Democratic Republic under articles 4 and 6 (hereinafter cited as Constitution). For the full text, see Hodges, *Historical Dictionary,* pp. 307–309.

46. See Constitution, art. 8.

47. The Polisario Front has dispensed with surnames such as "son or daughter of" to further minimize tribal allegiances; see Lippert, *Saharawi Refugees.* Also, the Polisario Front has sought to eradicate slavery, which, though not widespread, had been confined to people of black African origin; see Hodges, *Historical Dictionary,* p. 322.

48. See Constitution, art. 7 and 8.

49. See ibid., art. 3 and 11.

50. For a complete discussion, see Anne Lippert, "Algerian Women's Access to Power: 1962–1985," in this volume.

51. *Africa News,* December 20, 1976, p. 7.

52. Since the international system is comprised of sovereign states, only states can be members of international organizations; see U.N. Charter and OAU Charter. Moreover, treaties are by definition agreements between states; see Vienna Convention on the Law of Treaties, opened for signature, May 23, 1969, art. 2, par. 1(a), U.N. Doc. A/CONF 39/27 (1969), p. 289.

53. Michael Akehurst, *A Modern Introduction to International Law,* Minerva Series of Students' Handbooks No. 25, 3 rd ed. (London: George Allen and Unwin, 1977), p. 58.

54. Thompson and Adloff, op. cit., p. 257.

55. Ibid., p. 258.

56. See Ian Brownlie, *African Boundaries: A Legal and Diplomatic Encyclopaedia* (Los Angeles: University of California Press, 1979).

57. See MERIP, p. 3.

58. See Anne Lippert, "Emergence or Submergence of a Potential State: The Struggle in Western Sahara, *Africa Today* 24 (1977): 41. See also *Western Sahara and the Struggle of the Saharoui People for Self-Determination: Dossier* (Rome: International League for the Rights and Liberation of Peoples, 1978).

59. Ibid. See also MERIP, pp. 4 and 6.

60. *League of Nations Treaty Series* 165: 19. See also *Restatement of the Foreign Relations Law of the United States* 4 (1965), which defines a state as an entity that has a defined territory and population under the control of a government and that engages in foreign relations. For a complete discussion, see James Crawford, *The Creation of States in International Law* (New York: Oxford University Press, 1979).

61. U.N. Doc. A/10481-S/11902 (1975), Annex, cited in A/31/23/Add., p. 13.

62. For a complete discussion of the legality of the Saharan Arab Democratic Republic, see *Hearings,* app. 1.

63. MERIP, p. 6.

64. The Polisario Front initially controlled two-thirds of the territory; see *African Research Bulletin* (November 1975), p. 3837.

65. Morocco and Mauritania asserted that the Saharans welcomed the annexations (*Africa News,* July 29, 1976, p. 12).

66. "Organe central du parti du Front de Libération Nationale," *Révolution africaine* 82 (June 1981): 82.

67. *Africa News,* December 15, 1980, p. 5.

68. An example would be the submission to the United Nations in the fall of 1976 of a list of 237 names of Moroccans killed in battle during the first six months of 1976. Also, submitted was a list of Moroccan and Mauritanian prisoners who, the Polisario Front stated, would be treated according to the Geneva Convention of 1949 on the Treatment of Prisoners (*Africa News*, February 21, 1977, p. 9).

69. Ibid.

70. MERIP, p. 6.

71. Algeria, Angola, Benin, Burundi, Guinea-Bissau, Democratic People's Republic of Korea, Madagascar, Mozambique, Ruanda, and Togo (U.N. Doc. A/31/23/Add. 5 [October 25, 1976], p. 18).

72. Eldon Van Cleef Greenberg, "Law and the Conduct of the Algerian Revolution," *Harvard International Law Journal* 11 (1970): 40.

73. See *Le Monde*, August 11, 1959, p. 5.

74. For the text of the Algerian accession to the Geneva Conventions of 1949, see *White Paper on the Application of the Geneva Conventions of 1949 to the French-Algerian Conflict* (New York: Provisional Government of the Algerian Republic, 1960), app. 6 (hereinafter cited as *White Paper*).

75. Greenberg, loc. cit., p. 44.

76. See Maurice Flory, "Algérie et droit international," *Annuaire français de droit international* 5 (1959): 826.

77. Ibid; see also Greenberg, loc. cit., pp. 42–43.

78. A news magazine correspondent reported that "the rebels can count on the encouragement, tacit support, or at least the silence of 8,000,000 Algerians" (*Time*, March 12, 1956, p. 30).

79. Greenberg, loc. cit., p. 46.

80. Morocco initially maintained that the situation in the Sahara was "normal." But on July 9, 1976, King Hassan stated: "The sons of the Moroccan people are dying every day in the Sahara." He named Algeria as the enemy and reiterated that the Saharans welcomed their Moroccan brothers (*Africa News*, February 21, 1977, p. 10).

81. Ibid., September 4, 1978, p. 11; see also *Jeune Afrique* No. 924 (September 20, 1978): 32.

82. *Africa News*, January 10, 1977, p. 12.

83. Ibid., March 30, 1979, p. 10.

84. Ibid., pp. 4 and 10.

85. Ibid., December 11, 1978, p. 10.

86. See *White Paper*, p. 12 and app. 4.

87. See Bedjaoui, op. cit, Chap. 2; see also Greenberg, loc. cit., pp. 41–42.

88. Bedjaoui, op. cit., p. 138.

89. Speech by M. Auguste, 14 sess., 1st commission, 1076th sitting, December 5, 1959, quoted in ibid., p. 140.

90. Ibid., p. 141.

91. *White Paper*.

92. These are even expressly enumerated as the purposes of the *White Paper* (p. 1).

93. Flory, loc. cit., p. 826.

94. Quoted in Jean Charpentier, "La France et la GPRA," *Annuaire français de droit international* 7 (1969): 867.

95. Greenberg, loc. cit, p. 45.

96. *Africa News*, November 15, 1976, p. 2.

97. Ibid., February 21, 1977, p. 9.

98. These values are even codified within the Charter of the Organization of African Unity. Moreover, the Organization of African Unity has even upheld the sanctity of colonial boundaries over secessionist movements; see *International Legal Materials* 6 (1967): 1234.

99. MERIP, p. 6.

100. U.N. Doc. A/31/23/Add. 5 (October 25, 1976), p. 18.

101. *Africa News*, January 10, 1977, p. 2.

102. Ibid.

103. Ibid., February 21, 1977, p. 9.

104. Ibid., March 7, 1977, p. 5.

105. Ibid., p. 6.

106. Ibid., pp. 5–6.

107. Ibid., June 13, 1977, p. 5.

108. Ibid.

109. Ibid., June 27, 1977, p. 6.

110. Ibid., July 18, 1977, pp. 3–4.

111. Ibid., August 1, 1977, p. 12.

112. Ibid., July 18, 1977, pp. 3–4.

113. Ibid., August 1, 1977, p. 12.

114. Ibid.

115. Ibid., July 18, 1977, pp. 3–4.

116. The first special summit was an attempt to mediate the fighting in Angola in 1975.

117. The summit was initially shifted from Zambia to Gabon due to security problems which Zambia was experiencing along its border with Rhodesia. Gabon subsequently withdrew its offer to host the summit due to lack of finances.

118. See Thompson and Adloff, op. cit., pp. 266–267; see also *Africa News*, October 16, 1978, p. 10, and March 20, 1978, p. 12.

119. *Africa News*, July 17, 1978, p. 2.

120. See *New York Times*, March 15, 1979, sec. A, p. 15; see also *Africa News*, February 9, 1979, p. 9.

121. Bedjaoui, op. cit, p. 139.

122. "Organe central du parti du Front de Libération Nationale," loc. cit., p. 82.

123. See Thompson and Adloff, op. cit, p. 261; see also *Africa News*, December 11, 1978, p. 4.

124. *Africa News*, December 11, 1978, p. 4.

125. Ibid.

126. See Thompson and Adloff, op. cit, p. 260. For discussion of Morocco's growing diplomatic isolation, see Tony Hodges, *Western Sahara: The Roots of a Desert War* (Westport, Conn.: Laurence Hill & Company, 1983), pp. 307–320.

127. *Africa News*, March 16, 1979, p. 12.

128. Ibid.

129. Ibid., July 27, 1979, p. 2.

130. Ibid.

131. For the text of the resolution, see *Report*, app. 3.

132. *Africa News*, August 3, 1979, p. 9.

133. *Report*, p. 9.

134. For the text of the treaty, see ibid, app. 2.

135. "Organe central du parti du Front de Libération Nationale," loc. cit., p. 82.

136. For the text of the declaration, see *Report*, app. 5.

137. For the text of the resolution, see *Report*, app. 5.

138. "Organe central du parti du Front de Libération Nationale," loc. cit., p. 82.

139. During the Organization of African Unity summit meeting, General Secretary Edem Kodjo even told a press conference that, if a majority of states indicated support for the Polisario in writing, it would be formally recognized (*Africa News*, July 6, 1981, p. 2).

140. See ibid., July 6, 1981, p. 2.

141. Ibid.

142. See *Report*, app. 4, p. 5.

143. See ibid., app. 3, p. 3.

144. See *Africa News*, January 4, 1982, p. 5.

145. Ibid., August 31, 1981, p. 4.

146. Ibid., p. 5.

147. See ibid., January 4, 1982, p. 5.

148. See ibid., October 26, 1981, p. 11; Hodges, *Western Sahara*, p. 290.

149. See *New York Times*, October 14, 1981, sec. A, p. 8, and October 15, 1981, sec. A., p. 8; see also *Africa News*, October 26, 1981, p. 11.

150. *Africa News*, October 26, 1981, p. 11, and January 4, 1982, p. 5.

151. After Guelta Zemmour was recaptured, a BBC reporter stated that there was no sign that Soviet-made tanks and missiles had been used. He also reported that the local Moroccan commander could not produce evidence of the tanks and missile launchers that Morocco claimed to have destroyed (ibid., October 26, 1981, p. 11).

152. *New York Times*, October 15, 1981, sec. A, p. 8; *Africa News*, October 26, 1981, p. 11.

153. Assistant Secretary of Defense Francis West justified increased military assistance because of SAM-6 attacks. The U.S. State Department, however, confirmed that no such attacks

occurred; see *Africa News,* April 5, 1982, p. 8. For a discussion of U.S. military assistance, see Hodges, *Western Sahara,* pp. 355–364.

154. See *Africa News,* February 15, 1982, p. 10.

155. Ibid.; Hodges, *Western Sahara,* p. 360.

156. After Guelta Zemmour, in December 1981, U.S. instructors began training Moroccan pilots in antimissile tactics (Hodges, *Western Sahara,* p. 360 . For the Polisario Front's allegations, see *Africa News,* February 15, 1982, p. 9.

157. See *Africa News,* March 1, 1982, p. 3.

158. Ibid., February 15, 1982, p. 10, and March 1, 1982, p. 3.

159. Francisco Villar, *El Proceso de autodeterminación del Sahara* (Valencia: F. Torres, 1982), p. 395.

160. *Africa News,* February 15, 1982, p. 10.

161. See ibid., January 10, 1983, p. 4. Moreover, on May 27, 1982, the U.S. and Morocco entered into an agreement for American use of Moroccan military facilities with both parties agreeing "to take all agreed measures for cooperation in the military field" (U.S. State Department, *Treaties and Other International Acts Series,* 10399).

162. See *Africa News,* March 1, 1982, pp. 2–3; March 22, 1982, p. 2; and January 10, 1983, p. 5.

163. See ibid., March 22, 1982, p. 6.

164. Ibid., p. 11.

165. Morocco resorted to attempting to deny the organization a quorum. Initially Morocco was aided by several countries, including Egypt, Somalia, and Uganda, who boycotted the summit in Tripoli, Libya, in protest of Muammar Quaddafi's policies (ibid., August 2, 1982, pp. 1–3).

166. Egypt, Kenya, Malawi, Mauritania, and Nigeria (ibid., March 22, 1982, p. 6).

167. Cameroon, Comoros, Ivory Coast, Djibouti, Gabon, Gambia, Guinea, Equatorial Guinea, Upper Volta, Liberia, Morocco, Mauritius, Niger, Central African Republic, Senegal, Somalia, Sudan, Tunisia, and Zaire (ibid).

168. See *Africa News,* March 19, 1984, pp. 4–5; Hodges, *Western Sahara,* p. 308.

169. See *Africa News,* November 19, 1984, p. 14.

170. See ibid., March 12, 1984, p. 12.

171. See ibid., November 19, 1984, p. 13.

172. *SPSC Letter* 6 (June 1985): 6.

173. *Algérie Actualité* 1032 (July 25–31, 1985): 11.

### Chapter 4    Absolutism, Bonapartism, and the Formation of Ruling Classes

1. For a more detailed version of this argument, see Thomas M. Callaghy, *The State-Society Struggle: Zaire in Comparative Perspective* (New York: Columbia University Press, 1984). On absolutism see: Pierre Goubert, *The Ancien Regime: French Society 1600–1750* (New York: Harper Torchbooks, 1969); Roland Mousnier, *The Institutions of France under the Absolute Monarchy 1598–1789: State and Society* (Chicago: University of Chicago Press, 1974); Theodore K. Rabb, *The Struggle for Stability in Early Modern Europe* (New York: Oxford University Press, 1975); Perry Anderson, *Lineages of the Absolutist State* (London: NLB, 1974); Robert Mandrou, *La France au XVII et XVIII Siecles* (Paris: PUF, 1967); Pierre Goubert, *L'Ancien Regime: les pouvoirs* (Paris: Armand Colin, 1973); Georges Pages, *La Monarchie de l'Ancien Regime en France* (Paris: Armand Colin, 1928); Hans Rosenberg, *Bureaucracy, Aristocracy and Autocracy: The Prussian Experience* (Boston: Beacon Press, 1958); and Theda Skocpol, *States and Social Revolutions* (New York: Cambridge University Press, 1979).

2. F. H. Hinsley, *Sovereignty* (New York: Basic Books, 1966), p. 26.

3. For Max Weber "patriarchal patrimonialism is mass domination by one individual" that requires an administrative apparatus and a coercive capacity (*Economy and Society,* vol. II, ed. G. Roth and C. Wittich [Berkeley: University of California Press, 1978], p. 1106). Weber distinguishes between several types of patrimonial rule. In the increasing scope given to the personal discretion of the ruler, they are: gerontocracy, decentralized patrimonialism, centralizing patrimonialism (patriarchal patrimonialism), and sultanism (a despotic form of patrimonial rule). Patrimonialization entails increasing the presence or weight of patrimonial phenomena in a given state. It applies to leadership characteristics, administration, legitimation, and economic consequences. In the contemporary African context, it means diminishing the bureaucratic characteristics of rulership and administration in particular, thereby increasing the scope for personal discretion and arbitrariness. It also results in the diminished effectiveness of administrative performance. On Weber's notion of patrimonialism, see *Economy and Society,* vol. II, Chapter XII, "Patriar-

chalism and Patrimonialism," pp. 1006–1069, and Chapter XIII, "Feudalism, Standestaat and Patrimonialism," pp. 1070–1110, and Callaghy, *The State-Society Struggle,* pp. 69–78.

4. F. Dumont, "French Kingship and Absolute Monarchy in the Seventeenth Century," in Ragnhild Hatton, ed., *Louis XIV and Absolutism,* (Columbus, Ohio: Ohio State University Press, 1976), p. 66.

5. Robert Mandrou, *Louis XIV en son temps* (Paris: PUF, 1973). p. 205.

6. Goubert, *L'Ancien Regime,* p. 19; my translation.

7. Alexis de Tocqueville, *The Old Regime* (Garden City, N.Y.: Doubleday-Anchor, 1955), p. 57; emphasis added.

8. Richard M. Morse, "The Heritage of Latin America," in Louis Hartz, ed., *The Founding of New Societies* (New York: Harcourt, Brace, 1964), pp. 155–157.

9. Claudio Veliz, *The Centralist Tradition of Latin America* (Princeton: Princeton University Press, 1978), pp. 80–82.

10. Alfred Stepan, *The State and Society: Peru in Comparative Perspective* (Princeton: Princeton University Press, 1978), p. 16; on the organic-statist approach to the state, see Chapters 2 and 3.

11. See Ralph Milibrand, "Marx and the State," *Socialist Register* (1965): 278–296.

12. Nicos Poulantzas, "The Problem of the Capitalist State," *New Left Review* (November–December 1969): 67–78.

13. For example, see Hal Draper, *Karl Marx's Theory of Revolution,* vol. 1: *State and Bureaucracy* (New York: Monthly Review Press, 1977), pp. 464–472. For a cogent critique of this tendency in recent work on the rise of the "modern world system," especially that of Immanuel Wallerstein, see Aristide Zolberg, "Origins of the Modern World System: A Missing Link," *World Politics* 33, 2 (January 1981): 253–281. Zolberg notes that although Wallerstein "acknowledges that the transformation entailed epochal changes in political and economic organization, he attempts in vain to demonstrate causal precedence of the one over the other. My comments . . . indicate that an alternative framework, positing interactions between two structural linkages–with the political as basic as the economic–would provide a better fit for the historical account under consideration." Zolberg correctly points out that we must "view political structure as a irreducible and relatively autonomous systemic element" (p. 275) and stresses the importance of international factors of a politico-strategic nature. Also see Peter Gourevitch, "The International System and Regime Formation: A Critical Review of Anderson and Wallerstein," *Comparative Politics* 10 (April 1978): 419–438; Gourevitch makes similar points about Wallerstein's work and also notes Perry Anderson's useful stress on international economic *and* political factors while correctly taking him to task for rejecting Engel's useful balancing notion of the absolutist state in favor of a view of it as a revitalized form of landed aristocratic domination. From my point of view, Anderson, like Poulantzas, nicely underscores the early modern, transitional nature of absolutism, particularly its state formation characteristics. Also see Theda Skocpol, ed., *Vision and Method in Historical Sociology* (New York: Cambridge University Press, 1984).

14. Frederick Engels, *The Origin of the Family, Private Property and the State,* in Marx and Engels, *Selected Works,* vol. 2 (London: 1968), pp. 290–291.

15. John Lonsdale, "The State and Social Processes in Africa," a paper presented to the Annual Meeting of the African Studies Association, Bloomington, Indiana, October 21, 1981, p. 34.

16. For Marxist views of absolutism, see Draper, op. cit., pp. 464, 475–482; Milibrand, op. cit., pp. 136–139; and the excellent discussion in Nicos Poulantzas, *Political Power and Social Classes* (London: New Left Books, 1973), pp. 157–167. Also see Anderson, *Lineages,* passim. For one attempt to apply Bonapartism to Mobutu's Zaire, see Nzongola-Ntalaja, *Class Struggles and National Liberation in Africa* (Roxbury, Mass.: Omenana, 1982), pp. vi, 47–48, 55, 74–75. Nzongola describes Mobutu as a "patrimonial leader" whose efforts have led to "the transformation of the form of the state, from a parliamentary-democratic state to an exceptional or crisis state of a Bonapartist variety . . . by unifying the bourgeoisie behind a heroic leader and by depoliticizing the masses" (pp. 47, 55). He uses Bonapartism with some unease, however: "The characterization of the Mobutu regime as 'Bonapartist' in the essays on Zaire has been challenged by Wamba-dia-Wamba and Makidi-ku-Ntima. Unable to resolve the theoretical question involved at this time, I leave the analysis as it is, while I continue to develop my own thinking on the matter and hope to learn from what other analysts will contribute to the debate" (p. vi).

17. Phillipe Schmitter, "The Portugalization of Brazil," in Alfred Stepan, ed., *Authoritarian Brazil* (New Haven: Yale University Press, 1973), pp. 184–190, and Guillermo O'Donnell, "Corporatism and the Question of the State," in James M. Malloy, ed., *Authoritarianism and Corporatism in Latin America,* (Pittsburgh: University of Pittsburg Press, 1977), pp. 60–62.

18. On Bonapartism, see Draper, op. cit., p. 482 and passim; Milibrand, op. cit., pp. 135–139, and Poulantzas, *Political Power*, pp. 281–285. On Louis Napoleon, see J. M. Thompson, *Louis Napoleon and the Second Empire* (New York: W. W. Norton, 1955).

19. Poulantzas, *Political Power*, p. 164; emphasis added.

20. Ibid., p. 163.

21. Ibid., pp. 165 (n. 13) and 167.

22. In particular, see O'Donnell, op. cit., pp. 50–53 and 77. While pointing to the long neglect of the state as a useful concept, particularly because of "societalist" viewpoints common to pluralist, systems, and Marxist analysis, he cautions that without care a focus on authoritarianism can go too far the other way, towards what he calls "politicism" or "statism." He calls for a middle ground that neither overlegitimizes, advertly or inadvertly, the state nor underemphasizes "the dynamic of civil society itself and its location in the international context" (p. 53). One additional comment is necessary. This reference to the new Latin American bureaucratic-authoritarianism is not at all meant to imply that such regimes are either "natural" or "inevitable." Peter Gourevitch makes a similar point for early modern Europe: "The range of forms into which these common features could be fitted was nonetheless considerable: constitutional England, republican Netherlands, absolutist France. So was the variance with countries . . ." (op. cit., p. 433). As the recent political histories of Ghana, Nigeria, and Senegal indicate, a similar point holds for Africa.

23. For Max Weber's notion of the modern state, see Reinhard Bendix, *Max Weber* (Garden City, N.Y.: Anchor Books, 1962), pp. 383, 417–418.

24. See Guillermo O'Donnell, *Modernization and Bureaucratic-Authoritarianism: Studies in South American Politics* (Berkeley: Institute of International Studies, 1973); "Reflections on the Patterns of Change in the Bureaucratic-Authoritarian State," *Latin America Studies Review* 13, 1 (1978): 3–38. "Corporatism and the Question of the State," loc. cit., and "Tensions in the Bureaucratic-Authoritarian State and the Question of Democracy," in David Collier, ed., *The New Authoritarianism in Latin America* (Princeton: Princeton University Press, 1979), pp. 285–318.

25. This does not mean that it is not heavily dependent on the world economy, however, for it is very susceptible to fluctuations of commodity prices, particularly of copper, cobalt, and diamonds. On the notion of African neomercantilism, see Thomas M. Callaghy, "The Difficulties of Implementing Socialist Strategies of Development in Africa," in Carl G. Rosberg and Thomas M. Callaghy, *Socialism in Sub-Saharan Africa: A New Assessment* (Berkeley: Institute of International Studies, 1979), pp. 126–128.

26. Goubert, *L'Ancien Regime*, p. 41; my translation.

27. Mushi Mugumorhagerwa, "Incidences ethniques sur la fonction administrative au Kivu (1960–1973)," *memoire* (senior thesis), *University Nationale du Zaire*, 1974, p. 113.

28. For example, Mobutu Niwa, President Mobutu's oldest son, received 1.5 million Belgian francs for being a "roving ambassador": *Africa Now* (March 1982): 14.

29. Jean Rymenam, "Comment le regime Mobutu a sape ses propres fondements," *Le Monde Diplomatique* May 1977; my translation. He uses this term despite the fact that he admits, "Il n'y a donc pas de bourgeoisie economique actuellement en formation au Zaire!" Jean-Pierre Langellier calls it "une caste de privilegies qui se recrute avant tout parmi le personnel politico-administratif" (*Le Monde*, June 8, 1977). In the Zairian context, the following analysts use the following terms: David Gould and Nzongola Natalaja—"national bourgeoisie"; Michael Schatzberg—"politico-commercial bourgeoisie"; and Crawford Young has used both "national mandarinate" (which misleadingly implies extensive education and training) and "politico-commercial class." I prefer the term "political aristocracy" rather than the more common "national bourgeoisie" or "bureaucratic bourgeoisie" because, in its historical sense, "bourgeoisie" connotes a productive social class which the African ruling class generally is not; it certainly is not in Zaire. Nor is it a "national middle class"; it is the top class, the ruling, dominating one. By its basic values, actions, and style of life, it more closely resembles a political aristocracy of the type that was the core of the French absolutist state, as opposed to the landed aristocracy of feudal origins whose power it emasculated. See Goubert, *L' Ancien Regime*, pp. 41–64. Perry Anderson, in *Lineages of the Absolutist State*, incorrectly fuses these two aristocracies in his analysis of French absolutism. The ruling group in Zaire is a political aristocracy by its basic values, actions, and style and because its power, including its economic base, results from its relationship to the state. Although his overall analysis is excellent, Frantz Fanon is a good example of this terminological problem. He uses the term "national bourgeoisie," but then notes the following: "In underdeveloped countries, we have seen that no true bourgeoisie exists" (*Wretched of the Earth* [New York: Grove Press, 1968], p. 175). "In underdeveloped countries the bourgeois phase is impos-

sibly arid" (p. 174; also see pp. 148–205 generally). He notes that this group fails "to fulfill its historic role of bourgeoisie" (p. 153). So why call it a bourgeoisie at all? The continued use of the term simply leads to conceptual confusion. In fact, Zaire is not in a "bourgeois phase" at all; the current situation is prebourgeois—a key reason why Bonapartism is not applicable to Zaire now. It is early modern; only a very nascent domestic bourgeoisie exists.

30. Rymenam, loc. cit. The precolonial Kingdom of the Kongo, much of which covered territory that is now part of Zaire, had a similar political aristocracy. As in contemporary Zaire, membership in it came through holding a state position: "All these titleholders formed the aristocracy and one who could not claim to be a *mani-* [a political title prefix] something or another was not an aristocrat. It is therefore clear that aristocrats would support the existing regime . . ." They could also be replaced at will by the king—an unusual trait for African precolonial traditional states: Jan Vansina, *Kingdoms of the Savana* (Madison: University of Wisconsin Press, 1966), p. 42.; also see Georges Balandier, *Daily Life in the Kingdom of the Kongo* (New York: Meridian Books, 1969).

31. Goubert, *L'Ancien Regime*, pp. 12, 14; my translation.

32. Rymenam, loc. cit.; my translation. For similar process in Nigeria, see Richard Joseph, "Class, State, and Prebendal Politics in Nigeria," in Nelson Kasfir, ed., *State and Class in Africa* (London: Frank Cass, 1984), pp. 21–38.

33. J. H. Peemans, "The Social and Economic Development of Zaire Since Independence, An Historical Outline," *African Affairs* (April 1975): 162; David J. Gould, "Disorganization Theory and Underdevelopment Administration," paper presented at the African Studies Association Annual Meeting, Houston, 1977; see also his *Bureaucratic Corruption and Underdevelopment in the Third World: The Case of Zaire* (New York: Pergamon Press, 1980); informant, Kinshasa, Zaire, May 26, 1975 (at the time the official exchange rate was one Zaire to two U.S. dollars; the black market rate was one to one); Jean-Pierre Langellier, "Le Zaire miracule," *Le Monde,* June 9, 1977; the subtitle of the article is "L'Article 15," which means "on se debrouille" (to take care of oneself).

34. Rymenam, loc. cit.; my translation.

35. Quoted in Langellier, loc. cit.; my translation.

36. Quoted in Crawford Young, "Zaire: The Unending Crisis," *Foreign Affairs* 57, 1 (1978): 172.

37. Michael G. Schatzberg, *Politics and Class in Zaire: Bureaucracy, Business and Beer in Lisala* (New York: Africana, 1980 , p. 121.

38. Quoted in ibid., p. 121.

39. Based on personal observation in the Bas-Zaire, Shaba, Kivu, and Kinshasa regions of Zaire in 1974–1975. On the various Zairianization processes and their consequences, see Schatzberg, op. cit., pp. 121–152; Edward Kannyo, "Political Power and Class Formation in Zaire," Ph.D. dissertation, Yale University, 1979; and Crawford Young and Thomas Turner, *The Rise and Decline of the Zairian State* (Madison: University of Wisconsin Press, 1985), pp. 326–362.

40. Max Weber, *Economy and Society* (Berkeley: University of California Press, 1978), p. 1095 [the second emphasis is added].

41. Ibid., pp. 240, 1095, 1091, 1029.

42. Ibid., p. 1098. Also see Thomas M. Callaghy, "The State and the Development of Capitalism in Africa," in Naomi Chazan and Donald Rothchild, eds., *The Reordering of the State in Africa* (Boulder: Westview Press, 1986). On the development of capitalism in Europe, see Maurice Dobb, *Studies in the Development of Capitalism* (New York: International, 1963); E. L. Jones, *The European Miracle* (Cambridge: Cambridge University Press, 1981); and Douglass C. North and Robert Paul Thomas, *The Rise of the Western World: A New Economic History* (Cambridge: Cambridge University Press, 1973).

43. In *Ideology and Development in Africa* (New Haven: Yale University Press, 1982), Crawford Young notes that "Zaire is a rather different specimen of the perverted capitalist state" (p. 242). To call it a "perverted capitalist state" is historically misleading; it is, in fact, just one variant of a historically common type—that of early modern patrimonial capitalism linked to a patrimonial administrative state. On the political economy of Zaire, see Guy Gran, ed., *Zaire: The Political Economy of Underdevelopment* (New York: Praeger, 1979); J. Vanderlinden, ed., *Du Congo au Zaire, 1960–1980* (Brussels: CRISP, 1980); Fernand Bezy et al., *Accumulation et sous-developpement au Zaire 1960–1980* (Louvain-la-Neuve: Presses Universitaires de Louvain, 1981; Young and Turner, op. cit., Chapters 10–12; and S. N. Sang-Mpam, "Peripheral Capitalism, the State and Crisis: The Determinants of Public Policy in Zaire, 1965–1980," Ph.D. dissertation, University of Chicago, 1984.

44. On the useful distinction between the status and role elements of administrative positions,

see Robert Price, *Society and Bureaucracy in Contemporary Ghana* (Berkeley: University of California Press, 1975). On class in Zaire, see Young and Turner, op. cit., pp. 100–137.

45. Frederick Cooper, "Africa and the World Economy," *African Studies Review* 24, 2/3 (June/September 1981): 46.

46. Ibid., pp. 20–21.

47. Colin Leys, "African Economic Development in Theory and Practice," *Daedalus* 111, 2 (Spring 1982): 113; Cooper, op. cit., p. 70, n. 168. Also see Sayre Schatz, "Pirate Capitalism and the Inert Economy of Nigeria," *Journal of Modern African Studies* 22, 1 (1984): 45–57.

48. Janet MacGaffey, "Class Relations in a Dependent Economy: Businessmen and Businesswomen in Kisangani, Zaire," Ph.D. dissertation, Bryn Mawr College, 1981, pp. 7, 8 [emphases added].

49. See Nicola Swainson, *The Development of Corporate Capitalism in Kenya 1918–77* (Berkeley: University of California Press, 1980); Gavin Kitching, *Class and Economic Change in Kenya: The Making of an African Bourgeoisie* (New Haven: Yale University Press, 1980); and Thomas J. Biersteker, *Multinationals, the State, and the Control of the Economy: The Political Economy of Indigenization in Nigeria* (Princeton: Princeton University Press, forthcoming).

50. Aristide Zolberg, "The Military Decade," in J. van Doorn, ed., *The Military Profession and Military Regimes* (The Hague: Mouton, 1969), p. 329.

51. Weber, *Economy and Society*, p. 1099. The research upon which this section is based was funded by the National Science Foundation, grant number SES 80–13453, "Third World Debt and the International System: The Case of Zaire." The bulk of the data here comes from confidential interviews with Western governmental officials, Zairian officials, officials of international organizations, bankers, and businessmen that were conducted in Washington, D.C., New York, San Francisco, London, Brussels, Paris, and Kinshasa in 1980–1985. For a more detailed look at Zaire's economic and debt crises, see Thomas M. Callaghy, "The Political Economy of African Debt: The Case of Zaire," in John Ravenhill, ed., *Africa in Economic Crisis* (London/ New York: Macmillan/Columbia University Press, 1986).

52. Young, op. cit., p. 177.

53. In a classic move of Mobutu statecraft, Nguza was permitted back into Zaire in June 1985, leaving much of the opposition he had led high and dry.

54. Erwin Blumenthal, "Zaire—Report on her international financial credibility," typed manuscript, April 7, 1982, p. 19.

55. Confidential interviews, Kinshasa, July 29, August 5 and 6, 1982.

56. Cooper, op. cit., p. 51.

57. Ibid.

58. Richard Higgott, "Africa and the New International Division of Labor," in Ravenhill, *Africa in Economic Crisis*.

59. On the "exit option," see Goran Hyden, *Beyond Ujamaa: Underdevelopment and an Uncaptured Peasantry* (Berkeley: University of California Press, 1980).

60. The general sources for this section are Young, "Zaire: The Unending Crisis"; F. S. B. Kazadi, "Zaire 1981: Recovery or Relapse," *Africa Report* (July–August 1981): 40–43; Irving Kaplan, ed., *Zaire: A Country Study* (Washington, D.C.: Government Printing Office, 1979); *Africa Confidential*, 1977–1982; *Africa Contemporary Record*, 1977–78, 1978–79, 1979–80, 1980–81; and various periodicals including *New York Times, Le Monde, The Times (London), The Observer, Washington Post, Africa Now, Africa Report,* and *South.*

61. *Africa Research Bulletin (Political),* February 1–29, 1980, p. 5579.

62. *AZAP* (the Zairian press agency), March 17 and 18, 1982.

63. Weber, op. cit., p. 1107.

64. Cooper, op. cit., p. 49.

65. Leys, op. cit., pp. 105, 115.

66. John Iliffe, *The Emergence of African Capitalism* (London: Macmillan, 1983), p. 5.

### Chapter 5    The Petty Bourgeoisie in the Ethiopian Revolution

1. Among such early studies were Blair Thompson, *Ethiopia: The Country that Cut off Its Head* (London: Robson Books, 1975), and Rodger Yaeger, *Ethiopia: The Fall of Haile Selassie's Empire* (New York: Africana Publishing Co., 1975).

2. Marina Ottaway, "Social Classes and Corporate Interests in the Ethiopian Revolution," *The Journal of Modern African Studies* 14, 3 (1976): 469–489, and Bereket Habte Selassie, *Conflict and Intervention in the Horn of Africa* (New York: Monthly Review Press, 1980). Other authors who have focused on a class or group interpretation of the revolution are Fred Halliday

and Maxine Molyneux, *The Ethiopian Revolution* (London: Verso Press, 1981); John Markakis and Nega Ayele, *Class and Revolution in Ethiopia* (Nottingham: Spokesman Press, 1978); and Michael Warr, "The Process of Class Conflict in Ethiopia," *Ufahamu* 10, 1/2 (Winter 1980/81): 116–128. Recent socialist analysts and critics of the revolution have concentrated far less on the class character, or lack thereof, of the processes by which the emperor was overthrown and replaced than on an assessment of both the revolutionary and/or socialist character of the Dergue, its institutions and its policies. See, for example, Rene Lefort, *Ethiopia: An Heretical Revolution?* (London: Zed Press, 1981), and Paul Kemelman, "A Critique of the Ethiopian Revolution," in Martin Eve and David Musson, eds., *The Socialist Register 1982* (London: The Merlin Press, 1982).

3. See Addis Hiwet, "Analyzing the Ethiopian Revolution," *Review of African Political Economy* 30 (1984): 32–47; C. Mahrdel, "Mass Movement and Popular Revolution in Ethiopia," in Gerhard Brehme and Thea Buttner, eds., *African Studies* ([East] Berlin: Akademie-Verlag, 1983), pp. 189–202; Negussay Ayele, "The Ethiopian Revolution," *Ufahamu* 12, 3 (1983): 36–66; Azinna Nwafor, *Revolution and Socialism in Ethiopia* (Roxbury, Mass.: Omenana, 1981).

4. While obviously not the crucial strategies in either struggle, the creation and development of a system of formal education contributed to both, and were elements of what some scholars have described as defensive modernization. See Dankwart A. Rustow, "The Development of Parties in Turkey," in Joseph La Palombara and Myron Weiner, ed., *Political Parties and Political Development* (Princeton: Princeton University Press, 1966), p. 114.

5. *Ethiopia Statistical Abstract, 1965* (Addis Ababa: Central Statistical Office, Imperial Ethiopian Government, 1965), p. 151. There were 15,803 employees listed as working for the central government, and another 9,461 listed as working for both autonomous authorities (and, thus, also government employees) and selected private firms. Since it is impossible to separate out these two categories, I have in the text provided the range 15–25,000. For supportive data, see Girma Amare, "Education and Society in Prerevolutionary Ethiopia," *Northeast African Studies* 6, 1–2 (1984): 61–80. The petite bourgeoisie as conceptualized here clearly overlaps partially with others' concepts of, on the one hand, the bureaucratic bourgeoisie and, on the other, the labor aristocracy. Yet neither of these concepts isolates quite the same group I am discussing.

6. *Ethiopian Statistical Abstract, 1965*, p. 63.

7. For a discussion of the background of military personnel prior to 1974, see Haggai Erlich, "The Establishment of the Dergue: The Turning of a Protest Movement into a Revolution," in Robert L. Hess, ed., *Proceedings of the Fifth International Conference on Ethiopian Studies, Session B, April 13–16, 1978, Chicago* (Chicago: University of Illinois Press, 1979), pp. 784–786; and Yohannis Abate, "Ethiopia: The Origins of Military Intervention," *Northeast African Studies* 2, 3 (1980–81), and 3, 1 (1981): 2–4, and "Civil-Military Relations in Ethiopia," *Armed Forces and Society* 10, 3 (1984): 382–384.

8. Ethiopian landholding patterns are extensively described in Patrick Gilkes, *The Dying Lion: Feudalism and Modernization in Ethiopia* (London: Julian Freidmann Publishers, Ltd., 1975), pp. 101–136, and John Markakis, *Ethiopia: Anatomy of a Traditional Polity* (Oxford: Clarendon Press, 1974), pp. 73–142.

9. For the history of formal education in Ethiopia, see Richard Pankhurst, "The Foundations of Education, Printing, Newspapers, Book Production, Libraries and Literacy in Ethiopia," *Ethiopia Observer* 6, 3 (1962): 241–290, and Girma Amare, "Government Education in Ethiopia," *Ethiopia Observer* 6, 4 (1963): 335–341.

10. See Markakis, op. cit, p. 148.

11. Richard Greenfield, *Ethiopia: A New Political History* (London: Pall Mall Press, 1965), pp. 404–406, discusses the student role in 1960. Donald N. Levine, *Wax and Gold: Tradition and Innovation in Ethiopian Culture,* (Chicago: University of Chicago Press, 1965), p. 215, mentions the disaffection of university students.

12. An analysis of the political attitudes of secondary students is provided in Robert D. Grey, "Education and Politics in Ethiopia," unpublished Ph.D. dissertation, Yale University, 1970, pp. 185–189.

13. Gabriel A. Almond and Sidney Verba, *The Civic Culture,* (Princeton: Princeton University Press, 1963), pp. 380–381. Lester Milbraith, *Political Participation* (Chicago: Rand-McNally, 1965), and Sidney Verba and Norman H. Nie, *Participation in America* (New York: Harper and Row, 1972), also emphasize such effects.

14. Almond and Verba, op. cit., emphasize these factors, as do the various voting studies from SRC.

15. Until recently, the link between the amount of education one acquired and both the likelihood of getting a job and the attractiveness of the job appeared to be close.

16. See Robert D. Grey, op. cit., pp. 182–198.

17. There are several studies which document subsequent activity. See Peter Koehn, and L. Hayes, "Revolution and Protest: Comparative Analysis of Student Anti-System Behavior in Ethiopia and Nepal," *Journal of Asian and African Studies* 13, 1 and 2 (Jan. and April 1978): 33–49; Legesse Lemma, "The Ethiopian Student Movement 1960–1974: A Challenge to the Monarchy and Imperialism in Ethiopia," *Northeast African Studies* 1, 1 (1979): 31–46; and Girma Amare, op. cit., pp. 74–79.

18. See Grey, op. cit., pp. 42 and 45.

19. Such indirectness has been identified by Levine as characteristic of Ethiopian communication (op. cit., p. 5).

20. Ibid., pp. 250–252.

21. *News and Views*, 1, 9, Main Campus Student Union, Haile Selassie I University, April 30, 1966, p. 1.

22. *News and Views*, 1, 10, June 1, 1966, p. 1.

23. Ibid.

24. The retail price of food increased by 67.5 percent between 1963 and 1971; further increases followed the drought. See Peter Koehn, "Ethiopian Politics: Military Intervention and Prospects for Further Change," *Africa Today* 22, 2 (April–June 1975): pp. 10 and 12.

25. Ibid., p. 10.

26. Most early demands were for government economic actions: to raise wages in the public sector, civilian and military, and to control or lower prices. The government yielded to many of these demands. See Marina and David Ottaway, *Ethiopia: Empire in Revolution* (New York: Africana Publishing Company, 1978), pp. 29–47.

27. There are many good histories of this period. See ibid., pp. 29–43, for a typical one.

28. Little literature exists on the Ethiopian worker. Seleshi Sisaye, in several articles, has attempted to detail worker attitudes and behavior, as well as the explanations thereof. See, for instance, Seleshi Sisaye, "Industrial Conflict and Labor Politics in Ethiopia: A Study of the March 1974 General Strike," *Plural Societies* (Summer 1977): 49–76, and Seleshi Sisaye, "The Political and Economic Perspectives of Union Members in Addis Ababa, Ethiopia During the 1974 General Strike," *Ethiopianist Notes* 1, 2 (Fall 1977): 45–58.

29. Markakis and Nega, op. cit., p. 97.

30. Ibid., p. 97, that is, the civilian left. It must be remembered that, despite the "widespread" involvement in political activism in the cities in the early months of 1974, this was solely an urban phenomenon, and largely a movement of the petite bourgeoisie, a small part of the total Ethiopian population.

31. See Ottaway and Ottaway, op. cit., pp. 29–43, and Markakis and Nega, op. cit., pp. 77–123.

32. Although not crowned until 1930, Haile Selassie had been politically dominant for the preceding decade.

33. Erlich, op. cit., p. 785.

34. Ottaway and Ottaway, op. cit., pp. 44–47.

35. It had demanded, and won, pay increases in the interim. See Yohannis Abate, op. cit., p. 4.

36. Ottaway and Ottaway, op. cit., pp. 44–58, and "Pliny the Middle-Aged," "The PMAC:Origins and Structure," *Ethiopianist Notes* 2, 3 (1978–79): 1–18.

37. "Pliny the Middle-Aged," op. cit., pp. 6–10.

38. The Dergue quickly repudiated the right of its electors to replace the initial representatives.

39. See Levine, op. cit., pp. 238–286.

40. Ottaway and Ottaway, op. cit., pp. 138–144.

41. Ibid., pp. 71–81.

42. Ibid., pp. 128–148.

43. Robert D. Grey, "Leninism, The Soviet Union and Party Development in Cuba and Ethiopia," *Northeast African Studies* 2, 3 (1980–81), and 3, 1 (1981): 171–182.

## Chapter 6   Class, Status, and Power in Postreunification Cameroon

This paper was prepared under the aegis of the National Endowment for the Humanities 1981 Summer Seminar on Race and Class in Africa under the distinguished directorship of Professor Irving Leonard Markovitz, Department of Political Science, Queens College, of the City University of New York. Parts have appeared in slightly revised form as "Ethnicity, Regionalism and Political Power: A Post-mortem of Ahidjo's Cameroon," in I. William Zartman and Michael G. Schatzberg, eds., *The Political Economy of Cameroon* (New York: Praeger, 1985). I would like to thank Lenny Markovitz for inviting me to participate in the seminar and the NEH, whose generous financial assistance made it so difficult not to accept Lenny Markovitz's gracious invitation. I express special thanks to my colleagues and to Drs. John and Ndombo Kale for their many helpful comments and suggestions; and I gladly share with them whatever merits this paper might contain while absolving them of any errors of fact and interpretation.

1. Mr. Ahidjo resigned as president of Cameroon in November of 1982 but remained as president of the CNU until August 1983. He was succeeded in both offices by Mr. Paul Biya.

2. The pride with which the national bourgeoisie attaches to its version of reality is only matched by the ferocious attacks it levels against those Cameroonians who seek to offer an alternative version of the truth. In the same policy speech President Ahidjo bitterly attacked those "nationals both at home and abroad *who aid and abet those who thirst for domination with the hope of bringing about the collapse of the fine structure of unity, stability and progress which we are patiently endeavouring to build*. We are aware of the subversive activities and the false and coarse propaganda of dreamers and ambitious persons who from their voluntary exile itch with envious nostalgia.. . . These subversive activities assume dangerous proportions when they are allowed to undermine the foundations of the solid and organized nation which we are proud to build in toil and perseverance" (emphasis added). It is clear that the national bourgeoisie has been engaging in a campaign of cynicism aimed at discrediting the bona fides of any Cameroonian who dares to stray from the official party line. Inherent in this cynical propaganda is the doctrine that only those inside Cameroon enjoy special perspectives and insights about that society to qualify them as its authentic "interpreters." These "insiders" claim that as a matter of epistemological principle only they—not the "outsiders," that is, those on "voluntary exile" abroad— have *privileged*, if not *monopolistic*, access to Cameroonian knowledge.

This peculiar strain of Cameroonian solipsism, like all other strains of solipsism, is intellec- tually unsound because it simply negates the most elementary processes of logical reasoning. It suggests that one cannot understand situations and conditions external to one's own immediate experience and objective location in space and time. It threatens to extend the single dimension of experience to a total equation of *experience equals understanding*; it makes the whole intellectually incomprehensible except through the atomized element of *being*. Carried to its logical extreme and as Robert Merton suggests, the catalogue of claims to privileged or monopolistic access of knowledge becomes indefinitely expansible to all manner of social formations (Merton, 1973: 99-136). For example, China would then exist only for those who have visited or, better still, lived in China. Only black South Africans living in South Africa are capable of *understanding* and *discussing* apartheid; mind you, not the Dennis Brutuses, Bloke Modisanes, Lewis Nkosis, Miriam Makebas, and Hugh Masakelas in exile abroad. At its most absurd, it allows for the argument that one must first live among swines before one can fundamentally understand and discuss that distinctive aroma that pigpens exude! Affirming this is tantamount to abdicating all claims to clear thinking. But this facile proposition, that only those Cameroonians domiciled in the country have exclusive claims to the understanding and interpretation of Cameroonian reality, has received the blessing of the ruling class. I, however, find it not only disingenuous but intellectually unsupportable.

Claiming lineal descent from this doctrine of exclusivity is a related one which consists of labeling anyone who publicly disagrees with government policies as subversive; of dismissing as revolutionary cant any form of criticism of the regime; and of treating the great helmsman—first it was Ahmadou Ahidjo and now Paul Biya—as an infallible deity criticism of whom amounts to an unpardonable act of *lèse-majesté*. Lost in all of this war of words is the fact that Cameroon transcends particular individuals and groups and is the collective patrimony of all living Cameroonians as well as the millions that have gone before and the many yet unborn and that no one person can appropriate this heritage for himself, thus making it the special obligation of every living Cameroonian to question and criticize the direction Cameroon is heading when such criticism is deserved.

3. This position has been most forcefully presented in a series of communiqués put out since 1979 by the Cameroon Action Movement, a clandestine organization made up of Anglophone Cameroonians (see *West Africa* 28 [January 1980]: 143).

4. The range represents the variation in figures given by different authors. Victor T. Le Vine (1971: 11) puts the number of Muslims in Cameroon at 600,000, and for the other religions he has 27 percent of the Anglophone population and 35 percent of the Francophone as Christians and 65 percent and 45 percent, respectively, as animists. Prouzet (1974: 103) estimates the Christian population in Cameroon to be 2 million and the Muslims 1 million. Azarya (1976: 55) points

out that only 43 percent of the total northern population is islamized; and Joseph (1977: 17) gives a numerical estimate of Muslims in Cameroon as 395,000.

5. Under the federal system, the country was divided into six administrative regions, each headed by a federal inspector of administration. West Cameroon was one of the six regions. The other five were in East Cameroon: north, east, south-central, littoral, and west. I shall retain this regional division as a framework for analysis.

6. Of the ten provincial governors under the present Biya administration, two are Anglophones (Yakum Ntaw in the north and Ngomba Mutanga in the north-west).

7. Banque des États de l'Afrique Centrale (BEAC), Banque Internationale pour l'Afrique Occidentale-Cameroun (BIAO), Banque Internationale pour le Commerce et l'Industrie du Cameroun (BICIC), Cameroon Bank Ltd. (Cambank), Société Camerounaise de Banque (SCB), and Société Générale de Banque au Cameroun.

8. Banque Camerounaise de Développement (BCD), Fonds National de Développement Rural (FONADER), Société Financière pour le Développement du Cameroun, and Société Nationale d'Investissement du Cameroun.

9. Cameroon Development Corporation (CDC), Mission de Développement des Cultures Vivrières, Maraichères et Fruitières (MIDEVIV), Mission de Développement d'Ombessa, Société Camerounaise des Tabacs (SCT), Société de Développement et la Transformation du Blé (SODEBLE), Société de Développement du Cacao (SODECAO), Société de Développement du Coton (SODECOTON), Société de Développement et d'Exploitation des Produits Animaux (SODEPA), Société de Développement du Haut-Nkam (SODENKAM), Société de Développement de la Riziculture de la plaine des Mbos (SODERIM), Société d'Etudes des Bauxites du Cameroun (SEBECAM), Société d'Expansion et de Modernisation de la Riziculture de Yagoua (SEMRY), Société Régionale des Zones d'Actions Prioritaires Integrées du Centre-Sud (ZAPI du Centre Sud), and Société Régionale des Zones d'Actions Prioritaires Integrées de l'Est (ZAPI de l'EST).

10. A list of all the provincial and divisional service heads was compiled from the various National Year Books and *Les Elites Camerounaises*. I then had six different Cameroonian students knowledgeable in Cameroon ethnography match the names of these administrators against their province of origin. Of the 181 names, we initially had agreement on 163. The remaining 18 names were then given to a former Cameroonian administrator who had worked in several of the provinces before leaving the service for further study abroad. He was able to match this last group of names. Because so few Cameroonians from the East province hold national office and because of the relative isolation of this region from the rest of the country, we had the most difficulty in identifying eastern names. My approach then was to classify administrators as of eastern origin if their names could not be positively matched against the other five regions. My figures therefore contain some margin of error; however, a more positive identification of *all* the names on the list would probably affect the distribution but *not* the general pattern as described in our analysis.

11. Both studies, however, only dealt with the Francophone sector. We know of no published work in either English or French that has utilized class analysis in the English-speaking sector of Cameroon.

12. Others who participated at various times in the critical negotiations leading up to the formation of the single party state were amply rewarded in the aftermath: D. A. Nangah (one of the most successful Anglophone businessmen, whose multimillion-dollar Nangah Company would have folded sooner than it did but for the endless stream of lucrative government contracts); Chief Victor Mukete (chairman of the CDC for over two decades, 1960–1983); Solomon T. Muna (president of the National Assembly since 1973 and before that prime minister of West Cameroon and vice president of the republic); P. M. Kemcha (deceased); J. N. Lafon (held a cabinet position in the West Cameroon government); J. Tatoh (no information).

13. These were Effiom, Endeley, Egbe, Ekangaki, Foncha, Fonlon, Jua, and Elangwe. They comprised almost one-fourth of the total membership of the Political Bureau.

### Chapter 7   Religion, Ideology, and Property in Northern Zambia

This article is based upon field research spanning a period of some eighteen years. The initial period of fieldwork was undertaken during the years 1963–1965, with shorter field trips in 1973, 1976, and 1981. The 1981 field research was made possible by a Maryknoll Fellowship, for which I wish to express my gratitude.

I wish to express my appreciation to the following for their useful and constructive comments on different drafts of this article. I extend my thanks to Professors Elizabeth Colson, Janet Dolgin, Gillian Feeley-Harnik, Clifford Geertz, Ward Keeler, Martin Kilson, Wyatt MacGaffey, Lucy Mair, Irving Markovitz, John Peel, William Shack, and Joan Vincent. Much of this paper was written at the Institute for Advanced Study and is part of a larger work in preparation. I wish to thank the institute for the opportunity to work on these materials.

1. For a more detailed discussion of ideological field see Barnett (1977) and, for one view of field, Turner (1974: 17).

2. The functional, equilibrium notions of the ecological materialism propounded by Vayda and Rappaport (1967), though intriguing and fundamental to multilinear evolutionary theory, need not, I think, detain us here, since within their framework religion is viewed as nothing more than a repressive mechanism restoring ecological balance or leading to a new one.

3. For further exposition of Van Binsbergen's argument, see Van Binsbergen's *Religious Change in Zambia* (London: Kegan Paul International, 1981), pp. 266–316 and Fernandez (1978: 212–214).

4. Yombe society is experiencing change and rules governing marriage payments are often contested. Men argue with their sons as to who is entitled to the bridewealth of their daughters. It should be remembered that Uyombe is an area of heavy labor migration and adjustments are made. Men may not always be present to assert their rights.

5. For a more detailed discussion of the generation councils and factionalism see Bond (1972).

6. The cooperative grinding mill is part of the process of change. It is part of two normative orders, the one bureaucratic and the other customary. One joins the cooperative, an organization that is supposed to run according to impersonal "rational economic" principles. And, yet the cooperative operates within the context of an established sociopolitical matrix based more on personal, particularistic relationships than impersonal, universalistic ones. There is a tension between the norms of the two orders, those of society and those of a formal organization.

## Chapter 8   Women's Politics in African States

1. The first quote is from an unidentified woman, cited in Agnes Klingshirm, *The Changing Position of Women in Ghana* (Dissertation, Marburg/Lahn, 1971), p. 230. The second quote is from the Queen Mother of Tsito, and is cited in Jette Bukh, *The Village Woman in Ghana* (Uppsala: Scandinavian Institute of African Studies, 1979), p. 93.

2. The public-private distinction is drawn from various intellectual traditions. For its use in Western political thought, see Jean Elshtain, *Public Man, Private Woman* (Princeton: Princeton University Press, 1981), and Zillah Eisenstein, *The Radical Future of Liberal Feminism* (New York: Longman, 1981), p. 25. Marxists have addressed the transformation of the family under capitalism, but they are vague on the specifics of state action; see Eli Zaretsky, *Capitalism, the Family, and Personal Life* (New York: Harper Colophon, 1973), and F. Engels, *The Origin of the Family, Private Property and the State* (Moscow: Progress Publishers, 1948; originally published in 1884).

An influential collection by anthropologists divides society into public and domestic (the latter, my use of private); see Michelle Rosaldo and Louise Lamphere, eds., *Woman, Culture and Society* (Stanford: Stanford University Press, 1974), and later reflections of Rosaldo, "The Use and Abuse of Anthropology: Reflections on Feminism and Cross-Cultural Understanding," *Signs* 5, 3 (Spring 1980): 389–417. Anthropologists' ahistorical twentieth-century descriptions of societies, divorced from their incorporation into the state, reinforce the notion that women are forever relegated to a private, apolitical sphere.

The state is defined as roles, institutions, and individual office occupants having particular drives, compulsions, and aims of their own relating to decisions binding upon all segments of society in a certain territory. This is a composite definition from Stephen D. Krasner, *Defending the National Interest: Raw Materials Investment and U.S. Foreign Policy* (Princeton: Princeton University Press, 1978), p. 10; Alison Jagger, *Feminist Politics and Human Nature* (Totowa, N.J.: Rowman and Allanhead, 1983), p. 169, and Eric Nordlinger, *On the Autonomy of the Democratic State* (Cambridge: Harvard University Press, 1981), p. 11, who all alone had definitions with questionable dimensions. While John Lonsdale, "The State and Social Processes in Africa," paper presented to the Twenty-Fourth Annual Meeting of the African Studies Association, Bloomington, Indiana, October 21, 1981, provides a staggering synthesis of research on the state in Africa, he only says that "women's studies has barely impinged upon studies of the state" (p. 5), as if statist theorists had no analytic responsibility. (Lonsdale's essay was published in *African Studies Review* 24, 2/3 [1981]: pp. 139–225.)

3. Some precolonial state, or Islamic societies, have also imposed a public-private dichotomy. Compensating men for their loss of autonomy with authority over women may be an essential

feature of establishing large-scale state societies, but that analysis is outside the bounds of this paper. See my "Anthropological, Feminist, and Statist Theories: The Construction of Gender in Colonial Africa," a paper presented at the American Political Science Association Annual Meetings, New Orleans, August 1985.

4. Agnes Akosua Aidoo, "Asante Queen Mothers in Government and Politics in the Nineteenth Century," in Filomina Chioma Steady, ed., *The Black Woman Cross-Culturally* (Cambridge, Mass.: Schenkman, 1981), p. 65. In the same volume, Steady reports how a contemporary Sierra Leonean political leader said, "We give birth to men so in a way we own them," "The Black Woman Cross-Culturally: An Overview," p. 34.

5. Niara Sudarkasa, "Female Employment and Family Organization in West Africa," in ibid., p. 52. Probably the most gender-egalitarian society ever described has been the stateless and nonhierarchical !King Bushmen; see Patricia Draper, "!Kung Women: Contrasts in Sexual Egalitarianism in Foraging and Sedentary Contexts," in Rayna Reiter, ed, *Toward an Anthropology of Women*, (New York: Monthly Review Press, 1975). For a good overview of women in Africa, see Margaret Jean Hay and Sharon Stichter, eds, *African Women South of the Sahara* (New York: Longman, 1984).

6. "The Dual Sex Political System in Operation: Igbo Women and Community Politics in Midwestern Nigeria," in Nancy Hafkin and Edna Bay, eds., *Women in Africa: Studies in Social and Economic Change* (Stanford: Stanford University Press, 1976), pp. 111–133.

7. Nina Emma Mba, *Nigerian Women Mobilized: Women's Political Activity in Southern Nigeria, 1900–1965* (Berkeley: University of California Institute of International Studies, Research Series #48, 1982), pp. 2–29.

8. Okonjo, op. cit., pp. 111–133. Mba, op. cit., pp. 24 ff; Nancy Leis, "Women in Groups: Ijaw Women's Associations," in Rosaldo and Lamphere, pp. 223–242.

9. Annie M. D. Lebeuf, "The Role of Women in the Political Organization of African Societies," in Denise Paulme, ed., *Women of Tropical Africa* (Berkeley: University of California Press, 1963), p. 113.

10. Carol P. Hoffer, "Madam Yoko: Ruler of the Kpa Mende Confederacy," in Michelle Rosaldo and Louise Lamphere, eds., *Woman, Culture and Society* (Stanford: Stanford University Press, 1974).

11. Delaziere, as cited in Judith Bryson, "Women and Economic Development in Cameroon," report submitted to the U.S. Agency for International Development, Yaounde, January, 1979, pp. 25, 114.

12. Patricia Stamp, "Perceptions of Change and Economic Strategy Among Kikuyu Women of Mitero, Kenya," *Rural Africana* 29 (Winter 1975–76): 19–44; E. Mary Holding, "Women's Institutions and the African Church," *International Review of Missions* 31 (July 1942): 290–300.

13. Aidoo, op. cit.; Lebeuf, op. cit.; Bukh, op. cit.; Mba, op. cit., pp. 2–24.

14. Aidoo, op. cit., p. 66.

15. Mba, op. cit., p. 8.

16. Bolanle Awe, "The Iyalode in the Traditional Yoruba Political System," in Alice Schlegel, ed., *Sexual Stratification: A Cross-Cultural View,* (New York: Columbia University Press, 1977), pp. 144–160; Mba, op. cit., pp. 6 ff.

17. Lebeuf, op. cit., p. 100.

18. Barbara Lewis, "The Limitations of Group Activity Among Entrepreneurs: The Market Women of Abidjan, Ivory Coast," in Nancy Hafkin and Edna Bay, op. cit., pp. 135–156; Jans D. Siebel and Andreas Massing, *Traditional Organizations and Economic Development in Liberia* (New York: Praeger, 1974); Achola O. Pala, "African Women in Rural Development: Research Trends and Priorities," Overseas Liaison Committee, American Council on Education, #12, December 1976; Kathleen Staudt, "The Umoja Federation: Women's Cooptation into a Local Power Structure," *Western Political Quarterly* 33, 2 (June 1980): 278–290; Margaret Strobel, *Muslim Women in Mombasa* (New Haven: Yale University Press, 1979).

19. Irving Markovitz, *Power and Class in Africa: An Introduction to Change and Conflict in African Politics* (Englewood Cliffs: Prentice-Hall, 1977). Some stratification theorists take gender-based inequalities as axiomatic, such as Leonard Plotnicov and Arthur Tuden, who remark that "unstratified societies are ranked merely on the basis of sex, age and kinship status," in their edited collection, *Essays in Comparative Social Stratification* (Pittsburgh: University of Pittsburgh Press, 1970), p. 5. Gerhard Lenski conceives of stratification as ranking on the basis of power, prestige, and privilege which results in differential rewards; see his *Power and Privilege* (New York: McGraw Hill, 1966), pp. 74–75.

20. "Engels Revisited: Women, the Organization of Production, and Private Property," in

Rayna R. Reiter, ed., *Toward an Anthropology of Women*, (New York: Monthly Review Press, 1975), pp. 220, 228–233.

21. Mba, op. cit., p. 39.

22. Ester Boserup, *Woman's Role in Economic Development* (New York: St. Martin's Press, 1970), is good on the many agricultural assumptions of colonial officials. Until the mid-1970s, many development theorists revealed assumptions like these (if they mentioned women at all in their analyses).

23. Sudarkasa, op. cit., p. 51.

24. Rattray, cited (p. 145) in Susan Rogers, "Woman's Place: A Critical Review of Anthropological Theory," *Comparative Studies in Society and History* 20, 1 (January 1978): 123–162.

25. Charles Tilly speaks of state formation in this way in "Reflections on the History of European State-Making," in Tilly, ed., *The Formation of National States in Western Europe* (Princeton: Princeton University Press, 1975), pp. 27, 71.

26. "The Changing Economic Position of Women in Rural Areas: Case Studies from the Kisumu District, Kenya" (Nairobi: University of Nairobi, Institute for Development Studies, Spring 1974), Working Paper #156, p. 22.

27. Arthur Phillips, *Survey of African Marriage and Family Life* (London: Oxford, 1953), pp. xx. C. P. Groves, *The Planting of Christianity in Africa*, Vol. IV (London: Lutterworth Press, 1948–1955), p. 113; Lucy Mair, *African Marriage and Social Change* (London: Frank Cass, 1969), p. 1.

28. Groves, op. cit., p. 281.

29. African Educational Commission, *A Study of West, South and Equatorial Africa* (New York: Phelps-Stokes Fund, 1922), p. 22; Lord Hailey, *An African Survey* (London: Oxford, 1938), p. 1256; T. J. Jones, *Education in East Africa* (New York: Phelps-Stokes Fund, 1924), p. 341; Lord Lugard *The Dual Mandate in British Tropical Africa* (London: Frank Cass, 1965; originally published in 1922), p. 457.

30. Mrs. R. H. C. Graham, "The Moral Impact of the Gospel: A Record of Years Work Amongst African Women," *International Review of Missions 9*, 33 (January 1920): 103.

31. Lord Hailey, op. cit., p. 1256 (rev. ed. 1953, p. 1186).

32. Regina Oboler, *Women, Power and Economic Change: The Nandi of Kenya* (Stanford: Stanford University Press, 1985), pp. 258, 278.

33. African Educational Commission, 1922, p. 24.

34. Jones, op. cit., p. 116.

35. Ibid., pp. 17–18, 26–27.

36. A. U.S. Department of Agriculture representative recognized women's agricultural participation, in Jones, op. cit., pp. 370, as did other parts of the report on pages 38, 240, 351, and 377. Lord Lugard recognized women's agricultural activities when he said that "female labour in the fields" should be replaced by men (op. cit., p. 517). Lord Hailey's quote is from the 1953 ed., p. 872. His other references to women farmers are found on pages 821, 872, and 1386.

37. Marcia Wright, "Technology, Marriage and Women's Work in the History of Maize-Growers in Mazabuka, Zambia: A Reconnaissance," *Journal of Southern African Studies* 10, 1 (October, 1983): 75.

38. "Women's Clubs in Uganda," *Corona* 4, 5 (May 1952): 184; Editorial, *Community Development Bulletin* 4 (Dec. 1952–Sept. 1953). The *Journal of African Administration* disseminated programmatic program models as well.

39. Marguerite Mikolasek, "Some Attempts at Feminine Education in Cameroon," *International Review of Missions* 41 (October 1952): 492–495. A similar school is described in Yvette Bergeret, "A Training Centre for Home and Family Life," *International Review of Missions* 41 (October 1952): 496–502.

40. Jane Bell, M.B.E., "Domestic Science in the Bush," *Corona* 12, 5 (May 1960): 177.

41. Vandra Masemann, "The Hidden Curriculum of a West African Girls' Boarding School," *Canadian Journal of African Studies* 8, 3 (1974): 479–494; Lois Weis, "Women and Education in Ghana: Some Problems of Assessing Change," *International Journal of Women's Studies* 3, 5 (1980): 431–453.

42. Audrey Wipper, "Equal Rights for Women in Kenya?" *Journal of Modern African Studies* 9, 3 (1971): 420–442.

43. G. M. Roddan, C.M.G., "The Key is Woman," *Corona* (February 1958): 58.

44. Eveline King, "On Educating African Girls in Northern Rhodesia," *Rhodes-Livingstone Journal* 10 (1950): 72.

45. Judith Van Allen, "Sitting on a Man: Colonialism and the Lost Political Institutions of

Igbo Women," *Canadian Journal of African Studies* 6, 2 (1972): 165–182; Mba, op. cit., Chapter 3.

46. Jean O'Barr, "Pare Women: A Case of Political Involvement," *Rural Africana* 29 (Winter 1975–76): 121–134.

47. Mba, op. cit., pp. 46–49, and 73, Chapter 4.

48. Barbara Dobson, "Woman's Place in East Africa," *Corona* 6, 12 (December 1954): 454–457.

49. Ibid.

50. Margaret Jean Hay and Marcia Wright, eds., *African Women and the Law: Historical Perspectives* (Boston: Boston University Papers on Africa, VII, 1982), p. xiv.

51. "Making Customary Law: Men, Women, and Courts in Colonial Northern Rhodesia," in ibid., pp. 53–67.

52. "Justice, Women, and the Social Order in Abercorn, Northeastern Rhodesia, 1897–1903," in ibid., pp. 33–50.

53. Hay and Wright, op. cit., p. xiii.

54. Margaret Jean Hay, "Women as Owners, Occupants, and Managers of Property in Colonial Western Kenya," in *ibid.*, pp. 110–124 (Wilson cite, p. 111).

55. Kenneth Little, *African Women in Towns* (London: Cambridge University Press, 1973), pp. 63–65, 70, 206–207; also see M. Dobert, "Liberation and the Women of Guinea," *Africa Report,* October 1970.

56. C. Fluehr-Lobban, "Agitation for Change in the Sudan," in Alice Schlegel, ed., *Sexual Stratification: A Cross Cultural View* (New York: Columbia University Press, 1977), pp. 127–143.

57. See Bukh, op. cit.; Louise Fortmann, "Women's Work in a Communal Setting: The Tanzania Policy of Ujamaa," in Edna Bay, ed., *Woman and Work in Africa,* (Boulder, Colo.: Westview, 1982), pp. 191–206; Carol Bond, "Women's Involvement in Agriculture in Botswana, 1974 (unpublished); Kathleen Staudt, "Agricultural Productivity Gaps: A Case Study of Male Preference in Government Policy Implementation," *Development and Change 9,* 3 (July 1978): 439–457; L. B. Venema, *The Wolof of Saloum: Social Structure and Rural Development in Senegal* (Wageningen: Center for Agricultural Publishing and Documentation, 1978), pp. 112–113.

58. Of course, it is difficult to place women on the class hierarchy. One cannot simply assume they derive their class status from husbands, given the tradition of income separation within households found in many African societies and the changed situation of women (if economically dependent on husbands) after separation or divorce. Divorce and remarriage are quite common in some areas. Sam Jackson reports that Hausa have three to four marriages before menopause; see her study of women agricultural laborers; "Hausa Women on Strike," *Review of African Political Economy* 13 (1978): 21–36. Bukh, op. cit., pp. 42–46, indicates that over two-thirds of her respondents reported being divorced at least once and 42 percent of households were female headed.

59. Barbara Callaway, "Women in Ghana," in Lynne Iglitzin and Ruth Ross, eds., *Women in the World: A Comparative Study,* (Santa Barbara: Clio, 1976), p. 197.

60. Little, op. cit., p. 73.

61. Wipper, op. cit., pp. 434–435. Priscilla Abwao had the idea of using "memsahib" for African women.

62. *Daily Nation,* November 13 and 23, 1979; October 18, 1974; and March 27, 1975. The leader was Jane Kiano, interviewed in *Viva* magazine.

63. Kathleen Staudt, "Class and Sex in the Politics of Women Farmers," *Journal of Politics* 41, 2 (May 1979): 492–512.

64. Klingshirn, op. cit., p. 227.

65. "Less than Second Class: Women in Rural Settlement Schemes in Tanzania," in Nancy Hafkin and Edna Bay, eds., *Women in Africa: Studies in Social and Economic Change,* (Stanford: Stanford University Press, 1976), p. 274.

66. "An Assessment of National Machinery for Women," *Assignment Children* 49/50 (Spring 1980) 61.

67. Lewis, op. cit.

68. Nici Nelson, "Women Must Help Each Other," in P. Caplan and Janet Bujra, eds., *Women United, Women Divided* (Bloomington: Indiana University Press, 1978), pp. 77–98.

69. Klingshirn, op. cit., p. 232; Hodgkin, as cited in Little, op. cit., p. 72.

70. Audrey Smock, "Ghana: From Autonomy to Subordination," in Janet Giele and Audrey Smock, eds., *Women: Roles and Status in Eight Countries* (New York: Wiley, 1977), p. 206.

71. Ilsa Schuster, *New Women of Lusaka* (Palo Alto: Mayfield, 1979), pp. 160-165.

72. Leslie Sophia McNeil, "Women of Mali: A Study in Sexual Stratification," B.A. thesis presented to the Department of Anthropology, Harvard University, March 1979, pp. 113-118.

73. *Female Power in African Politics: The National Congress of Sierra Leone Women* (Pasadena, Calif.: Munger Africana Library, California Institute of Technology, August 1975), pp. 25-26, 69.

74. M. Catharine Newbury, "Ebutumwa Bw'Emiogo: The Tyranny of Cassava A Women's Tax Revolt in Eastern Zaire," *Canadian Journal of African Studies* 18, 1 (1984): 35-54.

75. Barbara Isaacman and June Stephen, *Mozambique: Women, the Law and Agrarian Reform* (Addis Ababa: U.N. Economic Commission for Africa, African Training and Research Center for Women, 1980), pp. 29-30.

76. Klingshirn, op. cit., pp. 228 ff.

77. Baker cited in Joan Nelson, *Access to Power: Politics and the Urban Poor in Developing Countries* (Princeton: Princeton University Press, 1979), pp. 309-310. Mba, (op. cit., analyzes considerable activity, but more so among educated as opposed to market women).

78. Sidney Verba, Norman Nie, and Jae-on Kim, *Participation and Political Equality: A Seven-Nation Comparison* (Cambridge: Cambridge University Press, 1978), Chapter 12. The data base for Nigeria excluded the north.

79. "Female Political Participation in Latin America," in Lynne Iglitzin and Ruth Ross, eds., *Women in the World: A Comparative Study* (Santa Barbara: Clio, 1976), p. 63; Mba, op. cit., Chapter 9.

80. Cited from Joyce Stanley, "A Women's Participatory Project," U.S. Agency for International Development, 1979, in (and final quote from) Susan G. Rogers, "Efforts Toward Women's Development in Tanzania: Gender Rhetoric vs. Gender Realities," in Kathleen Staudt and Jane Jaquette, eds. *Women in Developing Countries: A Policy Focus* (New York: Haworth, 1983), pp. 23-42.

## Chapter 9  Algerian Women's Access to Power

1. A study of the revolution is very illustrative of this fact. Among books to be consulted is the four-volume set by Yves Courrières, *La Guerre de l'Algérie* (Paris: Fayard, 1976). See also William Quandt, *Revolution and Political Leadership: Algeria, 1954-1968* (Cambridge: The MIT Press, 1969).

2. Algerians, like the French, often speak of the "couches" of the society, but word change does not alter the reality of class/strata differences. An extremely useful book to examine with regard to origins of class differenciations in Algeria is that by Marnia Lazreg, *The Emergence of Classes in Algeria* (Boulder, Colo.: Westview Press, 1976). Also helpful is Kader Ammour and Christian Leucate, *La voie algérienne* (Paris: Maspero, 1974).

3. This is evident in some of the discussions and recriminations surrounding the Family Code, women's access to employment, demands that women hold important posts in state structures. In newspapers, television debates, study days on women, etc., women speakers talk about their expectations and cite state documents to support this expectation. See Fadela M'Rabet, *La femme algérienne suivi par Les Algériennes* (Paris: Maspero, 1969). See also Tariq Maschino and Fadela M'Rabet, *l'Algérie des illusions* (Paris: Maspero, 1973). Also see Nadia Ainad-Tabet, "Participation des Algeriennes a la vie du pays," *Femmes et Politique autour de la mediterranée* (Paris: L'Harmattan, 1980) , pp. 235-239. A continuation of this debate is found in Souad Khodja, *Les Algériennes au quotidien* (Algiers: ENAL, 1985), and in "Code de la Famille et diverses tendances," *Algérie Actualité*, No. 1016, April 4-10, 1985, pp. 8-9.

4. Juliette Minces, "Women in Algeria," *Women in the Muslim World* (Cambridge, Mass.: Harvard University Press, 1978), p. 159. See also Frantz Fanon, *Sociologie d'une révolution, L'an V de la révolution* (Paris: Maspero, 1972).

5. "20 août, hommage émouvant à la volonté et au sacrifice," *Révolution Africaine*, No. 1070, August 24-30, 1984, pp. 6-9.

6. Walid Awad and Khawlah Qal'aji, "Jamilah Buhrayd, Legendary Algerian Hero," *Middle Eastern Muslim Women Speak* (Austin: University of Texas Press, 1977), pp. 251-262.

7. Frantz Fanon, op. cit., pp. 48-50.

8. French newspapers and magazines of the period are excellent chronicles of the effectiveness of this "use" of women. Fanon, op. cit., talks of the women's cells of the FLN. Alistair Horne, *A Savage War of Peace* (London: Macmillan, 1977), goes into some detail about the roles of Zohra Drif, Djamila Bouhired, Samia Lakhdari, Djamila Bouazza, Hassiba Ben Bouali, and Nefissa Hamoud. Recent articles in *Algérie Actualité*, a weekly paper in French, have described the

work of some women militants during the war for independence. See, for example, *Algérie Actualité*, No. 1016, April 4–10, 1985, "Le Guide: Vie de Femmes," p. 2. Dalila Lakhdar talks about Meriem Belmihoub, a lawyer in Algiers, who with Safia Bazi and Fadila Mesli, was one of the first women to join the revolution.

9. Bouhired's case was widely known throughout the East and West. See Walid Awad and Khawlah Qal'aji, op. cit.

10. Gisèle Halimi, "La libération pour tous . . . sauf pour elles?" *Nouvelle Observateur*, July 10, 1978, noted in Naila Minai, *Women in Islam* (New York: Seaview Book, 1981), p. 76.

11. Djamila Amrane, "La femme algérienne et la guerre de libération nationale (1954–1962)," *Cahiers du C.D.S.H.*, No. 3 (Oran: C.D.S.H., 1980), p. 204. It must be noted that these statistics are postconflict. The registration of former Moudjahidines occurred after 1962.

12. Ibid., pp. 204–207.

13. An interesting treatment of women's roles in the war is the poetic novel by Yamina Mechakra, *La grotte éclatée* (Algiers: SNED, 1979). The heroine is a "doctor/nurse" for the combatants who finishes up the war, after her underground "hospital" is destroyed by the French, in Tunis. The poetic form of the novel is, perhaps, most effective in helping a reader to relate to the feelings of a woman involved very directly in the war effort. A second work, *Nora*, Témoignages-Nouvelles, Musée National de Moudjahid, ENAL, Algiers, 1985, is a collection of remembrances of men and women involved in the war and some fictional pieces. It, too, contains a number of contributions by women.

14. One of the problems of the FLN was what to do with the unmarried women. These were university students and others who fled from urban areas to rural areas to escape the French. Still, most figures reveal that the majority of the women militants were married.

15. Djamila Amrane, op. cit., pp. 204–207.

16. Official recognition by the Algerian government of those roles that Algerian women played in the revolution has notably increased in recent years. In the "Dossier:" Hommage aux Moudjahidine," *Révolution Africaine*, No. 1079, October 26–November 1, 1984, "Le Djihad d'un peuple," pp. 1–8, a writer reports that during the celebration of the thirtieth anniversary of the outbreak of the war, that is, November 1, 1984, medals were awarded to former participants in the war for liberation. Listed among the celebrated male "chahid" like Ait Hamouda Amirouche, Mohamed Larbi Ben M'Hidi, Mourad Didouche, and Si Cherif is Fatima Djaghouri. Yasmina Belkacen is listed as one of three recipients of the medal for those severely wounded in the war. Twenty-three women were awarded medals for their work in the ALN the liberation army, and twelve women active in the Resistance received recognition medals as well. The names are a feminine who's who of the war: Zohra Drif, Zhor Ounissi, Nassima Khelal, Leila Tayeb, Dalila Brahimi, Nafissa Hamoud, Zoulikha Boudjemaa, Malika Boudoukha, Djamila Boupacha, Djamila Bouhired, and others.

17. Zohra Drif, a very well-known woman militant, did receive an important post with *Révolution Africaine*, the party journal, after independence. (David C. Gordon, *Women of Algeria, An Essay in Change* [Cambridge, Mass.: Harvard Middle Eastern Monograph XIX, 1968], gives the names of Drif and of some other women placed in important positions during Ben Bella's tenure in office.) Drif has remained in the center of power. She is, it must be noted, the wife of Rabah Bitat, the Algerian government official with the greatest "staying power." He served as interim president following Boumédiène's death. It appears that support at cabinet level has protected some wives-directors.

18. Fadela M'Rabet, op. cit. See also Souad Khodja, "Les femmes algériennes et la politique," in *Femmes et Politique autour de la mediterrannee*, pp. 251–261. A number of women have spoken quite bitterly about their disappointment. Perhaps, they were the ones to take Fanon literally.

19. Fadela M'Rabet, op. cit.

20. Germaine Tillion, *Le harem et les cousins* (Paris: Editions du Seuil, 1966). See the argument developed throughout the book.

21. In looking at the televised debates (many of which were impromptu), it appeared that women's rights and corruption of officials shared center stage. The national press of that period addressed the issue of women. UNFA with the Ministries of Culture and of Information published *la femme algérienne* (Algiers: collection visages de l'Algérie, 1976), at that time. The thrust of the booklet was that the new struggle for Algerian women was to participate fully in the "new" Algeria. See also *Projet de Charte Nationale* (Algiers: El Moudjahid, 1976), 31 pp. Tabrizi Bensalah, *La République Algérienne* (Paris: Librairie Générale de Droit et de Jurisprudence, 1979), also discusses this question in pp. 361–389.

22. Bensalah, op. cit. The constitution is printed in full in these pages.

23. On February 4, 1985, President Chadli Bendjedid talked about the role of UNFA and Algerian women in general during a meeting of the heads and the professional staffs of the "organizations of the masses" and of the Central Committee of the FLN. Bendjedid's words describe the delicate balance he is trying to maintain among all factions in the country on this issue. References to the traditional role of the woman as educator are contained in the president's comments, but his words point out that full political participation by women continues to be a state goal. The following has been translated from *Révolution Africaine,* No. 1093, February 8–14, 1985, pp. 13–14. Emphasis is by the translator.

Dear brothers and sisters:
As for U.N.F.A., one must note that women make up more than half the population [of Algeria]. U.N.F.A. owes it to itself to fully play its organic role in order that the Algerian woman participate in the social development of the nation. Personally I believe in an efficacious role that women can play in the education of generations to come and in the building of a harmonious society attached to its authenticity and belonging to arabo-islamic civilization. This role is important for the woman can, through her position and the social environment, educate and orient the youth [of the nation] and thus influence the whole of the society.
That is why we have encouraged the Algerian woman. *She is a member of the political Bureau and the Government* [ministerial posts]. It is up to her to impose herself through her work as educator, director and guide, all this while respecting our traditions and our civilizational roots. The Algerian woman has a respectable place in the society of which she forms a half, *which* [place] *cannot be on the margins* [of the society]. She owes it to herself to always take into account the social-political environment and the ideological orientation of the spiritual values imposed by our belonging to an arabo-islamic civilization. *We have faith in the capacity of our civilization for openness and change.* Our idea of Islam goes beyond the framework in which colonialism wanted to confine it.

24. This article has caused some Algerian feminists to state that absolutely no progress has been made in women's rights. See Souad Khodja, op. cit.

25. Note an early discussion of the Family Code, "Algeria: Chadli's Consolidation," *Africa Confidential* 22, 23 (November 1, 1981): 5.

26. Koran IV:34. *Le Coran* (Paris: Gallimard, 1967), p. 98.

27. I lived in Algeria and taught at the University of Oran from 1973 to 1975. I returned to that country in 1976, 1977, 1978, 1979, and 1981. In conversations with women over the years, the importance of the Family Code has been a major topic of women's comments, and, for most women, the concern has been that the Code be "progressive."

28. Notes from interviews with women in September 1981.

29. *Le Monde,* December 25, 1981, p. 6. See also *Africa Confidential* 22, 23 (November 11, 1981): 5.

30. Interviews with Minister of Justice Boualem Baki in *Révolution Africaine.* Also comments from contacts in Algeria.

31. See "Conférence de presse du Ministre de la Justice," *Révolution Africaine,* No. 1062, June 29–July 5, 1984, p. 15.

32. This was the subject of much discussion when I visited Oran in the summer of 1976. Both male and female Algerian teachers were opposed to the regulation.

33. A complete copy of the Code is printed in *Révolution Africaine,* 1062, June 29–July 5, 1984. The special supplement is sixteen pages in length.

34. Boualem Baki referred to the divorce rate in his discussion of the Code in *Révolution Africaine,* No. 1062, and in *Révolution Africaine,* No. 1061, June 22–28, 1984, pp. 7–8.

35. The official text reported in *Révolution Africaine* shows the caps. It is not certain if this appears in all versions or was done for popular consumption.

36. A discussion of some of the difficulties of mixed marriages is found in Khadidja Zeghloul's article, "Couples mixtes, aux frontières du mariage," *Algérie Actualité,* No. 1004, January 10–16, 1985, pp. 36–37.

37. In her interviews with Walid Awad and Khawlah Qal'aji, Bouhired is slightly testy over the question of her husband's name (he has taken an Arabic name) and his religion (Christian).

38. Leila Aslaoui, a judge in the family court division in Algiers, discusses the Family Code and some of its weaknesses and strengths in *Algérie Actualité,* No. 1016, April 4–10, 1985, pp. 8–9. She notes that some of the greatest protests about the Code as enacted are in the areas of custody (of male children), the father's lack of obligation to pay for housing the children if the ex-wife and children return to a relative's home, adoption, and inheritance. She notes that the greatest benefits to the Algerian family is the existence of the Code, which halts arbitrary judicial

judgments based on individual jurist's interpretations of the Koran, which prior to the Family Code was the basis for legal opinion and decision. Further she points out that divorce judgments are no longer subject to appeal except for property dispositions and that full guardianship of children now goes to the mother in the event of the death of her husband. The Code, of course, continues to be debated and will be amended in time.

39. The question of the state's right to write and promulgate the Code is the matter of several articles in *Révolution Africaine*. The heading of the official text of the Code cites the specific articles of the constitution under which the National Assembly acted.

40. That is, it is sensitive or uneasy that Algerian women will descend upon the government in wrath.

41. Constitution, in Bensalah, op. cit., Article 66, p. 371.

42. Ibid.

43. Fatima-Zohra Sai, *Mouvement National et Question Féminine: Des Origines à la Veille de la Guerre de Libération Nationale* (Oran: CRIDSSH, 1984), pp. 1–52 followed by pp. 1–25.

44. *Algeria News Report*, bimonthly publication, from 1978 to 1981.

45. *Révolution Africaine* periodically describes the new school construction. An attempt has been made recently (1982–1986) to provide advanced training (university and technical institute) throughout the nation rather than to focus it in certain cities such as Algiers, Oran, and Constantine.

46. "1985–1989, La prochaine étape du développement," *Révolution Africaine*, No. 1063, July 6–12, 1984, pp. 14–15.

47. Tony Smith, *The French Stake in Algeria, 1945–1962* (Ithaca and London: Cornell University Press, 1978), p. 94. Smith refers to Robert Aron's *L'Algérie et la République* (Paris: Plon, 1958), pp. 18 ff.

48. David C. Gordon, op. cit., p. 79. A study by Abderrahmane Remili in *Intégration*, December 14, 1980, p. 81, indicates that women made up only 7 percent of the total university student population in 1963–1964. It is not clear if Remili's figures include European students. If his data are correct, then there has been a remarkable increase in access of Algerian women to university education.

49. David C. Gordon, op. cit., p. 79.

50. Ibid.

51. Ibid.

52. Ibid.

53. This view did not arrive with independence. The idea of the value of at least elementary school education (twelve years of age) was viewed by the Ulemas and the other groups as useful instruction for girls as preparation for marriage.

54. *Algeria News Report*, June–July 1980, Washington, D.C., Algerian Embassy, p. 16.

55. Ibid., p. 17.

56. "Dossier: Le travail au féminin," *Révolution Africaine*, No. 1088, January 4–10, 1985, p. 23.

57. *Algeria News Report*, June–July 1980.

58. "Dossier: Le travail au féminin," p. 23.

59. *La femme algérienne* (Algiers: Ministries of Information and Culture, 1976), p. 47.

60. *Algeria News Report*, December 15, 1978, Washington, D.C., Algerian Embassy, p. 15.

61. *Algeria News Report*, June–July 1980, pp. 18–19.

62. Ibid.

63. Articles have appeared in *El Moudjahid* and *Algérie Actualité*, among others. One of the longest articles, a three-part discussion of these women workers, appeared in *Algérie Actualité*, No. 743, January 10–16, 1980. See also "Dossier: La travail au féminin," pp. 20–26.

64. Souhil Chennouf notes in "Dossier: Le travail au féminin," that "Women in Algeria like those in all other countries of the world are employed in teaching, the textile industry and the electronics industry, thus in those sectors of high intensity work and low remuneration." See page 23 of the article.

65. One effort of the state has been to provide trained medical personnel to areas of the country lacking this personnel. Women doctors accompanying husbands who are professionals in other fields (engineering) have frequently been used to staff out-of-the-way health care centers.

66. The difficulties facing a woman working in the United States today face the Algerian woman as well. Most women have the major responsibility for the care of the home and the children along with their professional responsibilities. The problem for most women is getting everything done, even if the Algerian woman can, perhaps, more easily find someone to assist with domestic chores.

67. Fatiha Hakiki, "Le travail féminin, emploi salarié et travail domestique," *Cahiers du C.D.S.H.*, No. 3, (Oran, C.D.S.H.: 1980), p. 59.

68. Ibid., p. 60.

69. Ibid., p. 40.

70. Ibid.

71. Ibid., p. 37.

72. Ibid., p. 66.

73. Ibid.

74. M'hamed Boukhobza, "La mobilité féminine à travers les rélations ville-campagne," *Questions de sciences sociales* (Algiers: O.N.R.S., September 1978).

75. *Annuaire Statistique de l'Algérie,* 1979 (Algiers: Ministère de la Planification et de l'Aménagement du Territoire, November 1980), p. 30.

76. Fatiha Hakiki, op. cit., p. 66. 1977 is the date of the last general census in Algeria; hence the most complete information on the work force comes from that data.

77. In discussions of the Sonelec plant experiment, this particular problem was raised.

78. An informant in her mid-thirties in Algeria noted that her grandfather was a paramedical. Her mother was sent to a boarding school for some elementary education while her uncles became doctors, dentists, engineers. Her mother stopped her education because she feared that with too much education her chances of marrying would be fewer. The grandfather encouraged his female grandchildren to get an education so as to have a career. The father-in-law of this same informant was also a paramedical. His daughters are teachers, although one is in training to be a doctor. Education is seen on both sides of the family as a means to rising in status and has been used by several generations to this end.

79. Claude Talahite, "Femmes à l'usine dans Algérie-Actualité," *Cahiers du C.D.S.H.*, No. 3 (Oran: C.D.S.H., 1980), pp. 353–386.

80. Ibid. In 1985, 1920 women worked at Sonelec.

81. One of the reasons for state interest is to balance segments in the state: religious leaders, women, party militants, etc.

82. Souhil Chennouf, op. cit., p. 26.

83. *Révolution Africaine* started a new rubric, "L'invitée de la semaine," in 1985. A woman police officer and a variety of other professional women have been featured. *Algérie Actualité* regularly carries articles on women artists, writers, and professionals in other fields. This has become an almost weekly feature since 1984. It must be remembered that there has been considerable interest by women in the arts. *Révolution Africaine,* No. 1097, March 8–14, 1985, carries an article by Mimi Maziz which relates that women make up 30 percent of the 500 members of the National Union of the Plastic Arts.

84. M'hamed Boukhobza, op. cit.

85. This was the case for many "maids" in the Oran area, those working in both Algerian and expatriate homes.

86. Fatiha Hakiki, op. cit., p. 70.

87. Leila Baghriche and Claudine Chaulet, "Le travail de femmes dans l'agriculture," *Cahiers du C.D.S.H.*, No. 3 (Oran: C.D.S.H., 1980), pp. 115–117.

88. This study was analyzed in the April–June 1984 issue of *Revue Statistique,* No. 3, O.N.S., in an article entitled, "L'activité féminine: un indicateur des mutations socio-économiques." The article noted, of course, that paid employment for women is primarily an urban phenomenon. Genia Boutaleb discusses the study as well in a special issue of *Algérie Actualité,* No. 1012, March 7–13, 1985, published to commemorate International Women's Day. The article is on pp. 14–15.

89. Abdelkader Hammouche, "Femmes: Inégalite Sociale ou Salariale," *Algérie Actualité,* No. 832, September 24–30, 1981, pp. 6–7.

90. Ibid.

91. Ibid.

92. K. Cherit, "SGT, Payer en fonction du travail," *Révolution Africaine,* No. 1091, January 25–31, 1985, pp. 14–19.

93. *Projet de Charte Nationale,* op. cit., p. 12.

94. See National Charter and Constitution.

95. At least it was not true in practice. Only in 1983 did the UNFA decide that all UNFA leadership was to hold FLN membership as well.

96. See National Charter and Constitution.

97. This has been particularly noticeable with the UNFA. A male Political Bureau member is assigned to work with the U.N.F.A. and to coordinate the National Congresses and meetings.

(In 1978 this individual was Mohamed Salah Yahiaoui. In 1985 it was Mohamed Cherif Messaadia.) This oversight occurs in part, perhaps, because of the independence of the UNFA.

98. "La femme algérienne: une participation qui s'affirme," *Révolution Africaine*, No. 527, March 29–April 4, 1974, p. 12.

99. National Charter, op. cit., p. 9.

100. Fatiha Hadri, "L'Algérienne en 20 Ans," *El Djazaïria*, No. 34, 1973, p. viii.

101. Discussions with Algerian women in 1973–1979 and in 1981. See also Helene Vandevelde Daillière, *Femmes Algériennes* (Algiers: Office des Publications Universitaires, 1980), p. 331, a valuable study of Algerian women in the Constantine area.

102. "U.N.F.A., un rôle réellement efficient," *Révolution Africaine*, No. 1030, November 18–24, 1983, pp. 16–17 and 20–23.

103. Tabrizi Bensalah, op. cit., p. 220. See also *4ème Congrès de l'U.N.F.A.* (Algiers: *El Djazaïria*, 1978).

104. "U.N.F.A., un rôle réellement efficient," p. 17.

105. Ibid.

106. The language of the resolutions is faithfully reported in *Révolution Africaine*. It must be noted that a male member of the Political Bureau continues to take part in U.N.F.A. Congresses.

107. Ibid.

108. At one point Boumèdiene is reported to have told UNFA women clamoring for a greater role in the state that their best contribution was to have children for the state.

109. A special report on "Démographie: Danger . . . Ralentir" appeared in *Révolution Africaine*, No. 1057, May 25–31, 1984. The report is thirty-four pages in length and deals with all aspects of the Algerian question. *Révolution Africaine*, No. 1043, February 17–23, 1984, also carried a long interview with Mme. Ounissi, minister for social protection, on the issue of family planning. Two other issues of *Révolution Africaine*, Nos. 1086 and 1087, December 21–27, 1984, and December 28, 1984–January 3, 1985, contain a two-part thirty-two page document on "Demography, Decisive Stakes." Of particular interest is the reliance on Islamic tradition to suggest that births should be spaced thirty-three months apart. The document reports that in 1967 there was 1 family planning center. In April 1984 there were 399. In 1975, 31,782 women came to family planning centers for contraceptive assistance. In 1983, the total was 779,318. State policy on family planning/birth control is clearly evident in the document and in the statistics that are now being collected on this issue.

110. The party is attempting to consolidate its power.

111. *La femme algérienne*, p. 58.

112. *4ème Congres de l'U.N.F.A.*, p. 47.

113. See *Algeria News Report*, June–July 1980.

114. "A la hauteur de l'importance de l'étape," *Révolution Africaine*, No. 1066, July 27–August 2, 1984, pp. 6–7.

115. *Algeria News Report*, November 15, 1978, Washington, D.C., Algerian Embassy, p. 14.

116. See earlier discussions of these points.

117. The names of members of the Central Committee were published in *Révolution Africaine*, No. 1036, December 31, 1983–January 5, 1984, p. 11.

118. The list of ministers was published in *Révolution Africaine*, No. 1040, January 27–February 2, 1984, pp. 8–9.

119. Fatima-Zohra Sai, "Les femmes dans les institutions representatives," *Cahiers du C.D.S.H.*, No. 3 (Oran, C.D.S.H.: 1980), pp. 227–291.

120. Ibid.

121. Ibid.

122. Ibid., p. 280.

123. "A.P.C.-A.P.W. 84," *Algérie Actualité*, No. 1000, December 13–19, 1984, p. 12.

124. Fatima-Zohra Sai, op. cit., p. 280.

125. "Z.G. l'avancée de la democratie," *Révolution Africaine*, No. 939, February 19–25, 1982, pp. 4–7.

126. "A.P.C.-A.P.W. 84," p. 12.

127. In 1980 Assia Kebir was named director of the University Center of Tiaret. Several Algerian women hold prominent positions in education, in the ministries, and in the universities and schools. The state has been as generous with women as with men in providing scholarship funds for study abroad for advanced degrees. University faculty members are provided released time to work on these degrees. Union activities have evidently helped assure this support.

128. "Le projet de statut personnel," *Révolution Africaine*, No. 1028, November 4–10, 1983, p. 18.

129. Interview with Boualem Baki, *Révolution Africaine*, No. 1061, June 22–28, 1984, p. 7.

130. The appearance of these films is accompanied by debates in the press and on TV.

131. The Centre de Recherche et d'Information Documentaires en Sciences Sociales et Humaines in Oran has provided impetus and support to this research and has published a number of studies.

132. This has been partly effective. Fatima Zohra Sai's *Quelques remarques à propos de la codification du droit de la famille* (Oran: CRIDSSH, 1983), may well have influenced lawyers in the Ministry of Justice. Certainly, the studies have been useful to advocates for women's rights.

133. Studies done by women at CRIDSSH on divorce, contraception, and family life would be available to Mme. Ounissi and would provide her ministry with studies on which to base approaches and recommendations.

### Part V  The *Encadrement* of the Population

1. Irving Leonard Markovitz, *Power and Class in Africa* (Englewood Cliffs, N.J.: Prentice-Hall, 1977), p. 20.

2. Richard Franke and Barbara J. Chasin, *Seeds of Famine: Ecological Destruction and the Development Dilemma in the West African Sahel* (Montclair, N.J.: Allanheld, Osmun, 1980).

### Chapter 10  From Nationalism to Marxism

I would like to thank the Department of Political Science at the University of Wisconsin—Madison for its practical support in 1980, when the earliest draft for this paper was being written. The following people have since provided valuable comments or information: Barbara Chasin, Steve Feierman, Dick Franke, Allen Isaacman, Lenny Markovitz, Barry Munslow, Dave Wield, and Ben Wisner.

1. Frente de Libertação de Moçambique.

2. FRELIMO, Programa e Estatutos (Maputo: Departamento de Trabalho Ideológico da FRELIMO, 1977), p. 8. Translations from this and all other Portuguese documents and speeches cited in this paper are mine.

3. Movimento Da Resistência Nacional. Apart from damaging roads, bridges, supply depots, etc., MNR activity has been explicitly directed at social targets. In 1982 and 1983, the MNR is said by the government to have destroyed, among other things, 840 schools, 212 health posts, 900 shops—as well as burning or otherwise destroying over 200 villages. See Joseph Hanlon, *Revolution Under Fire* (London: Zed Press, 1984), p. 255.

4. The main clauses of the Accords are reproduced in Hanlon, op. cit., p. 290.

5. John Saul, ed., *A Different Road: The Transition to Socialism in Mozambique* (New York: Monthly Review Press, 1985), p. 397.

6. *Relatório do Comité Central ao 3° Congresso* (Maputo: Departamento do Trabalho Ideológico da FRELIMO, 1977). This document is hereafter cited as *Report*.

7. Eduardo Mondlane, *The Struggle for Mozambique* (Hardmondsworth, Penguin Books, 1969), hereafter cited as *Struggle*.

8. Ibid., p. 101.

9. For more details of these early movements, see Ibid., pp. 118–121; T. H. Henriksen, *Mozambique: A History* (London: Rex Collings, 1978), pp. 168–170; Allen and Barbara Isaacman, *Mozambique: From Colonialism to Revolution. 1900–1982* (Boulder: Westview Press, 1983), pp. 79–84. Many members of the early movements had lived for so long outside Mozambique that they could no longer speak Portuguese. Mondlane discusses this in "The Struggle for Independence in Mozambique," in J. A. Adams and J. K. Barker, eds., *Southern Africa in Transition* (New York: Praeger, 1966), p. 203.

10. Itself one of the most economically backward states in Europe, Portugal could not afford the luxury of decolonizing when France and Britain did. See James Duffy, *Portugal in Africa* (Harmondsworth: Penguin Books, 1962); William Minter, *Portuguese Africa and the West* (Harmondsworth: Penguin Books, 1972); James H. Mittleman *Underdevelopment and the Transition to Socialism. Mozambique and Tanzania* (New York: Academic Press, 1981), especially Chapters 3 and 4.

11. For a discussion of the systematic use of state repression against labor, especially in urban centers, see Jeanne Penvenne, "Here Everyone Walked with Fear," in Frederick Cooper, ed.,

*Struggle for the City: Migrant Labor, Capital, and the State in Urban Africa* (Beverly Hills: Sage Publications, 1983), pp. 131–164. For a discussion of plantation labor, see L. Vail and L. White, *Capitalism and Colonialism in Mozambique* (Minneapolis: University of Minnesota Press, 1980).

12. These ethnic differences reflected the patterns of Mozambican labor migration, for example, from Tete Province into nearby Nyasaland, and from the more southerly province of Manica and Sofala into Southern Rhodesia. Recent—rather exploratory—research by Edward Alpers on the class composition of MANU suggests that, in that organization at least, membership was composed of peasants who had to some extent "got ahead" by leaving Mozambique, and whose aspirations were in no way revolutionary. The future they would have been most likely to desire was one of untrammeled African petty commodity production. See, "To Seek a Better Life," *Canadian Journal of African Studies* 18, 2 (1984): 367–388.

13. See Dos Santos, "FRELIMO faces the future," interview in *African Communist* 55 (4th Quarter, 1973): 35. Dos Santos was vice president of FRELIMO at the time of this interview.

14. In R. Chilcote, ed., *Emerging Nationalism in Portuguese Africa, Documents* (Stanford: Hoover Institute Press, 1972), p. 449.

15. "FRELIMO faces the future," p. 35.

16. In Chilcote, op. cit., p. 451.

17. "The Struggle for Socialism in Mozambique," in Carl G. Rosberg and Thomas M. Callaghy, eds., *Socialism in Sub-Saharan Africa* (Berkeley: Institute of International Studies, 1979), pp. 267–295. There are in fact earlier public statements than those Alpers cites which suggest a commitment to socialism. A speech by FRELIMO's representative in Paris, published in the *Boletím Informativo* 6 (March 1964) contains the following passage:

> We want to transform Mozambique from a dependent, oppressed and exploited country into a free and prosperous country, in which all exploitation of man by man will be completely eliminated.

18. See his essay "Ujamaa—The Basis of Socialism," *Ujamaa—Essays on Socialism* (Dares-Salaam: Oxford University Press, 1968), pp. 1–12. Nyerere argued that class conflict is a specifically European phenomenon and that African societies can build socialism on their past traditions of mutual aid and the extended family, once colonialism has been ended.

19. Interview with Helen Kitching, *Africa Report* 12, 8 (Nov. 1967): 31–32, 49–51.

20. Ibid., p. 51.

21. "FRELIMO Faces the Future," p. 67.

22. *Report*, p. 11.

23. It began in the extreme north, in Cabo Delgado Province, which borders Tanzania at the Rovuma River. Tanzania permitted FRELIMO to have bases, etc., within its borders.

24. "Mensagem por ocasião do 3° aniversário da luta armada de libertação nacional," in *A Vitória Constroi-Se, A Vitória Organiza-Se* (Maputo: Imprensa Nacional de Moçambique, 1977), p. 10.

25. "Mensagem por ocasião do 4° aniversário da luta armada de libertação nacional," in *A. Vitória Controi-Se*, pp. 34–35.

26. *Mozambique Revolution* 38 (March–April 1969): 2.

27. *Report*, p. 12.

28. Ibid., p. 14.

29. For an account of these events, see T. H. Henriksen, *Mozambique*, pp. 168–183; and B. Davidson, *In the Eye of the Storm* (London: Longman, 1972), pp. 225–230. See also Walter C. Opello, Jr., "Pluralism and Elite Conflict in an Independence Movement: FRELIMO in the 1960's," *Journal of Southern African Studies* 2, 1 (Oct. 1975): 66–82.

30. *Report*, p. 13.

31. Ibid., p. 14.

32. Machel, "O processo da revolução democrática popular em Moçambique," in *A Nossa Luta* (Maputo: Imprensa Nacional, 1975), p. 231.

33. Little data is available on this, outside FRELIMO's own rather general account. Isaacman and Isaacman conducted interviews with inhabitants of the former "liberated zones" in 1979, which seem to provide some confirmation of FRELIMO's account (op. cit., p. 95).

34. *Report*, p. 17.

35. Machel, "O processo," p. 215.

36. For example, Leo Milas, expelled from FRELIMO in 1964, publicly complained about the movement's multiracialism: "Jorge Rebelo, a leading member of the Central Committee is an Indian from Goa," while "much of the direction of FRELIMO is carried by Helder Martíns, a Portuguese, and Janet Mondlane" (Mondlane's white American wife): *Daily Telegraph* (Lon-

don), Sept. 21, 1966, cited in Isaacman and Isaacman, op. cit., p. 88. At the Mozambique Institute in Dar-es-Salaam, white Mozambican teachers became the particular target of racist attacks in 1967 and 1968. See ibid., pp. 96–97, and Opello, op. cit., pp. 74–75.

37. Mondlane, *Struggle*, pp. 28–29.

38. Machel, "O processo," p. 206.

39. *A Voz da Revolução*, Sept. 1965.

40. Mondlane, *Struggle*, p. 168.

41. Mondlane, *Struggle*, p. 220. Dos Santos, the vice president, was to strike a parallel note some years later: "Even now for us the basic problem is not guns; the Portuguese have guns, too, but that does not make a revolution. The problem is man. It is not because you give a Mozambican a rifle that he becomes a revolutionary, the problem is a political one" ("FRELIMO Faces the Future," p. 25).

42. Mondlane, *Struggle*, p. 183.

43. "Resolutions on foreign policy," cited in ibid., p. 195.

44. Ibid., p. 220.

45. Cited in ibid., p. 191.

46. "Resolutions on the administration of the liberated zones," cited in ibid., p. 191.

47. "Resolutions on social affairs," cited in ibid., p. 194.

48. "Resolutions on national reconstruction," cited in ibid., pp. 192–194.

49. This, it should be remembered, at a time when the more overtly Marxist struggle in Vietnam was at its height.

50. A. de Bragança, paper (untitled typescript) presented in Uppsala, Summer 1976, p. 16 ("Noyau marxisant," in the French original). De Bragança now directs the Center for African Studies at the Eduardo Mondlane University in Maputo.

51. Taped interview given in Algeria. Published in A. de Bragança and I. Wallerstein, eds., *Quem é o Inimigo?* (Lisbon: Initiativas Editoriais, 1977), Vol. 2, p. 200.

52. A. de Bragança, Uppsala paper, p. 11.

53. Machel, "O processo," p. 208.

54. *Mozambique Revolution* 38 (April–March 1969), pp. 2, 10–11.

55. "Gloomy Situation in FRELIMO," unpublished typescript, Dar-es-Salaam, Nov. 1969. Cited in Isaacman and Isaacman, op. cit., p. 98.

56. Unlike Mondlane, Machel was not an intellectual. Starting out as a nurse in the main hospital in Lourenço Marques, he was one of the first volunteers sent to Algeria to receive military training, soon after FRELIMO was formed. He rose through the military wing of FRELIMO, becoming secretary of defense in 1966.

57. "Os Graves Acontecimentos de 1968 e as Divergências Ideológicas," Dar-es-Salaam, Mimeo, 1969; cited in Opello, op. cit., p. 80 (my emphasis).

58. As given in his opening speech to the first conference of the Organization of Mozambican Women. "A Libertação da mulher é uma necessidade da revolução," in *A Nossa Luta*, pp. 69–92. (The conference was in 1973.)

59. A codified position on the "woman question" was developed in the early days of the Third International and has since been generally accepted in Third World revolutionary movements and states. See Maxine Molyneux, "Women in Socialist Societies," in Kate Young et al., eds., *Of Marriage and the Market* (London: 1981), pp. 175–177.

60. "A Libertação," p. 79.

61. Ibid., p. 80.

62. Ibid., pp. 80–82.

63. FRELIMO started to involve women in military activities by 1968, with the establishment of the "Destacamento Feminino," the Women's Detachment, of the army.

64. "A Libertação," pp. 82–83 (my emphasis).

65. See, for example, "Produzir é aprender," *A Nossa Luta*, pp. 9–23, and "Estabelecer o poder popular para servir as massas," *A Nossa Luta*, pp. 97–139. For speeches since independence, demonstrating the same ability, see Barry Munslow, ed., *Samora Machel: An African Revolutionary* (London: Zed Press, 1985).

66. FRELIMO started military action in Tete in 1968, as a response to the decision to build the dam. They failed to stop the dam from being built, but by 1970–1971 Tete province had become another major war zone—as evidenced by the frequent missionary reports about Portuguese atrocities against the civilian population. See *Terror in Tete* (London: International Defence and Aid Fund, Special Report, No. 2, 1973) and A. Hastings, *Wiriyamu* (London: Search Press, 1974).

On the opening of the front in Manica and Sofala province, see *Mozambique Revolution* 53 (Oct.–Dec. 1972): 2. The editorial discussed the implications of opening a new front in an area of the country with "highly urbanized areas with a high concentration of white population."

67. Machel, "No trabalho sanitário materializemos o princípio de que a revolução liberta o povo," in *A Nossa Luta*, p. 53.

68. *Mozambique Revolution* 53 (Oct.–Dec. 1972): 2.

69. *Report*, p. 89.

70. *Mozambique Revolution*, 58 (Jan.–March 1974): 3.

71. Ibid.

72. For example, one anonymous cadre described in *Mozambique Revolution* 51 (April–June 1972) how, as early as 1962, he heard about FRELIMO from someone he met on a train and decided to join. The man worked on the Sena Sugar Estates in the central province of Manica and Sofala. He described his tasks as propaganda, "to explain to other people about FRELIMO— its aims, the need for everybody to join the struggle," helping people trying to leave to join FRELIMO in the north, helping clandestine workers traveling south and carrying propaganda materials.

A. Hastings, in his article "Some Reflections Upon the War in Mozambique," *African Affairs* 73, 292 (July 1974): 263–276, suggests that although FRELIMO never had "liberated zones" in the center of the country, they were highly active and enjoyed widespread support by 1973. He argues that FRELIMO was able to move south so rapidly in 1973 and 1974 because they had there probably greater popular support than they had in the north of the country. He attributes this support to the fact that there was a very long tradition of resistance to colonialism in Tete and Manica and Sofala provinces and also to the fact that much of FRELIMO's leadership were southern in origin.

By early 1974 the district governor of Beira admitted that some areas under his authority were "controlled by FRELIMO terrorists" and Hastings says there is evidence that FRELIMO was operating well south of Beira before the April coup. It is hard to know, however, how wide FRELIMO's areas of operation were. In an interview given early in 1974, the Portuguese commander-in-chief, General Machado, confirmed that FRELIMO had been able to carry out "spectacular actions against targets of a non-military nature" in the Beira region. See K. Swift, *Mozambique and the Future* (London: Robert Hale and Co., 1975), p. 83. See also Barry Munslow, *Mozambique: the Revolution and its Origins* (London: Longman, 1983), pp. 119–120.

73. *Report*, p. 65.

74. As Mondlane himself had earlier remarked; see p. 15 above.

75. Calculated from *I° Recenseamento Geral da População: Informação Pública* (Maputo: Republica Popular de Moçambique, 1980), Tables 11A, 11B, 11C.

76. On the dynamics of mine labor and rural household economies, see Ruth First, *Black Gold: The Mozambican Miner, Proletarian and Peasant* (Brighton: The Harvester Press, 1983).

77. See Penvenne, op. cit., and Vail and White, op. cit.

78. See Barry Munslow, "Proletarianisation in Mozambique," in Barry Munslow and Henry Finch, ed., *Proletarianisation in the Third World* (London: Croom Helm, 1984), pp. 77–98.

79. *Documentos da 8ª Sessão do Comité Central* (Maputo: Departmento do Informação e Propaganda da FRELIMO, 1976), p. 40. This meeting analyzed both the political and economic situation in Mozambique and called for "a generalized political and organizational offensive on the front of production." It also decided to hold the Third Congress, which took place a year later.

80. *Report*, p. 74.

81. *8ª Sessão*, p. 13.

82. Ibid., p. 17.

83. It has been estimated that the Portuguese population was about 200,000 in 1973 and between 50,000 and 60,000 by early 1976. See T. H. Henriksen, *Mozambique* p. 226.

84. It has been estimated that the abandonment of settler farms led to a 55 percent fall in agricultural production between 1973 and 1975 and that *marketed* peasant production fell by 60 percent in the same period. See M. Wuyts, *Peasants and Rural Development in Mozambique* (Maputo: Centro dos Estudos Africanos, 1978), p. 30.

85. Interview I conducted with irrigation technicians in the Limpopo Basin, August 1975.

86. *Report*, p. 63.

87. Interview I conducted with one of the administrative directors of "Cajuca," a cashew processing plant, Maputo, August 1976.

88. By early 1977, 319 commercial and industrial enterprises had been "state intervened,"

but most of them were very small—only 47 had more than 100 workers. See D. Wield, "Mozambique—Late Colonialism and Early Problems of Transition," in R. Murray, C. White, and G. White, eds., *Socialist Transformation and Development in the Third World* (Brighton: I.D.S., 1983).

89. For a fuller account of the crisis and of FRELIMO's measures, see A. Isaacman, *A Luta Continúa, Creating a New Society in Mozambique* (Binghamton, N.Y.: Fernand Braudel Center, South Africa Pamphlets, No. 1, 1978). See also, J. Saul, "Mozambique: the New Phase," *Monthly Review* 30, 10 (March 1979): 1–19.

90. Some rural work-based "dynamizing groups" were also established—for example, in cooperatives and in private plantations. In addition, residential "dynamizing groups" emerged in some sectors of towns. The plan has been, since 1978, to phase out "dynamizing groups" as party cells have been established.

91. *Report*, p. 63.

92. For a description of them, see J. Saul, "Free Mozambique," esp. pp. 15–17; also Isaacman and Isaacman, op. cit., pp. 116–120.

93. I have drawn primarily on the first two chapters of the *Report* in examining FRELIMO's account of its own historical evolution. Chapters three to five provide the policy statement.

94. *Report*, p. 93.

95. See "The Arusha Declaration," parts Four and Five, in Nyerere, *Ujamaa—Essays on Socialism*, pp. 35–36. See also, L. Cliffe, "Underdevelopment or Socialism? A Comparative Analysis of Kenya and Tanzania," in R. Harris, ed., *The Political Economy of Africa* (Cambridge, Mass.: Schenkman, 1975), pp. 174–175, on the party in Tanzania.

96. *Report*, pp. 95–97.

97. "O processo," pp. 209–210.

98. As Forças Populares de Libertação de Moçambique (Popular Forces for the Liberation of Mozambique).

99. "O processo," pp. 224.

100. *Report*, p. 90.

101. Ibid., p. 89.

102. Ibid., pp. 90–91.

103. Ibid., pp. 92–93.

104. *8ª Sessão*, p. 42.

105. *Report*, pp. 108–109; p. 74.

106. Ibid., p. 74.

107. Ibid., p. 92.

108. Ibid., p. 111.

109. Ibid., p. 97. For a discussion of the development of a conception of leadership in FRELIMO which should ensure noncorrupt leaders, see B. Munslow, "Leadership in the Front for the Liberation of Mozambique," Part I, in C. R. Hill and R. Warwick, eds., *Southern African Research in Progress, I* (York: University of York, 1974), esp. pp. 144–148.

110. Maputo, FRELIMO Party, 1983.

111. See, Allen Isaacman, "FRELIMO's Fourth Party Congress: Returning to the Grass-roots," *In These Times*, June 1–14, 1983, pp. 8, 11. Also, Barry Munslow and Phil O'Keefe, "Rethinking the Revolution in Mozambique," *Race and Class* 26, 2 (1984): 15–31.

112. See "O Processo."

113. *Report*, p. 107.

114. Ibid., p. 111.

115. Ibid., p. 149.

116. Ibid., p. 150.

117. Isaacman and Isaacman, op. cit., pp. 128–132.

118. *People's Power* (London) 10 (Oct.–Dec. 1977): 10–14; 11 (Jan.–March 1978): 22–28.

119. *Out of Underdevelopment*, p. 101.

120. Ibid.

121. See, for example, the report of the speech by the Portuguese foreign minister, Dr. Nogueira, *Southern Africa*, May 14, 1965, pp. 356–357. Nogueira asserted that the war was really against Communist outsiders and not against elements of the population.

122. "Pluralism and Elite Conflict."

123. "Scientific Socialist Regimes in Africa: Political Differentiation, Avoidance and Unawareness," in Rosberg and Callaghy, op. cit., pp. 133–173.

### Chapter 11  Power, Class and Traditional Knowledge

Support for the research on this paper was provided through a grant from the National Endowment for the Humanities Summer Seminars for College Teachers, under direction of Professor Irving Leonard Markovitz, and by a 1981 grant from the Released Time for Research Committee, Montclair State College.

1. The Dogon also have special, institutionalized relationships with the Bozo fishing specialists of the Niger River bend (not to be confused with the Bouzou farmers described in the previous section of this paper). See Paulme (1940: 22–23), Griaule and Dieterlen (1954: 107–110), and Roberts (1981).

2. The Human Relations Area Files entry on the Dogon has only one page under the heading "classes" and a very small section on social stratification in general, mostly the age groups and castes. Information on castes in Mali appears in Diop (1971) and N'Diayé (1970b).

3. Another important tree in Sahel food production is the baobab, whose leaves and fruits are rich in those vitamins lacking in millet (Pélissier, 1966: 265; Owen, 1973).

4. According to Fulani legends, Ba's vassal at Macina, the Ardo Ngourori, said of Amadou: "In my eyes he will remain nothing but a house to house beggar while I am like an eagle" (Ba and Daget, 1955: 107).

5. Gueladio, one of Amadou's opponents and a vassal of the king of Segou, escaped from Amadou's control through treason by one of Amadou's confidants. Gueladio was able to raise an army and carry on a debilitating seven-year war against the Dina before being eliminated (Ba and Daget, 1955: 119).

6. For detailed examples and additional references, see Franke and Chasin, (1980: 63–83).

7. For cautionary examples from similar parts of the Sahel, see Franke and Chasin (1980: 192–194 and 207–214).

8. An even more superficial analysis led one animal health specialist to propose that "Cattle are of such cultural importance in Africa that means must be found for limiting the ecological damage that they cause. . ." (Ormerod, 1978: 377). Refutation of the logic on which this argument is based as well as empirical data contradicting it can be found in Franke and Chasin (1979; 1980: 84–108, 120–122).

9. Some critical comments on ranching in the Sahel are contained in Beauvilain (1977), Dunbar (1970); and Gallais (1979).

10. For some of the evidence supporting the characterization of the political motivations in Sahel development and their possible effects on the trajectory of the program, see Franke and Chasin (1980: 145, 148–164, 192–194).

### Chapter 12  Transnational Corporations and Party Realignment

This essay is part of a larger work which attempts to reconceptualize the nature of dependency relationships among the states of southern Africa (Libby, 1987). I wish to express my appreciation to Irving Leonard Markovitz, C. van Onselen, Leonard Thompson, Jeffrey Butler, Heribert Adam, and Hermann Giliomee for helpful criticism and suggestions for revision. Special thanks to Jeffrey Butler for his detailed comments. However, the views expressed herein are solely the responsibility of the author.

1. The states in the southern African region which by definition have important regional economic interests include South Africa, Zimbabwe, Botswana, Lesotho, Swaziland, Namibia, Zambia, Malawi, Mozambique, and, to a lesser extent, Zaire and Tanzania.

2. For the results of a survey of white opinion on how best to cope with "hostile" black states on South Africa's borders, see Geldenhuys (1982).

3. For a discussion of the role which representatives of large corporations had in planning South Africa's "total national strategy," see Geldenhuys (1984: 140–141, 149–155, 160–165). For an elaboration on the theme of the NP's political alignment with large-scale corporations, see Prinsloo (1984: 20–42), Innes (1983: 171–183), Wolpe (1983), O'Meara (1983: 248–256), and Davies and O'Meara (1985).

4. Giliomee (1985) questions the proposition that white political opposition to the NP flows from the latter's political alliance with large industrial capital. Instead, he argues that their opposition to the NP is based upon ending state subsidies for lower-income whites through inflated white salaries and job reservation. According to this logic, the state undertook the change out of the recognition that it had to modernize "racial domination." However, there is evidence that

working-class whites are threatened by the NP's support for large-scale corporations in South Africa. For example, Geldenhuys (1984a: 219) notes the fact that the NP launched the process of labor reform in the 1970s (leading to the Wiehahn Commission enquiries), which the white working class regards as a major threat, partly in response to the disinvestment campaign directed at multinational corporations in South Africa. In other words, in order to protect the interests of large corporations in South Africa, the NP was prepared to sacrifice the interests of the white working class. Adam (1978: 95) explains the government's "anti (*White*) union action" in terms of the state's "survival politics" in which national survival must come before avoiding class cleavages within the Afrikaner ruling group.

5. Giliomee (1983: 47) argues that the National Party split of 1981–1982 can be explained in terms of class divisions. He attributes the split to the need for nonwhite skilled labor (presumably needed by large corporations), increased social services for urban blacks, support for the mining industry, and the withdrawal of state support for white agriculture. This was said to have eroded the economic position of lower-class Afrikaners. The Afrikaner working class thus supported the "right wing opposition" (i.e., the HNP and the CP) while the middle class supported the NP. Therefore, the political contest among Afrikaners, as Giliomee sees it, is over control of the Afrikaner lower middle class (presumably contested by the NP and the CP), with most of the CP's support coming from marginal farmers, lower-income state employees, and small businessmen (Giliomee, 1985).

6. O'Meara (1983: 255) argues that the NP's nationalist class alliance has virtually collapsed. In the guise of a "Total Strategy Doctrine" a political alliance has been formed between the military and the "most powerful sections of the capitalist class" in opposition to the right wing of the NP. The right wing of the party has opposed reforms of apartheid such as scrapping influx control, recognizing black trade unions, and job reservation.

7. The managing director of the UF, Dr. Robin Lee, has pointed out that 95 of South Africa's 100 largest corporations are its regular supporters (*The Star* [Johannesburg], July 8, 1985).

8. "Transnational corporations" in the South African context refers to South African affiliates of multinational corporations as well as to large South African conglomerates and firms which have investments in, produce for, or have retail outlets in South Africa and other countries in the region. Examples of South African–based multinational, transnational corporations are CALTEX Oil (S.A.) (Pty.) Ltd., British Petroleum Southern Africa, G.M.-South Africa (Pty.), Ltd. (General Motors), General Electric Co. [Pty.], Ltd., Masonite Africa Ltd., and American Hospital Supply Corporation of South Africa, Ltd. Major South African transnationals include Anglo-American Corporation, Barlow Rand, Premier Milling, African Explosives and Chemical Industries, Fed Food Ltd., Pick 'n Pay, and OK Bazaars.

9. For an elaboration of CONSAS, see Botha (1979). The objective of CONSAS was given as encouraging regional economic integration based upon the "growth-generating potential of the South African economy to be realized throughout the region and beyond" (Leistner, 1981: 349). Official policy envisaged the inclusion of the following regional states in CONSAS: Botswana, Lesotho and Swaziland, Zimbabwe, Zambia, Malawi and Mozambique, and possibly Angola. Geldenhuys (1984b: 117–118) has argued that Botha's initial constellation plan had to be scaled down to include only an "inner constellation" of South African homelands—Transkei, Bophuthatswana, Venda, and Ciskei, the so-called SATBVC states—when the original targeted states refused to join and instead formed their own economic association designed to reduce their economic dependence upon South Africa. However, the nonaggression pacts which South Africa has signed with Mozambique, Angola, Swaziland, Zimbabwe, and Lesotho have undoubtedly revived South Africa's hopes for the at least partial achievement of the original constellation plan.

10. The government's Reynders Commission of 1972 pointed out, for example, that heavy intermediate and capital goods industries in South Africa require large markets and economies of scale to remain economically viable. The report recommended that the government follow an export-led strategy of industrial growth and that southern Africa be regarded as an "economic unit" for that purpose (See Nedbank Group Limited, 1983: 200–201).

11. One such effort, inaugurated in 1960, was the decentralization policy. In the guise of free enterprise capitalism, the major representatives of large firms have attacked the policy. For example, the 1967 Physical Planning Act (No. 88) has been criticized on the grounds that it is wasteful and penalizes established industries by discouraging urban development. The Federated Chamber of Industries (FCI), the umbrella organization representing large industries in South Africa, for example, has opposed this act (Myers et al., 1980: 67).

12. Houghton (1976: 178) has estimated that in 1970, South Africa exported 17 percent of its total exports to African countries.

13. The Southern African Coordinating Conference (SADCC, 1984: I.2) has reported a two-way trade between South Africa and African countries of US$1.5 billion in 1981, with about 75 percent of that trade (i.e., US$1 billion) comprised of South African exports. The South African government has reported a trade surplus of over US$413 million with African countries (excluding Southern African Customs Union [SACU] countries) in 1983 (*New York Times*, September 15, 1985). The South African Foreign Trade Organization (Safto) estimates that South Africa's total exports to Africa for the first half of 1985 was R1.3 billion (*Financial Mail*, August 16, 1985: 108).

14. The South African Foreign Trade Organization has noted a tremendous surge in South African manufacturers' interest in exporting to Africa. They attribute this to the recession in South Africa and the fact that "exporters are taking the logical route of exporting to our closest neighbours first" (*Financial Mail*, August 16, 1985: 108–109).

15. Three reasons are usually advanced to explain the inability of South African manufacturers to penetrate the markets of its principal industrial trading partners. The first reason is unequal exchange in trading relationships in which South Africa's costs of production have risen more rapidly than those of its major trading partners. Hence the manufactured exports are not competitive on international markets. The second reason is that South Africa's small domestic market has made it impossible for its manufacturers to take advantage of economies of scale, which gives major international firms a comparative advantage over South African manufacturers. The third reason is that increased domestic demand tends to coincide with recessions overseas and South African manufacturing exporters tend to shift away from export markets and toward satisfying domestic demand.

16. In 1985, Fiat, Chrysler and British Leyland halted car production and the remaining car manufacturers were operating at below 50 percent of capacity (*Chicago Tribune*, October 25, 1985, and *Finance Week* [Johannesburg], August 22–28, 1985: 591–592).

17. Marais refers to these exports as "forced exports" and argues that they may have been responsible for the increase in South Africa's exports of paper, paper products, chemicals, iron and steel products, and capital equipment between 1956 and 1975.

18. The South African Small Business Advisory Bureau has defined a small business as being independently owned, independently operated, having an annual turnover of not more than R1 million, consisting of not more than five operating units, having assets of not more than R0.5 million, and no more than 100 employees (Ernst W. Neuland, "Small Business Enterprises: Strategies for the 1980s," in *S.-Afr. Tydskr. Bedryfsl.* 13, 1 [1982]: 1–2). In 1982 one Rand = US$0.923.

19. The average number of employees in industrial establishments in South Africa in 1976 was eighty-eight and the average investment per establishment in capital equipment was R151,800, which indicates that most of these firms were labor intensive (Nattrass, 1981: 163).

20. The groups are the Anglo-American Corporation, SANLAM, Barlow Rand, SA Mutual, Volkskas, Barclays, Stannic, Rembrandt, United Building Society, Liberty Life, S.A. Breweries, and Anglo-Vaal.

21. In 1983 it was estimated that whites constituted 22.7 percent of the entire manufacturing work force, while contributing only 5.8 percent of the workers employed in the clothing industry, 13.7 percent of the food industry, 8.9 percent of the textile industry, and 13 percent in construction. By contrast, whites constituted 34 percent of the chemicals industry, 40 percent of the basic metal industry, 37 percent of the machinery industry, 44 percent of the printing and newspaper industry, 77 percent of banking, and 68 percent of the insurance industry (SAIRR, 1984: 144–163; see also SAIRR, 1985: 262–300).

22. The UF began its activities in 1977 during black urban unrest. The ostensible purpose of the foundation was to raise R25 million over a five-year period in order to finance the construction of low-cost housing for urban blacks who were de facto permanent residents (i.e., so-called section tenners who were gainfully employed in the "white urban areas") as well as improving their overall living environment. However, the real purpose of the UF was to set in motion a process of co-opting the black middle class into the South African economy and thereby help stabilize the social order.

23. Nafcoc succeeded the African Chamber of Commerce in 1955. Its purpose was to promote the commercial interests of Africans in the entire country.

24. The black urban market was estimated to be US$4.5 billion dollars a year in 1985 (*African Business*, September 1984: 25).

25. This is not to say, however, that the large corporations have not targeted black areas as major growth points in their marketing strategies. For example, four of Total South Africa's top ten service stations are owned and operated by blacks and its biggest station in southern Africa

is owned and run by a black dealer in Bophuthatswana (*Management*, March 1984: 36–38). Caltex and Shell have projected a "burgeoning black market" due to blacks' improved living standards and growing vehicle ownership (*Management*, March 1984: 39).

26. According to a study of black businesses carried out in 1982, there were only 7555 registered black business enterprises in black residential areas catering to over 4 million people. Over 40 percent of these businesses (i.e., 3030) were general dealers or corner shops (J. Kroon, " 'n Strukturranalise van Swart Sakeondernemings in die Republiek van Suid-Afrika" *S.-Afr. Tydskr. Bedryfsl.* 15, 3 [1984]). There is also estimated to be a sizable informal sector in black residential areas (between 10 to 20 percent of the urban population).

27. The co-founder of the UF, Anton Rupert, the head of Rembrandt, took the initiative in establishing the Small Business Development Corporation (SBDC) in 1979. Both the UF and the SBDC are seeking a massive injection of R5 billion by the government into black urban areas in the form of financing new black enterprises from sewing cooperatives to industrial parks (*The Star* [Johannesburg], August 26, 1985).

28. According to one study of the problems confronting small businesses, legal restrictions accounted for 80 percent of black business failures, compared to below 50 percent of white business failures (*The Star* [Johannesburg], July 15, 1985).

29. The large white retail chains such as OK Bazaars and Pick 'n Pay along with the large industrial corporations have supported efforts to deregulate commercial and industrial undertakings in order to facilitate the entry of black entrepreneurs. The dominant position of the large retail chains in the commercial sector (OK Bazaars alone carries more than 65,000 lines of products) plus the small size of most black businesses minimizes any serious competitive threat to the chains for a long time to come (*The Star* [Johannesburg], July 29, 1985).

30. Black traders and retailers have borne the brunt of intimidation, arson, looting, and attacks by agitators in the black townships. However, black industrialists have been largely untouched by the disturbances (*Financial Mail*, August 23, 1985: 110–111).

31. An indication that the government has as yet not been willing to finance the reform strategy of the large corporations is the meager appropriation for new housing for urban blacks. For example, from 1977 to 1982 only 45,030 new houses were provided by the government (including administration boards) for urban blacks (SAIRR, 1984: 268). However, it is estimated that over the next twenty years, 4 million new housing units will be required (Saul and Gelb, 1981: 68).

32. The government has announced its intention to allow blacks who already have ninety-nine year leases on property to own land (*New York Times*, December 5, 1985).

33. The apparent abandonment by the large corporations of Botha's "limited change" reform strategy after the massive two-day strike, by an estimated 500,000 black workers, in Johannesburg in November 1984 has apparently not been recognized by conservative white opposition leaders.

34. Arrie Paulus, the general secretary of the white Mineworkers' Union, has referred to elements of the Wiehahn report as "the worst betrayal of the white workers in South Africa since the days in 1922 when white mine workers were shot down by General Smuts." Paulus has called for the resignation of members of Parliament representing white mining constituencies who support the scrapping of job reservation on the grounds that the Wiehahn proposals had been implemented after the last general elections in 1981. He argues that voters have not had an opportunity to express their views on it (*The Star* [Johannesburg], July 15, 1985).

35. For a detailed account of the split within the NP in 1982, see Lawrence Schlemmer and David Welsh, "South Africa's Constitutional and Political Prospects," *Optima* 30, 4 (1982).

36. In the Transvaal, the CP enjoys the support of the faculties of education and theology at the Afrikaans universities of Pretoria and Potchefstroom. The influential Professor Hennie Maree, head of the Transvaal Teachers' Association and the rector of the Pretoria Teachers College also supports the Conservative Party.

37. Constitutional development and planning received the second largest allocation in the 1985 budget, second only to finance. Constitutional development received over R5.3 billion while finance received R5.5 billion and defense, R4.3 billion (*Rand Daily Mail*, March 19, 1985).

38. According to a recent poll carried out by *Rapport*, a Sunday newspaper, the government had risen in the estimation of 40 percent of English-speakers while 42 percent of the Afrikaners polled perceived a decline (*SA Digest*, August 2, 1985: 683).

39. At a series of secret meetings between business leaders and cabinet ministers, government officials put forward the argument that unless business comes to the rescue of the National Party, there is little prospect that the government will be able to produce the kind of reforms for which big business has been lobbying (*Rand Daily Mail*, June 29, 1982).

## Chapter 13　Managing Class Structures in South Africa

1. Harry Oppenheimer, "Why the World Should Continue to Invest in South Africa," International Monetary Conference, Mexico City, May 22, 1978.

2. Colin Bundy, "The Emergence and Decline of a South African Peasantry," *African Affairs* 71, 285 (October 1972): 373–377; Monica Wilson, "The Growth of Peasant Communities," in Monica Wilson and Leonard Thompson, eds., *The Oxford History of South Africa*, Vol. 2. (New York: Oxford University Press, 1971), pp. 68–70.

3. Surplus Peoples Project, *Forced Removals in South Africa. Transvaal*, Vol. 5 (Pietermaritzburg: 1983), p. xiv.

4. Harold Wolpe, "Capitalism and Cheap Labour-Power in South Africa: From Segregation to Apartheid," *Economy and Society* 1, 4 (November 1972), and "The Theory of Internal Colonisation—the South African Case," Institute of Commonwealth Studies, University of London, 1973, p. 13; John C. Cell, *The Highest Stage of White Supremacy: The Origins of Segregation in South Africa and the American South* (Cambridge: Cambridge University Press, 1982), p. 199.

5. See the Appendix for a descriptive account of the field research and procedures.

6. These impressions are based largely on interviews conducted with labor bureau and TEBA officials in Lebowa, Gazankulu, KwaZulu, and Transkei in April 1982. Further quotes will not be footnoted.

7. See interview documents, Sterkspruit Tribal Labor Bureau, Student Rural Labor Control Project, University of the Witwatersrand; also Gavin Maasdorp and Andrew Gordon, "Unemployment in the Transkei," Department of Economics, University of Natal, Durban, November, 1978, p. 13.

8. See Aninka Claasen, Field Research Report, and interview documents, Mapumulo Offices, Student Labor Control Project.

9. See Greenberg and Giliomee interviews and interview document, ACRO official, Student Rural Labor Control Project.

10. Colin Murray, *Families Divided: The Impact of Migrant Labour in Lesotho* (Johannesburg: Ravan Press, 1981).

11. See Greenberg and Giliomee interviews with Claasen, Field Research Report, pp. 3–5.

12. Charles Simkins, "The Demographic Demand for Labour and Institutional Context of African Unemployment in South Africa: 1960–1980," Working Paper No. 39, Southern Africa Labour and Development Research Unit, University of Cape Town, Cape Town, August 1981, pp. 28–31.

13. Johann Maree and Janet Graaff, "Men Without Choice: A Sample Survey of African Workers in Cape Town 1975–76," *Social Dynamics* 4 (1978): 5.

14. *The Buthelezi Commission. The Requirements for Stability and Development in KwaZulu and Natal*, Vol. II (Durban: 1982), pp. 155–161. A similar pattern can be found in rural Lesotho. There, income from migrant remittances rose from 43 percent in 1970 to 59 percent in 1974 to 71 percent in 1976 (Murray, *Families Divided*, p. 95).

15. Charles Simkins, "Measuring and Predicting Unemployment in South Africa, 1960–1977," in Simkins and Duncan Clarke, *Structural Unemployment in South Africa* (Pietermaritzburg: University of Natal, 1978), p. 5.

16. See the discussion by Norman Bromberger, "Unemployment in South Africa: A Survey of Research," *Social Dynamics* 4 (June 1978): 18–20.

17. Simkins, "Measuring and Predicting Unemployment," in Simkins and Clark, *Structural Unemployment*, pp. 34–35.

18. Ibid., p. 33.

19. Republic of South Africa, *Economic Development Programme*, p. 27. Only with a projected real growth rate of 5 percent, which the Economic Development Programme itself sees as problematic, is the rate of unemployment held reasonably constant at 11.5 percent. But even in this optimistic scenario, the absolute number of unemployed persons rises from 903,000 in 1977 to 1,262,000 in 1984 (p. 123).

20. Maasdorp and Gordon, "Unemployment in the Transkei," p. 16.

21. The principal author on other occasions conducted field research related to this work that has been incorporated where appropriate.

# Select Bibliography

Abubakar, Saad. *The Lāmībe of Fombina: A Political History of Adamawa 1809–1901*. New York: Oxford University Press, 1979.

Adams, William Y. *Nubia: Corridor to Africa*. Princeton: Princeton University Press, 1977.

Adamu, Mahdi. *The Hausa Factor in West African History*. New York: Oxford University Press, 1979.

Adedeji, Adebayo, ed. *Indigenization of African Economies*. New York: Africana Publishing Co., 1981.

Adelman, Kenneth L. *African Realities*. New York: Crane and Russak & Co., 1980.

Ainad-Tibet, Nadia. *Femmes et Politique autour de la mediterranée*. Paris: L'Harmattan, 1980.

Ake, Claude. *Revolutionary Pressures in Africa*. London: Zed Press, 1978.

———. *A Political Economy of Africa*. New York: Longman, 1981.

Albright, David E., ed. *Communism in Africa*. Bloomington: Indiana University Press, 1980.

Allen, Christopher, and Williams, Gavin, eds. *Sub-Saharan Africa*. New York: Monthly Review Press, 1982.

Altbach, Philip G., and Kelly, Gail P., eds. *Education and Colonialism*. New York: Longman, 1978.

Amsden, Alice H., ed. *The Economics of Women and Work*. New York: St. Martin's Press, 1980.

Armstrong, John A. *Nations Before Nationalism*. Chapel Hill: University of North Carolina Press, 1982.

Ayres, Robert L. *Banking on the Poor: The World Bank and World Poverty*. Cambridge, Mass.: MIT Press, 1983.

Azarya, Victor. *Aristocrats Facing Change: The Fulbe in Guinea, Nigeria and Cameroon*. Chicago: University of Chicago Press, 1978.

Bager, Torben. *Marketing Cooperatives and Peasants in Kenya*. New York: Africana Publishing Co., 1980.

Banerjee, D., ed. *Marxian Theory and the Third World*. New Delhi and Beverly Hills: Sage Publications, 1986.

Barkan, Joel D., ed. *Politics and Public Policy in Kenya and Tanzania*. New York: Praeger, 1979; 2nd rev. ed., 1984.

For works published before 1977, see bibliography in Irving Leonard Markovitz, *Power and Class in Africa*, Englewood Cliffs, N.J.: Prentice Hall, 1977.

Barker, Jonathan, ed. *The Politics of Agriculture in Tropical Africa*. Beverly Hills: Sage Publications, 1984.

Barongo, Yulamu, ed. *Political Science in Africa: A Critical Review*. London: Zed Press, 1983.

Bates, Robert H. *Markets and States in Tropical Africa: The Political Basis of Agricultural Politics*. Berkeley: University of California Press, 1981.

Bates, Robert H., and Lofchie, Michael F., eds. *Agricultural Development in Africa: Issues of Public Policy*. New York: Praeger, 1980.

Bauer, P. T. *Equality, the Third World, and Economic Delusion*. Cambridge, Mass.: Harvard University Press, 1981.

————. *Reality and Rhetoric: Studies in the Economics of Development*. Cambridge, Mass.: Harvard University Press, 1984.

Baumgart, Winfried. *Imperialism: The Idea and Reality of British and French Colonial Expansion, 1880–1914*. New York: Oxford University Press, 1982.

Bay, Edna G. ed. *Women and Work in Africa*. Boulder, Colo.: Westview Press, 1982.

Beck, Lois, and Keddie, Nikki. *Women in the Muslim World*. Cambridge, Mass.: Harvard University Press, 1978.

Bell, Roseann P., et al. *Sturdy Black Bridges: Visions of Black Women in Literature*. New York: Anchor, 1979.

Belloncle, Guy. *La Question Paysanne en Afrique Noire*. Paris: Editions Karthala, 1982.

Bender, Gerald. *Angola Under the Portuguese: The Myth and the Reality*. Berkeley: University of California Press, 1978 and 1980.

Beneria, Lourdes, ed. *Women and Development: The Sexual Division of Labor in Rural Societies: A Study*. New York: Praeger, 1982 and 1985.

Bernstein, Henry, and Campbell, Bonnie K., eds. *Contradictions of Accumulation in Africa*. Beverly Hills: Sage Publications, 1985.

Beveridge, Andrew, and Oberschall, Anthony. *African Businessmen and Development in Zambia*. Princeton: Princeton University Press, 1979.

Bezy, Fernand. *Accumulation et sous-développement au Zaire 1960–1980*. Louvain-la-Neuve: Presses Universitaires de Louvain, 1981.

Bideleux, Robert. *Communism and Development*. New York: Methuen and Co., 1985.

Bienen, Henry. *Armies and Parties in Africa*. New York: Africana Publishing Co., 1978.

Bienen, Henry, and Diejomaoh, V. P., eds. *The Political Economy of Income Distribution in Nigeria*. New York: Holmes and Meier, 1981.

Biersteker, Thomas J. *Distortion or Development? Contending Perspectives on the Multinational Corporation*. Cambridge, Mass.: MIT Press, 1978.

Bingen, R. James. *Food Production and Rural Development in the Sahel: Lessons from Mali's Operation Riz-Segou*. Boulder, Colo.: Westview Press, 1985.

Blomström, Magnus, and Hettne, Bjorn. *Development Theory in Transition: The Dependency Debate and Beyond: Third World Responses*. London: Zed Books Ltd., 1984.

Bolton, Dianne. *Nationalization: A Road to Socialism? The Lessons of Tanzania*. London: Zed Books Ltd., 1985.

Bond, George. *The Politics of Change in a Zambian Community*. Chicago: Chicago University Press, 1976.

Bond, George, Johnson, Walton, and Walker, Sheila, eds. *African Christianity: Patterns of Religious Continuity*. New York: Academic Press, 1979.

Bonner, Philip. *Kings, Commoners and Concessionaires: The Evolution and Dissolution of the Nineteenth Century Swazi State*. Cambridge, Eng.: Cambridge University Press, 1983.

Brantley, Cynthia. *The Giriama and Colonial Resistance in Kenya 1800–1920*. Berkeley: University of California Press, 1981.

Bukh, Jette. *The Village Woman in Ghana*. Uppsala: Scandinavian Institute of Africa Studies, 1979.

Bundy, Colin. *The Rise and Fall of South African Peasantry*. Berkeley: University of California Press, 1980.

Callaghy, Thomas M. *The State-Society Struggle: Zaire in Comparative Perspective*. New York: Columbia University Press, 1984.

Caplan, Patricia, and Bujra, Janet, eds. *Women United, Women Divided: Comparative Studies of Ten Contemporary Cultures*. Bloomington: Indiana University Press, 1979.

Cartwright, John. *Political Leadership in Africa*. New York: St. Martin's Press, 1983.

Cell, John W. *The Highest Stage of White Supremacy: The Origins of Segregation in South Africa and the American South*. New York: Cambridge University Press, 1982.

Chabal, Patrick. *Amilcar Cabral: Revolutionary Leadership and People's War*. New York: Cambridge University Press, 1983.

Chazan, Naomi. *An Anatomy of Ghanaian Politics: Managing Political Recession, 1969–1982*. Boulder, Colo.: Westview Press, 1983.

Chinweizu, Onwuchekwa Jemie, and Ihechukwu Madubuike. *Towards the Decolonization of African Literature*. Washington, D.C.: Howard University Press, 1983.

Clapham, Christopher. *Third World Politics, An Introduction*. Madison: University of Wisconsin Press, 1985.

Clapham, Christopher, Campbell, Ian, and Philips, George, eds. *The Political Dilemmas of Military Regimes*. Totowa, N.J.: Barnes & Noble Books, 1985.

Clarence-Smith, W. G. *Slaves, Peasants and Capitalists in Southern Angola 1840–1926*. New York: Cambridge University Press, 1979.

Clarke, W. Edmund. *Socialist Development and Public Investment in Tanzania 1964–73*. Toronto: University of Toronto Press, 1978.

Cock, Jacklyn. *Maids and Madams: A Study in the Politics of Exploitation*. Johannesburg: Raven Press, 1980.

Cohen, Abner. *The Politics of Elite Culture: Explorations in the Dramaturgy of Power in a Modern African Society*. Berkeley: University of California Press, 1981.

Cohen, Nicholas and Dumont, René. *The Growth of Hunger: A New Politics of Agriculture*. London: Marion Boyars Publishers, 1980.

Cohen, William B. *The French Encounter with Africans: White Response to Blacks, 1530–1880*. Bloomington: Indiana University Press, 1980.

Colin, Murray. *Families Divided: The Impact of Migrant Labour in Lesotho*. Johannesburg: Raven Press, 1981.

Collier, Ruth Berins. *Regimes in Tropical Africa: Changing Forms of Supremacy, 1945–1975*. Berkeley: University of California Press, 1982.

Colvin, Lucy G. *The Uprooted of the Western Sahel: Migrants' Quest for Cash in the Senegambia*. New York: Praeger, 1981.

Connor, Walter D. *Socialism, Politics and Equality: Hierarchy and Change in Eastern Europe and the U.S.S.R.* New York: Columbia University Press, 1979.

Cosentino, Donald. *Defiant Maids and Stubborn Farmers: Tradition and Invention in Mende Story Performance*. New York: Cambridge University Press, 1982.

Cooper, Frederick, ed. *Struggle for the City: Migrant Labor, Capital, and the State in Urban Africa*. Beverly Hills: Sage Publications, 1983.

Coquery-Vidrovitch, and Lovejoy, Paul E., eds. *The Workers of African Trade*. Beverly Hills: Sage Publications, 1985.

Crisp, Jeff. *The Story of An African Working Class: Ghanaian Miner's Struggles, 1870–1980*. London: Zed Press, 1984.

Crummey, Donald, and Stewart, C. C., eds. *Modes of Production in Africa—The Precolonial Era*. Beverly Hills: Sage Publications, 1981.

Dalby, David, and Church, R. J. Harrison, eds. *Drought in Africa: Report of the 1973 Symposium*. London: School of Oriental and African Studies, 1973.

Daniel, Philip. *Africanization, Nationalization and Inequality: Mining, Labor and the*

*Copperbelt in Zambian Development.* New York: Cambridge University Press, 1979.

Davies, Carole Boyce, and Graves, Anne Adams, eds. *Ngambika: Studies of Women in African Literature.* Trenton, N.J.: Africa World Press, 1985.

Davis, Eric. *Challenging Colonialism: Bank Misr and Egyptian Industrialization, 1920–1941.* Princeton: Princeton University Press, 1983.

Dinham, Barbara, and Hines, Colin. *Agribusiness in Africa.* Trenton, N.J.: Africa World Press, 1984.

Drewal, Henry John, and Drewal, Margaret Thompson. *Gelede: Art and Female Power Among the Yoruba.* Bloomington: Indiana University Press, 1983.

Du Toit, Bettie. *Ukubamba Amandolo: Worker's Struggles in the South African Textile Industry.* London: Onyx Press, 1978.

Dudley, Billy. *An Introduction to Nigerian Government and Politics.* Bloomington: Indiana University Press, 1982.

Dumont, René, and Mottin, Marie-France. *Strangehold on Africa.* London: Andre Deutsch, 1983.

Dunn, John, ed. *West African States: Failure and Promise: A Study in Comparative Politics.* New York: Cambridge University Press, 1978.

Dunn, John, and Robertson, A. F. *Dependence and Opportunity: Political Change in Ahafo.* London: Cambridge University Press, 1973.

Edsman, Björn. *Lawyers in Gold Coast Politics, 1900–1945: From Mensah Sarbah to J. B. Danqua.* Uppsala: Scandinavian Institute of African Studies, 1979.

Eicher, Carl K., and Baker, Doyle C. *Research on Agricultural Development in Sub-Saharan Africa: A Critical Survey.* East Lansing: Michigan State University, 1982.

Eicher, Carl K., and Staatz, John M., eds. *Agricultural Development in the Third World.* Baltimore: The Johns Hopkins University Press, 1984.

Eisenstein, Zillah. *The Radical Future of Liberal Feminism.* New York: Longman, 1981.

Emecheta, Buchi. *The Joys of Motherhood: A Novel.* New York: George Braziller, 1979.

———. *Double Yoke.* New York: George Braziller, 1983.

———. *The Rape of Shavi.* New York: George Braziller, 1985.

Esman, Milton J., and Uphoff, Norman T. *Local Organizations, Intermediaries in Rural Development.* Ithaca: Cornell University Press, 1984.

Eyinga, Abel. *Mandat d'Arrêt pour cause d'élections: De la démocratie au Cameroun: 1970–1978.* Paris: Editions L'Harmattan, 1978.

Faure, Y. A., and Medard, J. F. *Etat et Bourgeoisie en Côte-D'Ivoire.* Paris: Editions Karathala, 1982.

Firebrace, James with Stuart Holland. *Never Kneel Down: Drought, Development and Liberation in Eritrea.* Trenton, N.J.: The Red Sea Press, 1985.

First, Ruth. *Black Gold: The Mozambican Miner, Proletarian and Peasant.* New York: St. Martin's Press: 1983.

Fogel, Daniel. *Africa in Struggle: National Liberation and Proletarian Revolution.* Seattle: Ism Press, 1982.

Franke, Richard W., and Chasin, Barbara J. *Seeds of Famine: Ecological Destruction and the Development Dilemma in the West African Sahel.* Montclair, N.J.: Allanheld, Osmun, 1980.

Fransman, Martin, ed. *Industry and Accumulation in Africa.* London, Exeter; N.H.: Heinemann, 1982.

Freund, Bill. *Capital and Labor in the Nigerian Tin Mines.* Harlow, Eng.: Longman Group Ltd., 1981.

———. *The Making of Contemporary Africa: The Development of African Society since 1800.* Bloomington: Indiana University Press, 1984.

Gann, Lewis H., and Duignan, Peter J. *The Rulers of Belgian Africa 1884–1914*. Princeton: Princeton University Press, 1979.

Garcia-Zamor, Jean-Claude, ed. *Public Participation in Development Planning and Management: Cases from Africa and Asia*. Boulder, Colo.: Westview Press, 1985.

Geldenhuys, Deon. *The Diplomacy of Isolation: South African Foreign Policy Making*. New York: St. Martin's Press, 1984.

George, Susan. *Feeding the Few: Corporate Control of Food*. Washington, D.C.: Institute for Policy Studies, 1979.

————. *Ill Fares the Land: Essays on Food, Hunger and Power*. Washington, D.C.: Institute for Policy Studies, 1984.

Gershoni, Yekutiel. *Black Colonialism: The Americo-Liberian Scramble for the Hinterland*. Boulder, Colo.: Westview Press, 1985.

Ghai, Dharam, ed. *Rural Development in Women in Africa*. Geneva: International Labor Office, 1984.

Ghai, Dharam, and Radwan, Samir, eds. *Agrarian Policies and Rural Poverty in Africa*. Geneva: International Labor Office, 1983.

Giele, Janet, and Smock, Audrey, eds. *Women: Roles and Status in Eight Countries*. New York: John Wiley, 1977.

Gilkes, Patrick. *The Dying Lion: Feudalism and Modernization in Ethiopia*. London: Julian Friedmann Publishers, Ltd., 1975.

Girvan, Norman. *Corporate Imperialism: Conflict and Expropriation: Transnational Corporations and Economic Nationalism in the Third World*. New York: Monthly Review Books, 1978.

Gould, David J. *Bureaucratic Corruption and Underdevelopment in the Third World: The Case of Zaire*. New York: Pergamon Press, 1980.

Graham, R. *Monopoly Capital and African Development: The Political Economy of the World Aluminum Industry*. London: Zed Press, 1981.

Grainger, Alan. *Desertification: How People Make Deserts, How People Can Stop and Why They Don't*. Washington, D.C.: Earthscan, 1982.

Gran, Guy, ed. *Zaire: The Political Economy of Underdevelopment*. New York: Praeger, 1979.

Greenberg, Stanley B. *Race and State in Capitalist Development: Comparative Perspectives*. New Haven: Yale University Press, 1980.

Grundy, Kenneth. *Soldiers Without Politics: Blacks in South African Armed Forces*. Berkeley: University of California Press, 1983.

Gutkind, Peter C. W., and Waterman, Peter, eds. *African Social Studies: A Radical Reader*. Portsmouth, N.H.: Heinemann, 1977.

Hafkin, Nancy, and Bay, Edna, eds. *Women in Africa: Studies in Social and Economic Change*. Stanford: Stanford University Press, 1976.

Halliday, Fred, and Molyneux, Maxine. *The Ethiopian Revolution*. London: Verso Press, 1981.

Hancock, Graham, *Ethiopia: The Challenge of Hunger*. London: Victor Gollancz Ltd., 1985.

Hanlon, Joseph. *Mozambique: The Revolution under Fire*. London: Zed Press, 1984.

Harms, Robert W. *River of Wealth, River of Sorrow: The Central Zaire Basin in the Era of the Slave and Ivory Trade, 1500–1891*. New Haven: Yale University Press, 1981.

Harris, Joseph E., ed. *Global Dimensions of the African Diaspora*. Washington, D.C.: Howard University Press, 1982.

Hart, Keith. *The Political Economy of West African Agriculture*. New York: Cambridge University Press, 1982.

Hay, Margaret Jean, and Stichter, Sharon, eds. *African Women South of the Sahara*. New York: Longman, 1984.

Hay, Margaret Jean, and Wright, Marcia, eds. *African Women and the Law: Historical Perspectives*. Boston: Boston University Papers on Africa, VII, 1982.

Henriksen, Thomas H. *Mozambique: A History*. London: Rex Collings, 1978.

Heyer, Judith, Roberts, Pepe and Williams, Gavin, eds. *Rural Development in Tropical Africa*. New York: St. Martin's Press, 1981.

Hill, Polly. *Dry Grain Farming Families: Hausaland (Nigeria) and Karnataka (India) Compared*. New York: Cambridge University Press, 1982.

Hilton, Anne. *The Kingdom of Congo*. New York: Oxford University Press, 1985.

Hindess, Barry, and Hirst, Paul Q. *Pre-Capitalist Modes of Production*. London: Routledge and Kegan Paul Ltd., 1975.

Hlophe, Stephen S. *Class, Ethnicity, and Politics in Liberia: A Class Analysis of Power Struggles in the Tubman and Tolbert Administrations, from 1944–1975*. Washington, D.C.: University Press of America, 1979.

Hogendorn, Jan S. *Nigerian Groundnut Exports: Origins and Early Development*. Oxford: Oxford University Press, 1979.

Horne, Alistair. *A Savage War of Peace: Algeria 1954–1962*. London: Macmillan, 1977.

Houghton, D. Hobart. *The South African Economy*. Cape Town: Oxford University Press, 1976.

Howard, Rhoda. *Colonialism and Underdevelopment in Ghana*. New York: Africana Publishing Co., 1978.

The Hunger Project. *Ending Hunger: An Idea Whose Time Has Come*. New York: Praeger, 1985.

Hyden, Goran. *Beyond Ujaama in Tanzania: Underdevelopment and an Uncaptured Peasantry*. Berkeley: University of California Press, 1980.

———. *No Shortcuts to Progress: African Development Management in Perspective*. Berkeley: University of California Press, 1983.

Iglitzin, Lynne, and Ross, Ruth, eds. *Women in the World: A Comparative Study*. Santa Barbara: Clio, 1976.

Iliffe, John. *The Emergence of African Capitalism*. London: Macmillan, 1983.

Irele, Abiola. *The African Experience in Literature and Ideology*. Portsmouth, N.H.: Heinemann, 1981.

Isaacman, Allen, and Barbara. *Mozambique: From Colonialism to Revolution, 1900–1982*. Boulder, Colo.: Westview Press, 1983.

Isaacman, Barbara, and Stephen, June. *Mozambique: Women, the Law and Agrarian Reform*. Addis Ababa: U.N. Economic Commission for Africa, African Training and Research Center for Women, 1980.

Isichei, Elizabeth, ed. *Varieties of Christian Experience in Nigeria*. London: Macmillan, 1982.

Jackson, Robert H., and Rosberg, Carl G. *Personal Rule in Black Africa: Prince, Autocrat, Prophet, Tyrant*. Berkeley: University of California Press, 1982.

Jeffries, Richard. *Class, Power and Ideology in Ghana: The Railwaymen of Sekondi*. New York: Cambridge University Press, 1978.

Joseph, Richard A. *Radical Nationalism in Cameroun: Social Origins of the U.P.C. Rebellion*. London: Oxford University Press, 1977.

Kahler, Miles. *Decolonization in Britain and France: The Domestic Consequences of International Relations*. Princeton: Princeton University Press, 1984.

Kaplan, Irving, ed. *Zaire: A Country Study*. Washington, D.C.: Government Printing Office, 1979.

Kasfir, Nelson, ed. *State and Class in Africa*. London: Frank Cass, 1984.

Kea, Ray A. *Settlements, Trade and Politics in the Seventeenth Century Gold Coast*. Baltimore: The Johns Hopkins University Press, 1982.

Kennedy, Paul T. *Ghanaian Businessmen: From Artisan to Capitalist Entrepreneur in a Dependent Economy*. Munich: Weltform Verlag, 1980.

Kibreab, Gaim. *African Refugees: Reflections on the African Refugee Problem.* Trenton, N.J.: Africa World Press, 1985.

Kiros, Fassil G., ed. *Challenging Rural Poverty: Experiences in Institution Building and Popular Participation for Rural Development in Eastern Africa.* Trenton, N.J.: Africa World Press, 1985.

Kitching, Gavin. *Class and Economic Change in Kenya: The Making of an African Petite Bourgeoisie 1905–1970.* New Haven: Yale University Press, 1980.

Klein, Martin A., ed. *Peasants in Africa: Historical and Contemporary Perspectives.* Beverly Hills: Sage Publications, 1980.

Kofele-Kale, Ndiva, ed. *An African Experiment in Nation Building: The Bilingual Cameroon Republic Since Reunification.* Boulder, Colo.: Westview Press, 1980.

————. *Tribesmen and Patriots: Political Culture in a Poly-Ethnic African State.* Washington, D.C.: University Press of America, 1981.

Kuklick, Henrika. *The Imperial Bureaucrat: The Colonial Administrative Service in the Gold Coast 1920–1939.* Stanford: Hoover Institute Press, 1979.

Kuzwayo, Ellen. *Call Me Woman.* San Francisco: Spinsters Ink, 1985.

Lamb, David. *The Africans.* New York: Random House, 1983.

Lan, David. *Guns and Rain: Guerrillas and Spirit Mediums in Zimbabwe.* London: James Curry Ltd., and Berkeley: University of California Press, 1985.

Lappe, Francis Moore, and Collins, Joseph. *Food First: Beyond the Myth of Scarcity.* New York: Ballantine Books, 1978.

Lappe, Francis Moore, Collins, Joseph, and Kinley, David. *Aid as Obstacle: Twenty Questions About Our Foreign Aid and the Hungry.* Washington, D.C.: Institute for Food and Development Policy, 1980.

Law, Robin. *The Horse in West African History: The Role of the Horse in the Societies of Pre-Colonial West Africa.* London: Oxford University Press, 1980.

Lazreg, Marnia. *The Emergence of Classes in Algeria: A Study of Colonialism and Socio-Political Change.* Boulder, Colo.: Westview Press, 1976.

Lecaillon, Jacques, et al. *Income Distribution and Economic Development, an Analytical Survey.* Geneva: International Labor Office, 1984.

Lefort, Rene. *Ethiopia: An Heretical Revolution?* London: Zed Press, 1983.

Legum, Colin, et al. *Africa in the 1980's: A Continent in Crisis.* New York: McGraw-Hill, 1979.

Leo, Christopher. *Land and Class in Kenya.* Toronto: University of Toronto Press, 1984.

Leonard, David K. *Reaching the Peasant Farmer: Organizing Theory and Practice in Kenya.* Chicago: University of Chicago Press, 1977.

Leonard, Richard. *South Africa at War: White Power and the Crisis in Southern Africa.* Westport, Conn.: Lawrence Hill and Co., 1983.

Le Vine, Victor T., and Luke, Timothy W. *The Arab-African Connection: Political and Economic Realities.* Boulder, Colo.: Westview Press, 1979.

Lipman, Beata. *We Make Freedom: Women in South Africa Speak.* Boston: Pandora Press, 1984.

Lloyd, Peter. *A Third World Proletariat?* London: Allen & Unwin, 1982.

Machel, Samora. Ed. by Barry Munslow. *African Revolutionary, Selected Speeches and Writings.* London: Zed Books, Ltd., 1985.

MacShane, Dennis, Plaut, Martin, and Ward, David. *Power! Black Workers, their Unions and the Struggle for Freedom in South Africa.* Boston: South End Press, 1984.

Magubane, Bernard. *The Political Economy of Race and Class in South Africa.* New York: Monthly Review Press, 1979.

Mahmoud, Fatima Babiker. *The Sudanese Bourgeoisie: Vanguard of Development?* London: Zed Books Ltd., 1984.

Mamdani, Mahmood. *Imperialism and Fascism in Uganda.* Trenton, N.J.: Africa World Press, 1984.

Manning, Patrick. *Slavery, Colonialism and Economic Growth in Dahomey, 1640–1960*. Cambridge, Eng.: Cambridge University Press, 1982.

Marcum, John. *The Angolan Revolution, V. II, Politics and Guerilla (1962–1976)*. Cambridge, Mass.: MIT Press, 1978.

Marcus, Harold G. *Ethiopia, Great Britain and the United States, 1914–1974: The Politics of Empire*. Berkeley: University of California Press, 1983.

Marcussen, Henrik Secher, and Torp, Jens Erik. *The Internationalization of Capital: The Prospects for the Third World, a Reexamination of Dependency Theory*. London: Zed Press, Biblio Distribution Center, 1982.

Markakis, John, and Ayele, Nega. *Class and Revolution in Ethiopia*. Nottingham: Spokesman Press, 1978.

Markovitz, Irving Leonard. *Léopold Sédar Senghor and the Politics of Négritude*. New York: Atheneum, 1969; London: Heinemann, 1970.

———. *Power and Class in Africa*. Englewood Cliffs, N.J.: Prentice-Hall, 1977; 6th printing, 1984.

Marks, Shula, and Rathbone, Richard, eds. *Industrialization and Social Change in South Africa; African Class Formation, Culture and Consciousness, 1870–1930*. Harlow, Eng.: Longman Group Ltd., 1982.

Mazuri, Ali A. *Africa's International Relations: The Diplomacy of Dependency and Change*. Boulder, Colo.: Westview Press, 1977.

Mba, Nina Emma. *Nigerian Women Mobilized: Women's Political Activity in Southern Nigeria 1900–1965*. Berkeley: University of California Institute of International Studies, 1982.

McHenry, Dean E., Jr. *Tanzania's Ujaama Villages: The Implementation of a Rural Development Strategy*. Berkeley: Institute of International Studies, 1979.

Meillassoux, Claude. *Maidens, Meals and Money: Capitalism and the Domestic Community*. New York: Cambridge University Press, 1981.

Miller, Norman H. *Kenya: The Quest for Prosperity*. Boulder, Colo.: Westview Press, 1984.

Mittelman, James H. *Underdevelopment and the Transition to Socialism: Mozambique and Tanzania*. New York: Academic Press, 1981.

Mohiddin, Ahmed. *African Socialism in Two Countries*. Totowa, N.J.: Barnes and Noble, 1981.

Munslow, Barry. *Mozambique: The Revolution and its Origins*. New York: Longman, 1983.

Munslow, Barry, and Finch, Henry, eds. *Proletarianization in the Third World: Studies in the Creation of a Labour Force under Dependent Capitalism*. London: Croom Helm, 1984.

Myers, Desaix, III, Propp, Kenneth, Hauck, David, and Liff, David. *U.S. Business in South Africa: The Economic, Political and Moral Issues*. Bloomington and London: Indiana University Press, 1980.

Nabudere, D. Wadada. *Imperialism and Revolution in Uganda*. London: Onyx Press, 1980.

Nafziger, E. Wayne. *The Economics of Political Instability: The Nigerian Biafran War*. Boulder, Colo.: Westview Press, 1983.

N'Diaye, Bokar. *Les Castes au Mali*. Bamako: Editions Populaires, 1970.

Ndongko, Wilfred A. *Planning for Economic Development in a Federal State: The Case of Cameroon, 1960–1971*. Munich: Weltform Verlag, 1975.

Nelson, Harold, D., et al. *Area Handbook for the United Republic of Cameroon*. Washington, D.C.: U.S. Government Printing Office, 1974.

Nelson, Nici, ed. *African Women in the Development Process*. London: Frank Cass, 1981.

Ngara, Emmanuel. *Art and Ideology in the African Novel: A Study of the Influence of Marxism on African Writing*. Portsmouth, N.H.: Heinemann, 1985.

Ngugi, Wa Thionga. *Petals of Blood*. New York: E. F. Dutton, 1978.

————. *Barrel of a Pen: Resistance to Repression in Neo-Colonial Kenya*. Trenton, N.J.: African World Press, 1983.

Nnoli, Okwudiba, ed. *Path to Nigerian Development*. Dakar, Senegal: Codesria, 1981.

Nolutshungu, Sam C. *Changing South Africa: Political Considerations*. New York: Africana Publishing Co., 1982.

Nore, Petter, and Turner, Terisa, eds. *Oil and Class Struggle*. London: Zed Press, 1980.

Obbo, Christine. *African Women: Their Struggle for Economic Independence*. London: Zed Press, 1980.

Oboler, Regina. *Women, Power and Economic Changes: The Nandi of Kenya*. Stanford: Stanford University Press, 1985.

Odetola, Theophilius Olatunde. *Military Politics in Nigeria: Economic Development and Political Stability*. New Brunswick, N.J.: Transaction Books, 1978.

Offiong, Daniel A. *Imperialism and Dependency: Obstacles to African Development*. Washington, D.C.: Howard University Press, 1982.

Ofonagoro, W. Ibekwe. *Trade and Imperialism in Southern Nigeria: 1881–1929*. New York: Nok Publishers, 1979.

Olaniyan, Richard, ed. *African History and Culture*. New York: Longman, 1982.

O'Meara, Dan. *Volks-Kapitalisme: Class, Capital and Ideology in the Development of Afrikaner Nationalism, 1934–1948*. Cambridge, Eng.: Cambridge University Press, 1983.

Onimode, Bade. *Imperialism and Underdevelopment in Nigeria: The Dialectics of Mass Poverty*. London: Zed Press, 1982.

————. *Neo-Colonial Capitalism and Underdevelopment, 1960–1980*. London: Zed Press, 1982.

Oppong, Christine. *Middle Class African Marriage: A Family Study of Ghanaian Senior Civil Servants*. London: George Allen & Unwin, 1981.

————, ed. *Female and Male in West Africa*. London: George Allen & Unwin. 1983.

Ottaway, Marina, and David. *Ethiopia: Empire in Revolution*. New York: Africana Publishing Co., 1978.

Ouologuem, Yambo. *Bound to Violence*. Portsmouth, N.H.: Heinemann, 1971.

Owusu, Maxwell, ed. *Colonialism and Change: Essays Presented to Lucy Mair*. The Hague: Mouton, 1975.

Oyediran, Oyeleye, ed. *Nigerian Government and Politics Under Miltiary Rule, 1966–79*. New York: St. Martin's Press, 1979.

Patterson, Orlando. *Slavery and Social Death: A Comparative Study*. Cambridge, Mass.: Harvard University Press, 1982.

Peace, Adrian J. *Choice, Class and Conflict: A Study of Southern Nigerian Factory Workers*. Atlantic Highlands, N.J.: Humanities Press, 1979.

Pipes, Daniel. *Slave Soldiers and Islam: The Genesis of a Military System*. New Haven: Yale University Press, 1981.

Rahmato, Dessalegn. *Agrarian Reform in Ethiopia*. Uppsala: Scandinavian Institute of African Studies, 1984.

Ranger, Terence. *Peasant Consciousness and Guerrilla War in Zimbabwe: A Comparative Study*. London: John Curry Ltd., and Berkeley: University of California Press, 1985.

Reefe, Thomas. *The Rainbow and the King: A History of the Luba Empire to 1891*. Berkeley: University of California Press, 1981.

Resnick, Adrian H. *The Long Transition: Building Socialism in Tanzania*. New York: Monthly Review Press, 1981.

Reynolds, Lloyd G. *Economic Growth in the Third World, 1850–1980*. New Haven: Yale University Press, 1985.

Rimmer, Douglas. *The Economics of West Africa*. New York: St. Martin's Press, 1984.

Robertson, Claire C. *Sharing the Same Bowl: A Socioeconomic History of Women and Class in Accra, Ghana*. Bloomington: Indiana University Press, 1984.

Robinson, David. *The Holy War of Umar Tal in the Senegal. The Western Sudan in the mid-Nineteenth Century.* New York: Oxford University Press, 1985.

Robinson, Pearl T., and Skinner, Elliot P. eds. *Transformation and Resiliency in Africa. As Seen by Afro-American Scholars.* Cambridge, Mass: Harvard University Press, 1983.

Rogers, Barbara. *The Domestication of Women: Discrimination in Developing Societies.* New York: St. Martin's Press, 1980.

Rosaldo, Michelle, and Lamphere, Louise, eds. *Women, Culture and Society.* Stanford: Stanford University Press, 1974.

Rosberg, Carl G., and Callaghy, Thomas M., eds. *Socialism in Sub-Saharan Africa: A New Assessment.* Berkeley: Institute of International Studies, 1979.

Rosenberg, Nathan, and Birdzell, L. E., Jr. *How the West Grew Rich: The Economic Transformation of the Industrial World.* New York: Basic Books, 1985.

Rotberg, Robert I., and Rabb, Theodore K., eds. *Hunger and History: The Impact of Changing Food Production and Consumption Patterns in Society.* New York: Cambridge University Press, 1985.

Rothchild, Daniel, and Olorunsula, Victor, eds. *State Versus Ethnic Claims: African Policy Dilemmas.* Boulder, Colo.: Westview Press, 1982.

Rothchild, Donald, and Curry, Robert L. Jr. *Scarcity, Choice and Public Policy in Middle Africa.* Berkeley: University of California Press, 1978.

Saffioti, Heleieth I. B. *Women in Class Society.* New York: Monthly Review Press, 1978.

Samuels, Michael A., ed. *Africa and the West.* Boulder, Colo.: Westview Press, 1980.

Sandbrook, Richard. *The Politics of Basic Needs: Urban Aspects of Assaulting Poverty in Africa.* Toronto: University of Toronto Press, 1982.

Saul, John S. *The State and Revolution in Eastern Africa: Essays.* New York: Monthly Review Press, 1979.

———, ed. *A Difficult Road: The Transition to Socialism in Mozambique.* New York: Monthly Review Press, 1985.

Scarritt, James R., ed. *Analyzing Political Change in Africa: Applications of a New Multidimensional Framework.* Boulder, Colo.: Westview Press, 1980.

Schatz, Sayre P. *Nigerian Capitalism.* Berkeley: University of California Press, 1977.

Schatzberg, Michael G. *Politics and Class in Zaire: Bureaucracy, Business and Beer in Lisala.* New York: Holmes and Meier, 1979.

Schneider, Harold K. *Livestock and Equality in East Africa: The Economic Basis for Social Structure.* Bloomington: Indiana University Press, 1979.

Schwab, Peter. *Ethiopia: Politics, Economics and Society.* Boulder, Colo.: Lynne Rienner Publishers, 1985.

Seidman, Ann. *The Roots of Crisis in Southern Africa.* Trenton, N.J.: Africa World Press, 1985.

Selassie, Bereket Habte. *Conflict and Intervention in the Horn of Africa.* New York: Monthly Review Press, 1980.

Sen, Amartya. *Poverty and Famines: An Essay on Entitlement and Deprivation.* Oxford: The Clarendon Press, 1981.

Sertima, Ivan Van, ed. *Black Women in Antiquity.* New Brunswick, N.J.: Transaction Books, 1984.

Shaw, Timothy M., and Heard, Kenneth A., eds. *The Politics of Africa: Dependence and Development.* New York: Africana Publishing Co., 1979.

Shenton, Robert. *The Development of Capitalism in Northern Nigeria.* Toronto: University of Toronto Press, 1986.

Smith, Anthony D. *The Ethnic Revival.* New York: Cambridge University Press, 1981.

Smith, Tony. *The French Stake in Algeria, 1945–1962.* Ithaca and London: Cornell University Press, 1978.

———. *The Pattern of Imperialism: The United States, Great Britain and the Late-*

*Industrializing World Since 1815*. New York: Cambridge University Press, 1981.

Soyinka, Wole. *Ake, The Years of Childhood*. New York: Random House, 1981 and 1983.

Staudt, Kathleen, and Jaquette, Jane, eds. *Women in Developing Countries: A Policy Focus*. New York: Haworth, 1983.

Steady, Filomina Chioma, ed. *The Black Woman Cross-Culturally*. Cambridge, Mass.: Schenkman, 1981.

Stein, Robert Louis. *The French Slave Trade in the Eighteenth Century: An Old Regime Business*. Madison: University of Wisconsin Press, 1979.

Steinhart, Edward I. *Conflict and Collaboration: The Kingdom of Western Uganda, 1890–1907*. Princeton: Princeton University Press, 1977.

Stichter, Sharon. *Migrant Labor in Kenya: Capitalism and African Response 1895–1975*. Harlow, Eng.: Longman Group Ltd., 1982.

———. *Migrant Laborers*. New York: Cambridge University Press, 1985.

Stren, Richard E. *Housing the Urban Poor in Africa: Policy, Politics and Bureaucracy in Mombasa*. Berkeley: University of California Press, 1978.

Strobel, Margaret. *Muslim Women in Mombasa: 1890–1975*. New Haven: Yale University Press, 1979.

Swainson, Nicola, *The Development of Corporate Capitalism in Kenya 1918–77*. Berkeley: University of California Press, 1980.

Sweetman, David. *Women Leaders in African History*. Portsmouth, N.H.: Heinemann, 1984.

Tangri, Roger. *Politics in Sub-Saharan Africa*. Portsmouth, N.H.: Heinemann, 1985.

Thomas, Barbara P. *Politics, Participation and Poverty: Development Through Self-Help in Kenya*. Boulder, Colo.: Westview Press, 1985.

Thompson, Robert F. *Flash of the Spirit: African and Afro-American Art and Philosophy*. New York: Vintage Books, 1984.

Timberlake, Lloyd. *Africa in Crisis: The Causes and the Cures of Environmental Bankruptcy*. Washington, D.C.: Earthscan, 1985.

Tordoff, William. *Government and Politics in Africa*. Bloomington: Indiana University Press, 1984.

Tosh, John. *Clan Leaders and Colonial Chiefs in Lango: The Political History of an East African Stateless Society, c. 1800–1939*. New York: Oxford University Press, 1978.

Toyin, Falola, and Ihovbere, Julius. *The Rise and Fall of Nigeria's Second Republic, 1979–84*. London: Zed Books Ltd., 1985.

Tutu, Desmond. *Hope and Suffering Sermons and Speeches*. Grand Rapids, Mich.: William B. Erdmanns, 1983.

Uchendu, Victor C., ed. *Dependency and Underdevelopment in West Africa*. Netherlands: E. J. Brill, 1980.

Urdang, Stephanie. *Fighting Two Colonialisms: Women in Guinea Bissau*. New York: Monthly Review Press, 1979.

Vail, Leroy, and White, Landeg. *Capitalism and Colonialism in Mozambique: A Study of Quelimane District*. Minneapolis: University of Minnesota Press, 1980.

van Binsbergen, Wim, and Geschiere, Peter, eds. *Old Modes of Production and Capitalist Encroachment: Anthropological Explorations in Africa*. London: Routledge and Kegan Paul Ltd., 1985.

Van Onselen, Charles. *Studies in the Social and Economic History of the Witwatersrand 1886–1914*. 2 vols. Harlow, Eng.: Longman Group Ltd., 1982.

Vercruijsse, Emile. *The Penetration of Capitalism: A West African Case Study*. London: Zed Books Ltd., 1984.

Vincent, Joan. *Teso in Transformation, Peasantry and Class in Colonial Uganda, 1890–1927*. Berkeley: University of California Press, 1982.

Vogel, Susan, ed. *For Spirits and Kings: African Art from the Paul and Ruth Tishman Collection*. New York: The Metropolitan Museum of Art, 1981.

Wai, Dunstan M. *The African-Arab Conflict in the Sudan*. New York: Africana Publishing Co., 1981.

Wallerstein, Immanuel, ed. *Labor in the World Social Structure*. Beverly Hills: Sage Publications, 1983.

Walt, Gillian, and Melamed, Angela. *Mozambique: Towards a People's Health Service*. London: Zed Press, 1983.

Waterman, Peter. *Division and Unity Amongst Nigerian Workers: Lagos Port Unionism, 1940–60's*. The Hague: Institute of Social Studies, 1982.

Watts, Michael. *Silent Violence: Food, Famine and Peasantry in Northern Nigeria*. Berkeley: University of California Press, 1983.

Weiskal, Timothy C. *French Colonial Rule and the Baule Peoples: Resistance and Collaboration 1889–1911*. New York: Oxford University Press, 1980.

Weissleder, Wolfgang, ed. *The Nomadic Alternative: Modes and Models of Interaction in the African-Asian Deserts and Steppes*. The Hague: Mouton, 1978.

Whitaker, Jennifer Seymour, ed. *Africa and the United States: Vital Interests*. New York: New York University Press, 1978.

Wijkman, Anders, and Timberlake, Lloyd. *Natural Disasters, Acts of God or Acts of Man?* Washington, D.C.: Earthscan, 1984.

Wiking, Staffan. *Military Coups in Sub-Saharan Africa: How to Justify Illegal Assumptions of Power*. Uppsala: Scandinavian Institute of African Studies, 1983.

Wilks, Ivor. *Asante in the Nineteenth Century: The Structure and Evolution of a Political Order*. London and New York: Cambridge University Press, 1975.

Willis, John Ralph, ed. *Studies in West African Islamic History*. Vol. I: *The Cultivators of Islam*. London: Frank Cass, 1979.

Wilson, Graham K. *Business and Politics: A Comparative Introduction*. Chatham, N.J.: Chatham House Publishers, 1985.

Wolfers, Michael, and Bergerol, Jane. *Angola in the Front Line*. London: Zed Press, 1983.

Wolpin, Miles. *Militarism and Social Revolution in the Third World*. Totowa, N.J.: Allenheld and Osmun, 1981.

Yaeger, Rodger. *Ethiopia: The Fall of Haile Selassie's Empire*. New York: Africana Publishing Co., 1975.

Yansane, Aguibou Y., ed. *Decolonization and Dependency: Problems of Development of African Societies*. Westport, Conn.: Greenwood Press, 1980.

Young, Crawford. *The Politics of Cultural Pluralism*. Madison: University of Wisconsin Press, 1976.

———. *Ideology and Development in Africa*. New Haven: Yale University Press, 1982.

Young, Crawford, Sherman, Neal P., and Rose, Tim H. *Cooperatives and Development: Agricultural Politics in Ghana and Uganda*. Madison: University of Wisconsin Press, 1981.

Young, Crawford, and Turner, Thomas. *The Rise and Decline of the Zairian State*. Madison: University of Wisconsin Press, 1985.

Zartman, I. William, ed. *The Political Economy of Nigeria*. New York: Praeger, 1983.

———. *Ripe for Resolution, Conflict and Intervention in Africa*. New York: Oxford University Press, 1985.

# INDEX